THEATRICAL MANAGEMENT

IN THE WEST AND SOUTH

FOR THIRTY YEARS.

INTERSPERSED WITH

ANECDOTICAL SKETCHES:

AUTOBIOGRAPHICALLY GIVEN

BY SOL. SMITH,

RETIRED ACTOR.

WITH FIFTEEN ILLUSTRATIONS AND A PORTRAIT OF THE AUTHOR.

"The web of life is of a mingled *yarn*—good and ill together."

SHAKSPEARE.

NEW YORK:

HARPER & BROTHERS, PUBLISHERS,

FRANKLIN SQUARE.

1868.

Dedication.

To HENRY MARSH, Esq.,

THE BEST DECIPHERER OF OBSCURE, INTERLINEATED, AND INTERPOLATED MANUSCRIPT I HAVE EVER MET WITH,

WHO PRESIDES AS FOREMAN, IN THE UPPER STORY, OF THE IMMENSE INSTITUTION KNOWN AS THE PRINTING HOUSE OF

HARPER & BROTHERS,

AND WHO HAS OCCUPIED THAT EXALTED STATION

(ONE HUNDRED AND SIX STEPS UP TO IT AT PRESENT)

FOR FORTY YEARS OR MORE,

This Volume is most respectfully Inscribed

BY HIS OBLIGED FRIEND AND BROTHER TYPO,

THE AUTHOR.

INDEX TO THE ANECDOTICAL SKETCHES, ETC.

APPENDIX.

ILLUSTRATIONS.

PREFACE.

In times past, when we performed long journeys in stage-coaches, it was not unusual for passengers to pass a good portion of a night in telling stories and singing songs. Sometimes a new passenger would come into the coach after dark, and when he found that story-telling and singing were the order of the night, and when gently informed it was "his turn," he would most willingly and cheerfully contribute his quota to the general amusement, and possibly become considerable of a favorite even before his fellow-travelers had seen his face. Of course all sorts of conjectures were indulged in as to the personal appearance of the new-comer, and all were anxious for daylight to appear, so that his face might be disclosed. I have sometimes been that new passenger, and my desire to see the face of each passenger with whom I had been conversing, or whose stories or songs I had been listening to in the darkness, was as great as theirs to see mine. We were to be fellow-travelers for several days and nights, perhaps, and what more natural than that we should wish to become acquainted with each other, and to know how each other looked? And when daylight came, disappointment in some instances followed the general revealment of features; for it was not unfrequently found that a bass voice belonged to a slightly-made, effeminate youth, with a smooth chin, while a fine tenor voice had proceeded from a Susini-looking individual, "bearded like the pard."

When we read a book, especially an autobiography, we naturally want to know what sort of a person is the writer. What sort of a *looking* man is he?—or woman, if the author be of that denomination.

Now, my reader, as you have purchased this volume, or mayhap taken it out of the library, I take it for granted you are going to read it, in which event we are thrown together as companions for several hours at least. I am going to do my level best to AMUSE you on the way we are to travel; and, that you may have some notion beforehand what sort of a looking man is talking to you—for, in the nature of things, I must do all the talking, while you must necessarily be but a passive listener—I here present you, transferred to *wood* for your especial benefit, MY PHOTOGRAPH, by a fine artist. On the same card you will perceive that I have given you my AUTOGRAPH, which has been much sought for heretofore—so much, indeed, that answering letters asking "the favor of your [my] autograph" has occupied valuable time which might have been more usefully disposed of. All I need to say hereafter in answer to autograph seekers will be, "Dear madam, buy my BOOK, and you will not only have my AUTOGRAPH, but you will also become possessed of my PHOTOGRAPH and AUTOBIOGRAPH." (I know not if there be any such word as the last, but it will serve for the occasion.) I can have this brief, and, I trust, satisfactory answer printed or lithographed, ready to send to all applicants; and, if it were possible, I would have a *lock of my hair* lithographed, to go with it.

It will be seen that, in preparing these memoirs for the press, very little regard has been had to the length of the *Acts* or of the *Chapters*, the whole being huddled together somewhat heterogeneously. There is scarcely any uniformity of arrangement; but in relating my simple story I have endeavored to employ plain language, and to make use of as few words as possible to express my meaning, and those words are mostly English. It will also be perceived that I have proceeded on the hypothesis that one can possibly write amusively without *mis-spelling* words, as some of our modern humorists consider it necessary and proper to do; and, farther, that I have generally called persons and things by their right names—as instances, men are called men and gentlemen, and women are called women and gentlewomen, not *lords* and *ladies;* for we have no titled gentry born here, and the Constitution forbids our acceptance of any title of nobility from foreign governments or potentates.

I do not think proper to say any thing of the EGOTISM which must necessarily pervade a book of this kind—an autobiography, except that I remember reading something to this effect: *There is not a person living upon the face of the earth, be he ever so insignificant or humble in station, whose history, if truthfully written, would not be interesting, and even* INSTRUCTIVE.

One thing more, and the reader may go to the prologue. Elderly readers may come across some anecdotes in this little book which they have read before. I have heretofore (in 1845 and 1855) published two small volumes, which in their day had considerable circulation: some of their contents are here; and, moreover, a few of the sketches which I herein give are reclaimed from BURTON'S ENCYCLOPÆDIA OF WIT AND HUMOR, in which they were inserted with my consent; and they will probably be considered none the worse for having been bound up for a dozen years in the same volume with the humorous writings of such men as Washington Irving, Thorpe, Longstreet, Wendell Holmes, and Hooper.

"These things premised, you have my full consent," gentle Reader, to accompany me through my wanderings, if you think proper to do so; and I hope you will not have cause to regret the journey.

SOL. SMITH.

Clarendon Hotel, Long Branch, N. J.,
September, 1868.

THEATRICAL MANAGEMENT

IN THE

WEST AND SOUTH,

WITH

ANECDOTICAL SKETCHES.

PROLOGUE.

1801—1823.

CHAPTER I.

My early life, until I had arrived at the age of about thirteen years, was passed in Solon, Courtland County, New York, with the exception of about one year at the beginning, when Norwich, Oswego County, was my abiding-place—that village having been the residence of my parents when I made my first appearance. My father was a fifer in a volunteer company at the battle of Bunker Hill, at the age of thirteen or fourteen years. After his discharge from the volunteer army he served a regular apprenticeship to the trade of a goldsmith, and on coming of age he received from the government a patent for forty acres of land, which he afterward located in the military tract in New York, then almost a wilderness. He married early in life, and in due time became the father of a large family of boys. My excellent mother's maiden name was Hannah Holland. She was every thing a wife and mother should or possibly could be; and although she seemed to have more than her due share of troubles, she went through all unfaintingly, and never faltered in the performance of those onerous duties which Providence required her to undertake in the wild Western country which government had set apart for the citizen soldiers who had fought the battles of the Revolution.

My first remembrance is of a log house about twenty feet square, in which we all lived—the "big boys," as we children called the elder brothers, sleeping up stairs in the garret (up *ladder* would perhaps express the fact more accurately), while the two youngest of us occupied a trundle-bed, which in the daytime was shoved under the parental resting-place. A loom, two spinning-wheels, and under one of the three windows a work-bench, with the innumerable tools of a goldsmith, together with nicely-arranged "dressers" (shelves) for plates, platters, mugs, tea-cups and saucers — chairs, a table or two, pots, kettles, gridiron, and sauce-pans, filled the one room tolerably well. One side or end of the room, or at least two thirds of it, was occupied by a huge fire-place; but this took up but little space in the house, as the chimney was built mostly outside. Ah! the tremendous fires we have had in that old-fashioned fireplace! My father had engaged a man to clear half an acre of land, build the house, and dig and stone up a well, for which work, well and faithfully done, he paid him one hundred dollars in money, which was a rather scarce and valuable article in those days and in that part of the country. We took with us from Norwich a very fine milch cow and calf, a wagon and span of horses, and a colt—also a good dog (his name was Bose), and a cat.

There were seven boys of us when we moved into the "tract," named Josiah, Silas, Oliver, Holland, Cicero, Martin, and Solomon (the undersigned). Another, the eldest of all, Wright, had gone to sea some time previously, having shipped on the Constitution frigate, Commodore Rodgers, as a drummer, and at the time I am writing of filled the duties of drum-major—continuing in the service until the end of the Tripolitan War in 1805, when with his "grog money," which he had not drawn for the whole term of his service, he set up a store on a small scale in Charlestown, Massachusetts, from which city he removed over to Boston, where in a reasonable time he became a thriving merchant. Meanwhile the five "big boys" at home worked like beavers clearing land, and my father, by his constant labor at the bench and forge (I forgot to say the forge was out-of-doors), kept the women and girls supplied with ear-drops, beads, and finger-rings for forty miles 'round, receiving in return corn, wheat, and all other provisions, as well as "store-goods" from the merchants in Homer, Cincinnatus, Tioga Point, Cayuga, Scipio, and other places. My noble hard-working brothers, besides clearing our farm, went occasionally "out to work," particularly in harvest time. I was old enough to remember that my brother Josiah chopped twelve acres for a Mr. Wildman, his compensation being a yoke of oxen. "Chopping" consists of felling the trees, cutting them into logs 12 feet long, and piling the brush!

In due time three other boys were added to the family, Orrin and Samuel Sherwood (twins), and Levi, afterward re-named Lemuel. Of course for many years the five younger boys could assist but little, if any, in the labors of the place, and must have been a burden. But still my parents labored on, never complaining. Father had received a wound in battle, and, I believe, carried a British bullet in his body during his life; therefore he could only work at his trade, leaving the heavy work out of doors to the boys. Mother, besides the usual duties of housekeeping, carded the wool, spun the yarn, and wove the cloth from which she made our garments. We young ones did what little we could to help her through her laborious task, but that was little enough, so far as I was concerned, for I was only eight years old when I went forth from my home to earn my own living. But I am anticipating.

Besides being great workers on the farm, my brothers were "mighty hunters," and supplied our table with plenty of bear-meat and venison, as well as partridges and ducks. Father sometimes took a shot; but whatever shooting he did was mostly at the "licks," where the deer came to get salt which had been placed there for their enticement, the hunter being concealed in a clump of bushes hard-by. I suppose my father was one of the best shots that ever held a rifle. I have seen him several times lay on his back and bring down a hawk that was soaring so high that my young eyes could barely see it. The Indians who sometimes visited our place called him Hawkeye. (This was very long before Cooper wrote his "Pioneers.")

Our nearest neighbor one way lived three miles off. His name was Moss. The other way, over Mount Roderick, lived Colonel Wheeler, about two miles off.

At what date I can not exactly say, but it was after the great solar eclipse of 1806, a couple of strangers called in one day and told my father *he had located on the wrong land!*—that, in point of fact, our land laid on the other side of the road, and the place our people had cleared and cultivated with so much toil belonged to *them!* I shall never forget the shock this intelligence gave my parents and brothers. Having become satisfied the claim of the strangers was a just one, there was not a moment's hesitation in resigning the place. A barn had been built by this time—also a shop for father, separate from the house. All our people asked was time to clear a few rods of land on the other side of the road, and build another log house. A well was not needed, as there was a fine spring near the spot where the new house was to be located. The time was readily conceded, and, what's more, a fair equivalent was allowed in money and stock for all the improvements. In six months we took possession of our new log cabin, and our "boys" went to work clearing land again. If my blessed father and mother, and those glorious "boys," are not now enjoying in Heaven the reward for their long-enduring toils, there is no meaning in the promise made to mankind that "their works do follow them."

In the course of a few years a new frame house was built—the first in that part of the township, and the talk was that "Uncle Levi Smith was getting along in the world." But before the achievement of the new dwelling—that is, before it was quite finished, the writer of these pages had gone forth, as above intimated, to seek his own livelihood, and this at the tender age of eight years! I earned the first pair of shoes that ever inclosed my feet. Before this time I had worn only moccasins, made of raw deer-skins in winter, and "gone barefooted" in summer. It so happened that a family in "Twelfth Town" *wanted a nurse*, and I was engaged for the place! I remained a month, and received a pair of shoes for my wages.

Several of my brothers had gone to Boston to "tend store" for brother Wright, "taking turns" in the farm work and clerking; and it was thought *I* was quite old enough, God help me! to earn my own livelihood; so I was "put out," as it was called, to Mr. Eli Wildman, who resided three miles from our house in a straight line through the woods, and six miles in the usual course of travel by roads. Before leaving my early home, however, I must here say that if there is any good in me at all, I owe it to my mother's teaching. It is to her I am indebted for the moral culture which has taken me through all temptations and difficulties unscathed to a tolerably old age, and saved me from ever committing a dishonorable act. Oh! how much do we owe our mothers!

One morning I was started off, alone, to find the new home where I was to remain four years, and learn the trade, mystery, and calling of a Farmer. My little heart was heavy at leaving my real home, and I dragged myself but slowly up Mount Roderick on my way to the forks of the road, where I was to turn sharp to the left and soon be at Mr. Wildman's, as my father told me. But as I saw the sun slowly but surely descending in the west, it suddenly occurred to my mind that I couldn't possibly reach my destination before dark, and where, I inquired of myself, could I stay all night? I sat down on a fallen tree and reflected seriously—seriously for an eight-year-old boy, what had better be done under the circumstances. The thought at last flashed upon me that the best way would be to return home and stay *there* all night—and I did. On my arrival home about sundown, my father was, or pretended to be, somewhat offended at my disobedience of orders. "What on earth brought you back, Solomon?" inquired he. "Well, sir," I answered, "I felt pretty sure I couldn't travel six miles in one day, so I thought I would make two days of the journey, and came back to stay all night at home; besides, if I was caught out in the night, I was afraid of catamounts." My explanation was received with good-humor, and I spent that evening and the next morning in great happiness with my mother. Next day I made another start, and accomplished my journey in about ten hours, arriving just before dark at Wildman's farm.

I am not going to give an extended account of my sojourn with the Wildmans. Suffice it to say that they were passably good people, and treated me as well as I probably deserved. *I learned to work* pretty fast, and soon became useful to Farmer Wildman. At the age of nine years I regularly went to mill at Homer (14 miles), or Cincinnatus (6 miles). In winter I went to school, 2¾ miles, besides cutting wood, assisting in milking, feeding the cattle, and doing up other "chores." My mother had taught me the first rudiments, and at school I was invariably "at the head." This is boasting, but it is the simple truth. I feel I have a right to mention it, for three quarters' schooling is all I ever had; and when persons have written to me asking the particulars of my life, what books I have written, what papers I have edited, and particularly what college I graduated at, I have invariably and truthfully answered the last question by saying, "At a log school-house in Solon, Courtland County, New York." Whatever few acquirements I am master of, beyond what I learned there, have been picked up in the great school of the world.

I was allowed occasionally, say once a year, to visit my family, going in the morning and returning the same night—generally on a Sunday, so as not to neglect my work—and this I could easily do, as one of my brothers took the trouble of blazing the trees on the route by the short cut through the woods.

At 12 years of age I could take a yoke of oxen into the forest, and this in dead of winter, cut down and cut up trees, and "snake" them to the farm. I could and did drive the team to Cincinnatus, carrying on a pair of wheels and dragging huge logs to the mill to be sawed into boards. I could reap and bind, plough, rake hay, mow a little, chop wood, shear sheep, pull flax, assist to build stone fences, sing psalms and anthems, teach the children their letters—in fact, make myself useful generally, and I did all these things with right good will; there not being, as I verily believe, a lazy drop of blood in my veins at that time. I served faithfully for nearly four years, when my father took me home for some supposed ill usage on the part of Mr. Wildman. I don't pretend to say whether I really was ill used or not; but my father decided that I should return to the family mansion; and when I did return, what a change was there! The old gentleman was quite alone! My brothers, one by one, had entered into business in Boston, and, becoming prosperous, had invited our dear mother to visit them for the winter, and she was now with them, enjoying a rest from her toils in the wilderness. I went to school again, but soon felt such an unconquerable yearning to see my mother and brothers (for the young ones had accompanied her on her visit, and intelligence had been received that mother had been taken ill), that it was decided to let me go to Boston as fast as my legs could carry me; so, with five dollars in my pocket, some jewelry in a little box, a "pass" from Uncle Elihu Holland, who was a justice of the peace, and a pack containing a few shirts and any quantity of "crullers," contributed by my dear Aunt Jerusha, wife of the J. P., I commenced my walk of three hundred miles! Not quite thirteen years of age, I found my uncle's "pass" an indispensable document to have along. On the very second day of my journey I was taken up as a runaway by a man driving a sleigh and horses, and carried back at least three miles. This man could not and would not believe my story that I was going to Boston to see my mother. After a good cry, I bethought me of the pass, not knowing exactly what virtue it might possess, and asked him to read *that*, and "see if I was a runaway." Its effect was magical. The horses were stopped and turned round, the man was overflowing with apologies, and I was carried to the place of my capture, and *two miles beyond*, where the good man dismissed me with his blessing and a quarter of a dollar, as he said Squire Holland's pass requested "all who see these presents to aid and assist the bearer on his way." I took the quarter without scruple and with great thankfulness, though it is quite certain the good justice who wrote the pass never had contemplated *pecuniary* assistance would be afforded me. Just as we were parting there happened to come along a sleigh going my way, and, on learning of my being carried back, and carefully reading my pass, the owner said, "Jump in, little boy—I'll take you as far as Unadilla;" and he did, in pretty quick time, too, insisting on my staying all night at his house (a tavern) free of charge. At parting next morning I insisted on making his daughter a present of a pair of ear-rings as an acknowledgment of the kindness bestowed upon me; but the landlord wouldn't listen to it, though he was willing to gratify his daughter with the ear-rings, and insisted on paying me the full price for them, which I think was eighteen pence, they being of a very ordinary kind. Thus I pushed on toward Boston, getting free rides, and sometimes free lodgings and diet, though always ready to pay my bill like other folk. (It was the "pass" that did it.)

I shall never forget the sensations of wonder and surprise I experienced on entering Albany, the first large city I had ever seen. It was nothing like what it is now, but it was a grand sight to me. The trial of General Hull for treason was concluded on the day I was there. I remember I, child as I was, thought he deserved hanging for his conduct at Detroit, which post he surrendered without striking a blow. In consideration of his services in the Revolutionary War, his life was spared, and he was only cashiered for cowardice.

Arriving at Pelham (Massachusetts), I learned from an uncle that my beloved mother had gone to her long home, and I was never more to see her in this world. My feelings on receiving this sad intelligence can not be written. Her beautiful form could never more be encircled by these arms, but her TEACHINGS I could and would always retain and act upon. I have tried to do so; and I never repeat the prayers SHE taught me without adding a heartfelt wish that I may be found worthy of joining her in those realms of bliss which I know she inhabits. * * * I got to Boston at last, and entered into a new world.

I was taken into the store of my brother Silas, in Ann Street, and soon learned to be of use there. My brother Wright had a store in Milk Street, and Josiah and Oliver kept another at the corner of Kilby Street and Liberty Square. We kept open until 9 o'clock at night, and it was my duty to close the store at that hour. I remember one night closing it much earlier, in order to go and assist the Republican boys in tearing down the State-house, because the Federalists had illuminated it in honor of the downfall of Bonaparte, and his banishment to Elba. We were on the side of Bonaparte, you see—I mean we Boston boys, North-enders and South-enders, and we had made up our minds to tear down the State-house as aforesaid. We went to the Common, but didn't tear down any thing at all; but we chased all the niggers off the Common, as was usually done on occasions of gatherings, except on what was termed "nigger 'lection," which I don't know the meaning of to this day. I only know that on *that* day the colored people were permitted to remain unmolested on Boston Common.

One Sunday in that summer (1814) news came that the Constitution frigate (Old Ironsides) was chased by two frigates and a seventy-four into Marblehead. This being the vessel in which my brother had served five years (*and* saved his grog), and, moreover, being a general favorite with the whole people, there was a great stir when the news was spread of her danger. Without saying a word to any one but my brother Sam, who happened to be with me in our cellar in Wharf Street, I placed a large club in the hands of that patriotic youth, seized an old musket which was rusting in a closet under the stairs in the hall, which musket was destitute of any lock or ramrod, and saying "Follow me!" rushed forth into the streets, closely followed by brother Sam, and we pushed for Marblehead, to afford what little aid we could to the noble old Constitution. We ran at great speed through Broad Street, across State Street, down Flagg Alley, passing Faneuil Hall (with all its great memories), through Ann and Prince Streets, to Charlestown Bridge, which we half crossed, when we met some acquaintances, who, after learning our patriotic intentions, informed us that the Constitution was safe, and our assistance was not needed. We sneaked back to Wharf Street, our ardor having abated, and deposited our arms in the back cellar. On the following Sunday the buildings on Long and India wharves were crowded with people to see the gallant old Ironsides sail majestically into the harbor, and to send up cheers of joy for her safety, which cheers were answered by the glorious crew, who, under Hull and Bainbridge, had a short time previously captured the "Guerriere" and sunk the "Java."

In the fall of 1814 we all removed to Albany, where I served as clerk in my brothers' stores (changing about as wanted) for three years, all the time learning something of business and informing my mind. My leisure time was mostly spent in reading Shakspeare's Plays, with which I became familiar long before I ever saw a play acted.

CHAPTER II.

THE first theatre I ever entered was situated in Green Street, Albany, and was under the management of John Bernard, an actor of considerable celebrity both in England and this country. I purchased a check at half price, and witnessed the performance of the HIGHLAND REEL—not as we see it represented now, "cut" all to pieces, but the whole comic opera, as written by O'Keefe. Bernard played *Shelty*, the piper; Mr. Drake, *Sergeant Jack;* Sam. Drake, *Captain Dash;* Henry Placide (then quite a boy), *Charley;* Mr. Garner, *Sandie;* and Julia Drake and Mrs. Young the female characters. The impression made upon my youthful mind was strong and lasting, and I remember the airs of that comic opera to this day. My head was full of acting from that time forward; my duties at the store became irksome to me; in brief, I became, as thousands had become before me, and thousands will become after me—stage mad!

My brothers refusing me permission to visit the theatre, my only chance was to visit it by stealth—for see the play I would. I contrived to make an acquaintance with the young Drakes, by whose influence I obtained free admission behind the scenes; but then the difficulty was, how to leave home every play-night without the knowledge of the family. My room was in the second story, and opened on a shed, which was occupied as a wood-house and hen-coop. I was in the habit of letting myself down from my window, by means of sheets and blankets, to the shed, from which I could easily jump to the ground, and after clambering over old barrels, piles of wood, and a high fence—always causing a great sensation among the hens and other live-stock—thus gain the street. After luxuriating on the scenic feast, I was obliged to return the same way, generally waking up the whole family of fowls, but luckily never disturbing *our* family.

From witnessing the performances, I soon felt an ardent desire to participate in them. I accordingly applied for and obtained leave to enroll myself in that useful but much-despised class of individuals, indispensable in all theatres, called "supers," or, more politely speaking, "auxiliaries."

One night, having bedaubed my countenance with a plentiful supply of burnt cork and oil, to make myself a fit associate of the renowned *Three-fingered Jack*, it being late when the performance concluded, I forgot to wash my face previous to returning home. I went to bed black as I was, and in the morning, as usual on such occasions, overslept myself. My seat being vacant at the breakfast-table, a servant was desired to awaken me, when judge of her astonishment on seeing my black face peeping from under the bedclothes as I lay snoring! The poor girl ran down stairs three steps at a time, and declared there was a *nigger* in Sol's bed! This announcement brought the whole family to my room; an explanation was inevitable; and I visited the playhouse no more that winter.

At the close of the season Mr. Drake and his family wended their way westward. Miss Denny (afterward well known in the West and South as Mrs. Drake) made her first appearance on any stage in the village of Cherry Valley, personating the character of *Amelia Wildenheim.* Mr. Drake, with a small but talented company, proceeded to Kentucky, where he established theatres.

Funeral of King Henry VI.

The next season (1815–16) the members of the company were all strangers to me, consequently my free admission did not continue, and as my brothers did not allow me funds for the purpose, I had considerable difficulty in procuring admission. For hours together I have concealed myself behind old pieces of scenery in the carpenters' gallery, waiting for an opportunity to slip into the front of the house, satisfied with what I could *hear* of the dialogue going on below. At length, of even this poor privilege I was deprived; for the carpenters having discovered my retreat, I was ordered, with awful threatenings, to leave the premises, and never to make my appearance in that part of the house again. I was literally turned out. But would I *stay* turned out? Not by any manner of means. RICHARD THE THIRD was advertised for performance--*Richard* by Mr. Somebody, I forget who now, but it was some great actor. I could not resist the attraction: go I must, and go I did.

About six o'clock P.M. I entered the back door, which happened to be unguarded at the time, and went up to my old quarters in the carpenters' gallery. I felt my way in the dark until I found something which appeared to be a large box, into which I popped without the least hesitation, and closed the lid. For more than an hour I lay concealed, safe, as I thought, from discovery. At length the bustle of the carpenters and tuning of instruments in the orchestra announced that the operations of the evening were about to commence. The curtain rose, and I ventured to peep down upon the stage. I was delighted; I could see all that was going on, myself unseen. The second act was about to begin, and I was luxuriating on the pleasure I should derive from the "courting scene" of *Richard* and *Lady Anne*, when I heard four or five men making their way directly to my hiding-place. I had barely time to enter my box and close the lid, when I found, to my utter dismay, that the box was the object of their search; in short, as you will already have anticipated, *I was shut up in King Henry's coffin!* Here was a situation for a stage-struck hero! The coffin was taken up, the men remarking "it was devilish heavy," and I felt myself conveyed down stairs and placed upon the bier. Since I had been carried so far, I made up my mind to carry the joke a little farther. So I lay as quiet as the "injured king" would have lain had he been in my place, and was carried by four strong supernumeraries on the stage, followed by the weeping *Lady Anne* and all the court. Little did the lady imagine she was weeping over a living corpse! For my part I perspired most profusely, and longed for an opportunity to escape. When I was carried off "to Whitefriars" to be interred—that is to say, in stage parlance, when the procession moved off "L. H. U. E."—the supers were desired to replace the coffin in the carpenters' gallery. Being awkward (did you ever see supernumeraries who were not?), and finding their load rather heavy, they turned and tumbled it about in such a way that I could not bear it any longer, and was obliged to call out. The men dropped their precious burden and ran away in affright, which gave me an opportunity to make my escape from the coffin and my exit through the back door. I afterward heard that the affair had made a great noise in the theatre at the time of its occurrence—the four men declaring that a hollow voice had issued from the coffin bidding them to "put it down and be d—d to them!" and the carpenters affirming, on the contrary, that when they opened the coffin they had found it empty.

The four supernumerary gentlemen never visited the playhouse again, but immediately joined the Church. One of them, I believe, has become a notorious preacher, and never spares the theatre or theatrical people in his sermons, telling his hearers that he had a most mysterious warning when he was a young man!

For some time after the adventure just detailed, I dared not venture within gunshot of the theatre; I therefore gratified my passion for the drama by collecting together a number of boys in a neighboring cellar, where I recited such speeches as I could remember, arranging matters with the boys so that I was sure to receive a suitable number of "rounds" at the end of each speech. On these occasions I had several lads who acted as supernumeraries, and were very serviceable in the characters of *Peruvian soldiers* and *Venetian senators*. One of them, who afterward arrived at some eminence as an actor, and was at one time manager of the Albany Theatre, but is since dead, excelled all the rest in personating the unfortunate sixth *Henry*, while I, as *Richard*, was murdering him in the Tower. He omitted the speaking, it is true, but when I growled out the awful sentence, "Down, down to h—ll, and say *I* sent thee there!" and stuck him with a lath, Duffy had a way of falling from the woodpile in a most masterly and dignified manner, to the great amusement of the boys, and at the imminent risk of breaking his royal neck.

We carried on our work, or rather play, for some weeks, until we were ordered out by the owner of the cellar, who found we were likely to make too warm a business of it, having introduced a large quantity of India crackers among the wood for the purpose of blowing up *Grindoff's* mill. So "my brave associates, partners of my toil, my feelings, and my fame," and myself, were obliged to capitulate, and yield up our underground theatre.

During the season I saw Bernard in some of his best characters—*Timothy Sharp*, *Nipperkin*, *Kit Casey*, *Bras de Fer*, *Sadi*, *Sheva*, *Benjamin* (MAGPIE AND MAID), and a great many others. I saw Henry Placide play a *monkey*, and Andrew J. Allen *Abælino, the Great Bandit.*

For the season of 1816–17 the theatre was leased to a Mr. Mortimer, who, being inexperienced in theatrical management, in a few weeks lost the little capital he had invested in the busi-

FUNERAL OF HENRY VI. (See page 14.)

ness. I remember nothing of him except that he had a pretty wife. Mr. H. A. Williams was stage-manager and principal actor. A queer little fellow, named Joey Williams, played the eccentric comedy, and a Mr. Thornton the comic old men. Mrs. H. A. Williams (afterward Mrs. Maywood) was new on the stage, and played all the *Dollies*, *Pollies*, and *Peggies*. Mr. Price (son-in-law of Mr. Bernard) acted during this season, as did Mr. Bernard, Mr. H. Placide, and Mr. Hop Robinson.

Mrs. Burke, then a young and very pretty actress and singer, came to play a few nights, and appeared in *Rosina*, *Agnes*, and *Lothair* (ADRIAN AND ORILLA). A Mr. Phillips was the representative of *Octavian* and *Adrian.* I saw young Bernard make his first appearance in the character of *Dick the Apprentice.*

Near the close of the season, H. A. Williams and his wife left the Albany Theatre for the Park. Mr. Mestayer and his family arrived, and the season was eked out by the performance of harlequinades and pantomimes, intermixed with slack-wire arrangements. These were the last days of the old Albany Theatre previous to its being converted into a church, in which capacity it served for over thirty years; but I am happy to learn that it has recently resumed its theatrical character, and is now open as a temple of the Drama. The season ended in something like a row, and part of the company, with Mortimer at their head, went to Troy, with the vain hope of "making a raise," as they termed it.

After the departure of the theatrical people from Albany, I became more and more dissatisfied with my situation of clerk in my brother's store, and more and more desirous of becoming an actor. Having completed the study of *Young Norval*, so far as the words were concerned, I made up my mind and a small bundle one afternoon, and, instead of posting up my books, I posted off to Troy to "join the show-folk," not doubting for an instant that I would be received with open arms by manager and actors. Poor, mistaken individual that I was! The members of the company, who in Albany were "hail-fellow well met" with me, and were loud in their praises of my precocious talent for the stage, in

Troy scarcely recognized me! I had no money, not deeming it at all necessary to provide such an article, as I supposed (of course) that I should immediately be placed upon the salary list. Alas! I soon found that salaries were out of the question, and that the actors I had so envied, supposing them to be rolling in riches, had some difficulty to obtain food enough to keep soul and body together! Over a pot of porter I prevailed upon Mr. Thornton to speak to the manager in my behalf. An interview was granted; the matter talked over; another pot of porter drank; and the result of all was, that *Young Norval* dwindled down to the *Waiter* in Raising the Wind, and my debut was agreed on. The eventful night came, but, for some cause or other—probably *Jeremy Diddler* had made too free at the bar—the piece was postponed! Next morning, to my utter horror and amazement, I found that the manager had taken down his scenery and decorations—the theatre had vanished, and "he himself wandered away, no one knew whither!" The actors were in a state of consternation, being left entirely destitute of means to follow their leader, even if they had known his course. They made off as fast as possible, each determining in his own mind to "stand no farther question," and all fearing that their retreat might be cut off by those faithful followers of genius, the constables.

Being left in sole possession of the field, I began to reflect a little on my peculiar situation. My landlord hinted that I was in his debt for two weeks' boarding and lodging, and sundry pots of porter and Albany ale; that he had lost a good deal by the actor folk, and, having seen me frequently in their society—in short, his rules required payments weekly! I heartily wished myself back to No. 26 State Street, corner of Dock; but wishing did no good. My tavern bill must be paid. After much difficulty, I raised the amount by selling two of my best coats and a vest, paid my landlord, and trudged off toward Saratoga, where I arrived next morning. I had no particular object in view. I dared not go back to my brothers in Albany; "I must eat;" but how to obtain a dinner was a question difficult to be answered. While these thoughts were ranging about in my head, and hunger thumping away in my stomach, I happened to see some men *carrying stone* in the street. I asked one of them if I could be engaged in the business, and at what wages. A bargain was struck—fifty cents a day (and found!) was the price, and at it I went, determined at least to earn my dinner. I had been at work in my *new line of business* (the "heavy business") but about an hour when I saw a Mr. Garrow, who was a regular customer at our store in Albany, walking directly toward me. From a false pride I dreaded his discovering me in my honest employment, so, dropping a load of stone I was carrying, I seized my coat and ran off, my fellow-laborers hallooing after me for an explanation of my unaccountable conduct.

I had no dinner that day. During the afternoon I met Mr. Garrow, who recognized me at once, and asked me what brought me to Saratoga. I said I was out on a collecting tour. He replied that he was glad to meet me, as he had a payment due at our store the next day, and meeting me would save him the trouble of remitting. Hereupon he took out his pocket-book, and began counting out tens, twenties, and fifties, to the amount of three hundred dollars. I hesitated, but it was for an instant only, and refused to take the money. He insisted; but my mind was made up. By way of excuse for declining to receive the debt, I told him I was going to the western part of the state, and should not return for some time. On relating this circumstance to my brothers, some months afterward they informed me that Garrow failed the very next day, and they lost the whole amount!

I made my way on foot to Schenectady, where I remained three days literally without bread. Being heartily tired of my adventure, I wrote home for leave to return, like the prodigal son. The next day I received an answer from one of my brothers utterly refusing to receive me. I shall never forget my feelings when I received that letter. I felt alone in the world. To that letter I attribute all my wanderings in after life. Had I been permitted to return when I saw the folly of my conduct in leaving home, I should have been cured—I felt I should—of my infatuation for the stage, and should have become a steady merchant, lawyer, preacher, or something else equally as estimable in the eyes of the world. I may as well mention here that my brothers were not quite so hard-hearted as they may appear to have been. The letter was intended to have the effect of punishing me for running away, and the next day they sent for me; but it was too late; I had left the town in less than five minutes after receiving my sentence of banishment.

CHAPTER III.

I bent my course westward, and in about a week arrived at Solon (the place where I was "raised"), the clothes I had on my back constituting my whole stock of valuables, the bundle I took away from Albany having entirely vanished in exchange for eatables and lodging on the road. My father was away from home, and I did not see him. My Uncle Holland suffered me to remain at his house for a week or two, my labor on the farm being considered equivalent to my daily bread. Here one of my brothers visited me, and explained the Schenectady affair. The whole family were about removing to the GREAT WEST, and he appointed a place to meet me in about a month's time, when he expected to be on his Western journey.

A Hog Story.

There are extant any number of dog, horse, cat, rat, and fish stories. I am going to write a HOG STORY. It may not interest the reader; but, I assure you, the circumstance on which it is founded interested *me* for a whole month, and even *now*, whenever the recollection of it crosses my memory, feelings of remorse punish me considerably.

On the Cayuga Lake, east side, stands a beautiful village which is happy in the name of Aurora. One mile north of that lovely village lived, in 1817, a substantial farmer named Stott. With this Stott, a most worthy man, the writer of this engaged to work in the harvest-field *one month* for six bushels of wheat; each bushel of wheat was estimated to be worth one dollar, so that I had six dollars in prospect at the end of the month; and with these six dollars, added to five I had in my pocket, I intended to journey to the Great West, *then* a great distance off.

I went to work like a good fellow, mowing and raking hay, binding up wheat, and making myself useful in various ways—happy all the time, and joyous as the fish that sported in the smooth and clear lake in which we harvesters bathed every evening after sunset—delighted with the prospect of a rich reward for my labor, and dreaming of the "Far West," the goal of my hopes and wishes (then situated about Pittsburg, *now* away off to and over the Rocky Mountains), and glorying in the thought that I, a boy of sixteen, would be the pioneer of the great Smith family in the Western regions.

All went on smoothly. One day, as I was pitching, bundle by bundle, a load of wheat into the mow, I saw enter the barn, rooting and grunting along, a very large, fat, lazy, long-eared sow. I can't to this day account for the devilish feeling which induced me, without a thought, to throw the pitchfork into this unoffending old creature; but I DID IT—*instantly* did it! The handle was scarcely out of my hand before I repented of the deed; and in less than three minutes I was wondering what could have prompted me to such an act. Ah! many, very many hours, in the stillness of night, did I lie upon a sleepless couch and ruminate upon my crime! Bitter tears of repentance trickled down my youthful cheeks, sinner that I was! What had the poor beast done to deserve such a fate?

The poor surprised sow gave a horrible squeal (I hear it *now!*) and ran with all her might out of the barn and out of the yard, the pitchfork still sticking in her quivering pork. The instrument of torture was afterward found about three hundred yards from the place where the fatal deed was committed; but the old sow—the unoffending, innocent old sow—had disappeared in the thick undergrowth of a neighboring wood, and had doubtless ended her days in solitude, with no pitying relative near to close her eyes, or render the last sad offices to the dying innocent.

As for me, the perpetrator of the horrid crime, what a month did I pass! My mind was tortured with horrible images of ghastly hogs bristling up before me. The poor old murdered sow actually *appeared* before my half-waking and half-closed eyes, dressed in a shroud, walking on her hinder legs, shaking her right paw into my face, and pointing her left, with a "most piteous action," to two bleeding pitchfork wounds in her ribs! In vain I tried to shake off these fantasies; the more I shook, the more they wouldn't go. I was miserable—I was a murderer—I had committed *sow*icide!

As a compensation to the farmer, I had made over to him the proceeds of my six bushels of wheat, but *that* did not ease my mind in the least. I had done a deed which a thousand bushels of wheat could not atone for. The phantom sow, with the winding-sheet trailing after her, as she stalked around my bed in the garret, drove sleep away from my pillow, and deprived me of all chance of rest. I grew weary of life. I didn't care any more about traveling West. The idea frequently crossed my mind of sacrificing myself to the manes of the poor feminine hog.

My month was up.

Two Quakers came along and inquired for seed-wheat. I offered them my six bushels, and they purchased it, at a dollar and a quarter a bushel. I listlessly received the money, and passed it over to the honest farmer in payment for the murdered sow, and was just bidding farewell to my kind employer and his family, when a little urchin came running in, screaming with all his might—

"Oh, daddy! daddy! just come out here and

see something! If here isn't our dead sow comiug up the lane!"

Horror-stricken, I huddled on my pack with the utmost speed, and prepared to depart, dreading to meet the spectre which I doubted not was coming to upbraid me for my brutal butchery! I started off at full speed toward the gate, when —can I express my joy at the sight which met my view?—there was the veritable sow that I had for a month mourned as dead, alive and rooting!—somewhat thinner than when I pitchforked her, but apparently enjoying remarkably good health; and by her side marched sixteen clean, elegant little offspring, joyously grunting as they capered along up the lane. Oh what delight I experienced at this sight! A millstone had been taken from my neck—I was not a murderer—I was free from crime! I could have hugged that veritable old hog—I could!—and I believe I *did* kiss half a dozen of the pigs. I was completely happy.

Farmer Stott insisted that, inasmuch as I had *paid* for the supposed defunct sow, she belonged to me, and that I was also proprietor of her progeny—the whole being worth, at the lowest rate of hog's flesh, at least twelve dollars, which sum he offered to pay me. I utterly refused to receive any thing more than the price I had paid for the elder animal. Happy in the contemplation of the swinish family group, composed of the mother lying on her side, and furnishing an early breakfast to her sixteen young uns, I passed out at the gate, and wended my way westward.

By some accident my brother was prevented meeting me as appointed; and supposing he had gone on, and that his letters had miscarried, on I pushed to Olean Point, where I purchased a skiff, which I launched upon the waters of the Alleghany River, and floated and rowed until I found myself in Pittsburg, a distance of five hundred miles from the place of embarkation. Here my purse gave out; for, after paying my tavern bill and purchasing a pit ticket for the theatre, not one cent remained. Behold me, then, one thousand miles from home (if I can with propriety say I had any home at all), among strangers and in a strange land.

I went to the theatre. Mr. Entwistle was the manager, and Mr. Hutton and Mrs. Entwistle were his principal performers. Mr. and Mrs. Legg were members of the company. The LADY OF THE LAKE was the play, and the farce TURN OUT. The scenery was good, and the pieces were well played. Next morning I went to the stage-door for the purpose of applying for employment, but could not obtain an audience of the manager. Being asked my business by one of the performers, I had not the courage to make my wishes known, and I was *turned out!*

Hearing no tidings of my brother, I took passage on a flat-boat to work my way to Marietta. Not much liking the slow floating of the ark, I changed into a skiff owned by an elderly gentleman, who wanted a working passenger. He had a young wife and a beautiful child. I soon found I should not be very comfortable with them; for, although his young wife's conduct was in all respects considerate and proper, the old gentleman had a tincture of jealousy in his disposition, which would break out now and then, particularly when people mistook me for the young woman's husband, which they frequently did. I remember what a stew the old fellow was in one night, when the landlord of an inn lighted us up stairs, and, pointing to two doors, said to me, "You and your wife will occupy that room, and *your father* can sleep here."

The old fellow flew into a violent rage, and told the landlord he was entirely mistaken; that he himself was the husband of the lady, and I was *only a passenger!*

At Marietta I commenced a fruitless search for my brother. I traversed the whole valley of the Muskingum, actually subsisting on apples and peaches, and sleeping in barns! One day I happened in at Mr. Hall's bakehouse. Mr. Hall, his mother, wife, sister, and brothers, had lately arrived from Connecticut. They were all Methodists; and a more worthy family I have never known. After a very short acquaintance, suspecting my destitute situation, they inquired into my circumstances. I told my story, and was immediately invited to make their house my home until I could communicate with my brothers at Albany. I accepted their invitation with joy and gratitude, and endeavored, by my labor and attention to their business, to repay their kindness.

Years have passed—not a few, but many—and my gratitude to that family remains as warm and sincere as it was at the time they sheltered the poor wanderer!

I soon learned, by a letter I received, that the brother whom I had supposed ahead of me in my journey, had been compelled, by the sickness of his family, to turn back, and his letters to me, informing me of the fact, had miscarried.

In about two months, however, another brother and his family passed Marietta on their way to Cincinnati. I was taken on board their *ark*, and we all proceeded happily along down the beautiful river. My brother established himself at Cincinnati, where he was joined eventually by the whole brotherhood.

OLD HUSBAND AND YOUNG WIFE. (See page 18.)

The reader, if he is much acquainted in and about Cincinnati, will perceive that the writer forms *one tenth* of the family so well known in the Western country as the "*Sixty-feet Smiths.*" Alas! there are now (1868) but *twelve feet* of us remaining!

For myself, my wandering propensities soon returning, I proceeded as far as Louisville, where I engaged myself to H. Deming as an apprentice to the printing business. I was carrier of the *Herald*, and remember to this day the residences of the old citizens—the Galts, the Bullits, the Prathers, and the Oldhams, whom I served twice a week with the news fifty years ago.

The theatre was open. I renewed my acquaintance with the family of the Drakes, and, as at Albany, had free admission behind the scenes. The company consisted of Messrs. S. Drake, Savage, Blissett, Alexander Drake, S. Drake, Jr., J. O. Lewis, James Drake, and Cornell; Mrs. Lewis, Miss Julia Drake, and Mrs. Mongen. I saw Blissett in nearly all of his best characters, and a most admirable actor he was.

The FORTY THIEVES and the MILLER AND HIS MEN were performed frequently. In the last scene of the latter piece the *explosion* was omitted. *Lothair* used to say, "Confusion! the train has failed! Well, manly courage nerve my arm, and crush the tyrant!" A desperate combat ensued, which ended with the death of the *Miller*, of course.

Manager Drake had a singular propensity for altering titles, or, rather, adding second titles to plays. To the HONEY MOON he would add, "*or the Painter and his Three Daughters.*" He always announced the HUNTER OF THE ALPS with this addition: "*Or the Runaway Horse that flung its Rider in the Forest of Savoy.*" I will add one more specimen of his second titles, and proceed:

"RICHARD THE THIRD, *or the Death of Young Edward at Tewksbury, and of King Henry the Sixth in London; the Courtship of the subtle Duke Richard, and Marriage with Lady Anne; Unnatural Murder of the Children of Edward Plantagenet in the Tower; the Coronation of the Usurper; Rise of a formidable Rebellion in*

Wales; Overthrow of Buckingham, and his Decapitation; Death of the Tyrant at the Battle of Bosworth Field, and Accession of Henry the Seventh to the Throne of England!"

CHAPTER IV.

Becoming dissatisfied with my situation in the printing-office, *after the actors left the city*, and imagining Mr. Deming was a little unreasonable to expect me to rise at five o'clock in the morning, after working until two hours past midnight, "I gave him something, and we parted." I stored my pockets with provisions, and "broke for high timber;" in other words, I trudged off to the westward. While my provisions lasted, I was tolerably comfortable and happy; my *lodging* was "cheap and airy"—generally on the ground floor, and for three or four days I footed it merrily along through the wilds and prairies of Indiana; but when my provisions gave out, my spirits gave out also. Apples and peaches there were none; my only resources were to beg, starve, or impose on the people. I chose the latter alternative, and trumped up a story—I forget what it was now—which induced the good folk of the Hoosier State to give me corn-bread, bacon, and thick milk enough to keep soul and body together, *on a credit.* After many days of hardship, fatigue, and mortification, I arrived at Vincennes, on the Wabash River. When I left Louisville I had some faint hopes of finding a company of theatricals at this place, but there being none, I began to look about for something to do for a livelihood. I soon found a farmer a few miles from town who wanted a hand, and immediately engaged myself to him for twenty-five cents per diem to hoe corn! For about a week I toiled under an almost tropical sun, following the example of my fellow-laborers, and stripping myself, all but my pantaloons, by which means my back, arms, neck, and hands became blistered. In a few days I literally *shed my skin.* I could not stand this: to be *skinned alive* was rather too much. I left the farm, and engaged myself to Elihu Stout, Esq., proprietor of the *Western Sun* newspaper as an apprentice. Mr. Stout was a very worthy old man, a little too fond of card-playing, but one of the best-tempered men I have ever known. His wife—but the less we say of her the better; she was kind in sickness, and that, with me, covers a multitude of faults. This lady had been "raised" in Kentucky, and having been in the habit of commanding slaves, and the laws of Indiana not permitting her to own any of those convenient appendages to a household, she made use of her husband's apprentices in place of them. She had one negro—his name was Thompson—who had been brought from Kentucky under indentures. He was to be free at the age of twenty-one, and he was now at least thirty-five! Mrs. Stout made him believe he was but fourteen, and that he had yet seven years to serve. Thompson used to ask us boys in the office if we didn't think he was fifteen years of age. Of course we could not encourage him in such abolitional ideas. So he served on in blessed ignorance, and whether he has yet arrived at the desired age of twenty-one I am not informed. I don't know how it was, but Mrs. Stout acquired a complete ascendency over us all. With all her faults, as I said before, she was kind in sickness. If one of us complained ever so little, she would send for us, place us in a bed (we had not the luxury of a bed when in health), and nurse us with the greatest care until we completely recovered; then dismiss us to our type-setting with a hearty—blessing; and then her tyranny would be resumed, and continued sans intermission until we were fortunately taken ill again.

My fellow-apprentices were James A. J. Bradford, now of the army, John Thompson, since dead, and William H. Johnson, afterward proprietor of a paper in Louisville. The latter soon left the office, his apprenticeship having expired; the other two remained during my apprenticeship. In a short time I became so expert in the "art and mystery of printing," that by common consent I was declared foreman of the "Sun" office. I took a side in politics—and, of course, went with the "Sun." Party spirit ran very high in the little village of Vincennes. My mistress became so exasperated at the editor of the opposition paper (a Dr. Macnamara) that she one night buckled a belt around her waist, stuck in it two large horse-pistols, concealed a cowhide in her sleeve, and, thus equipped, commanded me to arm myself and follow her, to see fair play while she inflicted summary chastisement on the doctor! It was with much difficulty I could persuade her to "let the doctor off," and not until I had promised to blaze away at him in the next "Sun."

A Thespian Society was formed. Mr. Stout was appointed one of the managers, and Bradford and I were allowed to become members. The comedy of John Bull was cast, and the character of *Lady Caroline Braymore* assigned to my fellow-apprentice, Bradford, while I was called on to personate a *servant* attending on *Sir Simon Rochdale.* At the first rehearsal, finding I knew something of plays, the managers changed the cast, so as to allow me to play *Dan*. Another rehearsal made so favorable an impression that the afterpiece of 'TIS ALL A FARCE was selected, and the character of *Numpo* assigned to me. The performance of these two characters did my business for me—I was acknowledged as *the* low comedian of the society. I appeared successively and (as the people thought—so did I too, then) successfully in the characters of *Farmer Ashfield*, *Old Doiley*, *Robin Roughhead*, *'Zekiel Homespun*, *Stephen Harrowby*, and several others. I can remember the names of only a few of the members of the association—Dr. Shuler, Mr. Stout, Dr. Decker, and my fellow-apprentice, Bradford, were prominent actors. A Mr. Dillworth played the old women and Dr. Ollapod. The winter passed off pleasantly; indeed, notwithstanding the treatment I received from my mistress, the winter was all *spring* with Bradford and myself.

I had been an apprentice in the "Sun" office about a year, when one night, about 12 o'clock, we were alarmed by the cry of fire! After carefully locking up the form, which we had just finished correcting, we very leisurely went into the street to ascertain where the fire was, when we soon had light enough on the subject—it was our printing-office which was in flames! The people were running toward us frcm every direction—all was confusion. The family, who occupied the part of the building directly under where the fire was raging, were yet asleep. Our first care was for them—the next to preserve the printing materials. For my own part, after I had carried out, by main strength, several of the family, including Mrs. Stout, who was a load for any one, I went to work assisting the people to get out the press and types. I found the crowd industriously engaged in emptying the types on the floor, and rushing out with the *cases!* In the confusion and noise, I lost all recollection, but continued, as I was afterward told, to run in and out of the burning building, long after the crowd of people had entirely desisted, expecting the roof to fall in every moment. I was frequently warned against my foolhardiness, as they very justly termed it; but I heeded not—heard not—the warning. I continued to bundle out the cases, paper, imposing stones, and presses at a d—l of a rate. The first recollection I have is of hearing a tremendous shout or scream, as of a thousand voices. I gave a spring, and immediately found I had escaped the most awful of deaths. The roof fell in while I was passing from the printing-room, through a small entry, into the street. At first it was thought I was buried in the flames; but the momentary check the falling timbers met with when they reached the floor of the second story of the building gave me time to save myself.

In a few days our "pi was distributed," our press put in order, and the "Western Sun" rose in full splendor and in a new dress. But its rays gave no warmth to me. I was unhappy; for our Thespian society had been dissolved! I longed for an opportunity to tread the boards again; and, hearing that there was a company at Nashville (only three hundred miles off), I determined to set off for that place forthwith, without troubling my worthy master or mistress about the matter. Bradford had relations in Nashville, and as he also was tired of his situation, he agreed to accompany me. So off we started, in the middle of a night, and actually *ran* nearly fifteen miles, fearing I know not what—unless it was that Mrs. Stout should follow and take us up, runaways as we were. We heroically resolved not to be taken alive, if fifty *men* should attempt to apprehend us; but I verily believe, if the old woman had appeared, we should have surrendered at discretion.

Arrived at Nashville, I was doomed to be disappointed in my theatrical hopes. The company had just left the city for St. Louis, five hundred miles distant! As I had not five hundred cents to take me to them, I gave up all idea of becoming an actor for the time being, and consoled myself by spending the greater part of my Sundays in the old warehouse, which had been occupied as a theatre. There were the seats, the stage, the trap-doors, the banners! How I gloried in those banners! The last play performed had been BUNKER HILL, and the banners of both parties had been left upon the field of battle.

I engaged myself as a journeyman printer to Mr. Wilson, then just establishing the Gazette. Here I became slightly acquainted with General Jackson, who, being intimate with my employer, frequently visited the office. In about a month, my brothers at Cincinnati having got wind of my erratic movements, and having ascertained my whereabouts, sent me an earnest invitation to return home. I accepted it joyfully, took leave of my kind employer and his excellent family, and *walked* off to Cincinnati, a distance of three hundred miles. Here ended my wanderings for a while.

CHAPTER IV.

AT Cincinnati, among my numerous relations and friends, I spent a very happy winter. The evenings were delightful—singing meetings, debating societies, religious gatherings, oratorios, family parties, and politics, served to fill up my time rather agreeably; added to which, I attended a series of law lectures, performed the duties of clerk in one of my brothers' stores, on a salary of eight dollars per month, and played the organ in the New Jerusalem church three times every Sunday, and every Thursday evening, besides teaching a whole lot of young New Jerusalemites the art of psalmody two evenings each week.

Toward spring, finding I had a little time to spare, I joined a Thespian society, who held their meetings in a building belonging to Elmore Williams, in upper Market Street. I was the hero of the corps, and enacted *Young Norval.* A Mr. Sweeney (afterward justice of the peace) was *Lady Randolph*, and he acted the character very well, considering that his voice was decidedly a baritone, and he had not shaved for a week! The "meditating maid," *Anna*, was personated by Mr. George Row, a tall, lank carpenter, who chewed tobacco, and was obliged to turn aside every now and then to spit. *Glenalvon*, Mr. Davis, who afterward attached himself to the stage, but with no success. Of all the members of that society, I know of but one—leaving myself out of the count for others to judge of—who did not go to the devil! And it may not be thought improper here for me to say a word or two on the subject of *amateur theatricals.*

I never knew any good to come from Thespian societies; and I have known them to be productive of much harm. Performing a character with success (and Thespians are always successful) inevitably begets in the performer a desire for an enlarged sphere of action. If he can please his townsmen and friends, why should he not delight a metropolitan audience? He becomes dissatisfied with his profession or business, whatever it may be, applies to a manager for a first appearance in a regular theatre—appears—fails—takes to drink, and is ruined. Then to see the inordinate vanity of those amateurs who occasionally "volunteer" for some charitable purpose; the airs of consequence they give themselves; the ignorance they betray of a profession which they degrade by adopting even for a single night; the consummate impudence with which they strut before the public in the highest characters; not a shadow of fright about *them*—oh no! Their friends are in the house to applaud them, whether they deserve applause or not. Their success is not doubtful; the thing is settled; they *must* succeed; and they generally *do*, for applause is bountifully and indiscriminately showered upon them, and they are, in their own minds, immensely great actors before they have the slightest knowledge of the first rudiments of the profession.

A *gentleman* actor once told me that he had asked Mr. Booth's opinion of his acting in the character of *Richard*, and that Booth had acknowledged *himself beat!*

The foundation of the Columbia Street Theatre was laid this year, and the company of Messrs. Collins and Jones performed for a short season in the second story of Burrows and Tunis's store, corner of Columbia and Walnut Streets.

Late in the winter of 1820 the new theatre opened with WIVES AS THEY WERE. *Sir William Dorillon*, Mr. Collins; *Bronzely*, Mr. Jones; *Lord Priory*, Mr. Lucas; *Miss Dorillon*, Mrs. Groshon. Mr. Collins was an excellent actor; so was Jones. Mrs. Groshon was deservedly a great favorite. I had never seen her superior in *Lady Macbeth.* James M. Scott (afterward known as Big Scott, or Tragedy Scott, but better as *Long Tom Coffin*) was a leading member of this company. Mr. Garner, then a vocalist of some pretensions, performed a starring engagement, opening and closing in THE DEVIL'S BRIDGE. It was in this piece that old Fred Henderson first began to be appreciated by the audience. In after years he became an immense favorite, not only in Cincinnati, but in all the Western towns. It was a treat to see him and Alexander Drake in the farce of TURN OUT!

When the theatre closed for the season (1820) I felt my wandering propensities returning. Without much ceremony of leave-taking, I pushed for the westward again, and, strange as it may seem, bent my course for Vincennes. Arriving, I found my quondam master had farmed out his printing-office to a Mr. Osborn, with whom I immediately engaged as a compositor. I was kindly received by Mr. and Mrs. Stout, the latter declaring that she liked me all the better for the spirit I had shown in running away. In about a month's time my type-setting was interrupted, and my ideas all thrown into *pi*, by the arrival of my old friend, Alexander Drake, with a small company of comedians from St. Louis. They were to play in Vincennes during the summer months. The company was very small. I was four hundred miles from home. The temptation was too great to withstand. I applied, was accepted, and here I made my first attempts at acting upon a regular stage. My salary was fixed at six dollars per week.

The company consisted of Messrs. A. Drake, S. Drake, Jr., Palmer Fisher, Douglas, Jones, *Sol. Smith*, and Mesdames Mongin, Fisher, and three or four little female Fishers.

With a company so limited in number, it will

be supposed our range of pieces must have been extremely circumscribed; but this was not the case; we grappled at PIZARRO, the POOR GENTLEMAN, and other equally full plays.

By a lamentable casualty, our number, small as it was, was destined to be reduced. It was a custom with us to bathe in the Wabash River just previous to retiring for the night. Our hotel being on the bank of the river, we undressed in our rooms, and, wrapping ourselves in sheets or blankets, we so proceeded to our bath. One morning Douglas was missing; several remembered he had been with us in the water, but none had any recollection of seeing him when we came out. His clothes were found in his room, but there were no signs of his bed having been occupied that night. A search was immediately commenced, and resulted in finding the dead body of our friend two miles below the town.

We had now but four men and two women, and with this number we played PIZARRO. To those unacquainted with *country theatricals* the *cast* will be a curiosity:

Pizarro, the Spanish general, *Ataliba*, king of Quito,	..Mr. S. Drake.
Rolla, the Peruvian leader, *Las Casas*, a Spanish priest,	....Mr. Fisher.
Alonzo, joined with the Peruvians, *Orozembo*, an old cacique,	....Mr. A. Drake.
High Priest of the Sun, *Almagro*, a Spanish officer, *Blind man*, *Sentinel*, *Valverde*, secretary, *Guards*	....Mr. Sol. Smith.
Peruvian boy....................	Miss Fisher.
Elvira, *Priestess of the Sun*,	............Mrs. Fisher.
Cora............................	Mrs. Mongin.
Child..........................	Miss A. Fisher.

Thus Sam Drake (as *Pizarro*), after planning an attack on the unoffending Peruvians while engaged in worship "at their ungodly altars," and assigning his generals (*me*) their "several posts," in the next act is seen (as *Ataliba*) leading the Indian warriors to battle, declaring that "straight forward will he march until he sees his people free, or they behold their monarch fall!" He is victorious, and goes to offer up thanks to the gods therefor—when, presto! on comes the same man again (as *Pizarro*), smarting under the stings of defeat!

Fisher (as *Las Casas*) calls down a curse on the heads of the Spaniards, throws off his cloak, drops his cross, doffs his gray wig, and appears in the next scene as the gallant *Rolla*, inciting his "brave associates" to deeds of valor! Alexander Drake, as *Orozembo*, in the first scene gives an excellent character of the youth *Alonzo*, pronouncing him to be a "nation's benefactor;" he is then stuck under the fifth rib by a Spanish soldier (that's me again), and is carried off by his murderer; he then slips off his shirt and skull-cap, claps on a touch of red paint, and behold, in the next scene, he is the blooming *Alonzo*, and engaged in a quiet *tête-à-tête* with his Indian spouse!

For my own part, I was the Spanish army entire! but my services were not confined to that party. Between whiles I had to officiate as *High Priest of the Sun;* then lose both of my eyes, and feel my way, guided by a little boy, through the heat of the battle, to tell the audience what was going on behind the scenes; afterward, my sight being restored and my black cloak dropped, I was placed as a sentinel over *Alonzo!* Besides, I was obliged to find the sleeping child, fight a blow or two with *Rolla*, fire off three guns at him while crossing the bridge, beat the alarm drum, and do at least two thirds of the shouting! Some may think my situation was no sinecure; but, being a novice, all *my* exertions were nothing in comparison with those of the Drakes, particularly Sam, who frequently played two or three parts in one play, and, after being killed in the last scene, was obliged *to fall far enough off the stage to play slow music as the curtain descended!*

Our stage was ten feet wide and eight feet deep. When we played pieces that required bridges and mountains, we had not much room to spare; indeed, I might say we were somewhat crowded.

I generally "went on" for what is termed the youthful business—*Henry* in SPEED THE PLOUGH, *Henry* in the MAGPIE AND MAID, *Belville* in the COUNTRY GIRL, and other characters of a similar grade, but almost always had to "double" them with something else. I recollect going on for *Frederick* and *Stephen Harrowby* in the POOR GENTLEMAN. We played mostly from the Dublin (*doubling*) edition.

The season lasted about eight weeks. The company proceeded to Louisville, and I footed it back to Cincinnati, declining the offers of the Drake family for a permanent engagement, being fearful of the disapprobation of my brothers, who as yet knew nothing of the manner of employing my time in Vincennes. Being partially satisfied with my few weeks' experience as an actor, I now determined to "study the law." I was taken into the justice's office of Daniel Roe, and had the advantage of the books and instruction of Mr. Todd, an excellent lawyer and a worthy man, since dead. Here, and by attending the law lectures of William Greene, Esq., I picked up what little I know of that "intricate science," as it is termed by Sir Walter Scott. Mr. Drake came to Cincinnati soon after, and opened our Thespian House, under the style of the Haymarket Theatre; but the concern was unsuccessful, and the company returned to Louisville.

In the winter of 1821, the Columbia Street Theatre was managed jointly by Mr. Drake and Mr. Collins, the partner of the latter gentleman (Mr. Jones) remaining with a company in the southwestern towns. The drama of the FORTY THIEVES was produced with great splendor, and many other novelties were offered; but the season was an unproductive one. The company was indifferent, and the patronage worse than indifferent.

I continued to study the LAW.

CHAPTER V.

THE Cincinnati Theatre was opened by Messrs. Collins and Jones for the season of 1821–2 with the following company: Messrs. Collins, Jones, Cargill, Hays, Henderson, Bruce, Miss Denny, Mrs. Groshon, Mrs. Jones, Mrs. Hanna, and Miss Seymore (afterward Mrs. Cargill). I made application for the situation of prompter, and was engaged in that capacity.

First Appearance of Miss Peggy.

Mr. Cooper, then the leading tragedian of this country, performed an engagement during this season. On the first night of his engagement the following whimsical incident occurred: OTHELLO was the play:

The fame of the great tragedian had drawn a crowded audience, composed of every description of persons, and among the rest a country lass of sixteen, whom (not knowing her real name) we will call Peggy. Peggy had never before seen the inside of a playhouse. She entered at the time *Othello* was making his defense before the duke and senators. The audience were unusually attentive to the play, and Peggy was permitted to walk in the lobby until she arrived at the door of the stage box, when a gentleman handed her in, without withdrawing his eyes from the celebrated performer, and her beau, a country boy, was obliged to remain in the lobby. Miss Peggy stared about for a moment, as if doubting whether she was in her proper place, till, casting her eyes on the stage, she observed several chairs unoccupied. It is probable this circumstance alone would not have induced her to take the *step* she did, but she observed the people on the stage appeared more at their ease than those among whom she was standing, and, withal, much more sociable, and, as fate would have it, just at the moment, *Othello*, looking nearly toward the place where she was situated, exclaimed,

"Here comes the lady."

The senators half rose, in expectation of seeing the "gentle *Desdemona*," when lo! the maiden from the country stepped from the box plump on the stage, and advanced toward the expecting Moor! It is impossible to give any idea of the confusion that followed. The audience clapped and cheered—the duke and senators forgot their dignity—the girl was ready to sink with consternation—even Cooper himself could not help joining in the general mirth. The uproar lasted for several minutes, until the gentleman who had handed her into the box helped the blushing girl out of her unpleasant situation. It was agreed by all present that a lady never made her début on any stage with more éclat than Miss Peggy.

At the close of the season I withdrew from the theatre and got married. The gentlewoman who honored me with her hand was Martha Therese Mathews, daughter of Edwin Mathews, a musician of considerable repute at that time, and teacher of music. Miss Mathews was principal soprano singer in the Haydn Society, of which I was also a member. When I commenced married life I had exactly four dollars and sixty-two cents, which I handed to the minister as his fee. A month passed away very happily at a brother's house, after which it occurred to me one day that some means must be thought of by which to obtain eatables and drinkables. One morning I strolled over the river into Covington. I roamed about the hills back of the town, humming and whistling a variety of tunes, and was as happy as a lark. On a sudden it occurred to me that I possessed some knowledge of the *science of music*, and next I thought to myself, "Why may not I turn that knowledge to account?" *I will open a singing-school*—I WILL! Full of the idea, I ran into the town, crossed the Licking, and asked the first person I met if he thought a singing-school could be gotten up in Newport. "Well, stranger," he answered, "I don't know but you mout get one a-going; there are a heap of young people here, and nary a school for teaching to sing." "Enough!" said I; "next Saturday I open a singing-school at the Court-house." Proposals were soon written, and in the course of the afternoon I obtained fifty subscribers, at a dollar a head, payable at the end of the quarter. Full of confidence in the success of my scheme, I returned to Cincinnati, and purchased four dozen of Flint's edition of "Sacred Harmony," with which I returned, on the following Saturday, to commence my school. I found the grand jury-room crowded, and had no difficulty in disposing of my stock of books *on a credit* (that was the way I *purchased* them), and at it we went, singing psalms. I practiced my school in raising and falling the "eight notes" for about two hours, then "fa-sol-la'd" the men, women, boys, and girls, separately and together, for an hour more, and wound up at sundown with a touch of "Old Hundred" and "Vital Spark." Appointing the next Saturday as the second meeting of the school, we separated, apparently mutually pleased with each other. On Sunday I was at my post playing the organ in the little "Temple," and I related to my brother Sam and my fast friend Southerd Holmes, both leading members of our singing society, the success which had attended my attempt to establish a school among the Kentuckians, and received their warmest congratulations.

About the middle of the following week it occurred to me, while sitting reading a newspaper in a printing-office, that a *new paper* was very much needed in Cincinnati. Without saying a word to any one, I took a composing-stick and set up ten lines of types, proposing to establish a weekly newspaper, to be called the *Independent Press.* I worked off twenty copies of my ten-line prospectus, and, taking one of them, went up Main Street and obtained ninety subscribers. Next morning I called at John P. Foote's type-foundery and selected $200 worth of types, which he very readily agreed to let me have on a liberal credit, and, borrowing a wheelbarrow, I packed my types into it, and wheeled them up to Mr. Oliver Farnsworth's printing-office on Main Street. Leaving my wheelbarrow at the door, I entered the office, and asked Mr. F. if he would, for a proper compensation, permit me to print a paper there. He consented, the terms were agreed on, and I pulled off my coat and went to work setting up the type for the first number of my paper.

By dint of hard labor, night and day, the "Independent Press" made its appearance on the 4th of July, 1822. On the day of the first publication the subscription list increased to three hundred, and in a few weeks swelled to seven hundred! I shall say little about this paper. It carried considerable influence with it. I can truly say I was honest in my editorial course, and I believe at this day all who were opposed to the establishment will admit that my *intentions* were good. There was a series of letters published during the first six months which caused great excitement, inasmuch as they bore heavily (under fictitious names) on some of the oldest inhabitants, exposing many transactions for years supposed to have been forgotten. I was threatened with all sorts of punishments, and was several times attacked by persons who thought themselves aggrieved, but, somehow or other, always happened to come off with unbroken bones and a whole skin.

Almost a Street Fight.

One little incident, which amounted almost to what might be termed a "street fight," I must relate. A candidate for office, whose name I change to Bubble, complained of a communication published in my paper, and demanded the name of my correspondent. I told Bubble that I would see the writer, and in the afternoon of the same day would either surrender his name or assume the responsibility of the article myself. It so happened that, for certain reasons of a personal nature, the author of the communication wished not to be known (as frequently happens in such cases), and with a good nature which I *now* consider scarcely commendable, I agreed to shoulder the responsibility and screen the writer.

Meeting Mr. Bubble on the south side of Main Street, I told him that his demand for the name of the author of the obnoxious article could not be complied with, but that, of course, I was responsible to the law for any thing that appeared in my paper. I soon found it was not *to the law* I was to be held amenable; it was to Mr. Bubble *personally* (a tall, stout, heavy man, of nearly twice my size: I was very thin then) that I must account. I shall not attempt to give the language used on the occasion. It is sufficient to state that we were both of us very polite at first, but gradually my friend Bubble changed his tone —all the time keeping the up-hill side of me, by-the-by—until, in a very short time, he so far lost his temper as to tell me *I lied.*

Now I don't know how the reader may view my conduct on this occasion. I knew I had *not* lied, and I knew his *saying* I lied did not hurt me a jot; yet—consider I was only twenty-one years old at the time—under the circumstances, knowing that a fight was exactly what Bubble was after, and being quite certain I could not escape from him even by running, and, moreover, entertaining the foolish idea (being, as I said, young) that no man should "take the lie," my left fist somehow or other very suddenly came in contact with Bubble's forehead, exactly between his eyes and over his nose, and that gentleman found himself sprawling in the gutter then and there. The result of the blow astonished the giver more than it did the receiver, and an awful drubbing was what I fully expected as soon as my opponent should rise. So it occurred to me that it would be as well to guard against such a disaster by following up my first blow with sundry other blows, as he was endeavoring to regain his feet. By the means last indicated, I managed—though considerably frightened, I acknowledge—to keep my opponent in the gutter until our mutual friends rushed in and separated us; and greatly rejoiced I was when they did so, I give you my word. As for Bubble, he raved and tore like a madman, cursing his friends for separating us, and declaring that he had not yet got a lick at me, which (luckily for me) was the very truth. It is my belief to this day that if I had permitted my opponent to rise, as I suppose in a fair fight I should have done, he would have used me up in very short order; for he was noted for several "rough and tumble" fights, in which he had invariably come out victorious. My victory must be attributed solely to the fact that I was too much frightened to allow Bubble to hit me at all.

Thus began and ended all my fighting while engaged in the editorial line—that is to say, all fist-fighting. Bubble spread my fame throughout the district, saying that if I could whip *him*, there was no use in others trying their hand with me.

Besides writing the editorials of the Independent Press, which I did at home, after working hours, whenever there was an end to them—for oftentimes the working hours continued through night as well as day—with but one assistant (my young brother Lemuel), I did all the work of the office. Many a time on a Sunday have I played the organ in the New Jerusalem temple for the opening services, consisting of a hymn and a couple of chants, and then, seeing the good old Mr. Hurdus well under way in one of his long sermons, slipped away to the office and helped my brother "work off" the first side of the paper, returning to the temple in time—with not very clean hands—to accompany "Strike the Cymbals," the "Hallelujah Chorus," or some other stirring piece at the close of the services.

Moses Dawson and myself were the two first editors who raised the standard of General Jackson in Ohio. "Brother Mosey," as I used to call him in our affectionate editorial intercourse, battled away in the cause of Democracy for many years—was "rewarded" with the nomination to an office which the Senate would not advise and consent to—lived to a good old age, and died of joy on hearing of Polk's election in 1844.

One morning, as I was walking very fast up Main Street from the post-office with a bundle of exchange papers under my arm, a gentleman in a Kentucky jean coat and white hat nearly started from the sidewalk when he met me. Wondering at the man's surprise, and his countenance appearing somewhat familiar to me, I turned, after passing him a few steps, and observed he stood precisely in the same place as when I first noticed him, with one foot on the curbstone and the other in the centre of the gutter. "Do you know me, my friend, that you stare at me so?" I inquired, returning toward him a step. "That's what I want to find out," he replied; "I *think* I've seen you before; if I mout be so bold, mout your name be *Smith?*" "It is, sir—you want to subscribe to my paper, I suppose—come up to the office." Without uttering a word, he followed to my office, where I took down the subscription book and inquired his name. The fellow continued to stare at me for some time without answering, and at length, with a ghastly sort of smile, said, "Excuse me if I'm mistaken, but are you or are you not our *singing-master?*"

The truth flashed upon me in an instant; I *had forgotten all about my singing-school!* "Old Hundred" had been *pressed* from my memory, and the "Vital Spark" had not once entered my mind since I had become an editor!

My friend in the jeans and white hat informed me that my failure to meet my appointment had caused great consternation in Newport; that the scholars had continued to meet for several Saturday afternoons, in the continued hope of my reappearance, and that at last, reluctantly giving me up as lost, they had dissolved the school, singing "Old Hundred" and "Vital Spark" to my memory out of the four dozen of "Flint's Sacred Harmony," which they despaired now of ever having an opportunity to pay me for.

Late in the winter of 1823 Messrs. Collins and Jones again opened the Cincinnati Theatre. The members of the company this season were: Messrs. Collins, Jones, Scott, Forrest, Davis, Eberle, Henderson, Groshon; Mrs. Pelby, Mrs. Riddle, Miss Riddle, Miss Fenton, and Miss Eliza Riddle, then but a child. The opening play was the SOLDIER'S DAUGHTER, the part of *Young Malfort* by Mr. Edwin Forrest. Being editor of a paper, I was, *of course* and *ex-officio*, a judge of theatrical matters; but when I gave a very favorable opinion of Forrest's acting in the comparatively trifling character of *Malfort*, my brother editors laughed at me—and afterward, when he played *Richard* for his benefit, I prophesied his future greatness, they set me down as little less than a madman. They said I would "spoil the lad"—"he *was* a clever boy, certainly, but puffing would ruin him." Mr. Pelby acted as a star during this season, as did Mr. Pemberton, Forrest playing *Titus* and *Icilius* to their *Brutus* and *Virginius.*

In the summer the company proceeded to Louisville; but a party of them soon returned and opened the Globe Theatre on Main Street. This party consisted of Messrs. Forrest, Scott, Cargill, Woodruff, and Davis; Mrs. Riddle, Miss Riddle, Mrs. Cargill, and Mrs. Hanna. At this house Forrest played *Othello* and many other characters for the first time, but with scarcely any knowledge of the text, his taste generally leading him to prefer the low comedy characters! I recollect seeing him play *Blaise* and *Lubin*—and very well he played them too. Finding he was trifling away his time, I advised him to write to New Orleans for an engagement, which he did, and closed with Mr. Caldwell for the ensuing winter season, at a salary of eighteen dollars per week.

My brother Martin wrote a petit comedy for the Globe Theatre, entitled MODERN FASHIONS, which was quite successful, Forrest and Scott playing a pair of dandies in it. I wrote a sort of a farce called the TAILOR IN DISTRESS, in which a well-known merchant tailor in Main Street figured as the hero, and in which Forrest performed the part of a *negro.* Business being bad, and believing our two pieces played together might produce the expenses, I engaged the house for one night, agreeing to pay each performer the sum of two dollars. Thus Edwin Forrest acted a dandy in the first piece, a *negro* in the second, and *Sancho Panza* in the concluding pantomime, all for the sum of two dollars!

Business failing altogether in the Globe Theatre, the members of the company scattered in different directions. Forrest and Davis, with the Riddle family, made an excursion into the country, and performed in the small towns of Ohio with no success. At Lebanon, or Dayton, Forrest was obliged to pledge a trunk of stage wardrobe for his bill at a boarding-house or tavern; and whether he has yet recovered it I am unadvised. One day the party traveled on foot from Lebanon to Cincinnati—twenty-two miles —crossed the river to Newport, and played DOUGLAS and MISS IN HER TEENS to a house of seven dollars! They contrived to get through the summer, and in the fall they all joined Collins and Jones at Lexington, in Kentucky.

When I had published seventy-two numbers of the "Press" I began to find carrying on a newspaper without capital was a bad business. My notes fell due; subscribers were delinquent: I could not live on politics, and *I sold out.* The "Press" was merged in the "National Republican," which became a firm supporter of Andrew Jackson for the presidency, as my paper had been. Elijah Hayward, who succeeded me in the chair editorial, on the accession of General Jackson in 1828 was appointed Commissioner of the General Land-office. My last words to the readers of the Independent Press were, "*Live honestly, serve God, and take the newspapers.*"

Shortly after disposing of my paper, I made a tour into Kentucky for the purpose of making collections. Mr. Drake was performing with his company at Frankfort, the seat of government, where he had established a theatre as early as 1816. Mr. William Jones came down from Lexington to act *Falstaff* for the benefit of a friend, and I took a seat with him in his gig on his return. On the way he told me Mr. Collins and himself were about to retire from management, and he suggested that it would be a good opportunity for me to commence a business he knew I was attached to. I had never thought of such a thing as becoming manager of a theatre; but, the idea once in my brain, it was hard to banish it. I played one night in Lexington the character of *Numpo*, Forrest doing the part of *Myrtyllo.* Somehow or other it got reported among the actors that I was there for the purpose of forming a company for Cincinnati, and several applications were made for engagements before I had made up my mind to enter into the speculation. In my hap-hazard way I decided to venture, and engaged several performers; among others, "old Henderson" and the Riddle family. Forrest wished to form an engagement with me, but, as he was under a previous contract with Mr. Caldwell at New Orleans, I consulted his interests rather than my own, and refused to receive him. In vain he urged that he could easily compromise with the Southern manager, and that he would rather be with me at ten dollars per week than with a stranger at more than twice the salary; all would not do. I was steadfast in my refusal. In a pet with me, he went to the Circus, and made an engagement with the proprietors to go with them as a *rider* and a *tumbler* for a year! I heard of this arrangement just as I was about to leave Lexington, and my mortification was great. I called in at the Circus, and, sure enough, there was Ned in all his glory, surrounded by riders, tumblers, and grooms. He was a little abashed at seeing me, but, putting a good face on the matter, he said he had made up his mind not to go to New Orleans, and, having been refused an engagament at ten dollars a week by me, he had engaged "with these boys" at twelve. To convince me of his ability to sustain his new line of business, he turned a couple of flip-flaps on the spot. I asked him to walk with me to my lodgings, where, by dint of hard lecturing and strong argument, I prevailed on him to abandon his new profession, and commence his journey to New Orleans immediately.

Here ends my prologue. From this time (1823) for thirty years I followed the precarious occupation of a THEATRICAL MANAGER, with what results will be seen by following me through my checkered career, as recorded in the FIVE ACTS (or eras) into which this skimming history is divided.

ACT FIRST.

1823—1827.

CHAPTER I.

I PROCEEDED to Cincinnati with my company, and, after the usual troubles and vexations (increased by inexperience in my new business), commenced my managerial career in the "Globe." The company was composed of the following individuals: Messrs. Henderson, L. Smith, Davis, Sweeney, G. Rowe, Eberle, Joey Williams, Sturdevant, Sol. Smith, Mrs. Riddle, Miss Riddle, Miss Fenton, and Miss E. Riddle.

Joey Williams was *destroyed by wolves* in Florida a year or two after. He was traveling on foot from Pensacola to St. Augustine, and, being benighted, camped out in one of the everglades of that region. The only vestige found next morning by his professional companions was a quantity of tickets strewn about, and some wigs and stage properties torn into small pieces.

The once celebrated Jack Dwyer performed an engagement of six nights. The season failed, as I might have expected it would, and we removed to the Columbia Street Theatre, which I rented of Mr. Collins; but no better success awaited us there. My funds ran out, and most of my actors scattered, as actors generally do when they find no money is to be had—and they are right, for they can not live on air—though *I* have almost done so on several occasions. At the close of the theatre I found myself in debt eleven hundred and fifty dollars. Rather an unfortunate beginning.

With a remnant of my company I proceeded to Wheeling, where we fitted up a room and played a few nights with very indifferent success. The people were indifferent to our indifferent performances. The same at Steubenville. After numerous hardships and adventures, we arrived at Pittsburg, when I rallied my broken forces, and opened the theatre with a very good company.

Outwitting a Sheriff.

On our way from Wheeling to Steubenville we passed through the small village of Wellsburg, Virginia. Being urged by the inhabitants to perform one night, and hoping to raise a sufficient sum to pay our wagon and carriage hire, we consented. A room was soon fitted up, and bills were issued. The time fixed upon for the curtain to rise was "eight o'clock precisely," as the bills have it. "Eight o'clock precisely" came precisely at eight o'clock, but there came not one living being in the shape of an auditor! On inquiry, our landlord informed us that the price of admission was too high, and the Wellsburgers were unanimously determined that we should come down with our price of tickets before they would come up to our room. There was no alternative—the price of tickets was reduced to "twenty-five cents each, children half price," and the Virginians "came at last to comfort us," to the number of full sixty. Between the play and afterpiece (the *play* was the BLUE DEVILS, and the afterpiece the POOR SOLDIER), the landlord, who acted as doorkeeper for the time, informed me the sheriff wished to see me for the purpose of serving a writ, a complaint having been entered that we were *showing* without license. Our receipts were fifteen dollars—the penalty we had unwittingly incurred was forty dollars. *Paying* it was out of the question. I could not think of going to prison. Outwitting the sheriff was my only chance. It was Saturday night. I directed the doorkeeper to invite Mr. Sheriff to take a seat among the auditors, and I would attend him soon as our performance should conclude. This was satisfactory to the officer. He seated himself and enjoyed the entertainment very much. By introducing a few additional songs, I contrived that the curtain should not fall until after twelve o'clock. The good-natured sheriff was then invited behind the scenes, and he proceeded to execute the writ, apologizing for the necessity which compelled him to perform the disagreeable duty. "My dear sir," said I, leisurely proceeding with my undressing arrangements, "don't apologize—these things must be done; but why did you not serve your writ some minutes ago? You are now too late." "Too late! How so?" "Why, my dear sir, it is *Sunday*, and I make it a rule never to transact business, particularly *law* business, on the Sabbath." The sheriff here consulted his

OUTWITTING A SHERIFF.

watch, and found he had been overreached. "Sure enough, it *is* past twelve, I do believe, and I don't think I can touch you. Well, curse me if I can be angry with you, Mr. Darby. Come, all hands, and take a drink." On Monday morning we were in Ohio, where old Virginia could not reach us. We performed a few nights at Steubenville, Ohio, but our audiences were small.

Nearly arrested as Pirates.

On our journey from Steubenville to Pittsburg we put up for the night at a very small village on the Virginia side, about midway between the two places. My father-in-law, my wife, my brother, and myself supped at a private table. At supper our conversation turned on the performances of the night previous at Steubenville, which had consisted, among other things, of the pantomime of DON JUAN.

The girl who waited on us at table was very attentive to our conversation, in the course of which I observed that Davis, after *murdering Don Guzman*, was too slow in getting to sea—there was time enough for the whole town to be alarmed; that the *combat* with *Ferdinand* was shockingly bad, and that if he did not improve in *fighting* he had better leave the profession. My father-in-law remarked of Mr. Lucas that he had *murdered Doctor Pangloss* a few nights before, and that on another occasion he was too drunk to guard the prisoner *Alonzo*. A good deal of similar chit-chat took place, to hear which did the waiting-maid seriously incline. Next morning, when about to pursue our journey, we were surprised to see quite a crowd collected about our baggage-wagon. Having occasion to open one of my trunks, I noticed that the *gentlemen* composing the crowd watched me rather more closely than I thought was necessary for the gratification of mere curiosity. Being in Virginia, it occurred to me that the Wellsburg sheriff was not far off. I determined to know my fate at once; so, after unlocking one of my boxes and raising the lid, I turned suddenly to the crowd and asked, "Gentlemen, is there a sheriff among you?" "No," answered a big-whiskered fellow, "we are none of us sheriffs, but there'll be a *constable* here presently, who will do as well." My Wellsburg friend has sent on the writ to one of his deputies, thought I. "Well, gentlemen, if none of you are sheriffs, I will thank you to retire; I don't know what you can want about my luggage." "Why, stranger," again spoke the big-whiskered Virginian, "there's no use your getting mad, you've got to stop here—*we know you*, and you'll not get off in a hurry, *I* promise you." "Not get off? You have no right to detain me; I have incurred no penalty *here*." "No, I don't know that you have, *here*; but you may have to pay the penalty *here*, if so be our court has jurisdiction of your case." Curse those licenses! thought I to myself; they will be the ruin of me yet! I determined to settle the matter at once. "Look you, my friends, you say I shall not get off. *I* think I shall, as I believe you have no right whatever to detain me. I outwitted your sheriff at Wellsburg, and I think the deuce is in it if I can't get clear of your constable."

I called to my father-in-law to follow in the carriage with my family (as I supposed they would not trouble *them*), and began to whip the horses of my baggage-wagon at a furious rate; but before the animals had made a start the reins were seized by three men, and big-whiskers thus addressed me: "Stranger, you are in old Virginia, and you mustn't think of getting off. We don't mean to let *pirates* pass through here, no way, no how." "PIRATES!" exclaimed I: "do you then take us for pirates?" "No," answered whiskers, "*we* don't *take* you at all, but the constable will; and we only intend to *keep* you until he comes." I felt relieved. We were not to be arrested for the *tax*, at all events. "What reason have you for thinking us pirates?" I ventured to ask. "What reason?"—whiskers was still the spokesman—"that's a good one! In the first place, what can *honest* people do with such a heap of plunder as you are toting in that wagon? Nextly, your confessions last night before Peggy Duncan, while you were eating supper. Didn't one of your men like to have been taken before he escaped to the ship, after killing a Don? Didn't you threaten to discharge him because he fought so bad? Then that 'ere doctor which one of your people murdered 'tother night in Steubenville—Dr. Panglosh, I believe, was his name—and then got so drunk on the strength on't that he couldn't guard one of your prisoners. Reason, indeed! But there's one thing you can't get over, I reckon—that there figurin' and letterin' on the back of that box, to say nothing of the queer-looking clothes you've *got in it*." Wondering what he could mean by the "figurin' and letterin'," I turned up the box, when, to my utter confusion, the following inscription appeared, as near as could be imitated with Venetian red, in *letters of blood:*

"By thee I fell, thy fate's decreed;
Heaven will avenge the bloody deed."

And underneath, as if to place the matter beyond a doubt, the following:

"DON GUZMAN
MURDERED BY DON JUAN, AUGUST, A.D. 1464."

The truth of the matter was this: we had played DON JUAN at Steubenville the night before, and the property-man had painted up the back of this very box to make it answer for a pedestal for Don Guzman to *stand* on—there being no horse for him to *sit* on—and the letters remained, a damning proof of our guilt. I did not stop to comment on the absurdity of the villagers in supposing we would publish our misdeeds on our boxes, even had we been pirates, but thought it best to explain matters to my friend with the whiskers, and leave him to settle the matter with his neighbors, for, truth to tell, I did a little dread the arrival of the officers, still remembering the *tax* business. I accordingly took whiskers aside and explained that we were *actors* instead of pirates, and thus accounted for our conversation at supper, and the mysterious inscription. He roared with laughter, and slapped me on the back until I was quite sore. By the time we were ready for a start, the crowd had been made aware of their mistake, and had dispersed. The only one who remained—and he only staid, as he said, to see us off—was my whiskered friend, who continued inspecting our "plunder" to the very last.

While awaiting at Pittsburg the arrival of the recruits we expected from Louisville, Lucas, Davis, and my brother Lemuel made a trip to Greensburg, thirty-two miles distant, where they gave an entertainment, consisting of Scenes from RICHARD, songs, recitations, and SYLVESTER DAGGERWOOD. Davis strutted on for *Richard;* Lucas "doubled" *King Henry* and the *Earl of Richmond;* and my brother enacted *Catesby*, the *Lieutenant of the Tower*, *Buckingham*, and a few other characters, *all in one dress. Richard* wore a common soldier's coat, the royal *Henry* a Scotch kilt, and *Catesby* a Roman shirt. As they had no curtain, *Catesby* was ordered to bear off the body of *King Henry*, after that unfortunate monarch was murdered in the Tower; and the same ceremony took place with the tyrant himself, after his disaster in Bosworth Field, *Catesby* doing the "heavy business" in both cases. The murdered *King Henry the*

Sixth lived again in the *Earl of Richmond*, both characters being personated, as I said before, by Lucas. It was remarked that the family likeness was very striking, only the dresses were different, the aspiring earl wearing a sailor's jacket and Turkish pantaloons, surmounted by a large damask table-cloth, and a very fine officer's hat and plume. By this performance, such as it was, the three strolling gentlemen made enough to pay for their lights, lodging, and supper, and returned the next day poor as they went.

When the company was organized, it consisted of Messrs. Scott, Jones, L. Smith, Davis, Lucas, G. Rowe, Singleton, Eberle, Sol. Smith, Mrs. Pelby, Mrs. Jones, Mrs. Rowe, and Miss Pelby. I need not say, with such a company, pieces were well played; indeed, I doubt whether the people of Pittsburg, before or since, have had a better company, yet the receipts fell far short of the expenses, and I was obliged, prematurely, to close the season. My *own* debts I managed to pay, but security debts I found it utterly impossible to discharge.

Dodging the Constables.

My benefit came off, and a bumper it was! The street in front of the theatre was literally crowded with people long before the doors were opened, and such scrambling for seats I had never seen. The fact was, many of my creditors, foreseeing a very small chance of getting their money, had applied for tickets, which I paid out with a liberal hand, without much regard to the size of the house. The consequence was that I had a most crowded audience, and but thirty-three dollars were received at the box-office! I had taken places in the stage-coach for Philadelphia, and expected to be off the morning after my benefit; but the "warrants were out" ("curse on all such instruments!"), and I was warned by my friend Butler that after the performance I was to be put into durance vile. Not wishing to stay and contest the point, I told my friend of my wish to escape the fangs of those worthies, the constables, who, to do them justice (I speak now of those of Pittsburg), are the most indefatigable set of personages I ever met with. My friend and I arranged that, so soon as the curtain fell, I should descend through the trap-door, and there remain in darkness and solitude until he should warn me, by a signal agreed on, that all was safe.

The performance proceeded, and I could observe my watchful friends becoming momentarily more eager for their prey. At length the curtain fell, and down I went through the trap-door (it was what actors call a *Vampire trap*) before any one was aware of my intentions. I was scarcely out of sight before I heard earnest inquiries made for me above, but no one knew what had become of me. My brother, being questioned, answered, without the least hesitation, that I had jumped over a fence at the back of the theatre, dressed as I had performed my part, and he supposed I had gone home the back way. The faithful ministers of the law immediately jumped over a very high fence, and started off in full cry. After waiting in the dark about an hour, I heard my friend Butler's signal, and very willingly groped my way out of my hiding-place. He took me to his house, where he had already conducted my wife and child. The surprise of Mrs. Butler, when she saw me enter the house dressed in full for the *Doctor*, in ANIMAL MAGNETISM, may be guessed. She had a good supper prepared for us; after partaking of which we were shown to an elegantly-furnished apartment, where we were to stay until an opportunity should offer to smuggle us off in the stage. Next morning Mr. Butler went out to arrange such business for me as remained unsettled, and he was told I had most mysteriously disappeared the night before. Some said I had gone down the river in a steam-boat; others suggested I had gone in the stage eastwardly, but this was denied by the constables, who said they had watches ready to intercept me if I had attempted to go that way. At length the matter was settled by a man who declared he had seen me start down the river in a flat-boat, which I had chartered some days previously, to his certain knowledge. We remained a part of two days in our concealment. Toward evening of the second day, my friend came to the door with a close carriage, into which we got, and he accompanied us five miles out of town (having previously arranged for the stage to take us up the next day), furnished me with money for my immediate necessities, and we parted.

There are many versions of the *trap* story extant among my brother actors. One version is that I was playing the *Grave-digger* in HAMLET, and seeing the bailiffs waiting at the wings, and ready to pounce upon me when I should make my exit, I popped down into the grave, and never was heard of in that part of the country again! Others say I was actually put into a coffin and buried, to avoid the constables, and arose from the tomb by the assistance of my friend Butler, and fled the country! Both of these versions are very good, certainly, but, as *Sir Benjamin* says, "mine is the true one."

I am not the only actor who has been "hard run" at Pittsburg. Some years since, a Mr. Langton, and two or three other unfortunates, had recourse to the following expedient to raise the wind: They engaged themselves to the proprietor of a museum to dress and stand up in the show-cases for *wax figures!* Langton personated *General Jackson*, and was much admired for his natural appearance. He has since told me that he never "went on" for a character which proved so difficult to personate as the old hero. He was about "throwing up the part" several times, but the prospect of his dollar and a half restrained him; so he stood out his three hours and got his money, though he says, "by the eternal!" he would not do it again for twice the sum.

CHAPTER II.

On our way to Philadelphia, my wife and I gave concerts at Greensburg, Bedford, and Chambersburg, with some success—that is, we contrived to pay the expenses of our journey. Arrived in Philadelphia, I lost no time in making application to Mr. Wood, manager of the Chestnut Street Theatre. He received me kindly, and treated me with politeness, but he could give me no encouragement in regard to an engagement, as the theatre was on the eve of closing for the season. I witnessed that night the performance of the FORTRESS and A ROLAND FOR AN OLIVER. The afterpiece was a rich treat to me. How could it be otherwise, with such a cast as the following?

Sir Mark Chase	Mr. Warren.
Fixture	Mr. Jefferson.
Sir Alfred Highflyer	Mr. Wemyss.
Selbourne	Mr. Darley.
Maria	Mrs. Darley.
Mrs. Selbourne..................	Mrs. Wood.
Mrs. Fixture	Mrs. Jefferson.

Failing to obtain an engagement at the Chestnut Street, I next day applied to the manager of the Tivoli Garden Theatre, who gave me to understand that in a few days I could have an appearance at that establishment. Fearing the worst, I wrote to one of my brothers at Cincinnati, asking him to forward me fifty dollars by mail. In less than a week I received a message from the Tivoli acting-manager (Mr. Charles Porter) that I could commence my engagement next day; but, *as a favor*, he wished me to go on that night (it was then five o'clock P.M.) for *three parts*, in place of Mr. Crampton, who had suddenly withdrawn. I huddled my things together, and went on for *Sheepface* in the VILLAGE LAWYER, the MOCK DOCTOR, and something else which I can not now remember. I continued to play for a week, and, on application at the treasury, was referred back to the manager, who told me that he had no idea I expected to be paid, and *play all the best parts too!* Good parts without bread and cheese not answering my purpose, and my landlady beginning to look rather *dun*-nish (her name was Brown), I withdrew from the Tivoli, and accepted an offer of an engagement from my old Vincennes friend, Palmer Fisher, who, in conjunction with a Mr. Jones, was just opening a summer theatre in the Vauxhall Garden. I soon found my situation was not much improved by transplanting myself from one garden to the other. The mode of paying salaries at the latter house did not meet my approbation—indeed, it was a very singular one, and I will here state it, for the benefit of all *spirited* managers in time to come. On every Tuesday the proprietors of the garden issued to each performer a quantity of tickets, the number being proportionate to the salary of each, bearing on their face the following obligation:

GOOD AT THE BAR FOR ONE DRINK.

Not having occasion for drinks to the number of two hundred and sixty-six (my salary being rated at eight dollars per week), I declined to take my tickets, and was laughed at by my fellow-actors, who considered me a "leetle too d—d particular."

In due time the letter from my brother arrived, with the remittance; but I had no money to pay the postage. I tried the manager—no funds; my friend Porter, of the other house—"he would if he could, but he couldn't." As a last resort, I applied to Mr. Everdell, leader of the orchestra, who had been under my management in Cincinnati and Pittsburg, and who owed me about a hundred dollars. I asked him for a *loan* of fifty cents, but he had not the money to *accommodate* me! I must do him the justice, however, to state that he offered to let me have almost any number of *drink tickets* I might want.

I happened to meet a friend from Pittsburg, by the name of Shiras, to whom I had rendered some slight service. Of him I borrowed a small sum, and took out my letter. With my fifty dollars I paid board and lodging bills, and had five dollars remaining. With this we went to Trenton, where I advertised a concert, in conjunction with a Mr. Still. The concert was unproductive. Still returned to Philadelphia, and I hired a Jersey wagon (on a credit), which conveyed us to Princeton, where I delivered letters of introduction to the president of the college. A notice was *written* and posted up about the college-yard, announcing that "Mr. and Mrs. Smith, from Philadelphia, would give a vocal concert" on such a night, "to consist of a great variety of songs and duets, sentimental and comic." I had but nine cents remaining of my five dollars, and with this sum I purchased oil sufficient to set a large lamp burning in the centre of a school-room which I had rented for the proposed concert. I engaged boys to bring some additional benches from a neighboring church, promising them payment for their trouble in the evening. Having lighted my lamp about sundown, I waited for nearly an hour, doubtful whether a single individual would honor my concert by attending. Just as I was about shutting up the room in despair, one young gentleman came to the door, handed me half a dollar, and walked in. "What! nobody here yet?" "Not *yet.*" "Any tickets sold?" "Don't know—probably—left some for sale at the hotel." Never mind—I'll go and rouse up the boys;" and off he went. I called a lad who was loitering about the door, and dispatched him with the half dollar to purchase candles. The room lit up, I began to be haunted with misgivings that we should have no audience, and that I should be required to refund the half dollar to the young man who had gone to "rouse the boys." I was soon relieved from my suspense, however, for the young collegian returned with a dozen of his fellow-students.

Seeing I had no door-keeper, my first customer proposed to take that office, advising me to go and prepare myself for the performance, *as the house would soon be full.* Most readily accepting his services, I retired into the little closet set apart for our dressing-room, where my wife was awaiting my coming with trembling anxiety. Soon I heard a great stir in the room—moving of benches, rustling of silk, opening of windows, and all the indications of people gathering. At length our volunteer door-keeper came sweating to our closet, and announced that he believed "they had all come." We commenced our concert, and our eyes were gladdened with the sight of a room full of joyous-looking persons of both sexes, fanning themselves for dear life. The concert went off finely, notwithstanding it was exclusively *vocal.* When it was concluded, our amateur door-keeper made his returns, and we found ourselves in possession of the very handsome sum (in our circumstances) of forty-seven dollars!—quite a fortune!

Delighted with our great success, we next morning set off for Brunswick, where we arrived the same evening. This was my wife's native town, and here we found a great many relations—aunts, uncles, and cousins, but principally aunts. Leaving my wife and child with their relations, I took a boat for New York, with the hope of obtaining a situation at the Chatham Theatre. I visited the Broadway Amphitheatre and witnessed the representation of LOCK AND KEY and the TURNPIKE GATE, *Ralph* and *Crack* by Mr. Joe Cowell, both inimitable performances.

Presenting a letter of introduction from Mr. Pelby to Mr. Kilner, stage-manager of the Chatham Theatre, I was received and treated civilly by that gentleman. In answer to his inquiries, I told him I had been on the stage but a short time; that I was willing to engage for *utility*, in the fullest sense of the term, and that six dollars per week was the sum I rated my services at. The old gentleman seemed pleased with what he called my modesty, and promised me an introduction to the proprietor, Mr. Barriere. I waited in the garden for the arrival of that great personage. In about two hours I saw a little saffron-faced fellow approaching, and was informed by one of the waiters that *he* was the man. He looked more like a cook than the director of a theatre; however, I had nothing to do with his looks. It was getting late, and I was obliged to return to Brunswick that evening, so I ventured to introduce myself to the important individual, without waiting for Mr. Kilner, who was busy on the stage at the time. I accosted him respectfully. He returned my salutation with a most killing look, and the question, in a tone something like the bark of a spoiled poodle, "What you vant?" I told him what I wanted in as few words as possible, he walking away all the time, and I following. He cut the conversation and my hopes of an engagement short by saying, in the same barking tone, "I don't vant you, sair! I have too many actors now; you may go, sair; I don't vant you." Without waiting for a word of explanation or expostulation, the little-great man strided away, leaving me standing near the fountain, looking for all the world as if I had been stealing, and fearing to look one way or the other, lest my repulse had been witnessed by some person—and, confound the fellow, he talked so *loudly* too! Is there any necessity for treating an applicant in this way? I know, by experience, managers are frequently—very frequently annoyed by applications from novices, but I could never see any reason why they should be treated with rudeness. On the contrary, it is my opinion that it is one of the most delicate duties a manager has to perform to give a refusal in such terms as will modify the harshness which all novices imagine they are treated with when their services are declined, as declined they most generally must be.

Returning to New Brunswick, we gave a concert, which was profitable in a small way. We then went to New York, and spent a week with a cousin of mine, Mrs. Card, residing in Pearl Street. My funds again running low, I thought it high time to be doing something to recruit them. I took a shop in Hudson Street, and purchased (on credit) a lot of earthen-ware, which occupied, and nearly filled all the shelves; and agreed with a Mr. Sage to sell books and music on commission. This Mr. Sage had a tremendous bass voice, and could reach double C with the greatest ease. Of Mr. Silas Harvey, an old friend of our family, I borrowed the sum of twenty dollars, and of a Mr. Childs, a baker in Hudson Street, also an old friend, and member of the New Jerusalem Church, I borrowed a bed, two chairs, and a few other articles of furniture. At the back of the shop was a room eight by twelve feet in size, in which we lived; and I now declare, that for a couple of months I have never been more happy. Our means were slender enough, it is true, and some days we were somewhat stinted in our eatables; but we were industrious, saving, attentive to business, and contented. The books sold slowly—I let a few of them out on hire—and I kept on my own account, independent of my "commission business," some toy-books and fruit. The stock of crockery-ware remained good, as I did not sell a single article. My little capital of twenty dollars could not last forever. With all my exertions to keep it good, it dwindled away, little by little, until I found myself nearly destitute again.

Mr. Simpson, manager of the Park Theatre, passed by my door every day, and after much rallying of my courage, I wrote and handed him a note, expressing my wishes to attach myself, in a situation ever so humble, to his establishment. Next day, as he passed, he handed me a note, stating that his company was full, and that he regretted it was not in his power to meet my wishes.

This season (1824) the CATARACT OF THE GANGES was brought out at the Park with great splendor. I went to see it once. At the Chatham Garden PIZARRO was the great card, and filled the house, for a great number of nights, to overflowing. Mr. Hughes played *Pizarro;* Mrs. Entwistle, *Elvira;* Messrs. Pelby, H. Wallack, and others, *Rolla.* At this theatre I had the pleasure—purchased for twenty-five cents, the price of a pit ticket—to witness the representation of the ROAD TO RUIN, with the following cast of characters:

Goldfinch (first time)..........Mr. G. H. Barrett.
Dornton......................Mr. Kilner.
Harry Dornton................Mr. H. Wallack.
Sulky.........................Mr. Burke.
Silky..........................Mr. Spiller.
Jacob.........................Mr. Simpson.
Milford.......................Mr. Moreland.
Hosier........................Mr. Allen.
Mr. Smith....................Mr. Somerville.
Sophia........................Mrs. Burke.
Widow Warren................Mrs. Walstein.
Jenny.........................

The afterpiece that night was the DAY AFTER THE WEDDING, the character of *Lady Elizabeth* being sustained by the beautiful Mrs. Henry, afterward Mrs. Barrett. I saw OTHELLO played, with H. Wallack in *Othello;* Finn, *Iago;* Barrett, *Cassio;* Mrs. Henry, *Desdemona.* The season at the Chatham was very successful.

Star-gazing in Broadway.

My friend the baker, who loaned me the bed and kitchen things, had a *telescope* of great magnifying power, which was a source of considerable profit to him. He was in the habit of taking it up to the corner of Broadway and Chambers Streets, and exhibiting the moon through it at sixpence a sight. His receipts were generally from two to three dollars a night. One evening he came to my door with the telescope on his shoulders, and, setting it down while he rested himself, complained of a severe headache. I told him if he did not feel well I would take his telescope up to his stand for him, and do the best I could, and he might return home. He thankfully accepted my offer, and said I should have half the receipts for my trouble. I accordingly shut up shop, shouldered the telescope, and marched off to the appointed spot. I had observed, on a former evening, when I had accompanied my friend, that considerable time had elapsed before he could get any one to look through the telescope; but after one or two had taken a peep, others ventured. I therefore, on *my* night, had scarcely planted the telescope on the sidewalk and raised it up, pointing it to the moon, before twenty boys were squabbling for the first peep. I had promised them all a sight *gratis*, and by this means a crowd was instantly collected to see what was going on; and before the *free-list* was half served, there were dozens waiting with their sixpences ready to "pay for peeping." I took good care, when a party of ladies and gentlemen were passing, to be lecturing on the appearance of the moon—how distinctly the *land* and *water* could be distinguished—remarked upon the fine appearance of the *volcanoes*, and spoke of the *snow* that could be seen upon the tops of the *mountains*—all of which was eagerly caught at by the crowd. Business was very good for two hours, after which it suddenly fell off, for then the *moon went down!* My fortunes were suddenly obscured; an *eclipse* had taken place, and I was in the dark. It was but ten o'clock, and I tried to rally the crowd by telling them the evening-star presented a fine appearance through the telescope; but it would not do. They deserted me. I had not counted my sixpences; but my pockets felt pretty heavy, and I was far from being dissatisfied with my two hours' work; so, shouldering the instrument of my momentary good fortune, I wended my way homeward. As I was passing through Leonard Street, I met three men, who proved to be a captain of a vessel and two of his sailors. They hailed me, and demanded what sort of craft I had in tow. I told them it was a powerful telescope, with which I had been viewing the *stars* (I knew the *moon* was out of the question, and had been for at least half an hour). "The stars! I say, shipmate, let's have a squint at them stars." "Certainly, sir; six cents a squint." "Very well. I say, capt'n, and Jack, let's have eighteen pence worth of stars. Up with your jury-mast." "Yes." "That's it—steady!" "What star will you have, gentlemen?" "Capt'n, what star will *you* have?" "What star? why, let's see—Venus!" "Oh yes! Wenus, by all means." I raised up the telescope, and pointed it to the brightest star I could find, and when I had turned the screws to regulate the focus, they commenced star-gazing. After satisfying themselves with *Wenus*, they wanted to see *Saturn*, *Jupiter*, and a host of others. I gratified them, at sixpence each, until the receipts from my nautical customers amounted to three dollars! They were very tipsy, and I believe they would have given me their custom until daylight if I would have consented to stay with them. When they had viewed a great many planets and fixed stars, my astronomical knowledge began to give out, and I was obliged to show the *same planets* two or three times over, taking care to change the focus so as to give them a different appearance. It was nearly one o'clock in the morning. I proposed to my customers to close the exhibition, which they reluctantly agreed to; not, however, until I consented, in consideration of their being liberal patrons, to "throw in" a *couple of planets* for good measure. Next morning I divided with my friend the baker *eighteen dollars and sixty-two cents!*

At length my capital entirely gave out. Cold weather was coming on, and I thought it full time to look out for winter quarters. A proposition was made to my landlord to receive back the crockery-ware. Mr. Sage received his books. My landlord received a note for the rent, and I removed to New Brunswick, and took a furnished room from one of my wife's grand-aunts. What to do for bread and butter I did not know. Another concert was out of the question, my wife not being able to assist. At length, learning that Mr. Fitz-Randolph, editor of the "Fredonian," was a member-elect of the State Senate, and that he would necessarily be in attendance on the Legislature at Trenton nearly three months, I offered my services as editor during his absence, and was engaged at six dollars per week—to commence about Christmas, a month from the time when the contract was made. I felt perfectly satisfied with this arrangement as regarded the future, but it was a matter of some difficulty to know how we were to subsist until Christmas. My money was all gone, and I always had an indescribable horror of being considered poor *when I was so*. Indeed, I believe I would suffer from hunger a long time before I would let any one know I was in need of a dinner. It may be called a foolish pride—I believe it *is*—but I can not help it. When I have been induced to apply for loans of money, I have generally been refused. If I had been willing to let it be known that I was in need, I could probably have found something to do that would have afforded us the means to obtain bread; but I was ambitious to be thought independent.

One day I went to the printing-office and printed a few hand-bills, announcing to the inhabitants of [*blank*] that Mr. Sol. Smith, from the Philadelphia and Western theatres, would give a *concert of vocal music* on [*blank*] evening, to consist of a great variety of sentimental (!) and comic songs, price of admission twenty-five cents. With these bills, and a bundle containing some music-books, a pair of breeches, and a red wig, I embarked on board a steam-boat for Perth Amboy. I had previously borrowed a York shilling of my grand-aunt-in-law to pay my passage. I arrived at Amboy in the evening, and issued my bills for the next night. The people did not know what to make of it. The next night came, and seven people (men and boys) came also. The room was lighted, the tickets given at the door, and I began my songs. I never felt less disposed to sing—but I was in hopes my receipts would at least pay the tavern bill. It was a very cold night; and after I had sung two or three songs, my auditors proposed I should come and *sit with them by the fire*, which invitation I accepted very willingly (as I saw there was plenty of room), and finished my concert with my heels cocked up over the fireplace! Next morning I found my receipts would not satisfy my landlord's bill, there being a deficiency of more than a dollar. The landlord very generously offered to let me go to New York and borrow the money, loaning me a shilling to pay my passage thither, provided I left my baggage with him in pledge. As the steam boat passed I got on board, and at five o'clock P.M. I was in New York. I immediately went to Mr. William Mathews, my wife's uncle, a rich grocer, and told him my situation. He listened very attentively, and seemed quite sorry for me, but made no offer. After waiting an hour or so, I "screwed my courage to the sticking-place," and asked him for a loan of five dollars. He humm'd and ha'd a moment, and *declined!*

I was doomed to another disappointment. There was an auctioneer in the city whom I will call *Wiggins*. The year previously he had been in Cincinnati, and many civilities had passed between us. He had been a contributor to my paper; we were on terms of familiarity, and he had frequently said, if business ever called me to New York, he hoped I would command his services. On my arrival in the summer I called on him; he appeared pleased to see me, inquired about Cincinnati, and when he found I had abandoned the "*press*," advised me to establish a paper in New York, at the same time promising me his custom and influence in the way of auction advertisements. While I was carrying on my little shop in Hudson Street he called on me twice, and always expressed great anxiety for my welfare and prosperity. Was I wrong in thinking this man would befriend me, so far as to give me the use of *five dollars* for a month? After a severe struggle with my pride, I went into his auction-room; it was crowded with people, for he had a night-sale. I could not get an opportunity to speak to him, so I wrote him a note, of which the following is a copy:

"MR. WIGGINS: DEAR SIR,—I am in immediate want of *five dollars*. Will you loan it to me?

"P.S.—I can not return it under a month.

"Yours, SOL. SMITH.

"Tuesday evening."

In about an hour, seeing I did not leave the room, he wrote the following answer:

"MR. SMITH,—Times are hard, and money scarce. I find it difficult to carry on my business. However, if you will *give me security*, I will oblige you with the loan you ask.

"Yours, etc., —— WIGGINS."

It was half past ten o'clock when I received this answer. My first impulse was to tear it to pieces, and throw the fragments into the writer's face; but when I got into the cool air the question occurred to me, "Where shall I sleep to-night?" I reflected that I had already humbled myself as much as possible, and that my only chance was to comply with Wiggins's terms. I walked (or rather ran) from the auction store, which was in some street east of Broadway, to the house of my friend, the owner of the telescope, in Hudson Street, awakened him, wrote a note, signed, and asked him to endorse it, which he readily did. Hastening back to the auction store, I was told Wiggins had retired. I persuaded the shop-boy to take him a letter, in which I inclosed the indorsed note, naming the address of the indorser, and in about an hour after received a letter inclosing a five dollar bill, with an apology for putting me to so much trouble, but really times were so hard, and all that, etc., etc. It may be wondered at that while at the baker's (the owner of the telescope) I did not ask *him* for the money. I can scarcely tell *why* I did not *give him the preference;* probably I felt some little pride to show Wiggins there was at least one man in the city who had confidence in me. Perhaps I thought the worthy baker was unable to spare the money; or, what is more likely, I did not wish to let my destitute situation be known to him, after meeting with such rebuffs from two individuals; for I recollect I trumped up a story to the telescope-man that the note was for the accommodation of an acquaintance of mine, to whom I was willing to loan the money, but had it not with me. Well, I got the money, and went to the City Hotel and slept. In the morning, after paying six shillings for my lodging, I embarked on board a steam-boat at six o'clock, touched at Perth Amboy, paid my landlord his money, and returned to New Brunswick.

I was very impatient for the time to arrive when I should begin my task in the newspaper office. It was a custom with me to pass a portion of my time in the editorial room, being fond of reading the news. The carrier, or *devil*, as he is technically termed, wished me to write a New-Year's address, offering me one half of the proceeds of sale. I declined, for the simple reason that I had never perpetrated a rhyme in my life.

When within about a week of the time my editorial services were to begin, I took it into my head (not having the fear of failure before my eyes) to give a vocal concert (a *concert* with one performer!) at Elizabethtown. Having a few of my bills left, off I went in a steam-boat, and, arriving about noon, advertised my performance for the same night. This concert was attended by *five persons.* I had here the advantage of a piano, on which I accompanied myself in some of my *sentimental* songs. Only imagine, my Southern and Western friends, "Old Sol" singing sentimental songs!

Next morning, saying I had business in New York city (and so I had!), I told my landlord I would call on my return and settle my bill, at the same time asking him to *permit my trunk to remain,* with which request he very willingly complied. Arrived in the city, I went to a lottery-office with a quarter ticket I had purchased some months previously, which I sold at a small discount, and in this way raised one dollar and fifty cents. Hastening back to Elizabethtown, I discharged my bill, leaving myself not one cent with which to pay my passage back to Brunswick. It was no time for ceremony. I embarked on the first boat, trusting to Providence for the means of paying for the trip. Providence sent relief in the shape of a very clever young man who had formed a fifth part of my audience at the concert, and who was traveling for the purpose of obtaining subscribers to some periodical. He had seen some numbers of my Cincinnati paper, and seemed anxious to cultivate an acquaintance with me. While we were busy discussing some literary subject, the bell rang as a signal that it was time for the passenger-money to be paid. It appeared to me that it was *tolling* rather than ringing. I moved not, neither did my companion move. Pretty soon the clerk came bustling along, taking the shillings. He approached us —my literary friend handed him a quarter, and his hand remained extended, waiting for the change. Now was my time—life or death. "Let him keep it," I stammered out; "I will hand you the shilling." "Certainly," said he, and the thing was settled for the present, and we continued the conversation as if there had been no interruption. I presume but few of my readers can appreciate my feelings on this occasion; I can only say, my face burned like a coal of fire, and that it seems to me I would sooner submit to being shot by a file of soldiers than go through the same scene again. Yet there was nothing to create such a feeling. Nothing is more common (even among strangers) than making the very request I made; yet the fact of my having no cash in my pocket made me feel like a criminal. People may talk of the worthlessness of money—of its being the "root of all evil," and all that sort of thing; I say it is the talisman which unlocks all hearts; the balsam that heals all wounds; the creator of respect, esteem, friendship, love! Without it, a man is neglected, abandoned, and scorned; *with* it, he springs into rank, is courted, fawned upon, worshiped. Talk of respect gained by a long course of good deeds, and honest actions, and just deportment! Give the veriest wretch MONEY enough, and he may discard all the virtues, and yet retain the respect and admiration of the world. Money worthless! Nonsense. I have seen it unchain a criminal; change the made-up opinion of juries; sway the judge. The priest pretends to be laboring for the good of the souls of his flock: he is not—he is laboring for his fifteen hundred dollars a year. The patriot blusters and storms at "the powers that be" only to get the place of another, and with it the salary. The player—but why particularize, where ALL are striving for money! money!! money!!! We continued in conversation until the boat touched the wharf at Brunswick, and, just as I was leaving my fellow-traveler, I mentioned that I would call at his lodgings in the course of an hour or two and pay him his shilling, for I happened just to discover *that I had no change about me* (I never told a greater truth). He gave me his address, and we parted; he to get subscribers, and I to get the shilling. Without seeing my wife, I went to the printing-office and inquired for the *devil.* He made his appearance, and I told him I was ready to come to an arrangement with him; in other words, I was willing to write his *New-Year's Address*, if he still wished it. He was much surprised at my changing my mind, but was delighted that I had concluded to undertake it. "But stop, my lad —what terms am I to write it on?" "Half the proceeds," proposed the boy. "That won't do," said I. "What will you give me, cash down, for the address, and you take all the risk and all the profits?" "Why, I don't know—I generally get five or six dollars, and sometimes eight." "Well, I'll strike a bargain with you: give me three dollars, and I'll write your address." "Done!" said the devil, and away he flew to borrow the money of his brother-in-law. Being desperate, I went to work at making rhymes. I happened to know many local events which had latterly transpired, and I bundled them all in, higgledy-piggledy; touched off the presidential question; boarded the steam-boat lines; dug into the oyster-planting scheme; suggested action for the Legislature, and mixed up some few personal matters, which altogether formed forty-two lines. The boy returned in twenty-five minutes. "There are your three dollars," said he, handing me the money. "There's your address," replied I, giving him the scribbling. I need not tell the reader that the shilling was pretty soon paid to my traveling companion. I then went home and related my mishaps to my wife, and she laughed heartily at my manner of getting out of the difficulty, never having suspected me of possessing the smallest spark of poetic genius.

The sequel to this little affair was highly gratifying to my feelings. New-Year's day arrived, and the carrier came home in the evening, joy beaming in his ruddy countenance, and told me the *address* had produced a receipt of *thirty-six dollars*—thirty more than he usually received on similar occasions! The grateful boy insisted that I should receive *half*, according to his first offer; but I could see no justice in doing so, and of course refused.

The boy's name was Melancthon Carman. If he has not proved to be a good man, I was no prophet in 1824.

By the time I had expended the three dollars, I took possession of my new situation in the printing-office, and was comparatively easy in my circumstances. The first thing I did was to send the five dollars to my *generous friend* Wiggins, some days before it was due.

During my residence in New Brunswick I had formed many acquaintances, particularly with church-going people. This arose from the fact that I played the organ occasionally in the Episcopal church. There was a singing-school in the place, and, being invited by the teacher, I attended one evening, when it was discovered that I could *read music!* This was looked upon as a wonderful accomplishment, and I was immediately offered a school, if I would take one. I declined; but told the young gentleman who applied to me (William Duryie) that if gentlewomen and gentlemen, to the number of twelve of each, would form themselves into a class, I would very cheerfully devote one evening in each week to their instruction in the science of music, confining their practice to anthems and set pieces, and leaving the singing-master in undisputed possession of the psalm tunes and hymns. This was joyfully acceded to, and the class formed, with the understanding that, in consideration of my instructions, they were to sing for me *one night* at a select oratorio. We accordingly had meetings every Wednesday night, and my scholars were soon so far advanced in their musical education that they were proud to invite their friends to the meetings. It must be remembered that no one had any idea that I was connected with *the stage*. If they had known I was an actor, my reception and treatment in New Brunswick would most likely have been widely different. My pupils improved apace, and I only waited for my wife's recovery, after her confinement, to give my oratorio. I proposed to give one third of the receipts to a charitable institution.

In the mean time politics raged high. The President was to be elected by the House of Representatives, the electoral colleges having failed to make a choice. The struggle was soon over —HENRY CLAY decided the contest. He threw his vote and powerful influence into Adams's end of the scale, and Adams became the President. At this time began the great political struggle which ended in the election of Andrew Jackson BY THE PEOPLE in 1828.

But to leave politics, with which in these pages I have nothing to do, let me return to my winter quarters in New Jersey, where my twenty-four scholars have so far progressed as to be nearly ready for the oratorio. In New York I engaged a few musicians. Mrs. Smith recovered from her illness, and took her place as principal soprano; the oratorio was advertised and performed. The receipts, beyond all expenses, were upward of *one hundred dollars!* What a windfall! Considering that the price of tickets was only twenty-five cents each, the amount must be considered very large. I inclosed a third of the proceeds to the charitable institution named in the bills, and the next day it was returned, with a note of thanks from the gentlewoman who presided over it, saying that their funds were amply sufficient for the purposes of the institution. I paid off my debts in New Brunswick, and made preparations to depart. Our intention was to make our way to the Western country; but first, being now in rather better trim than I had been the fall before, I resolved on making another and last "desperate offer" of my services to Mr. Simpson, of the Park Theatre.

Attiring myself in my best suit, I went to New York, where I took cheap lodgings, and for three several days pondered on the best mode to prefer my request to the metropolitan manager. On the fourth day, about eleven o'clock A.M., I went boldly up to the box-office, where I found Mr. Price. I asked for Mr. Simpson. (It is probable, if Mr. Simpson had been there, I should have asked for Mr. Price.) "He was on the stage; had I any business?" "Yes; wished to see him particularly; would call again." "Very well." At two P.M. I saw Mr. Simpson go into the office, and, marching boldly up the steps, I made known my wishes. Mr. Simpson smiled at my apparent confusion, and said if I would call about four o'clock he would then have leisure to talk with me. The time from two to four was passed by me in the most feverish anxiety. Punctual to my appointment, I called at the theatre, and was told that Mr.

Simpson was on the stage, and would be glad to see me there. He received me kindly, but I soon found that there was no hope for me. My pretensions were of the most moderate kind. I was willing, and told Mr. Simpson so, to engage as chorus-singer at *six dollars per week*, and to make myself "generally useful" on the stage. He did not want chorus-singers then. After much consideration and walking up and down, he said all he could do for me was to give me a chance in his company connected with the Circus, then performing in Philadelphia under the management of Mr. Cowell. The *chance* was this: his principal tragedian and melo-dramatic performer had just left, or was about leaving, and they were in want of a *Timour!* I could have a trial in that part, and, *if successful*, would be placed upon the salary list. I had just learned enough of my profession to be sure of my unfitness for tragedy, and declined the attempt as hopeless. Mr. Simpson, who really seemed anxious to do something for me, finding I would not answer his purpose, very kindly dismissed me, proffering me the freedom of the house while I remained in the city.

In 1835, while performing a starring engagement at the Park Theatre, I recalled this interview to the memory of Mr. Simpson. He laughed heartily at the remembrance of my embarrassment, and good-naturedly said, "Well, Mr. Smith, it is probably a lucky thing for you I declined your services; *you have, doubtlessly, done better.*" Well, I had.

CHAPTER III.

FINDING there was no hopes of an engagement in the metropolis, I applied for and obtained a situation in the company of Mr. H. A. Williams, then about to commence a circuit in the western towns of New York. My salary was to be eight dollars per week. I took leave of my New Brunswick friends, who had been very kind to me and mine, and proceeded to Albany, where I joined my new manager. Our company performed three nights in Schenectady, and about a fortnight in the town of Little Falls with tolerable success; after which we took up our summer quarters at Utica, where we converted a circus into a theatre. I soon became convinced that my *nine dollars* a week (for my salary had been raised to that sum) would not support my family, and the little fund, the proceeds of my winter's exertions, was fast melting away. In this emergency my wife consented to go on the stage. She made her first appearance as *Norah* in the POOR SOLDIER. How far she succeeded as an actress, and to what eminence she attained in her profession, the Southern public can better say than it becomes me to write; but this much I will aver, being the best judge of the matter—there were two characters she sustained to admiration, those of a faithful WIFE and MOTHER.

From Utica we went to Saratoga Springs, where we made a season of eight or ten weeks. *De Witt Clinton* attended my benefit at this place.

It was here that I got even with my New York friend Wiggins. He was at the Springs on a visit, and had, in a gambling scrape, lost all his money. He came to me, and asked me to loan him a hundred dollars, which I did, borrowing the money for the purpose, and taking his own bill, without an endorser, for the amount. When I handed him the money, he began to express his gratitude in very strong terms, but I cut him short. "Wiggins," said I, "being in great pecuniary distress, I once asked you to loan me five dollars; you consented, on condition that my bill for the amount should be *indorsed* by a good man in the city. *You* now happen to be pushed, and ask a loan of *me;* there is the money; my obligation to you for the loan in New York I consider canceled. Wiggins, I have done with you." And so I had, for I have never seen or heard of him since, though it is but an act of justice to say that his bill was duly honored.

Learning, on our return to Utica, that the projected new theatre would not be ready for us in less than two months, we visited some of the small towns, Syracuse and Auburn among the rest. At the latter place my wife and myself withdrew from the company of Williams, and proceeded to Rochester, where we had been invited by the manager. We performed during the season, and had good benefits. At this place I sung the "Hunters of Kentucky" forty-one nights, and on the last night *forgot some of the words*, and was prompted from the boxes! We next went into Upper Canada, where I took an interest of one half in the management of a temporary theatre, and lost what little I had scraped together during the summer. Our first essay in his majesty's dominions was at Niagara, where our performance was interrupted by a dozen well-dressed fellows, who took a room immediately adjoining ours, and amused themselves and annoyed us by roaring out "God save the King," "Rule Britannia," and other loyal tunes. All this was done because they could not obtain admission to our performance at *half price!* We sent a remonstrance, but our messenger was treated with insult, and they declared unequivocally that their intention was to drive off the d—d Yankee vagabond actors. We finished our play and farce, and then proceeded to the bar-room in a body, determined to "thrash them," for our American blood was up. The party soon heard of our intention, and, re-enforcing their number with three or four boat hands—I will not call them boat *men*—some half-breed Indians, and a couple of negroes, they came upon us, armed with clubs and bludgeons. Our little band met the attack manfully; but it was a hard battle, and was going against us, when a large, fat, red-faced Englishman—he *was* an Englishman, the others were *colonists*—rushed in between the combatants, and, bellowing forth the word "Stop!" all desisted for a moment. "What the h—ll is all this rumpus about?" asked John Bull. "We are going to whip the d—d Yankees," responded twenty voices. "Upon 'em, lads!" and they were coming upon us like a hurricane, when John again interposed his "Stop!" Another pause. "You say you are going to whip the d—d Yankees"—here off went his coat—"and you are twenty to twelve"—his handkerchief. "These are Yankees, and you pretend to be Englishmen" —waistcoat—"whoever heard of an Englishman taking odds against an enemy? Stop! hear me out; what, you are determined, are you? Very well, boys, just as you please. I fought against the Yankees during the war (d—n me if I think any of *you* did!). I am a true Englishman; these Yankees are STRANGERS on our shores, and therefore entitled to kindness and protection. *You* are twenty, without the niggers; *they* are twelve. Boys (addressing us), do your best; I am on your side, and you are now a 'baker's dozen!'" The parties met. The Englishman dealt his blows right and left, and fought like a hero, as he was; and the colonists, sailors, lords, half-breeds, and negroes were routed!

We took passage in a schooner for Little York (now Toronto), where we made a most miserable season. Our bills were printed by Mr. Mackenzie, afterward so notorious for the part he took in the Canada rebellion.

In the hopes of bettering our business, and at the urgent solicitation of my partner in the management, I consented to accompany him to the governor's house to "request a bespeak." It was very much against the grain, I assure you; but I had been told a "bespeak" from "his excellency" would fill the theatre; and I felt it was my duty, for the sake of the company, if not for my own sake, to lay aside my republican pride on the occasion. After we had cooled our heels for the best part of two hours in an anteroom, an adjutant, or major, or something appeared, and wished to be favored with our business. I told him we wished to see the governor on a matter of importance. Receiving our names, he left us waiting another half hour. At length we were told the governor would see us, and we were conducted into the great man's presence. There were thirteen or fourteen people in the room, all whispering in corners, and looking like so many scared rabbits. My partner having pushed me forward as the speaker, I began: "Several citizens having suggested that you would like to visit the theatre if a box were fitted up for your reception, we are come, Mr. Maitland, to know when—" "You may save yourself farther trouble, *Mister* Smith," interrupted his excellency, "I do *not* wish to visit your theatre; when I do, I will make my pleasure known; good-morning." "But, Mr. Maitland, I was told—" "But, *Mister* Smith, I do not wish to hear any more on the subject." And he bowed us out of the room. "Confound your republican notions!" whispered my partner, as we sneaked along the hall to the street door, "that cursed *Mister* of yours has ruined all!" "Why, what ought I to have said?" I inquired. "*Your excellency*, of course, or your *lordship*, or your highness," replied he. "Well," I remarked, "this is the first time I ever invited any of the nobility to visit the theatre, and, please God, it shall be the last!" And it was.

The once celebrated Jack Dwyer was at this place teaching elocution. One night he came to the theatre in company with about thirty gentlemen of the place, who were, like himself, "full of wine." We had dismissed our audience that night (two men and a boy), but the jovial party insisted we should light up and go through with the performance, for which they would give us thirty dollars. We consented, and played the BROKEN SWORD, and some afterpiece. Having no painter attached to the company, we were at a loss how to make a bust of the murdered *Luneda.* Several had tried their hands at it and failed. As a last resort, I directed a Mr. Thomas to *whiten his face*, wrap a sheet around him, and stand up behind the pedestal. This answered the purpose very well. He did *move* a little occasionally, it is true, but the auditors thought the appearance of moving was caused by the wine they had been drinking. Between the pieces several tunes were called for—"God Save the King," "Rule Britannia," "Auld Lang Syne," "Exile of Erin," "*Hail Columbia*," and "*Yankee Doodle.*" According to custom, the audience stood uncovered while the British national tune was being performed; and, from mere playfulness, a Captain Matthews insisted that the same ceremony should be observed while the orchestra were playing "Hail Columbia." Some objected, and several hats were knocked off; but I considered it all a joke, and so, I believe, did all the persons concerned in it. I was not a little surprised, two or three years afterward, to see in a London paper at least a dozen columns occupied by an account of the trial of Captain Matthews for his share in the frolic!

Our next town was Ancaster, at the head of Lake Ontario. Here was a Thespian society, which had been in existence about two years. Two hundred pounds had been subscribed by the members for purchasing scenery, wardrobe, and books. The association met one night in each month for rehearsal, their first play intended for performance being SHE STOOPS TO CONQUER. They had met probably twenty times, and never had progressed in the rehearsal farther than the second scene in the comedy, for the following reason: The landlord of the hotel where the meetings were held was cast for the landlord in the play, and furnished the Thespians with *real* *liquor*, and that of the very best kind, so that, before the actors could get through the scene, they were *too tipsy* to proceed any farther, and generally broke up in a row. I learned these particulars from one of the members, who came to request we would perform that comedy, which we did, receiving three hearty cheers when we got through the first act.

The company next proceeded to Rochester, where we performed with indifferent success for a month, and then to Auburn. Here we opened the theatre with DAMON AND PYTHIAS. I remember the opening play from this circumstance: My partner, who was stage manager, came to me just before the time of beginning, and asked me to take a look at the supernumeraries, and say how I liked their dresses. I looked, and behold! he had twelve strapping fellows drawn up for my inspection, dressed in Roman shirts, and with *bare legs!* Not having sandals prepared, he permitted them to wear their own coarse brogans, and as they stood ranged on the stage, stooping down to make the shirts reach below the knee, their appearance was irresistibly

SYRACUSAN SENATORS AND SOLDIERS.

ludicrous. Instead of the burst of admiration Davis expected, I gave way to a fit of laughter, assuring him it would not do to let them appear before the audience in that plight. "Why not?" argued the stage director; "no one can deny that it is the correct costume; the fleshings which are usually worn are intended to represent the *bare flesh*, and here I have the *real thing*, natural as life." I would not be convinced, and the curtain could not be raised until the Syracusan senators had time to make themselves fit to be seen in the senate-chamber.

Leaving the company in charge of my partner, I returned to Rochester, and superintended the fitting up of a new theatre next door to the Mansion House, and near the canal. On my way I was mistaken for General Jackson, and treated with a great deal of attention by the passengers. In due time we opened our new establishment, and for a time succeeded tolerably well; but, becoming dissatisfied with my partner, I withdrew, leaving him the whole concern. I intended to set out immediately for the Western country, but my quondam manager, Williams, offering us excellent terms to remain a few weeks with him in his new theatre, just about opening, I entered into an engagement. I remember our bringing out the (then) new comedy of SWEETHEARTS AND WIVES, in which I played *Billy Lackaday* six successive nights, and for my benefit on the seventh. Mr. Maywood performed an engagement with us this season—a very successful one. It was here I first met Mr. John Bates, afterward a millionaire, and proprietor of a theatre in Cincinnati. He was barkeeper of Williams's new Rochester theatre.

CHAPTER IV.

AT the close of my engagement I got together a few people, and formed a small traveling company, intending to play our way to Cincinnati. I shall not attempt to describe this truly strolling expedition, but content myself with touching lightly on a very few of the incidents attending it. Our little party performed in Lockport, Black Rock, Niagara Falls, Fredonia, Westfield, Mayville, and Jamestown. Near the latter place we breakfasted with a man who believed he should *live forever!* He had been in the habit, for several years, of making *burnt-offerings* of cattle, sheep, fowls, dogs, and cats, and he told me it was his intention, some day, to offer up one of his children! He had only delayed making this last sacrifice because the Almighty had not yet told him *which* child would be the most acceptable! So firm was the old man in the belief that he would never die, he gave one hundred pounds (two hundred and fifty dollars) for the insertion of a clause, in a deed of a farm which he sold to a neighbor, entitling him (the long-lived) to re-enter and take possession of the land at the end of nine hundred and ninety-nine years, provided he came *personally* to claim it! I have not heard of this singular madman since. He may be living, and likely to live, for aught I know. If he *can* live forever, I am sure I have no objection.

The murderous Alleghanians.

At Warren our little company embarked on board two large skiffs, prepared for the purpose, and floated down the beautiful Alleghany. Proceeding on our journey, the boat or skiff containing the young men of the company was considerably in advance of us, with the understanding that if they came to a town worth "taking," they were to leave a flag flying on the bank of the river as a signal that the town was taken, or, in other words, that they had made arrangements to perform there. Toward night, on the third day, a storm threatened, and we saw no shelter at hand. The night thickened upon us, the lightning flashed, and the thunder muttered at a distance, warning us to seek a shelter. There were five of us in our little bark—Mr. and Mrs. Francisco, Mrs. Smith, our child, and myself. We held a consultation, and came to the conclusion we would run the boat ashore, strike a light, and fortify ourselves as well as we could against the storm and wild beasts. Just as we were about heading for the shore, a light was discovered some distance below, which gave assurance that a dwelling of some kind was near, and we pulled for it with all our strength. When arrived opposite the light we hallooed, and after a short pause received a "halloo" in answer. In a moment more the boat touched the land, and three stout, ugly-looking fellows welcomed us ashore. We had heard of banditti infesting these wilds, and appearances were not very favorable to our hosts. They seemed, as we thought, rather too anxious to accommodate us, assuring us that there was not another house short of fourteen miles! Mr. F. and myself, with our wives, and little Frank (that was my son's name), proceeded to the cottage, a few rods up a steep bank of the river, the three men carrying our trunks on their shoulders. "The devil!" muttered one, "they have a smart chance of plunder!" "Yes," replied another, "these boxes are confounded heavy; wonder which of 'em's got the specie in it?" In the cottage we found a female, who did not seem at all pleased with our visit. While we were seeing that our luggage was all safe, we could hear the woman expostulating with her husband, telling him they had no accommodations for travelers, no provisions in the house, nor any place for them to sleep. "Oh, never mind," answered the eldest of the three rob—the three cottagers, who really appeared good-natured and accommodating, albeit he had a monstrous black look, his face seeming to have *cut* all acquaintance with razors and soap—"we shall get along well enough. Bring some more pine knots, boys, and let's have a rousing fire." His commands were almost instantly obeyed, and a bright pine-knot fire imparted a cheerfulness to the scene, which for the time banished all gloomy apprehensions. Somehow or other, the women had from the beginning taken the idea into their heads that our entertainers were robbers—which idea the reader will have entertained ere this—and, indeed, their rough and uncouth appearance seemed fully to justify the supposition.

We seated ourselves by the fireside, and the three men and the woman began to consult about supper and lodging. We could catch a sentence or two of their colloquy occasionally, which did not serve to quiet the rising fears of the females of our party. "What success had you this evening?" asked the younger *boy.* "None at all," answered the father: "havn't killed a *living* crittur to-night, though I've been watching ever since dark. I came very near *knocking over* one fine fellow, but he was alarmed at the hallooing of these strangers, and made his escape before I could get a *crack* at him." "Thank heaven," whispered Mrs. F., "we have been the means of saving a fellow-creature's life!" "How are we to provide for these people?" asked the woman of the house. "That will be easy enough," answered her husband, "if the men-folks will consent to be *separated from their wives.* Let the two women and the child have your bed (for, poor things, I pity *them*), and we will find a *resting-place* for the men, never fear." "A resting-place!" groaned Mr. F.; "I dare say you will." "Dick and Pete," continued the old man, addressing the *boys*—their consultation being ended—"take the spade and that basket, and do as I told you." The two sons obeyed, first supplying themselves with a torch of pine. The two females, having by this time persuaded themselves we were all to be made mince-meat of, insisted that we should leave the house. In their alarm they were heartily joined by Mr. F., who could see nothing but "dagger, rope, and ratsbane" in the looks of our entertainers. He proposed to reconnoitre the proceedings of the "*boys,*" who had gone out, as he supposed, to *dig our graves.* Concealing himself behind a sort of natural hedge, he had an opportunity of seeing their operations and hearing their conversation, himself unobserved. They were *turning up the fresh earth,* and their dialogue was as follows—we being, evidently, the subject of their discourse: "This will be quite a windfall for us; these strangers seem to be rich, and will pay us well for our trouble." "Yes; how cursed heavy that black trunk of theirs is; they must be *very* rich." "I am sorry we can't give 'em better fare than what we are *providing for them!*" "Oh, never mind the fare; their *lodging* will be rather rough, to be sure, but they will be *sound asleep* in a couple of hours, and to-morrow it will make no difference to them what they sup on, or how rough their lodging is to-night." "Sound asleep!" thought poor F.; "no sound sleep for us this night; we'll not go to bed and get our throats cut!" By this time the *boys* had finished their digging, and they prepared to return to the cottage. Francisco hastened back before them, and related what he had overheard. We were watching the cottager and his wife, whose movements appeared suspicious. The women renewed their entreaties that we would leave the place at once, and abandon our property to the brigands; but before we could decide how to act, the cottagers were heard returning. "There," said the elder son, throwing down the spade, and handing a basket to his mother, "that job's over; we've finished our digging; if father's killed the *crittur,* we shall soon be through our night's work." At this moment the father appeared at the door, with his hands and garments *covered with blood,* a ghastly smile on his ugly countenance, and *holding a bloody knife in his hand!* "Here, boys," he bawled out, "I've *cut his throat;* come and help me drag him up!" The sons went out to assist the old cut-throat in his *bloody business.* We presently heard them return, and saw through the open door they were *bearing a dead body!* The blood curdled in our veins as we sat staring at each other, not knowing how to act. By this time the woman had placed a large kettle on the fire. The old man and his hopeful *boys* were employed *cutting up the dead body* outside the door, mingling with their occupation remarks like the following: "What a pity to kill the poor fellow!" "people must eat;" "if travelers call at our house, they must be *provided for;*" "it does go against my grain to *kill one so young!*" * *

Notwithstanding the dangers that surrounded us, I fell into a doze in the chimney-corner, and visions of blood and murder passed rapidly before my closed eyes. The two *boys* had me by the throat; the old sinner of a landlord held a knife at my breast, while he seized me by the hair; the fatal knife was raised, and the blow about to fall; suddenly I sprang from my seat, shook off my intended murderers, and was preparing for a desperate defense, when the old man exclaimed, "Stranger, SUPPER'S READY." I rubbed my eyes, and, staring about the room, saw our party seated at the table, with every trace of fear banished from their countenances. "Come, stranger, take this *cheer* [chair] at the head of the table, and help your people. You will find these potatoes, which the *boys have dug for you*, first rate. My wife has made a piece of the *lamb we killed* into a stew. I should have given you some venison, but your hallooing frightened off a fine buck I was about getting a *crack* at. My old woman here objects to my killing the young mutton, but I was determined you should have the best we could get you. So come; sit up, and eat hearty." It is unnecessary to say we did full justice to our good cheer. After an excellent night's rest, we paid our bill, which was quite reasonable, and floated on our way.

A Theatre in the Woods.

I have said the young men of the company who preceded us in our downward course were to display a flag as a signal to us whenever they had "taken a town." One day we discovered a white handkerchief flying at the end of a pole on the river-bank, where there was not a house (much less a *town*) to be seen. We obeyed the signal and pulled to the shore; but there was nobody to meet us. After waiting half an hour, and concluding we were hoaxed, it was agreed we should pursue our way down the river. We had not proceeded more than twenty rods when we saw the boat of our companions lying high and dry upon the shore. This convinced us that the party was not far off, and we accordingly made another halt. Before we reached the land we were hailed from the top of a high bluff—"Halloo! the boat! Pull ashore; this is the town you are to stop at; your actors are up at my house waiting for you!" The person who spoke soon came down to us, and, sure enough, we found we were advertised to perform that same night at Lewiston. "Yes," continued the man, whose name was Cartwright, "it's all fixed—look at the bills *posted on the trees*—you'll have a good house; the citizens are delighted with your visit." He had a conveyance (a one-horse wagon) for the women and child, and Francisco and myself walked up the hill in search of the town of Lewiston. But no town could we see. "Oh, you are looking for the houses! Bless ye, they are not *built* yet; but we *shall* have some splendid buildings shortly. Here is Broadway; Wall Street runs down in this direction; and do you see the blazed tree yonder? there's *to be* our court-house; and a little beyond, the jail. Oh, Lewiston is destined to be a place." Thus spoke our guide and landlord as he drove his little wagon through the but partially cleared paths toward his house. We arrived at length, and found our party very comfortably situated in a double log cabin, which was literally covered with playbills, which playbills most respectfully announced to the inhabitants of Lewiston and vicinity that Mr. Sol. Smith and his dramatic company would perform on such an evening the comic opera of the POOR SOLDIER, with the afterpiece of LOVERS' QUARRELS. I scarcely knew what to think of the whole proceeding. An audience seemed to me out of the question. Where they were to come from I could not imagine. "Come up and look at the theatre," invitingly spoke the landlord, when he had introduced our wives to his wife. I followed him up stairs. "You see we have fitted up this room pretty neatly," said he—and so they had. The room was twelve by sixteen, and the scenery and curtain were rigged up in one end of it—while three large benches represented the boxes and pit. Whether it was all a joke, or whether the man was mad, I did not stop to inquire, for dinner was announced, and there was "no mistake" in that; it was a first-rate one. We found that our landlord was a New Yorker, just settled in the new town of Lewiston, which he imagined would soon rise into a place of great consequence, and become the emporium of Lewis County. Being passionately fond of theatricals, and accidentally falling in with our pioneers the day before, ten miles above *the town*, he had persuaded them to stop and give an entertainment. Dinner over, we soon found it was really expected we should play; for the audience began to assemble from every direction—the men and women all coming on horseback. An unexpected difficulty now presented itself—*there was not a candle in the town*—that is, in the house! What was to be done? Night was coming on; we could not act in the dark, that was certain. The landlord hit upon an expedient at last. He tore up some linen, of which he made wicks, and, rolling them in tallow, soon made six decent candles. He thereupon took half a dozen large potatoes, and, boring holes in them, converted them into candlesticks, placing them on the floor in front of the curtain for *foot-lights!* He next called his neighbors up to the bar by proclamation, and told them the *box-office* was open. In ten minutes they were all supplied with tickets (mostly on a credit), and he proceeded to *open the doors*—acting himself as door-keeper—informing all who entered that *checks* were *not transferable*, and no smoking was allowed in any part of the theatre—"*and*, gentlemen, no admission behind the scenes under any pretense whatever!" When our audience was seated, he announced the fact to us, and admonished us that the curtain was advertised to rise at "eight o'clock precisely." In our narrow quarters, a change of dress, after we once entered the theatre, was not to be thought of—there was no getting to the dressing-rooms without passing among the auditors—there being but one door to the room. So *Norah* and *Leonora*, being played by the same person, wore the same dress; and so with the other characters—*Patrick* and *Carlos*, *Darby* and *Sancho*, *Father Luke* and *Lopez*, *Kathleen* and *Jacinta*, etc. Mr. Cartwright was enthusiastic in his applause, declaring to his friends and neighbors that the performances were nearly equal to those at the Park—only in the latter establishment, he was free to admit, the scenery and decorations were a shade better than those of the Lewiston theatre. The benches being all occupied, he squatted himself down by the potato foot-lights, and, at intervals, amused himself by snuffing the candles. At length, one by one, the lights began to give out, and we were in danger of being left in total darkness! Observing the state of affairs, I thought it time to bring the farce to a close, which I did by cutting LOVERS' QUARRELS rather short, reconciling the parties in the middle of the piece, and speaking the "tag." Down came the curtain, and out went the last candle! The potatoes were all tenantless; so was the room in a few minutes, the auditors making their way down stairs the best way they could, highly delighted with their entertainment. Mr. Cartwright and his worthy wife soon raised a sort of lamp, constructed out of a piece of twisted linen and some hog's lard in a saucer, and after listening to our landlord's critical remarks on the whole performance, and discussing an excellent supper, we retired for the night.

Next morning, while breakfast was preparing, Mr. C. took me about *the town*, pointing out the different embryo streets and the sites for the public buildings—a *theatre* among the rest. His nearest neighbor resided at the distance of three miles, but he was sanguine in his expectations that Lewiston would *in time* be a great town. Well, it *may*, "in time;" but, I fear, not in Cartwright's time, nor in mine. The charge for dinner, supper, lodging, breakfast, and the theatre (including the *lighting* of the same) was a mere trifle, and we parted from our host with regret. He was a perfect original. "Farewell, Mr. Manager," said he; "hope you have been pleased with our town, and will visit Lewiston again next season, when I hope to have the new theatre finished for you."

We were persuaded to stop and perform for "one night only" at a village called Freeport. If one good or honest man resided there, I had not the pleasure of seeing him or hearing of him. A cabal was formed against us on account of the high price of admission, and the out-door audience, by far the more numerous, made up their minds to use the *window* for an entrance instead of the door. They procured a ladder, and one strapping fellow, mounting on it, made his appearance at the window just as I was singing "Good-morning to your nightcap"—my first song in the POOR SOLDIER. I made a sudden spring to the window, and, seizing the interloper by the hair of his head, dragged him across the room in front of the audience, out at the door, and tumbled him down stairs in a much shorter time than I have occupied in writing an account of the proceeding. The turned-out man crawled away to his fellows, and I concluded my song as though nothing had happened.

I expected an attack when the performance was concluded, but was agreeably disappointed—the mob had dispersed.

At Franklin and Kittaning we performed short periods, and in due time arrived at Pittsburg. What actor, who has visited this city, will ever forget it?

I sought my friend Butler, but he had removed from the place. I had no other friend to inquire for, and was about pushing off my little skiff, when I was seized by my old and indefatigable tormentors, the constables. The constables of Pittsburg never forget an old friend. When I left the place a little more than two years before, I had surrendered all the personal property I then possessed to one James Mackey, to be sold on an execution he held against me. Finding some very good beds, curtains, watches, and other desirable articles in the lot, he thought proper to appropriate them to his own use instead of offering them at vendue, and I now found myself in custody for the very debt the proceeds of those articles were intended to pay. To be brief, I gave him all the money I had scraped together in my trip down the Alleghany, except ten dollars, and then the sum fell short about twelve dollars, for which he very kindly consented to receive two watches worth sixty. Heartily disgusted with a place where I had met with nothing but ill luck, I disbanded my little company, gave them letters of recommendation to the manager who was to open the Pittsburg theatre in a few days, and embarked with my wife and child on board my covered skiff. I never ceased to "tug at the oars" until Pittsburg, with its smoke, was lost in the distance: then I was happy!

"Is he a chaste actor?" inquired a manager who wished to ascertain the professional qualifications of an applicant. "I can not say, exactly," was the reply. "When he performed in Pittsburg he was a *chased* actor."

I shall not attempt to describe the tedious journey of five hundred and twenty-six miles, performed in the heat of summer, on the Ohio River. It is enough for the reader to know we got through it at last. The water was too low for steam-boats. We stopped at Marietta, where we were treated with the greatest attention by the Hall family. We gave an entertainment at Wellsborough, and our receipts were eleven dollars! At Galiopolis we intended to give a concert, but the people all mistook me for a *preacher*, and treated me as such. At bedtime we were shown into the best room. A Bible, prayer and hymn books were placed on the table; candles snuffed with great care; a deep sigh breathed by the landlady; in short, every thing indicated that I was mistaken for one of those godly individuals who perambulate the country converting sinners, and eating the best the land affords. I thought it a pity to undeceive our entertainers. If they chose to deceive themselves, why should I say any thing that would take away from their satisfaction? In the morning I offered to pay my bill, but not a cent would the landlord receive. So we departed without saying a word about the concert.

Early in October, 1826, we arrived at Cincinnati, having been absent about two years and a half—without a dollar in my pocket.

CHAPTER V.

Mr. Drake's company, which we now joined, consisted of Messrs. Drake, Sr., A. Drake, Henderson, Sol. Smith, L. Smith, Kelsey, Greene, Grover, and Carter; Mesdames Drake, Fosdick, S. Smith, L. Smith, Carter, and S. Drake. Business falling off, the manager proposed to place the company on a *sharing* system, with the understanding that if the receipts each week should fall short of the expenses, we should *share;* but if they should amount to *more*, we should receive our *salaries only*. Not perceiving the entire justice of this arrangement, it being somewhat on the jug-handle principle, all on one side, Kelsey, my brother, and myself, joined by Henry R. Crampton and family, leased the Frankfort Theatre of Mr. Drake, and opened it for a short season. It failed; and, disbanding the company, with the exception of a small traveling party (consisting of self, L. Smith, Greene, Winship, Matthews, and Woodruff; Mesdames S. Smith, L. Smith, and Greene), we proceeded to Georgetown, where we played three or four nights. Poor little Greene! What a figure he cut! He fancied himself a great *tragedian*, and was the most *comic*-looking genius I ever beheld. He made his first appearance as *Prince Rodolph*, in the Blind Boy, and wore a dress, the trunks of which reached to his feet. The dress was made for my brother, who was full six feet high, and little Greene was not more than four! I laughed till I cried, and the audience seemed equally delighted.

We next proceeded to Paris, and opened with the Honey Moon. I observed that a countryman entered the theatre before the candles were lit, and seated himself on the centre of the front bench; presently, as the audience began to congregate, he became surrounded by females, who seated themselves each side of and behind him. He did not turn his eyes to the right nor to the left, but kept them fixed on the performers. When I came on as the *Mock Duke*, I observed him sitting in the manner described, with his face leaning on both his hands. As I seated myself to hear the complaint of *Juliana* against her husband, he and I were not more than six feet apart, facing each other. He leaned farther forward than usual, straining his eyes to take a still closer view of my features. At this juncture I could not resist the temptation to give my admiring friend a quiet wink, when he jumped up, and, striking his hands together with great force, exclaimed aloud, "*I'll be d—d if it's wax!*" The uproar this occasioned among the audience caused the gentleman to look round; he seemed to be sensible, for the first time, where he was; his ludicrous appearance on making this discovery caused a still louder laugh, which presently increased into a real *Kentucky yell;* and the uproar did not subside until the cause of all this mirth had made a retreat.

While performing the same play in Port Gibson in 1829, when the *Duke*, in answer to a knock at the door, bids his wife to "see who it is that knocks," a gentleman, who happened to be standing near the stage-door, very composedly opened it, and, peeping out, turned to the *Duke* and answered, "It is nobody but one of the actors—Mr. Tatem, I believe." In Nicolesville, a few weeks afterward, we were performing the farce of LOVERS' QUARRELS. The theatre was in the ballroom, and the landlord was in the habit of going behind the scenes to witness the performance. On account of his belonging to the Church, he did not wish to be seen in front. In the first scene, when *Carlos* was making a present of his watch, purse, etc., to *Jacinta* for her good news, I (as *Sancho*) advised him to save something with which to pay his board. At this moment our religious landlord popped his head on the stage and said, "Mr. Smith, don't mind your board; go on with your play just as you would; if you haven't the money at the end of the week, I'll wait." He was honored with a thundering round of applause as he *backed out*, bowing.

After playing at Paris a week, we bent our course toward Maysville. The roads at that time were intolerable, and almost impassable. My brother and myself were crossing a field (to avoid the mud), when we met a beggar who demanded alms. We concluded to give him a dollar, and accordingly handed him a dollar note on the Commonwealth Bank, and were passing on, when he called on us to stop a moment. He put on a dirty pair of spectacles, and, holding up the bill to the light, examined it a moment; then holding it toward me, said, "We don't take that 'ere money except at a discount." Admiring the fellow's impudence, I asked him at what rate he took Commonwealth paper? He replied, "It is not worth more nor seventy-five cents on the dollar. I've lost a great deal on that kind of money, and don't like to take it, no how; but if you have no other, I won't be difficult with you; I'll take it at twenty-five discount." For the joke of the thing, we actually gave the fellow a silver quarter to make good the depreciated paper!

At Maysville we performed a week to good houses, and then disbanded and retired to summer quarters at Cincinnati.

Near the close of the summer (1827) we reorganized, and perambulated the different villages in Kentucky. Mr. Crampton joined us at Lexington, where we acted about three weeks, and had during the whole time but one good house, and that was when *Henry Clay* attended the theatre. On this occasion we borrowed portraits of President Adams and Mr. Clay, and hung them up over the stage. I recollect a curious item in the property man's bill; it was as follows:

"For rope to HANG *Adams* and *Clay*, thirty-one cents."

From Lexington we proceeded to Harrodsburg Springs, where our business again failed. We made a precipitate retreat, leaving Crampton (whom we considered a sort of theatrical Jonah), and performed in Nicolesville one week.

We played one week at Versailles, where we visited poor Collins's widow, daughter, and GRAVE, and then raised our standard at Georgetown; but the Methodists had raised *their* banner before us, and had got possession of all the money and all the hearts of the young folk. They fairly conquered us, and drove us from the field! I here received a visit from my old fellow-apprentice, Bradford, who ran away with me from Vincennes. He had received a military education and a commission at West Point, and had just been detailed for active service.

At Shelbyville we closed the campaign, having determined to accept an offer from Mr. James H. Caldwell, and join his company at Nashville. We proceeded thither, and arrived just as the season had commenced. The theatre opened that fall with TOWN AND COUNTRY—Mr. Caldwell acting *Reuben Glenroy*, which character I have never seen better played than he played it. My wife made her first appearance as *Diana Vernon*, and I mine in *Billy Lackaday*. CHERRY AND FAIR STAR was brought out with great splendor: *Cherry*, Mrs. Hartwig; *Fair Star*, Mrs. Rowe.

On the occasion of General Jackson's visiting the theatre, an original song was assigned me to sing. It was a political affair, contained sixteen verses, and the tune was "Gee-ho-Dobbin!"

Toward the close of the season, a branch of the company, consisting of eight men and five women, was sent out to Russellville, Hopkinsville, and Clarksville under my management. While performing the STRANGER at Clarksville, one of our auditors became so interested in the last scene that he got up and addressed my brother as follows: "Come, Smith, look over what's past and take back your wife, for I'll be d—d if you'll get such another in a hurry!"

At the close of the Nashville season we were taken up by Mr. Caldwell in the steam-boat Friendship, and away we went down to New Orleans.

ACT SECOND.

1827—1835.

CHAPTER I.

THE English Drama was introduced into the city of New Orleans in December, 1817, by a commonwealth company.

The performances took place in the St. Philippe Theatre, afterward the Washington Ballroom. In 1818 Mr. Aaron Phillips took a company to New Orleans, and performed in the French Theatre, Orleans Street. Mr. James H. Caldwell came the same year with a company from Virginia, and occupied the St. Philippe Theatre, afterward removing to the French Theatre, which he occupied three evenings of each week, alternating with the French company—a compromise having been effected with Mr. Phillips, who, with the principal members of his company, enlisted under Mr. Caldwell's banner. The then great tragedian, Cooper, performed an engagement this season, receiving, as I have been informed, $333 per night!

The foundation of the American Theatre, Camp Street (now the Armory Hall), was laid in 1821, and it was opened in an unfinished condition. In 1824 it was finished and regularly opened, with a company competent to give proper effect to the regular drama. The season was a profitable one to the manager, and satisfactory to the public.

In 1825–6 the theatre again enjoyed a prosperous season. My youngest brother, Lemuel, was a member of the company. Mr. Edwin Forrest was engaged (then but nineteen years of age), and opened in *Jaffier* (VENICE PRESERVED).

The season of 1826-7 I know nothing about, but have no doubt it was as successful as the preceding.

In the summer of 1827 Mr. Caldwell proceeded with his company to St. Louis, Mo., where he converted a salt-house on Second Street into a theatre, and performed with considerable success for about three months, proceeding from thence to Nashville, Tenn., where I joined him, as heretofore related.

I now proceed with my personal narrative, beginning with the opening of the American Theatre, Camp Street, in the fall of 1827. I am enabled to give a list of the New Orleans company of this season:

Messrs. J. H. Caldwell, Anderson, Jackson, Sol. Smith, Lem. Smith, Sam. Jones, R. Russell, Gray, Lear, Hartwig, Lowery, Higgins, Cambridge, Palmer, Crampton, McCafferty; Mesdames Hartwig, Russell, Rowe, Bloxton, Johns, S. Smith, L. Smith, Jackson, Higgins, Crampton, and Miss Russell (now Mrs. Farren).

Out of those twenty-seven members three only remain—all but Mrs. Russell, Mrs. Farren, and myself having taken their departure to

> "The undiscovered country, from whose bourn
> No traveler returns."

On the second night of the season, Mrs. Smith and myself made our first appearance in New Orleans—she as *Diana Vernon* in ROB ROY, and I as the sentimental *Billy Lackaday*, in the comedy of SWEETHEARTS AND WIVES. With the exception of the character of *Delph*, in the farce of FAMILY JARS, which I performed a great number of nights during the season, and the part of *Carlitz*, in a new one-act drama entitled LOVE IN HUMBLE LIFE, I had very little to do calculated to give me a position as an actor; yet I was kept busy enough, always being required to walk in processions, sing in choruses, and shout in armies, besides fighting in all *general* battles.

During this winter (1827-8) Mr. Booth came to perform an engagement, and was highly successful. I should say these were his best days. It was my luck to "support" him as the *Physician* in KING LEAR, the *Lord Mayor* in RICHARD THE THIRD, and one of the *Citizens* in each of the Roman pieces. After his engagement at our theatre was finished, he performed *Orestes* twice in the French Theatre to crowded houses and the great delight of the French population.

The season being over, the company received orders to proceed at once to Natchez, then full 300 miles distant—now, by reason of a "cut off," shortened to 275 miles—from New Orleans. We took passage on the splendid steamer Caravan.

Slow traveling by Steam.

Does any one remember the Caravan? She was what would now be considered a slow boat; *then* she was regularly advertised as the "fast-running," etc. Her regular trips from New Orleans to Natchez were usually made in from six to eight days; a trip made by her in five days was considered remarkable. A voyage from New Orleans to Vicksburg and back, including stoppages, generally entitled the officers and crew to a month's wages. Whether the Caravan ever achieved the feat of a voyage to the Falls (Louisville) I have never learned; if she did, she must have "had a *time* of it!"

It was my fate to take passage in this boat. The captain was a good-natured, easy-going man, careful of the comfort of his passengers, and exceedingly fond of the *game of brag.*

We had been out a little more than five days, and were in hopes of seeing the bluffs of Natchez on the next day. Our wood was getting low, and night coming on. The pilot on duty *above* (the other pilot held three aces at the time, and was just calling out the captain, who "went it strong" on three kings) sent down word that the mate had reported the stock of wood reduced to half a cord. The worthy captain excused himself to the pilot whose watch was below and the two passengers who made up the party, and hurried to the deck, where he soon discovered by the landmarks that we were about half a mile from a wood-yard, which, he said, was situated "right round yonder point." "But," muttered the captain, "I don't much like to take wood of the yellow-faced old scoundrel who owns it; he always charges a quarter of a dollar more than any one else; however, there's no other chance." The boat was pushed to her utmost, and in little less than an hour, when our fuel was about giving out, we made the point, and our cables were out and fastened to trees alongside of a good-sized wood-pile.

"Halloo, colonel! how do you sell your wood *this* time?"

A yellow-faced old countryman, with a two-weeks' beard, strings over his shoulders holding up to his armpits a pair of copperas-colored linsey-woolsey pants, the legs of which reached a very little below the knee, shoes without stockings, a faded broad-brimmed hat which had once been black, and a pipe in his mouth, casting a glance at the empty guards of our boat, and uttering a grunt as he rose from fastening our "spring-line," answered,

"Why, capting, we must charge you *three and a quarter* THIS time."

"The d—l!" replied the captain (captains did swear a little in those days). "What's the odd *quarter* for, I should like to know? You only charged me *three* as I went down."

"Why, capting," drawled out the wood merchant, with a sort of leer on his yellow countenance, which clearly indicated that his wood was as good as sold, "wood's riz since you went down two weeks ago; besides, you are awar' that you very seldom stop going *down;* when you're going *up* you're sometimes obleeged to give me a call, becaze the current's against you, and there's no other wood-yard for nine miles ahead; and if you happen to be nearly out of fooel, why—"

"Well, well," interrupted the captain, "we'll take a few cords under the circumstances," and he returned to his game of brag.

In about half an hour we felt the Caravan commence paddling again. Supper was over, and I retired to my upper berth, situated alongside and overlooking the brag table, where the captain was deeply engaged, having now the *other* pilot as his principal opponent. We jogged on quietly, and seemed to be going at a good rate.

"How does that wood burn?" inquired the captain of the mate, who was looking on at the game.

"'Tisn't of much account, I reckon," answered the mate; "it's cottonwood, and most of it green at that."

"Well, Thompson—(three aces again, stranger—I'll take that X and the small change, if you please—it's your deal)—Thompson, I say, we'd better take three or four cords at the next wood-yard; it can't be more than six miles from here—(two aces and a bragger, with the age! hand over those V's")."

The game went on and the paddles kept moving. At eleven o'clock it was reported to the captain that we were nearing the wood-yard, the light being distinctly seen by the pilot on duty.

"Head her in shore, then, and take in six cords, if it's good. See to it, Thompson; I can't very well leave the game now—it's getting right warm. This pilot's beating us all to smash."

The wooding completed, we paddled on again. The captain seemed somewhat vexed when the mate informed him that the price was the same as at the last wood-yard—*three and a quarter,* but soon again became interested in the game.

From my upper berth (there were no staterooms then) I could observe the movements of the players. All the contention appeared to be between the captain and the pilots (the latter personages took it turn and turn about, steering and playing brag), *one* of them almost invariably winning, while the two passengers merely went through the ceremony of dealing, cutting, and paying up their "*anties.*" They were anxious to *learn the game*—and they *did* learn it! Once in a while, indeed, seeing they had two aces and a bragger, they would venture a bet of five or ten dollars, but they were always compelled to back out before the tremendous bragging of the captain *or* pilot; or, if they *did* venture to "call out" on "two bullits and a bragger," they had the mortification to find one of the officers had the same kind of a hand, and was *more venerable!* Still, with all these disadvantages, they continued playing—they wanted to learn the game.

At two o'clock the captain asked the mate how we were getting on.

"Oh, pretty glibly, sir," replied the mate. "We can scarcely tell what headway we *are* making, for we are obliged to keep the middle of the river, and there is the shadow of a fog rising. This wood seems rather better than that we took in at old Yellow Face's, but we're nearly out again, and must be looking out for more. I saw a light just ahead on the right—shall we hail?"

"Yes, yes," replied the captain: "ring the bell, and ask 'em what's the price of wood up here. I've got you again—here's double kings."

I heard the bell and the pilot's hail: "What's *your* price for wood?"

A youthful voice on the shore answered, "Three *and* a quarter!"

"D—n it!" ejaculated the captain, who had just lost the price of two cords to the pilot—the strangers suffering *some* at the same time—"three and a quarter again! Are we *never* to get to a cheaper country? Deal, sir, if you please—better luck next time." The other pilot's voice was again heard on deck—

"How much *have* you?"

"Only about ten cords, sir," was the reply of the youthful salesman.

The captain here told Thompson to take six cords, which would last till daylight, and again turned his attention to the game.

The pilots here changed places. *When did they sleep?*

Wood taken in, the Caravan again took her place in the middle of the stream, paddling on as usual.

Day at length dawned. The brag party broke up, and settlements were being made, during which operation the captain's bragging propensities were exercised in cracking up the speed of his boat, which, by his reckoning, must have made at least sixty miles, and *would* have made many more if he could have procured good wood. It appeared the two passengers, in their first lesson, had incidentally lost one hundred and twenty dollars. The captain, as he rose to see about taking in some *good* wood, which he felt sure of obtaining, now he had got above the level country, winked at his opponent, the pilot, with whom he had been on very bad terms during the progress of the game, and said, in an under tone, "Forty apiece for you, and I, and Jemes (the other pilot) is not bad for one night."

I had risen, and went out with the captain to enjoy a view of the bluffs. There was just fog enough to prevent the vision taking in more than sixty yards, so I was disappointed in *my* expectation. We were nearing the shore for the purpose of looking for wood, the banks being invisible from the middle of the river.

"There it is!" exclaimed the captain: "stop her!" Ding, ding, ding! went the big bell, and the captain hailed:

"Halloo! the wood-yard!"

"Halloo yourself!" answered a squeaking female voice, which came from a woman with a petticoat over her shoulders in place of a shawl.

"What's the price of wood?"

"I think you ought to know the price by this time," answered the old lady in the petticoat—"it's three and a qua-a-rter! and now you know it."

"Three and the d—l!" broke in the captain: "what! have you raised on *your* wood too? I'll give you *three*, and not a cent more."

"Well," replied the petticoat, "here comes the old man; *he'll* talk to you!" And, sure enough, out crept from the cottage the veritable faded hat, copperas-colored pants, yellow countenance, and two weeks' beard we had seen the night before, and the same voice we had heard regulating the price of cottonwood, squeaked out the following sentence, accompanied by the same leer of the same yellow countenance:

"Why, darn it all, capting, there is but three or four cords left, and *since it's you*, I don't care if I *do* let you have it for THREE—*as you're a good customer!*"

After a quick glance at the landmarks around, the captain bolted, and turned in to take some rest.

The fact became apparent—the reader will probably have discovered it some time since—that WE HAD BEEN WOODING ALL NIGHT AT THE SAME WOOD-YARD!

CHAPTER II.

THE Natchez Theatre was opened under Mr. Caldwell's management in the spring of 1828 with scenery and company brought from the "American," in New Orleans. Here it was the cognomen of "Old Sol" began to attach itself to me, in consequence of my being frequently called upon to perform the characters usually personated by "Old Gray," who was generally *indisposed* about these days. I was then twenty-seven years of age.

The new theatre in Natchez was situated at the extreme end of the main street, and in a grave-yard. Two hundred yards of the street leading to it had been cut through this "last receptacle of humanity," and every day, in going to rehearsal, our sights were regaled with the view of leg-bones sticking horizontally out of the earth ten or twelve feet above us, the clay having gradually washed away and left them thus exposed.

The dressing-rooms for the gentlemen were under the stage, the earth having been excavated to make room for them. Human bones were strewn about in every direction. The first night, the lamplighter being a little "pushed" for time to get all ready, seized upon a SKULL, and, sticking two tallow candles in the eye-sockets, I found my dressing-room thus lighted.

In digging the grave of Hamlet, I experienced no difficulty in finding *bones* and *skulls* to "play at loggats with."

A young man, named M'Cafferty, was a member of the company, combining the duties of scenic artist and second low comedian. Being very drunk one night, he wandered forth among the tombs, and, after diligent search for him next morning, he was found quietly reposing in a ruined vault, where he had passed the night! Poor M'Cafferty! A few years afterward a Mr. Gamble and himself *took a bottle of whisky to bed with them* one night, and they were found dead the next morning!

A watch was stolen from my dressing-room in the theatre, and a negro boy was taken before Justice Tooley on a charge of having committed the larceny. Being sworn, I began to give in my testimony, to the effect that on the previous night, while I was officiating as *High Priest of the Sun*—

"How's this? how's this?" interrupted the magistrate—"High Priest of the Sun? Pray where did all this happen?"

"At the theatre, sir. I was officiating as High Priest, and—"

"At the THEATRE!" screamed the justice; "served you right, then—served you right! Boy, you may go; I dismiss the case."

The individual charged with this theft was no less a personage than a negro boy named Carey, who afterward became somewnat notorious as an Indian chief under the name of Oakah Tubbee. Nearly twenty years afterward this individual came to St. Louis, where he achieved considerable popularity as a serenading flute-player. Mr. Bailey, our treasurer, on the occasion of his benefit, wished Carey to play a tune between the play and afterpiece, but it did not seem exactly proper for a *negro* to appear on the stage. Being a bright mulatto, it was thought he might be passed off "for one night only" as *an Indian.* When the bill was being made out, Bailey came up into the director's room to ask me what *name* we should give our newly-created Indian.

"Name? Ah! yes, he must have a name," I replied; and, casting a look through the window over to the "Cross Keys," a large oak tub under a spout caught my eye. "There is an oak tub; let the Indian's name be Oakah Tubbee;" and Oakah Tubbee it has been ever since.

He soon went up into the Indian country, where, passing himself off as a Choctaw chief, he married a very likely squaw, and commenced traveling and giving concerts! I am sorry to hear lately that Tubbee has deserted his Indian wife and taken a *white* squaw, who fell in love with him at Niagara Falls. I suspect Tubbee is considerable of a rascal, though he was probably innocent of the larceny charged on him in Natchez.

Mr. and Mrs. Russell, at the close of the season here, proceeded to Boston, where Mr. Russell had received the appointment of acting manager of the Tremont Theatre.

The season, though short, was moderately profitable to the management, and nearly all the performers had good benefits.

Our next movement was to St. Louis, Missouri, then a village containing less than 6000 inhabitants. Here I made my first appearance in the character of *Kit Cosey* (TOWN AND COUNTRY), and was warmly received by the audience. Our theatre was an old salt-house in Second Street, mentioned as having been fitted up for dramatic purposes by Mr. Caldwell the year before, and was generally well attended. Our manager had gone "East" to recruit the Southern company, and play a starring engagement at the Park Theatre. The management was placed in the hands of Mr. James S. Rowe, the treasurer of the establishment, and the season was a paying one. The comedy of the HYPOCRITE was acted a great number of nights, Mr. Barry performing the character of *Dr. Cantwell*, and the writer of this that of *Mr. Mawworm.*

I remember with grateful feelings that the late Governor Clarke and most of his family made it a point for many years to attend my benefits, which were always profitable and flattering to my professional pride. The drama of the GAMBLER'S FATE was produced this season with great success, and I think with considerable moral effect.

Those were jolly times in St. Louis!

The Manager and the Planter.

In the days I am now writing about, it was customary for Southern managers to perform a journey once a year to "the North," for the purpose of forming engagements with "stars," and filling up the ranks of their stock companies, which yellow fever and the expiration of engagements had thinned.

During the stay of Mr. Caldwell at Cincinnati, on one occasion he was besieged, as usual, by actors of all grades, who were candidates for a Southern engagement. It happened that he wanted a man capable of taking the stage management.

By one of those strange coincidences that will sometimes occur (as if to help a fellow out with only a tolerable story) a rich planter from the vicinity of Natchez, Mississippi, put up at the same hotel with Manager Caldwell, and he bore the *same name!* This planter wanted to engage an *overseer* for his plantation, and he was told an advertisement in the Cincinnati papers would soon draw from Kentucky (opposite) plenty of applications.

The following notice appeared in the Evening Post:

"*An Overseer Wanted*—by the undersigned. To a capable man, good wages will be given. Apply personally, or by letter, at the City Hotel, to J. H. CALDWELL."

And the following in the Cincinnati Gazette:

"*Theatrical Notice.*—The undersigned will remain at the City Hotel, Cincinnati, until to-morrow morning at ten o'clock. Performers of acknowledged talent, who wish to engage for the Southern theatres, will please apply immediately. J. H. CALDWELL."

It is not my business to state the result of these notices farther than it relates to two individuals. A Mr. Henderson, better known as "Old Henderson" (there are a great many of us called *old* now, alas!), had long cherished a desire to visit New Orleans professionally; and a Mr. Jackson, of Newport, was anxious to engage as an overseer at the South. Both of these gentlemen called at the City Hotel about the same time for the purpose of making their applications.

The would-be overseer, on inquiry at the office of the hotel for Mr. Caldwell—he knew of but one, having seen no newspaper but the "Post"—was shown to the manager's room, while Old Henderson was conducted to that of the Mississippi planter.

If the reader will please take a seat in Manager Caldwell's private parlor, he will witness a specimen of equivoke that would not make a very bad scene in a farce.

Overseer (entering). Is this Mr. Caldwell?

Manager. The same, sir. Be seated.

O. I come, sir, in consequence of your advertisement in the newspaper.

M. Ah! yes; your name, sir, is—

O. Jackson, sir.

M. A very good name for the South, sir. Where have you acted?

O. Mostly in the western part of Virginia—latterly in Kentucky.

M. What is your line of business?

O. Line of business? I have always managed the slaves, and made it a point to get all the work out of them I could.

M. If you engage with me as acting manager—and I suppose that to be your aim—I would advise you not to call my people *slaves;* they will certainly take offense.

O. Take offense! Why, what would they expect to be called but slaves?

M. I assure you, sir, there are *some* who consider themselves, and are considered by others, gentlemen.

O. Then, sir, perhaps your "gentlemen" would object to being *whipped?*

M. Most undoubtedly they would. Is that your mode of carrying on business?

O. Where I have managed heretofore it has been impossible to get on without whipping, I assure you.

M. Well, sir, that mode might answer in the western part of Virginia, but it would not be prudent to try it at the South.

O. Sir, if the business *can* be carried on without it, I shall have no objection; but if I engage with you, and find any of your people obstinate, I must insist on giving them thirty or forty each. How many hands do you work?

M. We have something like seventy people in the establishment, besides musicians.

O. Pretty strong-handed. But what occasion have you for *musicians?*

M. I don't see how we could very well get on without them, sir.

O. Well, sir, that is a matter which concerns you, and not me. How do you *feed* your people?

M. They generally board at hotels.

O. They do? Board at hotels? Have *music;* and you never whip?

M. Never; they wouldn't stand it.

O. What wages do you propose?

M. Thirty dollars per week is the salary I paid my last acting manager.

O. That would be satisfactory to me. Of course, I should have a room at your house.

M. (becoming a little fidgety). No, sir; you would be obliged to furnish your own boarding and lodging.

O. My last employer boarded me, furnished me a horse to ride, and a servant to attend on me.

M. (wishing to bring the scene to a close). To be plain with you, Mr. Jackson, I doubt whether you would answer my purpose. Your method of enforcing authority by *whipping* would cause a rebellion at once.

O. Very well; if I don't suit you, there's no more to be said. Good morning.

M. Good morning to you, sir.

[*Exit Jackson.*

While this scene was progressing in the manager's room, Old Henderson was pressing his suit with the planter in another part of the house.

Actor. I have seen your advertisement in the paper, Mr. Caldwell, and have come to offer my services.

Planter. You wish to engage to go South?

A. I do, sir; and I have long wished to do so. You have a large establishment, I am told.

P. Tolerably extensive; work a good many hands.

A. Yes; I've been told you have a large company.

P. Pray, sir, what wages do you expect; and what would be your system of carrying on an establishment like mine?

A. Would you wish me to take charge of the acting department?

P. Most undoubtedly; I should wish you to *oversee* the whole concern; my people would be placed entirely under your direction.

A. You don't say so! I did not expect this; but, if you think me worthy of such a trust, I shall do my best to give satisfaction. By the way, what is the price of boarding at your place?

P. Indeed I don't know. If you engage with me, you will live in my house, of course.

A. Sir, you are very polite, I'm sure. How many have you in your company?

P. About one hundred.

A. A very large company, indeed. Many *musicians?*

P. Oh, I believe there are several of our people who play the *banjo*—I can't say exactly how many. Are you good at *whipping?*

A. Whipping, sir?

P. Yes, whipping; you do not expect to get along without some whipping, I suppose?

A. Why, sir, I must say I have never seen that system pursued where I have acted.

P. What! no whipping! My dear sir, it is impossible to carry on business in our country without it, I assure you.

A. And don't the people object to be treated in that way?

P. Object! Bless you, no; they are used to it. Besides, it depends upon *themselves* whether they are whipped or not; if they behave themselves as good slaves ought, they need not fear punishment.

A. Slaves! Do you call your people slaves, then?

P. Assuredly. What else can they be called?

A. (sidling toward the door). And if they don't *act* well, you have them *whipped!*

P. Undoubtedly; and if they continue obstinate, and are insensible to the *benefits* of kind treatment, and can not be reformed by severe punishment, I SELL THEM.

A. (at the door). Sir, I—I believe I must decline an engagement in your establishment; your "Rules and Regulations" are a d—lish deal too strict for me, so I wish you good-morning.

[*Exit Old Henderson in a hurry.*

We next proceeded to Natchez, with the intention of making a fall season previously to opening the Camp Street Theatre in New Orleans. On our way down the river, my brother and myself, with our wives, together with a Mr. Cambridge and a Mr. Wilkie, were induced to stop and perform a few nights at Port Gibson, in the State of Mississippi, and a most pleasant and lively time we had of it, the theatre being crowded every night we remained in that spirited little village. We opened with the HONEY MOON, and, not having a large stock of performers, we were obliged to adopt the *doubling* system. It thus fell to my lot to enact the *Mock Duke*, *Rolando*, *Doctor Lampedo*, and *Neighbor Lopez!* It being our first appearance in the town, and we all strangers to the play-going community, it was never suspected that each character announced in the bill had not a separate representative. My share of the characters in the comedy was announced thus:

Rolando (a woman-hater).......Mr. Smith.
Jacques (the mock duke).......Mr. Sol. Smith.
Dr. Lampedo...................Mr. S. Smith.
Lopez.........................Mr. S. F. Smith.

It was remarked next day that "there appeared to be a pretty smart chance of Smiths in the company"—which indeed was a fact; there did *appear* to be a good many, every character but two in the comedy having a Smith opposite to it.

When we had concluded our season of four nights in Port Gibson, it was found impossible to procure carriages to convey us to Natchez, so we had recourse to a large road wagon, drawn by six horses, which carried the company and baggage. Not being desirous to make much of a parade in leaving the town (in such a conveyance), Pitts, the proprietor of the wagon, was requested to be ready a little before daylight, that we might *quietly* take our departure. Pitts was punctual, but he came dashing down the street with his six horses rigged out in loud-sounding sleigh-bells! On being remonstrated with, he innocently answered that he didn't intend to *charge us for the extras.* After much persuasion he took off the bells, but doing this delayed our departure until after sunrise, and we were attended to the end of the town by quite a respectable number of the rising generation, all anxious to get a last peep at the "show folk." At Washington, six miles from Natchez, we took the precaution to make a halt, and send honest Pitts ahead with our baggage, while we awaited the arrival of a couple of carriages which he was commissioned to send out to us.

At Natchez we found several new members of the company awaiting the opening of the theatre; among the rest, George Hernizen, H. Pearson, and Mr. and Mrs. Crooke (formerly Mrs. Entwistle). It was here I again met my old New York strolling manager, Mr. H. A. Williams, who was engaged by Mr. Caldwell as principal low comedian, to supply the place of Mr. Russell.

A theatrical Dentist.

Most of the company had assembled nearly a week before the theatre opened. Time hanging rather heavily on their hands, they set to amusing themselves as well as they could. There was a Mr. Tooley in the town, a justice of the peace, a member of the Church, and a violent opposer of the theatre. On the previous season he had connived at the escape of a negro thief merely because he committed the felony in the theatre, telling the sufferer (who was no other than myself) that he was served rightly, and it was a pity he had not lost every thing he possessed, so that he would thus be prevented following his *criminal profession!* Among the new engagements this season was a Mr. Carr, a kind of "rough-shod" vocalist, a Cockney Jew, who could bellow out "Oft in the stilly Night" like a clap of thunder, and warble "Wha'll be King but Charlie?" like a bull. We learned that this vocalist had been a *dentist*, and he had communicated his intention of singing and drawing teeth in the Western metropolis on his arrival there—in short, he expected to charm the lovers of harmony with his *wocal* powers, and line his pockets by the exercise of his dental acquirements. These two persons were the ones chosen by the lovers of mirth as the *dramatis personæ* for the joke which was to make the time pass lightly for at least a day.

In due time Dr. Carr received the following note:

"Natchez, November 28, 1858.

"Sir,—For some years past our town has been visited by *quacks*, who have passed themselves off for dentists, imposing on the people and pocketing their money without rendering them any essential service.

"My wife has for a long time been in need of having a very difficult operation performed on her teeth and jaws, which I have been unwilling to employ any of the numerous pretenders who have visited this place to do, hoping that some skillful dentist would arrive with whom she might be intrusted with safety. I have been told by a friend from Philadelphia that you stood very high in that city as a professor of dentistry, and the object of this note is to request that you will favor me with your company to dinner at half past one, bringing your instruments; and I assure you I will make it worth your while to perform the operation required, as money is no object to me in comparison with Mrs. Tooley's comfort.

"Your having adopted the theatrical profession is an additional inducement for me to employ you, as I am always glad to have it in my power to *benefit* those engaged in it, considering it, as I do, the noblest profession on earth! Your complying with this request may be *beneficial* to you in more ways than one. Be punctual at half past one.

"Yours respectfully, J. Tooley."

When this letter was handed to Carr by a negro boy he was enraptured. Several of us *happened* to be present; he immediately excused himself to us, and, saying he had an appointment, began to prepare for his visit. He had swallowed the bait, hook and all. A few minutes before the time appointed, the performers (*by mere accident*) again happened to be strolling along the street which led to the justice's house. Punctual to his time, Dr. Carr was seen bustling along, with a miniature chest of drawers under his arm, and dressed up in the finest manner. Every one asked him to stop on some pretense or other. All we could get out of him was that he "'ad a werry himportant haffair hon 'is 'ands, and he vas afraid of being too late." Precisely at the time appointed he knocked at the justice's door. A servant inquired his business. "Tell the squire that Dr. Carr vishes to see him." "The squire is just sitting down to dinner." "Yes, I know it; please to deliver my message." In a few minutes the servant returned, and asked him to walk in. The doctor accordingly stepped into the dining-room, bowing and scraping. After the usual salutations, the justice inquired his business. "I'm Doctor Carr." "Ah! Doctor Carr, how do you do? Well, Doctor Carr, how can I serve you?" "I am Doctor Carr, from Philadelphia, you know." "Well, doctor, to what am I indebted for this visit?" "Vy, you know, I have come to see you; I've brought my hinstruments." "Brought your instruments?" "Yes—I belongs to the theatre, you know—I've brought my hinstruments. I'm going to dine with you, and then I'm going to hoperate on your vife!" At these words the justice seized a chair, and, raising it over the poor doctor's head, exclaimed, "You infernal play-actor, if you don't instantly leave my house, I'll perform an operation on your head!" As he was about to suit the action to the word, the doctor, in utter surprise, made a precipitate retreat, roaring murder. At the street door his foot slipped, and he fell headlong down the steps, his instruments flying in every direction.

On being questioned in the evening about his "appointment," poor Carr, with an exceedingly chop-fallen countenance, replied, "Gentlemen, that 'ere hinvitation, and the 'ole concern, was a *wile 'oax!*"

The season at Natchez was short and unprofitable, so we proceeded to New Orleans earlier than was intended.

CHAPTER III.

Mr. Booth was nominally our stage-manager the early part of this season. His "eccentricities" began to crop out about this date, and interfered somewhat with the interests of the theatre. Mr. George Holland made his début, and a great hit, in the burletta of a Day after the Fair, and Mrs. Knight played and sung a very successful engagement.

The rival Vocalists.

Mr. Still was for some years the principal singer in the Camp Street Theatre, New Orleans. He had a very pretty ballad-singing voice, and answered very well for the *Captain Somervilles* in farces and the singing heroes in melodrama. Mr.—I beg his pardon—*Doctor* Carr was this season engaged, also, as a singer. He had a thundering voice, and what he lacked in musical skill he more than made up in impudence and assurance.

The actors, with one accord, determined to set these vocalists by the ears. By retailing to each the pretended sayings of the other, in a few weeks they began to treat each other coldly, and presently they dropped all intercourse. From the time they ceased to speak to or recognize each other, it took but a very short period to make them deadly foes, and many were the threats made on both sides. When we had got their jealousy and hatred excited to a proper pitch, it was agreed that a regular "blow up" between the two should end the joke. It had been a part of the system to make them believe that there was a great excitement in the town about the talents of the two rivals. One night, having learned in the box-office that the farce of the Sprigs of Laurel, or the Rival Soldiers, was to constitute a part of the entertainment for a holiday night, I went into the greenroom, where the two vocal heroes were sitting, and addressed one of the principal performers thus, pretending not to see the two *captains*, as we called them: "This excitement about the two singers has grown to such an alarming extent, that the manager has determined to have a 'trial of skill' between them, and the one who loses is to be discharged." The vocalists pricked up their ears. Captain S. was incredulous at first, but C. was caught at once. "Vell, *I'm* ready any time; *I* an't afraid to meet the gentleman that vay, or any hother." He here cast a most killing look at his rival, who was Adonising before the large greenroom mirror. "What piece is selected for the occasion, and when is the trial to take place?" asked old Henderson, who was always in the front rank of jokers. "The Rival Soldiers, I believe, is the piece, and the 8th of January is selected as the most appropriate day for the contest," answered I. Just at that moment, as if to confirm my story, the call-boy entered, and wafered up a cast of the very piece spoken of, with Mr. S. set down for the character of *Sinclair*, and Dr. C. for that of *Lennox.* This settled the matter in their minds; there was no joke in it, *for the manager never joked.* The songs were selected, rehearsals gone through, and the glorious 8th arrived. The house was crammed, as it always was on that anniversary, and the bets ran high among the actors as to the result of the trial of skill.

For the purpose of clearing their voices, C.

provided a large orange, and S. had procured some mixture in a four-ounce phial. The mischievous actors contrived to fill C.'s orange with *snuff*, and to substitute *pepper vinegar*, from an oyster-stand, for S.'s mixture in the phial. The moment arrived when their fate was to be decided by the impatient public. The two singers were looking askance at each other in the glass, with no very friendly eyes, when the call-boy bawled out at the door, "Sinclair and Lennox—all the act!" Away went the rival soldiers; but, before mounting the steps which led to the stage, each hastened to his dressing-room to take a last "clearer" of his throat—a suck at the orange, and a portion of the pepper vinegar. They met at the steps which led to the stage. The vinegar and the snuff began to be tasted. "Vat the 'ell 'ave you been putting into my horange?" shouted the doctor. "What d—d stuff have you been putting into my phial? I'm poisoned," replied S. "By G—d! I'll vip you ven I come off the stage," continued C. Here the prompter's voice was heard exclaiming, "The stage is waiting for Lennox and Sinclair." Away they went, and met on the stage *as friends*, though their side glances were any thing but amicable. The cue for S.'s song was given to the orchestra, and, after clearing his throat as well as he could, he began, interlining the words of the poet with some expressions of his own, thus:

"Oh, my love is like the red, red rose,
That sweetly springs in June—
[*Just wait till I catch you out, that's all.*
My love is like the melody
[*I'll be d—d if I don't lay a cane on your back.*
That sweetly plays in tune;
[*I believe it's poison.*
And I will love my bonnie lass,
[*My throat is all raw.*
So deep in love am I;
[*Oh, you big-mouthed villain.*
That I will love thee still, my dear,
[*I can't stand it.*
Though all the seas gang dry. [*I shall choke.*
Though all the seas gang dry, my dear,
Though all the seas gang dry;
[*Can't some one get me a glass of water?*
And I will love thee still, my dear,
[*I can't sing the second verse.*
Though all the seas gang dry."

Next came C.'s turn; the snuff began to make him disposed to vomit:

"March to the battle-field,
[*I'll fight you, by G—d.*
The foe is now before us;
[*Ugh! I will—I'll be d—d if I don't.*
Each heart is freedom's shield,
[*Confound the snuff, I shall throw it up.*
And Heaven is smiling o'er us.
[*Look out, young man, ven ve gets off the stage.*
The woes and pains, [*Ugh! my stomach.*
the galling chains,
[*It's worse than the poison you talk about.*
That keep our spirits under,
[*I think a drop of something vould 'elp me.*
We will drain our dearest veins,
[*You bloody rascal, you.*
To break our bonds asunder.
[*I'll break your infernal 'ead.*
March to the battle-field," etc.

Their *side speeches* to each other, while going on with their *friendly dialogue*, were equally amusing, but the above is a fair specimen of the whole scene. When they came off the stage we all expected a regular set-to; but, somehow or other, their anger died away as the effect of the snuff and vinegar ceased to be felt. The next morning they exchanged mutual pledges of their innocence in regard to the "'*oax*," as the doctor termed it, became excellent friends for the remainder of the season, and sung in concert ever after.

The company was divided about the middle of the season, and a part sent to Natchez, under the direction of Mr. Booth, who exhibited many of his "eccentricities" to the people of the Bluff City.

Before the close of this season, my brother and myself obtained leave to withdraw from the company, for the purpose of organizing a small strolling concern, intended to operate on the principal towns of Mississippi and West Tennessee, commencing at Port Gibson, where our reappearance was warmly greeted by the inhabitants. After performing at this village for a couple of weeks, we proceeded to the flourishing town of Vicksburg, where a small theatre was erected by a Thespian society, and leased to us. Here we acted for four weeks with unvaried success, and, after returning for a week or two to our starting-point (Port Gibson), where we played with but moderate success, we proceeded to Memphis, then a very small river town at the mouth of Wolf Creek, in West Tennessee. Here we performed in a *room*, fitted up for the occasion, in the house of Mr. Young, next to his large warehouse, then on the banks of the river. Old Mississippi has since moved away about a quarter of a mile, and Uncle Sam's Navy Yard now occupies the ground where the Father of Waters formerly traced his channel. Memphis, in 1829, contained about six hundred inhabitants, and was considered a "thriving place." Look at it now!

Our operations were commenced in Memphis on the 23d of May, 1829, and we performed eight nights, closing on the 3d of June, the total receipts being $319!—an average of less than $40 per night.

On leaving this city our "*journey-work*" commenced in reality. The conveyances to be obtained at this early date were any thing but elegant. Common road wagons, drawn by from four to six horses each, bore this small band of Thespians through the "Western District," if not in very great style, certainly in great safety, and at an extremely moderate pace. Our first stopping-place was Somerville, where the inhabitants insisted on our giving an entertainment, which was attended by the whole village, the receipts amounting to $39. We gave them the DAY AFTER THE WEDDING, and a variety of songs and dancing, *without scenery*, and with a very small supply of *lights*. Bolivar was our next station, and here a room was very nicely fitted up for our performances, which were fully attended, considering the size of the village. The people seemed to *come out of the woods;* but they gathered every night in such numbers that in a week and a half the receipts amounted to $349, which was an average of nearly $37 per night.

The Landlord's Disappointment.

Some business detaining me at Bolivar, I sent the company ahead, and followed the next day in the stage. I arrived at about twelve o'clock at night at the small village of Middleton—I won't be certain that it is the name of the place, but it will do for the purposes of this sketch—and found considerable of a crowd awaiting the arrival of the stage. The landlord came out to light us, and I noticed that he stuck the lantern literally into the face of each passenger, apparently with the intention of becoming acquainted by a short cut with his new guests. I was the last to alight. The landlord handed me out with a very slight examination of my features, and then, poking the lantern into the coach, clambered up the steps to take a particularly good view of the inside. *He was evidently looking for some one.* After a hasty examination he returned to the sidewalk, where the passengers were waiting to be shown into the house, and took another view of each passenger's features with the help of the lantern, which he moved about so as to throw the light upon our several faces in turn.

"Why, he is not *here!*" exclaimed the worthy landlord, turning to his neighbors, who were surrounding our party. "The h-ll he ain't!" growled a carroty-headed fellow in his shirt-sleeves, who was smoking a pipe an inch and a half long. "Then you've kept us up till the middle of the night for nothing," he exclaimed. "Look at the way-bill," suggested a slim, pale-faced youth, who might be a clerk in the post-office. "Ay, look at the way-bill," confirmingly advised the crowd.

The landlord hereupon took out of his vest pocket a pair of greasy spectacles, and with the aid of his lantern began to scan the way-bill, which the pale-faced youth had by this time brought down from under the driver's seat.

"There's his name—yes, there's the old villain's name; but where is *he?*" This last inquiry was addressed by the landlord to the passengers, while his little gray eyes peered over the green spectacles, the eyes and spectacles together assuming the appearance of two italic interrogation points reversed. As I was standing nearest him, I ventured to ask who was expected—what "old villain" was referred to, whose non-arrival seemed to cause such disappointment? "*Who?*" sharply replied the landlord—"WHO was expected? Why, the *old fellow himself*—the old chap that has been cutting such a swarth at Bolivar. There's his name on the way-bill. Curse his old picture, here have I and my neighbors been waiting since eight o'clock to get a peep at the old fellow. His company went through here yesterday, and they said *he* would be along to-night! How is it?" Not wishing to be annoyed by the old gentleman's attentions, and not being in a mood to undergo the gaze of the smoking and tobacco-chewing crowd, I asked him to name the individual he was speaking of. "The *individual!* yes, he is an *individual*, certainly, though they tell me he can take any shape he pleases, and that he is one person to-day and another to-morrow, assuming as many characters as suits him; and he makes people *pay* for seeing him perform his tricks. Some people say he is as good as a caravan!"

"But *who* is it?"

"Why, *who* should it be but OLD SOL? There's his name on the way-bill—how is it that he is not *here?*"

"I believe I can explain this matter," I answered. "The old gentleman you mention *did* intend to come on in the coach this very night; but he is a changeable sort of a fellow, as I know. You are aware there are other routes to Jackson. At all events, finding the seat vacant, *I* took it, and am here in his stead."

"Well, stranger," said the old man, moving toward the supper-room, "I don't wish *you* any harm, and I don't wish to be uncivil to any gentleman; but I wish *you* had taken t'other route instead of *Old Seventy-six.* Confound all such don't-know-their-own-mind sort of fellows, I say!" and he led us into the supper-room. After discussing our midnight meal, I asked our muttering landlord where I was to sleep. (We had four hours' rest here, and the coach was to move on again at daylight.) He took up his everlast-

THE LANDLORD EXAMINING THE WAY-BILL. (See page 58.)

ing lantern and led the way to the best room in the house. "Here," said he, lighting a candle and setting it on the table, "you can sleep here. This room was intended for the *old sinner* we have all been waiting to see. I'll never prepare another room for the old ragamuffin—never!" and away went my worthy host and his lantern. The last I heard, as he groped along the passage, was, "Curse me if there is but one other man on earth I would have staid up for, AND THAT'S GENERAL JACKSON HIMSELF!"

Jackson was our next town, and here, for the first and last time, we performed in a *log* theatre. A tax was required to be paid for the privilege of performing in this village; but the municipal government promptly met and repealed the ordinance which classed the drama with shows and rope-dancing exhibitions. All honor to them for it. Their example might be followed, without discredit, by the corporations of older and larger cities. Our receipts in twelve nights amounted to $480—about $40 per night.

The citizen of whom we rented the log building which we temporarily converted into a temple of Thespis bore the name of Cloud. *Caleb Quotem* would have been a more appropriate appellation for this gentleman, for his occupations were as various as the individual so named, if not "more so." He was town constable, clerk of the market, auctioneer, nuisance-master, painter (sign and ornamental), carpenter, joiner, negro-whipper, tyler of a masonic lodge, sexton, hair-cutter, shaver (of bank-notes and chins), grocer, whitewasher, proprietor of the theatre, gauger of spirituous liquors, baker, and deputy sheriff!

A Mr. Rudicel was not far behind his neighbor Cloud in the number of his callings. He was a dealer in dry goods and groceries, saddle and harness maker (all at different stores), tanner and currier, trunk manufacturer, tinner, butcher, boot and shoe maker, brewer, carpenter, justice of the peace, member of the town council, and had a monkey to show!

In the town of Florence, Alabama, which was our next place of stopping, we played in the *garret* of the principal hotel (the largest room in the place), but with poor success, our total receipts in seven nights amounting to but $251.

At Tuscumbia we fared still worse, receiving only $150 for six nights' performances.

Our "journey-work" was suspended for one month at Huntsville, where we played eighteen nights in the beautiful little theatre which graces that city, to but a trifle over an average of $50 per night. We performed only four nights in the week; but I find by a memorandum made at the time that there was "preaching every night." The preachers carried the day—and the *night* too, and we were very glad to escape from Huntsville without a serious pecuniary loss. Yet our performances were not without their moral effect, though the preachers endeavored to make their hearers believe that all who visited the theatre would certainly be eternally roasted in the hottest sort of fires, the heat of which were to be intensified by liberal supplies of brimstone! During the performance of that most thrilling drama, the GAMBLER'S FATE, where *Albert Germaine* and his family are represented in a state of actual starvation, a country gentleman in one of the side boxes suddenly rose up: "I can not stand this," said he, in a voice loud enough to be heard all over the house. "Gentlemen, I propose we make up something for this woman." He was here admonished by certain "hushes," "set-downs," and "orders," that his proposition did not meet with much favor; on the contrary, it was received with considerable laughter, while a whispered intimation came to his ear from a friend at his elbow that the distress of the family was all *sham!* "Gentlemen," continued the charitable country auditor, "you may 'hush' and 'order' as much as you please; for my part, I don't see any thing to laugh at; you see the woman hasn't any thing to eat; and that poor little child of hers seems almost famished: now I wouldn't give the rascal, her husband, the first red cent; he doesn't deserve any pity; but really the woman hasn't deserved this distress; she has followed her husband through all his wanderings, and left her friends, where she was comfortable, to follow this scamp. Gentlemen, you may laugh, but here goes my V!" And, sure enough, he threw a pocket-book. "There, my good woman—*Mrs. Germaine*, or whatever your name may be, take that! Send for something to eat, and make yourself comfortable; but let me advise you not to let your husband know any thing about it, or he'll lose it at the first faro-bank he meets with, as sure as h—ll! and now," continued the philanthropist, settling himself in his seat, "now go on with the play."

My brother Lemuel and his wife withdrew from the company at the close of the season here, and went to Cincinnati, where he started a little "journey-work" on his own hook, progressing as far as Pittsburg, where he disbanded his forces the following spring without making a fortune.

For myself and family, with the traveling band of strolling dramatists, we pursued our way southwardly, and in due time brought up at the seat of government, Tuscaloosa, where we played, with slight interruptions, from the 9th of September until the 8th of January, to houses which barely paid expenses, without giving a dollar to the manager by way of profit.

Alarm of Fire in a Theatre.

The cry of "FIRE!" in a theatre is a most alarming sound. It is alarming any where, but *in a theatre* particularly so. Ever since the burning of the Richmond Theatre, whereby a great number of persons perished, the least alarm of any kind among a large assemblage is attributed to *fire*, and a rush is sure to be made for the doors, the "Richmond fire" being uppermost in the minds of all.

Among the expedients resorted to during the somewhat protracted season at the seat of government of Alabama, while awaiting the assembling of the Legislature, to draw audiences to our little theatre, was the production of the pantomime of DON JUAN, or THE LIBERTINE DESTROYED, with all the "accessories" of snakes spitting flames, fiends with torches, red fire and blue blazes in the last scene, which was represented in the bills of the day to be no other than the INFERNAL REGIONS, into which the amorous *Don* was to be cast without benefit of clergy!

This was all very well "in the bills;" and the boys about town were curious to know what sort of a *place* it was they had heard so much about, but never yet gotten a glimpse of. They ran home to their daddies and mammies, and told them all about the "great preparations" going on at the theatre—their daddies and mammies told their neighbors—and by the middle of the afternoon it was pretty generally known about town that "H—ll" was to be played at the theatre that night. The consequence was—a very full house.

Every thing went well until the "last scene of all." *Don Juan* clambered into upper windows (six feet high); committed divers murders; escaped in a ship; was cast ashore; had a dance with the peasantry; was invited to sup with a spectre on horseback; did the honors of the table with great propriety, and accepted in return an invitation to sup with the marble statue in a grave-yard. *Scaramouch*, the Don's attendant, had *his* fun too; and what with riding on the back of a dolphin, dancing with fishermen's wives, and eating maccaroni, he had rather a pleasant time of it.

"Every body for the last scene!" was called out in the greenroom; the fiends sprang to their places, the snakes were wriggled into their situations behind each wing, the pots of red and blue fire were manned, and a brilliant ending of the pantomime was anticipated, when suddenly an alarm of fire was heard in the front of the house! Confusion followed, of course; the auditors tumbled over each other, all pushing for the openings, and I am happy to say that *all but one* got safely out. I will tell you presently about that one; but first it is proper to explain the cause of the alarm, for this time it *had* a cause, which was nothing more nor less than *the burning of one of the wood wings*, the fire having communicated from one of the pots of blue fire, the ingredients of which had not been properly apportioned. On the instant of the alarm the curtain had been lowered, and in less than a minute the burning wing had been torn down and the fire extinguished, not, however, until the canvass had been burnt from the frame. In the hottest of the rumpus, a man named Somerville cut his way through the curtain, and in endeavoring to stamp out the burning piece of scenery, the pot of blue fire being unseen by him, he *put his foot in it*, and the lower part of his leg was very badly burned. He was confined to his room for several weeks.

Next day after the fire—or the *alarm* of fire—the town rung with an account of the danger encountered by the audience the night previous. The whole affair was greatly exaggerated. It was said that, in an attempt to represent the "infernal regions" on the stage, the scenery had caught fire, the whole theatre only escaping utter destruction by the intrepid daring of young Somerville, who had barely escaped with his life. The bigoted portion of the Tuscaloosans seized upon the circumstance, and held it up as a warning to all play-goers, and, shaking their heads ominously, said they knew all along that no good could possibly come from encouraging profane stage-plays in a Christian community. The tide of public sentiment was fast setting in against our poor little theatre, and I felt it was incumbent on me to do something to stem it. My plan was soon laid and immediately executed.

I must here state that, the instant the fire had been extinguished and the house cleared of the alarmed public, I called the scene-painter, and told him I would give him a week's salary if he would produce a wood wing the next morning exactly similar to the one burned. This he undertook to do, and accomplished.

During the afternoon of the next day "I mixed with the people," and ascertained that all were fearful of witnessing a repetition of DON JUAN; indeed, it seemed to be a pretty well understood thing that no audience could be collected together in that building again! What was to be done? The new theatre at Montgomery (my next stand) was not yet finished, nor would it be in less than four or five weeks.

My plan was this: I must convince the people that there had *been no fire*—that what they had seen was *only an imitation!*

Collecting together a committee of respectable citizens, we all took a drink and proceeded to the theatre. "Gentlemen," said I, after seating them on the front bench, "it has been reported, much to the injury of my interests and the interests of the drama, that *there was a fire here last night*. My object in asking you hither is to disabuse you, and, through you, the public of Tuscaloosa on this subject." Here one of the cutest of the committee observed, "Come, Smith, that won't exactly do; I was here myself, and there certainly *was* a fire—*something* of a fire; for, before the curtain was lowered, I saw one of them *wings*, I think you call them, all in a bright flame."

"My worthy friend," I replied, "I don't in the least doubt you *think* you saw it in a bright flame, as you say; but my object is to convince you that you labored under an optical illusion."

"Optical h—ll and d—n!" exclaimed rather hastily the aforesaid speaker; "I tell you I saw with my own eyes that scenery which stood down there at your left all in a blaze."

"Excuse me, my dear sir," calmly replied I; "you *think* you saw it; but I'll convince you in one moment of your error."

Here I called the carpenter, and asked him to place the first wood wing in its appropriate groove. This he did almost instantly.

"There, gentlemen," I said, pointing to the newly-painted piece of scenery triumphantly, "I believe you will recognize that; you have seen it often enough."

A close examination now took place, the result of which was the firm belief that it was the same wing they had supposed to be destroyed by fire. The committee of citizens unanimously agreed that the *imitation* of fire the night previous had been most perfect, and gave me a certificate, which I published in an extra poster, that they had investigated the whole subject, and had come to the conclusion that there had been a FALSE ALARM of fire in the theatre, and that there was no danger whatever in visiting that admirably conducted establishment. DON JUAN had a "run," and was the most successful piece of the season—the *last* scene being particularly applauded for its truthful representation of the infernal regions.

* * * * *

But poor Somerville—where was *he* all this time? He had heard of the reports about town that the fire was *all a sham*, but he was confined to his room from the effects of this sham fire. One day he came limping to the theatre:

"Look here, old fellow!" said he, "what is all this they've been telling me about your sham fires? Do you mean to say that this burn I've got on my leg was inflicted by sham fire?"

"My dear sir," I replied, gravely, "I don't know *how* you got your hurt; I remember seeing you in here during the alarm, and, if you got injured in your efforts to extinguish what you *supposed* to be the flames, I regret it exceedingly."

"But," expostulated Somerville, "do you mean to say that one of your wings was not in a bright blaze?"

"I mean to say," replied I, "that one of the wings might have *appeared* to be burning, but there is the wing to speak for itself," I continued, pointing it out.

It was a somewhat remarkable wing. It stood front of all the rest, and was therefore familiar to the view of the audience. It was, moreover, of a peculiar kind, being composed principally of the body of a large tree, with a dead limb on one side and a tremendous knot-hole on the other. It was a wing to be remembered.

Somerville took a good look at the renovated wing—went around it, viewed it in every light—*felt* of it, and at last, being apparently perfectly satisfied, observed, as he limped away,

"Well, I'll be d—d if that fire wasn't the best *imitation* I ever saw!"

CHAPTER IV.

PREVIOUS to this time I had made a contract with Mr. Caldwell to lease from him the Natchez Theatre for a spring season, and it was now time to wend my way to open that establishment, in order to "catch the stars" as they passed up from New Orleans to the cities of the Western country; but receiving from Montgomery a warm invitation to visit that town, and occupy for a limited period a beautiful new theatre just erected by a Thespian society, instead of taking a boat for Mobile on our way to Natchez (through New Orleans), we once more betook ourselves to the large road wagons, and in five days found ourselves, "bag and baggage," at the place which is now the seat of government of Alabama.

Here I became acquainted with John H. Thorington, a lawyer of great practice, who possessed all the qualities requisite to constitute a good man. He is no longer living to read my praises, but it affords me a melancholy pleasure to record his unvarying kindness to me and mine. As mayor or intendant of the town, some years afterward, he took a decided stand against the *gamblers* who congregated in Montgomery in great force, and he was persecuted by them in various ways, until he concluded to leave the place and remove to the Western country. In Iowa he was afflicted with a disease consequent upon the severe climate, which settled into his limbs, causing paralysis, and threatening his life. In hopes of relief, he was taken to New Orleans, and placed as a boarder in the Charity Hospital, where he ended his days. I was with him while he was lying on his death-bed, and afforded him at least the satisfaction of knowing he had a friend near him. Poor Thorington! He could not *speak* his thanks; but the pressure of his hand, even after he had lost the ability to raise his arm, told me that his stout Irish heart retained its warmth to the last pulsation.

There were other warm and true friends that I made in Montgomery—George Whitman for one. At the time I write of, Mr. Whitman was one of the first merchants of the place, and owned real estate sufficient to make him a millionaire, which he would undoubtedly be at this moment—*if he had held on to it.*

The *currency* in circulation here was made up of all sorts of what was termed *foreign* paper—*mostly counterfeit.* The first night of the season, Mr. George Whitman went into the box-office with me to assist in selling tickets, as I was quite ignorant about what money I could safely take. A gentleman, *with his wife on his arm*, asked for two tickets, and handed in a five-dollar bill, which I instantly returned, pronouncing it to be *counterfeit.* The gentleman flew into a terrible passion, and insisted on my handing him the tickets and three dollars in change. "My dear sir, I tell you the note is counterfeit." "Well, sir, and *suppose it is;* what difference does *that* make? A pretty fellow *you* are, to come here and attempt to regulate our currency! Come, give me my tickets; don't keep me waiting; don't you see I've got a lady on my arm?" My friend Whitman here interfered, and said, in a low voice, "You had better take it; it is about as good as any." "What!" remonstrated I, "take counterfeit money?" "Yes; we all take it here," replied George. Well, thinks I, if *they all take it here*, I am safe enough. So, without more objection, I handed the gentleman his two tickets and *three silver dollars* I happened to have in my pocket, and the affair ended for that night. Next day I had occasion to purchase some small articles at a store, and I went directly to my friend Whitman's. Selecting what I wanted, which amounted to a few shillings, I handed the clerk the identical V received from the gentleman the night previous. The clerk looked at the bill, and immediately discovered it was a bad one. He was in the act of returning it to me, when Mr. Whitman, who was mounted on a step-ladder showing some goods, turned his head, and, nodding to me, said to the clerk, "All right; take it;" which command was instantly obeyed, and four dollars and some cents handed to me by the clerk.

The Montgomery Theatre opened, in an unfinished state, the latter part of January, 1830. The attendance was good for two weeks, which was the limit of our stay, in consequence of my engagement at Natchez. Madame Feron, the great singer, performed with us two nights, and as we were without a regular orchestra, various means were resorted to for an accompaniment to her songs. A piano-forte was introduced upon the stage, and she accompanied herself in some pieces—in others she pressed me into the service. Thus, in the farce entitled OF AGE TO-MORROW, the dialogue was necessarily changed a little from the original text:

Maria. I had a lover once.
Baron. A lover? Twenty, I dare say.
Maria. But he deserted me.
Baron. Deserted you? Impossible. What had he to say for himself?
Maria. He said nothing; but [*if you'll have the kindness to seat yourself at that piano, and give me an accompaniment*] I'll tell you what I said to *him.*

Suiting the action to the word, the accommodating *Baron Willinghurst* (personated by the writer hereof) seated himself at the piano, and the beautiful song, "As I hang on your bosom," was gloriously breathed forth by the great prima donna of European Opera, in a theatre surrounded by uncut trees, and occupied by an audience whose appreciation was as warm as that of the dilettanti of Italy. In the farce of NO SONG NO SUPPER, to account for the presence, in *Farmer Crop's* house, of so rich an article of furniture as a piano-forte, *Crop* was constrained to say that a rich neighbor had *stored* it there until he could get his new house ready for its reception. Thus accounting for the instrument being there, it was an easy matter to ask *Margaretta to play upon it;* then a *song* was asked for, and after that another, and so on. Madame Feron entered into the spirit of the scene, and seemed to enjoy herself very much, imparting her good humor to all around, both before and behind the curtain. Mr. Maddox, since manager of the Princess's Theatre, London, accompanied Madame Feron as her man of business. From Montgomery she proceeded to New Orleans, where she had an engagement.

In two weeks we received in Montgomery the sum of $883, out of which I paid Madame Feron $101 for her two nights' acting and singing.

At the moment of departure from this village I had a pleasant interview with Mr. Thomas S. Hamblin, who was returning from a Southern engagement.

We proceeded next to Selma, a very small village on the Alabama River, where we performed nine nights in a ballroom fitted up for the purpose, to receipts of exactly $70 per night. The number of inhabitants did not exceed 400, white, black, and children. Those who visited the theatre visited it *every* night. The sheriff, being one day compelled to leave town on business, came and *left his dollar* at the bar of the hotel where we performed!

Arrived at Mobile, I was strongly urged to remain there and open the theatre, a shell of a place in St. Francis Street, which was offered to me by those who represented the interests of the owner; but, considering myself bound to open the Natchez Theatre, I pushed on to that city.

The Natchez Theatre opened under my management on the 10th of March, 1830, with the following company — Messrs. H. A. Williams, Crooke, Kidd, Campion, Marks, Myers, Tatem, Cole, Anderson, Perry, Sol. Smith; Mesdames Smith, Crooke, Honey, Prescott, Graham, and Voss—which was afterward augmented by the arrival of my brother, Lemuel Smith, on his return from his unsuccessful traveling expedition to Pittsburg and other Ohio River towns, where he experienced the usual vicissitudes which almost invariably attend "schemes" of that kind.

Having at this time accumulated a sufficient sum (about $1100) to *pay all my debts in Cincinnati, with interest*, I was very anxious to proceed thither, and accomplish the object of my seven years' toil. But I soon found that my hard earnings were likely to be swept away by a failing season of a few weeks in Natchez. I now became sensible of the folly of leaving my "journey-work," hard as it was, for the luxury of the "regular theatre." At the close of the first week, the receipts fell $150 short of the expenditures, and it was very evident that there was no likelihood of an improvement in the business. In this emergency I ventured upon a bold plan to save myself from loss. It was this: I divided my forces, placing my old New York manager, H. A. Williams, in command of a detachment for Port Gibson, where they opened the theatre, and continued to perform three nights in the week for nearly five weeks, at the same time that the Natchez concern was in operation four nights in the week! Even this bold manœuvre came near failing to accomplish the object I had in view, the receipts falling far below my anticipations in the then thriving village of Port Gibson. At the end of the first week's trial there, the following letter from my lieutenant general was received:

"Port Gibson, March —, 1830.

"MY SOVEREIGN,—This expedition must be a failure unless I have re-enforcements. I have only squeezed out of the Gibsonians $162 in three trials, which, after paying for transportation and fitting up the house, gives but about $50 with which to liquidate a salary list of $200 and upward, to say nothing of rent and printers' bills. Might I suggest, mighty sovereign, the kind of force best calculated to retrieve our lost ground here, I should say, COME AND ACT YOURSELF. 'The king's name is a tower of strength,' and if you will authorize me to announce you for Wednesday, as *Captain Copp*, I promise you a rich return from the treasury.

"Your faithful subject, H. A. WILLIAMS,
"*Gen. of 2d Division, or Forlorn Hope.*"

The following was my reply:

"Theatre, Natchez, Sunday, March —, 1830.

"GEN. WILLIAMS,—I'll try it. Wednesday—*Captain Copp.*

"Yours truly, SOL. SMITH."

The journey of fifty miles was easily performed on horseback, and the result was highly satisfactory, the treasurer's return being for that single night $166—four dollars more than the entire receipts of the previous week! My reception was enthusiastic in the extreme; and being called before the curtain at the close of the comedy of CHARLES II., I promised a second visit.

Returning to Natchez the next day, and acting in play and afterpiece at night, the Friday morning found me stiff and nearly done up; nevertheless, I pushed on to the fulfillment of the promise made to my friends at Port Gibson, and performed *Delph* on Friday night to a house rising $100. Acted again at Natchez on Saturday night; and finding by the meagre receipts at Port Gibson on the same night (less than $20!) that my performing the journey every day between our two towns would probably *save me from loss on the season*, I resolved to encounter the fatigue, and made arrangements for a relay of horses, by which means I could perform the journey in five hours. This feat I actually accomplished—traveling fifty miles every day in the week except Sundays, and acting every night for nearly a month! *It almost killed me*, and I feel the effects of such exertions to this day. But my object was gained; my profits at Port Gibson equaled my losses at Natchez, and I was enabled to carry out my long-cherished wish to PAY MY DEBTS.

It may be interesting to some of the hard-working "stock" of the St. Charles, who consider it something of a hardship to rise in the morning in time to attend a 10 o'clock rehearsal, and who can scarcely accomplish the labor of studying a new part once in a week, to learn how I managed to get through the labor above mentioned. Premising that the roads in those days were somewhat *muddy* and *deep*, I give a short

Extract from my Journal.

Wednesday. Rose at break of day. Horse at the door. Swallowed a cup of coffee while the boy was tying on leggins. Reached Washington at 8. Changed horses at 9—again at 10—and at 11. At 12 arrived at Port Gibson. Attended rehearsal—settled business with stage manager. Dined at 4. Laid down and endeavored to sleep at 5. Up again at 6. Rubbed down and washed by Jim (a negro boy). Dressed at 7. Acted the *Three Singles* and *Splash*. To bed at 11½.

Thursday. Rose and breakfasted at 9. At 10 attended rehearsal for the pieces of next day. At 1, leggins tied on, and braved the mud for a fifty miles' ride. Rain falling all the way. Arrived at Natchez at half past 6. Rubbed down and took supper. Acted *Ezekiel Homespun* and *Delph* to a poor house. To bed (stiff as steelyards) at 12.

Friday. Cast pieces—counted tickets—attended rehearsal until 1 P.M. To horse again for Port Gibson—arrived at 7. No time to eat dinner or supper! Acted in the MAGPIE AND MAID, and NO SONG NO SUPPER, in which latter piece I managed to get a few mouthfuls of cold roasted mutton and some dry bread, they being the first food tasted this day! etc., etc., etc., etc.

BUT I PAID MY DEBTS!

CHAPTER V.

THE season over, and all matters settled up with the company, who proposed to visit some of the Louisiana towns, enlisting, for the time being, under the banner of my brother Lemuel, I left Natchez with a light heart, and $1200 in my pocket, for Cincinnati, taking Vicksburg in my way, where we performed (my wife and self) with Manager Jackson for one third of the nightly receipts, clearing $175 in three nights.

Arrived at Cincinnati, the manager of the Columbia Street Theatre offered me an engagement for a few nights, which I accepted, and played *Mawworm* for my benefit. This engagement was not remunerative either to the manager or myself, the benefit night being the only one which yielded a profit.

A summer's rest placed me on my legs again, and with the coming of the fall season of the year came the desire to resume the duties of my arduous profession. Previous to going South we accepted an offer from Mr. Parsons, acting manager for Mr. Drake, to perform twenty nights in Louisville, receiving for our services the sum of $220. Mr. T. D. Rice was a member of the company here, and was busily engaged in composing and arranging his *Jim Crow* songs, which afterward raised him to the topmost wave of popularity, both in this country and England. Charles B. Parsons, the acting manager, took upon himself the leading characters in tragedy, and played *Hamlet*, *Brutus*, *Virginius*, and *Rolla*, and pale-face-hating aboriginal characters, "written expressly for him," much to his own satisfaction and that of the public. I have since heard him give copious extracts from the speeches of *Hamlet in the pulpit*, without, however, having the candor to acknowledge the *name* of the poet whose words he was transplanting into his sermons. As a Methodist preacher, Mr. Parsons succeeds better than he did on the stage—at least I *think* so; and, what's more and better, I believe him to be a sincere Christian.

Miss Eliza Petrie, daughter of the Mrs. Petrie who had traveled with me through Tennessee and Alabama as actress of the old women of the drama, was the young girl of the Louisville company. She possessed a good voice for singing, and was beginning to become popular with the public. Mrs. Rowe was the "old woman," and her husband performed the duties of prompter. Old Henderson was here "at home," and very popular. Mr. and Mrs. Charles Muzzy were useful members of the company, as were Mr. and Miss Clarke. My wife played what is termed the singing business, with some parts in comedy, which rendered her a favorite, and insured her a good benefit, on which occasion she personated the *Countess* in a play entitled MY OLD WOMAN. My benefit was also a good one, after taking which, our engagement being over, we proceeded to Nashville, where we were engaged to act six or eight nights, with Messrs. Rowe, Gray, and Mondelli, who temporarily had the management of the theatre. All I remember of this engagement is this: a great number of "stars," so called, were playing, and the houses were awfully empty! The names of Mr. Caldwell, Mr. and Mrs. Pearman, Mr. Geo. Holland, and (to make matters worse) the writer hereof and his wife, were all announced in flaming capitals at the head of the bill on one occasion, without attracting to the house *forty dollars!*

My First and Last Sermon.

The title of "reverend" has frequently been tacked to my name on letters addressed to me, and reports have been circulated that, during my peregrinations, I have been in the habit of holding forth to congregations of sinners. The truth of the matter is, I never preached but *one* "regularly-built" sermon in my life. With the exception of an address to the Encampment of Patriarchs and Lodges of Odd Fellows from the pulpit of the Unitarian Church in Mobile, and a few brief remarks to a congregation of passengers on the occasion of taking up a collection for a poor woman on the Alabama River many years ago, the following sketch will contain a true and faithful account of my whole ministerial experience.

As a preliminary, it must be known that my brother, who had succeeded me as the manager of the West Tennessee theatres, while I had gone to Cincinnati to spend the summer and pay my debts, in answer to the numerous and pressing inquiries respecting the whereabouts of "Old Sol," had uniformly asserted that I had been *converted*, and had commenced *preaching!* By this answer he got rid of any farther inquiries from the anxious West Tennesseeans, who had been accustomed to laugh at my stage jokes; for wonder succeeded to curiosity, and many a lurking smile accompanied the shake of the head and holding up of hands which the astounding information caused. "*Is* it possible?" "*Who* would have thought of *his* turning preacher?" "I can scarcely believe it!" "I would like to hear him try his hand at it!" were some of the exclamations heard by my brother on his impartment of the news of my conversion. Requesting the reader to remember that I was totally ignorant of these reports of my backsliding from the stage, I proceed with my story:

My brother and his company were at Memphis, where I had an engagement of six nights. A week before the close of the season in Nashville, I obtained leave to commence my Southern journey, giving myself time to fulfill my promise to my brother, and yet be ready at my post at the commencement of the campaign in New Orleans, where I had an engagement for the season.

About three o'clock one afternoon, the stage-coach stopped at the little town of Bolivar, where I had performed the year before, and where I was well known by every man, woman, and child for six miles round. The landlord of the hotel expressed great joy at meeting me, and ushered my wife and myself, with great respect and ceremony, into the family parlor, where he left us for a few minutes to attend on the other guests. The landlady and her daughters received us with great cordiality, but I could not help observing a sort of seriousness in their countenances which I had never seen before. My cloak was hung up, my overshoes taken care of, the fire stirred up, and—in short, I found myself very comfortable, and felt assured, by every action of my host and his family, that I was considered *somebody*. Dinner was soon announced, and we arose to join the general rush for the dining-room; but the landlady interposed a pressing invitation that we would join the *family* dinner, which would be ready in about ten minutes. A most superior meal soon engaged our attention in a room adjoining the parlor, with a cup of excellent *tea*, than which I know of nothing more refreshing while traveling. I noticed that when we had taken our seats at the table, "an awful pause" took place, while all eyes were turned toward *me;* but, at the time, it did not appear very singular that the assembled family should wish to have a "good look" at one who had so often ministered to their amusement.

Dinner over, I was mysteriously beckoned into a private room by Boniface, who said he wished to have a few words with me. We took seats. The worthy landlord here indulged in a long look at me, the corners of his mouth and twinkling of his eyes indicating, by certain twitchings and winkings, that a *laugh* was on the point of breaking through all restraints, and making itself seen and heard. After sundry "hems" and "ha's!" and moving his chair a little this way and a little that, my friend cleared his throat, and thus began a conversation, which resulted in a most singular adventure:

"You *must* excuse me—I can't help thinking what a change has taken place in you; but I must do you the justice to believe you are *sincere* in your professions. Will you tell me candidly, Mr. S., whether you like your *present mode of life* as well as you did that of last year, when you used to travel through this country with your company, and make us laugh ready to kill ourselves with your comicalities?"

Supposing my questioner merely wished to ascertain whether I was satisfied with a regular engagement in New Orleans, after indulging in the excitements and adventures incident to the life of a perambulating manager, I answered,

"I must confess, my friend, that the change is very agreeable to me; and a southern climate is essential to my bodily health in the winter."

"You are, then, stationed *permanently* in New Orleans during the winter?" inquired the landlord.

"Permanently," replied I, wondering what could be the object of these questions.

"But the *income*"—pursued my friend—"the *income!* that's the point! Do you *make* as much, in your present line of life, as you did in managing theatres?"

"Well," I responded, "that is somewhat doubtful; but in management there are a thousand cares and vexations which I now escape; and if my income is not quite so large, it is now fixed and certain—*my salary being sure.*"

"Ah! yes," chuckled the landlord, "I believe *all of you* take pretty good care about the salary, and it is all right you should; 'the laborer is worthy of his hire.' But how do you look, *now*, upon the *morality* of your past life?"

"Why, as to that," I answered, "it is not for me to speak. I have *endeavored* to do *what is right* in all my transactions as manager and actor, and I assure you I do not look back with any regret on my past life."

"Well, come, I like you all the better for *that.* I always told my neighbors that you never would 'run down' your former profession, and I believe you *are* honest in your present course," said the landlord, "and I will now proceed to business."

I was somewhat mystified, I confess, with the conduct and conversation of my landlord, but determined to wait patiently for a solution of his meaning.

Giving his chair an extra hitch, and assuming a more serious air, the landlord came to the point by saying,

"The fact of the matter is just here: the citizens of Bolivar, hearing of your arrival, have expressed an ardent desire—they have a hope, indeed—a wish—I may say a unanimous wish—that is, if you've no objections—and I am commissioned to request—solicit—that you will *stop here to-night, and* 'HOLD FORTH' at the court-house."

"Hold forth at the court-house!" echoed I. "What! give an *entertainment?* Impossible. I am announced at Memphis for to-morrow night, and must go on in the stage."

"My dear sir," persisted the commissioner from the inhabitants of Bolivar, "you can not conceive how very anxious we all are to *hear you* —indeed, indeed, you *must* gratify us—you can not imagine the excitement your arrival has caused; and the people are *determined* to have you stop and—"

"It is out of the question," I remonstrated. "My engagement at Memphis is imperative; I *must* be there to-morrow."

"So you *shall* be, my dear sir," answered mine host; "we have arranged all that. Before it was decided on to let the stage go without you—"

"What!" I exclaimed, in alarm, "has the coach departed, and left me here to—"

"Been gone three quarters of an hour," replied my determined friend, deprecatingly; "but don't be alarmed; Squire Jones has agreed to hitch up his team of horses to-morrow morning before daylight, and by two o'clock you'll see the Mississippi River."

In the early part of my professional life I had been compelled, as I have said elsewhere, to "give entertainments"—"solitary and alone;" but for several years I had abandoned this disagreeable mode of "raising the wind," and hoped I should never be compelled to resort to it again; consequently, I felt a great repugnance to the proposition of the citizens of Bolivar. Lectures had not at that time come into vogue, else I might have easily fudged up something for the occasion. Songs and recitations were all I could depend on for the entertainment of an audience.

After a moment's reflection, during which I took into consideration the fact that my means of proceeding on my journey were cut off (by a "pious fraud," as the landlord called it), and that my finances were in a state that required replenishing, I suddenly inquired of the landlord *what I should make by the operation.*

"Why, as to that," he readily answered, "I can't exactly say; but I am sure our citizens will be liberal. One thing I can assure you of—you will have the greatest congregation ever assembled in this burg."

"But there is no notice given," I argued.

"Isn't there?" triumphantly inquired the landlord; "just step to this window, *if* you please."

It *did* please me to step to the window and look out, but I can not say much for the pleasure I experienced when I saw a crowd around the court-house door, which stood but a few paces off, reading a written placard, two lines of which only could I decipher, one of which was,

"SOL. SMITH,"

and the other,

"THIS EVENING."

This seemed to settle the matter. I concluded to GIVE THE ENTERTAINMENT, and trust to Squire Jones's horses and wagon for the fulfillment of my engagement at Memphis on the morrow.

To my suggestion that some little "fitting up" of the court-house would be required, my accommodating entertainer cut me short by saying,

"Leave that to me: the house shall be lighted, the seats arranged, *a place fitted up for you*, and every thing fixed as it ought to be for the occasion; give yourself no trouble about it, my friend, but retire to your room at once, and *prepare yourself.* At seven o'clock I will go with you to the court-house, and if you don't find the greatest gathering you ever *did* see, I will never make another *call* on you to hold forth in this village again."

Thus assured, I retired to my room, and, after sketching a programme for the night's entertainment, I indulged in a refreshing nap for a couple of hours, at the end of which time I was waited upon by my landlord, who was accompanied by two pious-looking individuals, and conducted to the scene of my proposed labors for the evening.

On entering the court-house, closely attended by the two pious-looking individuals and the landlord, I found his expectations in regard to a large audience were more than realized. The crowd was immense. Every nook and corner of the court-room was occupied, and I was pleased to see that the fair sex of the village were numerously represented. The press for admission had evidently been so great that the door-keeper had abandoned his post, for I saw no one acting in that capacity.

I ascended to the judges' seat, and my two attendants took their seats in the clerk's place beneath.

I bent down my head behind a sort of screen that was in front of me to call to my recollection the words of my first song. I had been in this situation but a few moments when my ears were greeted with the following words, uttered by one of the pious-looking gentlemen beneath me:

"*Let us commence our worship by singing the one hundredth psalm, long metre!*"

If I had been struck with a thunderbolt I could not have been more astounded, unless utterly annihilated. Before I could recover from my stupefaction the reading of a psalm had been gone through with, and the whole audience commenced singing it to the tune of Old Hundred.

I raised my eyes to the desk before me, and found there a Bible, a hymn-book, and a glass of water. The landlord being near me, I beckoned him to me, and asked him, in a whisper, what was expected of me. "*Expected* of you?" he answered, with glistening and expecting eyes —"*expected* of you? Why, we expect a first-rate, right up-and-down orthodox SERMON, and I don't reckon we'll be much disappointed either!"

The murder was out. I saw through it all. But what was I to do? To gain time (the singing being concluded), I leaned forward and requested one of my *deacons* to go ahead with a prayer, during which I called my thoughts about me, and most sincerely prayed for a happy deliverance from my singular situation. Before the conclusion of the prayer I had made up my mind to "try my hand" at preaching—*and I did it.*

I had no time to select a text, but, opening the Bible at hap-hazard, read the following words, which I announced as the groundwork of my discourse:

"We are perplexed, but not in despair."—2 *Cor.*, iv., 8.

I will not attempt to give even an outline of my discourse. I spoke with the utmost sincerity, and soon found that, taking TRUTH for my guide, there was no great difficulty in my new undertaking. I will not say any thing of the *orthodoxy* of my sermon, but I trust there was nothing advanced from that temporary pulpit, by that temporary preacher, calculated to lead any of that crowded congregation out of the path to heaven.

At the conclusion of my discourse a hymn was sung, during which I heard considerable of a clattering, which sounded very much like coin falling into platters, and with a strong voice I pronounced the benediction, dismissing the congregation to their several homes.

The landlord and my deacons reported that they had collected forty odd dollars, which, to their great surprise, I directed them to apply to "charitable uses." At five o'clock the following morning Squire Jones was ready with his wagon and team. The landlord would not take any thing for our dinner, supper, and lodging, declaring himself more than paid by what he was pleased to term my excellent discourse.

Let not bigots and the *regular* clergy accuse me of making a mock of religion, or of scoffing at its forms. I spoke not a word, during my forced ministry of one night, that I did not religiously believe to be TRUE; and should I ever leave my present profession for the pulpit (which I shall certainly not do unless under a solemn

MY FIRST AND LAST SERMON.

conviction of duty), I shall remember without any feelings of regret MY FIRST AND LAST SERMON.

* * * * * * *

We arrived at Memphis in time to commence our *theatrical* engagement on the night following, and were greeted by a large audience, though by no means so *crowded* a one as that which witnessed my *first appearance* in the pulpit.

We played a week, with a profitable result, in a temporary theatre, under the management of my brother Lemuel, who at this point concluded his strolling summer season. My brother and the principal members of his party joined Mr. Caldwell's company, and after a delay of two weeks, waiting for a boat (we are not obliged to wait so long nowadays), the combined theatrical forces made their way to the Southern emporium on an unusually slow boat called the "Rapid."

CHAPTER VI.

THE veteran tragedian, Cooper, came to New Orleans this season to act a fortnight. I remember seeing him play *Virginius*, *Beverly*, *Sir John Falstaff* (first time), and *Cardinal Wolsey*. He was not very successful. In HENRY IV. Mr. Holland and myself were cast for the *carriers*, Holland being announced at the head of the bill as a star!

Mr. Pelby also played an engagement, and had some disagreement with the management, which led to a personal encounter between him and the stage-manager, Cowell. A large portion of the company sided in opinion with Mr. Pelby, supposing him to be ill used *on account of his being an American;* and the matter frequently forming the subject of discussion in the greenroom, the prompter one night became confused, and instead of calling the Roman citizens to the stage as "*All the plebeians*," bawled out, "*All the Pelbians!*" which caused a great laugh at the time. A lawsuit was the result of the misunderstanding between Mr. P. and the manager, and that eventuated in a verdict for—I don't know which of the parties, and *now* I don't care.

The play of HENRY VIII. was produced with great splendor.

Mr. Cooper appeared twice as *Jack Falstaff*, which character he personated, according to my poor judgment, better than any individual who had at that time undertaken it on the American stage since the days of Cooke, whose style he followed as nearly as he could.

It became the policy of the management to make a season at Natchez, for the purpose of sending thither some of the "stars" who visited New Orleans. A detachment of the company was accordingly detailed for that city. My brother Lem and myself, with my wife (Lem's wife remained at Cincinnati), were among the unhappy *conscripts*. With great reluctance we departed for the City of the Bluffs, for we had provided ourselves with comfortable winter quarters in the Crescent City. However, there was no appeal from Manager Caldwell's decisions; and if you attempted to remonstrate with him on any subject, he was sure to *convince you* that you were in the wrong! So we went to Natchez.

In consequence of what I then considered and do yet consider the injustice of the management toward my wife in Natchez, I withdrew her from the theatre during the early part of the season, and she consequently did not appear again until my benefit, which was a very great one, yielding a receipt of two hundred dollars more than that of any other member of the company. During the season Miss Clara Fisher, Mr. and Mrs. Plumer, Mr. Charles Kean, and Mr. J. M. Scott, performed starring engagements, which were more or less profitable (generally *less*) to the proprietor. Upon the whole, the season could not be said to be a successful one.

Involuntary Pugilism.

It has been my good fortune to pass along through the world without being engaged in many personal conflicts with my fellow-beings, which fact I attribute to three causes: *first*, my great dislike to quarrels of all kinds, because they *are* quarrels; *second*, a great reluctance I have always felt to inflict an injury on the person of any human being; and, *third*, a still greater reluctance I have continually felt to *receive* injury from my opponent, whoever he might happen to be. So, with the exception of the case mentioned as having transpired in Cincinnati while editing a paper, the one I am now going to relate, and a few slight skirmishes not deemed worthy of record, I have happily escaped fightings of all kinds. The two exceptions referred to ended well enough for me; but, good gracious! I was frightened nearly out of my wits while the fights were going on, and right glad when friends interfered to prevent farther hostilities.

The party with whom I was reluctantly engaged on this occasion I shall call O'Rourke—I did not know his name at the time — an Irishman, rather short in stature, but brawny, wide across the shoulders, sinewy, and every way just such an individual as a somewhat timorous person like myself would be entirely willing to avoid "locking horns" with.

My brother Lem, the year previous to the one mentioned, had rented a room from a Mrs. Langdon, with whom this Irishman lived, and he and I were in the habit, when speaking of him, of calling him Langdon, from the fact (supposed) that they two, Mrs. Langdon and Mr. O'Rourke, were soon to be made one by the holy bands of matrimony—though why we should have given the poor fellow *her* name instead of giving her *his*, under such circumstances, can only be accounted for by considering that we were always taking the oddest kind of notions into our heads, which, if any other person had entertained them, he would have been thought almost insane. We had never called this man Langdon to his face; but one day, as we were going from rehearsal, seeing him coming toward us, my brother said, "Here comes Langdon." It struck me that it would be very funny to speak to him as Langdon, and see the effect it would have upon him. As he was coming on the side of the pavement next to Lem, I whispered him, "Speak to him as Mr. Langdon." No sooner said than done. "Good-morning, Mr. Langdon," said Lem, blandly, as we met and passed. The Irishman returned the "good-morning" almost before he heard the name he was saluted by; but when the name "Langdon" did reach his ear, a scowl instantly covered his face, and he passed on. I saw at once that he was offended, and became satisfied we had done wrong. We talked the matter over, and both regretted the sorry joke we had foolishly perpetrated. However, there was no help for it now. We would apologize at the first opportunity. I say *we*, for, though Lem spoke the words, it was I who prompted him to speak them, and I took the blame exclusively upon myself. My brother and I parted at my door, he taking his way to Bailey's Hotel, where he boarded, and I going in to dinner, which was waiting my coming.

I had scarcely seated myself at table when a smart rap was heard at the door. "That's Langdon," said I. I felt sure it was he—and it was. As I opened the door, there he stood, with a very pale face, and his hand behind him, holding something, as I imagined, concealed under the tail of his coat.

"Ah! Mr. La—I haven't the pleasure of knowing your name—how do you do?" said I. "Walk in."

He stood right still, and, peering into the room, inquired,

"Where's your brother?"

"At his hotel," I answered. "Gone to dinner."

"*What* hotel does he stay at?" he asked.

"Bailey's," I answered, promptly, without thinking that I was putting this blood-seeking fellow on my brother's track.

On receiving this answer, he turned to go.

"I want to say a word to you," said I, calling after him, fully intending to explain and apologize.

"I want to see your brother," he answered back, and sulkily marched away.

"This won't do," said I to myself; "I must manage to warn my brother of his danger;" and, telling my wife I had a sudden call on business, I left her and the children to dine without me, and hastened by a short cut to Bailey's, and up stairs into Lem's room in the second story of the house. Lem was at dinner. Taking a card, I hastily wrote upon it:

"Your Room, 2 o'clock P.M.
"*Beware! Langdon is waiting for you.* S."

Ringing a bell, I sent this, by the answering servant, to the dining-room. In about a minute and a half I received the same card back, with the following line directly under mine:

"At Dinner, 2 1-60 P.M.
"*You can't come it, Smith!* L."

What was to be done? He thought I was playing a joke on *him*. We oftentimes did such things with each other. No time was to be lost. As he came out from dinner, he would inevitably be attacked by the enraged Irishman, and though, if warned, there was little to fear for Lem in a fair encounter, we both felt so thoroughly ashamed of the *cause* of the man's anger that it was desirable, in every point of view, that the foolish affair should be settled in a different way. I immediately dispatched another note to my brother to this effect:

"I tell you seriously that Langdon has been to my house inquiring for you, and I believe he is at this moment waiting for you in the sitting-room. Come up here at once."

This brought him. His voice was soon heard upon the stairs, and—oh, horror!—that of the Irishman also!

"Come up into my room, if you want to speak to me," said Lem, as he passed along the gallery.

"D—n your sowl!" growled the Irishman, "we can settle it here. Stop—stop, I say!"

But there was no "stop" in Lem then; on he came along the gallery, followed by Paddy, and entered the room, which was one step down from the floor he came over.

As the Irishman came to the door, and was about accepting my brother's invitation to "walk in," he saw me sitting composedly smoking a cigar (I smoked then, I don't now)—me, whom he had left not five minutes before at my house in a distant street, just in the act of sitting down to dinner. He started back a pace, and I improved the opportunity to step to the door and commence an explanation, telling him the exact truth of the matter, taking the whole blame upon myself, and offering the most full apology. He listened impatiently, evidently intent upon a fight, and replied, "I have nothing against *you*, but your brother there knew my name well enough, and he insulted me purposely, and he shall fight me, by——." "Oh, very well," says Lem; "if he won't accept of our apology, and will have a fight, I must accommodate the gentleman," and he threw off his coat. "Come on," says Paddy: "that's hearty," and off went *his* coat. "Stop!" said I, interposing between the two—one in the room behind me, the other on the gallery before me—"this must not be; it is folly to fight about such a trifle; we did not know your name, nor do we now know it." "That's a lie," asseverated the Irishman; "you both knew it." I couldn't stand "the lie," so off went *my* coat. "Look here," said Lem, "I'm not going to let you fight this fellow for my words. Stand aside, and let me give the gentleman satisfaction." There was no time for farther parley; the belligerent Irishman came at me like a mad bull, with head down and arms extended for a hug. He was on the gallery, as I have said; I was on the floor of the room, just one step, say twelve inches, below him, bringing us very nicely together, considering the difference of our heights. I would have given one hundred dollars willingly to have got out of the business, but there was no help for it; I was "in;" so, bracing myself firmly on my right foot (having forcibly pushed my brother back upon the bed, where he lay laughing during the combat), I met the enemy's charge by planting a left-handed hit between the eyes, which sent him reeling against the banister. Quickly recovering, he came at me again, again spreading out his arms and striking wide, cursing and swearing all the time, and was met by another blow very much like the first, and with like effect. By this time a crowd was gathered, and oh! how I did wish somebody would take my opponent off; but, confound them, they liked the fun, and insisted on the fight proceeding. As for Lem, seeing that the Irishman had no science, and that I was getting along very well, he contented himself by clapping his hands and ejaculating such sentences as these: "That's right, Sol! Go it, old fellow! He *would* have it, now let him have enough of it!" I never was so anxious to be relieved of an adversary as in this case. I felt sure that if he once got hold of me I was a goner! But he *didn't* get hold of me, nor did he strike me a successful blow. Every time he came up he got a lick fairly in the face, and in about two minutes *he was blind!* His face (poor fellow!) had lost all its distinctive features, and it is my belief that his own mother would not have known him then. After the crowd had made up its mind that my adversary had been punished sufficiently, they carried him down stairs to the pump. The fight was ended, and I had not received a scratch; but I was terribly frightened all the time, and was continually praying for a separation.

My brother and I (feeling really guilty) expected nothing else but that we should be mobbed, or hissed off the stage by the Irishman and his friends, and for three or four weeks were in mortal dread of the reappearance of our determined foe.

One morning a message from the box-office was conveyed to me upon the stage that a gentleman wished to see me.

"What sort of a gentleman?" I inquired.

"A short, stout gentleman—an Irishman, I think," replied the boy.

"It is Langdon," I said to my brother.

"Yes," said Lem, "there is no doubt about it: he has come to take his revenge."

"Well," said I, "there's no use trying to avoid him; I must go and meet my fate."

"Very true," assented my brother; "but I shall go with you; and remember, it must now be distinctly understood, it is *me* he is to deal with this time; you took the matter out of my hands on the first occasion—my turn has now come."

This as we walked along through the lobby.

Arriving at the box-office, we saw our man (it *was* he, sure enough) sitting inside, apparently quite cool and composed. Putting on as much calmness as I could—standing outside the door—I saluted him civilly, saying,

"Good-morning, sir; I hear you wish to see me."

As soon as he heard my voice, he started up and returned the salute with perfect good-nature, adding the usual inquiry as to my health. This being satisfactorily answered, he reached out his hand, and, seeing me hesitate about taking it, he said,

"Oh, Mr. Sol, don't hold back; and your brother there, that wanted to get at me so while you and I were settling the general dif-*fic*-ulty, let me have a shake of *his* hand too: it was no fault of his that you stood up in his place. I want to feel of you," he continued, after shaking us both by the hand for some time; "I want to see what the divil you are made of, any how, that you can lick Paddy O'Rourke all into smithereens without receiving a rap in return."

Hereupon he felt of my rather small hands and arms till he was perfectly satisfied that *science* had done the whole thing.

"That's it," said he; "I told my friend so afterward — it was the science, and not the strength, that did it."

As soon as I could get in a word, I re-tendered the apology I had offered at the hotel, and expressed a hope that he would *now* accept it.

"Divil an apology will I accept," said he. "Didn't we fight it out? and didn't I get beautifully whipped? No apology—none; unless *I* owe one for getting never a lick at you while you were punishing me so ilegantly."

After some little farther conversation in the same strain, Mr. O'Rourke said:

"Now I'll tell you what I'm come for: I've made a bet with some fellows that you can whip any man in Adams County. The question is, will you fight for me and let me win this wager?"

I assured him I would *not*.

"Oh bother! don't say no! You are sure to win for me. *I* can whip any man in the county but yourself. You see they haven't got the *science*."

I persisted in my refusal, and he rose to depart, saying, "I like you—I like you all the better for the punishment you gave me, for you did it genteelly, standing up to it like a man. By-the-by, when is your benefit?"

I told him when.

"Look out for a smasher," said he; "I'll see that the Irish turn out on the occasion;" and he went away after another general shaking of hands with my brother and myself.

He kept his word at my benefit night—there *was* a smasher—an immense house; and when I retired from before the curtain, after responding to a call for a speech, amid the shouts which greeted me, I recognized my friend's voice crying out, "Go it, old boy! You desarve all you have got to-night, and more too! It's the *science* that did it!"

Accepting a re-engagement with Mr. Caldwell, we next went with the company to St. Louis, where the season was an utter failure. I find, by reference to some scraps of memoranda, that the theatre closed in July, and the main body of the dramatic forces proceeded to Louisville, while I, with a small party gathered together in haste, opened the theatre *at half price*, and did a thriving business for two weeks. The newly-organized company consisted of Messrs. L. Smith (leading actor in tragedy and light comedy), Pearson, Carter, Baily, Short, Palmer, Jones, Wilkins, Mrs. Sol. Smith (leading actress), Mrs. Carter, Mrs. Palmer, and Miss Carter. Baily was the most useful man I ever employed. Besides acting, and singing between the pieces, he was "property man," and attended entirely to the fitting up of our temporary theatres while we were journeying. St. Louis at this time contained less than 7000 inhabitants.

CHAPTER VII.

Our first halting-place in this our new campaign was Memphis. Here we performed seven nights with indifferent success, and then departed for Bolivar, where my former landlord received me with open arms, having found out that the report of my having retired from the stage and *taken to preaching* was all a mistake. I think, however, my "first and last sermon" must have converted a good many of the Bolivarians, for they no longer flocked to the theatre, as on the occasion of our former visit. Our total receipts in six nights amounted to but $151. We left, and I have never visited that village since, either as an actor or as a preacher.

In Florence we fared no better, the receipts averaging about the same as at Bolivar. We tried a week over at Tuscumbia; but a religious excitement prevailing there at the time (one lady, a Mrs. Goodlow, hanged herself in her ecstasy), we played but six nights, to an average of $42 per night, and quit. The only other incident of interest during our stay in this place was the evident impression I made on the susceptible heart of some young girl, which caused her to break out in the following paraphrase of some old verses through the newspaper:

TO "OLD SOL"—*The Western Comedian.*

BY A YOUNG LADY OF TUSCUMBIA.

Let bigots rail against the stage,
  In senseless declamation dull;
They ne'er, with all their rant and rage,
  Could calm a heart like thee, "*Old Sol!*"

Let others praise the *Forrest* green,
  And some their *Booths* will yet extol;
But to expel the blues or spleen,
  You're for my money yet, "*Old Sol!*"

Let dandies stay at home and gaze
  Upon some automaton doll;
Such senseless beings some may please,
  Because they've never seen thee, "*Sol!*"

And lovers, too, be highly pleased
  While pleading to some Pegg or Poll—
I'd with such nonsense ne'er be teased
  While I could hear thee plead, "*Old Sol!*"

Farewell; and may it be thy lot,
Where'er you go, t' have houses full;
And when you come this way, I wot,
We'll treat you with a *bumper*, "SOL!"

Our next town was Columbia, Tenn., where we acted twelve nights in a very neat little theatre, owned by a histrionic association, and our receipts reached $60 per night. I find, on reference to my cash-book, that the comedy of the HYPOCRITE was the most attractive piece we played about these days.

At the spirited little town of Pulaski we performed a week, in the theatre belonging to the Thespian Society, to very good houses. Previous to commencing, we attended a representation of the society by invitation, and I must say I have seldom enjoyed a performance more than on that occasion. The theatre was about sixty feet long and thirty wide. No boxes—all pit. Over the curtain were two ill-proportioned mermaids, or some other nondescript animals, blowing trumpets, and supporting a scroll with these words inscribed upon it:

"THE WORLD IN MINIATURE."

Underneath this motto was painted what was intended to be a representation of a pile of drums, trumpets, fiddles, guitars, and cannon balls; the remainder of a very high proscenium, tapering off at the top like the gable-end of a house, was painted to resemble *brick!* This embellishment was hugely admired by the Pulaskians, and I was called on for *my* opinion of the *decorations.* Of course I admired them very much. The Thespian performances consisted of the SOLDIER'S DAUGHTER and THREE WEEKS AFTER MARRIAGE. The costume adopted by the amateur actors was ludicrous in the extreme. The reading and acting were equally so. The gentlemen wore their hats pulled down over their eyes during the whole evening, as if fearful of being known. The females (made of large boys) strided about in a very peculiar and unfeminine manner. Young *Malfort* entered through a back window! and justified the *step* by the language of the text, which makes him say, "I believe I have mistaken the apartment." *Frank Heartall,* in expressing his extravagant joy at finding his supposed rival is a *brother* of the widow, instead of making use of the language selected for that purpose by the author, broke out in the following strain: "I am so happy that I could jump over the Ohio, wade up the Mississippi, and tow two steam-boats over the falls at Louisville!" In the afterpiece *Sir Charles Rackett* changed the game of whist to that of *poker*, as being a game better understood in that section of country, and swore at his wife at a terrible rate, using the profane expression, "By G—d!" at least fifty times!

A fair-haired girl, sixteen years of age, followed us to this place from Columbia, with a determination to join the company and become an actress. I dissuaded her from her purpose, but she persisted. I placed her under the care of the landlady of the house where we boarded, and promised to give her an answer to her application in a week. In the mean time I wrote back to her parents, stating the circumstances of the girl's elopement, and begging them to come or send for her. The day before we left the town her brother arrived, and, after much persuasion on his part, and a positive refusal to receive her into the company on mine, she consented to return to her anxious parents.

The night previous to our departure we were complimented with a serenade by all the musicians of the place.

A Black Crowd.

My brother and myself were in the habit of playing off all sorts of jokes at the expense of whoever happened to come in our way, and occasionally on each other. We left Pulaski on a Sunday morning. The women were provided with a carriage, while Lem and myself rode on horseback. The carriage started early, and was many miles on the road before we left the hotel, where I was detained an hour or two in settling up the bill, and closing the business of the little season. Lem managed to slip off a few minutes before me, promising to wait my coming up a couple of miles from the town. He *did* wait for me. As I was descending into one of the beautiful valleys of that region, I saw before me a little army of negroes, some on horseback and others on foot, drawn up across the road, as if to interrupt my progress. I paid but little attention to this, as I knew the slaves were mostly at liberty on Sundays, and I supposed they had a gathering for some frolic of their own. The only thing that puzzled me was the fact that there was my brother, riding up and down, marshaling the negroes, addressing them earnestly, and frequently pointing toward *me* as I descended the hill. I was not left long in doubt as to their intentions; for, when I had arrived within about ten yards of the crowd, my brother called out to me, at the top of his voice, "I charge you, in the name of General Jackson and the State of Tennessee, to surrender!" To carry on the joke which I supposed he was playing on the negroes, I answered, "I will not surrender with life." Upon receiving this answer, he instantly turned to the crowd, and, addressing it in a very earnest manner, said, "This is the murderer of my brother Sol—seize him!" The negroes made a rush toward me, and, urged on by my mischievous brother, attempted to seize my bridle-rein. Finding there was no escape but in flight, I put spurs to my horse, and, upsetting some of the foremost of the gang, made my way through the crowd, and set off at full speed toward Huntsville. I was closely followed by my brother and the *black crowd* several miles, the hue and cry bringing out fresh forces from every plantation we passed. By hard riding I at length distanced my pursuers, all but Lem, who, of course, zealously pursued the supposed murderer of his brother, until the negroes were left far behind. We then enjoyed a most hearty laugh; but both of us resolved to leave off such practical jokes against each other, lest we might some day raise a storm we could not quell, which was nearly the case in the present instance.

At Huntsville we made a season of four weeks, and our receipts averaged only $60 per night. This was my last professional visit to this thriving city. The drama *may* flourish here at some distant day, but it will be when religious meetings and faro-banks shall have lost their attractions.

A journey of one hundred and eighty miles brought us to Tuscaloosa, where the state Legislature was in session, and where we opened on the 19th of November, 1831, with the SOLDIER'S DAUGHTER and the TWO GREGORIES.

"Here's your Blood."

On the second night we performed PIZARRO, my brother acting the part of *Rolla*. In the last act, after seizing the child, and as he was rushing up toward the bridge, he observed a tall negro holding a teacup full of *blood* (rose pink), which was wanted almost immediately on the other side of the stage. As he passed he said to the negro, "Here, boy, carry that blood round to me on the other side; I want it the moment I cross the bridge." Away dashed *Rolla*, bearing the child aloft, amid a volley of Spanish musketry; and, turning to cut away the bridge with his sword, what was his horror to see the tall negro walk deliberately upon the stage, between the "waters," and in full sight of the audience, holding the cup in one hand and stirring up the contents with the forefinger of the other, and hear him exclaim, "Heah, Master Smith, here's your blood!" I ordered the drop to be lowered immediately, to shut in the ludicrous scene.

Lobbying for a Benefit.

Toward the close of the season the *night sessions* of the Legislature interfered considerably with the interests of the theatre—so much so, indeed, that whenever a night session was held our hall was nearly deserted.

My benefit was announced for the closing night of the dramatic season, and I did hope that on this particular occasion a night session of the Legislature would be dispensed with, as many influential members of both houses had assured me they would do all in their power to make my benefit a good one.

The election of bank directors, by joint ballot, had been postponed from day to day for nearly a week—one house resolving on meeting the other on such a day, and the other *amending* the resolution by proposing another, and so on, until the very day of the night on which my benefit was announced to take place. Just as the House was about to adjourn in the afternoon, the resolution of the Senate appointing that very day for the election of directors was amended by substituting "at night," and it was generally understood by senators, representatives, and citizens that the Senate would meet and *concur* in the amendment of the House, and that immediately thereupon the Senate would proceed to the hall of the House of Representatives, and the election would be proceeded with. No one unacquainted with Alabama politics can form the least idea of the absorbing interest created by these elections by the Legislature in joint session. Every thing else is forgotten: the galleries are crowded with spectators; the whole town turns out *en masse*, as though the affair could not be gotten through with without their general and particular attention. As for myself, I saw at a glance that "it was all up with me," unless I could, by a bold and successful *coup d'état*, upset the whole arrangement of the "collected wisdom" of the Commonwealth.

"Here goes," said I to my brother, as I sallied out after a late and hasty dinner; "nothing like trying! Go to the theatre, and have every thing ready for a punctual beginning."

"All right," answered Lem; "I'll have every thing ready, you may depend on *that;* but I fear we shall have to play to empty benches."

"Perhaps not," I replied;

> "'If I fail not in my deep intent,'

we shall play the HYPOCRITE to a good house yet." So saying, I departed on my lobbying mission.

During two seasons in Tuscaloosa it may be

supposed I had made many friends, both among the members of the Legislature and the citizens. As I hurried through the streets on my present errand, I met many of the latter, who shook their heads in a peculiarly sorrowful and discouraging manner, saying, "Ah! Sol, old fellow, your benefit to-night—meant to attend—but this election—must go and see *that*—very sorry," and words of like import. All seemed to agree in one thing—*there would be nobody at the theatre, and I had better postpone;* but I had no idea of giving it up so, as I had contracted with a boat, which was to leave the next morning, to take the company to Mobile. "I'll have a full house yet," I said to myself, as I mounted the steps of the State-house, where the members and spectators were already beginning to assemble in large numbers. I stationed myself in the lobby of the Senate chamber, where I soon had an opportunity of seeing Judge Perry, an influential member of the Senate, who had frequently professed himself my friend, and willing to serve me if in his power.

"Judge," said I, hastily seizing him by one of his coat buttons, "you have it in your power to do me an essential service."

"Glad of it," answered the judge. "What can I do for you, friend Sol?"

"My benefit takes place to-night," said I—

"So it does," replied the judge; "I recollect—Hypocrite—Mawworm—ha! ha! ha!—wanted to be there; but this confounded joint session—it will kill your house—can't you postpone?"

"No—must start for Mobile to-morrow—passages engaged. *Can't you postpone this joint session?*" demanded I, looking him boldly in the face.

"Oh, no—no; impossible. It is an understood thing—the election will certainly come off to-night—no getting over it," said Judge Perry, evidently sorry that he could not oblige me.

"But, judge," persisted I, "the Senate has not yet concurred in the amendment of the House."

"That's true," he replied; "but it *will* concur—mere matter of form—that will be the first business; and we then proceed to the House, where the people are now assembled waiting for us."

"Well, judge, you have often expressed a wish to serve me—you now have it in your power."

"How?"

"Thus—*vote against concurring in the amendment of the House.*"

"My dear fellow, it will be of no use whatever; *one vote* against concurring can not be of any service to you; the election will certainly go on."

"Never mind that; if you wish to manifest your friendship, promise me that you will vote in the way I wish."

"Well, well, I do; you have my promise for that," were the concluding words of the judge, as he left me to take his seat in the Senate chamber; "but, rely upon it, the election will go on."

Having thus secured the judge, I turned my attention to another senator, who, under the supposition that *one vote* would make no difference in the intended action of the Senate, pledged me that *he* would vote against concurring with the House amendment. I then attacked another senator with the same result, and another, and so on, until I had the pledges of thirteen senators, each supposing he was the *only* one who had promised me to vote in the negative. *I had thus secured a majority* when the president's hammer called the Senate to order.

"The first business before the Senate, gentlemen," spoke the president (Mr. Pickens, I think), "is the amendment of the House to the resolution appointing a joint session for the election of bank directors; the question is on concurring with the amendment—is the Senate ready for the question? As many as are in favor of the amendment appointing this evening for the joint session will signify the same by saying Aye."

A considerable number of "Ayes" responded—enough, as it was generally supposed, to carry the question in the affirmative. As a mere matter of form, however, the president continued,

"As many as are of a different opinion will signify the same by saying No."

To the astonishment of every person in the hall, a considerable number of "*Noes*" were heard. The president thought there was some mistake (so well was it understood that the election was to take place that night), and required that those who voted in the affirmative should RISE. Twelve senators stood up, who, after being carefully counted, were directed to resume their seats. The negative vote was then called in the same way, when THIRTEEN members rose to their feet, looking around on each other with evident surprise at finding so numerous a vote in the negative.

The president, after counting the negative vote twice over, to make sure, announced that the amendment was LOST. A motion to *adjourn*, made by my friend, Judge Perry, was now carried by acclamation, and in less than three minutes the House followed the Senate's example, and streams of people were seen issuing from the State-house, chatting to each other, and asking what in the world it all meant.

My benefit was a most brilliant one, and a few "extra licks" I threw into the character of

Mawworm told immensely with the audience, particularly with the thirteen non-concurring senators.

Next day, January 15, 1832, we embarked on board the American, Captain Hammond, which in three days carried us safely to Mobile, a city which I had long wished to visit professionally.

The first person I met on landing was Thaddeus Sanford, one of the very best men I ever knew, and a true friend.

A small theatre was fitted up *over a billiard-room* in Royal Street, and the first season of my theatrical management in Mobile commenced on the 25th of January, 1832, with the comedy of the SOLDIER'S DAUGHTER and farce of the LYING VALET.

The company consisted of Messrs. L. Smith, Palmer, Pearson, H. A. Williams, Carter, Madden, Morton, Baily, Davidson, Trower, Donaldson, and Sol. Smith; Mesdames Sol. Smith, Carter, Sizer, Williams, and Miss Carter.

Henry J. Finn came and played an engagement of six nights, much to the delight of the Mobilians.

Mr. Ned Raymond also performed a starring engagement, and made money. He made his first appearance on any stage in Rochester, N. Y., in 1825, in the character (or charac*ters*) of the ACTOR OF ALL WORK. His ambition was then to become a low comedian—now he aspired to tragedy, and figured in *Virginius* and *Brutus.* A year or two afterward, in a fit of mania a potu, he committed suicide by throwing himself from one of the wharves in Boston. Raymond was not his real name; *that* I withhold in consideration for the feelings of his surviving relatives, who reside in the city of New York.

This was considered a most *successful season,* and it *was* moderately so. As it was my *first* in Mobile, and was the stepping-stone to my future operations in that city, an accurate account of the business of the season may not be entirely without interest to the reader:

First	week, Receipts	(4 nights)...	$320 00
Second	" "	(6 nights)...	660 00
Third	" "	(" ")...	820 00
Fourth	" "	(5 nights)...	543 00
Fifth	" "	(" ")...	505 00
Sixth	" "	(6 nights)...	1279 00
Seventh	" "	(" ")...	764 00
Eighth	" "	(2 nights)...	255 00
Total receipts of the season			$5146 00
My expenses during the eight weeks, including $575 paid to stars, and without reckoning traveling expenses to and from Mobile, amounted to			5121 00
Leaving me a profit of............			$25 00!!

If any citizen of Mobile had been asked to give an estimate of the profits of the theatre that season, *ten thousand dollars* would probably have been the very least sum thought of! And so it is with nearly every outdoor estimate of the business of theatres. For my own part, I must confess that the remembrance of my first professional visit to Mobile causes none but pleasing sensations. The audiences were easily pleased, and the actors exerted themselves to the utmost in their several roles, in gratitude for the leniency of the public.

Toward the close of the season's operations, Mr. Purdy Brown, by his agent, Mr. James P. Baily, opened, in an unfinished state, and with a very meagre company, a new theatre in St. Emanuel Street, and I withdrew my forces to Montgomery, deeming it better to leave the field to the invading army than to fight a battle in which both parties must inevitably be losers.

A most disastrous season my friend Brown had of it, commencing as it did late in February, and closing in the spring with a heavy loss, notwithstanding the attempts to retrieve the fortunes of the day by bringing on the field a large force of *cavalry.* Poor Purdy! I have some reminiscences in store respecting him which I may or may not put on paper for the amusement of the reader. He is gone to another scene of action, where I trust he is free from the annoyances of theatrical management, which, to say the truth, he was every way unfitted for, while, as a manager of a *circus,* no one was more capable.

I have not preserved the records of our season at Montgomery; but it was quite successful, yielding a handsome profit. It was from this point I made my arrangements for the *invasion of Georgia,* which event was to take place in the month of May of this year.

But, before proceeding through the Creek nation to that old and patriotic state, we were induced to pay a short visit to Selma, where we were welcomed by the same generous support ($70 per night) which had been extended to my former company the year before.

In an unlucky hour I listened to the urgent solicitations of several of the most influential citizens of Cahawba to give a week's performance at that ancient village, formerly the seat of government of the state; but the "lovers of the drama" were too few in number to remunerate us for our trouble, and, after playing five nights to wretched business, the steamer Herald heaving in sight, I "pulled up stakes" in double-quick time, and we embarked, bag and baggage, for Montgomery.

"Halloo! Smith," cried one from the crowd, as the last bell rang for starting, "you are not going to leave us in this way?"

"Yes I am," answered I from the hurricane deck. "Your town don't pay expenses—must go."

"But," persisted my friend on the shore, "the people have all been holding back for the *last night*. They will be greatly disappointed."

"Can't help it," I replied; "*they* have disappointed *me* five nights, and must become reconciled to my disappointing *them* once." And off we went.

We made another short season in Montgomery, and then, our arrangements for traveling being completed, we wended our way through the Creek nation into Georgia.

Adventure in the Creek Nation.

The company traveled in barouches, and the baggage was sent in a large Pennsylvania road wagon. We passed through the Creek nation about five years previous to the commencement of the disturbances which ended in sending the Indians to Arkansas. One afternoon we halted for refreshment at the residence of a chief, where about one hundred Indians were assembled, drinking and carousing. One of our number, by name John Carter, who had undertaken to perform the duties of general caterer for the party, purchased a gallon of milk, and the usual quantum of sugar and rum, of which ingredients, with the addition of a little grated nutmeg, he was busily engaged in forming that delicious mixture well known by Southern travelers as *milk punch.* Now it happened that John had been dreading this journey for some months, having taken up the idea that we should most assuredly be attacked and robbed (if not murdered) while traveling through this same Creek nation. My brother and myself formed a plan to have some sport out of his fears, and proceeded to execute it thus: I went to the chief, and offered to give a dollar to four Indians who would run a mile, and "keep up" with the Jersey wagon which I pointed out to him, at the same time showing him the man who was to drive. The chief immediately agreed to the proposal, and called four young men from their sports to give them their instructions. While this was going on, my brother called John mysteriously aside, and asked him what he had been saying or doing to the Indians. "I have not said a word to them," replied John, innocently, "except to ask them for these materials, which they furnished me willingly, and charged a pretty good price for too. There, taste that, and say if you don't approve of it: you won't get such a bowl of punch as that again in a hurry, I can tell you." At this juncture I came up and asked our worthy caterer the same question previously propounded by my brother, and added, "The Indians seem to have taken offense at some one of our party." This caused John to open his eyes a little, and his looks became somewhat disturbed. "I can't imagine who has been saying or doing any thing to offend them." "Nor I either," said John, "unless the tarnal fools have taken offense at my saying that ninepence a quart was a devilish high price for milk." "That's it," replied I, "to a certainty; these natives are very tenacious of their character, and can not bear to be charged with extortion." Here John cast some anxious glances toward a group of Indians, who seemed observing us attentively, and talking aside, every now and then pointing toward John, and then looking at the Jersey wagon which belonged to him and his family. "What do they mean by that, I wonder? They seem to direct their attention entirely to *me* and old *Copp*"—(that was the name of the horse)—"I don't know what to make of it, I'm sure." Thus spoke John, while big drops of sweat began to be apparent on his brow. "I do really begin to think they have some hostile design upon you," said I; "and, now I think of it, I recollect an expression of one of them, just as I passed those fellows with the hatchets, which confirms me in the opinion that they mean something." "What expression—what did the bloody-minded rascals say?" demanded John, in a tremor of apprehension, not a little increased by certain flourishes of hatchets by the savages, and a low murmur which met his ear, and which his fears interpreted into a death-song. "I don't understand the Creek language perfectly," was my reply, "but, from what I could gather, I am disposed to think they are highly offended at something; that tall fellow observed to the others that *ekrecrlculakahoochichopetehick*—which, translated into English, means, *if people don't like the price of milk, they had better not drink it;* to which that fellow who is now looking this way replied, *Chackledamnationuphillanddowntumbleum—chooh!* which, as near as I can make it out, means, *they'll follow you to the Chattahoochie River but they'll have revenge!* By this time John's fears had got the better of his love for punch, and he began to look round for his hat and gloves. Every movement was watched by the four savages, who had their instructions to chase the wagon a mile. "Here—stop a bit—I think, for fear of accidents, I'd better be off. If you'll take care of the ladies and pay for the punch, I'll quietly take old Copp and put." We agreed with him that perhaps it was best, for fear of accidents, that he should effect his escape, as *he* appeared to be the only one of the party the savages had any designs against. So, without even tasting the excellent punch he had brewed, he slipped round the barn and put the bridle on Captain Copp. The four Indians kept him in view all the time, but the fugitive appeared not to notice them. When he had fairly got the reins in his hands and mounted the Jersey, he cast one last look toward us and the bowl of punch, another (of quite a different kind) toward the four hostile savages, and gave the whip to old Copp. The crack of the whip was followed by a short whoop from the Indians. Off started the Jersey, with John standing up and lashing old Copp at every jump, and off started the four Indians in pursuit. Such a race has seldom been seen in the Creek nation.

Having drunk and settled for the punch, we pursued our journey at leisure, forming various conjectures how far our frightened companion would travel that night. About half a mile from the starting-place we found John's traveling-cap, and began to fear some accident might have befallen its owner; three quarters of a mile farther we found the four Indians dancing in the road, and tossing up in the air something which resembled a *human scalp!* "Heavens and earth!" I exclaimed, "is it possible our foolish joke has ended in the destruction of our poor friend?" On approaching the Indians, our worst fears were removed by one of them throwing us the scalp, which turned out to be John's *scratch*, that valuable article having been lost in the race! We paid the Indians the promised dollar, and, in return, they gave us a parting yell through their fingers which made the pine forest ring again.

About eight miles farther on we found our friend sitting on a log by the road-side, the perspiration bursting from his bald head in drops as large as bullets; Captain Copp was in a complete foam. "Thank God!" exclaimed the poor fellow, as we approached, "you have escaped the blood-thirsty savages. If General Jackson don't take this matter up, he's not the man I take him for, that's all." Having restored John his wig, and removed his fears of immediate danger by telling him we had met the Indians returning from the chase, we began to question him concerning his miraculous escape. "Gentlemen," said he, "it's all owing to that glorious horse, Captain Copp, who is the greatest animal living: it took him to take me through the dangers of this day. The infernal villains poured in upon me from all quarters; there was one behind every tree ready to intercept me; and then their outrageous yells and whooping—they ring in my ears yet. I lost my hat and wig in the strife, for at one time there were about a dozen in the wagon endeavoring to scalp me; but, knocking over five of the foremost of the ruthless villains, and laying the whip boldly on to old Copp, I managed to get out of their infernal clutches, and am still alive."

Some days after this adventure, one of our party asked John how many Indians he thought there were in pursuit of him. "I can not be certain," replied he; "I had but little time to think of counting them at the time; but, from a calculation I have made since, I think that, without taking into the account the squaws and papooses, who are considered non-combatants, there couldn't have been much less than FIFTEEN HUNDRED."

I could fill volumes with accounts of this and other journeys through this then uncultivated country; but I spare the reader all details, and carry him straight through, barely stopping by the way to say that we "put up" the second night, on this particular occasion, at the BLACK WARRIOR'S, where the warrior's wife (the warrior himself being off on a hunt) gave us rather "lenten fare," but fed our horses well; bad beds, well peopled with fleas and bed-bugs; and made enormous charges for our accommodation. At Mr. Elliott's, twelve miles from Columbus, we fared much better, being served with an excellent supper of fish, which the landlord informed me he caught in great abundance—sometimes as many as 300 a night—in a trap!

Sunday morning, May 20th, 1832, we crossed the Chattahoochie River, leaving Alabama behind us.

CHAPTER VIII.

GEORGIA! generous, hospitable Georgia! How well do I remember my sensations when first entering upon your soil! It was Sunday, and the streets of Columbus were filled with gayly-dressed citizens and Creek Indians. The arrival of a theatrical company created a decided sensation.

"When do you open?" was the general question.

"Next Thursday," was the response.

"*Where* do you open?" was the next and most natural inquiry.

"In the NEW THEATRE," was the brief but somewhat puzzling reply.

Having taken possession of apartments in the

Columbus Hotel, then kept by Messrs. Pomeroy and Montague, I asked that a message should be sent to the most expeditious contractor in the city. A Mr. Bates soon appeared, and in twenty minutes he had my directions. On the next Saturday the following *true* paragraph appeared in one of the newspapers:

"EXPEDITION.—A theatre, 70 feet long by 40 wide, was commenced on Monday morning last by our enterprising fellow-citizen, Mr. Bates, and finished on Thursday afternoon, in season for the reception of Mr. Sol. Smith's company on that evening. A great portion of the timber, on Monday morning, waved to the breeze in its native forest; fourscore hours afterward, its massive piles were shaken by the thunder of applause in the crowded assemblage of men."

Here began my acquaintance—may I not say friendship?—with Mirabeau B. Lamar, Esq., afterward President of Texas. He was a candidate for Congress—not nominated on the ticket of either party, but "on his own hook"—merely for the "excitement" it afforded him. With the same object he traveled through Texas, fought at the battle of San Jacinto, eventually submitted his name to the people of that redeemed country as a candidate for the highest office in their gift, and was elected.

Unusual Ceremonies in the Temple of the Sun.

PIZARRO was one of our most popular stock plays. My brother Lem's *Rolla* was his best tragic character; when dressed for the part he *looked* every inch an Indian chief. At Columbus we produced this tragedy *with real Indians for the Peruvian army*. The effect was very *striking*, but there were some unrehearsed effects not set down in the bills. I had bargained with a chief for twenty-four Creek Indians (to furnish their own bows, arrows, and tomahawks), at fifty cents each and a glass of whisky. Unfortunately for the entire success of the performance, the whisky was paid and drank in advance, causing a great degree of exhilaration among our new *supes*. They were ranged at the back of the theatre building, in an open lot, during the performance of the first act, and on the commencement of the second they were marshaled into the back door, and posted upon the stage behind the scenes. The entrance of *Rolla* was the signal for a "shout" by the company, carpenters, and scene-shifters; the Indians, supposing *their time had come*, raised such a yell as I am sure had never before been heard inside of a theatre. This outburst being quelled, the scene between *Alonzo*, *Cora*, and the Peruvian chief was permitted to proceed to its termination uninterrupted; but when the scene changed to the Temple of the Sun, disclosing the troops of *Rolla* (his "brave associates, partners of his toil, his feelings, and his fame") drawn up on each side of the stage in battle array, the plaudits of the audience were answered by whoops and yells that might be, and no doubt were, heard a mile off. Order being partially restored, *Rolla* addressed his army, and was greeted with another series of shouts and yells even louder than those which had preceded. Now came *my* turn to take part in the unique performance. As *High Priest of the Sun*, and followed by half a dozen virgins and as many priests, with measured step, timed to slow music, I emerged from behind the scenes, and "with solemn march" perambulated the stage, in dumb show called down a blessing on the swords of *King Ataliba* and General *Rolla*, and in the usual impressive style, looking up into the front gallery, commenced the Invocation to the Sun. Before the time for the joining in of the chorus, I found I was not entirely alone in my singing. A humming sound, at first low and mournful, and rising gradually to *forte*, greeted my ear; and when our chorus *did* join in the strain, it was quite overpowered by the rising storm of *fortissimo* sounds which were issuing from the stentorian lungs of the savages; in short, *the Indians were preparing for battle* by executing, in their most approved style, the Creek war-song and dance! To attempt stopping them we found would be a vain task; so that, after a moment or two of hesitation, the virgins made a precipitate retreat to their dressing-rooms, where they carefully locked themselves in. The *King*, *Rolla*, and *Orano* stood their ground, and were compelled to submit to the new order of things. The Indians kept up their song and war-dance for full half an hour, performing the most extraordinary feats ever exhibited on a stage, in their excitement scalping *King Ataliba* (taking off his wig), demolishing the altar, and burning up the sun! As for Lem and I (*Rolla* and the *High Priest*), we joined in with them, and danced until the perspiration fairly rolled from our bodies in large streams, the savages all the time flourishing their tomahawks and knives around our heads, and performing other little playful antics not by any means agreeable or desirable. At last, to put an end to a scene which was becoming more and more tiresome as it proceeded, an order was given to drop the curtain. This stroke of policy did not stop the ceremonies, which proceeded without intermission until the savages had finished their song and dance, when, each receiving his promised half dollar, they consent-

INDIAN WAR-DANCE IN THE TEMPLE OF THE SUN. (See page 79.)

ed to leave the house, and our play proceeded without them. Next night the same troupe came to the theatre and wanted to *assist* in the performance of MACBETH, but I most positively declined their "valuable aid."

After a season of two weeks, we made a move for Macon, where another temporary theatre was put up in little less than a week's time. Here we performed to respectable and very discriminating audiences for about five weeks, after which we raised the dramatic flag at the capital of the state, Milledgeville. The theatre was erected here as early as 1817, as I was told; but, at the time we took possession of it, the famed Augean stable must have been a carpeted parlor in comparison with it. Thirty barrels of lime were used in the cleansing of this temple of Thespis, and even then it always retained a rather unsavory odor. Our visit was hailed with delight by the noble-hearted Georgians, and for one week our audiences were large and fashionable. It being about "Commencement" time at Athens, we posted off to that classic village, where another new theatre—built in three days—was prepared for our reception.

My brother Lem was not with us here. He had obtained leave of absence for a brief period to visit Cincinnati, where he performed a starring engagement in a new theatre opened that season by our former manager, Mr. Caldwell. He also performed a brief engagement at Louisville.

At Athens our success was but meagre. The exercises of "Commencement" engrossed the public attention, and we closed our doors after a season of one week.

At this place I experienced the great pleasure of becoming acquainted with A. H. Pemberton, Esq., one of the ablest editors of the state, and author of the best *Defense of the Drama* which ever came under my notice.

At a small town called Madison we "hung out our banner" for a week, and performed in the ballroom of a tavern kept by a Mr. Campbell, a large fat man—"fat as butter"—who fed and slept us well, and *charged* us accordingly. Total receipts for the week, $205! The barber who shaved me in this village, a very black negro, had a light mulatto wife. They had several children of the proper shade of color, and one, the youngest, almost *white*. Being asked the reason of the last child's being so much whiter than the others, the barber very innocently answered that it was all owing to his wife's having followed the advice of a white lady during her pregnancy, and *taken a great deal of magnesia and chalk to cure the dyspepsia.*

Our fat landlord was a very religious individual—a great hand at revivals and camp-meetings—and it was only by dint of hard persuasion the town's people could obtain his consent to receive into his hall the sinful actors. But it so turned out that Mr. Boniface, after taking a few peeps behind the scenes, became greatly taken with the plays, so much so that one night he boldly walked into the front among the audience and took a conspicuous seat, determined to "see it out." The people welcomed him with a round of applause which he did not take to himself, but, turning around before seating himself, he said, "Oho! you talk of *my* making a noise at camp-meetings—I've got you now—*you* make a plaguy deal more noise here at the show than I ever did there." Another "round" greeted our fat landlord, and the curtain went up.

Our next town was Monticello, where we performed in the dining-room of Mr. Stovall, and occupied one of his best parlors for a greenroom. Receipts for the week precisely the same as at Madison, after paying $25 tax, which the commissioners demanded for the privilege of leaving about $100 more in their town than we received. We had here *one* auditor, a constant attendant, who evidently appreciated our performances—a cat! Every night she found her way into the theatre, and, seating herself immediately in front of the foot-lights, watched and listened to the performances from beginning to end!

We returned to Milledgeville and performed two weeks with poor success, closing on the 1st of September.

Opened at Macon Monday, September 3d, and performed one week only; after which we pushed on to Columbus, where we managed to stay three weeks, the policy being to pass the time away until the meeting of the Legislature in Milledgeville.

Being up and out on a walk early one morning—this was at Macon—I strolled to the Methodist Church, where I heard singing. Stepping in and taking a seat, I found assembled six negro men, one mulatto girl, and two white men. A lazy-looking young fellow, one of the white men, seemed to conduct the affair, asking his *white brethren* and *black brethren* to pray alternately. I staid to hear one *white* and one *black* prayer, and it is difficult to say which was better of the two. The *black man* prayed in something like the following words:

"O most holy and significant Fader! thou spencer of ebery precious and deliberate gift, look down on your poor miserable *children*, and bless us with thy sacred and devoted power—*if it be thy will.* O most holy Fader, we humbly pray for the instigation of thy wrath throughout dis deboted land; bless all who hab turned out to dis praar meetin' and dem dat habn't—*if it be thy will.* May thy mercy and vengeance smile upon our white bredren, who are prayin' and preachin' for us poor sinners, and in reliance upon the precious blood of Jesus Christ—*if it be thy will.* O bless de poor heden, and larn dem to examine de doctrines of thy Word, which is a sharp two-pointed sword, goin' out of the mouth of dy servants—*if it be thy will.* May de Gospel spread like de cholera through de earth, spreading vastation and castigation around—*if it be thy will.* We pray thee, O holy Christ, the fader of the 'maculate Virgin Mary, to cleanse us ob our sins, and scrub us with the scrubbin'-brush ob corruption, till we are the sanguine dye of thy holy truth; and though our sins be as wool, may dey be made white as scarlet with thy most precious lamb, which was killed on Mount Sinai for our sallivation—*if it be thy will.* And, O most holy Jesus, send thy Spirit upon us this morning, that we may sing thy praise and worship thee with meekness and compunctuation; and when we give up our immortal existence in this immaculate world, wilt thou receive us to thy bosom—*if it be thy will*—when we will gib all de glory, and honor, and power to our holy medidator and Savior foreber and eber after—Amen."

During our stay at Columbus, at the earnest solicitations of a Mr. Childers, he was permitted to make his "first appearance on any stage" as *Tony Lumpkin*, which he performed tolerably well for a new beginner. His figure was better fitted for *Don Quixote* than the character he chose for his opening, being very lean and bony; but *Tony Lumpkin* he had studied, and *Tony Lumpkin* he played. After the performance he made a regular application for a situation in the company. I declined entering into the proposed engagement, and wrote him a long letter, urging him not to persist in his determination to become an actor, and advising him to continue his studies in the law. With great reluctance he followed my advice, became in time an eminent lawyer in Alabama, and died many years afterward in Mobile, of which city he was once elected mayor.

Returned to Macon, and performed a very few nights to very small audiences; but remained a couple of weeks, it being considered quite useless to open in Milledgeville so early in the season. Time hanging heavy on my hands, as the saying is, I entered into a little "speculation," just for amusement, which I will now proceed to relate.

Speculation in Whiskers.

There lived in Macon a dandified individual whom I shall call Jenks. This individual had a tolerably favorable opinion of his personal appearance. His fingers were hooped with rings, and his shirt bosom was decked with a magnificent breastpin; coat, hat, vest, and boots were made exactly to fit; he wore kid gloves of remarkable whiteness; his hair was oiled and dressed in the latest and best style; and, to complete his killing appearance, he sported an enormous pair of *real whiskers!* Of these whiskers Jenks was as proud as a young cat is of her tail when she first discovers she has one.

I was sitting one day in a broker's office when Jenks came in to inquire the price of exchange on New York. He was invited to sit down, and a cigar was offered him. Conversation turning on the subject of buying and selling stocks, a remark was made by a gentleman present that he thought no person should sell out stock in such-and-such a bank at that time, as it *must* get better in a few days.

"I will sell *any* thing I've got, if I can make any thing on it," replied Jenks.

"Oh no," replied one, "not *any* thing; you wouldn't sell your *whiskers!*"

A loud laugh followed this chance remark. Jenks immediately answered, "I would; but who would *want* them? Any person making the purchase would lose money by the operation, I'm thinking."

"Well," I observed, "I would be willing to take the speculation, if the price could be made reasonable."

"Oh, I'll sell 'em cheap," answered Jenks, winking at the gentlemen present.

"What do you call cheap?" I inquired.

"I'll sell 'em for fifty dollars," Jenks answered, puffing forth a cloud of smoke across the counter, and repeating the wink.

"Well, that *is* cheap; and you'll sell your whiskers for fifty dollars?"

"I will."

"Both of them?"

"Both of them."

"*I'll take them!* When can I have them?"

"Any time you choose to call for them."

"Very well—they're mine. I think I shall double my money on them, at least."

I took a bill of sale as follows:

"Received of Sol. Smith *Fifty Dollars* in full for my crop of whiskers, to be worn, and taken care of by me, and delivered to him when called for. J. JENKS."

The sum of fifty dollars was paid, and Jenks left the broker's office in high glee, flourishing five Central Bank X's, and telling all his acquaintances of the great bargain he had made in the sale of his whiskers.

The broker and his friends laughed at me for being taken in so nicely. "Never mind," said I; "let those laugh that win; I'll make a profit out of those whiskers, depend on it."

For a week after this, whenever I met Jenks, he asked me when I intended to call for my whiskers.

"I'll let you know when I want them," was always my answer. "Take good care of them—oil them occasionally; I shall call for them one of these days."

A splendid ball was to be given. I ascertained that Jenks was to be one of the managers—he being a great ladies' man (on account of his whiskers, I suppose), and it occurred to me that before the ball took place I might as well call for my whiskers.

One morning I met Jenks in a barber's shop. He was Adonising before a large mirror, and combing up my whiskers at a devil of a rate.

"Ah! there you are, old fellow," said he, speaking to my reflection through the glass. "Come for your whiskers, I suppose?"

"Oh, no hurry," I replied, as I sat down for a shave.

"Always ready, you know," he answered, giving a final tie to his cravat.

"Come to think of it," I said, musingly, as the barber began to put the lather on my face, "perhaps now would be as good a time as another; you *may* sit down and let the barber try his hand at the whiskers."

"You couldn't wait until to-morrow, could you?" he asked, hesitatingly. "There's a *ball* to-night, you know—"

"To be sure there is, and I think you ought to go with a clean face; at all events, I don't see any reason why you should expect to wear *my* whiskers to that ball, so sit down."

He rather sulkily obeyed, and in a few moments his cheeks were in a perfect foam of lather. The barber flourished his razor, and was about to commence operations, when I suddenly *changed my mind.*

"Stop, Mr. Barber," I said, "you needn't shave off those whiskers just yet." So he quickly put up his razor, while Jenks started up from the chair in something very much resembling a passion.

"This is trifling!" he exclaimed. "You have claimed your whiskers—take them."

"I believe a man has a right to do as he pleases with his own property," I remarked, and left Jenks washing his face.

At dinner that day the conversation turned upon the whisker affair. It seems the whole town had got wind of it, and Jenks could not walk the streets without the remark being continually made by the boys, "*There goes the man with old Sol's whiskers!*" And they had grown to an immense size, for he dared not trim them. In short, I became convinced Jenks was waiting very impatiently for me to assert my rights in the property. It happened that several of the party were sitting opposite me at dinner who were present when the singular bargain was made, and they all urged me to *take the whiskers* that very day, and thus compel Jenks to go to the ball whiskerless, or stay at home. I agreed with them it *was* about time to *reap my crop*, and promised that if they would all meet me at the broker's shop where the purchase had been made, I would make a call on Jenks that evening, after he had dressed for the ball. All promised to be present at the proposed *shaving operation* in the broker's office, and I sent for Jenks and the barber. On the appearance of Jenks it was evident he was much vexed at the sudden call upon him, and his vexation was certainly not lessened when he saw the broker's office was filled to overflowing by spectators anxious to behold the barberous proceeding.

"Come, be in a hurry," he said, as he took a seat, and leaned his head against the counter for support; "I can't stay here long; several ladies are waiting for me to escort them to the ball."

"True, very true—you are one of the managers—I recollect. Mr. Barber, don't detain the gentleman; go to work at once."

The lathering was soon over, and with about three strokes of the razor *one side of his face was deprived of its ornament.*

"Come, come," said Jenks, "push ahead; there is no time to be lost: let the gentleman have his whiskers—he is impatient."

"Not at all," I replied, coolly, "I'm in no sort of a hurry myself—and, now I think of it, as *your* time must be precious at this particular moment, several ladies being in waiting for you to escort them to the ball, I believe *I'll not take the other whisker to-night.*"

A loud laugh from the by-standers, and a glance in the mirror, caused Jenks to open his eyes to the ludicrous appearance he cut with a single whisker, and he began to insist upon my taking *the whole of my property!* But all wouldn't do. I had a right to take it when I chose; *I was not obliged to take all at once*, and I *chose* to take but *half* at that particular period; indeed, I intimated to him very plainly that I was not going to be a very hard creditor, and that, if he "behaved himself," perhaps I should *never* call for the balance of what he owed me!

When Jenks became convinced I was determined not to take the remaining whisker, he began, amid the loudly-expressed mirth of the crowd, to propose terms of compromise, first offering me ten dollars, then twenty, thirty, forty—fifty! to take off the remaining whisker. I said, firmly, "My dear sir, there is no use talking; I insist on your wearing that whisker for me for a month or two."

"What will you take for the whiskers?" he at length asked. "Won't you sell them back to me?"

"Ah!" replied I, "now you begin to talk as a business-man should. Yes; I bought them on speculation; I'll sell them if I can obtain a good price."

"What is your price?"

"One hundred dollars—*must* double my money."

"Nothing less?"

"Not a farthing less—and I'm not anxious to sell even at *that* price."

"Well, I'll take them," he groaned; "there's your money; and here, barber, shave off this d—d infernal whisker in less than no time: I shall be late at the ball."

Near the end of October we opened the Milledgeville Theatre for the season, hoping great things from the fact that the Legislature was soon to meet. My brother Lem rejoined me here, and the season commenced auspiciously.

During our journeyings the past summer we were accompanied nearly the whole time by Mirabeau B. Lamar, Esq., who was a candidate for Congress, and who received a very large vote, but was not elected, not being on either the Union or State Rights ticket. I have never in my life met a more gentlemanly man. He was a good speaker—rather too vehement in his manner, perhaps; but, being well read, and possessing a good face and person, he enchained the attention of his auditors. He was at that time rather dyspeptic, but seemed to enjoy life reasonably. He could appreciate a joke and a good dinner; had Shakspeare at his tongue's end, and could quote him correctly and at pleasure; fenced well, and was otherwise highly accomplished.

Finally, he was a great lover of the stage. I dedicated a book to him, and on his marriage in 1851 (nearly twenty years after the events I am noting) he promised to name his first child after me; but, unfortunately, it turned out to be a girl, and the idea of naming *her* "Solomon" was given up at once.

During this season we produced the play of THERESE, translated from the French by John Howard Payne, and I must say I have never to this day seen it so well played as by the "Georgia company." My wife personated the part of *Mariette*, and my brother that of *Carwin*. It is not in my province to speak of the talents of my wife and brother (now no more), but, as they both occupied, while living, a prominent place in the dramatic company of which I was manager, and as many persons in Georgia may yet live who have seen them act, it may not be amiss to insert here a brief extract from a criticism published in one of the newspapers of the day, written (I am permitted to say now, though I did not know it at the time) by Gen. Lamar:

"Mr. Lem. Smith has the advantage of a fine person (he beats his brother in that), a good eye, and a flexible voice, not of the greatest compass, but sufficiently strong to be heard distinctly. He succeeds equally alike in comedy or tragedy, and extremely well in both; conceiving his characters properly, and never overstepping the modesty of nature. His powers, we think, are considerable, and his genius versatile. There is much refinement in his manners when in comedy, and much dignity and force in his appearance in higher characters, such as *Tell*. We have seen him in a great variety of parts, and find it difficult to decide in which his success is greatest."

* * * * * * * *

"One we have yet to name—the star of her profession—it would be censurable not to hold up to the admiration of our readers, as she has often presented herself to her gratified audience. We mean Mrs. Smith. It is far from our intention to enter into any minute analysis of her acting—setting forth her peculiarities; lauding what is good, and apologizing for what is otherwise, but shall speak of her merit in the aggregate, reserving our more detailed and definite criticism for some future number. To say that she is a first-rate actress would be giving her nothing more than her due, but we should probably not be believed, because she had not been brought up at the Park or at Drury Lane. Stars we have seen of the first magnitude who have shone with unrivaled lustre upon both these boards, and can say that they have afforded us no greater pleasure than we have derived from the performances of Mrs. Smith. If it be at all true that the merit of an actress may be justly estimated by the effect which she produces, her claims will be found inferior to few; for we have never yet heard the first person declare himself disappointed or dissatisfied—we have never seen one who did not admit that she always had a just conception of the part she played—that she entered deeply into the spirit and feelings of the character she represented, and that her look, gesture, and attitude were always graceful, natural, and appropriate; and if these, added to other qualities which she possesses—a melodious voice and eloquent delivery—do not constitute the perfection of the histrionic art, then we are at a loss to know what does. All these excellencies are universally conceded to her. In what character she succeeds best we could never decide for ourselves; she seems to be qualified by her versatility equally for the grave and the gay—'for farce, comedy, and tragedy.' We saw her once, on a benefit night, in the SOLDIER'S DAUGHTER, and concluded she appeared best in that part; but when she subsequently appeared in the ORPHAN OF GENEVA, we thought no character became her as *Therese*, and now our present decision is that her greatest efforts have been in *Elvira*."

While I am about it, it may be as well to give the general's opinion of *myself*, particularly as I think it is a tolerably correct one in the main. Here it is, segregated from the same article the foregoing extracts are taken from:

"Now then for 'Old Sol.' But, before entering upon the trial of this 'head and front' of the battalion, it may be proper to settle a preliminary question upon which his acquittal or condemnation chiefly rests. The heart will sometimes laugh in defiance of the sober decrees of the head, and when this is the case, which is in the right? Who has not had his risibility irresistibly excited by a joke which his judgment could not sanction? Shall the joke therefore be condemned? 'That is the question.' We answer, no. Now this is exactly 'Old Sol's' situation. His acting we can not approve as being always in good taste, yet he will extort the laugh from us in despite of our disapprobation. Shall we therefore condemn him? We answer, no. Our objection to him as an actor is, that he often lowers comedy to a farce, and brings farce to the borders of buffoonery. The approbation which we have to bestow is that which we have just admitted—his absolute dominion over our risible propensities. He never fails to accomplish the end and aim of all comic performances, that of exciting involuntary laughter and applause. This, however, is not his only merit. He possesses a lively fancy and a good fund of original wit, which enable him to introduce many seasonable jokes, acceptable to all, and offensive to none. This practice, it is true, is liable to abuse, and stands reprobated by authority no less than Shakspeare; but, with all due deference to the Bard of Avon, we must still adhere to our infallible rule, to censure nothing and praise all that produces a happy effect; by virtue of which 'Old Sol' is entitled to our high commendation and a full absolution for all faults, which we do hereby freely award him."

On the 12th of December the tragedy of DOUGLAS was performed, it being the LAST AP-

PEARANCE OF MY BROTHER, who personated the character of *Glenalvon*.

[In an appendix to this volume I propose to give some account of the MURDER of my beloved young brother.]

The season in Milledgeville was brought to a close on the 23d of December, the Legislature adjourning about the same time. The actual profits of the six months preceding this date are set down, in a business memorandum I kept at the time, at $1500, which sum, considering the labor performed, the journeys made, and wear and tear of the constitution, can not be considered over payment for the services of my wife and myself.

Macon was again tried on our way to Alabama, where we received for twenty-four nights' performances, in a cold theatre, $1580, being an average of about $66 per night—and this was considered good business.

Passing on toward Montgomery, our next stopping-place was Columbus, where we acted two weeks to an average nightly receipt of $56, closing on the 9th of February, 1833.

I purchased in Columbus some real estate at a cost of about $2000, which raised on my hands, and was eventually sold for nearly $20,000.

On Saturday, 16th of February, our standard was raised in Montgomery, Alabama, to a house of $140. The people appeared well pleased at our return. Business continued good here, and several "stars" (so called) shone forth during the season—Mrs. Knight and Mr. Forbes among the rest. My theatrical year ended on the 22d of March.

I subjoin a statement of the actual result of this year's "journey-work" in dollars and cents, as it appears in my cash-book of that day:

We must have traveled at least 5000 miles during the year. All traveling expenses were paid by the manager.

Total receipts—46 weeks—$20,885. Average per week, $454; per night, counting the actual number of nights played, to wit, 262 nights, $79 70. Profits of the year about $4000.

Mr. and Mrs. Lyons joined me at this time, and the season was prolonged a week, after which the theatre closed with my benefit, which was very largely attended.

CHAPTER IX.

AT the conclusion of this season I resolved to gratify a desire, long entertained, of visiting Cincinnati, the home of my brothers and numerous other relations. The company being disbanded, Messrs. Palmer and Lyons, members of the late organization, proposed to rent the Georgia theatres, and I consented to give them the use of my wardrobe and properties, with the understanding that, if they were successful in their speculation, they should have the privilege of purchasing my interest in the circuit at a given price; but if unsuccessful, they should return the properties in the ensuing fall. The result of this attempt of Messrs. P. and L. will appear hereafter.

Leaving the new managers to push their fortunes in the South, I made my way, with my family, toward Cincinnati, where we proposed to spend the summer; not, however, until Mrs. S. and myself had performed a short starring engagement in Mobile, under the management of Mr. Purdy Brown. I could relate hundreds of anecdotes relative to Manager Brown, but do not feel much disposed that way. A few lines must comprise all I have to say about him.

Manager Brown.

Mr. Brown's knowledge of theatrical matters was extremely limited; consequently, he was liable to be imposed upon by the actors, who, as a class, are never backward in furthering a joke. Mr. B. appeared on the stage occasionally, and when he did it was generally his wish to enact some important character—some person of rank in the drama—it being very much against the grain to appear *as a supernumerary*. Reading plays not being much in his way, he was in the habit of asking the actors what characters they thought would best suit him, and he was generally advised to study such parts as *Count Luneda* in the BROKEN SWORD, *Timoleon* in the GRECIAN DAUGHTER, *Beverly's Uncle* in the GAMESTER, and others of that sort. When, after a diligent search, poor Brown informed his friend, the actor who had advised him, *that no such character could be found in the play*, he was gravely informed that he had been searching in the wrong edition!

Manager B. had an abiding faith in horses—indeed, he had good reason for his faith—*they* never deceived him or played practical jokes upon him. Whenever he perceived that a play—be it tragedy, comedy, or melodrama—appeared to "drag;" or, to speak more intelligibly, to "hang fire;" or, to make the expression still more easily understood by the general reader, "go off dull," he ordered out his whole stud of horses and circus riders, and sent them on "to end the piece." Thus it is said (I confess I did not see this) that on the occasion of the performance of the SOLDIER'S DAUGHTER he sent on his circus troupe, dressed as Turks or Arabs, who performed a "grand entree" on the stage, driving the *Widow Cheerly*, *Governor Heartall*, and company down to the foot-lights, where they were obliged to stand for a mortal half hour and witness the cavalry evolutions, the whole winding up with a grand tableau, illuminated by red fire!

Mr. B., on one occasion, was compelled to assist in the performance of DAMON AND PYTHIAS—the company being short in numbers—and, finding the character which he chose (*Dionysius*—*King* Dionysius) too long for his study, which was none of the best, he was prevailed on to take that of *Procles*, which he was told was a sort of *Captain* in the Syracusan service. He proposed to act the part on horseback; but Webb, who was the *Damon*, dissuaded him from this, and the worthy manager consented to do it on foot. Some wag, to whom he applied for advice as to the manner of acting the part, told him that *Procles* was a fierce and spirited warrior, and when he was spoken to by *Damon* in the streets of Syracuse, and branded as a traitor, he should *seize the senator by the throat*. At the proper time, placing himself at the head of the supernumerary soldiers, "high heaped with arms and plunder," he rushed upon the stage with his shouting troops. When Webb, as *Damon*, came to these words,

> "And thou,
> Who standest foremost of these knaves,
> Stand back and answer me—what have ye done?"

Captain *Procles* looked daggers at him, but restrained himself so far as to wait for his "cue," which receiving at length in these words,

> "Thou most contemptible and meanest tool
> That ever tyrant used,"

he rushed upon *Damon* like a tiger, seizing him by the throat, and holding his neck between his hands as in a vice. Webb struggled and swore—in vain! "Let me loose! you are strangling me!" exclaimed the infuriated *Damon*, in a hoarse whisper. "Of course I am," answered *Procles*; "it is the business of the part!" And it was not until *Pythias* interfered in his behalf that he could be persuaded to loosen his hold.

On the last night of our engagement I enacted *Scaramouch*, in the pantomime of DON JUAN. In the last scene the amorous Don is seized by demons and cast into the infernal regions, as the bills have it, through a trap-door. At rehearsal, I told the manager that about twelve demons would be required at the wings to seize *Don Juan*, and cast him down the trap. "*And*" (I added in a joke) "*you must be ready under the stage, at the head of a troop of devils with pitchforks, to torment him until his numerous sins are burnt and purged away, as Shakspeare says.*" As I was leaving the theatre, the manager followed me to the back door, and asked me to repeat some direction I had given relative to the banquet in the pantomime. He afterward said something which induced me to think he wished to carry on the joke about the demons I had spoken of, to be stationed under the stage.

"How many demons did you say, Mr. Smith?" he asked.

"A dozen will do," I replied, laughing.

"Yes, a dozen *on* the stage, I know; but how many of those *tormenting* fellows underneath?"

"Oh," I answered, "as many as you like; the more the better; and be sure you have plenty of red fire."

"Never fear that," he replied, as he turned to go away.

Scaramouch is not a very easy character to perform, particularly when attempted by one like myself, unused to gymnastic feats; so that when I had gone through the dancing, the shipwreck, the riding on a dolphin, the eating of maccaroni, the frights at seeing the ghost on horseback, and other little incidental exercises, and had bid good-by to my master, the Don, in the grave-yard, it may be supposed that I lost no time, "distilled with fear" and perspiration as I was, in hastening to my dressing-room, with the view of disrobing as quickly as circumstances would permit. I had in part accomplished this, and was busily engaged in rubbing the upper part of my perspiring body with a coarse towel, when the call-boy knocked violently at the door, and begged me to step down to the stage, as the manager wished to see me particularly. Throwing a cloak about me, I hastened to the late scene of action, nearly suffocated with the smoke from the red fire, which was ascending in thick volumes, and found, on looking down the trap, that my friend Brown was there with thirty or forty fiends, all dressed in red flannel, and *armed with pitchforks*, waiting for the descent of *Don Juan!* It seems that, in the concluding scene of the pantomime, the performer who enacted the part of *Don Juan* (Mr. Heyl), finding a thick column of "sulphurous and tormenting flames" ascending through the trap-door, would not consent to be "plunged in," as required by the stage direction, but, on the contrary, had burst from the supernumerary fiends and escaped to his dressing-room. The curtain was lowered, and the piece was considered ended by all but the worthy manager, who was in the regions below, with his army of fiends, waiting for his victim. It was some time before he could be persuaded to abandon his post, and not until he had declared his determination to discharge the contumacious actor who had refused to take the "fatal plunge."

Mr. Edwin Forrest passed through Mobile while we were there, on his way to New Orleans. Ten years had elapsed since we had parted in Lexington, Ky., he to join Mr. Caldwell at the South, I to commence my managerial career in Cincinnati.

We were succeeded by Mr. James Wallack—*the* Wallack—the very best *Iago* I ever saw—I can not pay him a higher compliment. I witnessed his performance of *Rolla* and *Dick Dashall*, considered by the public as his best characters. Ah! what an actor he was! To see his personation of *Don Cæsar de Bazan* was worth a pilgrimage to New York.

On board the steamer Ohio, Captain Haggerty, I embarked with my family at Mobile on the 11th of May, 1833, bound for Cincinnati by way of the Gulf of Mexico and the Mississippi River. Arrived at New Orleans the next day without accident.

We remained in New Orleans two days and nights, and had the opportunity—which we improved, of course—of witnessing the performance of the GLADIATOR (for Forrest's benefit), and CINDERELLA on the first appearance of Madame Brichta. Mr. J. M. Field, a young actor of considerable promise, enacted *Phasarius*, the secondary part in the GLADIATOR, and the next night appeared as the *Prince* in CINDERELLA.

The production of CINDERELLA at New Orleans formed an era in theatrical annals. Though a hodge-podge (made up of Rossini's original work of the same name and other productions of that composer, WILLIAM TELL being largely drawn upon), it was the first attempt at the grand opera *in the English language* at the South. All previous attempts had been confined to what is termed the *comic* opera — the BARBER OF SEVILLE (an English adaptation), MARRIAGE OF FIGARO, LOVE IN A VILLAGE, DEVIL'S BRIDGE, etc. The cast of CINDERELLA, as originally produced in New Orleans this season, was as follows:

Prince..................Mr. Field.
Dandini................Mr. Caldwell.
Baron Pompolino.......Mr. Thorne.
Alidoro................Mr. Iforgethisname.
Pedro..................Mr. Russell.
Cinderella.............Miss Jane Placide.
Clorinda...............Mrs. Russell.
Thisbe..................Mrs. Rowe.
Fairy Queen...........Miss Nelson.

Thus cast, and with the advantage of beautiful scenery and appointments, its success was very great.

This year Mr. Caldwell sold out his managerial interests to Messrs. Russell and Rowe, and turned his attention to lighting the city with gas.

On the 16th we re-embarked on the Ohio, and off we steered for Cincinnati. It is not my purpose to attempt a description of the scenes witnessed on this boat — the CHOLERA raging! Nevertheless, I will briefly notice a few incidents. After supper, the second day out, I counted *eight card-tables*, surrounded by persons playing the game of "brag!" At the same time persons were scattered around the floor and in the staterooms groaning, complaining, beseeching for assistance — *dying* with the cholera! In one instance I saw a man fall from his chair in a fit, clenching his cards in his hands, and die in a few minutes! Another fell back on the floor from the card-table, was taken up senseless, and carried to his state-room, where he lingered until the next day, and then died, having in the interim made his will, disposing of a very large property in Virginia. This last one I became slightly acquainted with, and rendered him all the assistance I could. Just before he died we put him into a warm bath, which seemed to revive him very much. When we laid him on his mattress, he looked up into my face and asked,

"What is your real opinion, Mr. Smith? Will I get over this?"

I answered, "Upon my word, I think you will; you are evidently much better." This was my most candid opinion.

"I am glad—I am glad to hear you say so," he responded faintly, looking up into my face with a smile; and with that smile on his face he almost instantly ceased breathing.

The sick Frenchman.

In nearly every voyage I make, especially if there be sickness among the passengers, I get the name of *Doctor*, probably from the fact that I am always willing to lend a hand to assist the sick. It was so in this case. Captain Haggerty, the clerk, and myself seemed to be the only persons on board who knew any thing about the medicine-chest, and the *quantities* proper for a dose of the various articles therein contained. A little Frenchman, as healthy a man as there was on board of the boat, took it into his head that *he* was attacked by cholera, and sent for me to attend to his case.

"Oh, Docteur, Monsieur Docteur!" he exclaimed, "I am vaire sick—much malade! My stomach vaire much ache! Do sometings for me, docteur, do sometings vaire much quick, for I sal die—oh!"

I found his pulse regular, and became convinced he was in excellent health. I told him so, and for a time he appeared reassured; but presently he sent for me again, and begged me in the most piteous tones to do "sometings" for him. Satisfied that nothing ailed the man but fright, I went to the medicine-chest and made him up a pill of gum arabic, which I requested him to swallow, assuring him that he would soon be better. For about two hours this seemed to quiet my little Frenchman, and I was at liberty to attend to other cases. When next called to Monsieur he said he felt a little better, but "weak from the operation of de medecin."

"The pill has operated, then?" I remarked.

"Oui, oui—operate vaire much—*make me sleep*—ah ha! Un opiate, ha?"

I let him think it was an opiate, and telling him to keep quiet during the night, left him. The following morning my patient seemed much better, and partook of a hearty breakfast and a large portion of a bottle of claret. Card-playing continued during the day, and Monsieur took a hand, losing considerable money. He retired early, and I was in hopes he had entirely recovered from his fright, and that I should not be called on to attend him any more; but I was mistaken. He was not at supper, and hearing a groaning in his state-room as I passed, I opened the door and looked in. There lay my little Frenchman, writhing with pain, and evidently experiencing the effects of the "premonitory symptoms" pretty strongly.

"Ah! Monsieur Docteur," he said, as he saw me coming in, "I am vaire glad you come; I have got him *now* certainement; you must give me some leetle peel encore; I sal die if you don't give me sometings vaire quick!"

Poor fellow! he *had* the dreaded disease beyond a doubt—the symptoms were unmistakable. Feeling his pulse, and saying a few encouraging words, I left him to make up a dose a little more efficient than *gum arabic*, for I was convinced he had frightened himself into the cholera. While preparing the medicine, a crash was heard that seemed to shake the boat to the very centre. At first all supposed an explosion had taken place. Confusion reigned for a few minutes, the passengers rushing hither and thither in "wild disorder." My first care, of course, was for my wife and children, the latter being at the time eating their supper at the second table. The crash was caused by the breaking of the *fly-wheel*, the fragments of which were thrown with great force through the cabin floor and hurricane roof, scattering the dishes on the supper-table, as well as pieces of the table itself, in every direction. It providentially happened that no one was hurt. My boys I found seated on the brink of the chasm where the table had been. The oldest boy, then five years of age, was holding an empty saucer in his hand, and when he saw me he exclaimed, "Pa, look here; they've spilt all my coffee!"

But to return to my patient—I found him busily engaged dressing himself.

"By gar, Monsieur Docteur," said he, "I sal not stay on dis boat any longer; such dam crashing I never sal hear again no more nevaire; did you hear him? It was like heaven and earth sal be coming togedder!"

"It was a tremendous crash," I replied. "The fly-wheel is broken—can not be mended short of Pittsburg; the passengers are most of them preparing to leave."

"Leave! leave! I believe you, Monsieur Docteur," he said, as he proceeded with his toilet; "I sal no stay one moment, by gar; I sal be off in de first boat, ha! I sal not stay in dis d—n cholera boat any more at all."

A boat bound up the river was by this time alongside, and nearly all were making their arrangements to go on her.

"How do you feel now, Monsieur?" I at length inquired, when he had finished dressing. "Here is the medicine I have prepared for you; will you take it?"

"Take de medecin?" he answered; "no, by gar, I want no medecin. I am well—*tres bien*—never sal be better in my life."

"What! not got the cholera?" I inquired.

"No, by d—n: dat confounded crash knock de cholera out of me, *tout de suite!*"

And so it had; fright had brought it on, and fright had sent it off. I met him afterward in Cincinnati. He shook me warmly by the hand, and thanked me for my doctorly care, but declared that if it had not been for that "grand crash," he should have been a dead man to a certainty, and I firmly believe he was right in his opinion.

It was during this trip, and before the "crash," that I witnessed a game of faro, in which a negro man named Fred was staked and played for. A negro trader, having lost all his ready money, offered to stake his servant on the game. The dealer agreed to this, and Fred was ordered by his master to mount the table and stand upon the ace. During the game he was "split" twice—got "out of split," being ordered to move about on the various cards to suit his master's views—and at last was lost on the corner of the deuce! The dealer very quietly told Fred to step down on *his* side of the table, and the negro was thus transferred to a new owner!

It was soon ascertained that the damages sustained by the boat could not be repaired without going to Pittsburg, and during the night all the cabin passengers except a Mrs. Miller, her sister, and our family, took their departure on various boats. Next morning Captain Haggerty announced to his few remaining passengers that in a day or two he thought the boat could proceed *with one wheel.* We concluded to abide by the fortunes of the vessel, and I believe it was well for us that we did, for the cholera entirely disappeared with the crowd of passengers, and all on board enjoyed health the remainder of the journey, arriving at Louisville on the 30th of May.

Arrived at Cincinnati on the 1st day of June, just three weeks out from Mobile, and met a most cordial reception from our numerous (almost innumerable) relatives and friends.

The great pleasure derived from meeting with my relations and friends at Cincinnati on this occasion, and *always*, may be mentioned, but it is not a subject to interest the general reader, so I pass on, in my skimming way, to theatrical matters.

The Columbia Street Theatre was open, under the management of Messrs. Cabell, Forrest, and Muzzy. A Mr. Judah was playing as a "star." Went to see him enact *Richard III.* Have seen better *Richards*—and worse. Witnessed Fletcher's representation of *Ancient Statuary.* Very good. Also witnessed the extraordinary acting of Monsieur (!) Gouffe, the "Man Monkey," for the first time.

One of the most comic pieces of acting ever witnessed by me was Mr. Wm. S. Forrest's personation of *Alonzo*, in the REVENGE, at this theatre.

A Floating Theatre.

The "Chapman family," consisting of old Mr. Chapman, William Chapman, George Chapman, Caroline Chapman, and Harry and Therese Chapman (children), came to the West this summer, opened a theatre at Louisville, and afterward established and carried into operation that singular affair, the "Floating Theatre," concerning which so many anecdotes are told. The "family" were all extremely fond of fishing, and during the "waits" the actors amused themselves by "dropping a line" over the stern of the ark. On one occasion, while playing the STRANGER (Act iv., Scene 1), there was a long wait for *Francis*, the servant of the misanthropic *Count Walbourgh.*

"Francis! Francis!" called the Stranger.

No reply.

"Francis! Francis!" (a pause:) "Francis!" rather angrily called the Stranger again.

A very distant voice—"Coming, sir!" (a considerable pause, during which the Stranger walks up and down, à la Macready, in a great rage.)

"Francis!"

Francis (entering). Here I am, sir.

Stran. Why did you not come when I called?

Francis. Why, sir, I was just hauling in one of the d—dest big catfish you ever saw!

It was some minutes before the laughter of the audience could be restrained sufficiently to allow the play to proceed.

It is said of this Floating Theatre that it was cast loose during a performance at one of the river towns in Indiana by some mischievous boys, and could not be landed for half a dozen miles, the large audience being compelled to walk back to their village.

The season at the theatre in Third Street, under the management of Messrs. Russell and Rowe, successors of Mr. Caldwell, commenced on the 15th of June. The company consisted of Messrs. Scott, Field, Russell, Judah, Page, Hernizen, Charnock, Lyne, Powell, Gilbert, Thorne; Mrs. Rowe, Mrs. Russell, Mrs. Ludlow, Mrs. Salzman, Miss Petrie.

Mr. Edwin Forrest commenced an engagement on the 17th of June.

The Ravel family appeared during this season, and the opera of CINDERELLA was produced, Mrs. Knight playing the part of *Cinderella.* Mr. Page performed *Dandini;* and the cast was otherwise as in New Orleans.

Cholera broke out in Cincinnati, and raged violently. It did not pass over *our* humble home without taking its victims. When we recommenced our wanderings, two only daughters were missing from the family group; two boys remained (Lemuel and Marcus), and they are living at this day, each a happy husband and father; and there are five more boys now grown up into manhood.

Of Messrs. Russell and Rowe's company, Mr. Charnock and Mr. Page fell victims to the epidemic. Mr. Page died singing the music of the opera in which he last appeared!

CHAPTER X.

RECEIVING no remittance or intelligence from Messrs. Palmer and Lyon, my successors in Georgia, about the 1st of August I deemed it prudent to commence preparations for resuming my managerial sway in the Southern regions. The cholera continuing its ravages, there was no difficulty in enlisting a few recruits for the winter season in Georgia and Alabama, with the understanding that for their services while traveling, and until the commencement of the fall season in Georgia, their traveling and other expenses should be paid by me. I purchased two wagons and teams, a set of scenery, and a small lot of wardrobe; engaged a small party, consisting of Mr. and Mrs. Delmon (late Miss Charlotte Crampton), Mr. Coney, Mr. Lyne, Mr. Gamble, and one or two others, and on the 12th of August, 1833, leaving the cholera behind us, as we hoped, we started for Georgia, through Kentucky, *via* the Cumberland Gap.

Our first stopping-place (for business) was Paris. It was plainly to be perceived that, although no cholera actually existed there, the *fear* of it kept people from assembling together in large numbers. Our receipts were next to nothing, and I soon found that paying the boarding and traveling expenses of the company was a bad speculation; and, worst of all, I had provided myself with only three hundred dollars for the journey, supposing that we should certainly be able to "play our way" triumphantly into Georgia.

Our next town was Richmond, which was reached by traveling through a most romantic country, crossing the Kentucky River at a point where it was necessary to unload our wagons and "tote" the trunks up a hill at least half a mile, the horses being barely able to haul the empty vehicles.

At Richmond the receipts were rather better than at Paris, but nevertheless very small; and the authorities of the place charged rather a heavy tax on our performances, which did not set us forward any. Here began dissensions between Mr. Delmon and his wife, which ended in the departure of the former for Cincinnati. The real name of this young man was Delmon Grace, but he dropped the Grace when he adopted the stage as a profession.

With my fund considerably diminished, we took our departure from Richmond on Sunday, the 1st of September, and on Tuesday passed through the town of London (containing five houses and a half), arriving at Barboursville, at the foot of the Cumberland Mountains, on Wednesday. Here we were persuaded to give a concert, and the Barboursvillians turned out to the number of twenty-two, at 25 cents each (all they would pay for *any* "show," they said), giving us a sum total of $5 50—about half the amount of our tavern bill.

After paying toll next day at a gate on our way through the mountains, my "ready money" had become reduced to the inconsiderable sum of eight dollars and fifty cents! Rather a discouraging situation we were in, the reader will probably think—and we were.

On the 6th we passed over and through what is called the "Cumberland Gap," and arrived at Tazewell. The encouragement here for a concert was very small indeed; and a theatrical performance was out of the question, there being no room large enough. Our announcement of an entertainment, consisting of songs, recitations, etc., brought forth a demand by some public functionary of fifty dollars for license! After considerable search, I found an old statute which exempted theatres and concerts from the operation of this license law, and we were permitted to proceed with our concert *un*licensed.

Our performance was given in the dining-room of the hotel where we stopped. The auditory, about twenty in number, were seated on chairs in the room, while we, the performers, sung and spoke on a sort of landing-place or gallery, about six feet long, and two and a half feet wide. From this landing-place, which was four feet higher than the floor of the room, three doors opened, one leading to our retiring, or green-room, one to a sitting-room, and the other to the stairway which led to the rooms above; besides, there were steps leading down from each end of the platform into the dining-room. Persons were passing from one room to the other continually, and the performer was obliged to *move* whenever any one passed.

Mr. Lyne, our heavy tragedian (afterward a celebrated Mormon preacher), undertook, as his share of the entertainment, to give Shakspeare's "Seven Ages," from the comedy of AS YOU LIKE IT. I here attempt to give a portion of the recitation, as spoken on this occasion, with the "side speeches" or interpolations of the reciter, caused by the frequent interruptions he was subjected to:

All the world's a stage,
[*Sir (to the landlord, a fat man, who entered at the moment, shoving the actor against the wall), I'll thank you not to crowd me so—our stage is very small.*
And all the men and women merely players:
[*Don't—don't crowd me off!*
They have their exits and their entrances;
[*Indeed, sir, if you keep going in and out in this way, I can not go on with my speech.*
And one man in his time plays many parts,
[*Now, sir, if you'll shut that door, I'll be obliged to you. "Certainly, sir, go on."*
His acts being seven ages.
[*Thank you, sir. Now, pray, sit down.*

At first, the infant,
Mewling and puking in the nurse's arms;
[*If you can't stop that child's crying, madam, I respectfully recommend that you retire with it into another room, and furnish it with some refreshment suited to its tender years.*
And then, the whining school-boy, with his satchel,
[*You needn't snuff these candles just now, boy.*
And shining morning face, creeping like snail
[*I shall never get through if you keep jambing me in this way.*
Unwillingly to school.
[*Waiter, bring me a julep.*
And then, the lover;
Sighing like furnace, with a woful ballad
[*I think the singing takes better than recitations.*
Made to his mistress's eyebrow.
[*It's devilish hot.*
Then, a soldier;
Full of strange oaths,
[*I shall swear, presently, if that child is not taken out.*
And bearded like the pard,
Jealous in honor, sudden and quick in quarrel,
[*Set down the julep—I'll pay you when the performance is over.*
Seeking the bubble reputation e'en in the cannon's mouth.
[*Sucks julep through a straw—pronounces it very good.*
And then, the justice, etc., etc., etc.

Next morning, after settling our tavern bill, I had not enough money left to pay for our breakfast, which was to be partaken of about ten miles ahead. Our *avant courier*, nevertheless, was directed to order the usual morning meal, and on went the vehicle, containing the majority of the party, while I remained behind a little, in order to "raise the wind," if possible, to pay for the expected repast. As my wagon was brought to the door, I asked the landlord if there was such a personage in the town as a pawnbroker. He did not understand me. "A money-lender," I explained—"one who lends money on pledges."

"Well, yes—I reckon there is; our postmaster, Mr. ——, sometimes lends money in that way."

I soon found Mr. Postmaster, and opened the negotiation. Offering him a gold chain which cost $40, I asked a loan of $20 on it for one month. He looked at the chain, weighed it in his hand, and declined.

After considerable haggling, the worthy postmaster offered, out of pure *friendship* (as he said), to let me have $15 if I would return him $20 in a month, and leave my gold watch, worth $200, as security. *I* declined this time, and we parted.

Desperately I whipped up the horses, urging them on toward our breakfast place, my appetite entirely gone, but fully believing that I should come across some one who would furnish me with the required loan. I felt very certain of this, and told my wife so; and, sure enough, just before reaching the dreaded haven, we overtook a Mr. Burns with a drove of horses—a person we had frequently passed, and been passed by, during the journey. "That's my man," said I, as we neared him.

"Good-morning, Mr. Burns."

"Good-morning, Mr. Smith."

"Where do you breakfast this morning?"

"At this place just ahead."

"So do I. Can I speak to you one moment?"

"Certainly." And in less than three minutes my immediate wants were supplied by the transfer of a twenty-dollar bill from his pocket-book to mine. It turned out that, although our personal acquaintance was slight, merely from casual meetings as we progressed in our journey, he knew me very well, and was perfectly satisfied with my responsibility. Indeed, he wished me to take a hundred or two; but I positively declined, feeling great confidence that at the Warm Springs, which we were now nearing, we should retrieve our fortunes, and be in funds again. My appetite returning, we all made a hearty breakfast, and pursued our journey with renewed vigor and spirits.

Crossing Clinch Mountain, from which there is the most magnificent view I ever looked upon, and partaking of some water from a strongly impregnated chalybeate spring at its base, we reached Bean's Station, in East Tennessee, on the evening of the 7th of September, and "put up" for the night.

A Concert in the Dark.

It soon became noised about that we were "show folk," and a very strong request was made by the citizens of the little settlement that we should give a performance in the parlor of the hotel or tavern. We acceded to the request after considerable persuasion, and quite a number of persons, male and female, collected about the house just before dark.

Remembering the difficulty I had experienced on a similar occasion many years previously, as heretofore related, when we were obliged to use potatoes for candlesticks, I made inquiry of our landlord as to the manner of *lighting the room* for the intended performance. The reader will scarcely credit me when I say that neither a candle nor a lamp could be procured in the neighborhood! Of course we expected this would end all idea of the proposed performance; but we were mistaken; the villagers insisted on the fulfillment of our promise to "give them a show," and at last, as a bit of fun, I told them that we would perform, if they would be satisfied that we should do so *in the dark*. The crowd agreed to this willingly, and I here record the fact that we gave an entertainment, consisting of songs, duets, recitations, and instrumental music, in TOTAL DARKNESS! The performance appeared to take well with the audience, the applause being liberally showered upon us. At the close I dismissed my "patrons" with the assurance that we charged nothing for our services on that occasion, which seemed to please them more than even the "entertainment" which had drawn them together, three tremendous cheers being voluntarily given for the "show folk" as the delighted Bean Stationers groped their way to the door, and the tired travelers felt their ways to their several dormitories.

Next morning we found that our hotel expenses had been settled by some of the leading gentlemen of the village, who had been instrumental in getting up the entertainment, and we wended our way toward the North Carolina Warm Springs.

A Tennessee Door-keeper.

At Greenville, East Tennessee, we made a halt, and determined to treat the inhabitants of that beautiful village with three representations of the "legitimate drama," in a carpenter's shop, hastily, but tastefully fitted up for the occasion.

The first representation was attended by just *six people*, making the total receipts of the evening THREE DOLLARS!

My landlord, the carpenter, attributed the slim attendance to a *camp-meeting* that was in successful operation about two miles from town, and "reckoned" that if I would "hold on" until that broke up, we should have full *shops* every night.

Thus urged, we did "hold on," and our next performance was rewarded with a receipt of TWO DOLLARS AND A HALF!

I proposed to decamp next morning, but the printer of the Greenville Expositor (who was on the *free-list* as a matter of course) remonstrated against so sudden a move, urging that a *third* performance must be successful, as it was quite certain the camp-meeting would break up that morning, and the young folk would all return to their homes.

I yielded, and advertised for "positively the last performance" the play of WILLIAM TELL, a favorite afterpiece, and a lot of comic songs.

At the time of beginning I was glad to find a crowded audience in waiting—the shop, work-bench and all, was literally crammed. One of the carpenter's apprentices, whom I had transformed into a citizen of Altorf for the occasion, told me that all but five or six of the people in front were *religious folks*, who had attended the camp-meeting faithfully to its conclusion.

The performance proceeded—the actors were in high spirits. Lyne bullied Governor *Gesler* with great fierceness; *Sarnem* whacked the carpenter's apprentice with a hearty good-will, while the latter was making a bow to the governor's cap, on a pole five feet and a half high—the arrow, aimed at the apple on *Albert's* head, flew, with remarkable exactness, into the horse-blanket held up as a target to receive it behind the scenes, and the play was received with shouts of satisfaction by the Greenvillians. The farce was honored by peal on peal of laughter, while the comic songs were doubly encored, every one of them.

The entertainment over, I observed there was a reluctance in the audience to depart—*they wanted another song.* I gave them one. Still they remained as if glued to their seats. I went before the curtain and thanked the people for their patronage, and informed them the performance had concluded. They did not move—they wanted yet *another song.* I gave them another, and again told them the entertainment of the evening was over, intimating, at the same time, that the stage-carpenter was waiting to take down the scenery. A gentleman in the gallery (the work-bench) here arose and addressed me as follows: "Mr. Sol. Smith: Sir,—I have been requested to express to you the unanimous wish of this meeting that you will *prolong your season.* The liberal patronage bestowed upon you this evening must have convinced you that we *can* make something of a turn-out here, and I feel authorized to say that, if you will give us a performance to-morrow night, you will have another house *as crowded as this.*"

A murmur of applause confirmed the opinion of the speaker, and I was greatly tempted to yield to their wishes; but, bethinking me of certain announcements for performances in towns farther south, I was obliged to decline the invitation of my kind auditors, and content myself with the eighty or ninety dollars which I supposed had been contributed that night to my ways and means. Finding me determined, the audience gradually dispersed, each individual casting wishful and sidelong glances toward the stage, which by this time was beginning to be dismantled.

Motioning the door-keeper to follow me into a sort of shed adjoining the theatre, I proceeded to open the ticket-box in his presence, while he sat down on a bench in the corner to wait for his wages. I found SEVEN TICKETS in the box, and, turning to the waiting door-keeper, who was busily engaged chewing tobacco and spitting, I asked him what he had done with the rest.

"They are all *thar*," he replied, with great composure, looking intently on a beam of the shed, and rocking his right knee, which he held in his clenched hands, and raised about half way from the floor to his chin.

"All *there*—where?" was the very natural question that I next propounded.

"*In the box* whar you *told* me to put 'em," he answered, still eying the beam or rafter.

"I find but seven here," I remarked: "I want to know where are the tickets for the one hundred and sixty or one hundred and eighty people that were in the house to-night."

"I tell you again they are all *thar*, sir," he answered, sturdily; "and I allow 'twon't be safe for any man to insinuate any thing agin my character," he continued, releasing his knee, and taking a large quid of tobacco from a rusty steel box and ramming it into his mouth.

"I do not wish to insinuate any thing against your character," I said, soothingly, "but I want to know what you have done with the tickets."

"They are *thar*," he again alleged—"every one of 'em thar; no one passed *me* without giving me a ticket, and the tickets are all *thar*."

I began to get a little pettish, and asked the tobacco-chewer to explain himself. "There were nearly two hundred people in the house," I urged.

"There war full that," he admitted.

"Well, then," I asked, finally, "where are the tickets? Will you explain this mystery?"

My friend, the tobacco-chewing door-keeper, here renewed his grasp on his raised knee, deliberately withdrew his eyes from the rafter, and fixing them, half closed, on mine, at length afforded me the desired *explanation*, thus:

"You engaged me to *keep your door;* and I performed my dooties to the best of my abilities, for which you are indebted to me three dollars, and I want my money. No person has passed me without a ticket. My character is above suspicion, and no one must say nothin' agin it."

"My good friend," I ventured to say, "I don't wish to say any thing against—"

"No, I should think *not*—you'd *better* not," he continued, "for I'm too well known here; well, as I was a sayin', you employed me as *door-keeper*—mark the distinction—I had nothin' at all to do with the WINDERS—*and thar's where your hundred and eighty people came in*, you 'tarnal fool to leave 'em open when there was sich a crowd comin' from camp-meetin'!"

I paid the fellow his three dollars, and next day was far on my road to the Warm Springs, in the famous county of Buncombe, where they raise the largest peaches and the yellowest children in all creation.

CHAPTER XI.

ON the 11th of September we reached the Warm Springs, Buncombe County, N. C. This is a beautiful place, situated in a lovely valley, surrounded by hills—mountains I might say. The river French Broad runs in front of the premises. The principal building, which is very spacious, is surrounded by beautiful white cottages for the accommodation of visitors. The Warm Spring is a great curiosity. The dining-room of the hotel is capacitated for the accommodation of 800 diners! We found we were too late in arriving here (just my luck!), nearly all the company having left the week previously. No matter; we determined to try our fortune with the few pleasure-seekers who remained, and were favored with the attendance at our first entertainment of an audience composed of *every person at the Springs*, including a numerous body of black servants belonging to the place, who occupied the "upper end of the hall," being admitted on the "free list."

Finding that our heavy tragedian and other "principal actors" could be of no use whatever in the concert line, I dispatched them in the stage to Greenville, S. C., and gave the next and last entertainment with the assistance of Mrs. Smith and Mrs. Delmon only. This was attended by *all* the visitors again—our total receipts the two nights amounting to twenty-two dollars and seventy-five one-hundredths.

I here sold one of my teams, pledged my $200 watch to Colonel Patton, our landlord, for $50 (never have had an opportunity to redeem it), paid our bill, returned the borrowed money to my friend Burns, the drover, and secured seats for Mrs. Smith, Mrs. Delmon, my two little boys, and myself, for Greenville, S. C., where we were told a splendid business might be calculated on.

Almost a Duel.

On getting into the stage-coach, I was greatly surprised to find two *men* on the back seat, naturally supposing the two women and children would have been permitted to occupy that place; but my surprise was still greater when, being remonstrated with by the agent, they *claimed* the seat, and expressed their determination to keep it. In all my travels, before or since, I have never met with a case like this, all *gentlemen* I have traveled with having ever been ready to yield the back seat in a stage-coach to gentlewomen. Not wishing to delay the coach, I requested the women and children to take the *front* seat, and, boiling over with passion, I ascended to the box, where I took a seat with the driver. At our breakfast-place, one of the occupants of the back seat came to me, and offered to resign his place to my wife, a sense of shame having overcome him on the way. The other person, who persisted in his claim, was a Mr. SMITH (it was such a singular name I shall never forget it!), a *preacher* from Charleston. While breakfast was getting ready, I went to the reverend gentleman and told him that *he must not think of riding inside the coach any farther;* that *I* had taken my turn outside, and I wished him to experience the pleasant sensation of riding in the rain for a dozen miles or so, as I had done. He turned very pale, but said nothing. Shortly after he took his co-occupant of the back seat aside, and, after some conversation between them, the latter came to me and said that if I persisted in my demand that Parson Smith should ride outside in the rain, he should espouse his cause, and see that no harm came to him—in short, that he would not permit the preacher, that individual being a non-combatant, to be treated with violence. I observed that in Georgia I had heard of a man who amassed a considerable fortune by minding his own business, and gently hinted that perhaps *he* might profit by confining his attention to his own affairs. This rather nettled Mr. Bobadil (I purposely suppress his real name), and he cut short our conversation by notifying me that if I offered to prevent the preacher's entrance into the coach, he should consider it a personal insult, and challenge me to mortal combat.

"Challenge me, will you?" said I. "I don't see how I can accept your challenge; I am bound by my oath, as an attorney-at-law, not to challenge to fight, fight, or accept a challenge to fight a duel with deadly weapons."

"You can resign your office of attorney-at-law, and can then accept my challenge," replied Mr. B.

"But I don't *want* to resign," persisted I; "I don't *want* to be at liberty to accept a challenge; I don't believe in fighting duels; in short—"

At this juncture breakfast was announced, and we all made a good meal before resuming the subject. Breakfast over, I conducted the women and children to the coach, and placed them in the back seat, after which I went to the clergyman and told him that if he went any farther by that conveyance he must ride with the driver. Mr. Bobadil came up and asked in a formal way if I intended to persist in my determination to make the clergyman ride on the outside. My answer was in the affirmative.

"Then, sir," said he, "I challenge you to give me the satisfaction of a gentleman."

I answered, "Sir, I have no cause of quarrel with *you; you* have resigned your seat to the females, as any gentleman ought; but I know the custom of this country will not permit me to decline your challenge, so with great sorrow I accept it."

"It is well," replied my opponent. "I have a pair of pistols, and we can settle this affair in five minutes."

"Hold, sir!" I interposed. "I have already told you I am principled against dueling; also, that I have taken an oath not to fight with deadly weapons. You have challenged me—I have accepted your challenge. If I am rightly informed in regard to your rules in matters of this kind, I, the challenged party, have a right to select the time, the place, and the weapons; am I right?"

"Undoubtedly," he answered.

"I avail myself of my right, then," I continued; "the *time* shall be NOW; the place HERE; and the weapons—FISTS."

A general laugh followed this announcement, a considerable crowd having collected by this time to witness the expected duel.

"Sir," said Bobadil, "the *time* I agree to; the *place* I make no objections to; the *weapons* I reject."

"On what grounds, pray?" inquired I.

"On the ground that they are not *gentlemanly* weapons," he replied.

"But I insist," said I, "that they *are* gentlemanly weapons."

"How do you make that out?" asked he.

"Thus," I replied: "You challenge me, by which act, according to your rules, you acknowledge me to be a gentleman. They are *my* weapons—*ergo*, they are the weapons of a gentleman, or, in other words, gentlemanly weapons."

Several of the crowd here began to take part with me, exclaiming, "Good—well argued—go it, lawyer!"

"I object to your weapons," persisted my opponent, "on the ground that they are *unusual*, and finally that, not being a pugilist myself, the chances would be greatly in your favor."

"Just the reason that I named them," I replied. "If I fight in the way proposed, I *expect* to conquer; whereas, if I should fight with your confounded pistols, it is ten to one I would get a bullet in my thorax, which would be vastly inconvenient, I assure you, particularly at this time, when I am under a pledge to the good citizens of Greenville to appear before them day after to-morrow night."

The laugh being entirely against Bobadil, he took new ground. He said if I persisted in a "fist-fight," he should avail himself of his right to postpone the battle, and procure a "champion" in three days.

"I refuse to fight any champion; it must be either yourself or the preacher," said I.

Finding that not much was to be made out of me in the talking line, Mr. Bobadil proceeded to the coach, where, taking out and cocking a pistol, he said to the preacher,

"Go into the coach—I am here to protect you."

The reverend gentleman hesitated.

"Don't attempt to go into the coach," said I, coming up to the other side of the door; "I am here to prevent you."

The parson hesitated just a moment, and then *mounted the box and took his seat with the driver.*

This ended all the difficulty. The fighting gentleman became as friendly as a "sucking dove," and long before our journey was over even the clergyman joined us in laughing over the adventure, and acknowledged his regret at having claimed the back seat, and of being the cause of any words between the South Carolinian and myself.

This little scene took place thirty-five years ago. At the time, and long afterward, I thought I was in the right during the whole of that altercation. I record it to say I was in the wrong—decidedly. My conduct toward the preacher was almost brutal, and I acknowledge it thus publicly, in hope, if these sheets should meet his eye, that with the same Christian spirit which impelled him to ascend to the top of the coach to endure a dripping rain for the sake of peace, he will forgive me the harsh words I was guilty of uttering on that occasion. On my part, with the utmost sincerity, I forgive him for his great impoliteness in taking the back seat in the coach to the exclusion of women and children, and feel certain he will never sin in that way again. And, while I am about it, I may as well accord him *my* forgiveness for a furious attack he afterward made from the pulpit, in Charleston, upon theatres and the theatrical profession. Amen.

Beyond all comparison, the road from the Warm Springs to Ashville is the most romantic I ever traveled—that is, for a road that *is* a road. Projecting rocks, some of them 200 feet high, crowd the traveler almost *into* the French Broad River nearly the whole thirty-seven miles. The river itself is something of a curiosity, being almost continuous rapids the whole way.

Ashville is a very small village, and is the county seat of the great county of Buncombe, which Congressmen speak to so often.

On the urgent request of many persons, we gave a concert here—couldn't give a "performance," in consequence of our baggage wagon not having arrived (we had passed it on the way)—and received from the generous villagers and fashionable strangers assembled there the sum of six dollars and seventy-five cents!

On Tuesday, the 17th of September, we arrived at the beautiful village of Greenville; and on Wednesday, having completed the necessary alterations in the masonic lodge-room, we opened it as a theatre, making our first appearance before a South Carolina audience in the comedy of the HONEY MOON (somewhat cut down), and the afterpiece of FAMILY JARS. The four nights of that week yielded us a receipt of about $150.

The Quarrel of Brutus and Cassius.

We performed two more nights in the following week. My quondam friend Bobadil (as I have called him) and another gentleman came to me on Tuesday morning, and expressed a wish to make their appearance on the stage in a tragedy! It was, of course, out of the question to get up a tragedy for their accommodation; but it struck me that the appearance of "two gentlemen of South Carolina, their first attempt on any stage" (or in any lodge-room), would be of considerable benefit to my exchequer, so I told them they might, if they thought proper, enact the celebrated quarrel-scene of *Brutus* and *Cassius*, in Shakspeare's JULIUS CÆSAR. This just suited them, as they were both familiar with the text, having at various times taken part in it at school. They went at it, hammer and tongs, rehearsing, while I sent out the performers of our troupe to make the fact known *confidentially*, to as many people as they could find, that Messrs. B. and G. were to appear that night. The house was crowded.

Perhaps the reader is not aware what tricks amateur actors are subjected to when they aspire (or *condescend*, as they consider it) to perform with regular actors. Some slight idea may be formed by the manner in which these gentlemen were treated on this occasion—all the actors lending a hand, of course, to assist in putting them through.

First, the dressing. (They had requested to

be so completely disguised that no one could know them.) *Cassius* (Bobadil) wore a gray tunic, a large spangled shoulder-cloak, slouched *hat and feathers;* stock, gray wig with a very long tail, black whiskers (painted with cork), mustaches turned up, large eye-brows, nankin

THE QUARREL OF BRUTUS AND CASSIUS.

pantaloons, boots, *spurs!* gauntlets, broad-sword, and truncheon. *Brutus*, his companion in arms (Mr. G.), was rigged out with a soldier's coat, Scotch kilt, large modern military hat, with enormous red and white feather, leopard-skin cloak, as worn by *Rolla*, blue military pantaloons, considerably too short for him, pumps and spurs (couldn't do without the spurs), red wig, black whiskers, mustaches turned down (as a contrast), a Turkish cimiter, two pistols in his belt, gauntlets, very high-standing shirt collar, white cravat, tied with an enormous bow, and ruffled shirt, displayed to the best advantage. Thus accoutred, they appeared before the audience, with a success unprecedented in *that* town, I'll venture to say, and probably not exceeded any where. *Cassius* ranted and stamped like mad, keeping his back to the audience, and crowding the "gentle *Brutus*" into a corner, where that personage quietly "took the word" from the prompter, and kept a bold front to the public until the dialogue was concluded. The applause and laughter of the audience shook the masonic hall to its foundations. The *gentlemen* actors were in high glee at their success, and Bobadil asked me if there would be any thing improper in volunteering a *comic song*. Consenting at once to this addition to the fun of the evening, I rang up the curtain, and *Cassius* gave a very passable song, entitled the "King and the Countryman." This pleased the excited public so well that they called for a song from the *other* gentleman. Mr. G. had begun to discover the joke, and was in the act of disrobing when this call was made, and nothing should induce him, he said, to make a fool of himself a moment longer; "besides," he added, "I never sung a song in my life." *Cassius* was somewhat enraged at his comrade's refusal to gratify the audience, and proposed, as the noise was kept up, that since *Brutus* would not sing, they should *act the quarrel-scene over again;* but *Brutus* positively declining, the fiery *Cassius* turned to *me* and offered to dance a hornpipe, if *that* would be satisfactory to our patrons. Putting on a grave face, I said,

"It is very plain to *my* comprehension that the audience do not want singing or dancing; what they want is a little more *tragedy.*"

"Do you think so?" said *Cassius.* "Well, what can we give them?"

"I know of nothing you can give them," replied I, "better, or more appropriate, or more likely to be acceptable, than the *death-scene of Cassius* on the plains of Philippi."

"Hah! the very thing!" agreed the excited amateur; "but I haven't studied it. What are the words?"

I put a volume of Shakspeare into his hands, pointing to the page, called our low comedian, Mr. Coney (dressed for *Diggory*), and told him he must perform the part of *Pindarus*, *Cassius's* freedman, which he very willingly undertook to do, "under the circumstances, at very short notice," and *Cassius* having, as he thought, mastered the few lines of the scene to be enacted, the curtain was again rung up.

Cassius had by some accident (or more likely by some contrivance of one of the actors) changed hats with *Brutus*, and he now appeared with the large military cocked hat which had sat so gracefully on the brow of the "noblest Roman of them all."

The scene which followed was ludicrous in the extreme.

Cassius. Come hither, sirrah!
In Parthia did I take thee prisoner,
And then I swore—I swore—
[*D—d if I can remember any more.*

Prompter. I swore—

Cassius. [*I've said that.*]

Prompter. And then I swore thee, etc.

Cassius. [*Yes, I remember.*] I swore thee, saving of thy life—

Prompter. That whatsoever I'd bid thee do—

Cassius. That whatsoever I'd bid thee do,
Thou shouldst attempt it. Come, now, keep thine oath.

Prompter. (*Cassius* repeating after him.)
Now be a freeman, and with this good sword,
[*Where is it? Oh, here, on the wrong side.*
That ran through Cæsar's bowels, search this bosom.
Here, take thou the hilts,
[*Coney takes sword and an attitude.*
And when my face is covered, as 'tis now—
[*How am I to cover my face? This surtout won't reach.*

Manager. Pull your hat over your eyes.

Cassius. [*Oh, very well; pulls the hat over his eyes and down to his nose.*] Guide thou the sword.

[*Coney stabs him several times, which Cassius not observing, being blindfolded, continues to stand with his arms extended, trying to run on the sword.*

Manager. (From the wing.) Fall!

[*Cassius falls with all his weight, half his body off the stage, still blindfolded.*

Manager. Now for the dying words.

Cassius. [*What are they?*]

Prompter. Cæsar, thou art revenged, etc.

Cassius. Cæsar, thou art revenged even with the sword that killed thee.

Manager. Now for the dying struggle.

Cassius. [*Gives several dying kicks—the curtain falls.*

Our next town was Pendleton, the very centre of the state, and then the hotbed of Nullification. After considerable difficulty the Farmers' Hall was procured for our performances, and the Pendletonians were treated to the first representation of a play and afterpiece in their town, *on a brick floor.*

We acted about a week in Pendleton, during the races, to very moderate houses, paying $5 per night to the town treasurer for the privilege, and then pulled up stakes, determined to get out of the state as soon as possible.

Monday, October 7th, passed through Anderson village, the seat of justice for the district, where we were urged to perform a few nights. No; positively no more acting by us in South Carolina, where they tax us about two thirds of our receipts. Tuesday night staid at a Mrs. Liddell's, where we had mush and milk for supper, "by particular desire!" When we seated ourselves at the table, the landlady raised her hands toward the ceiling and pronounced the following words instead of asking a blessing:

"Come all ye mush-eaters of the best,
Aloft your spoon-shanks raise,
And in the voice of melody,
Sing forth the mush-pot's praise."

Supposing it might be a custom of the country, we sang the lines to the tune of *Mear*, and then fell to.

Next morning, after paying a swinging bill (for poetry, mush, and lodging), we proceeded on to Abbeville Court-house, where we had the satisfaction of paying no tax for playing, for the simple reason that we did not play, though strongly urged to do so. Thursday morning we crossed the Savannah River, on each side of which, at our crossing-place, stands a *town*—Lisbon on one side, and Vienna on the other—and arrived the same night at Washington, in Georgia. Here we were announced to perform three nights; but, to our utter dismay, on the rising of the curtain we found that only *nine persons* constituted our entire audience! At the close of the performance I directed the carpenter to take down the scenery, and be ready for an early start in the morning. A great many people remonstrated against this hasty retreat, saying that now the citizens understood the performance was "respectable," they would crowd the room the other two nights; but I was firm in my determination to leave, and leave we did, without subjecting ourselves to the chance of such another mortification.

Two of our company, Mrs. Delmon and Mr. Coney, were married in this place—that is to say, the marriage ceremony was performed—I can not suppose there was any legality in it, as Mr. Delmon was alive at the time. Poor Coney afterward went to Texas, joined a military company, and was killed in battle. *Mrs. Coney*, after marrying several other gentlemen in the theatrical profession, is at present performing in Salt Lake City, under her maiden name of "Miss Crampton!" She is certainly a very talented actress, and in retaining, or, rather, *resuming* her maiden name, she is only following the example of hundreds of others, some of whom are "happy wives" and mothers of children. This sailing under false colors is a most ridiculous and disgraceful custom, and operates more against the respectability of the profession than any thing I know of.

Being returned to Georgia, I thought it time to make inquiry as to the whereabouts of my company, left in charge of Managers Palmer and Lyons. It had scattered! There were several "branches" of the original stock perambulating the state, but the *generals* had beat a retreat, and had "wandered away, no man knew whither!"

A Mr. Dyke, somewhat notorious as a strolling manager in Indiana and Illinois, having engaged one or two of my former company (a carpenter and door-keeper), announced his concern as one of my *branches*. Some years ago this same Dyke applied to my brother Lemuel for an engagement in the words and figures following, to wit:

"DEAR SIR:—I am informed u are in want of a woman. I can furnish you with my wife. She plays Mrs. Haller and dances the slack wire eleguntly—the vursatility of her talents you may perceive by this is astonishing; and I don't give up the mock duke to no actor in the country. if you want my wife you can have us boath on resonable turms, say ate (8) dollars for her and sicks (6) for me. Rite by return of male.

"Ures, WM. DYKE."

Pushed on to Milledgeville, where we arrived on the 18th of October, and commenced preparations for opening the theatre, which was no small task, inasmuch as Messrs. Palmer and Lyons had "managed" to destroy, scatter, and lose nearly every thing in the shape of wardrobe, scenery, and properties intrusted to them. Mr. Lyons I did not meet for two or three years afterward. Mr. Palmer came to see me during the time that we remained in Milledgeville; and in consequence of his having taken part with the murderer of my brother during my absence—that brother having always been a kind friend to him when living—I uttered this prophecy: "PALMER, YOU WILL DIE IN A DITCH!" Five years afterward he came to me here in St. Louis, a poor drunken wretch, begging for means to purchase bread. I gave him $5, and he left me. Next day I learned that, in crossing a gully on his way to St. Charles, he fell in, and actually died in the way I had prophesied! Lyons, about the same time (1838), formed a company for Texas, and, embarking on board a brig at New York, was lost, with all the company except two (Mr. Dougherty and another), the vessel being upset in a gale.

With a rather inefficient company, consisting of some few stragglers reclaimed from my "branches," and the recruits I had brought with me from Cincinnati, the Milledgeville Theatre was opened on Monday, the 28th of October, with the comedy of the SOLDIER'S DAUGHTER, and the standard farce of FAMILY JARS.

Business continued dull until the assemblage of the Legislature on the 4th of November, when the tide turned in our favor, and we continued to perform to good houses to the end of the session and season.

A. H. Pemberton, Esq., from Augusta, passed most of his time here during the session. This gentleman (now dead) was a very energetic political writer, and wielded a considerable influence in the affairs of the state. He was a warm advocate and able defender of the stage, and wrote in its favor whenever opportunity offered. In 1831 he received the thanks, in a series of resolutions, of Mr. Caldwell's company, then performing in St. Louis, for his able and masterly defense of the drama, and of a member of our profession, Mrs. F. Brown, against the attacks of a fanatic named Gilchrist.

Fire in the Capitol.

On the 16th of November there was an alarm of fire, and it was soon ascertained that the State-house was burning. Our company instantly suspended rehearsal and repaired to the spot, where all were engaged in carrying out the valuable documents, records, and the assets of the Central Bank of Georgia. I did not perceive that any persons were making attempts to extinguish the fire, which was in the upper part of the house—all seeming to be impressed with the idea "the house must go," there being no engines in the town. Meeting an acquaintance or two (I remember the names of Messrs. M'Elvoy and Williams), I proposed that we should go up and ascertain where the fire was. These gentlemen acceded to the proposition, and on our way, seeing a very large and strong negro man busily at work carrying out books, we enlisted him in our little band and proceeded to the roof, where we soon found that by energetic and prompt action it was yet possible to save the building. I am not going to describe the proceedings which took place; suffice it to say they were successful; the State-house was saved. The following article from the pen of Mr. Pemberton, in the *Augusta Chronicle*, will show that due credit was given to those who were happily instrumental in saving the government building:

"Great credit is due to Peter Williams, Esq., Sol. Smith, Esq., of the theatre, Mr. M'Elvoy, of the House of Representatives, and one or two others whose names we do not know, and a negro, for their intrepid and indefatigable exertions on the roof, to which mainly the preservation of the building is to be attributed. We trust the members of the Legislature and the people of Milledgeville, which latter have a deep interest in the preservation of the State-house, will propose a benefit to Mr. Smith, and give him a glorious bumper for his fearless and most valuable exertions on the occasion. He richly deserves it."

The "benefit" *was* proposed, at $5 a ticket, but I shrank from the acceptance of any such demonstration. The NEGRO, however (gods! how that fellow did work!), was rewarded by the Legislature with his freedom—or rather, I should say, it was the *intention* of the members to vote him his freedom, but in their hasty legislation they voted $1800 to *purchase* the man, and forgot to pass an act for his emancipation! It was only in the year 1852 that the governor discovered the omission, and the Legislature passed the necessary act. The noble fellow had been for nineteen years the property of the commonwealth, and had busied himself in taking care and keeping in order the building he had so efficiently assisted in preserving.

Now one word for myself. In that affair I lost a good (almost new) overcoat and a valuable pair of boots, which I took off while working on the roof. The coat I say nothing about; but the boots!—I don't think it would be at all out of the way if the State of Georgia were to make me a present of a *bran new pair*. Although I declined the proposed *benefit*, I will not decline the boots, if offered in a proper and considerate way.

Byrom, the Gambler.

"HENRY BYROM, the gambler, is shot!"

Such were the words which were passed from one to another on the morning of the 20th of November, 1833, at the seat of government of the State of Georgia. Henry Byrom, a young man of fine talents, and well educated, was a merchant in one of the small towns of Georgia, operating on a capital of $10,000 furnished by his mother. In an evil hour he entered a gambling-house, "just to see what was going on," and was induced to make some small bets on the game of faro. He was successful at first; but before midnight, stimulated by strong drinks with which he was plied, he not only lost all the ready money he had with him, but became deeply in debt to the keeper of the bank. Next day he was unfit for business and did not open his store, and when night again shrouded the earth he stealthily sought the gambler's den, determined to retrieve his fortunes or lose all.

"Here is the key of my store," said he to the banker, throwing it down upon the table; "in it is a stock of goods which cost $10,000; give me checks — I play until I win back my last night's losses, or you win all the store contains."

"Agreed," said the banker, and commenced turning the cards.

In two short hours all was decided; the key remained in possession of the banker, and Byrom rushed out into the square a ruined man!

"I swore an oath," said Byrom, when relating these occurrences to me, "that from that moment *I* would prey upon mankind; *I* would learn the devilish arts of the gambler, and turn them against my fellow-men. I have done so. Behold me now; I am no longer a merchant—no longer a respectable man. Can *he* be respectable—nay, can *he* lay any claim to a shadow of respectability who has gambled away his mother's all, and caused her death? No, no! I am —Byrom, the gambler!"

Traveling from Milledgeville to Athens in a stage-coach with a mother and her two daughters, his fine appearance and polished manners made an impression so favorable that when the coach stopped and he was bowing his adieu, the old lady expressed the hope that he would call on them if he should visit Macon, where they resided. He smiled languidly as he listened to the old lady; then, drawing himself up, he threw open his outside traveling-coat, and casting a piercing glance at the ladies, he laughed sarcastically, and exclaiming, "I am Byrom, the gambler!" walked away.

Byrom, when I knew him, was one of the most

expert of the "sporting men" in the state; he played high, drank deep, and was, in fact, a gentlemanly desperado. In an affray he killed a Mr. Ellis, of Macon, in 1832, and was now in Milledgeville pursuing his nefarious profession. On the night of the 19th of November, some difficulty occurring between a hotel-keeper (Mr. Macomb) and Colonel Ward, a friend of Byrom's, fire-arms were resorted to, and the colonel received a dangerous wound from a pistol-shot. Byrom became savage, and threatened vengeance on Macomb, who, it was universally conceded, acted only in self-defense. I heard the conclusion of a speech he made to a large concourse of people from the steps of the hotel where Macomb lay wounded. He denounced Macomb and all who sided with him as poltroons and cowards, and dared them, one and all, to "fight it out" with *him;* said that he would have the heart's blood of Macomb, and concluded by taking out his watch, and saying, "I APPOINT TWELVE O'CLOCK THIS NIGHT TO DIE, AND INVITE YOU ALL TO MY FUNERAL."

Macomb's friends had armed themselves, and stood ready, on the second floor of a back gallery, to repel any attack which might be made. Byrom continued to walk up and down the platform beneath the gallery, with a cocked pistol in each hand, until exactly twelve o'clock, when exclaiming, "Come, it is time!" he rushed up the steps, and was met by the discharge of a volley of musketry, which laid him dead. There I saw his lifeless body the next morning, the pistols still grasped in his clenched hands. Seven or eight buckshot had entered his brain—and that was the end of BYROM, THE GAMBLER!

A Victim of Circumstantial Evidence.

On Friday, the 22d of November, I witnessed the execution of the Rev. Mr. Johnson, convicted of murdering his wife's sister, a child about twelve years of age, by hanging her on a hackberry-tree. His guilt appeared undoubted, although the evidence was all *circumstantial.* On the gallows he seemed quite unconcerned. He had evidently made up his mind to die, all intercessions to the Legislature on his behalf for a pardon having proved unavailing. His wife, who was mainly instrumental in proving his guilt, was on the gallows with him, and seemed anxious that her husband should forgive her before he suffered. The poor man, whose hands were fast tied, could not embrace his wife, but allowed her to embrace *him,* and appeared rather pleased when she got through with her caresses. Mr. Johnson was then asked if he had any thing to say before he suffered the extreme penalty of the law. He turned and looked around on the crowd, and said, mildly, "I have nothing to say except that I hope all of you, my friends, who came to see this sight, when your time comes to die, may be as ready to meet your God as *I* am. I DIE INNOCENT." In less than a minute after these words were uttered his body was hanging a lifeless corpse, and the people were returning to their homes, wondering how any man—particularly a minister of the Gospel—could be so hardened as to die *with a lie upon his lips,* for probably not one in that large crowd gave credit to his dying words.

Reader, he *did* die innocent! Fourteen years afterward a negro was hung in Mississippi who on the gallows confessed that *he* committed the crime for which Mr. Johnson paid the terrible penalty.

On the occasion of my benefit—the closing night—I issued a "message," which undoubtedly had its desired effect, for the house was crammed in every part. I spare the reader a perusal of it.

CHAPTER XII.

OUR next move was to Macon, where, in consequence of bad weather, we made but a poor season. I remember nothing very *amusing* connected with my present visit to this city except the following:

A Challenge and a Blow-up.

During Christmas time, one night, our heavy tragedian got "tight," and kicked up "considerable of a muss" in one of the dressing-rooms, ending his manœuvres by attacking one of the employés of the theatre, and inflicting upon him many blows, cuffs, and thumps. This conduct entitled him, under our rules and regulations, to an instant discharge, which he instantly received; when, taking his bundle under his arm, and assuring me in an emphatic manner that I should "hear from him," the indignant tragedian went off, and the play went on. The piece was PAUL PRY AT DOVER, in which I personated the inquisitive *Paul.* Just as I was going on the stage in the third act, to be shut up in a box of fire-works, a note was handed to me by the call-boy. Not having leisure to read it at the time, I put it in my vest pocket, and proceeded with my part. In due time I was in the box, where (having a lighted candle with me) it was my business, at a certain "cue," to set fire to a fuse

or match communicating with fire-works. As I lay there waiting for my cue, the note I had received occurred to my mind, and I determined to read it. It was *a challenge from the discharged tragedian!* I burst into a violent laugh (I couldn't help it), and during my cachinnatory movements I upset the candle, which communicated to the fuse before the proper time, and the contemplated "terrible explosion" took place prematurely.

Moving southwestwardly (I forgot to say there was no duel—the challenge was withdrawn next day), Montgomery, in Alabama, was our next destination, leaving out Columbus this time.

Punch and Prayers.

Of the various stopping-places when journeying from town to town in Georgia, I remember none with more pleasure than the "Old Station"—Captain Crowell's. The arrival of our company, always announced by an *avant courier*, was the cause of a holiday with the jolly old captain and his amiable family. Such delicious fare as we had at the station! and with it, always such a hearty welcome!

The captain had a boy named Peter—rather an old *boy*—say between fifty and sixty years of age—a negro, in whose judgment he had great confidence. When in the least doubt on any matter he always appealed to Peter, who never failed to give his opinion honestly, bluntly, and immediately. Sometimes the traveling community crowded on him in such numbers that the worthy captain found it difficult, even with his "ample room and verge," to accommodate the late comers. After talking the matter over, he would appeal to his black oracle. "It don't seem to me we can possibly accommodate any more; every bed is engaged. Peter, what do *you* think?" "Put 'em on blankets by the fire," Peter would suggest, if favorably inclined to the travelers; if otherwise, his answer would probably be, "Can't take in anudder one;" and the captain always confirmed Peter's decision, exclaiming, "Peter is right."

It so happened on one occasion, when we were sojourners with Captain Crowell, that a traveling preacher came along rather late in the evening, and applied for accommodation.

"Don't believe we can take you in, stranger; mighty full to-night—got the play-actors here—jolly set! full, jam up!" said the captain.

"I regret exceedingly that you can not accommodate me, as I am fatigued and hungry, having been in the saddle since sunrise," mildly replied the preacher, as he turned his horse's head to pursue his journey.

The captain relented a little. "Fatigued and hungry! The devil! It won't do to turn a man off fatigued and hungry; what do *you* say, Peter?"

Peter, who had been waiting for the question, answered, "Better call 'um back"—which was instantly done.

"Halloo! stranger! Halloo! you with the saddle-bags! Come back and 'light; we'll see what we can do for you."

The preacher did not wait for a second invitation, but returned and dismounted.

"*I* don't like preachers much, nor Peter either; but mother and the girls have no objections to 'em," mumbled the captain, as he took the saddle-bags and put them safely away. "I'll be dot darned if I know what to do with him, though; every thing is full. What do *you* say, Peter?"

"Put him in de bar," answered Peter, and it was so arranged. "Peter is right!" exclaimed the captain.

After supper, the preacher proposed that we should have family worship, saying that Mrs. Crowell and the young ladies had accorded their consent to such a proceeding. The captain was taken completely aback. The truth is, he had ordered Peter to make a tremendous bowl of punch, and had calculated on passing the evening in a jolly and convivial way. The proposed "family worship" didn't seem exactly compatible; yet he disliked to refuse, as the females seemed to favor it.

"Well, stranger," said he, "I don't know what to think about this here business. I didn't expect, when we took you in, that you would knock up our fun—that is, I didn't exactly look for you to go in for any of your preachin' fixins; the fact is, we have company to-night (lowering his voice) who ain't much used to that sort of thing; in short—What do *you* say, Peter?"

"Let him go it," replied Peter at once, knowing that it would gratify his mistress.

So the travelers and family were gathered together in the bar-room, and the worthy Presbyterian commenced one of those extensively long prayers which appear to have no end, and in which the Almighty is *told what to do* with his creatures in all their varied walks of life. The captain stood it pretty well for the first quarter of an hour, but after a while he began to get mighty uneasy. Looking first one way and then another, his eye at length rested on Peter, who was standing on the outside of the door, bearing in his arms a large bowl. He had been tempted several times to stop the clergyman, but now he determined to submit the matter to an umpire that never failed to decide correctly. Accordingly, in a loud whisper, he propounded the question, "What do *you* say, Peter?"

"Better quit it," was the decision of Peter, who almost immediately added, "Punch is ready."

The captain gave a gentle jog to the long-winded Presbyterian, and said, "Peter thinks we'd better bring this matter to an end. We've got a splendid bowl of punch, and, as soon as you can conveniently come to 'Amen,' perhaps it would be as well to wind up."

The minister did "wind up" rather suddenly, and the "family worship" was over for that night. I feel compelled to add that the preacher, after a little urging, drank his full share of the punch, and the evening passed off pleasantly, ending with the stowing away of the worthy divine in the little room known as the "bar," where he rested as well, probably, as he would have done in the best bedroom, his long ride in a drizzling rain, assisted by the comforting contents of Peter's punch-bowl, predisposing him to a sound sleep.

It had been told me for a fact that Captain Crowell had said no man should marry his daughter who could not *outjump her.* At the time I traveled in that country, it was said she had outjumped all the young men who had come to woo her; but the captain felt pretty certain that when the *right one* should come *she wouldn't jump so well.* More than likely, long before this time she has been "won and wed."

Another famous stopping-place was General Woodward's, at Caleba Swamp. The general was a tall, noble-looking fellow, a rough likeness of George Barrett. He always gave us a hearty wolcome, and many a pleasant night I have spent at his house. A most eccentric man he was. A preacher putting up at his house one night complained of being disturbed by a fiddler who kept playing till midnight. (The "fiddler" was the general himself.) Next morning, as the travelers came up to settle their several bills, each was charged a dollar except the preacher, of whom a dollar *and a quarter* was demanded.

"Will you be kind enough to inform me why it is you charge me more than the others?" asked the preacher.

"Sartin," replied the general; "the extra quarter I charge you for—*the music.*"

It was General Woodward who, during the Indian troubles, sent a formal offer to the War Department that for $500 he would take as many rocks as he could carry in his pocket, and *stone the Creeks out of the nation.*

The consolate Widow.

Between Caleba Swamp and Lime Creek, in the "Nation," we saw considerable of a crowd gathered near a drinking-house, most of them seated and smoking. We stopped to see what was the matter. It was Sunday, and there had been a quarter race for a gallon of whisky. The first thing I noticed on alighting was the singular position of one of the horses of the party. He was kneeling down and standing on his hinder feet, his head wedged in between the ends of two logs of the grocery, and was stone dead, having evidently ran directly against the building at full speed, causing the house partially to fall. About five paces from the body of the horse lay the rider, quite senseless, with a gash in his throat which might have let out a thousand lives. As I said, most of the crowd were seated and smoking.

"What is all this?" I inquired. "What is the matter here?"

"Matter?" after a while answered one in a drawling voice, giving a good spit, and refilling his mouth with a new cud. "Matter enough; there's been a quarter race."

"But how came this man and horse killed?" I asked.

"Well," answered the chewing and spitting gentleman, "the man was considerably in liquor, I reckon, and he run his hoss chuck agin the house, and that's the whole on it."

"Has a doctor been sent for?" inquired one of our party.

"I reckon there ain't much use of doctors *here,*" replied another of the crowd. "Burnt brandy couldn't save either of 'em, man or hoss."

"Has this man a wife and children?" inquired I.

"No children, that I knows on," answered a female, who was sitting on the ground a short distance from the dead man, smoking composedly.

"He has a wife, then?" I remarked. "What will be her feelings when she learns the fatal termination of this most unfortunate race?"

"Yes," sighed the female, "it *was* an unfortunate race. Poor man! he lost the whisky."

"Do you happen to know his wife? Has she been informed of the untimely death of her husband?" were my next inquiries.

"Do I *know* her? Has she been informed of his death?" said the woman. "Well, I reckon you ain't acquainted about these parts. *I* am the unfortunate widder."

"*You*, madam! *You* the wife of this man who has been so untimely cut off?" I exclaimed, in astonishment.

"Yes, and what about it?" said she. "Untimely cut off? His throat's cut, that's all, by that 'tarnal sharp end of a log; and as for it's being *untimely*, I don't know but it's as well now as any time—*he warn't of much account, no how!*"

She resumed her smoking, and we resumed our journey.

The season in Montgomery this year (1834) commenced on the 16th of January. The celebrated George Holland joined me in the management, and the firm was "Smith & Holland."

George Holland came to this country under an engagement for three years at the Bowery Theatre. After performing in that establishment for a short time, he received so many offers of *starring* engagements that he *bought himself out*, and started on a tour through the States, making money at every step. In a year or two he accumulated sufficient means to purchase a cottage at Harlem, New York. Being fond of domestic comforts, he fitted up his place in the most tasteful manner — improved his grounds — had a boat — kept his gig and fast-trotting pony, and was really in a little earthly paradise. Being a very popular comedian in New York, and his cottage being always open to his friends, he had considerable company, who delighted in his society, his jokes, his dinners, and his Champagne. He lived thus for about two years, when some "d—d good-natured friends" persuaded him to fit up his place as a *house of entertainment*. He followed the advice, expended a large sum in preparing his premises for the reception of company, and—was ruined! Those *friends* who could find time to pass days at his cottage when it cost nothing, now found that their business in town suffered during their absence; the wine, which was drank with such *goût* before, was now discovered to be of the same kind as that kept at Niblo's in the city; the ice cream, ice punches, and strawberries could be got in New York, and the expense of the ride saved; the few who did visit the cottage found that Holland, the hospitable host of invited guests, was a different person from Holland the *landlord;* and though he had been always ready with his joke and repartee when entertaining friends at his own expense, his feelings shrank from giving an expected anecdote with a glass of cream, or a *bon mot* with a bowl of punch. *The speculation failed*, and George Holland was compelled to go out into the world again.

The veteran Cooper, Mr. Barton, and Mr. Holland made a professional tour, giving entertainments in all the principal towns from Baltimore to New Orleans. The anecdotes which might be related of this tour would fill a small volume. George gave loose to his love of fun, and the two tragedians were obliged to "stand it."

My business connection with George Holland was a very pleasant one. We parted at the close of the season with mutual good feelings, and he proceeded to New Orleans, where he soon became the principal clerk of James H. Caldwell, about that time extensively engaged in starting his gas company. In after years we were thrown into antagonistic interests, but not for a moment did either of us entertain any but the most friendly feeling toward the other. In prosperity and adversity he adhered to the fortunes and misfortunes of Mr. Caldwell until 1843, when that gentleman, as will be hereafter related, bade adieu to theatrical management. For a few months Mr. Holland traveled with Dr. Lardner as his agent and manager, and then attached himself to the Little Olympic, under Manager Mitchell, where he remained seven years, as great a favorite as New York ever knew. On the retirement of Mitchell from the management in 1849, Holland accepted an engagement offered him by Mr. Thomas Placide, manager of the "Varieties," New Orleans, where he enjoyed a popularity never perhaps achieved by any other actor in that city. Mr. Holland is now a fixture at "Wallack's," in New York, where he is deservedly esteemed both as an actor and a man.

The following is a list of our Montgomery stars: H. J. Finn, Mr. and Mrs. George Barrett, Mr. George Hill, and Miss Jane Placide. The season was a moderately good one, and closed on the 26th of April.

Mr. G. W. West, a tailor by trade, and a very sensible man, volunteered to perform the character of *Rolla* for the benefit of one of the actors; and I must here record the fact that he succeeded very well—better than any amateur actor I ever saw attempt the part. In the last scene but one, where he crossed the bridge, bearing Cora's child out of the Spanish camp, he met with an accident which might have been fatal to himself and the rescued child also. Whether, in the confusion created by the firing of muskets at the retreating hero, he became confused and missed his footing, or the joint of the bridge was dislocated too soon by the attending carpenter, I do not know, but certain it is that *Rolla* had an inglorious tumble into the waters below, still holding on to the child, which he bore aloft while struggling in the waves! Young Mark Smith was restored to his mother without a scratch, while the nose of West bore such unmistakable marks of violence from some quarter that no extra application of a bloody sponge was necessary to prepare him for his dying scene.

West received great applause for his performance, and many of his friends advised him to adopt the stage as a profession; but he had the good sense to adopt the advice of a better friend than any of those who so advised him, and he is now one of the first merchant tailors of St. Louis, respected by every body, with plenty of the world's riches to render him independent and happy. I don't know how Colonel West may relish my mention of his youthful freak, but he and I often talk over this *Rolla* affair with great pleasure. He has become quite portly, but the child he rescued from the Spaniards has outgrown him considerably; and he admits that an attempt *now* to carry Mark over a bridge would inevitably result in another tumble.

CHAPTER XIII.

A NEW organization of my forces was absolutely necessary. The past year's company was any thing but one to be proud of. Falstaff refused to "march through Coventry" with *his* company—*I* was determined I would no longer march through Georgia and Alabama with mine; so, repairing to New Orleans, the word was passed around that "recruits" were wanted for my last traveling campaign, and a very short time sufficed to fill the list, which is here annexed:

Mrs. Sol. Smith, Mrs. Gay, Mrs. Sullivan, Mrs. M'Donald; Messrs. J. M. Field, Spencer, C. W. Hunt, Langton, Gay, Washburn, Sullivan, Decius Rice, Flagg, and Rutherford. Leader of the orchestra, H. C. Walsh.

I note here the decease of Mr. J. Purdy Brown, manager of the Mobile Theatre, on the 7th of June, 1834, after an illness of only a few hours, caused, as it is supposed, by eating *crabs* for supper at a late hour.

Conceiving that too many details of the *business* must tire the reader (it certainly tires *me* to write them), I will confine myself to a very brief compendium of our proceedings during this year.

The company was certainly better, by several degrees, than any which had preceded it in the circuit, but the receipts fell far below those of previous seasons.

At Montgomery, to begin with, we played two weeks; at Columbus, four; Macon, six; and then proceeded to Augusta, at the earnest request of many of the most respectable citizens. Here I leased the theatre for one year, and occupied it one month, losing in that month $1000. The rent ($1000) was secured by a mortgage on a lot in Macon, which was eventually sold to pay the same. Two years afterward that lot was worth $11,000! So my month's management in Augusta was any thing but profitable.

A Manager for a Minute.

Charles W. Hunt was a member of my company at the time. He was then a promising young actor, aspiring to establish himself as a low comedian; but, young as he was, and *modest*, I think the reader will agree with me, when he reads what follows, that he exhibited a degree of *coolness under difficulties* worthy of an experienced veteran.

On the very first night of the season, this Hunt got into a difficulty with a Mr. Sullivan, a fiery, trodden-down young tragedian. A fight ensued, which ended in the breaking of poor Hunt's arm. A fight behind the scenes, being a most unusual occurrence in any well-regulated theatre, is always visited upon the party who is in the wrong by the utmost rigor of the "rules and regulations"—either an immediate discharge, or a heavy penalty in the way of stoppage of salary must be submitted to by the offender. Hunt stood in this predicament. He had brought the misfortune upon himself, and in an apologetic letter the next morning he acknowledged his fault to the fullest extent; but, inasmuch as he was suffering for his indiscretion, and would be prevented, at least for several weeks, from appearing on the boards, my mind was made up at once to treat him with great leniency; in fact, I determined to say nothing at all about the affair, and permit him to rejoin the company whenever his arm should be healed.

The season closed—so did the broken bone of Hunt's arm. The treasury was opened for the payment of salaries for the final week in Augusta. As was my custom at that time, I attended personally to this ceremony. Piles of silver and bank-notes were laid out before me on a table in the director's room; the receipt-book was ready, and the clerk was directed to admit the performers, "*one by one*," to receive their salaries. The door was opened, and the first individual that appeared was the broken-armed comedian, Hunt!

"Ah! is that you, Mr. Hunt? Good-morning"—thus I greeted him—"glad to see you out. Arm quite well?" I asked.

"Thank you, yes," he replied, taking a chair which I pointed to. "I have suffered greatly for my folly," he continued; "only catch me getting into a fight again, that's all!"

"That's the right feeling, Mr. Hunt," I remarked. "Such scenes are disreputable in every way. Let this be a lesson to you."

"It shall, most assuredly," promised the repentant comedian. The conversation here ceased, and I began to count over a "ten" pile, in hopes my visitor would take his leave and permit the payment of salaries to proceed, as I was in haste, intending to leave the city for Milledgeville the same afternoon. Finding the comedian did not exhibit the least sign of departure, after a few commonplace observations respecting the fine weather for traveling, I ventured courteously to suggest that I should be happy to see him *some other time*, it being "salary day," and a busy one for me—the people waiting—

"Ye—es," replied Hunt—"salary day; that's just the reason I came in at this very time. My salary has been lying in the treasury during the whole season of four weeks; and as we leave this afternoon, why, I thought—"

"*Your* salary, Mr. Hunt!" I exclaimed, with some surprise; "I was not aware there was any thing due *you*. If my memory serves me, every thing was settled at the close of the season in Macon."

"Decidedly," admitted Hunt; "every thing was paid up fair and square; but it is *this* season's salary I speak of, and which I have called to receive."

"My dear sir," I remonstrated, "you don't imagine, I hope, that you are entitled to salary during the time you have rendered no service? Your hurt was not received in the performance of your professional duties; on the contrary, you received it while engaged in a most unpardonable breach of the rules and regulations, which not only subjects you to a heavy fine, but renders you liable to an instant discharge, as you know and have admitted; and now—"

"That is all true," interrupted Mr. Hunt, "but—"

"Hear me through," I continued; "and now, instead of coming to ask leave to rejoin the company at Milledgeville, and perhaps *ask a loan* of a small sum, which very likely would not be refused under the circumstances, it appears you intend to set up a claim for salary during your confinement. Am I right in supposing such to be your intention?"

"Most indubitably you are," was my friend Hunt's reply; "that is," he continued, "so far as my claiming *something* in the way of salary, you *are* right. I do think you ought to allow me at least a *portion* of the amount which would now be my due, had not this untoward accident happened. Gentlemen of the army receive *half pay* when they are wounded or retire from service. What say you? Let us compromise this matter; give me *half* salary for the four weeks, and we'll have no more words about it."

The coolness of this proposition almost upset my temper. The rules and regulations which he had agreed to and signed stipulated that "no salary should be received during sickness or when no services were tendered;" and although I had always been in the habit of making some allowance in cases where performers received an injury while in the exercise of their duties in the theatre, I could not see the least reason why the treasury should be taxed in a case like this, where there had been a decided breach of the rules, and where the fault was acknowledged to be on the side of the party now claiming salary.

"I can not admit this claim," I said, firmly. "I intend to reinstate you in your situation at the next town, considering that your sufferings had atoned for your fault; moreover, I now profess myself ready to *loan* you some money, if you stand in need of it, to enable you to settle up your bills here and travel to Milledgeville. This is all I can or will do."

"Then I consider you act unjustly," replied Hunt, surlily, rising and taking his hat. "Here have I been suffering for a month, confined to my room, earning nothing, subjected to expenses of boarding, washing, and surgical attendance, and now to be fobbed off without any salary for four weeks—really it is too—"

"Fobbed off?" I rejoined—"fobbed, sir? Is it not enough that I should be deprived of your services during the whole of the season? Must I now be accused of acting unjustly because I do not entertain your absurd claim, and *pay* you for your improper conduct?"

The discussion was waxing warm, and there appeared to be no chance of coming to an understanding; the company were all waiting in the next room for their salaries. I became impatient, and at length proposed that we should call in two or three members of the company as arbitrators; but to this Hunt objected, saying that he thought he was capable of attending to his own affairs, and that he would not give up his own judgment for that of any person living.

"Well, then," I replied, "to *your* judgment and sense of justice I will submit the matter. Here, take this seat. You shall be the manager, *I* the actor. You shall be judge in your own case."

Mr. Hunt very readily took possession of the vacated chair, graciously remarking that my proposition convinced him that I was indeed the upright and just man he had always taken me to be. I felt quite confident that he would view the matter in a proper light when he came to see it in all its proper bearings.

Taking Hunt's late position in front of the table—

"Mr. Manager," I began, "the season being ended, I have come to request that the outrage I committed on the first night, and which has laid me up for a month, may not be in the way of my restoration to the company, inasmuch as I have suffered greatly from the serious hurt I received on that unfortunate occasion."

"Yes, yes," replied *Manager* Hunt, with a dignified wave of the hand, "that is all understood; join us at Milledgeville, and let us have no more such scenes; they are disgraceful in the extreme. What more?"

"Well, sir," continued I, still in the character of the suppliant invalid, "perhaps, as I have been so great a sufferer, you may not think it unreasonable that I should ask some pecuniary accommodation?"

"It is but reasonable," replied the manager *pro tem.*, promptly; "that matter has been thought of. Have you no other request to make?" he inquired, turning round in the chair and taking up a pen.

"Yes," I replied, hesitatingly, "I have been thinking—though really I am almost ashamed to mention it—that possibly you might allow me *half pay* during my confinement; in short, as it is a delicate matter, I leave it entirely to your own sense of justice to decide whether I shall receive *any thing* from the treasury or not."

"Ahem! yes, I understand," said my *locum tenens.* Casting a cursory glance over a copy of the rules and regulations which happened to lay before him, riveting his eye for a moment at the particular section which had been violated, and uttering two or three emphatic "hems," he then proceeded slowly to pronounce judgment in the case as follows:

"Young man, you have done very wrong—very wrong indeed; but, on the other hand, you have suffered very much—I am fully sensible *how* much; therefore we will let that pass. The offense has carried its own punishment with it. I have already told you that you are restored to your situation. In regard to your application for pecuniary assistance, I scarcely know what to say. You speak of *half* pay. This, I am disposed to believe, would scarcely reach your merits—certainly not your *necessities.* Your rapid improvement in your profession has not been unnoticed by the management; your conduct, with the single exception of the case under consideration, has been most exemplary; *your salary is not large*—and, in this connection, I may say *a small addition* to your weekly income has been thought of; but the season has been so unpropitious that this is not the proper time to carry out my intentions concerning you; therefore, taking every point into consideration, and acting upon the principle of returning good for evil, which, as a good Christian, I feel impelled to do—THERE!" (with great composure selecting six of the ten-dollar piles before him, and magnanimously pushing them, one by one, across the table)—"there, my boy, is the WHOLE OF YOUR SALARY TO DATE. Sign the receipt."

* * * * * * * *

The judgment was of course affirmed when I resumed the managerial chair. Hunt pocketed his sixty dollars, and retired perfectly satisfied with his brief term of management, and I proceeded with the payment of salaries to the other members of the company, who had been kept waiting by the enactment of this singular scene. Hunt afterward justified his proceeding by saying he acted on the golden rule—"DO UNTO YOURSELF AS YOU WOULD OTHERS SHOULD DO UNTO YOU."

At Milledgeville, during the session of the Legislature, we made a moderately successful season of seven weeks, performing all of the most legitimate tragedies and comedies before the intelligent Georgians to their perfect satisfaction. J. M. Field was a good leading actor, Mrs. Smith a great favorite, and the company fully equal to their support. The Shaksperian plays we gave were MACBETH, KING LEAR, ROMEO AND JULIET, MERCHANT OF VENICE, RICHARD III., and MUCH ADO ABOUT NOTHING. One of our best actors we parted with about this time for breaking his temperance pledge. I have something to say about this actor before parting with him.

Giving Entertainments.

Harry Langton was the theatrical name of a very honest, tolerably talented, and very eccentric fellow who, for several years was attached to the stage in the South. He was a worthy individual, a useful member of a company of actors, and was beloved by every one who knew him, yet he was cursed with one failing—*he would drink.* Well, he is gone now, and we will think only of his *good* qualities, which were numerous, and endeavor to amuse ourselves with his eccentricities.

I have elsewhere mentioned the fact that, being pushed for means whereby to live, he engaged himself to the keeper of a museum in Pittsburg, where he stood up in a glass case for two mortal hours as the *wax figure of General Jackson!* I intend, in this sketch, to give some other instances of his versatility of talent, by the exercise of which he overcame temporary pecuniary difficulties.

Harry Langton never let an opportunity slip of *giving an entertainment* where there was the least chance of success. Sometimes, indeed, I have known him to propose "trying it on" at places where the chance of profit was any thing but flattering. Traveling in a stage-coach, he was always looking out for eligible villages for his purpose, and I recollect that on one occasion he seriously proposed to issue bills for an "*entertainment*" at a place where we stopped to water the horses, though nothing in the shape of a dwelling could be seen, except a shanty of a stable!

"Why, Harry," one asked, "where do you expect your audience to come from?"

"Oh!" was his ready reply, "there are plenty of people hereabouts *somewhere*, I'm certain, for I've seen lots of cattle as we came along, and they've got owners, be sure on't. Let us put out some bills and 'try it on!'"

In two instances it has been *my* fate to *assist*, much against my will, in poor Langton's entertainments.

In the fall of 1830, the boat which conveyed the New Orleans company on its way from Nashville to its winter destination stopped a few hours at the then inconsiderable village of Vicksburg. Langton was on the look-out, of course, and, after taking a view of the town, came in, rubbing his hands, and with his face flushed with hope.

"Sol," said he, "here's a glorious chance for an entertainment. Theatre can be had—people all anxious—if the boat would only wait—"

"But the boat *won't* wait," I replied; "the captain has just told me he starts in half an hour, positively."

"I think he might be induced," persisted Langton. "It is now four o'clock; we can have the town billed in an hour, and we can put a hundred dollars in our pockets just as easy as nothing. What do you say to trying it on?"

"What do *I* say? I say it's all nonsense, even if the boat would wait. You could not get twenty people to the theatre at such short notice. Besides, you are an entire stranger here; nobody has ever heard of you."

"That's very true," he answered, nodding his head knowingly; "but they all know *you*—*you* have acted here."

"To be sure I have," I answered, "but you don't expect *me* to make a fool of myself in your proposed entertainment?"

"Make a fool of yourself! Not at all; but I expect you to make fifty dollars! Come, old fellow," he continued, beseechingly, "give us a lift. There are four of us going into the speculation, and we propose to give you half the receipts, if you will but permit your *name* to be used, and sing three songs."

"My dear fellow," I remonstrated, "I can't think of it. Besides, the captain won't wait, and, moreover, my wardrobe is at the bottom of the hold, and can not be got at. Your offer is very tempting, certainly—[half the receipts! Macready's terms!]—but put this entertainment out of your head."

"The captain *will* wait, and has already *promised* to wait till ten o'clock, so it all depends on *you*. As for wardrobe, I'll lend you a red wig and a pair of striped stockings. Come, old fellow, if *you* don't want to make a little money, *we* do, and it all depends on you whether we are enabled to do it or not."

After some farther holding back on my part, and considerably more urging on that of Langton, I consented to sing two songs, provided sufficient notice could be given to the inhabitants that the entertainment would take place.

"Leave the *notice* entirely to me," said Langton, as he vanished over the plank, and rushed up into town through the mud.

Langton won my slow consent about sundown. I had hopes that when he found the difficulty of lighting the house and giving notice to the citizens, he would give up the project altogether. Not so. Langton was not the man to be staggered by slight difficulties. The entertainment must be given; doors open at 7, curtain to rise at half past, and "no postponement on account of the weather."

After tea, without much devotion to the deed, I assure you—putting a wig and a pair of comic stockings in my pocket, I trudged off toward the theatre. On my way (in the dark), a negro bellman, who was the town-crier, stopped at a corner as I was passing, and, after shaking his bell for nearly a minute, put me out of all doubt in regard to the "notice" which was to be given of the proposed entertainment by promulgating, in a loud voice, the following proclamation:

"Oh yes! oh yes! *oh* yes! Every body take particular notice hereby dat *Ole Sol* has come back to dis here burg on his way to New Orleans, and, moreover, will exhibit hisself dis night at de the-*a*-tur as large as life! So dis is to certify dat you must all come and see him, by particular desire, for dis night only! Oh yes! oh yes! *oh* yes!"

I felt willing at that moment to sink into the mud even farther than I *had* sunk while listening to this proclamation, provided I could have availed myself of such an *accident* as an excuse for not "exhibitin'" myself pursuant to notice. However, I was in for it in more senses than one. I was engaged, and on starring terms! So I waded to the theatre, where I found Langton and his associates lighting candles, selling tickets, and sweeping off the stage preparatory to the grand entertainment. The house was tolerably well filled. SYLVESTER DAGGERWOOD was the drama performed on this memorable occasion. Two songs by your humble servant, and some recitations by the "rest of the company," completed the programme, and I returned to the boat, *declining to take my share of the proceeds*, and made a solemn determination never to be coaxed into such a scrape again.

"But who shall control his fate?"

I *was* again seduced to do the very same thing on another occasion, and by the self-same Langton.

It was at the little town of Benton, on the Alabama River, in 1832, that Langton saw a fine opportunity for giving an entertainment. (We were again traveling together.) The seducing villain made use of the very same arguments he had urged so successfully at Vicksburg: the boat would wait—the people were *so* anxious to see *me!*—such a crowd would be in attendance—fifty dollars, at least, he would be able to put into his pocket, and he was so in *need* of money—he was sure I couldn't have the heart to prevent his making such a handsome sum. I consented.

The room selected for the "entertainment" was exactly fourteen feet square. It was filled to overflowing, and we were obliged to give our songs and recitations on a table set outside of a window!

The only remarkable part of this performance was this: Langton gave the *comic* recitations and songs, while I gave the *tragic* recitations and *sentimental* songs!

By this queer entertainment, given through a window, Langton cleared over $40.

Poor Langton! He went to Texas in the beginning of the war of independence, and I have never seen him since.

In his last letter to me, giving a portion of his travel's history, he began by expressing his belief that I would find no difficulty in calling him to remembrance—shall I ever *forget* him?—said he had just returned from giving an entertainment in one of the Camanche villages on the northern frontier, where he narrowly escaped scalpation, and concluded with the following sentence:

"Sol, if you'll come to Texas, we'll make our fortunes—glorious chances here for giving entertainments—come out!"

Deciding to go directly to Montgomery, without stopping at Macon or Columbus, we made arrangements for our journey of three hundred miles, which we accomplished, after undergoing unheard-of hardships, in ten days, at an expense not much short of $1000, without reckoning the salaries of the company. At Caleba Swamp we found about three thousand persons waiting for the mending of a bridge. If any one is curious to know some of the incidents at this "watering-place," let him purchase J. M. Field's "Drama at Pokerville," and turn to the sketch entitled "A Night in a Swamp."

Opened at Montgomery on the 3d of January, 1835, with the HEIR AT LAW and 'TIS ALL A FARCE. Next night we played HAMLET and MY AUNT—*Hamlet*, Mr. J. M. Field, his first appearance in Alabama.

It has often been said of me that I have been "an actor of all work." It is measurably true. I had an opportunity, about the time I am now writing about, to exhibit the versatility of my talents in a new line of business. The members of the Episcopal Church had purchased a very nice *organ*, but, there being no one in the place who knew any thing about putting it up, it had lain in a basement room for a year or two, and the owners had about given up all hope of ever hearing it in operation. Accidentally learning the state of affairs, I volunteered to put up the organ, if two or three laboring men would lend me their assistance. Two of the church-members readily undertook to assist me, and in two days the instrument was ready to be played on. I had never done any thing of the kind before, but the pipes were all clearly marked, and I found no difficulty at all in putting them in their places. The organ being up and ready, the next thing was to find somebody to play upon it. After faithful inquiry, not a living being could be found who knew any thing of organ-playing, except a chap who said if it was a *hand*-organ he could turn the crank, he thought. At length, rather than that these good Episcopalians should go without music now they had an organ ready to be played on, I had to volunteer my own services for a few weeks, until Mr. Evans, my leader, could learn to play. My services were accepted with thankfulness by the whole congregation, and, a choir being immediately formed, the beautiful services of the Episcopal Church were given ever afterward with organ accompaniments, much to the gratification of the people.

During this season Mrs. Drake acted with us a starring engagement—so did Yankee Hill, and —last, not least—HENRY J. FINN.

Urged by the citizens of Wetumpka, I sent my dramatic forces, under the temporary command of Brev. Gen. J. M. Field, to that remarkably primitive city, where a considerable business was done in a billiard-room, hastily transformed into a theatre, during a season of two weeks. Mr. Charles Mason, a nephew of John Kemble, played here three or four nights, to good houses.

Haynesville, in the opposite direction, now claimed a visit; and in a large room in the academy, a little out of town, the drama shed forth its influences on audiences who gave no token whatever of their appreciation of our efforts. For twelve successive nights we exerted ourselves for their edification, and to this day I am in utter ignorance whether our efforts were satisfactory or not, for not a hand of applause greeted us during the whole time, neither did a smile—a laugh was out of the question—shed its ray, to cheer us on in our task. Yes, there *was* one attempt at a slight smile—indeed, I might say that a real jolly laugh was on the point of breaking out on one occasion; but it was checked in its incipiency. It was during the performance of the HYPOCRITE, Act v, where *Mawworm* mounts on a table behind a screen and gives an extemporaneous discourse, which on this particular occasion was interlarded with some local hits, which actually took effect upon one tall fellow standing in a corner near the stage. A premature "Ha! ha! h—" was bursting out, when one of the deacons of the Presbyterian Church arose from a chair with great solemnity, and addressed the *quasi* disturber of the assembly thus: "Mr. Thompson, you must quit that or leave the meeting." Mr. Thompson "shut up."

"Old Jack Barnes," with his wife and daughter Charlotte, came to play an engagement toward the end of the season in Montgomery, opening in the SCHOOL FOR SCANDAL, in the first scene of the second act of which, a fat negro wench, being told to hold up Miss Barnes's train until she got to the wing, *followed Lady T. upon the stage*, and remained there, holding up the train, during the ceremony of reception, which, under the circumstances, was an uproarious one, and reluctantly leaving, with a low courtesy, only when *Sir Peter* (Mr. Barnes) told her that her services were no longer required.

On one of "Yankee Hill's" nights (with shame I confess it), my name was associated with his in the committal of a horrid murder!—*Richard* and *Richmond* being the characters in which we perpetrated the dreadful deed.

Our prompter's name was Gay. He performed old men, personated marble statues, and danced comic hornpipes. On one occasion, the performances ending with DON JUAN, in which Gay enacted the part of the murdered governor on horseback (a statue), the audience demanded a *comic dance* before they would leave the house.

"What is to be done?" asked Gay, in a piteous tone, the perspiration bursting out through the Spanish whiting on his face. "It will take at least a quarter of an hour to prepare for a dance!"

"Not at all," replied I, promptly; "go on as you are."

"What!" said Gay, "go on for a comic dance dressed as a marble statue?"

"Yes—as the marble statue; it will be all the more comic"—and up went the curtain.

The audience relished the dance hugely; and I must say that the marble statue, dancing to the tune of "A frog he would a-wooing go," *was* a most original and mirth-provoking affair.

During the engagement of the Barneses we performed the farce of THREE WEEKS AFTER MARRIAGE. It will be remembered that there is in this piece a matrimonial quarrel about a game of cards. A fellow in the pit had listened to the dispute with much interest until the end of the first act, when, just before the fall of the drop, *Sir Charles*, in reply to his lady's invitation to go to bed, exclaims, "I'll not go to bed with any woman who don't know what's trumps." The man in the pit got up in utter surprise, and said, in a tone loud enough to be heard by the whole house, "Well, you're a cursed fool to quarrel about such a trifle! Blast me if *I* wouldn't confess to the diamond, and go to bed!" The drop scene again rose, and soon the newly-married couple were again engaged in their dispute about the game of whist, and, to convince his wife of her error, *Sir Charles* went up to the table and dealt out the cards. The man in the pit called out and asked "what's trumps?" *Sir Charles* just at that moment said "clubs!" and his lady "diamonds!" which appeared to be answers to his question; whereupon the auditor took up his hat and made for the door, exclaiming, "*I* sha'n't wait any longer; they've been quarreling here for half an hour about clubs and diamonds; I don't see as there's any likelihood of their coming to an understanding, so I'll go; it's getting late." This speech elicited a round of applause from the pit. Turning as he was about passing through the opening into the passage, he addressed *Sir Charles* and *Lady Racket*—"Young people, you'd better make up that little difficulty and let the play go on; it's of mighty little consequence *what* was trumps; make it up and go to bed!" Then, looking up at the audience, who were roaring with laughter, he made a low bow, and retired from sight, lit a cigar at a lamp in the passage, shook the door-keeper by the hand, and walked off.

Matthew Field, who afterward became a good actor, and somewhat celebrated as a writer (under his own name and that of *Phazma*), made his first appearance on any stage in Montgomery as *Hemeya*, in the tragedy of the Apostate, Mrs. A. Drake performing *Florinda*. The début was a successful one; but the "last scene of all in *that* eventful tragedy" was rendered somewhat ludicrously. If the reader is not aware of the fact, I must inform him that Mrs. Drake is what we term a *heavy* actress—how well I remember her a slim young girl in Albany, more than fifty years ago!—and *Florinda* dies and *falls* beside *Hemeya* at the close of the piece. Mat. Field had got through *his* troubles, and lay dead and stiff, congratulating himself on the success he had met with on his first attempt at acting, when he suddenly perceived that Mrs. D. was preparing for "a fall" in the immediate vicinity of his own resting-place. I was watching Mrs. D.'s splendid death, and it must be confessed that poor Mat. did appear in considerable danger of being *fallen upon* by the poisoned *Florinda*. At first there were sundry twitchings of the arms and legs of the dead *Hemeya*; then, as the body of the devoted *Florinda* was seen actually descending, a sudden spring of her lover's corpse placed it out of danger, and there they both lay, "faithful to each other even in death." When Mat. found that he was not crushed, it seemed to occur to him that it was not altogether proper or picturesque to turn his back to the lady, so he very deliberately *turned over*, and, stretching forth his dead arms, encircled her with them in a loving embrace, the curtain falling on the picture.

Mary Vos (afterward Mrs. Stewart) performed a few nights "previous to her departure for the Eastern cities."

The season and my "country management" ended on the 10th of June, 1835, with my benefit, which was very largely attended, notwithstanding the extremely hot weather; my Montgomery friends, without resorting to the humbug of a "complimentary," filling the house to its utmost capacity, and cheering me with their shouts and kindly greetings to the last.

Here ends my Second Act, and rather a long one it is; but I wanted to get through with my "management" in the rural districts before taking the reader with me into my metropolitan experiences, which I propose to hurry through with less regard to detail than has characterized the recital of the incidents of the first twelve years of my theatrical life.

ACT THIRD.

1835–1840.

CHAPTER I.

To begin with, and as a preliminary to the intended opening in Mobile, the reader, if he (or she) wishes to keep with me, must be my companion in a sort of starring tour to the North.

Negotiations, pending for some months, had resulted in an arrangement which was to sink my managerial individuality in a "firm" destined to exist, as it now appears, for eighteen years, wielding an influence in theatrical matters unequaled in the States. In the following fall this arrangement was to go into operation at Mobile. In the interim, it was necessary that I should "go North" to pick up a company and engage stars. A glance at this Northern trip must be brifly noticed.

Leaving my wife and children in a snug little cottage at Harrowgate Springs, near Wetumpka, I started on my Northern journey, in company with Mr. J. M. Field, about the middle of June, passing through Mobile and New Orleans, and embarked on the steamer Warren for St. Louis.

A friendly Game of Poker.

On the evening of our second day out from New Orleans I found myself seated at a card-table, with three of my fellow-passengers, playing at the interesting game of "poker." Card-playing was a very common amusement then (1835), and it was not unusual to see half a dozen tables occupied at the same time in the gentlemen's cabin of a Mississippi boat. I had sat down at the game *for amusement*, but on rising at ten o'clock I found my amusement had cost me about sixty dollars! "This won't do at all," said I, thinking aloud; "I must try it again to-morrow." "Of course you must," replied one of the poker-players, who happened to be an old acquaintance of mine from Montgomery, Alabama, where he had been a jailer for several years, and where he was considered a very respectable citizen. "You must not give it up so," he continued, following me out on the guard; "*to-morrow you'll get even.*" I entered into conversation with my old acquaintance, whose name was Hubbell or Hubbard—I don't remember which—we'll call him Hubbard—and he advised me by all means to try another sitting on the morrow. I suggested to him that a slight suspicion had crossed my mind that some of our card party might possibly be *blacklegs*—in other words, *gamblers.* He answered that the same thought had struck *him* at one time, but he had come to the conclusion that all had been fair. Before leaving me, my quondam friend told me that *he* had become a sporting man—he felt it his duty to inform me of it—but he assured me, upon his honor (!), he would not see me wronged. *Of course* I believed him, and it was agreed that we should try our luck again.

Next morning, soon as the breakfast things had been cleared away, I found Hubbard and *a friend of his* waiting for me at one of the card-tables, and I took my seat with the hope of *getting even*—a hope which has led many a man into irretrievable ruin. I felt quite confident of winning back my losings overnight, and my *play-mates* gave me every encouragement that I should be successful. At it we went, playing with varying luck for about two hours. At about eleven o'clock Hubbard's friend left us for a few minutes to "get a drink," and the jailer and myself were left playing single handed. When the third man left, we were using the "small cards," as they are called—that is, *sixes* and under; but Hubbard immediately proposed that we should take the "large cards" (*tens* and over), which I agreed to, as a matter of course. One thing I here observed—my friend, the jailer, dealt the cards *without shuffling.* This made me resolve to watch him closely. Taking up my cards, I was agreeably surprised to find I had an excellent hand. "Now," thinks I to myself, "now is the time, if ever, to get even; if my adversary only happens to have a decent hand, I shall do well enough."

[The reader who does not understand the game of "bluff," or "poker," as it is most generally called, may as well leave off here.]

I commenced the game by bragging a dollar. My adversary went the dollar, and five better. I went that and ten. He immediately put up the ten, and laid down a twenty, keeping his pocket-book out, as much as to say, "I am ready to go any thing you choose to bet." After a moment's reflection (all acting), I said, "I go that—and fifty." "All right," replied the jailer, "there it is; I go that and a hundred!" I here looked at my cards again, and affected to have great doubt whether I should go the hundred. "Take back your last bet," I urged; "it is too much for either of us to lose: I begin to think I have been rash; take it back, and let us show our hands for the money already down." "No," said Hubbard; "if you mean sporting, put up the hundred, or back out and give me the money." "Can't do that," I replied; "I don't come from a backing-out country; I must have a showing for the money that's down—so there's the hundred; and, as my pocket-book's out, and my hand's in, there's *another* C." This new bet seemed to please my friend Hubbard mightily. He answered it without a moment's pause, and went two hundred more! I now requested my opponent to permit me to show my cards to some of the by-standers, who were crowding around the table in great numbers to see the fun, all considering me most undoubtedly "picked up." Hubbard would not agree that I should show my hand to, or take advice from any one. "Play your own cards," said he, reaching over, and gently compelling me to lay my cards on the table before me. "Then," said I, "*you* tell me if THREE ACES *and two other cards* can be beat?" "Oh yes," he replied, smiling with a self-satisfied air, and using the spit-box, "they *can* be beat, certainly, but not easy." "*Not easy*, I think myself," replied I; "therefore, inasmuch as I believe you are trying to bluff me off, I go the two hundred." "You do!" "Yes, I *do;* there's the money." "Any thing better?" inquired my adversary, insinuatingly, and leaning over to make use of the spit-box again, all the time keeping his gray eyes fixed upon my countenance. "Why—yes," I answered, "since you've got me excited, I will go something better—I go two hundred better than you." Looking me steadily in the face, he said, "Well, you're a bold fellow, any how, for a novice: *it takes all I've got*, by hokey, but I go it; and, if you'll let me *bet on a credit*, I should like to go back at you." (Spit-box.) Feeling confident of winning, I consented that he *might* go what he liked, on a credit, provided I should be allowed the same privilege. "Well, then," said Hubbard, a little spitefully, "I go you five hundred better—on a credit." (Spit-box again.) "The devil you do!" exclaimed I: "this looks like *gambling;* but, since we're in for it so deeply, I go you the five hundred, and—a thousand better—on a credit." At this stage of the game the third hand returned, and seeing at a glance how matters stood, requested to look at Hubbard's cards. "No, *sir*," interposed I, "*you must play your own cards*," at the same time motioning my opponent to lay down *his* cards as I had laid down mine. The carpet began to suffer at about this time—the spit-box was disregarded. The excitement among the passengers was great, and my ears received many a whisper that I was "licked." Hubbard took a long and earnest look into my eyes, and said slowly but confidently, "I GO IT—AND—CALL YOU." "I suppose I'm beat," said I [hypocrite that I was! I *didn't* suppose any thing of the kind]; "but turn over your papers and let us see what you've got." With one hand he gracefully turned over FOUR KINGS and a Jack, and with the other tremblingly "raked down" the pile of bank-notes, gold and silver, while a groan burst out from the spectators, who all seemed to regret my bad luck. "You are as lucky as a jailer," I remarked, as my friend began to smooth down the V's, X's, L's, and C's. "By-the-by," he inquired, again resorting to the spit-box, and looking over patronizingly at me, "I forgot to ask what *you* had." "Well," I replied, calmly, "I think you *might* as well see my cards." "Ha! ha!—oh, I reckon you're beat, my friend," he answered; "but let's see your hand, at all events." "Here are the documents," replied I; "there's *my* hand!" and I turned over my cards one by one: "there's an ACE—and there's another—and there's another!" "A pretty good hand, young man," remarked Hubbard—"three aces! What *else* have you?" "What else? Why, here's a QUEEN." "And what *else?*" asked every body. "*Another* ACE!" —FOUR ACES!!! * * * I looked over the table and discovered the face of my lately elated FRIEND had lost all color; the tobacco-juice was running out of the corners of his mouth; the V's, X's, and C's were dropped, and amazement and stupefaction were strongly imprinted on his features. A shout went up from the by-standers, and all hands were invited to take Champagne at my expense.

It is scarcely necessary to say that the money *bet on a credit* was never paid, nor was it ever *expected* to be paid. My friend Hubbard recollected he had urgent business at Vicksburg, and *left the boat.* It so *happened* that the *stranger* who had played with us also disembarked at the same burg, where they met with a singular accident, being promiscuously hung, a few days afterward, by a mob! Hubbard died *game*, and *spat* upon the excited populace.

A FRIENDLY GAME OF POKER. (See page 112.)

About a month after the adventure above related, I met a gentleman in Cincinnati whom I instantly recognized as one of my fellow-passengers on the Warren. After inquiring the state of each other's health, he asked me if I had played any at the game of poker lately. "Not since the great game you witnessed on board the Warren," I replied. "Do not play any more," said he, assuming a serious air; "you are liable to be fleeced. I saw you were in the hands of swindlers," he continued, "and, when one of the fellows left the table, I noticed that he laid a pack of cards *he had been shuffling* near your adversary's elbow. As an experiment (passing by at the moment), *I took the top card from the pack and shoved it under the bottom*, by which means *you* got the four aces intended for his partner, while *he* got the four kings intended for *you;* and thus the sporting gentlemen were caught in their own trap!"

MORAL.—Poker is decidedly a dangerous game to play at, particularly with strangers; but when you find yourself in possession of *four aces*, GO IT WITH A PERFECT RUSH!

In due time we arrived at St. Louis, where we had an engagement, early in July. Here I was welcomed in the good old-fashioned way and had a good benefit.

Mr. Field opened in RICHARD THE THIRD, and was quite successful.

Cincinnati was our next town. Mr. Field was well known here, and was warmly received, though there was some little talk to the effect that they liked his comedy better than his tragedy. His benefit was a very fine one. For myself, falsifying the saying that a prophet is not without honor except in his own country, the people seemed determined to shower honors "thick upon me;" and my benefit—it was a "crowder." Mr. Field and I here took different routes, he proceeding to Buffalo, where I believe he played (afterward filling an engagement at Baltimore), while I went on to head-quarters —New York.

A Postmaster General in Disguise.

On my way, in company with several gentlemen of New Orleans, it happened that the stage in which we were passengers stopped for supper at a small village situated between the towns of Columbus and Zanesville, on the Cumberland Road, in the State of Ohio.

There was a great gathering of militia captains, lieutenants, ensigns, sergeants, and corporals, with a considerable sprinkling of privates, all of whom had been exhibiting their patriotism during the day by marching up and down the road, shouldering arms, carrying arms, presenting arms, and charging bayonets, preparatory to intended hostile operations against the neighboring State of Michigan, the authorities of which and those of the State of Ohio were at open war—almost—about *boundary*.

For the purpose of amusement, it had been agreed that the stage-driver should be informed *confidentially* that I was Amos Kendall, *Postmaster General of the United States*, traveling in disguise, and assuming the very common name of *Smith*, in order to discover abuses in the mail transportation department. With many mysterious hints, and under strict charges of secrecy, Jehu was made acquainted with the awful fact that he was actually driving the important individual above named. The reins almost fell from his hands! "What! Mr. Kindle—*Amos* Kindle!" exclaimed the astonished driver; "it can't be possible!" "It *is* possible," answered the gentleman who was imparting the information, and who was enjoying a cigar and an outside seat; "and it is his wish to be entirely private, in order to avoid the attentions that would otherwise be lavished upon him." The driver promised the most inviolable secrecy, and on our arrival at the stopping-place, after bowing me into the house with much ceremony, proceeded to curry down his horses.

We had not been long in the hotel before it was plainly perceptible that *something* was going on: curious glances were thrown into the barroom where we were sitting—militia officers flitted about and collected into groups—the landlord and his family began to spruce up; in brief, it was evident our secret had been confidentially imparted to half the village.

The first demonstration that was made consisted of an invitation to my friends and myself to accept the use of a private parlor. This being at once agreed to, the landlord ventured to suggest that, if it was not disagreeable to me, my fellow-citizens of the village would like to pay their respects to me and *take me by the hand.*

"No objections in the world," said I; "let the worthy citizens come in."

Then followed a scene of the richest kind of fun; but Dickens has since described a similar adventure, and I pass on.

Supper was announced. I was placed at the head of the table—all standing until I was seated; the richest viands and nicest kinds of preserved fruits were set in profusion before us. We feasted; and during the operation numerous female heads, or, rather, heads of females, were continually popping in at the windows and open doors, while the piazza was filled with boys of all sizes, who amused themselves by firing off Chinese crackers, sending up young rockets, and shouting "Hurra for Jackson!—*and* his cabinet!"

Supper over, we retired to the bar, and demanded our bill of expenses. The landlord smilingly answered that he was too happy to entertain us without compensation; he felt honored by my sitting at his board, and my friends were equally welcome. After much urging, *I* consented to receive his hospitality, since he *insisted* on it; but *my friends*, I would not consent that *they* should feast at his expense. *They* must be allowed to pay for their splendid supper. Well, if I *insisted*, he *would* take pay from *them*—and he did.

"Could I say two or three words to you in private?" asked the landlord, in a low voice, as he walked by my side toward the coach, which was waiting.

"By all means," I replied; and he led me a little on one side, into a dark part of the piazza. After two or three hems to clear his throat, the landlord commenced:

"Whatever *others* may think of you, sir, *I* consider you an *honest man.*"

"Sir, I feel very much obliged by the favorable estimate you have formed of me."

"Yes, sir; let the opposition say what they please, *I* believe you to be a conscientious individual—*I* do."

"Well, sir, considering this is the first time we have ever met, I must say your liberality is extraordinary; but I thank you for your good opinion."

"Ah! sir, though we have never *met*, I know you well; we *all* know you for a most efficient officer and a deserving man."

"It is true I am tolerably well known in the Western and Southern country, and as for my *efficiency*, I believe I do push ahead about as hard as a man conveniently can."

"That you do—all parties must acknowledge it. You have effected many improvements in your department."

"Yes, I flatter myself that in the *stage* department I have made some improvements."

"Your *removals* have met with general approval in this part of the country."

"Removals? Oh, yes, I do travel a great deal."

"Yes, you do, and to some purpose. Now I wanted to speak to you about the postmaster here."

"Indeed! Well, what of *him?*"

"Are you not aware that he is a Whig?"

"No! is he?"

"Yes, he is; and it is thought by the friends of the administration here that *he* ought to be removed, and a good Democrat appointed."

"What is the office worth?"

"About $500 a year."

"Who would be a proper person for the office?"

"Why, I couldn't exactly say; but if—"

"Would *you* accept the appointment?"

"Most willingly, if you should think me worthy."

"Well, I'll tell you what you'd better do. Write on to the department; state the matter as you've stated it to me, and perhaps—"

"If *you* would just make a memorandum it would be sufficient."

"My dear sir, don't depend on any thing that passes between us *here*. *Here* I am Sol. Smith, as you may see by the way-bill; but at Washington—you understand—"

"Yes, I understand. Then I'll write on to the department."

"Yes—write."

"Sir, I shall depend on your good offices."

"Sir, you may. Your supper was excellent; your attentions shall not be forgotten. Farewell. Write on to the department, by all means."

The worthy aspirant to the postmastership of the village accompanied me to the coach, carefully turned up the steps when I had entered, and then joined his fellow-citizens in three loud cheers, with which our departure was honored.

Arrived at New York, arrangements were soon made for my opening at the Park Theatre, Mr. Simpson very willingly according me an engagement as a star, although he had declined my services as a stock actor (at $6 per week) ten years previously.

I opened in the comedy of the HYPOCRITE, with the following cast of the characters:

Doctor Cantwell............Mr. Clarke.
Sir John Lambert..........Mr. John Fisher.
Col. Lambert..............Mr. John Mason.
Darnley...................Mr. Richings.
Seyward...................Mr. Wheatley.
Bailiff...................Mr. John Povey.
Mr. Mawworm.............Mr. Sol. Smith.
Old Lady Lambert.........Mrs. Wheatley.
Young Lady Lambert......Mrs. Gurner.
Charlotte.................Mrs. Hilson.

This engagement, although I was wedged in between the nights of the Woods, was moderately profitable to the management and myself; I soon received offers from Boston, Philadelphia, Baltimore, Pittsburg, and many smaller towns, all of which, for want of time, I was compelled reluctantly to decline, except that from Philadelphia, which I was enabled to accept, because I could perform alternate nights in that city and New York, which I did during a period of two weeks. My engagement at the Walnut Street Theatre, Philadelphia, closed on the 25th, and that at the Park Theatre, New York, on the 26th of September.

The following notice of the latter event is copied from the New York Spirit of the Times, edited by William T. Porter:

"*Old Sol's Benefit.*—On Wednesday evening Mr. Sol. Smith—or, as the Philadelphia play-bills call him, 'the Liston of the South'—took his benefit, and we were glad to see a crowded house. The performances went off admirably. His personation of *Kit Cosey*, in TOWN AND COUNTRY, was excellent. In the LYING VALET, Mr. S. kept the audience in a continual roar of laughter. Upon the whole, 'Old Sol' has every reason to be gratified with his visit to New York, for, not to say any thing of the fame he has acquired, the *profits* must have been something handsome. At the close of the performances Mr. Smith was 'called out' by the audience, when he addressed them nearly as follows:

"'LADIES AND GENTLEMEN,—In answer to your flattering and unexpected call, I can only say that, for the kindness and indulgence with which my efforts have been received during my brief engagement at this house, and for the very large attendance on this my benefit night, you are entitled to my heartfelt acknowledgments. If you can estimate an actor's feelings, you will not think me vain when I say that I shall always remember with honest pride that I have performed with a degree of success (however small) on the boards of Old Drury—the first theatre in the first city of the Union. I assure you it will be my constant endeavor, wherever my lot shall be cast, so to demean myself, as an actor, as a man, and as an American citizen, that I may deserve, and continue to deserve, your approbation. With these brief remarks, destitute of form as they are, but made with the sincerity of truth, I respectfully take my leave, not, however, without expressing the wish (to use the language of the honest citizen whose character I have this evening attempted to portray) that you may always be "*what I call comfortable.*"'"

CAST OF TOWN AND COUNTRY AT THE PARK THEATRE, 1835.

Kit Cosey (of the town).....Mr. Sol. Smith.
Peter Trot (of the country)..Mr. John Fisher.
Reuben Glenroy.............Mr. J. M. Field (volunteered).
Rev. Owen Glenroy..........Mr. Clarke.
Capt. Glenroy..............Mr. Wm. Wheatley.

Plastic......................Mr. Richings.
Jacky Hawbuck....................Mr. H. Placide.
Ross........................Mr. Povey.
Williams....................Mr. T. Placide.
Hon. Mrs. Glenroy..........Mrs. Gurner.
Rosalie Somers..............Mrs. Hilson.
Mrs. Moreen................Mrs. Wheatley.

The LYING VALET was cast thus:

Gayless......................Mr. Richings.
Timothy Sharp..............Mr. Sol. Smith.
Beau Trippet................Mr. T. Placide.

The great Charles Mathews was the last performer of the part of *Sharp* before me in the Park Theatre, as appeared by the cast-book; the other characters about the same as with me.

Embarking on the steamer Columbia, I in due time arrived at Charleston, S. C., and proceeded by railroad and stage (three nights without sleep) to Montgomery. Taking my family on board the Roanoke at Wetumpka, we were safely conveyed to Mobile, where I superintended the preparations for commencing the greatest season then ever made in that city.

CHAPTER II.

MOBILE, Ala., has at times been one of the best theatrical cities in the United States, and at other times the worst. When, in 1834, the death of Purdy Brown threw the theatre into the market, many managers were anxious to obtain it. Being on the most friendly terms with the administrator of Mr. Brown's estate, Thaddeus Sanford, Esq., and being possessed of some means, I have but little doubt I could have secured a lease of the house against all competitors, but I entertained a foolish idea that the person who had established the drama in Mobile, and who had been driven from the field by fire and bad seasons, had a sort of pre-emption right to the city; so I wrote to him, proposing we should take the theatre together, if we could get it, and carry on the management in partnership. The answer came promptly, agreeing to my proposition, and it was settled we should meet in Mobile the following October, there to perfect our plans and prepare for a vigorous campaign, combining our two companies for the purpose. Sickness in my family prevented my keeping the appointment we had made, but I wrote an authorization for my proposed partner to do for me all that might be necessary to secure a joint lease of the theatre, and assuring him that I would set out with my company at a day's notice for Mobile. My correspondent succeeded in securing the theatre for one season, but *he took it in his own name*, and I was thrown overboard! Some sharp correspondence followed, ending in nothing. He had the house for *that* season sure, and I was obliged to fulfill the engagements with my company in Montgomery and neighboring towns, instead of in Mobile, losing considerable money, while the "sole lessee" at the latter city made a handsome sum — sufficient, as he informed me afterward, to relieve him from heavy pecuniary embarrassments, occasioned by fires and other misfortunes.

I visited Mobile in the following spring, prepared to *purchase* the theatre at the then forthcoming sale of Brown's estate. This becoming known to the temporary lessee, he became not only willing, but quite anxious to perfect our original design of forming a partnership. Not being able to purchase the property without involving my friends as securities for part of the purchase-money (though they were quite willing to lend me their names), I consented to the following arrangement, which was eventually carried out: Mr. Charles Cullom, afterward joined by others, would purchase the theatre, make all necessary alterations and repairs, and rent it to us for ten per cent. on the cost.

I have not named the person with whom I joined my fortunes, nor do I intend to do so. I never have thought, nor ever shall I think, his taking the theatre on his own account, to my exclusion, was justifiable under any rule of fair dealing, but as I condoned the act by entering into partnership with him afterward, I consider myself estopped from taking any exceptions now, even if I were inclined to do so. There are other reasons — business matters which have transpired since the dissolution of our partnership — sufficiently cogent, in my mind, to keep the name of the individual referred to *forever out of my books*.

The season of 1835–6 opened on the 9th of November with the play of the HUNCHBACK, the cast of which I do not remember, except that Miss Riddle sustained the character of *Julia*, and J. M. Field that of *Sir Thomas Clifford.* Probably Matthew Field played *Master Walter*. Talented men were the brothers Field, and honorable in all their dealings. Miss Riddle was the original actress of *Julia* in America, having performed it with the author in Philadelphia. The receipts on that night amounted to $541 25; ROMEO AND JULIET, the next night, only produced $209 50; and VENICE PRESERVED, on Wednesday, yielded still less; WIVES AS THEY WERE, WIFE, and SCHOOL FOR SCANDAL, filled out the week, the total receipts of which amounted to the very moderate sum of $1655 75. The following week opened with a benefit to Miss

Riddle, which gave a total receipt of $352 only; after which began the first star engagement—that with Mr. Barton, then newly arrived in this country, afterward for several years acting manager of the St. Charles Theatre, New Orleans. I had known Mr. Barton before, at Montgomery, where he had acted with me, and where we had passed many pleasant hours drinking tea (yes, literally drinking tea!) and discussing the play of HAMLET.

William Tell Crushed.

Mr. Barton opened in WILLIAM TELL, and, bating that he had a weak voice, caused by asthma, and a rather imperfect utterance, the result of bad teeth, a noble representation of that hero he gave.

In the second act, it will be remembered, *William Tell* is seized by the Austrian troops, under the command of one *Sarnem*, and loaded with chains, by order of Governor *Gesler*. At rehearsal, as is usual, I called four of our "useful" people to do the seizing, but Mr. Barton requested that, instead of the actors doing this business, I would select four strong supernumeraries, and to *them* intrust the task of seizing and crushing him down.

"I always find," said Mr. B., "that supers do this business best; they are unused to the conventionalities of the stage, and therefore act *naturally*."

So it was arranged in that way.

"Instruct them to *crush me down*," added Mr. Barton; "let them understand that at the cue they are to rush upon me, and, not paying the least attention to what is said or what I do, they are to *c-r-rush me down*, and hold me there till the curtain falls."

"All right," said I; "we have some pretty strong fellows among our supers, and they will undoubtedly crush you down, and keep you down."

"The stronger the better," replied Mr. B.; "and be sure to tell them to *keep* me down when they have got me there."

"Never fear," I rejoined; "they will keep you down, undoubtedly."

At night I selected four of the strongest fellows I could find, and asked the stage manager to take charge of two of them on one side; I took the other two, and stationed them exactly opposite. Being extremely anxious that the scene should go well, and all depending on the final tableau, I was very particular to give the supers their orders—in short, they stood ready at the cue to leap like tigers upon their prey.

"Seize him!" exclaimed *Sarnem;* and they *did* seize him. As soon as they were told to "go," they were upon him! And oh! how quickly poor Barton found himself crushed down!

"Let me up; you are murdering me!" gasped the unfortunate *Tell.* But there was no "letting up" there—no, sir. They had been told not only to crush him down, but to *hold* him there, regardless of any thing that should be done or said, and they obeyed their orders most implicitly. In vain *Tell* struggled with his captors—in vain he swore they were killing him. There they held him, and there they would have held him during the remainder of the night, if the fall of the curtain had not put an end to the scene. Poor Barton, puffing and panting, breathing asthmatic curses against the strong supers, was carried to the greenroom, and the performance was delayed a full half hour for his recovery.

Here this anecdote should end; but I can not resist the temptation to add the following, to show how differently two persons sometimes may tell the same story:

About three years after this occurrence, I was dining with Caldwell, Barton, Finn, Holland, and a few other congenial souls in New Orleans, and was greatly amused by the recital of this anecdote by Mr. Barton. His version of it was very correct down to the time of the *crushing* business, which he gave in about the following words:

"Smith and his stage manager, each with a pair of Titans at the wings, were ready watching for the cue for seizing me. At length it was given, and, gentlemen, the four Titans, under the instructions of old Sol, who, I believe to this day, meant to murder me, r-r-rushed upon me like a tornado, and, seizing me by the arms and shoulders, *began to c-r-rush me down.* I called on them to wait, but there was no wait in them; down, down I felt myself going, and I found it was necessary to put forth my full strength to prevent being prematurely 'crushed to earth;' so, gathering all my energies, I planted myself firmly on my feet, and bracing myself up as well as I could, with a gigantic effort I threw them off, and before they could recover from their astonishment and the momentum they had received, I finished the few words I had to say, and then calmly submitted to my chains. I tell you, gentlemen, I never have fallen into the hands of such strong men as those four Mobile supers, and I assure you *it took all my strength* to get out of their clutches."

WILLIAM TELL "CRUSHED." (See page 117.)

The engagement with Barton was not very successful. Miss Vos, on whose account there was quite a cabal organized against Miss Riddle at first, opened to a fair house, but the receipts fell down to a low figure during her starring nights until her benefit, which was a good one; and then came that stroke of managerial policy of playing the rival actresses in the same pieces, when the admirers of each rallied and filled the house for nearly a week.

Mr. James E. Murdoch, who was a member of the company at the St. Charles, New Orleans, appealed to me to give him a chance of a starring engagement in Mobile, and I did so; and this was his "start" as a star. He performed his round of comedy characters for six nights. Even at that early period of his professional life, Mr. Murdoch was a very pleasing actor, and had very few, if any equals as a light comedian.

Attempted Row in Mobile.

Mr. and Mrs. Tiernan were the next stars, and they were successful in every way. It was during this engagement that a few discontented individuals attempted to get up a little "row" against the writer of these memoirs, which proved very amusing at the time, and the relation of the particulars of which may cause a laugh even at this distant day.

On the accession of the present management of the Mobile Theatre, we found a small cabal or "clique" regularly organized in opposition to us. The persons composing it had been in the habit of managing the former manager (the lamented J. P. Brown), and desired to manage *us* as they had *him*—claiming, as a collateral right, free access to the greenroom and dressing-rooms, with Champagne and punch, oysters, and other refreshments.

Just before the time of raising the curtain on

the first night, a paper was sent to the management anonymously, most respectfully announcing that the "performance would not be allowed to proceed" unless a satisfactory reason could be given why *Miss Vos* had not been engaged as leading actress. It had always been a custom with me to pay no attention whatever to anonymous letters; but, on consultation with my old friend Thaddeus Sanford, it was agreed that upon this particular occasion an explanation should be made, and it *was* made by the writer hereof, apparently to the satisfaction of every person in the house, to wit: that the lady had publicly announced, the previous spring, that she was going East to reside permanently; on the strength of which assertion the citizens of Mobile had given her a tremendous "farewell benefit." It was true, I said, she had afterward applied for an engagement with us, but she was too late, another actress (Miss E. Riddle) having already been engaged for the situation. "However," I concluded, "if Miss Vos comes here, as we are informed she intends to do, she can yet be received, if she is willing to share the leading parts with the actress who is to be introduced to this public to-night." I was dismissed with loud applause, and we hoped all trouble was over in *that* quarter; but we eventually found that the members of the above-mentioned clique were determined not to be fully satisfied with *any* thing. Miss Riddle, though welcomed warmly by the general audience, was saluted, upon her entrance, with a few hisses, which were occasionally repeated during the whole performance. At the close of the play, however, the applause was so overwhelming, and her triumph so unmistakable, that all opposition was given over, and the malcontents *appeared* to join in the verdict awarded to the debutante.

On the arrival of Miss Vos she was immediately engaged, and all went on satisfactorily for a while, the party feeling which sprung up among the playgoers—between the *Vos*-ites and the *Riddle*-ites—contributing not a little to increase the nightly receipts at the treasury.

The opposition, though silenced for a time, was not entirely abandoned; the "clique" only waited a fit opportunity to manifest their hostile feelings without the show of injustice.

In the musical afterpiece of a ROLAND FOR AN OLIVER, *Sir Mark Chase* is required to say, "My family are all mad, and I believe I shall soon be in the *family way* myself!" When I delivered this sentence, amidst the loud laughter and applause which followed, several *hisses* were perceptible. I thought nothing of it at the time, but the next day was told I had committed a monstrous outrage, and would be held accountable for it; that a respectable citizen had been obliged to take his wife out of the boxes in consequence of the personal allusion I had made to her *situation*, and that the first time I should appear on the stage it was determined I should be *hissed off!* The alleged offense was committed on Monday, 21st. On Friday, 25th, I was in the bill for the *Mock Duke*, in the comedy of the HONEY MOON, Mr. and Mrs. Tiernan appearing as the *Duke* and *Duchess of Aranza.* A few hisses were mixed with the applause with which my entrance was greeted; but the scene proceeded without interruption until the newly-married couple had had their hearing before the supposed duke, and retired to "wear out a month at least as man and wife," when a voice was distinctly heard from the second tier of boxes, pronouncing these words, "NOW, BOYS, GIVE IT HIM!" But the "boys" did not muster courage to let out the full force of their indignation while I remained on the stage, preferring to wait until I had finished my soliloquy and made my exit; *then* came the combined hiss of thirty-six people, which produced any thing but an agreeable sensation on my nerves. The general audience were astonished at this outbreak against one of their greatest favorites, and a considerable din was raised in cries of "Shame!" "Hush!" etc. Mrs. Tiernan met me at the side wing, and said, "Mr. Smith, whatever be the cause of this, you had better stop the play, and come to an explanation with your audience; *something* is the matter, and you may depend upon it you had better meet the affair at once." Without a moment's hesitation I ordered the curtain to be lowered; with a towel, and a little soap and water, removed the paint from my face, enveloped myself in a large cloak, and walked forth before the curtain to meet the storm. My appearance had the effect to produce a perfect stillness in the house. Bowing low, I began addressing the audience in the following words:

"LADIES AND GENTLEMEN,—I have had the honor of appearing before you at various times during several years past, and never before to-night have my efforts been visited with tokens of disapprobation. I have frequently attempted to act the part which I am attempting to-night, and I have always been rewarded with approbation, unmixed with those peculiar sounds I have heard on this occasion; hence I feel quite certain the disapprobation is not intended for my *acting.* I come before you to ask those who have thought proper to *hiss me* for the cause—"

A voice from the second tier. "Old Sol, you said you were in the *family way!*"

I continued, "Is that the charge against me?"

Several voices. "It is! it is! family way. You must apologize."

"Well," I continued, "I have heard the charge; I shall not pretend to misunderstand the accusation, for I have heard something of this out of doors. I do not deny having used the expression; on the contrary, I admit the fact, and I must say I don't perceive the least harm in the sentence. It is spoken by all who perform the character of *Sir Mark Chase*, and I can not see any reason why I should be called to account for speaking that sentence more than for any other speech of the author—"

Several voices. "It is not in the author; it is your *own* language"—"silence!"—"hear him!"—"turn 'em out!—"hush!"—"Sol, go on!"

"I think I heard some one say the objectionable sentence is not in the author?"

Ben Wilkins. "It is *not* in the author."

"I think—Mr. Wilkins—Mr. Benjamin Wilkins—*Squire* Wilkins—you said it was not in the author?"

Wilkins. "Yes, I did."

Voices. "Turn him out!"—"hurra for Ben Wilkins!"—"hurra for Old Sol!"—"silence!"—"hush!"

"Will the prompter please to procure a book of A ROLAND FOR AN OLIVER from the office?" I asked, slightly drawing aside the curtain.

Voices. "Yes! yes!"—"the book!"—"the author!"—"hurra for Old Sol!"—"hurra for Wilkins!"—"Wilkins, get on the stage!"—"the book!"—"turn 'em out!"

Here Benjamin Wilkins, Esq., a justice of the peace in and for the County of Mobile, jumped upon the stage, and commenced parading backward and forward near the foot-lights. His advent was greeted with cheers from his party and hisses from the general audience. The book came at length, and I began to turn over the leaves in search of the obnoxious speech, Wilkins all the time saying, "Yes, let's see it; you *say* it is in the author—*show* it to us—let us have it." It seemed like looking for a needle in a haystack, and at one time I almost began to think I had been mistaken, and that I should be convicted of interpolating my own language as charged. All this time my friends in front were offering to bet large sums that I would find the passage. *I did find it!* and, handing the book to Mr. Justice Ben, pointing with my finger to a certain passage, asked him to *read it to the audience.* Wilkins took the book and kneeled down to the foot-lights; then, laying the book on the stage, very deliberately took out and put on his spectacles, took up the book with a look of triumph, evidently with the full belief that *the passage was not there*, and began to pore over the page. At least a minute elapsed without his giving any indication that he was satisfied. The audience began to exhibit symptoms of impatience, and I confess the scene became a little tiresome to me. I ventured to repeat the request that he would read the passage to the audience. He looked up and replied, "When I find it, sir, I will." This raised the hopes of the clique considerably, and my friends began to think there was something wrong. However, we were not kept long in suspense, for Justice Wilkins soon appeared to be satisfied, shut the book, put away his spectacles, and, rising from his knees, said, "By G—d, gentlemen, we are wrong, and Old Sol is right." This announcement was followed by rounds and rounds of the most solid applause I have ever heard within the walls of a theatre. My triumph was complete. After the enthusiasm had subsided a little, some of the audience began to call out for a song from Ben Wilkins; others greeted him with hisses and groans. This enraged him very much, and he stamped with rage, exclaiming, "Gentlemen, I will challenge any man that hisses me." This created great mirth, and I took the occasion to say, "You can now judge how it feels to be hissed." "Yes," says Ben, in an undertone to me, "d—n me if I ever hiss any body again. Sol, get me out of this, for heaven's sake—let me out!" I made a short address to the audience, asking my friends to forget and forgive, which was good-naturedly responded to, and I helped Brother Ben up the same way he had come, through a private box. The play proceeded, and on the entrance of the *Mock Duke*, in the fifth act, there was a most thundering round of applause, *and no hisses.* The "clique" disbanded, and the members were my warmest friends ever after.

Miss Phillips, from Drury Lane, London, performed a good engagement.

Yankee Hill was moderately successful for a few nights. I have reason to remember *his* engagement for the following reasons, among others: He purchased some real estate, paying part cash and giving notes for the balance, which notes, amounting to some $800, *I* paid, Mr. H. having requested I should do so in case his funds to meet them did not come to hand. Mr. Hill's funds never did come to hand to pay the notes, and I am to this day that amount out of pocket. Years afterward I obtained a judgment against him for the amount, but did not get a cent, as the "Yankee delineator" took the benefit of the act for the relief of insolvent debtors; and that was the last I ever heard of *that* $800.

An engagement with Mdlle. Celeste was a very great one, eclipsing all other engagements of the season.

Daddy Rice (Jim Crow Rice, as he was called) played a few nights to fair houses, and had a fine benefit. I was playing in Louisville, Ky., in 1830, when Rice was composing his great song, and perhaps helped him a little in fixing a tune to it. This Jim Crow song, which afterward was so popular in this country and in England, was first sung by Rice in a little piece entitled the RIFLE, which was written, I have understood, by Solon Robinson, now and for many years past the agricultural editor of the New York *Tribune*.

Miss Meadows, a child under the tutelage of Mrs. Brown (a sister of Vincent de Camp), played successfully in starring parts. If that child had continued on the stage, she would have become one of the best actresses that ever trod the American boards. She married early, and was no more seen.

Mr. Charles Mason and sister were quite unsuccessful in drawing audiences, but gave great satisfaction to the judicious few who attended their representations. Charles Mason, one of the most gentlemanly actors I ever knew, is a nephew of the great Kembles. He is, I am happy to state, still extant, and "well to do" in the world. I had him by the hand a day or two ago, in Broadway.

Mrs. Clara Maeder (late Clara Fisher) performed a successful engagement. This admirable woman is one of the very few precocities whose popularity has survived their infancy.

Miss Nelson and Mr. Henry J. Finn played good engagements. Other persons of less note, or rather of no note at all, attempted to edify the good citizens of Mobile during the season, but failed to entitle themselves to even a mention here. The business of the season gave a profit of about $20,000.

CHAPTER III.

IN St. Louis, at the old theatre in Second or Church Street, commonly called the "Salthouse," a season was made with nearly the same company that composed the force in Mobile. The stars were Miss Riddle, Mr. J. M. Field, Miss Nelson, Mrs. Drake, Miss Meadows (quite successful), Mrs. Prichard, Mrs. Lewis, and Mrs. Duff, so called, though she was then married to J. Sever, Esq., a lawyer of New Orleans. This gentlewoman was the sister of the poet Moore, and, when quite young, became the wife of John Duff, who was so conspicuous a member of the old Philadelphia company. Mr. and Mrs. Duff for many years maintained their position at the head of their profession.

During this season Mrs. Ludlow, a gentlewoman greatly esteemed by all who had the good fortune to know her, took her farewell of the stage. She has since taken her farewell of the earth.

A new theatre was projected, which was to be built by subscription, to be located at the corner of Third and Olive Streets, much against the judgment of several members of the building committee, who thought Second Street "as far out" as we ought to go for a site, and rather inclined to Main Street, or Market Street, between Main and Second Streets, as the most desirable location. The foundation was laid and most of the scenery painted during the summer.

The season was successful on a small scale, and I laid out my share of the profits in the purchase—giving a bonus of $1200 to the original purchaser—of twenty acres of land in the St. Louis Common, which I was entitled to hold ninety-nine years, renewable forever, on paying five per cent. interest on the purchase-money, with the right to obtain the fee-simple title by paying, at any time, the sum of about $4000. I held this land and paid the interest for several years, when—wait, and I'll tell you how I came out on *that* speculation.

Wouldn't Eat his Breakfast.

I think it was during this summer that, as I was passing through Olive Street, I observed a large crowd assembled in and about the door of a justice's office, where a trial was going on for assault and battery. Inquiring of a by-stander the nature of the case, I found that my old friend Captain Alexander Scott was the defendant, and the prosecutor (represented by Charles D. Drake, now a U. S. senator) was one of the deck-hands on board of the Madison, then, and for years afterward, under Captain Scott's command. Having traveled with Captain Scott in the old North America as long ago as 1828, and having then formed a very favorable opinion of him as a commander and skillful pilot, I immediately began to feel an interest in the suit now pending. Taking a seat by the justice's side, in a whisper I asked leave to act as counsel for my old friend, which was most courteously and immediately granted. The counsel for the state examined a great number of witnesses, who all testified that Captain Scott had struck the prosecutor with a handspike *because he had refused to eat his breakfast.*

I sat silently observing the progress of the trial, and did not interpose a question to any witness until the prosecutor himself was sworn, who stated in substance the same facts that had been sworn to by the other witnesses, and was about taking his seat, considering the case made out, when I quietly desired him to remain and answer a few questions which I proposed to propound to him. The witness returned to the stand, not a little surprised to find a new *actor* in the scene. The prosecuting attorney seemed a little surprised too, and appeared disposed to demand oyer of my license to practice; but Justice Shepherd, in a whisper, told him it was all right, and I proceeded with my cross-examination. I asked questions at random (for I knew nothing of the case until I had heard the evidence for the prosecution), but, as luck would have it, hit upon the right chord, and made the poor fellow confess that he had been very turbulent on the morning of the assault, and for a day or two previous; and he repeatedly acknowledged, in reply to my questions, that Captain Scott had always been as a father to him, treating him with the greatest kindness until the very morning the assault was made upon him, and that even then he had struck him because he was obstinate, and *would not eat his breakfast.* I gave the prosecuting witness leave to retire, and, on being asked if there was any testimony for the defendant, promptly answered, "No, we rest the case here!"

Captain Scott seemed as much astonished as any one to see *the part I was acting;* he had forgotten me, and probably supposed I was some lawyer who had been retained for him by the owners of the boat. Mr. Drake suggested that if I intended to address the jury, now was the proper time, as "the state had the privilege of closing."

"Most undoubtedly, brother counselor," replied I, "it is my intention to make a speech." And I forthwith commenced addressing the jury. I first summed up the evidence fairly, and acknowledged the full force of its bearing against the prisoner. I then took a rapid sketch of Captain Scott's life, from the time he was employed as a "*hand*" on a flat-boat, when steam was unknown on the Western waters; his gradual rise to the situation of captain of a "*broad horn;*" his employment as pilot of the first boat which breasted the waves of the Upper Mississippi; his promotion to the captaincy of the same boat; his valuable and enduring services for years and years as commander of numerous proud steamers, now only remembered by the old citizens, several of whom I saw on the jury, down to the present time, when he stood in the front rank of that host of industrious and enterprising citizens known as RIVER MEN! I then put in a few touches about his kind-heartedness; his attention to the wants of his crew and passengers; his habit of always saying, "Come, boys," and never "go;" his good standing, not only in his profession, but as a man and a citizen. In short, I praised him for "no quality he had not," but set forth those he had in as fair a light as possible, at the same time representing the prosecutor as an ungrateful fellow, who, instead of being gently knocked down by my client, deserved to be *put in irons* for his mutinous conduct. I concluded by asking the jury if, with these facts before them, they could convict the prisoner?

I plainly saw the impression I had made upon the jury was favorable, and I patiently listened to the somewhat lengthy argument of the state's attorney, with almost a certainty that he was working up-hill. Justice Shepherd told the jury that, after the very *able* arguments they had been listening to, he felt it would be useless to add any thing, and the case was submitted. It was the custom then, and is now, for aught I know, for the court and spectators to *retire into the street,* leaving the "gentlemen of the jury" in possession of the court-room. We all left the office—prosecutor, defendant, justice, lawyers, and lookers-on—and I was making my way out of the crowd, when my attention was arrested by loud words from my client, who was hauling my brother counselor (Drake) over the coals for having called him "tyrant" during his argument.

"My dear sir," expostulated Charley, in his blandest manner, "no man has a greater respect for you than I have; *in courts,* we sometimes are obliged to use expressions like those you complain of, but I assure you no harm was meant."

"Ah! but that won't do," replied the captain. "Young man, you must steer clear of me in your speechifications, or mayhap you'll strike a snag! Now you didn't hear that other lawyer chap—I don't know who the h—ll he is, but he's a first-rater, any how—you didn't hear *him* say any thing to hurt a man's feelings."

I was looking on this scene with great composure, chuckling at the idea of Charley being in something like a scrape, and wondering how he would get out of it, when I was suddenly and roughly seized by the shoulder, and turned round like a turnstile, and who should stare me in the face but the veritable prosecuting witness.

"Look here, my chap," commenced he, ramming a huge quid of tobacco into his cheek with his thumb, "I think you told them there gentlemen of the jury as how I desarved being *put in irons?*"

Endeavoring to draw him aside, I began to soothe him as well as I could by telling him that "we lawyers" were obliged sometimes to make use of *figures of speech* to express our meaning, assuring him at the same time that no person had a greater respect for steam-boat-men than I had; that what I did was to serve my client, etc.; but he would not be pacified.

"As for figures of speech, old feller, I know nothing about 'em; but I mean to show you that in saying I ought to be *put in irons*, you have missed *your* 'figure;' for, d—n your infernal lawyer soul to d—nation, I'll let you know before I've done with you that—"

I can not say what might have followed this outburst of passion had not the court-room door at that moment opened, and the jury appeared. It was soon announced they were "hung," as the term is when they can not agree; so they were dismissed, and a new trial ordered. My client came to me to ask what was next to be done. Learning from him that "steam was up" on his boat, and that he was going to Alton, I advised him to "unhitch her" and "put out." He grasped my hand with great energy, swore I was the best lawyer he had ever fallen in with, and, after signing a bail-bond, in which I joined, followed my advice.

The new trial was to take place next morning; but, meeting the prosecuting witness before the hour appointed, I represented to him what a fool he had made of himself; urged upon him the policy of making up the matter with the captain, and, resuming his situation on board the Madison, dropping the law proceedings altogether. He was sullen and dogged at first, but by degrees he melted, and finally burst into tears.

"If he hadn't *struck* me," said he, blubbering, "I could look over all."

"Well, suppose he *did* strike you? He didn't hurt you bad. Come, think no more of it—besides, the captain is sorry enough for it, now his passion is over."

"Sorry? Does he *say* he's sorry?"

"*I*, as his attorney, say it *for* him."

"Do you? Well, give us your hand: if he'll take me back, I'll go."

"That's hearty; just step into the office and settle the costs, and *I'll* take care the captain will overlook all past differences, receive you back, and ask no questions."

The fees were paid, the deck-hand gathered his bundle, and we walked down to the landing, where the Madison had just arrived from Alton. The captain seemed a little obstinate at first, but when I told him of the penitence of the man, and assured him that the *law business* was at an end, he said,

"Well, Bill, come aboard; go to work, and behave yourself; but I give you one caution—*never again refuse to eat your breakfast.*"

CHAPTER IV.

On the 9th of November commenced our second Mobile season, which turned out (probably) the best ever made in that city. Vincent De Camp was stage-manager and representative of the "old men." J. M. Field, M. Field, and Tom Placide were prominent actors. Miss Riddle, Miss Vos, Miss Petrie, and Miss Emily Clarke were in the company, and pieces *without stars* were played in an admirable manner. We had for stars this season Mrs. Drake, Mr. Balls, a very clever light comedian from London, Mrs. Sol. Smith (to fill up a gap), Mrs. Pritchard, *a Mazeppa Horse*, Wallack, the Keelys, young Burke, Finn, Mrs. Lewis, and some others. It was a great treat to see Mr. and Mrs. Keely in the Loan of a Lover and the Swiss Cottage. Their acting has never been excelled—that's my opinion—in farces.

A grand military ball was given on the 22d of February in the theatre, for the use of which the committee paid two thousand dollars!

Toward the close of the season the opera of Cinderella was produced in a very gorgeous style as to scenery and appointments. The principal characters were cast thus:

Cinderella................Miss Eliza Petrie.
Prince....................Mr. Larkin.
Dandini...................Mr. J. M. Field.
Baron.....................Mr. De Camp.
Pedro.....................Mr. Tom Placide.

I had calculated greatly on this piece, it being the first opera ever presented with any completeness in Mobile. Music had always been my passion, and, if this opera succeeded, it was my intention to "go in" largely for the production of that species of entertainment. I had personally attended and directed the rehearsals for two months, and, while I am free to admit that first-rate musical talent was not there to *insure* success, I do aver that every note of the opera was sung and played, and the performance was highly creditable to all concerned in it. The success was undoubted, the applause enthusiastic, and (best of all, some may think) the house was crammed.

Next day after the first performance I threw myself in the way of a friend whose opinion I valued, and asked him candidly to say how he liked CINDERELLA.

"I like it well," he exclaimed, enthusiastically; "it was finely performed; you have hit the fancy of the people this time; nothing *could* be better—it is magnificent!"

"Glad to hear it," said I. "The performance took up rather too much time, but that will be remedied to-night. Now tell me, if you please, and I ask you as a friend to do so, is there any thing in the performance which can be improved? We frequently *cut* a piece after the first night, and make changes in business which experience teaches us may be beneficial and add to the effect. If you have any thing to suggest, now is the time."

"Well," replied my friend, "there *is* one suggestion I will make, since you ask me to do so, though please to understand I am entirely satisfied with the piece as it was performed last night, and so, I think, is the public." He paused, and seemed reluctant to name the proposed alteration; but, being urged again, he said, "You speak of its being not unusual to *cut* a piece when in the performance it be too long. I suggest, then, friend Sol, and I am quite sure I speak but the sentiments of the large audience in attendance last night, that you—*cut out the music.*"

Good heavens! here had I been toiling for months, drilling the choruses, rehearsing in the greenroom with the piano and on the stage with the full orchestra, and when at last the opera was before the people, and had received their plaudits, to be told I had better *cut out the music!*

On the 19th of May was produced, for the benefit of J. M. Field, an original tragedy, written by W. H. Smith (I do believe he is now Governor of Alabama), entitled AARON BURR, EMPEROR OF MEXICO, the author personating the character of *Burr*. It was a good play, but was never performed but once afterward. The author brought the parts to the theatre *ready printed.* The idea of carrying the action of the piece into Mexico, and there placing the hero upon the throne of the Montezumas, was a bold one, and well carried out. Field, I think, played *Blennerhassett*, and Miss Riddle *Theodosia.* If the author is the man I suppose him to be, and will send me a copy of this tragedy, I will exercise all the influence I possess to have it produced in one of our best theatres; and, if properly performed, I can not doubt of its success.

In the spring of 1837 a Mr. Ferry built and opened a new theatre on Government Street, of which more hereafter.

In an evil hour, and tempted, I almost think, by some very evil spirit, if not the old d—l himself, I bought a half interest in the Mobile "Mercantile Advertiser," the other half being purchased by Edwin Harriman. I paid part cash (one third) and gave notes for the balance. It was right in the commencement of bad times, and my losses by this speculation were considerable.

The new theatre in St. Louis, being so far completed as to allow of its occupancy, was opened on the 3d of July with a PRIZE ADDRESS, the HONEY MOON, and SIMPSON & CO. The company, nearly the same as in Mobile, was very strong in talent and numbers. The Prize Address was delivered by J. M. Field to an audience of about *ten people*, who thought it worth their while to go to the theatre in time to see and hear the beginning of the performance. It being summer-time, eight o'clock came only about half an hour after sun-setting; so, as nobody in St. Louis thinks of going to the theatre or any other amusement "before dark," it was all accident that there were a dozen or so of people (all strangers) present at the time advertised for the beginning of the exercises on this occasion—the opening of the first real theatre west of the Mississippi River; and among this dozen or so was the author of the Prize Poem, who happened to be in the city, and who went especially to hear the Address, which he had not the most distant idea was *his*. He had sent his poem to the committee months before, from Greensburg, Penn., giving his name as *Deacon Kurtz*, that being the name he used in writing for the newspapers in his section. His real name was Edward Johnson, and he was afterward Secretary of State of Iowa, then a territory. When he presented himself next morning and claimed the prize of $100, announcing his name as *Johnson*, I at first felt doubtful about "handing over;" but the matter was finally settled by requiring Deacon Kurtz to draw an order in favor of Edward Johnson, *in the handwriting of the poem*, and the money was then paid.

I insert the Prize Address, and seven of the rejected addresses, which this "committee of literary gentlemen" must have found it hard to *reject.* I call attention particularly to the truly poetic effusion of Caroline Hentz. Several others, in my opinion, possess decided merit, and deserve to be exhumed from their coffins—where they have slept for thirty-one years, even until their authors have nearly all left the earth—and restored to the light of day. With great pleasure I hand them to the type-setters.

There were seventeen addresses sent in. *One* of the "rejected" I reserve for the Appendix.

PRIZE ADDRESS

SPOKEN BY J. M. FIELD, ESQ., AT THE OPENING OF THE NEW ST. LOUIS THEATRE, JULY 3, 1837.

BY DEACON KURTZ.

When Freedom's flag was wide o'er Greece unfurl'd,
And Delphi was the centre of the world,
The Drama first uprear'd the rustic stage,
To smooth the manners and instruct the age;
And though hoar Time hath sped with ceaseless flight,
And crush'd the splendors of that age of light—
Though the famed monuments of that bless'd day
Have fallen to earth, and moulder'd in decay—
Though, vision-like, two thousand years have roll'd,
And Greece is not now what she was of old—
The Drama still, to kindly feeling true,
Loves the bright land where first her childhood grew,
Points to her *Thespis*, who, though rude in Art,
Touch'd the warm feelings of each generous heart;
To *Æschylus*, who madden'd while he sung,
And o'er the lyre a hand of phrensy flung;
To *Sophocles*, who, gorgeous and sublime,
Lives to this day, and only dies with Time;
And to *Euripides*, whose plaintive song
Seizes the list'ner as it floats along—
Leaves with the bosom liquid notes of woe—
Steals to the heart, and makes the tear to flow!
Where the rough Alps, with summits high and free,
Look o'er the plains of fallen Italy—
The Drama there a look of pity throws,
For there, in days of yore, her anthems rose;
For then were heard the mirth and laughter loud
When *Plautus*' muse address'd the Roman crowd;
When *Terence*, too, pour'd forth the comic song,
The cheers were high—the laughter loud and long.
Again she casts her searching eyes around:
"Beware!" 'tis whisper'd "this is holy ground!"
Why? 'Tis on Britain's Isle our footsteps stand;
Nay, it is more—'tis Shakspeare's fatherland!
Here did that Master all our feelings scan,
Each nook, each recess in the heart of man;
Here brilliant *Sheridan* Fame's laurel won;
Here *Johnson* put his "learned buskin" on.
Flush'd with fond joy, she turns with rapturous glance
To vine-clad hills and sun-bright vales of France;
Points to the Theatre with tragic mien,
And marks the passions of the stern *Racine*.
From those who pity, and who kindly feel,
She asks a tear—to shed with "*great Corneille!*"
Now, swift across the Atlantic wave she flies—
Where, reared 'mid wilds, her beauteous domes arise!
Each hill and dale her thrilling voice has heard,
And *Forests* echo to the native *Bird;*
Throughout our land, where'er she chance to roam,
She finds a *resting-place*—but here a *home!*
We dedicate to thee, oh! goddess bless'd,
This thy *first* temple in the far, far West!
Oh! fondly cherish this fair house of thine,
And shed around thy influence benign.
Let vivid images of by-gone things
Defile before our eyes like "Banquo's kings;"
Let *Lear* again enact his frantic part,
And sweet *Ophelia* steal the hearer's heart;
Let the kind audience feel a fond regret,
And weep with *Romeo* over *Juliet;*
Let *Spartacus*, again from bondage freed,
Not like a slave, but like a Thracian bleed;
Picture the scene where chaste *Virginia* fell,
And point to "freedom in the shaft of *Tell!*"
And may the sylph-like nymphs our joys enhance
By mystic trippings of the fairy dance
On Ariel's wing, and soft as brooklet's flow,
Their footsteps falling like the flakes of snow—
Let their lithe forms in mazy circles run,
And grace receive—what *Taglioni* won!
Let these fair walls with echoes soft prolong
The dulcet gushings of each soul-born song—
Sweet as the euphony of Heaven's bright spheres
Strike the bland warblings on the list'ner's ears.
Now to our audience—honor'd, learn'd, and gay—
The humble speaker hath one word to say:
If e'er loathed Vice should rear her hideous face,
Or in this tragic fane find dwelling-place—
If e'er this house with scullion jesting rings,
Or desecrated be to sinful things,
Let the bold actor his presumption rue—
Be cursed the player and his temple too.
But if the Muse, enlighten'd, never strays
Far from the pleasant path of Virtue's ways,
Then shall fair Learning sanctify this dome,
And Joy and Science fix their lasting home—
The tragic muse shall high her sceptre rear—
The sternest eye shall glitter with a tear.
Mild Thalia, too, shall all our griefs beguile,
And from the lips of sorrow steal a smile.
The rudest hearts shall feel the genial power,
And future ages bless this natal hour!
Then o'er the player be your kindness shed—
Pour out a golden shower upon his head;
And may this house be ever richly bless'd,
And *stars* arise hereafter in the *West!*

CHAPTER V.

I DEVOTE a chapter to a few of the rejected addresses.

ADDRESS FOR THE OPENING OF THE NEW THEATRE IN ST. LOUIS.

BY CAROLINE LEE HENTZ, FLORENCE, ALABAMA.

Why do we gather on this festive eve,
The wreath of genius and of taste to weave?
Why beam the walls with beauty's living flowers,
While music ushers in the gliding hours?
We come, the votaries of the heavenly nine,
To dedicate to them this virgin shrine;
Not with unhallow'd pomp and orgies loud,
With mystic rite and fragrance-breathing cloud,
But with those inspirations of the soul,
That, like all Nature's incense, heavenward roll.
In ancient days, when classic Greece was young,
Her bards the praises of the Drama sung,
And the sweet notes of that melodious age
Were breathed in loftiest numbers from the stage.
Have ye not read when, in the dungeon's gloom,
The vanquish'd Grecian warriors mourn'd their [doom,
The mighty master of the tragic lyre
Swept in the hostile camp its chords of fire,
The victors own'd the triumph of the strain,
Unbarr'd the bolts, and loosed the captive's chain?
Children of Freedom! could a nobler meed
Than *Freedom* crown and consecrate the deed?
'Twas the same genius, whose presiding ray
Illumes *this* scene, inspired that God-like lay.
Oh! by the memories clustering round each dome,
Where erst the muses made their hallow'd home,
By all the hopes that gild this lofty fane,
Preserve its unpolluted walls from stain.
If ever here the fair, unsullied rose
Of modesty, with wounded crimson glows;
If Virtue veil her angel-brow with shame
To see the fading of her heaven-born flame;
And oh! if here the shafts of wit are hurl'd
Against that *Faith* which glorifies the world,
Then may the hand of some avenging power
Destruction write on this devoted tower.
But no! a brighter vision dawns, to cast
The glowing future o'er the fading past.
The wave, that mirrors our exalted spires,
Bathed in the light of heaven's cerulean fires,
As here it rolls in gather'd grandeur by,
Shall long reflect it to the bending sky.
Ne'er, till this dome in classic beauty swell'd,
Have the bold dwellers of our land beheld
A temple, sacred to the Muses' rest,
West of the mightiest river of the West.
Roll on, in all thy opulence of streams,
Father of ancient waters! Tell the beams
That gild the Atlantic shores how pure the fame
Of this young city of illustrious name.
Yes, 'tis a high and honor'd name it owns—
St. Louis—the inheritor of thrones;
Star of the crusade—pilgrim to the shrine
Which kneeling nations worship'd as divine;
Louis—the glory of a later age,
The royal friend and patron of the stage.
Sons of St. Louis! while this name endures,
A proud, a kingly heritage is yours.
The flowers of genius and the gems of art
Shall blush and glitter in your crowded mart;
And as ye guard this now unsullied pile,
So shall those flowers in richest beauty smile.
Cold as the polar ice the heart that scorns
The ennobling scenes that tragic verse adorns;
Which darkly turns, and breathes its blasting ban
On that which may exalt the soul of man.
Oh! for a strain of such a magic spell,
The echoes in this vaulted roof shall dwell
When fades the brilliant pageant of the hour,
Whose inspiration speaks the Drama's power—
That power which ancient ages have confess'd,
And unborn millions here may yet attest.
Unslumbering guardians of the public weal,
'Tis yours the fate of this proud fane to seal;
To wake the voice of *censure* or *acclaim*,
And stamp this night with *glory* or with *shame*.

ADDRESS.

BY CHARLES HARRIS, JR., BOSTON, MASS.

Friends of the Drama! you of every age,
Who play your parts on life's eventful stage;
Free'd from its shifting scenes of endless strife,
With much of joy, but more of sorrow rife,
From every woe that makes existence drear,
We tender *all* a friendly welcome here.
If the poor actor in his nightly task
From secret vice remove the glitt'ring mask;
If he arouse within some potent voice,
Some hidden chord that makes the heart rejoice,
Or, faintly picturing forth ideal woe,
Bid the quick tear in silent rapture flow;
If he by skill, with modest merit join'd,
Seek to inform and elevate the mind,
May he not hope that you will kindly deem
His earnest efforts worthy of esteem,
And give the vot'ry of fair virtue's cause
His *dearest* recompense, your just applause?
He trusts he may; and now he asks of you—
Is it too much?—a friendly welcome too!
From the bleak regions of the stormy North
The fierce barbarian calls his legions forth,
And death and darkness, following in his train,
Drop their thick veil o'er Europe's fertile plain.
Her haughty fanes, her palaces are low,
And e'en "imperial Rome" is forced to bow!
Condemn'd to seek a more congenial home,
And o'er the world's wide wilderness to roam,

Sadly she look'd for *one* redeeming ray,
And for a time the Drama pass'd away.
But *dawn* is breaking on this starless night!
'Tis Nature rising in her native might!
What giant spirit on lone Albion's isle,
Breathing with life, and warm beneath her smile,
Grasps her chaste sceptre with a fearless hand,
And all her empire holds at his command?
Lo! rising fast, obedient to his sway,
Like Banquo's ghosts, a sad and grim array,
The mastering passions of the human breast,
In all their stern deformity confess'd!
What fairy beings from their "high estate"
Astonish'd gaze, and on his nod await!
What vast creations, opening into day,
Come at his call, and, while he wills it, stay!
Nature herself, to crown the matchless whole,
Gifts him with pure divinity of soul;
A fancy rich, with endless visions fraught,
Curbed by resistless energy of thought,
A fev'rish thirst the heart's still depths to prove,
And touch the springs that each affection move.
No darken'd leaf to this, her fav'rite, seals,
But freely all her hoarded stores reveals;
Wreaths him with laurel from Parnassus' height,
And dips his pen *in fount of living light;*
Then owns aloud, before admiring Earth,
Her mighty masterpiece in *Shakspeare's* birth!
Immortal spirit! deathless and sublime,
Thy name shall triumph o'er the wreck of time!
Shed its pure lustre o'er each coming age,
The brightest gem that decks the Drama's page!
Oh! ne'er shall cease the music of thy lyre,
Till glows the flame round "*Nature's fun'ral pyre!*"
To paint in vivid colors to the view
The varying pictures that his pencil drew,
Give to the study of ingenuous youth
Their thrilling force, their excellence and truth,
Shall be our pride; and if it be our lot
To call up feelings now almost forgot,
Kindle beneath the snowy breast of care
A spark that slumber'd *unsuspected* there,
Excite *one* lofty spirit still to soar
To higher virtue than attain'd before,
Bring back *one* wand'rer to the fold again,
Our best exertions will not be in vain.
But a few winters, and the wild wind sighed
Through the dark ravine and the forest's pride,
And the deep waters of yon river roll'd
Their worth unknown, their riches never told!
Heir of the West! NOW cast thine eye around!
See thy broad land with happiness abound!
See Art and Science all their treasures spread,
And wealth and honor shower'd upon thy head!
See *all* that man holds rational and dear,
In *one bright halo* meet around thee here!
From all that cheers and animates the heart,
The Drama comes to claim one little part;
Secure indeed, if she be *justly* tried,
Her trifling boon can never be denied.
She hopes that Taste and Talent *here* will meet,
And in these walls feel their communion sweet;
That Genius, Wit, and Fancy *here* may find
Food for their flight, agreeable and refined;
And last, *not least*, that Beauty's magic power
Will lend its witchery to this fleeting hour.
What were the actor's part—this noble shrine—
If stripp'd of that which makes them *half divine?*
Be with us, then; your cheering influence lend;
Be to the Drama all she asks—a *friend.*
Sustain her rights, and cherish *undefiled*
Her earliest altar in this Western wild.

PRIZE POEM FOR THE NEW THEATRE AT ST. LOUIS.

BY CATHARINE STEWART, BUFFALO, N. Y.

In that fair season when the blushing rose,
Bathed in soft show'rs, in freshest beauty glows;
When hawthorn blossoms whiten all the vale,
And send their balmy odors on the gale;
When babbling rills tell, eloquently gay,
How languid vines have kiss'd them on their way,
In a lone dell, beneath o'erhanging shade,
A dusky form, in native ease, was laid,
Whose polish'd symmetry and classic face,
Sculptor, as model for his art, might seize.
His bow and arrow, carelessly thrown by,
Bore language of his nation's archery.
A timid fawn that sported by his side,
Cropping the grass, by turns, the stranger eyed.
Bared to the breeze, the heavings of his breast
His high and bold imaginings express'd.
Deep slumber chained him; yet his restless mind,
Like his own native air, roved unconfined.
In vain his spirit wander'd forth to meet
Features familiar, which were wont to greet
His own! Alas! he missed the wigwam rude,
Border'd by rill, and skirted by green wood.
The deer he saw not in the flying race,
That oft had lured him. Brothers in the chase,
Where were they? Through thick copse and bloss'ming vale
His dog was not, that loved to scent the gale.
Forms pass'd before him, in the eager aim
Of other objects than the woodland game.
So many towering structures clustering stood
As left no room for musing solitude.
O'er the dark wave, where oft had floated light
His bird-like bark, what wonders met his sight!

Beings of breath and fire, in vapory pride
And graceful fleetness, triumph'd o'er the tide.
Convulsive motion quiver'd o'er his mien:
"Beauteous canoes!" he sigh'd—then dream'd again.
Years roll'd away: behold how changed the scene!
Beings of other hue the woodland green
Moved o'er. Low, 'neath the axe, the forest lies.
The sons of industry and bold emprise
With sinewy arm unlock'd the golden stores
Of wealth, and pour'd them o'er these wave-lash'd stores.
As the resistless tide of life rolls on,
Wave after wave, through Western wild-woods lone,
Satiate with Eastern climes, from her far home,
Pluming her wings, see Science onward come,
Radiant in smiles; settling her empire fair
Where Nature languishes for guest so rare—
Through new and blooming wildernesses moves,
Planting her altars in the Western groves.
In her bright train, the Histrionic Muse,
Allured by wiles, this gay emporium strews
Around, to woo the stranger to her bowers;
Fann'd by fresh breezes from her wastes of flowers,
Consents to pause a while, in dalliance gay,
'Mid the soft blandishments our smiles display,
To wake the trembling numbers of her lyre,
To warm us with her spirit-breathing fire.
A while she linger'd on our shores sublime,
With eye averted to her favor'd clime
Of love, of war, of story, and of song,
In her heart's memory cherish'd deep and long;
Thought of the pictured porch, the colonnade,
The bowers where grave philosophy has stray'd,
Then turn'd to us, piquant, and new, and fair,
With Oriental beauty to compare.
"Though *there* are softer airs and brighter skies,
And art, despoil'd, in splendid ruin lies,
Can glittering gems or polish'd marble vie
With all this fresh and youthful majesty?
Broad lakes, bold mountains, prairies, rock, and flood,
These Nature form'd in wild, fantastic mood,
Then careless, smiling, threw away her mould,"
She said, and plunged in Mississippi bold.
In all the lustre of her smiles and tears,
Pensive and gay as she by turns appears,
In all her versatility of powers,
Let us, then, bid her welcome to our shores,
Where she in hues faithful, and bright, and true,
Gracefully holds the mirror to our view;
Bid holy aspiration, hand in hand
With nature, draw her outlines free and grand.
And while to her this shrine we dedicate,
Let elevated feeling consecrate
Its classic walls. Let virtue frown severe
On vice and heartless pride; and let the tear
Of dew-eyed sympathy gush freely forth,
And innocent refinement chasten mirth,
While blushing garlands, twined from sweets so rare,
Give out their odors to the brow of care.
Let us then say, All hail to our new guest,
Welcome to this fair city of the West!

ADDRESS.

BY THOMAS H. GENIN, ST. CLAIRSVILLE, OHIO.

To fire the genius and improve the age,
See, sprung to life, the vice-subduing stage;
Another post whence Truth her rays shall send,
Fair Virtue with her monster foes contend,
And on the follies which the world annoy
Impressive Satire oft his darts employ.
Here Avarice, Vanity, Revenge, and Pride
Will oft their own true images deride,
As Truth's day-beaming hand each feature shows
In all its shame, and Virtue lovelier grows.
To mend, as please the public, we design;
Let wit and taste to aid our views combine,
Nor tyrant fashion wrong direction give;
For by conforming to her laws we live.
What you approve, such will the drama be;
'Tis ours to make it with your taste agree;
Like statesmen, follow where the people go,
Nor lead but when the general will we know:
The senseless farce, the punning, empty strain,
But wins attention from an age as vain.
Amusement hither, unrestrain'd by care,
Beset with Beauty's witchery, shall repair.
Before her bright-eyed Mirth shall blend his smiles
With ready sentiment and playful wiles;
Gay Comedy dispense her laughing strain,
Nor Tragedy bid tears to roll in vain;
The treasured genius of the world engage
To bless and elevate the list'ning age;
The gems with which th' historic mine is fraught,
Morality, by great examples taught;
For lo! ascending from the gloom of years,
The majesty of other days appears;
Stalks in its pride, yet bids earth's pilgrims trust
In heaven alone; 'tis but the shade of dust,
That, hov'ring o'er time's dark, sepulchral vale
Of man's mortality, repeats the tale.
Before her, Beauty, long in death confined,
With mimic life again shall please mankind;
The imposing firmness of the good and great,
Like mountains, moveless midst the storms of fate,

To loftiest tone exalt the noble soul,
And make the vital current brisker roll;
Revive the fire that burn'd on Bunker's Hill,
With generous rage the glowing bosom fill;
The patriot teach to bleed, the man to bear,
And poverty contentment's face to wear.
Let tyrants, hypocrites, and fools oppose—
It were reproachful were not these her foes.
Fell brood of darkness! know the stage ne'er drew
Her bread from ignorance, want, and fear, as you.
To man's important interests hers is wed:
Immortal genius has her progress led;
Nor was she in unletter'd ages born,
For laurel'd science graced her early morn;
Around her cradle all the Muses sung;
The rights of man employ'd her infant tongue;
With her, fair genius saw her honors grow,
And tuneful wit in brighter colors blow,
When ere, propitious to the mimic scene,
Was felt the presence of the happy queen;
Thine, lovely Nature! ever fair and young!
Still true to thee be every heart and tongue.
In vain will truth, love, valor, gild the stage,
If thy all-conqu'ring graces not engage.
Shakspeare's great tutoress! source of all the fair,
Grand, and pathetic, may we prove thy care
Obedient acting to thy easy laws,
And from the public gain deserved applause.

ADDRESS.

BY E. A. M'LAUGHLIN, CINCINNATI, OHIO.

The doors unbar, the silken drap'ries rise—
What manly forms—what beauteous, meet our eyes:
All that gives being bliss—life's fairest glow,
Adorns the circle, bright as Iris' bow:
Beauty with grace, and elegance with worth,
Virtue with youth, and innocence with mirth,
In one bright galaxy of living light,
Cheer and irradiate this festive night:
The Muse shall welcome all the brilliant train
Here met to consecrate Apollo's fane.
Hail! pure Intelligence, from Heaven that came,
And warm'd the spirit with celestial flame,
Tamed the wild, rough, and untaught sons of earth
With magic strains of more than mortal birth,
And, as they heard with transport and delight,
Unveil'd bright Genius to the wond'ring sight.
Crown'd with immortal bays he moves along,
And while the whispering dells the notes prolong,
The wood-nymphs list, the sylvan satyrs peep,
And blue-eyed Nereids hush the foaming deep.
The Muses saw, and loved the gifted youth,
And gently led him to the fount of Truth;
While to all lands—to every distant clime—
Fame bore his name upon the wings of Time.
Long in the Eastern hemisphere he stray'd,
And wooed the Sisters in the sylvan shade;
Till once, as in prophetic mood he lay,
Admiring Pallas caught the youth away—
On whistling winds o'er the Atlantic whirl'd,
And laid the slumberer in the Western world.
Beneath a fair magnolia's virgin flowers
Entranced he lay, unconscious of the hours,
Till came Refinement o'er the blooming land,
And touch'd the Sleeper with her magic wand;
He wakes to light and life—with starry eyes
Beholds new realms diverge, new states arise;
Fair flowing streams the fertile vales divide,
The clustering branches kiss the silver tide;
And Art and Science rear the stately dome,
Where the young stranger finds another home.
Cheer'd by your smiles, by your approval warm'd,
Here Truth shall triumph, Falsehood be disarm'd:
Virtue and Vice in the same mirror view'd,
Vice be avoided, Virtue be pursued;
Honor and Baseness weigh'd in even scale,
Baseness mount up, Integrity prevail.
The sea-born queen, led by the rosy hours,
Shall linger here as erst in Paphian bowers;
The attendant Graces round the goddess move,
And Beauty's presence charm the soul to love.
No more the gaunt wolf prowls the wint'ry wood,
No more the panther scents the vale for blood;
No more the savage war-whoop's fearful shriek
Wakes sleeping Innocence to death's last sleep!
The arts of Peace a smiling land renew,
Which yields its blossoms and its fruits for you.
So blooming Thalia spreads *her* festive board,
With Fancy's flowers and Reason's vintage stored;
And while the Muse invites you to the feast,
Oh may the viands please each welcome guest!

ADDRESS FOR THE OPENING OF THE NEW THEATRE AT ST. LOUIS.

BY JOHN THORPE HEMMENWAY, NEW YORK CITY.

When Alexander wept to find that he
Had no more realms to own his mastery;
Wept that his world of conquest was a span,
Its bound the sea, its conqueror a *man*,
He little dream'd that yet, beyond the flood,
A virgin world, unknown, unconquer'd stood,
In the first blush of her primeval charms,
Unstain'd by battle and unbent to arms—

A world of rock-built towers, gemmed caves,
Wide-spreading forests, and deep-gliding waves.
Here first amid the melancholy wood,
Its sovereign lord, the dark-eyed Indian stood.
From rock to tree his eagle glance was thrown;
The Indian claim'd it—felt it for his own.
For him the wild bird check'd its warbling breath;
For him the dun deer died upon the heath;
The hairy bison toss'd his mane and fled,
But fell beneath the Indian bolt well sped.
Here in wild wreaths arose his sacred fires;
Here in green graves were lain his swarthy sires.
Next came the bold, the stalwart pioneer,
In strength the lion, and in speed the deer;
Care flung behind—the new-found world before him,
A fertile sod beneath, and heaven o'er him;
No longer fear'd the hard-wrung tithe and tax,
The rocks give back the echo of his axe.
The startled Indian scouts upon the hill,
To mark the wonders of his strange fusil;
Sees at his will the chary bison fall,
And wanton birds drop willing in his thrall.
The pilgrim-priest next wanders in the wild,
Takes by the hand the forest's wond'ring child;
Tells him of hopes he little deem'd of;
Tells him of worlds he little dream'd of.
The Indian lists a while; but, like the wind,
He leaves the priest and rosary behind—
Away, away, o'er mountain-stream and plain,
The eagle-footed seeks his wilds again.
Yet, undismay'd, the pilgrim-priest will roam
Through suff'ring here, for recompense to come.
Now through the new-found earth a cry is thrown—
Oppression hath been here! The mutter'd groan
Is smother'd by the war-cry. Vale and hill,
Rock, stream, and forest with the echo thrill!
The nation wakes! The priest his gown throws by,
And starts a soldier at his country's cry.
From hill to hill the gathering call is toss'd,
Till in the wildwood's mystic depths 'tis lost;
And scarce eight springs on their own breezes fly,
Ere the same hills and woods resound with vict'ry.
When we, who now are lithe and strong, shall be
Sires and grandsires of stalwart progeny,
And to the shadowy grave be tottering near
(For life no sorrow, and for death no fear);
When our sons' sons shall lead us by the hand,
And fill for us the places where we stand;
When what are wild-woods now be cities then;
When lands, as yet scarce known to human ken,
Shall be the fertile field, the shaven lawn,
Or garden reeking in the dews of dawn,
Then shall we bless the hand that guided here
The patient priest, the sturdy pioneer.
Is it a dream, or wizard's cunning spell?
Or have I drunk a draught at fairy well?
That here, where erst the deer and wild horse grazed,
A temple to the Drama now is raised?
It is no dream. The temple riseth o'er us,
Its multitude of patrons full before us.
We'll seek the Drama o'er the sea no more—
We have an altar on our very shore.
Here *Puck* shall change the Indian's red papoose,
And *Ariel* flit amid Niagara's dews.
Descend, O Liberty! and crouch upon this dome,
Make this thy altar, dwelling-place, and home.
Guide us the right to show, the wrong to right,
Thou who hast guarded us in field and fight—
Thou who hast led us safe through murk and fear,
To win our way, and fix our banner here.
Give to this fane the shelter of thy wing;
Attune thy wild harp's music while we sing
The heart-born chorus of the free,
The full, resounding song of Liberty.

AN ADDRESS,

WRITTEN FOR THE OPENING OF THE ST. LOUIS THEATRE.

BY JAMES REES, NEW ORLEANS.

As Genius mused upon the historic page,
The world enshrouded in its darkling age,
Bright beam'd her eye; she gave to smiling earth
Beauty renew'd—the Drama's self a birth.
Her hallow'd form now shines more pure and bright,
Resplendent here, in richer, chasten'd light;
No blush shall tinge the cheek of Beauty here,
But warmer glow the sympathetic tear,
Or smiles of joy which Virtue well may claim,
To guard her vot'ries with a holier flame.
Chaste language here express'd, as Shakspeare taught,
Shall charm the ear with truth and virtue fraught,
And native bards to emulate, will raise
Our country's harp, and tune their joyful lays:
Thus step by step, to Thalia's temple soar,
And brighten age with legendary lore.
This stately pile, this rich and costly dome,
The Muses' haunt, bright Genius holds her throne,
Like magic raised, like magic still shall seem
The brighter vision of some fairy dream;
Here, where talent slumber'd cold and long,
And here, where silence mourn'd the loss of song,
And sigh'd alone, now claims no wish to roam,
But dwell enraptured on our own sweet home.
The time has been—but time is now no more—
When Genius slumber'd on our slighted shore:

The pen was silent, mind itself seem'd dead,
While flow'rets faded on their early bed.
The scene hath changed; a brighter radiance gleams
Over the place, and learning sheds its beams.
When you were nurslings in this forest land,
How did your hearts with patriot pride expand
When the fierce war-whoop thunder'd from the shore,
While stern *Missouri* echoed to its roar?
Now, midst its wild grandeur, mark what spires uprise,
What novel scenes on every side surprise;
Old Time his scythe delighted throws aside,
With a bright talisman its place supplied:
Where'er he moves, new wonders crowd the way,
Art triumphs now, and Time hath no decay.
The goddess smiles—what beauteous temples rise,
And, Babel-like, seem tow'ring to the skies;
Among them, now, the drama's temple sway
The sombre domes—to light the joyous way.
Like some lone pilgrim through this Western wild,
Fair THALIA comes, an unprotected child;
This is her temple—she dedicates to you,
To hold the world—the mimic world to view;
Here let her live—in all her pride to roam,
Here let the drama find a welcome home;
Let no dark cloud obscure its early light,
No other star shine on her path so bright,
Than those around her; other orbs may shine,
She asks no brighter than these orbs of thine.
Hail, holy temple! here let fancy dwell
In all her pride—thrice hallow'd be her cell;
Here shall the Muse, with fond and plaintive sound,
Breathe forth her notes, which Genius' self hath crown'd;
Here Europe's bards shall proudly tune the lyre,
Here shall our youth catch inspiration's fire;
Be this the Athens of the Western world,
Here let the banner proudly be unfurl'd;
Then bid it live—oh, let the modern stage,
By you protected, live in after age.

James Rees, the writer of the last address which I publish (of the "rejected)," is a very old and valued friend of mine and of the theatrical profession generally, which owes him a debt of gratitude—if it did but know it—for the many sound and wholesome theatrical criticisms which he, under the pen-name of *Colly Cibber*, has favored it with through the newspapers of New Orleans, Philadelphia, and New York during the last thirty years. He is not unknown in the field of literature, being the author of three books which have had a good sale, to wit: "Dramatic Authors of America," "Footprints of a Letter-carrier," and "Mysteries of City Life," of which latter work the London Athenæum said: "The author is one of the home missionaries of Philadelphia," and compared his scenes and sketches with the writings of James, the novelist. Mr. Rees has also written many plays, most of them successful in the acting, among which I remember LA TOUR DE NESLE, CHANGES (a comedy), PAT LYON, ANTHONY WAYNE, THE UNKNOWN, or the DEMON'S GIFT, CHARLOTTE TEMPLE, LAFITTE, the PIRATE OF THE GULF, THE MISTLETOE BOUGH, or the OLD OAK CHEST, and OLIVER TWIST. In the latter piece Charlotte Cushman played *Nancy Sykes*, and those who have seen her in the part say that it was a splendid piece of acting, as no doubt it was. I give one of Mr. Rees's pen-sketches in the Appendix, being myself one of the characters in it.

CHAPTER VI.

ST. LOUIS had not yet begun to feel the hard times, and our first season in the new theatre was moderately successful. The stars who had the privilege of shining during the inaugural season were Mrs. Drake, Master Burke, Mrs. Prichard, Mr. Parsons, Mrs. Baily, and Mr. Plumer. CINDERELLA was produced splendidly, and with the same cast as in Mobile, except Mr. Field took the character of the *Prince*, and your humble servant that of *Dandini*. Singularly enough, I received the same advice from a friend here, after the first performance, that I did from a friend in Mobile: "*Cut out the music!*" The fact is, the people of St. Louis had then very little taste for music in any form; but the scenery, which was splendid, they could appreciate. We have improved somewhat in our musical taste since that time, for be it remembered I am now writing of events which occurred more than thirty years ago. "Yes," said my friend, who was no other than Mr. E. H. Beebe, "cut out the music, Sol; it is tedious."

Miss Riddle, the Fields, De Camp, and myself had fine benefits, and the house closed on the 3d of November. Previous to their departure for the South, Miss Eliza Riddle and Mr. J. M. Field, leading actress and actor of the company, were united in wedlock.

An Unpublished Obituary.

I forgot to mention that about the middle of the season I had an attack of brain fever, and was cured (under Providence) by Doctor Marcy, then a young practitioner, now, I believe, Surgeon General of the United States Army, or something of the kind. He stuck to me like a brother, night and day, until the disease was conquered. I only mention this sickness of mine as introductory to a fact which I am about to relate. Before I had recovered my strength entirely, I took it into my head that change of air would do me good, and, without much preparation, took passage on a boat and journeyed to Louisville and Cincinnati, at both of which cities I learned that the player-folk had heard that I had died and been buried! How this report got out I don't know, but George Farren and George Hill, when I walked into the Louisville Hotel, took me for a ghost of myself. I *was* assuredly very pale and thin, but I soon convinced them and others that the figure they beheld was composed of flesh and blood; and when I appeared before my long-time friend and professional associate, Mrs. Fanny Drake, and convinced her that I was the veritable *living* being she had so long and so sincerely loved and esteemed, and whose untimely "taking off" she had been bewailing for at least two mortal days (so she said, but her daughter Julia, on being appealed to, did not remember any bewailing—bless the dear girl!), I was nearly crushed with her affectionate embraces. I arrived in Cincinnati just in time to "stop the press" of my old friend and brother typo, John H. Wood, who had prepared an elaborate obituary notice, a column long, of the person who is penning these lines. I shall never forget my sensations as I stood over the types which were to commemorate my many virtues. I actually shed tears upon them. I was not aware of the possession of the many shining qualities therein typified and set forth by my ardent friend. I now regret I did not take a proof copy of that able tribute to (supposed) departed worth; but I begged John to distribute the type immediately, which request he complied with, and that splendid "obituary" is lost to the world.

On returning to Mobile this fall, opening on November the 20th, we were agreeably surprised by being greeted with large audiences. George H. Barrett was the first star, followed by Mrs. Lewis, Mr. Hackett, the Ravel family (who performed ten nights to enormous receipts), Miss Ellen Tree (who also played to fine houses, her benefit being $1026), Mrs. Watson (vocalist), Cony and his dogs, Miss Clifton, Yankee Hill, Miss Nelson, Hodges, Jim Crow Rice, Mrs. Baily (vocalist), Mrs. Stuart, Mrs. Gibbs, and Mrs. Shaw.

The American Theatre (Mr. Ferry's) had rather fizzled out in the spring, notwithstanding his "liberal" mode of advertising and tremendous posters—printed at the "Advertiser" office at my expense, as it turned out, for he never paid his printer's bill; but somebody by the name of Wilkins—not *Judge* Wilkins, who made himself so ridiculous in the attempted row two years before, but his brother, I think; at all events, one of the Wilkinses—brought out a company and commenced operations this fall, with the avowed determination to shut up the Emanuel Street concern in one month. How far he succeeded will appear when it is stated that he came to me very early in the season and offered to turn over the whole Government Street concern *and quit management forever* if the engagements he had made with his company would be assumed by the management of the St. Emanuel. It was undoubtedly a great undertaking to assume those engagements; but, having a theatre unoccupied in St. Louis, *only* 1400 miles distant, the bargain was consummated, and the whole American Company, with some necessary re-enforcements, under the temporary management of Matt Field, were posted off to the Western City, "bag and baggage, scrip and scribbage."

Miss Petrie was deservedly a great favorite in Mobile, and when it leaked out she was to be sent to St. Louis, there was great excitement among the young men, and they determined *she shouldn't go*. The following remonstrance was handed in on the night of her "benefit and last appearance previous to her departure for St. Louis:"

"Mobile, December 20, 1837.

"*To the Managers of the Mobile Theatre:*

"GENTLEMEN,—At a meeting of a great many young men who often frequent your theatre, I was appointed a committee to inform you, as proprietors of the Mobile Theatre, that if what was laid before the meeting be true, viz., that Miss Petrie is about leaving for St. Louis, the meeting pledge themselves that they will never again darken the doors they have so often entered; and, furthermore, they will also do their best endeavors to forward the establishment of another in this city. We muster strong, so look out for the consequences. We hope you will alter your minds, and send some one who is less admired by the citizens of Mobile.

"Yours, etc., J. HAZWRELL.

("In haste.")

And the following found its way into Miss Petrie's dressing-room:

"Mobile, December 21, 1837.

"MISS PETRIE,—In behalf of the signers of the remonstrance against your leaving the city of Mobile, we have the honor to inform you that such remonstrance has been handed to the managers, and we respectfully desire your co-operation in the same.

"With the hope of your co-operation and acquiescence in the same, we remain, very respectfully, your obedient servants."

(Signed by a number of young men as "a committee.")

The fact happened to be that Miss Petrie *wanted to go;* and on being called out at the end of the play, and being called on for a "speech—speech—speech!" she very plainly told the public that while she thanked the writers of the letter for the interest in her welfare which she supposed prompted them to interfere in her affairs, she felt herself quite capable of attending to her own business arrangements. She concluded her little speech (which, I confess, I wrote for her at her own request) by saying, "I have engaged to go to St. Louis, and go I must and will." And go she did, the young men giving her up with more resignation than might have been expected under the circumstances, most of them declaring that without her co-operation and acquiescence it was useless to proceed any farther with the intended row; and all agreed that the little favorite didn't "co-operate" nor "acquiesce" worth a cent. So that was the end of the matter.

This was the last really good season in Mobile during my management, and as an *average* this was not particularly good. The house closed on the 5th of May, never to open again but for a very few nights. But let me not anticipate. Dark times were ahead.

Matt Field and the company wended their weary way to St. Louis. In due time—as soon as I could arrange the business so as to leave it —I followed, and found the river above Cairo closed to navigation, so I had to work my way by land.

Matt Field (as good a man as ever lived) proceeded with his company to St. Louis, where, after innumerable difficulties, he effected an opening about the middle of January. Lots of stoves were purchased, and every attempt made to warm the house—all in vain. The house couldn't *be* warmed, and the people wouldn't visit it—to be frozen. The business was horrible. Poor Matt, in his new position of manager, did all man could do to make the season successful; but with all his efforts, seconded by a rather ordinary company, taken for all in all, he could make no headway, the houses averaging no more than about $70 per night. He worried through eighteen nights, all the time praying for my arrival to relieve him of his managerial duties, and then succumbed—closed, with an announcement that the house would "reopen on the arrival of the manager, Mr. Sol. Smith." In one of his letters to his brother at Mobile he said: "I shall be miserable till Sol comes, and shall have bowels of compassion for managers as long as I live after this."

I did think of giving a history of my journey from Cairo to St. Louis by land, but I find I have not room for it. I arrived at last, and my arrival was welcomed by the company and their manager with unfeigned satisfaction. As for poor Matt, his manifestations of joy were extravagant and sincere, unmixed with a single atom of self-interest. Miss Petrie, I believe, was equally sincere in her joy at my arrival. The rest of the company (from the broken-up opposition house in Mobile) rejoiced greatly, also, for they knew I never closed on account of bad business. So, after a recess of three nights only (for which time the people were paid the same as if the house had been kept open), we resumed the season, and continued it to the end. Under my personal management, now in the coldest part of the winter, the first week of the reopening yielded only $350—not quite $60 per night! We played one night to a house which counted only $15 50. With the extra company brought to St. Louis was Mr. C. W. Mueller, a very talented musician, who was leader of the orchestra. At my request, he composed music for a new piece I had just received from London, entitled the PET OF THE PETTICOATS, and we performed it several times to the high gratification of the discriminating few who favored us with their presence on those cold nights. The character of *Job* suited me exactly, and Miss Petrie played *Paul the Pet* very prettily. We two were nightly encored in the song of the "Pious Child," which we sung to the tune of "Old Mear." Other musical pieces we gave; and, even in that dreadful season, desperately resolved to do *something* to draw out the people, (shall I write it?), CINDERELLA was revived! a Mr. Brunton assaying Joe Field's part of the *Prince*, and Matt Field, ever willing to aid in any way, studied the music of the *Baron*, and played it in a manner entirely acceptable, even after the truly admirable personation of the same character, a few weeks before, by De Camp. This opera raised the receipts a little for one night, when $150 were realized; but they fell down for the remainder of its representations to $52, $107, $86, etc. If we had "cut out the music," CINDERELLA *might* have drawn better; but my opinion then was, and now is, that nothing in the shape of tragedy, comedy, opera, or any thing else would have drawn paying houses.

On the arrival of Mr. and Mrs. Lewis (our first stars), the weather moderating at the same time, the business rose a little—almost to a paying point; and, on April 15th, the glorious Ellen Tree commenced an engagement, and carried us triumphantly through two weeks. Then came John Sefton (the celebrated *Jemmy Twitcher*), followed by Mrs. Gibbs, both of whom played moderately successful engagements, and the winter season closed at the end of May with the ever-attractive Ravel family.

[On the 4th of June, 1838, I experienced the greatest misfortune of my life in the death of my wife Martha, who had been my faithful partner for seventeen years.]

Most of the company departed at the close of the season just closed, their engagement being fulfilled, and, with the regular company from Mobile, the summer and fall season began on June 6th, with Miss Clifton as the star. During this engagement was produced Bulwer's LADY OF LYONS, for the first time in America, Miss C. of course personating *Pauline*, and Mr. Barton (the c-r-rushed down *William Tell*) *Claude Melnotte*. Then followed J. R. Scott, Mrs. Gibbs, Miss Nelson, Mr. Hodges, Mrs. Stuart, Mrs. Shaw, and Mr. Llewellen with a Mazeppa horse. The house closed, after a barely paying season, with a new piece from the pen of J. M. Field, entitled VICTORIA, in which the author personated an editor on his travels in Europe, intended for the celebrated editor of the *N. Y. Herald*.

CHAPTER VII.

I WENT ahead of the company to superintend the refitting of the Mobile Theatre (the old St. Emanuel), and, if possible, to sell out, get rid of, or throw into the river the *Mobile Mercantile Advertiser* establishment, which was involving me in losses I was little able to bear. I had already been compelled to buy out General Bates, a politician who had succeeded to the interest of Mr. Harriman; and the whole concern had cost me $18,000, besides the losses sustained in carrying it on. If it had not been for the faithful and able management of Mr. Keating, who had full control in my absence, my losses would have been much heavier than they were. Luckily, on the very night before the day on which I had determined to end the career of the *Advertiser* by tumbling the types, presses, and every thing pertaining thereto into the Alabama River, I found a couple of good fellows, Messrs. Langdon and Harris, who were willing to purchase the establishment, which had been long advertised, at the price I asked for it—$18,000—if I would take in payment what they had to give. "Any thing—any thing whatever," I exclaimed; "lands, notes, cash, *bull-pups*—any thing. Long credit, short credit; fix it your own way."

Finding me so easy to deal with, they made their proposition, which was to purchase the paper, office, and good-will at the price above named, payable in Illinois bounty lands at $4 50 per acre, a $5000 note of Broadnax & Newton, and to give their own notes for whatever balance might be due after the whole of their stock of Illinois lands had been turned over to me; it being agreed that they were to allow me, besides the price named, *half* the amount of debts on the books. Of course I closed with them at once, set a lawyer at work drawing up the papers, and, with all the clerks to assist, the new proprietors went to work ascertaining how much the debts on the books amounted to. Two hours were occupied in this latter business, when Langdon, with a very long face, came to me and demanded a parley. "Look here, Mr. Sol Smith," said he, in a serious tone, "how much do you suppose those debts on your books amount to?" "Haven't the least idea," I replied. "A considerable sum, I think, for I have collected scarcely any thing since I became proprietor here."

"A considerable sum, indeed," remarked Langdon, who really seemed awfully cut down by the result of his two hours' work in the counting-room. "I am afraid, friend Sol," he continued, seating himself on a high stool, "it will be impossible to carry out our trade, after all. We have not half land enough to pay for those debts. We have only gone through a few pages of the ledger, and they already amount to nine thousand dollars."

"Is it possible?" said I. "I had no idea that the whole would go much over *ten* thousand."

"Ten thousand!" echoed Langdon. "It is my belief, judging from the beginning we have made, that the debts on that one ledger will amount to considerably over $100,000."

I started up. I was amazed and frightened—frightened at the idea that Langdon and Harris were likely to back out from the proposed bargain.

"You must see, friend Sol," remarked Langdon, "that it will be out of the question to carry out our arrangement, the sum being so far above any amount thought of by either party."

"Look here, old friend," said I, looking my interlocutor straight in the eye, "there is no back out in *me*, and I hope there is nothing of the kind in *you*. *We must trade.* Your lands may fall short, but—have you any—bull-pups?" My friend knew the story on which my question was based, and laughingly answered that he hadn't such a thing as any kind of a pup to his name. Harris might have one or two, but he thought not.

"Well," said I, "bring in Harris, and we'll talk over this matter." Harris was called in, and I soon learned from the two that they could not or would not carry out the agreement to pay half price for all the debts due the office, so I addressed myself to getting the best bargain I could out of the new circumstances developed by the partial search of the pages of the ledger.

"You proposed to allow half price for all the debts on the books," I began. "You find those debts large in amount—much larger than you anticipated. So far as the examination has gone, they amount to $9000. I can not compel you to go on with the examination, but, as far as you have gone, *I hold you to.* Pay me for half the debts you have *already* found due, *and I throw the rest in.*" They accepted this offer very cheerfully, and the *Mercantile Advertiser* passed into their hands, while a bundle of patents, signed by James Monroe, fell into mine, and *remained* in my possession for many, many years, together with authenticated transfers of the same from brave soldiers of the War of 1812, long since dead and gone. I may as well finish up this Illinois land business by saying that in the course of about fifteen years I managed to get rid of the whole of them, some at as high a rate as $50 for 160 acres. The last purchaser was a Mr. Green, who offered me $150 for eight tracts of 160 acres each. For several years I had paid the taxes, but at the time I refer to I had neglected for a long time to notice the call of the tax-gatherer. I had, in fact, become very sick of the whole Illinois land business; so I said to Mr. Green, "If you will take all these papers away with you (about a bushel, more or less), and never let me see them again, I will give you a quit-claim deed for every inch of land I own in Illinois for the sum you offer." Green acceded, and I have never since had any thing to do with Illinois lands in any shape or manner.

Having rid myself of the incubus of the newspaper, which I had no business to purchase, but not of the debts I owed *for* the purchase—(the holders of my notes would not touch Illinois lands with a ten-foot pole)—I went to work finishing the redecoration of the theatre, which, in a bran-new coat of paint and costly upholstering, opened on the 10th of November. On the 20th of the same month, after the performance of the MILLER AND HIS MEN, the St. Emanuel was burned to the ground, together with all the scenery, properties, wardrobe, library, and every thing therein.

Without the least hesitation, it was resolved to fix up and open the Government Street Theatre (the "American" it had been called), that establishment having fallen into our hands by virtue of a sale under deed of trust and by compromise with Mr. Ferry, the builder and owner, and I went immediately over to New Orleans to purchase wardrobe, books, and music. These articles I luckily found, the property of the estate of Richard Russell, then recently deceased, and the theatre on Government Street, refitted and renovated, opened on the 1st of December, exactly ten days after the destruction of the St. Emanuel. This was certainly quick work, and it was so considered by the Mobilians; but the theatre-goers held back most provokingly, not considering Mrs. Stuart, late Miss Vos, and Mr. Forbes, who were our first stars, as worth their attention to any great degree. Dan Marble did a little better, and a troupe of horses did tolerably well in the way of *drawing;* but still the public held back, waiting for the "big stars." At length they came, the charming Ellen Tree in the van. It seemed at first the irresistible Ellen was going to fail in her attractive powers, for her first night yielded a receipt of only $296; but the engagement turned out a capital one, the twelve nights giving her for her share $2229 25, the share to the theatre being $3729 25, over $300 per night. Then came Forrest for fourteen nights (receipts averaging about the same as the Tree's), followed by Booth, who—on a "certainty," as it is called when managers take all the risk and pay the star a stipulated sum—played to any thing but good houses. He was paid $100 for each night's performance, and, with the exception of his *Richard* night, the receipts ranged thus: $295, $399, $295 50, $267, $202, $148, $93, $159 50, $170, the last being announced as his benefit. His *Richard* produced $690.

Master Burke followed Booth; then a troupe of Bedouin Arabs. Miss Meadows performed a few nights, and after her came the invincible Celeste, whose engagement was good, but not great this time; and last (and least) came Miss Jane Davenport, the "phenomenon" of Dickens, with her father, the veritable Crummles, immortalized by the same author. The engagement was a poor one, the benefit receipts only reaching $130. This Miss Davenport became a fine actress, and at the time I write (1868) is fairly rivaling the great Italian actress Ristori in performing the characters of *Elizabeth* and *Mary Queen of Scots.* The season closed with the benefit of Mrs. Field (late Miss Riddle); receipts $400. This theatre never opened its doors again, but was destroyed the following fall in the great conflagration which laid in ashes about a third of the city of Mobile.

During this year (1839) I took unto myself a second wife, Miss Elizabeth Pugsly. She still lives, a stout, healthy woman, and the mother of three sons, all grown to man's estate. As she never was on the stage, this is probably the only mention I shall make of her. Though not of the theatrical profession, she has acted well her part.

A Miss Hamblin (no relation of the New York manager, Tom Hamblin) was a member of the company this season. A tragic performance of hers will be hereafter mentioned.

Vincent De Camp, a very talented comedian, ended his engagement with us here. Who in Mobile does not remember De Camp in his milk-cart, a coffee-bag pinned over his shoulders, and his beard unshaven for three days? Poor De Camp! He was but a child, though nearly 70 years of age. He had been for many years a popular actor in London, but, having lost one of his eyes—*how* I never learned—he left the British metropolis for this country, where he had managed several theatres with varied success. He could not lay up any money, made he ever so much. In Montreal he was lessee and manager of a theatre for a season with very poor success. Being very much addicted to playing *Vingt-une* (a game with cards), he generally succeeded in winning a great portion of the salaries of his actors (this he told me himself), using *corn* for stakes, reckoning each corn at sixpence; so that, when salary-day came, it was a common thing for De Camp to say to an actor, "Ah! Mr. ——, let's see; your salary is so and so; your fines this week amount to so much, and here I have fifty *corns* which you are to redeem; that squares our accounts. Please send in the next."

Some money-making scheme was always running away with De Camp's reason and his professional earnings. In his latter years he went into speculations of various kinds, which were invariably unsuccessful, and kept him poor. One of his ventures (in 1837) was taking to Mobile from St. Louis a cargo of turkeys, chickens, ducks, geese, and cabbages. He invested all the money he could raise, besides employing his own credit and that of his friends, so far as they would permit him, and strewed the hurricane deck of the "Praire" with his poultry and vegetables. I can very well remember the squawking, cackling, and gobbling of the feathered cargo, intermingled with some cursing of the crew, which saluted our ears whenever we put forth our heads from the cabin. Besides the poultry and cabbages, he had managed to procure a few cows and a sheep or two, which were stowed below. Altogether, the decks of the "Praire" might be likened unto Noah's ark for the variety of its passengers. For the last three years of his life, *cows* were almost the sole object of his speculative attention. He labored assiduously in his profession, and received a good salary; but he laid all his money out in cows, and the cows kept dying about as fast as he got them.

As a last resort, this good old man and excellent actor went to Texas, with the intention of playing a starring engagement and establishing a dairy with the proceeds; but before he had accomplished either of his objects, the fell sergeant Death summoned him, and he obeyed the call without a murmur or protest, only regretting that he had not gone to Texas years before, being fully impressed, as he said on his death-bed, with the belief that in that splendid grazing country he could in a very short time have become one of the richest men in the South.

CHAPTER VIII.

Several weeks previous to the closing of the season in Mobile, I proceeded to St. Louis, where in a very short time an extra company was collected together—a pretty good one too—for the purpose of "playing the stars" on their way to the North. Among this extra company were Joe Cowell and daughter, Mr. Duff, Mr. Lennox, and Mr. Bateman. Mr. and Mrs. Farren afterward joined the company, under an engagement for three years. Mrs. Farren I had known from her childhood. She is the daughter of the late Richard Russell, manager of the Camp Street Theatre. She remained with me for eight years, and I may truly say that this excellent woman and fine actress always did her duty, and much more. Mr. Farren was a capital actor of old men. Mr. E. Woolf was leader of the orchestra —a fine musician and worthy man, besides possessing a fund of humor and a talent for pen-sketching, which enabled him to make others laugh, though I never saw on his own countenance any thing that approached nearer to a smile than a slight twitching of the lips.

This season opened on the 8th of April, with Mr. Forbes as the star, and the total receipts amounted, the first week, to $1617 50. Next week, without any star, the receipts were about the same; and on the 22d began the engagement of the glorious Ellen Tree, who played seven nights to such business that her pay, on sharing terms, amounted to just $300 per night. Her benefit was $1052.

Banishing Rosalind.

During this engagement a most ludicrous mistake of one of the actors, Mr. Duff, came very near putting a premature end to the performance of Shakspeare's AS YOU LIKE IT before the conclusion of the first act. Duff was cast for the character of *Duke Frederick*, and being detained from rehearsal by indisposition, he had only studied as far as the wrestling scene, supposing that was the end of the part; so, when that scene was ended, he quietly proceeded to his dressing-room and commenced disrobing. When he had got off all his stage dress but his "trunks," he heard a call made in the green-room, directly underneath, which sounded to his affrighted ear very much like "Duke Frederick and attendants!" Holding his "trunks" up by the waistband, he hurried down the stairs, exclaiming,

"It can't be *me*! I've finished my part!"

"But it *is* you," answered the call-boy, "and the stage is waiting for you."

Rushing forward to the first entrance, he heard *Rosalind* exclaim,

"Look! here comes the duke."

To which announcement *Celia* added,

"With his eyes full of anger."

But the *Duke didn't* come, and as for his eyes, they seemed more full of sorrow than of anger while he stood at the wing, with one hand employed in holding up his trunks (a sort of trowsers) and the other in expressive gesticulation.

"Here comes the duke," repeated *Rosalind*, at which inviting cue poor Duff clasped his hands together in anguish, releasing, for a moment, the waistband of his trunks, which immediately commenced falling, of course, exclaiming in a loud whisper,

"I can't go on in *this* way, you know."

As if in fear that he *would* go on in *that* way, Miss Tree turned to *Celia*, and saying, "Let us go and meet his grace," led the way from the stage, and the curtain was lowered amid a shower of hisses.

In a moment I was on the spot. The *Duke* was full of apologies; the fair *Rosalind* was full of mortification; I was full of perplexity, and the audience full of ill humor. What was to be done? It was clear the play could not go on without the banishment of *Rosalind* from the court, and equally clear that to raise the curtain for the few lines that remained to be spoken and then drop it again, as needs must be done to allow *Rosalind* to change her dress, would appear to be trifling with the patience of the public.

"I have it!" exclaimed I. "You, *Rosalind*, must be banished. I hereby pronounce sentence of banishment upon you. Go and put on your boy's clothes, and be ready to begin the second act."

"But," interposed Ellen Tree, "what will the audience think?"

"Never mind the audience," I answered; "leave me to settle it with *them*."

Away went Ellen to dress, and (a little bell being rung) out went I before the curtain.

"RESPECTED AUDIENCE,—Extremely sorry, etc., etc.; misconception of the gentleman cast for the *Duke*—indisposition, etc.; usual indulgence, etc., etc.; hope you will overlook the blunder, etc.; and as the play can not well proceed without the banishment of *Rosalind* from the court, I ask permission from you to pronounce the sentence which the *Duke* should have pronounced before his abdication."

General applause and laughter answering these apologetic remarks, I straightened myself up, and assuming, as nearly as I could, the voice and manner of the defaulting actor, I pronounced the sentence in the *Duke's* words—

> "Firm and irrevocable is my doom
> Which I have pass'd upon her. She is banish'd."

The now good-natured audience confirmed the sentence with loud applause, and the performance went on.

"After the storm comes a calm." Mr. C. Mason performed a week to horrible business, and on his benefit night, after playing a scene from MACBETH, refused to go on with the performance on account of the scarcity of people in the front of the house. He addressed the audience, thanking the few who were in attendance, but said he must decline to proceed any farther to such a small audience. The "small audience" took this speech very kindly, and, as Mr. Mason made his exit R. H., I made my entrance L. H., and assured the public that, notwithstanding the star's defection, if a wait of ten minutes were accorded, I would pledge myself, by substituting other actors in Mr. Mason's place, the performance should go on as announced in the bills. The public were entirely satisfied, and in precisely ten minutes from the time I left the stage the performance was resumed, and eventually carried through with entire success. The entertainments consisted of *acts* from various plays, and I found no difficulty in finding *Hamlets*, *Shylocks*, and *Richards* in abundance, very glad of the opportunity to exhibit their hidden powers; and, what was better than all, the house "picked up," and in the end the receipts amounted to nearly $200.

Mr. Forrest (for which he received $2157) played twelve nights, of course to fine houses, followed by Celeste, who, though not attracting so greatly as either Tree or Forrest, had a benefit which amounted to $1149 50, the highest receipts on any one night in that theatre.

Dan Marble played a moderate engagement, followed by a "combination," consisting of Barrett, Scott, and young Burke (not very successful), and the spring season of thirteen weeks closed with the performances for six nights of Mr. and Mrs. Sloman, the latter a very fine actress of tragedy characters, and the former a very excellent comic singer; but they didn't draw.

After a vacation of about five weeks the house reopened, and the first week's receipts amounted to only $748. After weeks of preparation, the JEWESS was produced with great splendor, and drew on its first representation $460, and then the receipts ran down to almost nothing.

During Mr. Forrest's engagement he was attended by A. J. Allen as costumer. I have some anecdotes of this gentleman, and I may as well conclude this chapter with them.

The Father of the American Stage.

Andrew Jackson Allen (now deceased) claimed to be the father of the American stage; that is to say, he supposed he had been on the American stage a longer period than any other living actor. This may be true. I have seen his name in the bills, and his person on the stage as long ago as 1815. He was Andrew Allen *then;* the Jackson has since been acquired—*how*, I do not pretend to say; but I believe it was laid hold of by, and conceded to him by the world, in consequence of the able manner in which he "got up" the *Battle of New Orleans* at his benefit, soon after the news arrived of the grand affair at New Orleans, performed on the 8th of January of the above-named year.

The first character I saw performed by the subject of this sketch was the *Laird of Raissy*, in the opera of the HIGHLAND REEL. I next saw him in a raw-head-and-bloody-bones mixture of pantomime and melo-drama, entitled the BLACK CASTLE, or the DISTRESSED MAIDEN, in which he enacted an extremely savage-looking confidential servant to a villainous usurper, with a slouched hat, overhanging feathers, broad belt, with a very wide brass buckle in front, short sword, and wide-sleeved gauntlets; and it was his peculiar province to attempt all the assassinations; to be most unmercifully beaten by men with clubs, and other rescuers of innocence; and to cry "Confusion! foiled again!" and rush off, shaking his dagger at the audience, and with a look at his intended victim which indicated, as plainly as looks *can* indicate, that it wouldn't be well for the aforesaid intended victim to let him catch her alone again—that's all. He made a great impression on me; and afterward, when I saw him in *Abœlino, the Great Bandit*, through the knot-hole of a pine board under the boxes, where I had stationed myself in the afternoon before the doors were opened, my admiration was excited to the highest pitch. This was in the old Albany Theatre, in Green Street, where he produced, or assisted in producing, a piece called the BATTLE OF LAKE CHAMPLAIN, the ships floating in *real water!* In this piece he played the character of a negro, and sung a song of many verses (the first negro song, I verily believe, ever heard on the American stage), two verses of which I give from memory:

"Backside Albany stan' Lake Champlain,
  Little pond half full o' water;
Plat-te-burg dar too, close 'pon de main;
  Town small—he grow bigger, do', herearter.

On Lake Champlain Uncle Sam set he boat,
  An' Massa Macdonough he sail 'em;
While Gineral Macomb make Plat-te-burg he home
  Wid de army, whose courage nebber fail 'em."

In the winter of 1816 the father of the American stage became the sole proprietor of the Shakspeare House, nearly opposite the theatre, previously occupied by one Morse, afterward proprietor of a Shakspeare Hotel adjoining the Park Theatre, New York. He still continued to act in the theatre, playing stern villains in dramas, and clowns in pantomimes. He took a benefit, and paid off an immense amount of debts, *in tickets*, leading each creditor to suppose that *he* was the *only one* who could be paid, and assuring him that the tickets could be easily disposed of. It leaked out during the day that every body had tickets for sale, and the price fell to almost nothing. I purchased a box ticket for six cents, and, by planting myself at the door at four o'clock, was one of the eleven hundred that were shoved into the house. The three or four thousand outsiders amused themselves by kicking up all sorts of rumpuses in the street. The "father" did not care for all this—he had the receipted bills of his creditors in his pocket.

Having paid all his debts in Albany, he proceeded to New York, where he engaged in the Park Theatre, and was moderately successful in his slouched hat, broad buckle, and short-sword characters, until his creditors—for he had a way of getting in debt perfectly surprising to young beginners — became somewhat impatient and troublesome. One, in particular, determined to try the virtue of a *capias ad respondendam*, and employed a well-known and afterward celebrated constable, by the name of Hays, to execute the same on the body of Father Allen. I may as well here state two things: first, my hero was partially *deaf;* and, secondly, he had a way of speaking which conveyed the idea that he was always laboring under the effects of a bad cold in his head, without a pocket-handkerchief to help himself with. The reader will please bear these things in mind.

Young Hays (he was then young) found Father Allen on the Park Theatre steps. "Good morning," said he, saluting the actor very civilly, but speaking in a very loud voice, for he knew the actor's infirmity, and pulling out a small bit of paper; "your name is Allen, I believe?"

"Yes, Addrew Jacksod Alled, at your service," replied the debtor, supposing the officer was an applicant for a front seat in the dress circle; "what cad I do for you, by friedd?" continued he, patronizingly, as he gently tapped the ashes from his cigar. "It is my bedefit, you see—Battle of Lake Erie, sir, with real water—great expedse—fide play—'we have met the edeby add they are ours,' you kdow—lots of doble ships, flags, guds, and smoke. Look at the bill, sir."

"That's just what I want *you* to do," replied the officer. "Here is a bill I want you to examine, and here is a writ requiring that I shall take your body forthwith before a squire."

It was useless to attempt to misunderstand this plain explanation, for, if he could not *hear* very well, he could *see* as well as any body, and it was equally useless to attempt to escape; so, after quietly examining the papers, the *beneficiaire* of the evening gave a puff or two more at his cigar, and then, with a nod of the head, intimated that he understood the whole affair.

"Let's see—yes, sevedty-two dollars exactly. Cursed ill-datured of by friedd Thobsod to trouble you with this busidess; I idtedded to pay it out of by bedefit bodey to-borrow. But dever bind; step idto Bister Sibsod's roob with be, and I'll hadd you the aboudt."

"Certainly, sir," answered Hays, and he followed the defendant into the theatre through a private door. I shall not attempt to describe the route they took, but it is said the officer was led up and down numerous stairways, over divers stagings, and through many dark passages and underground vaults, until he was completely bewildered. At length, in the midst of darkness, he was requested by his conductor to "hold on a minute." "Here's Bister Sibsod's roob," said he; "wait here till I see if he is at leisure." The officer stopped stock still as desired, for he had no idea which way to move, and waited patiently for the return of his prisoner, whose retreating steps told him that Mr. Simpson's room was not so near to where he stood as he had supposed. After waiting for about ten minutes, he began to call the name of his prisoner in a loud voice. Suddenly a trap-door opened immediately above his head, and, looking up, he distinctly saw Allen's face, lit up with a most benevolent smile. "Well," inquired the officer, "have you found Simpson?" "Do, by friedd, I haved't yet foudd that worthy gedtlebad, but I do dot despair of beidg able to beet with hib sobe tibe this evedidg. Be so good as to wait there, by idterestidg friedd, while I take a good look for hib; it is more thad likely I shall see hib sobewhere betweed here add Philadelphia, for which city I ab about ebbarkidg."

"Embarking for Philadelphia!" fiercely exclaimed the officer: "no you don't! you are my prisoner, and must not move."

"By dear friedd," replied Allen, who had not heard a word the officer had said, but saw by his movements he was inclined to leave the place where he had located him, "you'd better dot stir frob that spot till sobe of the labplighters arrive, for if you do, idasbuch as there are trap-doors all roudd you, you'll fall forty feet or so, add that bight hurt you, you know." The trap-door was closed with a loud noise, and the next that was heard of Father Allen, he was getting up The Battle of Lake Champlain in Philadelphia. I have never learned how the constable got out of the theatre, but I presume he was *turned* out. The return on his writ was, "Executed by taking in custody the defendant, who escaped by misleading me into the devil's church, and leaving me to get out the best way I could."

The next I heard of the father he was manager of a theatre in Pensacola, where he played *Abœlino* and *Caleb Quotem* with great success. In 1822 he was in Cincinnati, where I was editing a paper, and he was then engaged in sending up a series of balloons, in opposition to one Mons. Dumileau, and appealing in his advertisements to the patriotic feelings of the Cincinnatians to sustain *his* balloons, on the ground that they were the true *American* article, while those of Dumileau's were decidedly *French*.

He went into Virginia, causing balloons to ascend from every village. At one of his stands he found great difficulty in collecting together the proper materials for generating gas; nevertheless, he advertised that the exhibition would take place, and, providing a quantity of the spirits of turpentine to burn under the balloon, hired a large garden, into which the Virginians flocked in great numbers, each paying fifty cents at the gate. When the hour of ascension arrived, the exhibitor found that with all his exertions it would be impossible to cause the balloon to mount! He had a number of juvenile assistants, who were busy about the inner inclosure, and to them he addressed himself, first handing an old bull's eyed watch to the largest boy—

"Look here, by boys, I've got to go add purchase sobe bore *sulphuric acid:* you take this watch, add when the hadd poidts at the hour of two, set fire to this here turpedtide; do you hear?"

The boys said they *did* hear, and promised obedience. The master spirit made his way to the gate, where he requested the door-keeper to "hadd over the fudds, as there was such a crowd there was do tellidg what bight happed id the bustle." He then mounted a pony he had wisely provided for the purpose, and galloped off for the drug-store, but, mistaking the way, he found himself, at precisely two o'clock, on a very high hill overlooking the scene of his late operations. The boys were true to their promise, and communicated the fire to the turpentine at the appointed time; the *balloon went up*, but it was in small flaky fragments, and the humbugged Virginians began to look about for the operator, but in vain! With $600 in his pockets, he was wending his way toward some city where gas could be more easily generated. In giving an account of this affair, my venerable friend said: "Dab the idferdal ballood! I foudd there was do use id tryidg to bake it rise; so, as I dislike bakidg apologies, I thought I would bake byself scarce. Whed I got od that hill add looked back, the boys had set fire to the ballood, add such a sboke rose up! the whole village appeared to be od fire; d—d if it did'dt look like a youdg Sodob add Goborrow!"

When Mr. Edwin Forrest began to rise in his profession, Allen determined to rise with him, and attached himself to that tragedian as costumer, in which capacity, and that of a fighting gladiator, he traversed this country and Great Britain, always taking to himself a full share of credit for "the boy's" success; "for," said he, "what would be the use of taledt without the proper costube?" I am not informed of the cause of separation, but certain it is the great tragedian has managed to "get on" without the aid of the father of the American stage for several years past. During the latter years of his life, Mr. Allen earned an honest livelihood in New York by manufacturing silver leather. His last advertisement, or the last which I saw, begins as follows:

"☞ HUMBUGS AVAUNT!!! ☜

I AM NOT DEAD YET: ingratitude has not killed me—thanks to a clear conscience and a pair of *silver leather breeches.* All I want is work, that I may thrive by my *industry*, pay my debts, and die, as I always have lived, *an honest man.*"

Which he did, at a good old age, respected by all.

CHAPTER IX.

ONE of our company, Mr. Bateman (afterward married to Miss Sidny Cowell), was a good actor for the experience he then had, but somewhat belligerent at times. There was an editor named Foster to whom he administered a *caning* in return for some criticisms on himself or his wife which he considered unjust. Foster had Mr. B. arrested and taken before the mayor, who fined him $25, which Mr. B. and his counsel thought too much for caning an editor.

Mr. Primm (Counsel for Bateman) to Sol. Smith.

"St. Louis, November 30, 1839.

"SOL. SMITH, ESQ.:—DEAR SIR,—Will you have the goodness to call on the mayor and inform him as to the amount of salary received by Mr. Bateman weekly. The mayor has imposed on Mr. B. a fine, which I think disproportionate to his means. Your statement will doubtless have the effect of procuring a reduction to something like a nominal fine.

"Yours truly, WILSON PRIMM."

Dr. William Carr Lane (Mayor) to Sol. Smith.

"SOL. SMITH, ESQ.:—DEAR SIR,—I have received your favor of this date upon the subject of Mr. Bateman's salary. Please say to that gentleman that, after considering the subject in all its aspects, and with every disposition to serve him, I am of opinion that $25 is a very small sum to set off against a *caning* inflicted upon any sort of a gentleman, and that, according to my sense of duty, I can not reduce the *fine* without trampling upon *public justice.*

"Very respectfully, your obedient servant,

"WM. CARR LANE, Mayor of St. Louis.

"St. Louis, December 2, 1839."

This Mr. Bateman has since been a prominent man in the theatrical world. He is the father of the celebrated Bateman children, one of whom (Kate) is a reigning star at this time in England. Ellen married and retired young. To Mr. Bateman the Eastern cities are indebted for the introduction of the French *Opera Bouffe*, at this moment so popular in New York City. His wife (formerly Sidny Cowell) is the author of some successful plays—SELF for one.

The ICE WITCH was gotten up splendidly, scenery by Joe Cowell, Jr. Mark Smith, then ten years of age, was brought from the St. Louis University to personate the *Sun-God.* Cowell played *Magnus Snoro*, Mrs. Farren the *Ice Witch*, and Miss Sidny Cowell the chambermaid, whatever her name may be. In short, the cast was strong; nevertheless, the piece was weak in its attractive powers. The same may be said of the LADY OF THE LAKE, also produced in good style in every respect.

The house was kept open a full month longer than was intended, in consequence of the news coming that in the great fire which occurred in Mobile, the Government Street Theatre was (as before stated) swept away by the devouring element. So, while a new building was being erected, or, rather, an old building fitted up—at an expense of $12,000—we had to "hold on" at St. Louis, losing at the rate of $100 to $150 per day! Dan Marble, Dempster (the sweet vocalist), and Herr Cline were tried as stars, but all would not do. The last gasp of the season was given on the 11th of December, and the company embarked for the South.

But, before I take the reader to the new scene of loss and trouble, I intend to devote a short chapter to some letters, which, at the time they were written, kept the town in a continual grin for a week or two. Through the post-office one day I received the first of these letters, which I immediately handed to the editors of the "Republican." Next day it appeared in that paper, with prefatory remarks, as follow:

From the St. Louis Republican.

"We have been presented with the annexed letter, and publish it for the purpose of giving our readers an insight into the nature of the applications with which the managers of theatres are constanty afflicted. It is addressed to Sol. Smith, Esq., the worthy manager of our theatre.

"*Miss Eliza Pelling to Sol. Smith.*

"'St. Louis, October 7, 1839.

"'MR. SOL. SMITH: MY DEAR SIR,—I have taken the liberty of writing to you, as I am too timid to hold a personal interview with you, the modesty of my sex forbidding me to hold communion with one of yours; and I should now despise myself for the action but that I am a houseless wretch, scorned and despised by my relations, and am destitute of shoes and stockings, and am reduced to the necessity of soliciting of you what I have never solicited of human being before—an engagement at your theatre. I have read much, and have seen a great deal of acting in my time, although I am but eighteen years of age. Mr. Forrest, Esquire, was an intimate acquaintance of my father's brother, who became acquainted with him during a journey up the Hudson; and, indeed, he promised to call and see us, but he never kept his word; but my uncle says he is a very good sort of a man. He referred my uncle to Madame Celeste for his character—and my uncle went to Boston on purpose—and Madame Celeste said that he was a gentleman of very good parts, and spoke English very fluently. But to the point. I have been informed that you are in want of a leading actress. I am willing to engage with you to undertake that line of business at any time I may be called upon to act. I am unfortunate, and the landlady of my boarding-house holds me in pledge until I pay her for my board. She says that her behavior proceeds out of pure love toward me, but I do not believe her. I have been very unhappy since I ran away from my parents, who reside at Grand Gulf. They are of the Methodist persuasion, and abominate actors and all their tribe—but enough. You want to know what line of business I can act. I will tell you. I should like to play such parts as *Little Pickle*, and *Mrs. Haller*, and general light comedy parts. I am also very handy at my needle, and would willingly mend any lady's or gentleman's wearing apparel belonging to your establishment; and I would also wash for them, for I understand that they dirty a great many pairs of stockings in the course of the week, especially in the warm weather. I can also prick down tunes, and am willing to play supernumerary dancing-girls' characters, provided you will not desire me to dress in an indelicate manner, like the *Adam* and *Eve* exhibiting in this city. I have often blushed for the native modesty of my sex while gazing at Madame Celeste in the BAYADERE, and Mr. Forrest in SPARTACUS. I should like to play *Ariel* in the MIDSUMMER NIGHT'S *Tempest*, for I can sing "Where the Bee lurks there suck I," and "Round-a-round," and "Bonny Blue-cap," and "Fancy Bread." It has been my greatest misfortune in life to be attached to theatricals. I should have been married before this, and independent of the world, but that I abominate the cold formalities imposed upon us by our religion. Mr. Marble is a very handsome man, and so is Mr. Schinotti; but I think Mr. Marble is a better actor. I wish you could inform me if Mr. Marble is married, or if Mr. Schinotti is a widower. Don't say that I asked you. I have seen Mr. Schinotti bathing in Chouteau's Pond very often. I wish you would inform me if he has any children. He makes good properties. I don't think that Mr. De Gensen will ever be a great actor, although he looks very well in a helmet. Mr. Jones has the most expressive face I ever saw. I was in hopes that he would have played *Roderick Dhu* in the LADY OF THE LAKE. I have heard him read the part with so much feeling that he has frothed at the mouth. I have also seen him play *Kingerzu* in the UNACCLIMATED INDIAN. He made his first appearance in Boston as one of the front legs of the *Elephant* in BLUEBEARD, and the time of the choruses was to be directed by the motion of the proboscis of the elephant, to which was attached a string held by Mr. Jones. It so happened that he was seized with a fit of the chills, when, not having presence of mind to let go the string, the chorus singers were led astray, and sang so fast that Mr. Ostenelli broke three fiddle-sticks in his rage. Mr.

Rose is a nice man, and wears well. My uncle says that he remembers him forty years ago as the owner of a log hut near the Niagara Falls, and that he was the proprietor of a plantation of split peas near to that place, and that he domesticated bullfrogs and kept them in wicker baskets; he also vended quack medicines, and had remedies against the bites of fleas. Why do you not bring him before the public? I have hitherto seen him do nothing but lead processions. If you could see him in doublet and hose dance to the tune of "Peas upon a Trencher," you would lift up your hands with astonishment. He can play female characters very well, such as *Lady Macbeth*, *Crackajowler*, *Juliet*, and *Desdemona*. I should like to play *Othello* upon that occasion, for I would rather smother him than any other man living. Some few years ago he was bitten by a hydrophobic musquito, and for many months after he ran trumpeting about our house, occasionally dipping his nose into the raw-beef tub. I can not tell if he has altered since that time, but he was then distinguished by a small tuft of hair, like a furze-bush, growing in each nostril, and had the rudiments of whiskers. My landlady informs me that I shall not obtain more than from fifty to sixty dollars per night; but I do not believe her, for I can not imagine that you would insult the sensitive feelings of genius by making such a paltry offer. Should you feel inclined to avail yourself of my services, you will do well to direct your answer to ELIZA PELLING.'"

In the same number of the "Republican" appeared a communication from Miss Pelling's father. Here it is:

George Pelling to the Editor.

"St. Louis, October 9.

"*To the Editor of the Missouri Republican:*

"SIR,—My daughter, Eliza Pelling, having left me, her heart-broken father, to pine with sorrow in my old age, I have been searching for her every where, and have traced her to this city. I reside at Grand Gulf, and am in comfortable circumstances. I have ever been a kind and indulgent father to her. Her motive for leaving me I can not surmise, unless it be that she had a great love for the theatrical profession. I have every reason to believe that she is concealed in this city. My motive for writing to you is urged by the hope that you will give publicity to this letter by inserting it in your valuable journal. I am willing to forgive her and forget the past, so that she will return to her fond father's arms. Let me entreat you to publish this letter, so that it may reach her eye. She is the only prop of my declining years. I promise her that I will never revert to the past.

"By giving insertion to this communication, you will oblige your obedient humble servant,

"GEORGE PELLING.

"P.S.—If Eliza Pelling will address a few lines to X. Y. Z., and leave them at the Post-office, they will be gladly attended to."

"October 10, 1839.

"SIR,—Since the writing of my communication to you, I have discovered a clew that will probably lead to the recovery of my lost child. With many thanks for your proffered kindness, I remain your obedient servant,

"GEORGE PELLING."

In a day or two afterward two other letters were received by me from the lovely Eliza, one of them being an inclosure for Dan Marble, the popular Yankee delineator, who was fulfilling an engagement in St. Louis at the time. They were sent to the "Republican," in which paper they appeared with preliminary editorial remarks.

From the St. Louis Republican.

"ELIZA PELLING AGAIN.

"This interesting young lady, whose somewhat lengthy epistle to the manager of our theatre was communicated to the world through the columns of this paper, has been the subject of very general remark and inquiry during the past week. Her letter seems to have excited a wish in our young beaux to witness her first appearance on the boards, for we can not imagine for a moment that our gallant manager will hold out against the fair Eliza's pleading for an engagement. We have been favored with a perusal of two more letters—one, directed like the first, to the manager, the other to Dan Marble, the Yankee comedian, who is nightly convulsing crowded audiences with his Yankee drolleries. The *penchant* of the young lady for the stage and stage performers is obvious, and not to be concealed. We must earnestly recommend that the lovely Eliza be allowed to appear on the manager's benefit night.

"We subjoin a short extract from her second letter to the manager, and give her moving appeal to the fascinating Dan entire.

"'St. Louis, October 10, 1839.

"'SOL. SMITH, ESQ.: MY DEAR SIR,—By perusing this morning's paper, I find that my father, George Pelling, is in this city. He doubtless is in pursuit of me. Should he call upon you, I hope that you will not betray me by showing him my letter, for I am determined that I will never go home unless he will allow me to have a private theatre erected in his house, so that I may be enabled to entertain a select company of friends by the sole efforts of my theatrical conceptions. Nor will I return with him unless he will engage three or four of your actors to play parts with me. On this I am bent, for I am determined to act, and act I will; but let me request of you not to betray me unless you are compelled. I expected to have received an answer to my last letter, and sent to the Post-office for that purpose, but was sadly disappointed; you have not any of that gallantry which is so becoming a propensity of your sex—but I must forgive you. Your business doubtless prevented you from attending to my wants. But the means of making reparation is now in your power, and can immediately be performed by forwarding to me a brace of flannel petticoats and some pomatum; also three or four pairs of white stockings that have not been darned, with a gross or two of hair-pins. You can leave them for me at the General Agency Office, Pine Street.

should like to play *Belvidera* for Mr. S.'s benefit. I wish you would ask him. If he consents, you will save me much time and trouble by purchasing forty-three yards of black silk velvet for me, and a string of pearls. You can leave them for me at the Agency Office.

"'Yours everlastingly, ELIZA PELLING.

"'Do not betray me to my father.'"

"'Wednesday, October 16, 1839.

"'D. MARBLE, ESQ.: SIR,—Excuse the liberty I have taken in thus addressing you, for I am of a sensitive and delicate constitution, so that a harsh reply, especially from you, would cause me hours of unutterable anguish. I have lately been suffering from an attack of the spleen and tic douloureux, and for which my doctor's bill amounts to eighteen dollars and two bits. Do not imagine that I am about asking you to pay for it, for I would rather die than ask such a favor from you; but the awkward situation in which I am placed, and, above all, the extreme sensibility of my sex, causes the hectic blush to pervade my frame even to my finger nails. Would that I had never seen you! Yet you are not to blame. Had I never loved the theatrical profession I should never have adored you—pardon the expression—the susceptibility of my sex—the tears that bedew this paper. Oh! willingly would I become your seamstress and washerwoman, or hold the enviable situation of getter-up of your small linen, so that I could be under the same roof with you! Oh! how I did envy the lady who chewed gingerbread with you upon the stage! and oh! what horror ran through my susceptible frame when you jumped off the Niagara scene! I thought that you had killed yourself, for the breath that left your body agitated the sham water into very billows. But when I saw you arrive safe on shore upon the stage I went into a fit, and did not recover until forty-eight hours after. There are but few who love with a fervor like to mine. None but a hammerer of anvils can form an idea of the intensity of the heat pervading my susceptible heart. Yes, I own it. I should be ashamed to disclose the weakness of my sensitive nature to you but that I am driven forward against my inclination, for I believe myself to be right modest. There are but two extremes to which a susceptible heart like mine can be driven, and they are either hate or love; but I prefer the latter. It is fortunate for me that my landlady can not read, for she is now peeping through her spectacles over my shoulder, and her nose, resembling a full grown and well boiled beet, dangles to and fro, like an ill cooked pease-pudding, upon her puckered face. She imagines that I am writing a penitent letter to my father, with a request of a few hundred dollars, but she is mistaken. Little does she imagine the love that preys upon my heart; but, as I say in a poem that I have written upon my unfortunate passion,

Men are deceivers,
and
Women believers!

and in the concluding lines—

My fervent love, alas! away is thrown,
For, make the most of Marble,' tis but Stone.

Now I am so miserable in my mind that I have determined to punish myself by abstaining from the eating of animal flesh, and to appear abroad squalid and slipshod; nor will I comb my hair, nor know the use of nail or tooth-brush, and will wander around the city of St. Louis and the suburbs like a hairy phantom, unless you will grant me a boon—it is the last that I may ever beg of you—promise to meet me at Chouteau's Pond to-morrow evening between the hours of six and seven. I am anxious to hold a conversation with you. Can you be secret? Dare I trust myself with you? Alas! were I so inclined, the jealous scrutiny of my landlady would prevent it. It is probable that she will follow me, for she will never trust me out of her sight until I pay her for my board hire. I will conduct you to a retired dell where we may converse without the danger of interruption. Do not fail, as you value the peace of your unhappy

"'ELIZA PELLING.'"

I give the above as a *specimen* of the PELLING LETTERS, as they were called. Besides the genuine letters of Miss Pelling (exclusively in the "Republican"), other papers had spurious letters purporting to be from the same party. The "Pennant" spread itself on the "Pelling Letters," all spurious, but excellent imitations, and greatly increased its circulation by their publication. At length the height of absurdity was reached by the fair Eliza (the spurious article) offering to *attend the theatre on the occasion of my benefit*, if a box were offered her properly decorated for the occasion; and some young men did actually go through the farce of taking a *boy*, dressed up in a very gaudy and fashionable way, into the box prepared for Miss Pelling, amid the plaudits of the audience. During the delivery of *Mawworm's* extemporaneous address, I took occasion to mention the visit of Miss Pelling, when she rose and courtesied repeatedly, to the great amusement of the people.

I will give one more letter of Miss Pelling, and dismiss her for the present.

Eliza Pelling to Sol. Smith.

"St. Louis, November 27, 1839.

"TO SOL. SMITH, ESQ.:

"And is it true that you are about to quit St. Louis for the balmy South with your company of delightful players? Oh, do not go! I implore you, do not go! Your theatre is the solitary star of my destiny. How joyously my susceptible heart has throbbed when I have dwelt upon the fame I should acquire by acting in your theatre. I hope, for my sake, that you will consider what you are about to do. Oh, what would I not give were I permitted to show my peculiar talents upon the front boards of your stage—to hear the shouts of an enraptured audience—to blush with virgin modesty on beholding the waving of white cambric handkerchiefs of the ladies, and to cast my eyes to earth with becoming bashfulness upon being quizzed by the full-whiskered young men—to be called for at the end of my performance by the delightful spectators—to receive a coronet of white roses from an admiring swain, and sundry pairs of stockings from the sympathizing ladies: these are visions of glory the which I had hoped would have been realized; but now you are about to quench the flame of my happiness by closing the theatre.

"There are but two alternatives for me, the *stage* or the *madhouse.* Ah! call it folly, infatuation, or what you will, it is decreed—an actress I will be, or the precincts of a lunatic asylum will be my cloister. You might even now avail yourself of my valuable services, and gratify my most ardent wishes, by paying my landlady the small sum of *eighty-five dollars.* She would then suffer me to depart. Oh, thou most glorious shades of *Thespis* and *Melpomene*, together with the wandering ghosts of *Æschylus*, *Euripides*, *Terence*, and *Aristophanes*, I invoke thy aid. Is it possible that I am not worth eighty-five dollars? Did ever genius like to mine languish in obscurity for so small a sum? My beauty, like the blush of retiring eve, is fading away, and I am covered with black and blue pinches from my landlady's long fingers. Oh, you can not form an idea of her tyranny; and her frightful scowl at me through her spectacles inspires absolute terror. When she retires for the night, I am compelled to accompany her, for she has caused an iron ring with a chain to be fastened to my ankle; and upon her getting into bed, she uses the precaution to wind the aforesaid chain twice or thrice around her arm, allowing me sufficient length to slumber upon a bundle of raccoon skins placed upon the floor for my accommodation, so that escape is rendered impossible. My only consolation during the night is in reading tragedy play-books by the light of the moon, or in reciting Mrs. Haller's domesticated speeches in the dark. Occasionally I amuse myself by singing sweet and dulcet lays, and such songs as are best calculated for my shrill, bell-toned voice, viz., 'The Squire in Boots,' 'Trundle the Hoop,' 'Down the Fern, Davy, Love,' 'Penitential Groans,' and other well-known melodies. Oh, sir, if you really possess that philanthropy of soul for which you are famed, release me from my cruel thraldom, which noble and praiseworthy action can be easily accomplished by forwarding to me about one hundred dollars in specie (for I would not tax your kindness by accepting of Illinois or wild-cat paper bills, they being on a par with each other). With the surplus money remaining (after having satisfied my avaricious landlady) I can purchase a parasol, reticule, and other fancy articles; and, indeed, it is certain that I must have silk stockings to endure the inclemency of the winter.

"I implore you to keep open your theatre, if only to oblige me. I am sure that you will be a gainer by the venture, for I am convinced of my great talents; and even that modern Longinus, Quevedo (who is *suaviter in modo, fortiter in re*), would lift up his eyes and hands in an ecstasy of rapture, and his pen flourish forth praises upon the merits of ELIZA PELLING."

The last remark of Eliza, relative to "Quevedo," had reference to a writer in one of the daily papers who assumed that name.

CHAPTER X.

I FEEL strangely tempted to pass over this wretched season in Mobile (1839–40) in silence; and, were it not for some anecdotical recollections belonging to this particular era, I should do so.

Being in St. Louis, 1400 miles away, I had nothing to do or say in the selection of the site for the theatre which had been prepared for our reception. I *now* say, however, that the location was a most unfortunate one—away up in the "Orange Grove," among the cotton warehouses, and so inaccessible that several bridges had to be built to enable people to get to it. The house opened on the 31st of December, the night being fair, to a receipt of $75 50!

In consequence of detentions on the way, I did not arrive in person until the day after the opening, and I here declare that it was with considerable difficulty I found the new theatre! Nobody seemed to know where it was situated, though some few of whom I inquired seemed impressed with the idea that there *was* a new theatre somewhere. At last I found a man who had worked upon the building, and *he* told me it was "awa-a-ay up yonder, beyond the steam-boats and among the cotton presses." "Did it open last night?" I ventured to inquire. "Well, I haven't hearn," answered the man; "it *was* to."

I found the place at last—and such a place! * * * I can't describe it, and will not attempt to do so. The second (New Year's) night produced $66.

Stars this season, Conner, Le Compte, Mason, Marble, Balls, Herr Cline, and the Ravel family, which I went 500 miles—into Georgia—to secure. Le Compte and the Ravels were the only parties who could be said to have drawn even "decent" houses, and their houses were far, far below what would or could be called "paying," either to the manager or star.

The "Alhambra," a large ballroom in the city, was opened by the Chapman family with a very small company, and did a good business. J. M. Field played a starring engagement there, not being this year a member of our company, having (with his wife) accepted an engagement at the St. Charles, New Orleans. On his arrival in Mobile he came to the theatre to see me; it was in the night-time, and I shall never forget the plight in which he appeared before me in my dressing-room. He was literally covered with mud from the soles of his boots to his arm-pits. He had been told where he could find the theatre ("awa-a-ay up yonder, beyond the steamboats and among the cotton presses"), and Joe had pushed through the swamp, urged by the desire to take his old friend by the hand, striking a bee-line toward some lights which he rightly took for the street-lamps (only there was no *street*) in front of the theatre. After talking over old times for half an hour, I loaned him a monk's cloak to hide his nastiness, and furnished him a guide to his hotel.

During the season Miss Eliza Pelling again made her epistolary appearance, in the shape of a letter to the New Orleans Picayune, which the editors sent to me, not deeming it of sufficient interest to be laid before their readers, but which would most likely interest *me* to a very considerable degree, inasmuch as the lovely Eliza therein speaks of a certain report circulated to her disadvantage, that she "cherished a passion and nourished a design to captivate the heart" of the manager to whom she had addressed her previous appeals.

Eliza Pelling to the Editor of the Picayune.

"Pickinsville Theatre, Ala., Feb. 22, 1840.

"SIR,—I have observed, with all those proper feelings of female modesty for which my susceptible sex are so justly famed, that a report, or rather an insinuation, or something to that effect, has found its way into various newspapers, and from the which I have suffered somewhat a little materially, or perhaps a little more. I allude to an observation, or rather an oblique hint, that I have cherished a passion and nourished a design to captivate the heart of that worthy and excellent gentleman, 'Mr. Sol. Smith, Esquire,' comic actor and manager of two theatres, one at St. Louis and the other at Mobile. Now I do believe that it is well known to the world, especially to my learned and literary friends, that an idea of love for that most esteemed and celebrated individual has never entered my mind, except that a species of veneration and gratitude a well-disposed female ever feels for one who proffers kindness in the hour of distress and affliction can be so interpreted. It is, indeed, an authenticated fact that, when I visited the theatre at St. Louis upon the benefit night of Mr. Sol. Smith this last fall, he was pleased to pass some very flattering remarks upon me as I sat in the boxes, and promised me a situation the forthcoming spring at his theatre. He did this from the public stage, and before the audience assembled upon that eventful occasion; whereupon I arose, as I felt in duty bound, covered from head to foot with modest blushes, and acknowledged his kind proffer with a most reverent and becoming courtesy; upon which the ladies and gentlemen present testified their approbation by loud and continued applause, both with their hands and feet; and many gentlemen, both young and old, assembled in the parquet, kissed their hands and bowed to me, with various contortions of countenance, as if inspired by an ecstasy of rapture. Now, since this occurrence, and the publication of various epistles I had addressed to Mr. Sol. Smith, Esq., I have been accused of cherishing a passion for that facetious gentleman. Oh, sir, I would that I could impress upon your feelings what I have suffered since that report has found its way to Alabama! I am engaged as leading actress at the Pickinsville Theatre, at a very liberal salary, but, owing to the bad system of paper currency, I have not yet received any emolument for my services. Since I became a member of Pickinsville Theatre, an excellent opportunity offered itself for my future establishment and comfort through life. Mr. Ranter, our principal tragedian, made me a tender both of his heart and hand: he is a most excellent actor, and in impassioned scenes (actually and in a most natural manner) turns as red as a Philadelphia brickbat in the face. Our manager says that 'he is all nature.' He has a very bold voice and powerful lungs, and can sing the 'Bay of Biscay' in a stronger key than any person I ever heard; and his voice is sweet and powerful as a bass trombone. His regard for me was testified by very delicate and feeling attentions, such as procuring for me 'porter sangaree,' fried oysters, and buckwheat cakes between the acts, or copying a part from some particular play for my study, carrying my wardrobe, escorting me to the theatre and home again, and many other gracious little offices of kindness, and for which I began to feel more than grateful. I had also another admirer in the person of Mr. Timotheus, leader of the orchestra, who is a man of great abilities, and who, in addition to the violin, performs also upon the Cornish trumpet and occasionally upon the Pandean pipes. He is a perfect Orpheus, and would be more than endurable did he not, whilst performing on the violin, indulge the exquisite sensibility of his nature by closing his eyes and making the most hideous grimaces. He conducts the orchestra with great precision and judgment: it consists of a violin, a key bugle, a fife, and a long drum; they sound very loud, and can play 'Hail! Columbia' and 'Yankee Doodle' in any possible key. The band is very much admired here, and the discriminating audience frequently testify their approval and evince their musical taste by a simultaneous encore upon hearing those beautiful airs, 'Long-tailed blue' and 'Sittin' on a rail.' But I digress. I may, at some future opportunity, forward to you a description of our company and its capabilities. My object in writing this epistle is to convince you that, since the appearance of the before-mentioned ill-timed reports of the newspapers, I have lost the attentions both of Mr. Ranter and Mr. Timotheus; and, although I have vowed by '*Sol and the presiding stars*' that the worthy editors of the newspapers have been misinformed, they have nevertheless ceased to opportune me with their vows of affection. Trusting that, for the recovery of my reputation, you will give this letter publicity, so that my friends may sympathize with me, I remain, dear sir,

"Yours, etc., the unhappy ELIZA PELLING."

This is the last I heard from the stage-struck Miss Pelling; and I may as well say here that it was soon afterward discovered that the writer of the PELLING LETTERS, which caused so many hearty laughs, was no other than our musical director, E. Woolf, Esq.

Of all the seasons I ever had any thing to do with, this of 1840 in Mobile was the most unsuccessful. The company was good, the stars were those who had been attractive elsewhere. The losses of the season's business could not have been less than $1000 per week!

One afternoon during this unlucky winter, as I was passing the lottery-office of Mr. Gregory, I was hailed by that gentleman and invited to purchase a ticket in a Baltimore lottery, *the only one he had left.* "It is sure to draw a big prize," said Mr. Gregory, "and I want you to have it." "What is the price of the ticket?" I asked. "Fifteen dollars," he answered. "Come, take it; it will make up all your losses, and make you a rich man." I confess I felt a desire to take it, and, what's more, I felt a presentiment it *would* draw a prize. "Come, say quick; if not sold at four o'clock—and it now lacks but five minutes of that hour—I have got to mail it to Baltimore." I took out my pocket-book and recorded the numbers, but, on counting the money I had with me, found I had but eleven dollars and a half, and told Mr. Gregory so. He said, "That makes no difference; you can take the ticket and hand me the balance to-morrow." But against *going into debt* for a lottery ticket my mind revolted, and I decided not to take it. "You'd better," said Gregory. ' "No," I replied, firmly, "I'm in debt enough already." "You won't take it?" "No." "Positively?" "Positively." "Well, here it goes, then, into the letter, and off to the post-office." And off it went, and off *I* went, congratulating myself on having successfully resisted the temptation to gamble; but many times that night I caught myself thinking, "If it *should* turn out a prize!"

Ten days afterward I was passing along Royal Street, when I was again hailed by Mr. Gregory: "Smith, come in here." I went in there. "What did I tell you about that ticket I offered you—that *last* ticket?" "You said I would be sorry I didn't take it." "Yes, I did, and I think you *will* be sorry when I tell you that *that* ticket —that very ticket—drew the $75,000 prize." I looked at my memorandum of the numbers, and compared it with the official drawing which Gregory placed in my hand, and, sure enough, the ticket which I refused to purchase had drawn the highest prize, and I had escaped being made a rich man.

A Slim House.

In the course of my management, it may be well supposed that the receipts have on some occasions been very small, but it has seldom happened that a performance has taken place without the presence of a dozen or two who paid for their admission. It will be seen by what I am now about to relate that in *one* instance a performance took place (at least in part) before about the smallest paying audience on record.

It was a very rainy night. The play advertised was TORTESA, THE USURER, with Mr. E. Conner as the star, after which the celebrated Herr Cline was to go through with his wonderful feats upon the tight rope—the performance to conclude with the farce of the RENDEZVOUS. Conner was to receive, and did receive, $50 for his night's services; Herr Cline was to get one *clear third* of the receipts, and our nightly expenses were two hundred and fifty dollars. Contrary to my usual custom, I did not go to the theatre in the early part of that evening, having no part to play in the first piece, but at about nine o'clock I wended and *waded* my way thither, and found the curtain just falling upon TORTESA. Herr Cline, dressed for his performance, met me as I entered.

"Oh! for God's sake," said he, imploringly, "don't compel me to dance to this handful of people; the night is so bad, there are not twenty dollars in the house. Come, let me off; dismiss the audience, and let them go home."

In this petition he was joined by all the actors who had parts in the afterpiece.

"This is all very well," said I, "to ask me to dismiss the audience; but you forget that this 'handful of people' have come nearly a mile through the pitiless storm, on the promise held out in our bills. No, no; if they require the performance in full, they shall have it. I am willing, however, if they are entirely satisfied to receive their money back—but not otherwise—to abandon the rest of the programme and let you all go home. Before putting the question to the audience, however, I must "look into the treasury."

As I passed across the stage to the box-office, I cast my eye through a hole in the curtain, and could discover in front not more than a dozen faces, counting bar-keepers, dead-heads, and all. I found the ticket-seller sitting on a high stool in the office, looking as melancholy as an undertaker in a healthy season.

"What are the receipts?" I asked.

"Guess," said he.

I guessed fifteen dollars.

"You have gussed just fourteen dollars above the mark," said the treasurer, throwing down two half dollars upon the shelf where the money was taken in.

"Only one ticket sold?" gasped I.

"Only one ticket sold," remarked he, coolly, again jingling the two half dollars upon the shelf, to give me full assurance that what he said was entirely true.

"And a five act play has been given to the one discerning and discriminating purchaser of that single ticket," I remarked.

"Exactly so," said the treasurer. "You know your rule, "*No postponement on account of weather.*"

"Stop a little," I said; "I'll go and see this gentleman—he may be bought off;" and away I went into the front of the house. I soon found the gentleman, seated exactly in the centre of the parquette, listening very attentively to "an overture by the orchestra," which formed a part of the programme upon the bills of the evening.

"Quite a rainy night, sir," I said, addressing the attentive listener to the overture, seating myself at his side. He did not reply except by a polite inclination of the head.

"You will, I hope, excuse the request I am about to make of you," said I, as soon as the overture was finished (another nod from the gentleman); "but it being, as I remarked, quite a rainy night, our efforts here" (pointing to the stage) "have not been so well rewarded as the attractions offered might seem to deserve" (another nod). "In brief, sir, *you* are the only individual in the house who has paid for admission (nod); and we ask it as a favor that you will receive back your money, and relieve our actors from farther exertions to amuse you this evening."

Several emphatic nods, and one or two shrugs of the shoulders, were the only responses I received to this civil speech. After waiting a moment for an answer *in words*, I ventured to repeat my request that he would receive back his money, at the same time tendering the identical half dollars the treasurer had been jingling the whole evening. The gentleman stared at the money, and then at me, as if he was at a loss to understand the meaning of my words and action. It suddenly occurred to me that the gentleman might be a little hard of hearing; so, placing my mouth close to his ear, I again requested his acceptance of the money, and demanded his permission to omit the remainder of the performance. Thus adjured for the third time, the gentleman at length opened his mouth, set his tongue in motion, and spoke as follows:

"Monsieur, je ne comprends pas un mot de ce que vous dites; mais je suppose que vous parlez de l'excellente representation, et dans ce cas je suis d'accord avec vous—c'est superbe! Monsieur Conner est un jeune acteur charmant, et Madame Farren est delicieuse!"

(Sir, I do not understand a word you say; but I suppose you are remarking on the excellent performance, in which case I agree with you—it is superb. Mr. Conner is a fine young actor, and Mrs. Farren is great.)

Mustering up the very limited knowledge I possessed of the French language, after imparting to him the information that I was one of the directors of the theatre, I managed to let him know what it was I wanted of him, which he no sooner comprehended than he acceded to my request with the greatest readiness, so far as remitting his claim to the rest of the performance; but in my bad French I found it utterly impossible to persuade him to take back his dollar. The polite Frenchman lighted a cigar at the door, hoisted his umbrella, and went forth, calling back to me, "Bon soir, Monsieur le Directeur; je n'ais pas compris le language de votre piece; mais elle etait bien jouee—tres bien jouee. Madame Farren est une splendide actrice. Bon soir, Monsieur le Directeur."

(Good evening, Mr. Director; I did not understand the language of your play, but it was well acted—very well acted. Madame Farren is a splendid actress. Good evening, Mr. Manager.)

So there had been a large company of actors and actresses performing a play in five acts to the bare walls, two or three bar-keepers, a dozen dead-heads, and one paying auditor, *who did not understand a word of the English language.*

CHAPTER XI.

THE regular season was brought to a premature close about the 1st of March, and the company proceeded to St. Louis, where it was hoped better business awaited it. I remained in Mobile, where, as if I had not had enough of the infernal bad business in the Swamp Theatre, it was concluded that, with a few regulars and two or three amateurs, a short spring season should be made, for the purpose of receiving Mr., Mrs., and Miss Barnes; and they came; and they performed—to such houses! Oh! it is impossible to extract from the old cash-book of that day the wretched figures which recorded the receipts. But we had some fun, notwithstanding, old Jack and I. For instance, our orchestra in the after season being composed of negroes and mulattoes, who did not understand a note of music except "by rote," it was my lot to sit in the leader's chair and accompany old Barnes in his comic songs! Be it understood, however, that I always sent out the colored band before I took my seat in the orchestra. In the SPRIGS OF LAUREL (as *Nipperkin*), old Jack had these lines to sing:

"A lass is good, and a glass is good,
And a pipe to smoke in cold weather;
The world is good, and the people are good,
And we're all good fellows together."

Which he changed a little, singing thus:

"A lass is good, and a glass is good,
And a pipe to smoke in cold weather;
Old Sol is good, and his fiddle is good,
But we can't draw the people together!"

Any one who has seen Jack Barnes play *Nipperkin* can imagine how this "brought down the house," when informed that it was only in the *repeat* that he made the change, and that he accompanied the words with appropriate winks and blinks at poor me, as I sat all alone by myself on a high seat, playing as well as I could under such circumstances, and playing left-handed at that!

Mrs. Barnes and Charlotte (bless them!) made the best of every thing, and every thing was bad enough, that is certain—never complaining of the wretched support they received from our inefficient part of a company and the ambitious amateurs before mentioned. We got through at last, and the doors of *that* theatre were closed, never to be seen opened again by me.

In a tight place pecuniarily.

As I intimated just now, the company had departed for St. Louis, and I was left to settle up matters in Mobile. Yes, to "settle up matters," without any means to settle up matters *with*. I am not going to inflict upon the reader a detailed description of the hell upon earth I had to endure during the two months I remained South. One little incident must serve as a specimen of the many "tight places" I had to squeeze through, and I select *it* because in so doing I am enabled to make mention of *one* of the many acts of kindness which made up the life of Thaddeus Sanford, a man whom I am proud to call FRIEND—now no more.

In 1835, '36, and '37, individually, and as a member of our theatrical firm, I had been in the habit of "changing checks" with Mr. Sanford and *one other individual* in Mobile, to any amount when needed, and it is but the sheer truth to say that the balance of obligation (though I did not consider it in that light) was not on my side. The checks were always paid, and, as we received no interest on our deposits in bank, it was just as well those friends should have the use of money we did not for the moment want as to let it lie useless in the coffers of the bank. The crash of 1837 brought every body up "all standing," as the saying is. There was no more changing checks with any body. Poor Mr. Sanford was deeply involved for friends, and the "other individual" could barely weather the gale, with every disposition on the part of the bank directors to help him through; but he *did* weather it, and at the time I am now writing of was flourishing in business about as usual, while Mr. Sanford was straining every nerve to meet renewals of the paper of his friends on which his name appeared as indorser for their accommodation.

Mr. Sanford was at this time President of the Bank of Mobile. It so happened that, at the burning of the Emanuel Street Theatre in the fall of 1838, he was on a rent note of ours for $5000, which note was now in the course of payment by renewals and reductions every ninety days. Up to this time the payments had been met; but now, my partner having found it utterly impossible to remit the sum from St. Louis, and all my untiring exertions to raise the amount in Mobile having proved unavailing, the note went to protest. I give the following note to the reader, with the assurance that coals of fire poured upon my head could not have caused me more pain than did the words of which it is composed:

"Mobile, —— —, 1836.

"FRIEND SOL,—The note of your firm, on which I am indorser, having gone to protest yesterday (probably through some mistake of yours as to the date of its maturity), it will be necessary to attend to it this morning, if I am to take my seat at the board this afternoon.

"In haste, yours truly, T. S."

If I lived I must raise the sum required before three o'clock. I only wanted the sum for thirty days, being about to visit Columbus, Ga., where I knew I *could* raise some money by sacrificing certain town lots I owned there.

I went to every man in Mobile who had the reputation of having money to loan, offering a valuable negro woman as security, and proposing to pay *any* rate of interest, and, among others, that "other individual" spoken of as having had the use of our surplus funds—and do you think I could raise $500? *I couldn't!*

At a quarter before three o'clock, with feet sore with walking and heart sore at the discovery that those I thought my friends failed me as soon as it was in their power to serve me, I sought out Mr. Sanford. The moment I entered the office he saw I was suffering greatly in mind, and, pointing to a chair, asked what was the matter.

"What's the matter?" I groaned, casting his note upon the table before him; "the matter is this: Your name is under protest as indörser on our note; you are president of the bank, and *for us* must vacate your office. That's the matter; for if it were to save my life I could not raise $500 this day."

He remained silent about a minute, looking more serious than I had ever seen him; then, taking a pinch of snuff (the idea of taking snuff at such a moment!), and looking into my face, he said,

"So you can't raise money for this renewal?"

"Exactly so," I replied, desperately; "I can *not!*"

"You have been trying, I suppose?" he quietly asked.

"*Trying?*" answered I, bitterly; "I have been all over the town—asked every friend—"

"Oh!" said he. "You have asked every friend?"

"Yes," I continued, "asked every one I *thought* to be my friend—offered any security, any rate of interest, and all, all in vain. I am ready to make an assignment of every thing I have on earth—break, fail—any thing. In short, I am desperate."

"Well, well," answered Mr. Sanford, in a tone a little sarcastic, I thought, "you have been to every friend, you say?"

"Yes, I say again, every friend."

"And can't raise $500?"

"And can't raise $500."

He here took another pinch of snuff, and, turning in his chair—

"By-the-by," said he, "have you dined?"

"Dined?" said I—"dined? Do you imagine I can *dine*, with my heart stopping up my throat? No, I have *not* dined, nor do I intend to dine this day, or *ever*, unless I can get over this difficulty." And I rose to depart.

"Stop a moment, if you please," said Mr. Sanford, motioning me to resume my seat. "This renewal is not yet provided for."

"I have told you over and over again that all is over. I can not raise the money, even by pledging my life's blood."

"And you have applied to *all your friends?* Look here, Mr. Sol Smith, I have a word or two to say to you. You have used me badly."

"I know it. You are under protest on my account."

"Hear me through," interposed he, laying his hand gently upon my arm; "I say you have used me badly, and, for the first time during our acquaintance of ten years, I must accuse you of not telling the exact truth."

"Sir—Mr. Sanford—" I began—

"Now I have a little piece of advice to give you at this time," he resumed, "and it is this: *You had better go to dinner; Mrs. Smith will be uneasy at your absence.*"

I rose from my seat in utter amazement. The language and tone he had assumed was any thing but agreeable to my ears at that moment, and I was on the point of making a somewhat angry remark, when he rose from his seat, shut his snuff-box, and went on with what he had to say without farther interruption from me.

"Now are not you a pretty fellow? I ask you, are you not? Here have you been running around the town until you are tired to death; letting your dinner-time pass without even sending home word, I'll be bound, that you would not be there; been to *all your friends*, as you say, endeavoring—in vain—to raise $500 for thirty days! I say here to your face, you have *not* been to *all* your friends. There is *one* friend you have not applied to, and that is Thaddeus Sanford, editor of the *Register*, and President of the Bank of Mobile! Now, what have you got to say for yourself?"

I was so utterly overwhelmed that I could say nothing for several moments. When I did get my tongue, I said that, knowing his numerous involvements for friends, and the large sums he was obliged to raise daily, it had never occurred to my mind (and it hadn't) to ask *him* for assistance.

"Ah!" said he, taking his hat and cane, "that's it—that's what I complain of—that you should have left me out—*me*, that, in your prosperous days, you have often accommodated—me, that you should have come to *first*. As for the large sums I have to raise, that is all true; but this $500 is but a drop in the bucket. There's the note for the renewal. Sign it. I will see that it is all right. You will be in funds and can repay me in thirty days. Now go and eat your dinner."

Now, reader, have I made myself understood in the foregoing sketch? Not if you are not impressed with a most favorable opinion of my old friend. Thank God! he has never lost a dollar through me, or any one connected with me. As for the sentiment entertained by me for the gentleman whose name I have so freely used on the last page or two, it may be judged of from the fact that one of my sons, now twenty-eight years of age, bears his name, and I pray that he may be always worthy to bear it. As for his noble godfather, he has gone to his rest in that undiscovered country where there are no notes to be renewed, nor any "shinning" to be done.

After making a trip into Georgia, where I was persuaded to "*give evidence*" to a public meeting of citizens that General W. H. Harrison was not an abolitionist, I was selected by the Odd Fellows of Mobile to deliver an address to the fraternity on the occasion of the anniversary of the formation of the Order in America, which duty I performed to the best of my ability, in the Unitarian Church. If there is any true PRACTICAL CHRISTIANITY in this world, it is my belief it may be found in an Odd Fellows' lodge.

My old friend J. M. Field took a benefit at the St. Charles, New Orleans, about the time I was to pass through that city, and as "I owed him a night" since 1835, when he played for me at my benefit at the Park Theatre, as well as an abundance of good will, I accepted his invitation to "appear" for him in one of my comic characters, *Timothy Sharp*, in Garrick's farce of the LYING VALET. On the day of my appearance the following welcome appeared in the *Picayune*, from the pen of Matt Field, at that time one of the editorial staff of that paper:

SONNET TO SOL.

Sol-fa! sol-fa! Ut, re, mi, fa, sol, la!
La, sol, fa, mi, re! How are you, Old Sol?
Welcome to Orleans, worthy old soul,
With your grave-looking phiz and your cimical poll;
Three cheers and a welcome hearty and whole,
"Red fire" and "a flourish!" Sol-fa, sol-fa!
And why does *Sol* pause on his brilliant way?
What Joshua orders the light to stay?
A *Joe*, not a Joshua, wins the ray
That beams in the night as well as the day!
To-night in "the Temple" *Old Sol* will shine,
Will "the Temple" be thus a dome of the *Sun?*
May *Sol*, the mortal, be ever divine,
And his course be bright till his race is run!

PHAZMA.

The bills truly stated it was my first appearance in the Crescent City for nine years. Joe had a fine house, but whether the receipts were increased at all by my being announced to appear, this deponent saith not, for he don't know. This was my *only* appearance upon the boards of the first St. Charles Theatre. Next day, in a notice of Field's benefit, by George Wilkins Kendall, the following sentence occurred:

"Old Sol's reception on this occasion was one of the most enthusiastic things which has occurred at the temple during the present season."

On the 7th of June I embarked on the steamer Chester, Captain Cable, for St. Louis, and next day began to witness the effects of the terrible tornado which devastated the city of Natchez (Miss.) on the 6th, in the shape of floating barrels, hams, dead poultry, lumber, etc., which seemed to fill the river. Wrecks of boats were continually passing down. It is said 104 flat-boats were moored at the landing when the storm commenced, and when it was over not one of them was to be seen, nor were they ever heard of afterward! On the 8th we stopped at the devoted city, and I wandered through its desolate streets. Whole trees, blown from the opposite side of the river, were strewn in the streets; also the carcases of numerous dead cows, oxen, and horses. What a sight! The theatre, at the opening of which I "assisted" twelve years previously, and which I had afterward managed for a season, shared the fate of nearly every other building, and was in ruins. Fragments of scenery, palanquins, canvas cottages, gates, paling-fences, castles, thrones, and painted stone walls lay scattered about the old grave-yard in most "admired disorder." On our way up we saw thousands upon thousands of trees which had been torn up by their roots by the tornado, in strips half a mile wide, and other thousands upon thousands which had been stripped of their bark!

As I was personally present in St. Louis but a very short time during the season of 1840, I propose to omit nearly all particulars of its progress. I went to Cincinnati and played an engagement of six nights with no great pecuniary results, though my benefit was very largely and fashionably attended, the entertainment comprising OF AGE TO-MORROW, in which I played five characters, THREE AND DEUCE, in which I personated the three brothers, and the comedy of the HYPOCRITE, in which I appeared as *Mawworm*—nine characters in all. It was the year of the "Hard Cider" campaign, and theatricals were dull every where.

I went to Illinois to inquire about my lands, and found they were so covered up by *tax titles* that they were considered worth very little indeed—not more than 25 or 30 cents per acre, at about which price I eventually sold them. They nominally cost me $4 50 per acre, but I was as glad to get rid of them *at any price* as I was to get rid of my newspaper in Mobile, in payment for which I had received them.

The theatre opened March 26. The stars were Conner, Llewellen (and horse), Le Compte, Eaton, Sinclair, the Barneses, Barrett, A. A. Adams, and Dan Marble. Adams had the talent to rival Forrest, but he was addicted to putting that "enemy in his mouth that steals away the brains." It is said JACK CADE was originally written for him by Judge Conrad.

Finding our firm becoming more and more involved in debt, and being considerably behind with the salaries of Mr. and Mrs. Farren, I proposed to let them have a beautiful building site I had purchased from Henry Chouteau, consisting of about three acres, on which I had intended to build a home for myself, if I should ever have the means to do so. They accepted, and the deeds were made out in Mrs. Farren's name, and a clause inserted in the deed of trust to secure the deferred payments, that any debts due to them by the firm for salary and benefits should go as so much on the payment. This turned out a good bargain for Mrs. Farren, and she richly deserves her good fortune, for a better woman does not walk the earth.

The season was an unprofitable one, but I passed most of the summer in making arrangements which were to lift from us a portion of the heavy burden of debt by which we were crushed down, as will shortly appear.

On one of the several trips I made on the river, I had a little experience which I will now relate:

Doctoring and Piloting.

Western men will remember the Vandalia, which was for many years a popular and profitable freight and passenger boat on the Mississippi, and which only ceased running in 1842 or '43. She was an "eight-day boat," and, before the introduction of the Scotts, Whites, Missouris, Shotwells, and Eclipses, was set down as a "fast-running" vessel, being rated at our insurance offices A No. 1.

The incidents I am about to relate occurred in the summer of '40.

The river was low, and it was not thought advisable to "run nights"—at any rate, until we got below Memphis.

There was considerable sickness among the deck passengers, and *as I was the only physician on board*, my time was much occupied in weighing out grains, drachms, and scruples of calomel, jalap, and ipecacuanha from the medicine-chest. This I got along with very well, having a faithful assistant in the clerk, Thompson, who went the rounds with me, and took particular care that my prescriptions were attended to.

One evening the steward came to my state-room and said that Captain Small desired to speak with me.

"What!" I exclaimed, more than half asleep—for, truth to say, I was snatching an afternoon's nap, to make up for the loss of rest caused by my professional attendance on the lower deck—"is the captain taken sick? Well, bring me the medicine-chest. How was he taken—fever? Tell Thompson to give him the usual dose of ipecac to clear out his stomach, and I'll be with him before it operates."

"You are mistaken, doctor"—(they all called me so during this voyage)—"the captain is not sick; he wants to see you on particular business."

"Oh, that's a different matter; ask the captain to come to my state-room."

Away went the steward, and soon after the captain made his appearance. After the usual inquiries by me of "How do we get on?" and "How far have we run to-day?" and an apology from him for disturbing me, the worthy captain opened the business of the evening.

"I fear our first pilot's in a bad way; nothing will stay on his stomach," remarked Captain Small, taking a chair, and stretching out his legs in the easy way that captains of steam-boats will. "Can't you do any thing for him?" he asked.

"I fear not," was my answer; "I have tried every thing in the medicine-chest: there is no hope whatever of his being able to take his post at the wheel during *this* voyage; soon as we arrive at New Orleans he had better go to Stone's Hospital; a month's care in that excellent institution will probably restore him."

"This is very unlucky," grumbled the captain. "I wanted to 'run nights' after to-night, and the second pilot can not stand double watches. What's to be done?"

I quietly told him I didn't know *what* was to be done, and supposed the *business* was over; but Captain Small lingered, gave two or three "ahems," spat violently through the state-room door and over the guards, changed his position several times, and at length continued the conversation:

"Mr. Sol, I understand that during your life you've turned your hand to 'most every thing."

"Well, I have—"

"I have heard of your merchandising, your preaching, your acting, and your *doctoring;* did you ever try your hand at PILOTING?"

"Piloting? Never—unless occasionally lending a hand at steering a flat-boat may be considered piloting."

The captain looked somewhat disappointed when he received my answer, and rose to depart.

"What is it you want?" I asked.

Looking up in my face, he said, "I want a pilot; we can't run nights with *one;* Jim being down with the fever, and there being no hope of getting him up, I thought if you—"

"Am I to understand you that, failing to get

Jim on his legs, you wish *me* to stand watch as pilot?"

"Why, if you *would*—Thompson says you *can* if you will."

"But what would the insurance companies say in case of accident?" I inquired.

"That's the point," answered the captain; "I wanted you to take Jim's place at the wheel, and *assume his character* at the same time. If you will do this, we shall save at least forty-eight hours between this and New Orleans."

I pondered a moment, and then asked when he wished me to assume my new duties.

"At the commencement of the dog watch—six P.M. to-morrow," he answered.

"Enough said; I'LL DO IT! Consider me engaged, and be so good as to send Thompson to me."

The captain departed, rejoicing at my ready acquiescence, and that same evening a report went through the boat that Jim was much better, and would be able to resume his post at the wheel very shortly. Thompson came to me, and I arranged with him to give our patients a farewell dose all round, and pronounce them cured.

Next evening I visited the pilot's state-room, and just before six o'clock the tall figure of Jim was seen (or was *supposed* to be seen) enveloped in his great-coat, a large hat pulled over his eyes, and a bandana tied around his neck, coat collar and all, stalking up to the wheel-house. A supposed sore throat, the effects of salivation, was a sufficient reason for the pilot's taciturnity during the remainder of the voyage.

In my character of doctor I had some difficult duties to perform; as an actor and manager, my path had not always been strewn with roses; as a preacher, I had perspired "a few;" and as a lawyer, some *hard cases* had come under my superintendence; but this PILOTING was by far the most difficult job I had ever undertaken. It was observable that, while passing over "bad places," *Captain Small was always in the pilot-house*, which was somewhat strange, as Jim was known to be one of the most careful and competent pilots on the Mississippi; but this was accounted for from the fact that the captain was young at the business, and *wanted to learn the river*.

We arrived without accident at New Orleans, and I do assure you I felt much relieved *myself*, though, as a faithful physician, I felt it to be my duty to recommend that poor Jim, *being much worse, from his constant attention to his duties at the wheel*, should be sent to Dr. Stone's hospital for a month. I am happy to say that Jim recovered, and was ready to resume his post in the wheel-house on the very next trip of the Vandalia. He never meets me without calling out, "SOL, WHO'S AT THE WHEEL?"

ACT FOURTH.

1840–1845.

CHAPTER I.

Since 1818 Mr. Caldwell had enjoyed a monopoly of the theatrical business in New Orleans, and although often urged by personal friends to try my fortune in that city, my friendly relations with Mr. Caldwell forbade any serious consideration by me of their tempting propositions in regard to a new theatre. In 1834 the management of the American Theatre in Camp Street had passed temporarily (by lease) into the hands of Messrs. Russell and Rowe, Mr. C.'s long-time stage-manager and treasurer; and it was supposed the Pioneer of the Drama in the South, as he had been called—not altogether justly, I think —would be content to "repose on his laurels and losses," consoled for the latter by the splendid fortune which was just then opening to him in the shape of a charter for lighting the city with gas. A decided reaction for the better in the business of the theatre, however—the new lessees having realized a profit of thirty thousand dollars in one season—seemed to beget in Mr. Caldwell a desire to resume the reins of theatrical management; and, being now abundantly able, in a pecuniary way, to carry out his views, the magnificent St. Charles was projected, and in an incredibly short period of time opened to the public. This latter event took place on the 30th of November, 1835. The decease of Mr. Rowe by suicide in Nashville, followed by that of Mr. Russell by congestion of the brain in New Orleans, threw the Camp Street Theatre again into the hands of its original occupant and owner; so that, with the two American theatres, Mr. Caldwell once more held undisputed sway over the destinies of the English Drama in the Crescent City. But, after a trial of one season, finding that two theatres in the second municipality were too many by one, he concentrated his forces in the St. Charles, and turned the Camp Street house into a ballroom! I am deterred by shame from writing or speaking of the *character* of the balls given within those once-honored walls, as reported to me by respectable citizens. Suffice it to say that one season of that sort of entertainment in that municipality was as much as the people of that part of the city would stand, and the old American was closed as a theatre, never to be reopened.

New Orleans and Mobile being neighboring cities, and the managers on friendly terms with each other, many civilities and courtesies were exchanged between them; and it is but just to say that we were greatly benefited by the good understanding which existed between the St. Charles and St. Emanuel managements, particularly in the facilities afforded us of obtaining any quantity of *star*-light we might need, without going far for it. Yet it sometimes happened that the St. Charles desired to relieve itself temporarily of some of its "lesser lights" when it did not exactly suit the convenience of the St. Emanuel to permit them to shine upon its boards, and this occasional reluctance of the St. Emanuel to accommodate itself entirely to the convenience of the St. Charles led to some slight dissatisfaction in the mind of Manager Caldwell, who was so used to exercise unlimited sway in his own realm that he began to think of extending his dominion a little. During a visit of mine to New Orleans in the winter of 1838–9, directly after the burning of the St. Emanuel Theatre in Mobile, we had some serious discussions relative to a proposition made to me by Mr. C. for the occupancy of several weeks of our season, then progressing in the Government Street Theatre, by certain members of his stock company *as stars*— Messrs. J. R. Scott, J. S. Browne, H. J. Finn, and others—fine actors, undoubtedly, and fully entitled to any position they might aspire to, but not at that time, managerially speaking, worth engaging on starring terms, to the exclusion of Ellen Tree, Forrest, and Booth, who were all three in negotiation with us; and, in the heat of our argument, Mr. C. said:

"I must control the drama in Mobile. Several citizens, not altogether satisfied with your management, have already expressed a wish that I would build a theatre there; and if you will not co-operate with me, and receive such persons as I choose to send you, I *will* build a theatre at once in your city."

To which I answered:

"All right; Mobile is open to you and all other managers. Our theatre being burned down and we being obliged to occupy the Government Street concern, a new theatre in a good location would take the business, and we should be driven from our ground and compelled to seek some other city for our operations. New Orleans is near, and might support a second theatre, which Mobile can not do; so, if you build a theatre in our city, you must not be surprised if we should attempt a competition with you here."

"Oh! of course, of course," replied Mr. Caldwell, "you have a perfect right to open a second theatre here, though *one* can scarcely be supported, except out of the manager's pocket; and it is certainly quite likely you can find friends to erect a house for you here in New Orleans, while you acknowledge your friends have failed to assist in rebuilding the St. Emanuel."

I replied, "I have frequently been invited to this city by responsible individuals, who, 'not altogether satisfied with *your* management,' as strange as it may seem to you, are willing to assist in building a new house."

"Threats have no effect on me," said Mr. Caldwell — "twenty theatres in New Orleans could not affect the St. Charles a jot."

"If any threats have been made, *you* have made them," I replied. "If I come here, which I shall not think of doing unless driven by you from Mobile, which, as I have already said, can not sustain two theatres, while New Orleans possibly *can*, it will not be with the expectation or wish to 'affect the St. Charles' at all, but simply with the view of repairing the losses at Mobile, if possible, and accumulating something for the support of my family and the education of my children."

"Very well," said Mr. C., and

"Very well," said Mr. S.

Nothing came of this at the time except the sending over Mr. Finn to lecture on astronomy (with illustrations), and Mr. Holland to exhibit, through a magic lantern, some dissolving views, which speculation not succeeding very well, and as I observed no signs of a new theatre going up, I thought no more of the matter, and felt safe in the prospect of a monopoly in Mobile theatricals for some time to come.

More than a year passed. The season at the fudged-up theatre in the Orange Grove (the successor of the Government Street house) of 1839–'40 having proved, as I have heretofore said, a most disastrous one, it seems my friend Caldwell thought the time had come when he could strike the threatened blow effectively, it being now quite certain our crippled condition would not permit us to build such a theatre as was required in Mobile. He therefore caused proposals to be privately circulated for the building of a "splendid new theatre," and invited the citizens to take stock therein. (I can not learn to this day that one dollar was subscribed by the worthy citizens who had so strongly invited him to build.)

I was in Mobile at the time, settling up the winter's business, but did not hear of the movement for several days after the paper had been put in circulation; but when I found out, through a friend, that a demonstration was assuredly to be made—I was in Mr. Sanford's editorial room at the time; it was a quarter past 12 o'clock P.M.—I scribbled and sent a note to my wife informing her I should be off in the 1 o'clock boat for New Orleans, and asking her to send my valise and a couple of shirts. At 1 I was off, sure enough, and at 8 o'clock next morning I was eating breakfast at the St. Charles Hotel in the Crescent City.

On Poydras Street, between St. Charles and Camp Streets, and on the site of an old cooper's shop, there was in the course of erection a large stable and circus by Messrs. Dubois & Kendig. Taking a look at it, I found that, with certain alterations which could easily be made, a tolerably commodious theatre could be formed out of this building. I sought the proprietors, had a talk with them, and a consultation with a few friends, and before any dinner went into my mouth that day a contract was made for the erection of a theatre, of which I was to be the lessee for five years at $10,000 per year. I took it in my individual name, not feeling that I had a right to involve my partner in the speculation, he being at the time 1200 miles away, but reserving for him the right to become joint lessee with me if he should elect to do so, thus making what I call something of a Christian return for his conduct in regard to the Mobile Theatre in the fall of 1834, when he leased that house *on his own account*, excluding me from a participation in the business of that season, in violation of an understanding that we were to join our forces and become joint managers.

Next morning the lease was duly executed; and this was the way there came to be a new American Theatre in New Orleans in 1840.

The theatre on Poydras Street, corner of St. Francis Street, New Orleans, I named the New American. During the summer a very excellent dramatic company was engaged, and a circus company, under John Robinson, besides. The parquet seats were so arranged that they could be taken up in a couple of hours, and replaced in three or four hours; so that, if it was desirable to exclude the equestrian performances any night, no one, on entering the house, would suppose from its appearance that any *sawdust* had ever been there. While this theatre was being built, Mr. Caldwell was pushing ahead his new theatre in Mobile, and opened it during that fall. It gives me no pleasure to write that he never made any money there.

The New American opened for the season on the 10th of November, 1840, and the receipts on the first night were $981 25. On the second night they fell down to $179! The circus company was brought in on the 19th (together with dramatic entertainments), the receipts on that occasion being $624. The business was almost universally good the whole season, particularly so during the engagement of that charming actress, Mrs. Fanny Fitzwilliam, and that capital comedian, Mr. Buckstone, who played about fifty nights, the horses being, of course, dispensed with during their engagement. TIMOUR THE TARTAR, MAZEPPA, the FORTY THIEVES, EL HYDER, and CATARACT OF THE GANGES were the "horse pieces" produced. The great feature of the circus company was a little boy, adopted son of our equestrian manager, whose name I changed from Jimmy Robinson to Juan Hernandez. He was a wonderful child, not over eight years of age, and could execute the most difficult and dangerous equestrian feats, besides singing comic songs and acting children's parts on the stage.

I mention, as a great error in management, the engagement of Fogg and Stickney's company and stud of horses for three months of this season, paying them $9300, which might just as well have been saved. They attracted not one person to the house, as I verily believe, and the expense of keeping an extra stud of useless horses was a considerahle item in the outlays from the treasury. A letter of mine to my old friend Woolf, our sometime leader, I here insert, to save some writing.

Sol. Smith to E. Woolf.

(Extracts.)

New Orleans, February 7, 1841.

* * * * * * *

In return for your theatrical information from the East, I must tell you something of the doings in this region.

The St. Charles has not been doing well this season, except during the engagement of Power, and two nights of a brilliant star which burst out upon the boards of the "temple" of the legitimate, bearing the sparkling name of Dimond, a nigger dancer, whose benefit was good; and after that, under the auspices of Barnum, they got up a humbug dancing-match for a pretended wager of $500 a side, and introduced a supernumerary, with his face blacked, to dance with and be beaten by that jewel of dancers, which produced a return (I should think) of nearly $2000!

The weather has been awful for the past six weeks, and has injured the business at both of the theatres very much. "Our house" has held up its head in all weathers, and breasted the storms manfully, not having experienced one failing week; yet our expenses are enormous. Since I last wrote you, we have added Fogg and Stickney's equestrian company to ours, at an expense of nearly $1000 per week. We did this more to prevent their going to the other house than from any gain we expected to derive from the arrangement. I took a circus company, made up of selections from the two troupes, to Natchez, where they performed seven nights to a receipt of $1850, which relieved the concern here of the expense of twenty-three people and twelve horses for nearly two weeks. The two equestrian companies are now performing in the Third Municipality, down by the United States Mint, but are not "coining money," as the saying is; yet the receipts there lighten the expenses here, while Mrs. Fanny Fitzwilliam, the "bright particular" luminary, is cramming the American every night, and throwing from 900 to 1000 people into fits (of laughter), and causing them to forget the hard times, short crops, and every thing else of a disagreeable nature. Isn't she a darling of an actress?

Mr. Caldwell is playing an engagement at his own theatre, but with poor success, which I am sorry for, for he *is* a fine comedian, and we shall not soon "look upon his like again." Mr. Ranger failed signally at the St. Charles; Buckstone ditto.

Fanny Ellsler has not arranged with any of the N. O. managers yet, but all accounts agree she is coming here soon from Havana. She now asks only $1000 per night! and it is at present uncertain which establishment is to be ruined by her. I hope not ours.

If I had not known you, I should have stared at your getting up "Norma" in so short a time; but, having witnessed your efforts on former occasions, when *we* have been in a hurry to produce musical pieces, I shall not wonder at any thing you may hereafter do in the musical line.

* * *

Commend me to my old friend Thorne. His quondam partner, Scott, opens the Natchez Theatre to-morrow night—a new one, altered from a warehouse, or something of the kind. I don't think he has made much in Vicksburg this season. Mud six feet deep all the time—so he says.

Wishing you every comfort and all happiness, which you so well deserve, I am most truly yours, SOL SMITH.

The trip to Natchez mentioned in the above letter resulted in a positive loss. Performances under canvas in Lafayette, and in the lower part of the city, also involved a loss. It actually rained every night a performance was attempted out of the theatre!

Among the members of our dramatic company this season were E. S. Conner, leading actor; Charles Webb, heavy man; Mrs. Farren, leading actress; Geo. P. Farren, first old man; Ben De Bar, light comedian and eccentric comedy; Mrs. De Bar, singing business; Mr. and Mrs. John Green, Mrs. Maynard, Mr. and Mrs. James Wright, and a great many others of sterling talent. C. H. Mueller was leader of the orchestra, vice Woolf (gone to Burton in Philadelphia), and C. L. Smith scenic artist. I remember a Mr. Sanky, who, if he had lived, would have become one of the best actors of old men the American stage ever produced. He made a great hit in the character of *Kecksy*, in the IRISH WIDOW, Mrs. Fitzwilliam performing the title rôle. Poor Sanky, at the end of the season, was persuaded to join a company for the West Indies, and on the voyage thither, or on his return trip, he was shipwrecked and drowned.

Ben De Bar was a London actor not long in this country. He was brought over by Mr. Caldwell in about 1837. In the St. Charles Theatre he played *Mazeppa*, doing his own riding up the "runs," periling his life every night for $18 per week, and enacting "walking gentlemen" in farces the same night, which he thought rather tough, and I have seen the glasses hop and jingle on the table in a little drinking-house called the "Green-room," under the effects of certain emphatic thumps he administered while drinking beer and uttering his just complaints to his fellow-actors. De Bar's greatest character, by all odds, at that time, was *Strapado*, the drunken corporal. I do think I have gone to the St. Charles Theatre at least twenty times to see this truly wonderful performance, and, moreover, I have no hesitation in saying that if Ben had not grown so fat and unwieldy, I would go twenty times more to see him play the same part. From the time he joined our company he seemed to become a different man. He dressed his characters well, played them well, and—no more glasses hopped and jingled in coffee-houses by reason of any thumps the tables got from Ben.

The good business at the St. Francis (New American) did not particularly please my old friend and manager Caldwell, and I don't wonder at it. The fact is, the St. Charles, until the arrival of Tyrone Power, was almost deserted. That great actor, whose mantle has never yet found a wearer, played to very good business for perhaps twenty-five nights, and then, he being gone, down fell the houses to almost nothing. This greatest Irish comedian that ever graced the American stage was lost on the steam-ship President.

The St. Charles succeeded in securing Fanny Ellsler, whose engagement ($3 admission, and seats sold at auction) was a great success; but *our* Fanny (Fitzwilliam) fairly divided the houses with Fanny the divine, and filled the St. Francis to overflowing at regular prices.

A detachment of the St. Francis company was sent to Mobile for the support of Mrs. Fitzwilliam during an engagement at the *Swamp* Theatre, which she very cheerfully entered into, in consequence of Mr. Caldwell having failed to accede to what she thought reasonable terms for performing at his new Mobile Theatre.

About $12,000 of our Mobile debts were paid out of the proceeds of this season in New Orleans, notwithstanding the enormous expenses involved in carrying it through.

Another letter to my friend Woolf is all I shall add relative to the season of 1840–41:

Sol. Smith to E. Woolf.

(Extracts.)

New Orleans, April 15, 1841.

FRIEND WOOLF,—Yours of the 4th instant is just received, and, to-morrow being set apart as mourning-day for our good President Harrison—the theatres to be closed—I have an unusual amount of leisure upon my hands, which I proceed to occupy in answering your "ti-tum-ti" epistle. To begin, then, I like those ti-tum-ti letters of yours vastly. They are written in that sort of familiar style which smacks with my taste exactly. What is the use of a roundabout, rigmarole way of expressing one's ideas and sentiments to a friend? Why not *write* as one *talks?* For my own part, I go in for saying what one has to say in as plain and straightforward a way as possible; and if I have any "style" in writing, it is the *talking* style. As for system in writing, I never had any. Even when editing a newspaper, many years ago, my manner was so rambling that it puzzled my readers at first to find out what I would be at; but they soon got to liking my queer style, if I may judge by the great and steady increase of my subscription-list. It passed for *eccentricity*, and that made it all right.

Last week I went to Mobile on business. The

new theatre there (Mr. Caldwell's), from all I can learn, has not paid its way this season. We gave it a hard dig in the ribs by taking over Fanny Fitzwilliam for two weeks, during which we drew the town up to Orange Grove, where is situated our *magnificent* temple. By the way, speaking of temples, we have dismantled that unfortunate theatre, the location of which, so completely out of town, was my partner's selection, not *mine*, please bear in mind, and rented it for—oh! ignoble purpose—a cotton warehouse.

Mrs. Fitzwilliam has been seriously indisposed for three weeks at Natchez, but has just returned to us, and appears on Saturday. Buckstone plays with her during the ensuing engagement. Fanny has done immensely here. Her fourth engagement exceeded either of the other three, and *the* Fanny [Ellsler] playing at the St. Charles at the same time! Speaking of the St. Charles, that house closed its doors for the season two weeks ago, but was reopened one night for the benefit of J. M. Field, on which occasion Ellsler danced the "Smolenski" for him, thus putting into his pocket over $1000. Glad of it, for Joe's sake; but it was a singular move her dancing for him, after all the ridicule he had been heaping upon her in his "Straws," as well as in a little piece he wrote and brought out at the St. Charles, entitled "G—A—G." The "divine" is now dancing at the Orleans Theatre, but her influence is not felt to the injury of our theatre up here in the American quarter.

Yesterday part of our company departed for St. Louis, where the season is to commence immediately. I remain here until the 10th of May, when up I go too.

I agree with you entirely in opinion regarding Mrs. Fitzwilliam. She *is* indeed, as you say, a charming actress and most amiable woman. She is a great favorite of mine, I assure you.

I am truly sorry to hear that my old friend Eliza Petrie "seldom looks pleasant." What can ail the girl? She must recross the mountains, and try the "great West" and the "sunny South" again. I can not answer your question, "Why don't she marry?" On the contrary, I repeat it, Why *don't* she? I presume she *has* her reasons. I never knew a girl that hadn't. I know this, and tell it boldly, she has had *offers* enough to satisfy any reasonable woman; but they popped, and popped, and kept on popping, all to no purpose. She wouldn't have *any* of 'em. Her time will come.

Friday morning, April 16.

Half-hour guns are firing; flags are flying at half mast; crape is being worn on many left arms; the shops are closed; theatres ditto; in short, this is mourning-day—*by appointment.* Yet here am I with pretty much the same feelings I had yesterday. Can't help it—can't get up a solemn feeling for the occasion, if I should die for not doing it. And this want of feeling is not caused by any want of respect for the memory of the old general. On the contrary, I verily believe there is not a person in the city who regrets more the loss of President Harrison than I do. He was for many years a neighbor of mine, and I am proud (now he is gone) to say he was a personal friend. But I can't mourn; it isn't in me. I had the pleasure of taking him by the hand last summer in Cincinnati, when he was pleased to thank me for the exertions I had been making in behalf of his cause in the South. Those exertions consisted of making two or three speeches at political meetings in Georgia, when dragged like a martyr to the stake, in which I summarily disposed of the charge of *Abolitionism* brought against him by his opponents. I was considered a good witness, having twenty-two years ago been hotly engaged against him on that very ground—that is, having written against him, and succeeded with my single paper in preventing his election, when a candidate for Congress, because of his friendliness to the Southern "institution" of slavery. But what care *you* for all this? I can't mourn.

With kind regards to family, etc., yours very truly, SOL. SMITH.

P.S.—Have you heard lately from the lovely *Eliza Pelling?*

CHAPTER II.

THE St. Louis season of 1841 commenced on the 26th of April, the theatre having been altered so as to admit of equestrian performances in a ring constructed for the purpose. The first appearance of the equestrians attracted an audience that paid only $169, and their second but $41! To the eternal credit of St. Louis, equestrian performances *in a theatre* were not encouraged at all, and it was found expedient to send off Robinson and his troupe, "horse, foot, and dragoons," on a traveling expedition through Ohio, Kentucky, and Tennessee. In this very dull time, all expedients failing to attract paying audiences, a very absurd thing was done in the engagement of a queer sort of a fellow by the name of M'Cumber, for the particulars of which the reader is referred to an article in the Appendix, headed "The Committee on Authors and Actors."

The Rev. Artemus Bullard, an excellent man, now no more, felt called upon to preach a sermon on the occasion of the death of President Harrison, and in that sermon he took occasion to attack the theatre as an institution in such a way that I felt a reply was called for. That reply I attempted to make, as follows:

Sol. Smith to the Rev. Mr. Bullard.

Rev. Sir,—A pamphlet with a yellow cover, neatly printed and stitched, was placed in my hands a day or two ago by a friend, purporting to be a sermon preached by you "On the Death of William H. Harrison," our late President. Being a great admirer of General Harrison, whom I had the happiness of personally knowing for upward of twenty years, I took the earliest opportunity of perusing the sermon, supposing the public services and private virtues of the deceased, together with his well-known character for piety, would be the theme of your discourse. To say that I was disappointed would but faintly express the feelings with which I rose from the perusal of your sermon. Instead of pointing out the course of the deceased patriot and soldier as an example worthy to be followed, I find your talents were employed on that melancholy occasion in attempts to decry the institutions of your country, the policy of its government, and the habits of its people. Had your efforts been confined to the pulpit, many persons might have doubted the policy, on *such* an occasion, of denouncing, in set terms, our public men, and the several classes of people composing the community in which you live; yet none, perhaps, would have been disposed to call you to an account for the course you thought proper to pursue, respecting, as all do, the highly responsible situation you occupy as minister of an enlightened congregation of Christians. But, having sent forth your sermon to the world *in print*, you must expect to be guarded by no immunity pertaining to the sacred desk; your work is now fairly the subject of remark and criticism; and you must not be surprised, reverend sir, if members of certain professions and classes which have fallen under your denunciations shall attempt to refute some of the sweeping charges you have preferred against them.

The Press has already found an able champion in the editor of the Republican. Having been myself connected, in an humble way, with that branch of our national literature, I could not but feel highly gratified at the manly course of Colonel Chambers in relation to the sermon I have just been reading. Relying on the intimation he has given of his intention farther to pursue the subject, I do not feel called upon to discuss all the various topics which you have *stepped out of your way* to animadvert upon. Between you and I, reverend sir, it appears to me, *we* are not the most proper persons in the world to decide upon questions of governmental policy. Besides, no good could possibly come from such a discussion—we could never agree. For instance, you disapprove of the purchase of Louisiana and Florida; *I* have always thought the acquisition of this immense country, securing to us an outlet to the Gulf of Mexico, of incalculable advantage to the United States, to say nothing of the field it opened to the farmer, the mechanic, and professional man. Were it not for the purchases from France and Spain, I believe you and I would never have been heard of; we should probably have been, at best, but obscure individuals; whereas, the great West being open to us, we have both acquired some notoriety at least, if not popularity. Again, you do not approve of the "treatment of the Indians upon our borders," while I have always considered the policy pursued by the government toward them as humane and parental—always excepting the encouragement given to *missionaries* to reside among them. The illustrious individual whose funeral sermon you professed to be preaching went heart and hand with the government in the "treatment" complained of, and had a greater personal agency in forming treaties with them, extinguishing their titles to lands—which you term deluding them into a snare, where they could be robbed at pleasure—than any other man. I do not partake in your fears that "a war with England" would cause the "turning loose of thousands of abused savages," or have the effect of "arousing millions in our midst (meaning our slaves) to throw off their fetters," or that "a discussion of what shall or ought to be done with them (the negroes) may involve us in a civil war, or dissolve the Union," though I verily believe that such a result would be far from disagreeable to certain "brethren" at the East and North. Finally, while I have always believed TRUE RELIGION to be essential to the happiness (here and hereafter) of every individual in the nation, I have been and am so irreligious as to consider a "national religion" quite unnecessary. Entertaining opinions on these subjects so opposite to yours, a discussion with you on those points could result in no good. We should gain nothing, and might lose—our tempers. Leaving, therefore, political questions to those who are disposed to discuss them, I proceed to the main object of this letter, which is to notice four lines of your *funeral* sermon, which you have devoted to Theatres. They are here quoted:

"*Our theatres have become too degraded for any purpose but the exhibition of brute animals and the most abandoned of the human family, male and female.*"

Now, my reverend friend, this is rather a sweeping charge, for, in effect, it is pronouncing all persons connected with our theatres to be the "most abandoned of the human family!" And I feel called upon, in behalf of my professional associates, most solemnly to deny the accusation you have thus made against them as a class. You ought to know that the "profession" is not accountable for the actions of individuals attached to it more than you and other good men are accountable for the peccadilloes of wicked priests. If our theatres are degraded by the introduction of "brute animals," the degradation must be attributed rather to the taste of the public than to the wishes and inclinations of the directors.

In your denunciations against other classes you have thought proper to make "exceptions," but in the instance of theatres, "with one fell swoop" you denounce its professors as the "most abandoned of the human family." How do you arrive at this conclusion? Have you any personal acquaintance with any ONE of those beings who nightly "exhibit" themselves in the theatre of your own city? Have you HEARD any of them accused of crimes which place them in the *lowest* grade of the human race? If there be *one* of the ONE HUNDRED employed in the St. Louis Theatre who can be justly charged with any offense against the welfare of society—with any crime which would render him or her deserving of being termed the "most degraded of the human family," or with conduct calculated to bring disrepute upon the dramatic profession, *let the proofs be given*, and that individual shall be "cast out" from the community of players just as surely as you would "read out" an offending brother from your church.

In that excellent book which you seem to think has been "abandoned" by our chief magistrates for more than thirty years "until this spring," there is a sentence something like this: "Judge not, lest ye be judged." Did you think of this precept when you gave utterance to the above sweeping denunciation? Have you visited the theatre in this city? Have you *ever* visited a theatre? If not—as I shrewdly suspect is the case—do you consider yourself a proper judge of the conduct of those against whom you have passed sentence? "Let him who is guiltless cast the first stone!" was the mild sentence of the Master you profess to serve; but here are you casting a volley of stones into a community of individuals who never injured you in word or deed, without first ascertaining *their* guilt, and without reflecting that *you*, by the very act, may be offending against *his* precept.

As I said before, I do not wish to enter into a discussion with you. I content myself with a simple *denial* of the justice of the charge brought against the "community of players" by you in your pulpit, which charge you have repeated in an aggravated form by sending it forth to the world through the press. If you have any proof to offer in support of your charge, *produce it.* Until such proof be adduced, the conduct of those you style "the most abandoned of the human family, male and female," will weigh greatly against your unsupported assertions. "The tree is known by its fruits."

Recommending to you the cultivation of more charitable feelings toward your poor, sinful brethren of the human family, I remain, reverend sir, your well wisher, SOL. SMITH.

June 1st, 1841.

[The publication of the above letter elicited the following remarks from the New Orleans Picayune:]

"☞ A letter from Manager Sol Smith appears in the St. Louis Bulletin, in which the worthy humorist defends manfully his profession from the violent abuse of some ill-advised preacher, who, in pronouncing a sermon upon the death of the late President, found it necessary to denounce perdition upon a large class of his fellow-beings. Old Sol addresses the reverend gentleman in a strain of caustic but polished reproval, and the style, thoughts, and Christian-like spirit of his letter all present so forcible a contrast to the fire and brimstone character of the sermon, that, without close attention, one would be apt to mistake the preacher for the player, and the player for the preacher. It is a sad error theologians fall into in launching these loose and ill-considered thunder-bolts at the drama; they betray by it their superficial knowledge of the subject; for, were they aware of how much mental and moral force can at any moment be lifted in its defense, and the expanded minds that are ever ready to support it, they would be cautious of rushing into so blind a position. While we see the most enlightened expounders of the Christian faith constantly indebted to Shakspeare for sentiment and moral, it must surprise us to hear the lesser lights of the pulpit taking in hand the vengeance of the Most High to hurl at one of the oldest and most firmly rooted institutions ever cherished by civilization."

The fall season was a slight improvement on that of the spring and summer, the price of admission having been reduced; but still the profits amounted to but a few hundred dollars, to offset the loss of as many thousands up to the closing in the summer. Mr. Hackett played a fair engagement, and Mrs. Farren (as always) had a good benefit, which was really the only great house of the season.

I here insert a couple of letters written to my musical friend, who had followed the fortunes of Manager Burton from Philadelphia to New York, and in the latter city shared in the misfortune which overwhelmed all concerned in the National Theatre, Leonard Street:

Sol. Smith to E. Woolf.

St. Louis, June 25, 1841.

Your highly complimentary letter of the 15th instant is just received. You give me too much credit for my letter to the parson. It was scribbled off one morning during the bustle of business, and sent to the publisher without reflection. If I had had the slightest idea of its producing the "sensation" it did here, I should have composed it with more care. However, it answered the purpose intended — it wakened the people up a little; and my friend Cady, of the Bulletin, in which it appeared, sold 350 extra copies of the paper containing it, as he informed me. You are not the only one whose good opinion I value that has complimented me on this occasion. The New Orleans Picayune has spoken in very high terms of the letter, particularly of its *tone*. Well, let it go for what it is worth.

"Things go on most execrably here in Syracuse, my Pythias"—or, rather, in St. Louis — in the theatrical line. We have sustained heavy losses during the season just closing; and if we experience no favorable change during our fall season, the "fortune" every body insists we made in New Orleans, and every body can't be wrong, will be soon swept away by the expenses of this extensive establishment. By-the-by, speaking of extensive establishments, this *is* an extensive country, isn't it? — this America. Englishman as you are, confess it! We have very clever rivers out here in the West (for a new country), and first-rate prairies, and pretty large forests, and some tolerably large farms—is it not so? But, oh vain boast! * * * *

Fanny Fitzwilliam has brought us up a little during the present week. She and Buckstone "go it" together next week, and then we close for the season. You must not be very much surprised if I pop in upon you some July morning in New York, and frighten all the little Woolves with my woe-begone countenance.

If it please the Lord to let me out of the vortex of management next year, I intend to establish a newspaper office in which I can employ my boys, now increased to six, and I hereby bespeak you for a correspondent; therefore hold yourself disengaged, if you please.

Sunday morning, June 27.

I am sorry for poor Burton—no, not *poor* Burton; I beg his pardon. I see by the papers he don't like the adjective "poor" attached to his name, and I don't blame him. A curse upon the cold commiseration of the world, say I. It don't *mean* any thing. But when I say poor Burton, I mean nothing more than an expression of sympathy for him on the occasion of the destruction of the National Theatre by fire. I hope the newspapers magnify his losses.

We have a prospect of having Eliza Petrie in N. O. next season. The worst of it is that you Eastern managers give (or *promise* to give, which, in effect, is the same thing, so far as making engagements at the South is concerned) such high salaries that we Western and Southern managers are obliged to go beyond what our business is likely to afford, and our Eliza has got tolerably high ideas from the fact that she has been rated on Burton's salary-list at a pretty round figure. At Niblo's she does *get* a very good salary; but, that establishment aside, I do not conceive there is any Eastern theatre which should be made a guide for ours, inasmuch as they all (it appears to me) *close* whenever it suits the convenience of the managers, without the least consideration for their companies, while we go on sometimes at a loss of thousands. Respects to Mrs. Woolf and all the little Woolves, and I remain, etc., SOL. SMITH.

Sol. Smith to E. Woolf.

(Extracts.)

St. Louis, October 21, 1841.

* * * * * * *

The half-price system successful—gained $600 or $700 on the season, in place of *losing* as many thousands, as we did in the spring season. We hear of extensive arrangements by the "Emperor," but feel quite confident of being able to compete successfully with him in New Orleans, having a good stock company. Weather almost freezing; thermometer at 40°. I can not stay long *here*, fever or no fever *there*. Hackett begins to-morrow night, and closes to-morrow night week. Then two benefits are to *come* off, and then we are to *go* off, certain.

P.S.—Oh, I had nearly forgotten to tell you we have got up a most exquisite burlesque opera called SCHINDER ELLER, or the DOCTOR AND THE LITTLE DUTCH SLEEPER — words paraphrased from Cinderella by Matt. Field—music adapted from the opera. It was highly successful here for four nights, and we expect great things of it in New Orleans, where the scene is laid, especially if Ellsler goes to the St. Charles again. *She* is the *Cinderella*, and Dr. Stillman, the sarsaparilla-man, the *Prince*. It is very funny. It plays an hour and a quarter—in one act. We have bestowed considerable pains on the getting up of this piece, and some of the "effects" are ludicrous in the extreme. Only think of Dr. Mesmer (in place of the *Fairy Queen*) being projected out of an alligator's mouth, head foremost, and alighting on his feet in an attitude! *Schinderella* comes up standing in a tub of sarsaparilla! Frogs (very large ones, with glistening eyes, made of any quantity of foil leaf) are seen swimming in the swamp; steam-boats passing and repassing in the lake beyond; railroad cars running down and from the lake, etc., etc. In the last scene a magical change takes place. The doctor's laboratory is transformed into the ballroom of the St. Louis Exchange Hotel, and, after the Cracovienne by *Eller*, a *pas de quatre* takes place between two bottles of sarsaparilla sirup and two boxes of sarsaparilla pills! I take some credit to myself for the "effects," which are mostly of my own contriving. * * * *

Yours most truly, SOL. SMITH.

CHAPTER III.

THE St. Francis opened on the 20th of November, 1841, for its second and last season, with the comedy of the HEIR AT LAW and the farce of 'TIS SHE. Receipts, $400. The equestrian troupe, "rough and ragged" from their tour through Ohio, Kentucky, and Tennessee, joined us, on our way down the river, at Memphis, bringing no replenishment to our exhausted treasury, but, on the contrary, every equestrian had in his pocket lots of "bills receivable," signed by our agent, J. P. Baily, for salaries due. To be plain, the summer expedition of the equestrians had brought us in debt. The rich costumes with which they started out were threadbare and shabby on their return, and instead of entering the city in procession, as was their wont in country towns, they were smuggled off the boat at Lafayette, and quietly marched to the city during the darkness of night, and directed not to show themselves until refitted and reconstructed. It was a full week before the ambitious riders were allowed to "appear."

We found the St. Charles, on our arrival, "going it" exclusively with circus performances, Mr. Caldwell having engaged Fogg and Stickney, with their troupe of equestrians, who were to perform alternately in New Orleans and Mobile. This move of Mr. Caldwell resulted in a miserable failure. Equestrianism was at a discount in both cities.

Our excellent dramatic company was increased this season by the return of Miss Petrie, and the engagement of James Thorne for low comedy, and we played LONDON ASSURANCE, MONEY, and other new pieces in a style quite unexceptionable—in every instance getting ahead of the St. Charles in their early production.

We had Mr. Joseph Foster to "get up" showy pieces, and he got them up in the most extensive and expensive manner. The NAIAD QUEEN, NAPOLEON, DICK TURPIN, and other grand dramas, followed each other in "rapid succession," as the underlinings have it; and, though the houses were generally good, the profits were small, owing to the lavish expense bestowed upon the "getting up" of the great scenic pieces.

Sol. Smith to E. Woolf.

Natchez, Miss., January 2, 1842.

DEAR WOOLF,—After most sincerely wishing you and yours a happy New Year, I proceed to resume my part of the correspondence which has been happily established between us. "What the d—l!" you will say, on reading the date of this letter, "is the old fellow doing up at Natchez?" I'll tell you, my friend. I am up here with a troop of horse! In plain words, and not to keep you in suspense, I am here superintending the "fiscal" affairs of our equestrian company, now performing in the city of the tornado. We engaged Levi North for two weeks at a very high rate, and thought it would be better that he should perform half of the engagement here. I fear we were mistaken. My window looks out upon our canvas, which is actually covered with *snow!*

I suppose you will expect some account of New Orleans theatricals. Mr. Caldwell, imagining our great success last season was attributable to the *horses*, engaged Fogg and Stickney's *stud* for the legitimate St. Charles, and actually opened that splendid establishment with equestrian performances only! In about a month he began to mix in some dramatic pieces, and the lovers of the "legitimate," who thronged the temple at the rate of about 120 a night, were regaled with those finished productions of genius called farces, after witnessing the wonderful tricks of the horse "Champion," and listening to the refined songs (or national anthems) from a professor of Niggerology, interspersed with the chaste witticisms of the clown. The dramatic pieces thus produced were of the highest order, which you will readily admit when I tell you that the ever-to-be-remembered comedy of the RENDEZVOUS headed the list. The BATH ROAD, or TOM AND ELLEN, had a *run*, and the TURNPIKE GATE was produced with a new mug and first-rate great-coat (with extra capes) for *Crack*. HIS LAST LEGS (legs by Gentleman George) followed, and *ran* through a week. Then came the Dog-star Bruin, followed by Herr Cline, Master Wood, and a Swiss family; afterward Hackett, who drew a $600 house at his opening, played to $200 audiences during a week, and had $700 at his benefit. All this time the orchestra was led (?) by Signor Cioffi, a fine musician certainly, and an excellent player of the trombone, but about as fit to *lead* an orchestra as the writer hereof.

The American, finding the "San Carlos" going it so strong on the *horses*, opened and played during the first month *nothing but the legitimate* — comedy, tragedy, melodrama, OPERA (yes, you may laugh), and vaudeville were the order of the day. We sent the equestrians to Lafayette—to the Third Municipality—any where, to keep them away from the theatre. The copy of the comedy of LONDON ASSURANCE was received on a Saturday night. We rehearsed it, had new scenery and appointments prepared for it, and produced it in good style the next Sunday but one, anticipating its production at the St. Charles, where it had been underlined for a month. The comedy was eminently successful with us, being well acted throughout. Farren played *Sir Harcourt* most admirably; Mrs. Farren, *Lady Gay*, most dashingly; Miss Petrie, *Grace Harkaway*, most acceptably; Mr. Sanky, *Max Harkaway*, most respectably; Mr. Thorne, *Mark Meddle*, most excruciatingly, and Ben De Bar, *Dazzle*, most unexceptionably. We played it four nights to increasing audiences, leaving but three nights for the BARBER (which we had been rehearsing several weeks) before the commencement of the Ravel family. The St. Charles played it *five* nights to *de*creasing audiences, and gave it up, but it was revived at that house at a later period of the season with much better success and a much better *Dazzle*—J. S. Browne.

* * * * * * *

We have some idea of taking our equestrians to Havana. They are a dead weight to us here.

Ever truly yours, SOL. SMITH.

We went to Havana, the horses, equestrians, my son Mark, and I, and here is what came of it:

Don Hemit in Havana.

To insure a proper understanding of this sketch, it is necessary to explain that the uncommon name of "Smith" is pronounced by the Spaniards "Hemit." Bills posted at the corners of the streets in Havana, during the winter of 1842, announced, in good Spanish, that "los Cirque Olympique Americano" would open on such a night, by permission of the Captain General of Cuba, etc. It fell to my lot to go over to the Spanish island as "impressario" of a circus company, consisting of Levi North, *Otto Motty*, Young Juan Hernandez, John Robinson, Eaton Stone, Dennis ditto, and about twenty others of less note, together with a host of grooms, and something like forty horses. Instead of realizing a profit of $10,000, as we expected, we were obliged to submit to a loss of about $4000. But that is all over, and it is not my intention to dwell upon a subject so disagreeable to remember.

After the usual difficulties of custom-house inspections and examinations, we effected a landing—"horse, foot, and dragoons." In transacting business with the commercial house to whom we were consigned, I found that the name of Sol Smith had become changed to DON SOL HEMIT, in which style I was addressed, while on the island, by all who had occasion to transact business with the concern.

The first thing that strikes an American on arriving at Havana is the great difference between a free and a despotic government. It appears a little strange to a republican to meet a soldier under arms and on duty at every corner and at every crossing. If you visit a theatre, you see one of these interesting gentlemen stationed at the entrance of each box! They are quite inoffensive, however, and in a day or two they cease to annoy you; you pass them as you would so many posts.

The grand entrances of the private dwellings in the city serve for the ingress and egress of the family, servants, horses, and carriages! One morning, while a large party were at breakfast in our boarding-house, a splendid stud-horse was brought in by a groom and paraded around the table for the inspection of General Harney, who wished to purchase an animal of the kind.

It is the duty of the keepers of boarding-houses and taverns to report to the government every person they entertain and lodge each night, and they are accountable to the treasury of Queen Isabel the Second for the sum of fifty-two dollars for every one that dies in their houses. Whenever a foreigner leaves the island he is obliged to obtain a certificate from the *dead office* that he is alive, another from the custom-house that he is clear of *its* books, and yet another from the Captain of Partida (I think that is his title) *that he owes no debts!*

On the opening night of the "Cirque Olympique," a company of twenty soldiers, under the command of a sergeant, marched up to the box-office, and reported to *Don Hemit* that they came by command of the alcalde of the quarter to preserve order in the house, and to guard the box of the governor, for which service the sergeant intimated, through an interpreter, that he expected a *gratification* from Don Hemit. In reply, I directed the interpreter to say to the sergeant that there was no occasion for his or his soldiers' services; and that, if the governor's box required guarding, they were welcome to guard it, *but not at my expense;* and that, so far from *gratifying* them (which the reader ought to be informed meant making them a present of *an ounce* of gold), it would afford me, Don Hemit, a great *gratification* if they would march back to their quarters, and keep out of my sight for the remainder of their natural lives. The worthy sergeant touched his cap with the back of his hand by way of salute, wheeled his command to the right about, and marched off. After the departure of the soldiery, two *ministers* presented themselves, and demanded a gratification of a quarter of an ounce each for sitting each side of the alcalde's box, and this imposition I was obliged to submit to every night of performance.

The contract with *Otto Motty*, the man that plays with cannon balls, was to the effect that he was to perform four weeks in the island of Cuba, and receive for his services $1000. At the end of our second week I found that it would be policy to cut off the last week of our season, and by that means save about $1500. As a compromise with Motty, I proposed to pay him $750 for the three fourths of the time agreed on, and $250 on our return to New Orleans, where he should perform the other week. *This he agreed to;* but, after all arrangements were made to close up the disastrous season, and leave the island in the steam packet, he concluded to act the rascal, and demand the full amount of his bond. He accordingly filed his claim of $500 with the proper authorities, and the passport of Don Hemit was stopped! Here was a dilemma. I had procured (by the help of sundry ounces of gold) passports for the whole company and stud of horses, but Don Hemit was ordered not to depart the island until the demand of the thrower of the cannon balls was fully satisfied. It was the night previous to the day of our intended departure that the decree of the governor was communicated to me. What could I do? Obtaining a hearing of the case was out of the question, it appeared; and, even if the matter *could* be brought to adjudication, I had no proof of the compromise I had made with the Dutch Jew, the evidence of my son and clerk (who heard the new agreement) being excluded by the Spanish law, while he had our original contract which called for the fulfillment of its provisions *in Cuba.* At last, after much reflection, it occurred to me that if I should bring a suit against *him*, I could at least obtain an immediate *hearing* of the case, and possibly I might so *mix matters up* before the alcalde that the judgment might work a release of the prohibition to quit the island. I sought out a *minister*, and placing half an ounce of gold in his hand, desired him to arrest Otto Motty at the suit of Don Hemit for breach of contract, etc. In about a quarter of an hour the defendant was in the presence of the alcalde, whose attendance at that late hour was secured by means of *an ounce* sent into his private room by the *minister* whose services I had secured as above stated, and the trial began. And oh! *such* a trial! The lawyers, parties, and spectators all kept their seats while they made their statements. Otto Motty insisted upon his bond, and demanded $500 of Don Hemit (he had received $500, and there was really $250 due), while I demanded that he should go to New Orleans and perform a week before he should be entitled to the full amount which we had agreed to pay him. We sat and jabbered there about an hour, when, looking up, I discovered that *the alcalde had left the room!* My friendly minister informed me, on inquiry, that the worthy magistrate had gone to supper. Quietly slipping *an ounce* into the minister's hand, I desired that disinterested functionary to pass it in to the alcalde, with my compliments, and ask him if he was ready to decide the case. The minister returned almost immediately, and reported that the alcalde had *decided* that we must *arbitrate* the matter in dispute on these conditions: Don Hemit could not compel Otto Motty to leave the Spanish dominions, and Otto Motty could not compel Don Hemit to pay him for services which he had not rendered. The clerk instantly recorded this decision, or whatever it may be called, and I was informed that by paying $250 into the court I should satisfy the judgment, and be entitled to my passport. "Here is the money," said I, in high spirits at the result. "I shall not take it," indignantly replied old Motty: "I shall have my tousand dollars." "No you won't, old fellow," said I; "here is the decree of court." "But," pleaded the Dutchman, "I will go with you to Orleans and play the other week, as you proposed, and get the other $250." "Oh no," was my answer; "the judgment of this court is final: here is your money; take it, and be thankful." A question here arose about the *costs.* The clerk and ministers said Don Hemit must pay them, as the judgment was against him. I turned to Otto Motty and said, "*You* must pay these costs." Of course he declined; so I called to my minister to bring me a fee bill, which I found amounted to just two ounces ($32). I then asked for a bit of paper, and wrote as follows:

Don Otto Motty—

To Don Sol. Hemit, Dr.

For transporting cannon balls from ship to the Cirque Olympique, and thence to the Plaza de Toros, several times .. $32 00

Handing this to the minister, I told him to arrest Mr. Motty and *stop his passports.* In a moment the man of cannon balls saw the predicament he was in, and *agreed to pay the bill without farther question.*

Next day, at five o'clock P.M., all things were on board the good steamer Alabama, and we were ready for a start. Just as I was stepping on board the small craft which was to carry us to the ship, Otto Motty was seen hurrying down past the custom-house with a cigar in his mouth, and his passport, which he had with great difficulty obtained, in his hand. He spoke to some one of our party, and observed that he feared being too late. "Too late for *what?*" I inquired. "Too late for the steam-boat," he answered. I here commenced whispering with the circus people, pointing occasionally to Otto Motty, who was in a small boat alongside of us during our row out into the harbor. We entered the steamer at the same time, and Robinson (the equestrian manager) took Otto Motty mysteriously aside and whispered in his ear, "Beware!" The same warning was whispered by other members of the equestrian corps in various tones. Otto Motty at last ventured to inquire of one what he was to "beware" of. He was then gradually let into the secret that it was the intention of Don Hemit to throw him overboard during the voyage, with his cannon balls attached to his feet as sinkers! At first he was incredulous, but all the circus people assuring him in the most solemn manner that there was no mistake about it, he at length determined that he would not risk his life in the same ship with me. The last I saw of him, he and his cannon balls were in a small boat making their way toward the shore, while we were in our magnificent steamer, leaving the beautiful and unequaled harbor of Havana, and passing the frowning Moro Castle.

Arrived at New Orleans, I shaved off my whiskers and mustaches of a month's growth, and abjured forever the cognomen of DON HEMIT!

Sol. Smith to E. Woolf.

New Orleans, March 12, 1842.

FRIEND WOOLF,—I have been back to my own native soil nearly two weeks, and take some shame to myself for neglecting to reply to your last valued epistle. I may as well confess the truth, which is this: I had inadvertently permitted my *mustaches* to grow to such an enormous length while on the island of Cuba, that, when returned to the States, I found I could speak and write *nothing but Spanish!* I deemed it would be a useless shedding of ink to write you until I had parted with the aforesaid. They *came off* yesterday evening about gun-fire. So here I am again, restored to my vernacular, and ready to inflict three pages of scandal, or whatever else my pen may happen to run into.

You will no doubt expect a full and explicit description of Havana and the whole island of Cuba—its customs, amusements, etc. It is but a reasonable expectation, and I proceed to give it in as concise a way as I know how:

DESCRIPTION OF THE ISLAND OF CUBA.

Cuba is a Spanish island, governed by military people, 25,000 of whom favor the country with their presence. The inhabitants eat, sleep, smoke, and ride in volantes drawn by horses a good way ahead, with tails braided and hitched to the saddle-bows, which horses are ridden by black men dressed in livery, with jack-boots and long spurs. The amusements of the people consist of the opera, Spanish plays badly acted, bull-baiting, and cock-fighting.

END OF THE DESCRIPTION OF THE ISLAND OF CUBA.

We lost about $4000 by the expedition, and you may be sure your humble servant will not be in a hurry to repeat his visit to the "Queen of the Antilles."

The opera from Havana is in full blast at the St. Charles. The houses are pretty good, but the expenses must be enormous, and above the receipts. *Our* business is tolerable only—Mrs. Fitzwilliam and Buckstone, the reigning stars at present, as great favorites as ever. The St. Charles closes next Friday. We shall endeavor to keep open till May, but may not be able to do so. The banks are all bursting up! * * *

Tuesday morning, March 15.

The St. Charles Theatre and Arcade Baths were burned to the ground on Sunday night last! You will hear of this a day or two before this reaches you, but I could not send a letter without mentioning an event of such magnitude—an event deplored by every one, and, I think, by none more than the writer. The Gas Company lose $30,000 only, it is said, the balance being insured. They had purchased the building (taken it for debt) a short time before the fire. I have this from Dr. Rogers, superintendent of the Gas Works. Mr. Caldwell's loss (unless he is insured) is the wardrobe, scenery, and properties—probably $20,000. We offered the sufferers by the fire a free benefit, but it was promptly declined by Mr. Caldwell, *he* being, as he says, the *only* sufferer. The Opera Company applied for three nights in the week at our house, but, our nights for the three coming weeks being engaged, we were obliged to decline accommodating them. Fortunately for Signor Marty and his company, they kept their wardrobe out of the theatre, and thus saved it all. * * *

Yours most truly, SOL. SMITH.

I remember that, on the occasion of the burning of Mr. Wallack's theatre in New York, Mr. Simpson, manager of the Park Theatre, offered a benefit to the sufferers, to which offer Mr. Wallack returned a curt reply, *declining*. I give here the correspondence which took place between the managers of the surviving theatre (not *long* to survive) and the burned-out manager:

"American Theatre, New Orleans,
March 14, 1842.

"JAMES H. CALDWELL, ESQ.: SIR,—We respectfully tender a free benefit at this house to the sufferers by last night's calamity. If acceptable, we propose to devote Friday or Saturday next to the proposed benefit, and to pay the proceeds, without any deduction whatever, into your hands for distribution to the sufferers.

"Very truly yours."

(Signed by the managers.)

Answer of Mr. Caldwell.

"New Orleans, March 14, 1842.

"GENTLEMEN,—I know of no sufferers by the calamity of last night except myself. I have not heard of any. No one has said to me, 'I am a sufferer.'

"If, therefore, your offer of a benefit without any deduction whatever was intended for me, I most respectfully decline it.

"Yours respectfully,
"JAMES H. CALDWELL."

The old American Theatre, Camp Street, had a short time previously been destroyed by fire, leaving, however, the walls standing, and they were made available in the erection of an auction mart, with a concert-room in the upper story; so that was the end of the "old Camp," as we used to call it. It has never since, to my knowledge, been occupied as a theatre.

Mrs. Fitzwilliam and Mr. Buckstone returned this season, and played two fine engagements, producing during the second one an original piece (*monopolylogue* it was called) entitled the SNAPPING TURTLE, from the pen of Buckstone, written in this country. This piece, in which the talented Fanny Fitz played a great many characters—an American *Fireman* for one—was very successful, both in this country and (afterward) in England. Mrs. Fitzwilliam's greatest effort was in the capital burletta, written for her, entitled WIDOW WIGGINS. Mr. Buckstone, now manager of the Haymarket, London, is probably the most prolific writer of the age. It is said he is the author of over two hundred successful dramatic pieces. His acting is a treat to see. In 1859 I saw him play *Major de Boots*, in the comedy of EVERY BODY'S FRIEND, twice, and it is my belief that no living actor can approach him in that character.

Between the two engagements of the last above-named artists, they went to Mobile for a few nights to fulfill an engagement with Mr. Caldwell in his new theatre there.

Before giving a letter from Mr. Buckstone, briefly mentioning a tragic occurrence in the Mobile Theatre, I will state that the Miss Hamblin heretofore mentioned had been married to a Mr. Ewing, and they were this season members of the Mobile company.

J. B. Buckstone to Sol. Smith.

"Mobile, Saturday morning.

"MY DEAR SOL,—We are all *hors du combat* here. Our theatre was the scene of a terrible affair last night—the murder of one of the actors, a Mr. Ewing, who was acting with us in MY OLD WOMAN the part of *Colonel Girouette*. After the first act, a Miss Hamblin, also performing in the same piece (*Victor*, the page), went into the dressing-room and stabbed the young man. Of course we were obliged to dismiss the audience. * * * Truly yours, J. B. BUCKSTONE."

Strange as it may appear, this woman was cleared by a jury, under a charge from the judge who presided at the trial to the effect that he *might* have died from a disease of the heart, with which he was afflicted, if he had not been stabbed!

The divine Fanny (Ellsler) did not return to New Orleans this season as expected, so *our* Fanny (Fitzwilliam) had every thing her own way, as the saying is.

The Chevalier Wyckoff attended to Fanny Ellsler's business matters. They visited Havana, and, not being able to come to terms with Don Marty, Fanny rented the theatre Tacon from the old Don, and managed it to suit herself. The following letter from her agent to Mr. M. Field, one of the editors of the *Picayune*, will explain why the "divine" did not come to New Orleans this season, besides giving a description of an "ovation" which she quite *unex-*

pectedly (of course!) received on the last night of her performance in the Tacon, and which the veritable Wyckoff styles a "theatrical solemnity!"

Henry Wyckoff to M. Field.

"Havana, April 29, 1842.

"MR. FIELD: MY DEAR SIR,—I am greatly obliged to you for your polite letter, and reply to it in a great hurry, chiefly with a view to give you some intelligence that I fear will not be agreeable to an honest enthusiast, as I believe you to be, of the dance.

"It is quite clear and decided that Mlle. Ellsler will not go to New Orleans this year, and I may say it is therefore improbable she will ever go; and principally for these reasons she waives all intention of going now:

"The St. Charles has burned down, and the French Theatre has closed, consequently she is perfectly free of all engagements and compromise.

"The season is very far advanced, and she would be incapable of supporting in the small American Theatre the great heat of the climate.

"She has received lately the most magnificent offers from Mexico, and she is at this moment hesitating whether to go there or return to Europe direct from here. She will certainly do one thing or the other. She feels some objections to encountering all the dangers that assail the travelers in Mexico—first, the yellow fever at Vera Cruz, and next, the robbers on the road, together with the length and badness of the way and conveyances to the capital.

"Should she go, the results will doubtless be brilliant. She would like, she says, out of pure gratitude, to visit New Orleans, and again thank them for the enthusiastic kindness to her last year. She remembers it well, and never will cease to cherish a grateful recollection, in no matter what part of the world she goes.

"I would like to tell you something of her last adieu to Havana, a few nights ago. It was certainly the most imposing and affecting solemnity eye ever witnessed. After dancing with infinite grace and effect the island dance of 'Sapateado,' suddenly, without her knowing it, the whole decorations changed, representing Olympus. A person dressed to represent America came toward her; Terpsichore advanced with a wreath of white on the other side; the three Graces danced around her. Fanny was for a moment bewildered. A fine band of military music struck up at the same moment, and a choir of thirty persons concealed above chanted an ode in her praise. The effect on the house was overwhelming; but Fanny's exquisite behavior heightened it a hundred fold. She seized America (Madame Martin) in her arms, and lavished a thousand caresses on her, then put America's hand on her heart, who nodded to the sympathizing thousands that it beat loudly and fast. She knelt while a crown of grace was put on her head, and the stage resplendent with light of white and red that had lit up in all the wings. It was a sight worth seeing, and long to be recollected.

"In a hurry, yours truly, H. WYCKOFF."

There! If that can be beat by the paid puffers who accompany female stars of the present day, let us see it done, that's all. America "nodding" to the sympathizing thousands that Fanny's heart "beat loudly and fast," is decidedly good. The "white and red fire" could be excelled by the calcium light now in vogue to light up ballet-dancers with; but there is no such puffer now extant as the chevalier who wrote the above, and *for publication*, remember, doubtless without Fanny's "knowing it" any more than she knew of the sudden "change of decorations" in the "solemnity," or of the "thirty concealed choristers" who sung the "ode in her praise."

This season in Mobile, where the tragedy occurred, his second, was a very unprofitable one, and the last Mr. Caldwell ever made there. He next season rented the theatre to a Mr. Dumas, keeper of a restaurant, who, under the management of Mr. Hodges, cooked up the drama in various styles—boiled, fried, roasted, broiled, or on the half shell—involving a loss of whatever ready money he may have been possessed of—in fact, breaking him up. On invitation, I played a week's engagement with this new manager, and had a full and fashionable house on my benefit night, which was a stormy one.

But let me not wander. The season of the New American closed at the usual time, and here was an end of the engagement with the equestrians, thank goodness. They were a good set of fellows, and their manager, Robinson, was a trump; but I always had a prejudice against taking horses into a theatre. Robinson has become a wealthy man, and resides in Cincinnati, Ohio, where I had the pleasure of meeting him a year or two ago.

Our season, burdened with the losses at Havana, was a little short of a paying one, and we were obliged to leave $2400 of the rent unpaid, for which sum judgment was confessed in one of the District Courts, with stay of execution, with the understanding that we were not required to pay it until the following January. I only mention this fact here because, as will be seen, it influenced events to follow. We had, in the two seasons, accumulated a fine stock of scenery and properties, all of which, with the theatre containing it, was burned on the 30th of July following, leaving the English drama without a home in New Orleans. I was at Barnum's Hotel, in Baltimore, on my way to New York, when I heard of this last conflagration. Arrived in New York, I soon had letters assuring me Dubois & Kendig were going to rebuild immediately, they being fully insured, and that I could safely go on making the arrangements for the winter season, as we should certainly have the new house. These assurances were made by Mr. Dubois at St. Louis. What his partner, Kendig, was doing in New Orleans will presently appear.

The St. Louis season of 1842 was a miserable one. The first night's receipts barely reached $200, and those of the closing night to only $75 75. Mrs. Sefton (now Mrs. Wallack) and E. S. Conner played a tolerable engagement, and Mr. J. H. Kirby a very poor one. Martin Van Buren, on his visit to the house, though well advertised, only drew $477 50. And the worst of all was, *Corporation currency*, worth but sixty, fifty, and forty cents on the dollar, was the only money (?) in circulation. This Corporation currency was the stepping-stone to the fortunes of several rich citizens I could name. Thus: they managed to sink its value to the lowest point it would go, to wit, forty cents on a dollar, and then, through brokers, *bought it all up!* As soon as they got possession of the whole, some hundreds of thousands, they began to *run it up*, but would sell none, and very soon managed matters so that they induced the City Council to issue bonds bearing ten per cent. interest, which were ultimately paid in coin. I shall not mention the names of the lucky capitalists. Some are dead, and some are living. *One* of them, it is said, is going to give all he made in this way back to the city, and more too. Just look at the operation and its results. With $40,000 a purchase is made of $100,000 worth of the currency, which is funded, the bonds bearing ten per cent., *payable in coin*, which can be sold the instant they are received *at par*, giving a profit of $60,000, or 150 per cent. upon the $40,000 invested. Rather a nice operation for the capitalists, but a little hard on the mechanics and tradesmen who had to take the currency at par for their labor and goods, and sell it at 60 per cent. off its face.

It was about this time, I think, that the twenty acres of land in the St. Louis City Commons, which I acquired in 1836, for which I paid a bonus of $1200, and on which I had paid the yearly interest (as rent) for five years, became forfeited to the city in consequence of my inability to pay the small sum of about $200, one of the required yearly payments! I made up my mind all would have to go, and this among the rest. Could I have held on to this property until now, paying the yearly interest, or purchasing the fee-simple title at about $4000, which I had at any time the right to do, I should be at this time a tolerably rich man.

Soon after the forfeiture of the twenty acres—in fact, the very day the forfeited lands were resold (mine and others)—I ventured to bid off a small lot of four and a half acres away out in the woods, adjoining what is now Lafayette Park. I think the price of this was $350 an acre, the purchaser paying five per cent. interest on the amount for which it was bid off for ninety-nine years, renewable forever, with the privilege of purchasing at any time, and thus becoming the possessor of the fee-simple title. The following year a Board of Commissioners was appointed to "graduate" the price at which the purchase of common lands could be made. The price of my lot was "graduated" down to $130 per acre, and at that price I *purchased it*, managing to make the first cash payment, and giving my notes for the deferred payments. I have told you the result of my first speculation in city common lands; at the proper time I propose to tell you how I came out with *this*.

For reasons which will soon appear, the company stopped at Vicksburg during the month of December, and made a season of three weeks. The receipts were too small to appear in so large a book as this—too large the book is likely to be, by-the-by, unless I hurry on and give the balance of my trials with less detail in relating them than has characterized the foregoing pages, though really, it seems to me, I but skim along upon the surface of things, leaving hundreds of events unrelated that ought to be interesting, if *any* narrative of this kind *can* be made so, which I doubt. Well, I'll say nothing about this Vicksburg season except that *I was not there.* Where I *was* at the time I now proceed to mention.

CHAPTER IV.

Mr. Caldwell had endeavored to raise means for rebuilding the splendid St. Charles, and failed. Dubois and Kendig commenced rebuilding the American very shortly after its destruction. In September or October, an agent of theirs went to St. Louis and informed us that the house was nearly covered in, and advised that we should begin to prepare the scenery for it, which we accordingly did. The agent had not been long returned to New Orleans before reports came that *the American had been rented to Mr. Caldwell!* Mr. Dubois, who was in St. Louis, stoutly denied the truth of this report, and said there was no doubt about our going on with our lease, as if no fire had happened. I resolved to go to New Orleans at once. Dubois said he would go with me, and we went down on the same boat. Arrived in the Crescent City (on the 20th of October), my worst fears were realized; Mr. Caldwell was in possession of the new theatre sure enough, and was preparing scenery and decorations for an early opening. Upon consultation with friends, I found there existed a general desire that we should not "give it up so," but that *another* new theatre should be built, and that immediately. On the 21st I wrote the following statement, which appeared in the *Picayune* of the next day:

"THE AMERICAN THEATRE.

"'*Where the offense is, let the great axe fall.*'

"We have never obtruded our private affairs upon the attention of the New Orleans public. An excuse for making the following statement, it is believed, may be found in the fact that we have been connected, in the responsible capacity of managers, with a *public institution* which has been sustained and fostered by our '*resident population*,' as well as by the numerous residents of other parts of our country, who pass a part or the whole of the winter in this southern emporium, and in the other fact that by no fault of ours *our connection with that institution has ceased.*

"We have no wish to excite sympathy. Since 1837, blow after blow has fallen heavily upon us. We have been constrained to abandon one of our strong-holds (Mobile) for want of means to compete with a powerful professional contemporary, who, 'with appliances and means to boot,' has for many years aspired to control the destinies of the Drama in the entire South and West. In St. Louis we were enabled to maintain our position, the stockholders having refused to listen to his propositions for a lease of their splendid temple.

"We came to New Orleans as to a place of refuge. Although it appeared plain to us that we could not compete successfully with the theatre then building in Mobile by Mr. Caldwell—our last theatre in that city being in a comparatively bad location—we thought that *here* two theatres *might* be sustained. We opened the American. To the threats of our contemporary that he would *shut us up in a month* we made no answer; his sneers at our humble temple, which he endowed with the classical appellations of a 'dog-pit' and a 'shanty,' we heeded not; his statements in the public newspapers that 'the expenses of his orchestra alone exceeded those of our whole establishment,' we noticed not, though, at the time that statement was made, our orchestra contained *ten* more musicians than his, and our dramatic company was superior to his, both in number and talent, to say nothing of *two equestrian companies* which were attached to our establishment, and which certainly did not *lessen* our expenses. We pursued the 'even tenor of our way,' satisfied that our exertions were appreciated by the public and munificently rewarded. Affairs are changed; both theatres have been destroyed by fire. One (the 'Little American') is being rebuilt, and as the time approaches when we expected to resume our professional operations, we find our 'shanty' in possession of James H. Caldwell! And that is not all; he has managed, hard as the times are, to find means to *purchase a judgment*, which he holds *in terrorem* over our heads! We repeat, we do not wish to excite sympathy; we trust we have sufficient energy remaining to enable us to rise even from this last blow. We shall at least *make the attempt.*

"STATEMENT.

"On the 14th of January, 1841, we leased of Messrs. Dubois and Kendig, for the term of five years, computing from the 1st of July, 1840, all and singular that portion of ground situated on Poydras Street, in the second municipality of this city, which was leased by Dubois and Kendig from George Morgan and others, by an act passed before H. B. Cenas, a notary public in this city, on the 4th of May, 1840, together with all the buildings and improvements thereon, known as the American Theatre.

"A clause in the lease provides that, '*in case of the destruction of the said premises by fire or otherwise, the rent shall cease and be no longer payable.*'

"In virtue of this agreement of lease, we occupied the premises two seasons. On the 30th of July last the premises was set on fire by an incendiary, and burned to the ground, together with all our theatrical property in New Orleans, consisting of scenery, furniture, machinery, gas fittings, and properties of every description pertaining to a well-regulated theatre, and which cost over twelve thousand dollars. We were the only parties interested, who were utterly uninsured. When the intelligence of the destruction of the theatre reached St. Louis, one of our firm was in New York making engagements for the ensuing winter campaign; the other immediately communicated with Mr. Dubois, then at St. Louis, and it was distinctly agreed between them that if the theatre could be rebuilt with the insurance money, a contract would be made to that effect immediately, and we were to continue to occupy it until the close of the term of our lease. Neither party being in possession of a copy of the lease, neither was certain what stipulation it contained in regard to the contingency which had occurred; but Mr. D. observed that, whatever the stipulation might be, they should feel themselves *morally* bound to rebuild, if they had the ability so to do, and he considered we were *morally* bound to go to work with our occupancy; and Mr. Dubois departed for New Orleans. On his return he said he had not made himself acquainted with the 'stipulations in the lease,' considering it quite unnecessary to do so, as the rebuilding was contracted for, and we were to have the theatre as a matter of course. He said *an application had been made, immediately after the burning*, for a lease of the American, should it be rebuilt; but he laughed at the idea of any one supposing it could be taken out of our hands, after the great loss we had sustained. It being clearly and distinctly understood that the lease was to be held good by both parties, the partner in New York was so advised, and, placing implicit confidence in the honor of our old friend Dubois, we felt no uneasiness on the subject. The theatre was to be ours beyond a doubt.

"On the strength of this understanding, and without a suspicion of bad faith any where, we proceeded to make our arrangements for the ensuing winter—engaged performers, orchestra, artists, and machinists—commenced preparing scenery and fixtures—applied for gas fittings, and expected to commence business in the new house about the 20th of November.

"On the 24th of September the Commercial Bulletin contained the following editorial article, founded, as we have since learned, *upon information furnished by Mr. James H. Caldwell himself:*

"'We hear that Mr. Caldwell has leased the American Theatre, Poydras Street. There was a clause in the late lease by which it was stipulated that, in case the building was burned, the lease should end.'

"This article was republished, in substance, by nearly all the city papers, and in the papers of the Eastern cities, much to our injury, as we believe—though we most cheerfully acquit the Bulletin of any intention to injure us—holding out to professional people at the East who might be engaged to come to us the supposition that we should have no theatre at which to receive them. Seeing this paragraph in the newspapers, we had another interview with Mr. Dubois, and he assured us he knew of no such proceeding as the one spoken of, and *placed no reliance whatever on the report.*

"A confidential clerk of Messrs. Dubois & Kendig had been to St. Louis a few days previous to the above paragraph meeting our eye. He had two or three interviews with us, and did not say a word about any intention to lease the theatre to Mr. Caldwell or any one else. On the contrary, our conversation was exclusively confined to the progress of the new building; the preparations we were making to carry down scenery from St. Louis; the necessity of one of us proceeding to New Orleans in the course of a few weeks; and, finally, he promised to write us immediately on his arrival, and advise us of the state of the building, and when it would be necessary for us to commence work on the stage and machinery. Mr. Dubois informed us that the clerk had visited him for the purpose of raising means to go on with the building, in case one of the insurance companies should fail, as he feared it would, to meet the payments which would be due the contractor. He added that he had given the clerk authority to raise means from his personal friends, if they could be so raised, and if those means failed and the insurance company did not come up to the mark, he feared the *building must stop*, but said not a word about transferring the house into other hands.

"On the 9th of the present month we received intelligence that the new building had certainly been leased for our unexpired term to Mr. James H. Caldwell, and that he had obtained control over a judgment for $2418, which we had confessed in favor of Dubois & Kendig for a balance due on last year's rent. In short, we received the assurance that we had been 'headed' by Mr. Caldwell, trifled with by Mr. Kendig (for to this day we sincerely believe Mr. Dubois was no party to the transaction, and knew not of it; he assured us so himself), and our company, orchestra, artists, machinists, and all others who had formed engagements with us for the coming season, numbering nearly one hundred persons, were thrown on our hands, and we without a place to employ them in!

"One of us is here, and, to save the time and trouble of answering questions—for there does appear to be considerable curiosity to know the particulars of a transaction by which we have been thrust out of the American Theatre—this statement is thus publicly put forth. The community may think we have received ill treatment; indeed, we believe there will be but one opinion on the subject. We shall not occupy our time in useless complainings, but act. If our courts will afford a remedy for the injuries we have sustained, they may be appealed to, when leisure will permit us to 'wait the law's delay;' at present a new theatre must be prepared for the reception of our company. We shall exert every faculty and use every honorable means to resume the position from which we have been ejected by incendiarism, intrigue, and treachery. Notwithstanding the untoward circumstances in which we are temporarily placed, we confidently expect to be able to fulfill every engagement made for the ensuing winter.

"[Signed in the name of the firm.]

"New Orleans, October 22, 1842."

I made short work of building the new theatre, and shall make shorter work in relating *how* it was built. The site selected was that of the old St. Charles, on St. Charles Street. The ground was rented of the Gas Bank, and from that institution a portion of the means were procured to pay the workmen as the building progressed; but I here assert as a fact undeniable, that, without the efficient aid of Messrs. F. D. Gott, J. R. Pike, and Jamison & Mackintosh, the house could not have been built. Their kindness can never be forgotten. Another firm friend on this occasion was Patrick Irwin, an Irishman, with a heart large enough for any two reasonably good men.

I may say here that all my previous difficulties since I entered into theatrical management amounted to almost nothing when compared with those I now encountered; but I surmounted them all, and the new St. Charles rose like a phœnix from the ashes of its splendid predecessor. In *forty working days* (it rained nearly half of the time while the walls were going up) the new house was ready for the reception of the company. I am not going to relate the difficulties referred to, except one, an account of which I published at the time in the *Picayune* of the 26th of November:

THE NEW ST. CHARLES THEATRE.

Shylock. We trifle time: I pray thee pursue sentence.
Portia. A pound of that same merchant's flesh is thine.
The court awards it, and the law doth give it.
Shylock. Most righteous judge!
Portia. And you must cut this flesh from off his breast;
The law allows it, and the court awards it.
Shylock. Most learned judge! A sentence! Come, prepare.
Portia. TARRY A LITTLE—there is something else.
Merchant of Venice—Act IV.

"☞ The reader will recognize in the above quoted lines an extract from the celebrated case of Shylock *versus* Antonio, as reported by Shakspeare. The plaintiff in that case has always been looked upon as a hard-hearted fellow; indeed, he was pronounced by the Duke of Venice

"'A stony adversary, an inhuman wretch,
Uncapable of pity, void and empty
From any dream of mercy:'

And yet he only claimed the 'due and forfeit of his bond.' The duke, a very good sort of a gentleman, endeavored to soften his flinty heart, and even went so far as to advise the Jew to take off fifty per cent. of the amount unquestionably due him, in consideration of severe *losses* sustained by the defendant by shipwreck and other casualties. But Mr. Shylock was not to be moved by prayers or entreaties; on the contrary, he reproved the court for interfering in his affairs, and boldly threatened a forfeiture of their charter if they should refuse to grant a decree in his favor. He refused to allege a reason for his harsh proceedings except 'a lodged hate' he bore the unfortunate defendant. The 'strict court of Venice,' after hearing arguments on both sides, together with some pretty smart speeches from the by-standers, mostly friends of the defendant, proceeded to pronounce sentence in the words quoted at the head of this article. In accordance with the 'sentence,' the Jew was about to help himself to a pound of the defendant's flesh, when he was gently told by the 'learned judge' to 'TARRY A LITTLE.' Matters hereupon took an ugly turn for Mr. Shylock, and at the conclusion of the proceedings he sneaked out of court—a broken man.

* * * * * * * *

"About a week since, notices appeared in the *Courier* and *Bulletin* newspapers, in the English and French languages, announcing that the sheriff of the District Court had seized all our rights in a lease of the lot of ground on which the New St. Charles Theatre is being built, and that the same would be sold by public auction on the 30th instant, at the St. Louis Exchange, to satisfy an execution in favor of Dubois & Kendig, whose rights had been subrogated to Jas. H. Caldwell.

"It has been already stated that Mr. Caldwell purchased of D. & K. a certain judgment which we had confessed in their favor for $2418. When we confessed that judgment (it being what is termed 'a friendly suit'), they agreed to wait for the amount until January next; but when they broke their contract with us by leasing the American Theatre to Mr. Caldwell, it appears they 'made a clean sweep of it' by giving him control over the judgment against us, and left us entirely at his mercy. By examining the notarial act, we find that the amount of the judgment is added to the rent of the American, so that Mr. C. has *three years to pay it in*, the first payment (one eighteenth part) falling due in January, 1843. Having such easy terms himself, and having not only taken away 'the prop that did sustain our house,' but taken possession of the house itself, we expected that a proposition would be made that we should put him in funds to meet the payments as they should fall due. We were mistaken. The ink was scarcely dry with which we signed the lease of the ground on which we are building the new St. Charles before the sheriff was ordered to make a seizure. We do not suppose Mr. Caldwell *expected* to make the money out of us at the present time. He knew—'none so well as he' —that *burnt-out* managers can not be always ready for such a call as that made upon us by his order.

"It is proper to remark here that the *effects* of the seizure and advertisement of the lease have not been, we believe, *exactly* what were intended. Many persons have inquired, 'Has the building stopped?' but we are glad to say that the contractors have not been for a moment dismayed—the furnishers have not held back a single material—the work has not been delayed by the hostile proceeding a single hour; and it only remains for us to state, for the information of those gentlemen who have contributed to the building of the new theatre by taking stock or purchasing certificates for tickets, that we hold protested paper of Mr. Caldwell to an amount sufficient to pay the judgment against us; an INJUNCTION has issued to prevent the sale of our lease, and—the new manager of the American has been told to '*tarry a little.*'

"We feel no pleasure in making a statement that Mr. Caldwell has not been able, in all instances, to meet his pecuniary liabilities, and nothing should tempt us to make such a statement now but a desire to protect ourselves from the effects of the judicial proceedings instituted by him against us. The misfortunes we have both met with in the destruction of our theatres should beget any thing but ill feeling among the sufferers.

"To our friends and the general public we say again, 'the work goes bravely on.' Give us good weather for twenty days, and the NEW ST. CHARLES will open a week before the close of the year.

"[Signed in the name of the firm.]

"New Orleans, November 26, 1842."

The "protested notes" mentioned consisted of those given to the lamented Tyrone Power for his last engagement at the St. Charles, and some others owned by Mr. Irwin, which he had purchased from Fogg and Stickney, they having received them in lieu of cash for their engagement at the same theatre and in Mobile. I purchased the whole *on a credit*, the holders being willing to lend a helping hand to building of the new house.

On the 5th of December Mr. Caldwell opened the new American Theatre. I insert a portion of the lengthy address printed in the posters on that occasion, because Mr. C. therein gives, in his own peculiar style, some reminiscences of his early career in New Orleans which are interesting:

"NEW AMERICAN THEATRE, NEW ORLEANS.

"As I am about to commence a new career in the theatrical business, a few observations may be expected from me by way of address. In attending, therefore, to that presumed expectation, although I must necessarily touch upon matters as painful to my recollection as they have been injurious to my fortunes, I hope most sincerely that the public will acquit me of any desire to awaken their sympathies.

"I know that, generally, addresses to the public, how much soever the writers of them may aver to the contrary, are expressly intended to excite sympathy as well as interest, for the man who says to you that he wants no sympathy, asks for it in telling you so. I assert, however, that I am an exception to this general rule.

"It will be generally conceded, I believe, that I am the founder of the Drama in New Orleans. I built the 'American Theatre' in 1822, since termed the 'Camp Street Theatre,' which was recently destroyed by a vile incendiary, who, as yet, I have not been able to bring to justice, although I still live in hopes of that event.

"Such was the situation at that time of the Sixth Ward, which is now the Second Municipality, that the streets in which are some of the greatest monuments were scarcely even defined.

"New Levee Street was then a continuous line of ponds for more than a mile, and Tchoupitoulas and Magazine Streets could then boast of no better buildings than such as are denominated 'shanties,' with here and there the mouldering remains of a former plantation residence.

"Camp Street had only at that time a few tobacco and cotton warehouses, and St. Charles Street was best known to the boys, who sought in sport for snipe among the *latannier* in the marshes, which had never been disturbed otherwise in its original growth.

"The gradual rising of the walls of the first 'American Theatre,' which walls are still standing, excited a great deal of curiosity, and naturally so, for people, conceiving no mercantile use for such a building, speculated jocularly on the idea of its being intended for a fortification.

"For several years the people had to travel on gunwale sidewalks; and it is probably well remembered by several of our present residents, carriages could not be used after a heavy rain in places so far out of the way as Camp Street.

"The success attendant on my building the American Theatre rendered it a nucleus around which enterprise and commercial prosperity first began to grow to that importance which may be said to have settled and called into existence the Second Municipality.

"My enthusiasm in favor of the Drama, and my strong feelings in favor of New Orleans, induced me, in 1835, to build the 'St. Charles Theatre and Arcade Baths.' At this period I may state, merely for the purpose of explaining matters as I go along, that I had $176,000—one hundred and seventy-six thousand dollars, cash assets, in my grasp.

"Circumstances, of which all of us are, more or less, 'the most obedient humble servants,' have left the 'St. Charles Theatre,' the 'Arcade Baths,' and the 'Camp Street Theatre' 'among the things that were,' and myself with an accumulation of losses and misfortunes almost too serious to be reflected on.

"Now, however, I begin again; but instead of commanding my own large ship from my own quarter-deck, I have chartered a smaller vessel to embark for sea in search of another golden shore, from which I may gather means to erect another (for so I suppose I should)—another REAL St. Charles."

[He then gives his version of how he came to lease the "American," asserting that the lessees of the theatre burned down had no claim whatever on the house that was rebuilt upon its site, concluding as follows:]

"My claims upon the patronage of the public must rest, I well know, upon the attractions offered in this new establishment, and consequently my utmost exertions will most assuredly be devoted to that end. I will state, however, that I am far from expecting the success which, at the outset of my new career, I had anticipated, and from the conviction that two theatres for a similar order of dramatic entertainments can not be supported in the Second Municipality.

"Competition does not always secure the best services, particularly as regards the drama; for it raises the price of every thing connected with the stage, and fosters directly the most destructive system associated therewith—the starring system.

"But, despite all difficulties and annoyances, I take the field again, active and determined, hoping, like a prudent general, so to marshal my forces as not easily to be beaten from the field.

"It is more than probable that, had I expected the existence of a rival theatre in this municipality, I should have retired with my fortune of laurels and losses, and fed upon the reflection that I had spent twenty-three years of unremitting professional labor for the advantage of those who intrude upon my path, not kindly or courteously, but with enviousness and misrepresentations.

"The case is, however, otherwise, and I am now determined to bestir myself in such a manner as to render my new project in favor of the Drama, if not profitable to my purse, at least additionally laudatory of my character.

"JAMES H. CALDWELL."

As the end of Mr. Caldwell's theatrical career so soon followed the above announcement, it may be as well here to insert the following card, which appeared in the posters early in January, about six weeks after the opening of the new house in Poydras Street, and one week before the NEW ST. CHARLES was to open its doors. It will be seen that he did not wait to be "beaten from the field," but wisely retreated before his competitors fired a gun. It appears from his own statement that his "new project" had not been "profitable to his purse." It will be for others to judge whether it had been "laudatory of his character."

"AMERICAN THEATRE.

"This establishment will be closed for the season on Saturday, the 14th instant.

"The lessee is constrained to say that the situation of the times, to which alone he can attribute the nightly losses, compels him to a course unavoidable as it is painful to his feelings.

"Were the private fortune of the subscriber equal to what it was when he completed the late St. Charles Theatre, he would have been proud, as he then was, to sustain the losses which attended that beautiful temple; but all those means are gone—all in honor.

"His pride now has to sustain a shock unparalleled to him, but which will be appreciated by all honorable men. He can not now, without the public support, continue in his much-loved profession, and he is aware that the drama, not only in this country, but in the old country, has sustained a shock which can not be recovered from in a generation.

"It is now my painful duty to announce that I shall retire from the Drama altogether—it is no longer a profession for a sensitive mind to follow; and as to pecuniary profit, the following facts, I hope, will illustrate to the world that I have done for it what few men with capital would have thought of. From the day of the completion of the St. Charles Theatre, on the 30th of November, 1835, to its conflagration on the 13th of March, 1842, I have expended in the support of its losses $100,000.

"In the belief—a belief which was sustained by the whole population—that no other theatre than the present American would be built for several years, I was induced to enter in the field again. Unfortunately I did so; and, although no theatre was open, the expenses have not been met by at least $200 per night.

"Had I the means I should in very pride continue on, in the hope which constantly cherished me in the St. Charles, that better times would return, and that the Drama would meet with a competent support. Not possessing them, I must, though reluctantly, abandon it, and seek some employment by which I can live, for loss and double ruin is the inevitable result of a managerial career in the present day.

"JAMES H. CALDWELL."

CHAPTER V.

THE New St. Charles opened on the 18th of January, 1843, seventy-four days after the lot came into my possession, having been built in forty working days, as before stated, rain preventing work for thirty-four days. First night's receipts, $490 75.

The season was moderately successful, considering "the situation of the times" referred to by Mr. Caldwell; but we were borne down by pecuniary embarrassments the whole time, all creditors fully expecting to be paid out of the receipts of the house.

The "American" was carried on by a "commonwealth," under the nominal management of Mrs. Ann Sefton, but the season fizzled out ingloriously in a very short time. Mr. Dinneford then tried his hand at management, but he also failed, and we had the field to ourselves long before the usual time for the closing of theatres in New Orleans.

The stars who appeared at the St. Charles this season were J. H. Hackett, Dan Marble, George Vandenhoff, Miss Lee, J. M. Field, and Dr. Lardner (lecturer). Mr. Hackett, in addition to his usual characters, essayed *Richard the Third*, and *I* thought played it very well.

It may be supposed that I entertained no very friendly feelings toward Mr. Caldwell after the events above narrated. Such a supposition would not be justified by the fact. From the first moment I met him in 1827 until the day of his death, I entertained for him a warm friendship, and, except during the time of our rivalship in business, believe he reciprocated my feeling. When he retired from management, a very short time elapsed before we were on good terms again, and we so continued ever after. He soon came to take an interest in the new St. Charles, and was ever ready to advise with me (and I often consulted him) on difficult points which arose in its management. About the first *act* under the new (or rather restored) impulses which now inspired him was the offer to us of a lease of his new Mobile Theatre. Unfortunately, as it turned out, we took it, and lost a great deal of money there in after years. Relieved from the annoyances of management, Mr. Caldwell arose out of the embarrassments which were surrounding him, and eventually became a very rich man, principally by means of his gas companies in Cincinnati and Mobile. I will venture here to state it as my opinion that, averaging Mr. Caldwell's twenty-five years of management, he did not realize a profit of over $1000 a year; and when you get through reading these memoirs (only written to string anecdotes upon), you will know of another manager who worked with about the same result. The truth is, the business of theatrical management is very uncertain and fluctuating, and the profits of managers are greatly overrated.

I can express my opinion of Mr. Caldwell as an actor in no better way than by saying I have never yet beheld his equal as a light comedian. Murdock comes the nearest to him (of those that I have seen), and Charles Mathews next. In *Reuben Glenroy* he was so true to nature that, in the scene with the *Hon. Mrs. Glenroy*, he not only brought tears into *her* eyes, but into those of all the young mothers among the audience. Mr. C. played the whole range of tragedy, and but for some mannerisms, such as drawling out certain words as if he were running the chromatic scale of the gamut in music, no actor gave greater satisfaction to Southern audiences than he did. He was scrupulously guarded in giving the true text of Shakspeare when performing *his* characters. In the later years of his life he only appeared in comedy, and in that he was unapproachable.

Monsieur Matthieu.

In 1819 (I think that was the year) the above name appeared at the head of posting bills in Cincinnati, accompanied by a notification to the good citizens of that growing town that a concert would be given on a certain night, on which occasion the giver would sing a number of Italian, French, and English songs, accompanied by himself on the guitar. A tolerably numerous audience attended the ballroom of the City Hotel on the evening appointed, myself among the number, and for the first time I saw and heard the subject of this sketch. He was not much more than the shadow of a man in appearance, but had a pleasing countenance and a very pleasant smile, which won from his auditors a favorable reception. His voice was not powerful, but it was sweet (what there was of it), and he gave his simple ballads with considerable feeling. One of his own compositions, "Sweet at Evening's pensive Hour," still retains a place in my memory, though it has been confoundedly jostled about by all sorts of music since.

Mons. Matthieu visited the Western country accidentally; his journey happened thus: Soon after landing in Baltimore from a Havre packet, he heard of a great opening for a music-school in Petersburg, Virginia, and resolved to proceed thither without delay. At the stage-office the clerk registered his name for *Pitts*burg instead of *Peters*burg, and the monsieur did not discover the error until he had crossed the Alleghany Mountains and commenced his inquiries for the gentleman to whom his letters of introduction were directed.

"N'importe!" exclaimed the monsieur; "I vish to go to *Peters*burg—dey bring me to *Peets*-burg. Eh bien! I sal stay over de mountain—pour quoi?—because I can not make a raise of de vind to pay back my passage to Baltimore." So he made himself contented, and shipped on board a flat-boat bound for Cincinnati, where, he heard, it cost but little to live. "I hear," said he to me, "dat in dis Cincinnati de peops very mush fond of de musique, and de eat and de drink is *sheep* [cheap]; dat dey have de *cochon beaucoup*—plenty! Trois sous de pound, and de spare-rib throw him in, begar! and here I sal make some casting of my anchor, as de sailor say."

I felt an interest in the welfare of Mons. Matthieu, but soon lost sight of him. He dwelt for several years in Louisville, where he manufactured cigars, and led the orchestra in Jefferson Street. Jeffersonville, over the river, was his residence for a time. In 1833 he discontinued his business (confectionery and teaching music), and started off for the Yellow Springs, in Ohio, with the view of sending up a series of balloons from that fashionable watering-place. A friend of mine, a great lover of music, loaned him some money, to be repaid out of the *first proceeds* of the Yellow Springs balloon speculation, and he has been looking out for the balloons ever since, but has seen none, for the simple reason that "they are not yet in sight."

In 1836 (he had now a wife and a small houseful of children) he applied for and obtained a situation in the orchestra of the Mobile Theatre, in which he played the tenor violin. In addition to his musical duties, he made fire-works for all the explosions in Celeste's pieces. He was terrible, and sometimes *terrific* at explosions. Many a time and oft have I trembled for the walls of old St. Emanuel. I can imagine I see his jolly, sweaty face now, peeping out from a cloud of exploded powder, after some of his *rehearsals*, as he exclaimed, "Ah ha! what you tink of dat, ha? Good explosion, eh? Shake de house, ha?"

After our season closed, Mons. Matthieu hired a small farm about five miles from Mobile, and endeavored to raise potatoes and other vegetables; but, while the potatoes were growing, his children's jaws must be going, so he accepted an engagement as leader of two blind fiddlers at Mr. Ferry's new theatre in Government Street, his salary being fixed at eight dollars per week. The *weeks* came and went, but the eight dollars were not forthcoming—or, rather, were *always* forth *coming*, but never *came* forth. The leader was discouraged. "Sacre! I plant la pomme de terre—he no grow in five months; I make en-

MONSIEUR MATTHIEU LEADING A SMALL ORCHESTRA. (See page 173.)

gagement to play de feedle—I get no pay! Begar, I sal take up my bed and promenade—dam if I don't!" and, sure enough, he put off for Texas!

One morning in the winter of 1843, a card was brought to me in the director's room of the St. Charles's Theatre on which was written the name of the veritable Mons. Matthieu! I directed that he should be instantly shown up. On entering the room, he jumped so high that I was doubtful whether he would ever come down again.

"Ah ha! Monsieur Sol, I am too happy I see you again! Ah ha! you got one splendid theatre; I sal make application to be your leader, *tout de suite*, directly."

"Sit down, my old friend, and compose yourself. Where have you hid yourself for the last seven years?"

"Hid myself? I have been at Tex-ass, by gar. I fight some battel at St. Jacinto; I get so mush land as I can not *find;* I almost starve my family in that glorious country; and I come back to follow my profession in dis city for some bread to eat."

After some conversation, I asked him what he was doing in New Orleans.

"Doing? what I do here? I am at present *leading* for Mr. Adams, the conjuror," he replied.

"Leading?"

"Yes, leading the orchestra." He was the sole musician!

I have not seen the monsieur since. There was but little left of him; a strong wind would find no difficulty in blowing him away.

CHAPTER VI.

THE St. Louis Theatre was sold this spring (1843) under a deed of trust given by the stockholders to secure a loan of $20,000. It was bought in by Mr. George Collier, of whom we afterward rented it. The original cost of the lot and building was $78,000, and it was never finished.

The season opened May 20th, with Yankee Hill as the star, to a house of $157 75. Joe Kirby and Ben De Bar played brief engagements, and then came the English lecturer Dr.

Lardner. The only thing I remember about the doctor's engagement is that my old friend George Holland, having served Mr. Caldwell faithfully through all his difficulties to the end of his theatrical career, now appeared as Dr. Lardner's business agent and generator of his gases. Miss Ince, Mr. and Mrs. Brougham, and Seguin's Opera Troupe appeared during the season, which closed on a considerable loss. John Brougham can *almost* wear a certain "mantle" while playing Irishmen; and he has a mantle of his own while playing other characters which will be as long finding a deserving wearer when *he* goes as has been that of poor Power!

The Tremont Theatre in Boston was sold to a religious society this spring. Being in Boston on business—in fact, to purchase the wardrobe of the said theatre, I felt "called" upon to write and publish the following letter:

Sol. Smith, of St. Louis, Mo., to the Rev. Dr. Beecher, of Cincinnati, Ohio.

Boston, Sunday evening, August 13, 1843.

Sir,—The newspapers have given the substance of a discourse delivered by you at the Tremont Theatre soon after that building came into the possession of its present proprietors. When that discourse was delivered I was in St. Louis, nearly one thousand miles from Boston. Business has brought me here, and I take leave to address you a few lines on the subject of your address, conceiving there are some parts of it, if correctly reported, somewhat exceptionable—at least likely to be so considered by members of the theatrical profession.

I make no apology for addressing you through the columns of a newspaper. We are personally unacquainted with each other, and, to be plain with you—for "bluntness is my trade"—I am not very desirous of an introduction. *You* are a preacher of the Gospel; *I* am nothing but an actor, and a *poor* one at that, in every sense of the word. *You* are in possession of a princely income, as payment for advocating the cause of the meek and lowly Jesus; *I* am struggling for a precarious subsistence in my capacity of a stage-player, occasionally adding a little to my income by appearing "in the character" of a *lawyer* in our courts of justice. I may add that *you* stand at the head of a powerful sect of professing Christians in the United States, while *I* am content to claim membership in the lowest rank of artists called histrions. I presume, if I were to seek a conversation with you at your splendid mansion, I should be spurned from your door as unworthy to press your carpet with my unhallowed feet. The name of "Sol Smith, the actor," announced in your study, would probably be the signal for bolting your doors; indeed, if the report of your discourse at the Tremont be a true one—and I have no reason to doubt that it is—you must entertain a "lodged hate"—a "certain loathing" for all poor sinners of our class. Therefore it is that I do not seek a personal interview, but say what I have to say through these columns.

You are represented to have made your "first appearance on the Tremont boards" before a "house crowded from pit to gallery;" and it is said you "returned thanks to Almighty God for having changed the place *which was once the seat of Satan aud his works* into Christ's holy temple;" and prayed that "all theatres might soon become temples of God; and that Satan, their great head, might immediately be driven back to his appropriate home, the bottomless pit." You are said to have dwelt particularly upon the "BAD CHARACTER of actors and actresses," and to have asserted of theatres that "there was no redeeming quality about them—they were evil, and that continually—they were the fruitful source of ALL vice—[all!]—the great social exchange where sinners of all grades, colors, and descriptions assembled to barter away and sell their immortal souls."

Now, Mr. Beecher, read over the above quotations, while quietly sitting in your closet, and how do they look in print? Do not your denunciations strike you as being rather on the *wholesale* order? How different—how widely different was the language of your Master and mine while tabernacling upon the earth! Without the slightest attempt at proof to support your assertions, you throw out an accusation against the whole community of actors. You stand up in the pulpit (late the social exchange of sinners), and before three thousand people, drawn together by your great fame as a speaker, and by curiosity to witness the cleansing of the Augean stable by the river of your eloquence, and point at a large class of your fellow-citizens, and brand the whole of them as *bad characters!* Without particularizing their crimes—without affording them an opportunity of defense, you consign thousands of your fellow-mortals to infamy—or, in other words, *send them to the devil!* You must not be surprised, then, doctor, if the community you have so unsparingly denounced and slandered—yes, slandered!—do not sit calmly down under the imputation cast upon them. A worm, when trodden upon, will turn upon a giant.

In the name of my professional brothers and sisters, I deny that, *as a class*, they are obnoxious to the charges you have brought against them. I deny that the theatre is an exchange where sinners barter away their souls—and I am willing to take the late Tremont Theatre, with all its faults, as a specimen of all theatres in the United States—and I pronounce your attempt to foist upon all actors and actresses the title of "bad characters," uncharitable, unfair, and unmanly. To deny that the institution of the theatre is sometimes abused, and its objects perverted, or that some members of our profession are faulty, would be to deny that managers, actors, and actresses are human beings. But let the professors of the stage be compared with those of any other calling—nay, let them be compared (and I invite the comparison) with the occupants of the *pulpit*—let the moral character of each class be set side by side before the world, and the result need not be feared by the much-abused histrions.

If we thought proper to "carry the war into Africa," we might retort upon the pulpit, and point out instances (and not a few either) where all the wholesome restraints of society have been broken through and trampled under foot by preachers of eminence—where the sanctity of the domestic circle has been invaded; the obligations of the marriage vow have been broken; confidence has been betrayed, and fathers and husbands have been compelled to seek redress from courts of justice for injuries inflicted on their daughters and their wives by hypocrites who use religion as a cloak to hide their hellish propensities. One would suppose, doctor, to hear you, and such as you, speak of actors and actresses, that in *your* profession there is *no acting;* that, from the holy horror with which you pour forth your denunciations against the poor players, *you* would shrink from employing any of the arts you condemn so unsparingly in the actor. I assert that many of you make a *trade* of religion. To say nothing of the attempt that was made to *raise money* by exhibiting the *Tremont Theatre* as it stood when the wicked actors left it—in all its glare of splendid scenery, rich decoration, and gas-lights, you every week cunningly contrive out ways and means to gull the public and obtain money from sinners as well as saints—that at your meetings you resort to all manner of tricks to obtain contributions for pretended charities, and for the support of missions to distant countries, with the professed object of saving heathen souls, *while your next-door neighbor is perishing for bread;* that, contrary to the command of our Savior, who directed that we should receive the Gospel "without money and without price," you take care to confine your labors to such congregations as will *pay you a price*, and a very *good* price too; that you "accept of engagements," like the actors, where the highest salaries are given; that the *louder the call*, the more likely you are to *hear it;* and that, instead of treating your fellow-sinners kindly, and drawing them by affectionate remonstrances from what you consider their evil ways, you denounce them in a lot, and, so far as in you lies, shut the door of grace upon them!

It would appear to me, reverend sir, that on the occasion of taking formal possession of the Tremont Theatre—the late "seat of Satan and his works," since you will have it so—a temperate and forbearing tone would have been more becoming your character and situation. Considering that you had succeeded in turning old Satan and about one hundred sinners out of doors—the sinners to starve, perhaps, and Satan to look out for other quarters—the air of triumph you assumed, and the sentences of condemnation you uttered, were unworthy of you. You had hurled the Muses, neck and heels, from the premises; you had deprived their humble followers of the means of earning their bread—was *that* a time to indulge in scoffs and maledictions? was *that* the way to purify the unholy spot?

How is it, fellow-preacher, that our Lord Jesus Christ—for he is *my* Lord as well as *yours*—did not say a word against theatres when on earth? I do not find a sentence of his recorded which implies that there is any sin in social amusements; on the contrary, the Bible is full of injunctions to cultivate a cheerful disposition. I need only to refer to the fact of David's *dancing before the ark* to show that dancing is pleasing in the sight of God. Speaking of David—read his Psalms, and you will find in those incomparable poems that rejoicing and clapping of hands—playing upon instruments, of all the kinds then invented—skipping, and making "joyful noises," formed most of the themes of the mighty poet. If I am not mistaken (I have not my Testament with me to refer to), one of the apostles *took refuge in a theatre*, which proved to him a safe sanctuary when pursued by a ruthless mob. Our Savior dwelt among sinners, gently leading them into the paths of virtue. How different is the conduct of his pretended followers of the present day—how different from the course pursued by the apostles in the early ages of Christianity! Instead of "going forth into all the ends of the earth to preach the Gospel to all nations," without coin or scrip, your modern preachers must live upon the fat of the land, dwell in splendid mansions, be in receipt of stipulated salaries; and, instead of spreading the blessed tidings of the Gospel to the inhabitants of heathen lands, they confine their teachings to their own favored flocks—unless some temple of Satan is to be purified—*then*, indeed, a reverend divine can travel hundreds of miles — not, as in Pilgrim times, bareheaded and barefooted, but in steamers, railroad cars, and coaches, to fulfill a prophecy made by himself before he was "called" to the West! *Then*, instead of extending the hand of charity to the houseless individuals who have thought it no sin to "labor in their vocation," and, if he thinks their calling sinful, telling them to "GO AND SIN NO MORE," he can brand a whole community with infamy—pronounce them ALL "bad characters"—and can "sup after that!"

But stop—what am I about? Let me not fall into the same error I am condemning in others. *All* preachers are not to be answerable for the faults of a portion of them. I *have* known some orthodox preachers (and I record it with pleasure) who were honest, charitable, and Christianly. I only wished to show that, bad as actors are, or may be as a class, they will lose nothing by a comparison with preachers. In all the practices of active benevolence, I religiously believe they rank far above them.

I would suggest to you, my fellow-sinner, that if you really believe actors and actresses to be the "bad characters" you represented them to be in your sermon, it is your bounden duty to *preach* to THEM—point out wherein consists the sinfulness of their calling, reason with them, draw them from their evil ways, if they *are* evil, and, by treating them kindly, convince them that you are indeed the minister of that blessed Redeemer you profess to serve. During the year preceding the last Presidential election, I was sometimes called on to "speechify" at political meetings. Hard cider and coon-skins were all "the go," as the saying is; and, being a good Whig (I believe *you* went for Harrison too, doctor, but no matter for that)—well, as I was saying, being a good Whig, my stump speeches were "applauded to the very echo." I have frequently thought since that if I had avoided the "log-cabins," and made speeches at the meetings of the locofocos, my rhetoric would (or might) have had much more effect; for the Whigs were all right, and *thought as I did*, whereas it should have been our policy to convince the other party of their error; for it was to *them* we looked for votes to turn the scale in our favor. So with you preachers and professing Christians: if you and your congregations would *attend* theatrical exhibitions (for, depend upon it, doctor, you can not "put them down"), applaud the good sentiments, and express your disapprobation of every thing calculated to produce an immoral effect upon the audience—in short, if you and they would *co-operate* with us, and endeavor to purge the stage of its impurities, instead of endeavoring, as you do, to *exterminate* it, much good might be effected, and the drama might flourish as the adjunct of Christianity.

I did intend to say something about Satan, for I do think you treat that imaginary being rather cavalierly, taking into consideration the fact that he is always at hand as a convenient scarecrow to "drive the stray lambs into the fold," and that you could not carry on your business a week without him; but, upon second thoughts, I have concluded to say nothing in his behalf. Send him back "to the bottomless pit," doctor, as soon as you like, and a good riddance, I say.

At some future period I propose to discuss at some length the USEFULNESS OF THE STAGE. At present I fear I have wearied your patience with my desultory and disjointed strictures. I will conclude by recommending to your consideration the 7th chapter of Matthew, 1st to 5th and 21st to 23d verses.

Hoping you will receive this letter in as kind a spirit as that which dictates it, and advising you to cultivate Christian feelings, I remain, dear sir, your fellow-laborer in the vineyard,

SOL. SMITH.

CHAPTER VII.

THE new St. Charles, now finished, and well furnished with new scenery, opened for its second season November 15, 1843, with the HUNCHBACK and A ROLAND FOR AN OLIVER. Receipts, $369; certainly not a very promising beginning. Next night (GABRIELLE, MR. AND MRS. WHITE, and A LOVER BY PROXY) the receipts fell down to $77 75. Mr. Brougham, on his first appearance, attracted a house of only $99 75. When, on the next night, his wife appeared with him, the receipts were $269 50; and so went on the business for some time. H. Placide (first time playing as a star) brought the business up a little, his first house being $366 25. Mr. P.'s second appearance drew only $129 25; his third, $202 75; his fourth, $165 50; and his fifth (GRANDFATHER WHITEHEAD), $313 50. On Monday, December 4, Mr. Placide played in two pieces, CLANDESTINE MARRIAGE and DOUBLE BEDDED ROOM, supported by a company fully competent for their correct performance, to a house of $96! Next night GRANDFATHER WHITEHEAD, and the comedy of JOHN BULL, brought the receipts up to $444 25; but next night (Placide in two pieces, and another piece performed with them) the receipts fell down to $49 25!

Ole Bull, the great violinist, played three nights, at double prices of admission, to the following receipts: $1103, $1207, $883, and $953.

Vieuxtemps also played a few nights, but his attraction at our house was small, while at the French theatre he did pretty well.

We had a troupe of wild beasts, under the management of a Mr. Hopkins, and they performed in a piece entitled MUNGO PARK, in which a Mr. Shaffer played *Mungo*, I believe. Mr. Shaffer also went into the cage of wild animals. During this engagement I received a note one morning from Miss Edista Stora, in the following words:

"New Orleans, February 2, 1844.

"*To Sol. Smith, Esq., Manager, St. Charles Theatre:*

"SIR,—Understanding that you are in need of a female with sufficient nerve to act with the wild beasts in a new piece to be brought forward, I wish to offer my services for the purpose, if we can come to an understanding. I am no actress, never having been on the stage; but if the part has not much in it to say, I am confident I can acquit myself with credit as far as being with the wild beasts, or permitting them to climb upon or over me may require.

"An early answer by the bearer, stating when an interview can be had, is respectfully requested by your obedient servant,

"EDISTA STORA."

It seemed a strange notion of the young woman; but believing, from the amiable temper of the animals, that she would incur no danger, and that a woman appearing in the cage with wild animals would prove attractive, I drew up the following brief engagement, which she signed by making her mark:

"New Orleans, February 3, 1844.

"I do hereby engage with the managers of the St. Charles Theatre to go into the cage of wild animals with Mr. Shaffer, on Sunday night (to-morrow), in the said theatre, for the sum of ten dollars; also, if required, on Monday night, for the same sum.

her
"EDISTA × STORA."
mark.

This Lady of the Lions "went into the cage with Mr. Shaffer" two nights, but this apparently dangerous feat created no sensation, nor increase to the receipts at the treasury. The truth is, Hopkins's were very tame beasts, and it was a hard matter to get up an idea that they were in any way dangerous, *in* or *out* of the cage. In one scene of MUNGO PARK, the hero—*Mungo* himself—played by Shaffer, was to be jumped upon, while lying asleep, by a tiger, and a terrific struggle (so said the bills) was to take place between the man and the infuriated animal; but, all that the keepers could do, the animal would not become infuriated. It was something like Barnum's buffalo-hunt over in Hoboken—a failure. The tiger was dropped down through a hole cut in the scene, so arranged that she appeared to spring upon Shaffer from a thicket. A struggle ensued, but it was Shaffer struggling to hold on to the tiger so that she wouldn't run away!

Mr. J. W. Wallack—*the* Wallack, as he was called—was engaged for a few nights, but was not successful in drawing large audiences. Of this actor I must say that he was deservedly an immense favorite in this country since about 1820. He was very fascinating in his acting. No one could help admiring him. In London he was contemporary with Macready, and for many years considered by some his equal in tragedy, his superior in melodrama. Henry Clay told me he liked Wallack's *Hamlet* better than that of any actor he had ever seen perform the part, and he had seen all the great actors. *Rolla* was his most popular part in tragedy, but it afforded him no pleasure to be told so. He generally opened in *Rolla*, and *Dick Dashall*, in the farce of MY AUNT. Mr. Wallack never had his equal, I think, in such characters as *Martin Heywould*, *Massaroni*, *Michael* (ADOPTED CHILD), and *Don Cœsar de Bazan*.

On Wednesday, the 7th of February, took place the first appearance in New Orleans of Mr. Macready, who opened in HAMLET; receipts, $822. On Friday he appeared as *Macbeth;* receipts, 885. The houses did not keep up to that mark, but they were universally good. James H. Hackett played on what is termed the "off nights," but that unquestionably fine actor, backed up by H. Placide and the excellent stock company, was overshadowed by the "great tragedian." Only think of Hackett playing *Sir Pertinax Mac Sycophant* and *Mons. Mallet* to $118 50! and his benefit only yielding a hundred dollars more than that to his personation of *Rip Van Winkle*, *Col. Wildfire* (the KENTUCKIAN), and *Mons. Tonson!*

Mr. Macready finished his first fine engagement, and then played with us in the Mobile Theatre, which we rented from Mr. Caldwell that season.

Mr. Forrest followed Macready in the St. Charles, and played a good engagement, afterward going to Mobile.

On the finishing of a second engagement at the St. Charles, Mr. Macready went up with the company to St. Louis in the steamer Scott, Captain Swon. Some very amusing scenes were acted during this voyage, one of which I propose to relate.

An intimate Friend.

There is a class of individuals who claim to know every body. Actors particularly, and particularly *great* actors, are their most familiar companions. Macready, Forrest, and Booth are their most valued professional friends; they have known them *so* long and *so* intimately—interchanged *so* many civilities with them—been in their society under *so* many peculiar circumstances—indeed, they have known them from childhood—they consider them as brothers!

In 1844 one of this class happened to be a passenger on the Scott on her trip from New Orleans to St. Louis during the month of March. He was a jolly fellow, full of anecdote, and always ready with his joke, conundrum, repartee, or pun. Snatches of the fashionable negro songs—called, for fashion's sake, Ethiopian melodies—quaint sayings, and quotations from Shakspeare, were at his tongue's end. He was the life of the social hall. Not knowing his real name, we will call him Spriggins.

The great tragedian Macready had been performing an engagement at the St. Charles Theatre, and he was, of course, *the* subject of conversation in the cabin of all steam-boats leaving New Orleans. Spriggins had, according to his own account, attended the theatre every night Macready had acted.

"His *Macbeth* was great," said Spriggins, joining in a conversation by the stove in the social hall, where the passengers were picking their teeth and smoking, "his *Hamlet* superb, and his *Werner* magnificent! I have frequently said to him, at supper, after he has been personating the latter character—"

"You know him, then?" interrupted a passenger, who was at the moment lighting a cigar by Spriggins's.

"*Know* him?—know Bill Macready? Well, I should rather think I *do*—intimately—intimately—spent most of my leisure time with him while he was in Orleans. It was by *my* advice he came out to the South."

"Indeed!"

"Yes, indeed. It was a lucky thing for the managers that I happened to be in New York on Macready's arrival from England. He never would have visited the South had it not been for me."

"What sort of a man is he in private life?" inquired a gentleman.

"Oh," replied Spriggins, "he is devilish haughty and austere to strangers, but in his intercourse with friends he is a very companionable sort of a fellow, I assure you."

"Are you acquainted with Mr. Forrest?" asked a passenger.

"Acquainted with *him?* — Ned Forrest? Have known him since he was a boy. We were schoolmates in Philadelphia; saw him make his first appearance as *Young Norval* at the Chestnut Street Theatre. It was by *my* advice he adopted the stage as a profession. Great man Ned is, but, after seeing Macready, one doesn't relish Ned's acting as formerly. He is all very well as *Metamora* and *Jack Cade*, but when he attempts Shaksperian characters—" Spriggins concluded this criticism by shaking his head and slightly shuddering, as a man does when he has just taken a dose of salts.

"Did you see him act during his late engagement at the St. Charles?" asked one.

"No, I didn't," replied Spriggins. "Though I like Ned, I couldn't persuade myself to undergo his stentorian inflictions. He called to see me once or twice, and I dined with him three times, I believe, and that's the extent of our intercourse this season."

Spriggins went on chatting about actors and actresses till near dinner-time, giving very amusing accounts of their adventures during his long and intimate acquaintance with them. He knew them all "*like a book.*" The Southern managers were under great obligations to him for *advice;* indeed, they very seldom made any engagement of consequence without consulting *him.* He knew all the stars and principal stock actors and actresses. He had been the prime agent in getting up most of the complimentary benefits; he had written nearly all of the criticisms and puffs that had appeared in the New Orleans papers during the past theatrical season; in short, if his veracity might be relied on, he was the connecting link between the public and the theatre, and, to a casual observer, it would be a matter of wonder how theatrical affairs could proceed for a single week without him.

Who was he?

He knew every body connected with the stage, or who had been connected with it during the last twenty years. He dined with Mr. Caldwell twice a week. It was by his advice that gentleman had built the old St. Charles. We have already seen that he was on terms of intimacy with the two great tragedians of the age. Before the ringing of the dinner-bell, the congregated passengers in the social hall became aware that a few of the more humble followers of Thespis were also honored with Mr. Spriggins's acquaintance and limited regard. In reply to questions judiciously propounded by the cigar-smokers, it became known that the season at

New Orleans had closed, and that the company were about leaving for St. Louis; that *he* was bound for the same city, but he had declined the invitation of Bill Macready, Jim Ryder, Joe Field, Jack Weston, and Sol Smith to go with them in the J. M. White, in consequence of being obliged to stop on the way at several towns on the river. "Besides," he observed, "it is a relief to be by one's self during a journey of this kind; for I knew how it would be if I went with them—long sittings over the wine-bottle after dinner, late suppers, tedious stories, and professional reminiscences. I am *such* a favorite with them all that I should be bored to death with their attentions."

The bell rung out the summons to dinner. After the cloth had been removed, it was observed that five gentlemen remained, enjoying their wine, at the middle of the table. Spriggins cast a wistful look toward the party, but did not venture to move his chair up to the place occupied by the *bon vivants.* One of the five—a reverend-looking individual—observing that a gentleman lingered at the lower end of the table, after a short whispering consultation with his companions, sent the steward with the compliments of the party, and a request that Spriggins would honor them with his company, and partake of a glass of wine with them. He accepted the invitation with alacrity, and was soon the merriest of the group. During the "sitting," Spriggins imparted the information that he was connected with the press, and that he was on a tour through the river towns for the purpose of increasing the circulation of one of the New Orleans papers. He *might* proceed as far as St. Louis. Bill Macready was going to that place, and didn't know how he could get along in a city so far West without some friend to take care of him; but he didn't see, *he* didn't, how people could expect people to leave their business to attend to other people's business. Jim Ryder had insisted on his going; Joe Field had expressed a great desire that he would go, and assist him to establish his projected new paper; Jack Weston had said he *must* go, and Old Sol wouldn't take no for an answer.

"So," said Captain Swon, who had just joined the party, "you are very well acquainted with these actor folk, Mr. Spriggins?"

"*Acquainted* with actors? Oh, no; I don't know any of them—ha! ha! ha!" answered and laughed Spriggins, winking at the wine-drinkers all round; "never met any of them in my life."

At this moment the clerk of the boat happened to be passing by that section of the table where the party were enjoying themselves.

"What's that you say, Mr. Spriggins?—not know any of the actors!" said he. "Allow me to introduce you to a few: Mr. Macready, Mr. Spriggins; Mr. Ryder—Mr. Field—Mr. Weston—Mr. Sol Smith, Mr. Spriggins; Spriggins, Macready—Weston; Spriggins, Field—Ryder; Spriggins—"

The party rose to do honor to the introduction—all but Spriggins, who sat in his chair holding a wine-glass midway between the table and his mouth, the very picture of astonishment.

"Steward!" faltered Spriggins, when he found the use of his tongue, "bring forward my trunk; I get out at Natchez."

He *did* get out at Natchez, and I have been told that he now stoutly denies ever having been acquainted with any member of the theatrical profession.

Another scene I give in the words of Matt Field, as he wrote it out for the *Reveille*, a new paper which he and his brother, J. M. Field, and Charles Keemle, established in St. Louis this year:

"THE SECOND ADVENT.

"'A time, and a time, and a half a time—lo, a great time!'

"Not a great while since, there came, on one of our 'bully boats,' from New Orleans 'up,' a crowd of all sorts, and 'all sorts of a crowd' it proved to be; settees at a premium, and *standees* commanding attention; seats at the first table a romantic delusion, and second ditto a matter merely problematical. We will not say that there was any great degree of suffering from *ennui*, notwithstanding, for there were some 'good ones' on board, and plenty of *ice;* ducks in the river no one could hit; a lovely moon and ample boiler-deck, to say nothing of an occasional 'saw,' and a select library of De Koch novels! One day the strangely exciting intelligence was spread around that a 'live Millerite' had just turned up! A real live Millerite! And such, indeed, the stranger proved to be: a small-sized, middle-aged, transparent-looking gentleman, with a wandering eye, his hair combed back from a fine *slope* of forehead, a white cravat, and a black frock almost as transparent as his complexion. He was by no means backward in proclaiming his opinions, and a hand-bill was, in consequence, immediately put up at the bar, 'Wanted, a Mormon;' but, though one was discovered below among the deck passengers, he was too ill with an ague to confront the *fire-worshiper.* Such an opportunity on board a steam-boat was not to be lost, however, and, at request, the woe-commissioned one consented to explain his calculations and establish the proximity of brimstone immediately after tea. Tea dispatched, and all on tip-toe, the bell was rung, chairs were placed for the ladies, etc., when the Millerite appeared from his state-room (one of the berths in which a kind young gentleman had surrendered to him in reverence to his calling), bearing his *chart* and a wand *à la Lardner!*

"The chart was unusually large and awe-inspiring. When tacked up it covered two state-rooms. On one hand glared the figure of the Prophet's Vision, large as life, with its breast of gold and belly of brass, etc., etc.; then came the ram and the goat, the beast, the dragon, and the scarlet lady, with the array of units, tens, hundreds, and thousands fringing the edges mysteriously, as usual. After a rather self-satisfied and familiar request that Heaven would open the eyes of the benighted ones around him to a proper fear of the judgment which *might* arrive before morning, the learned lecturer began his explanations. He subtracted the bear from the dragon, added the goat to the beast, multiplied the horns by the legs, which, with the figure's 'ten toes,' Nebuchadnezzar, Napoleon Bonaparte, and the Clay Convention, gave the year 1844 as clear as mud!

"Smoking a cigar, gazing from the boiler-deck upon the glorious stars, perhaps pondering upon that mad mass, the human brain, the moments were passed till bedtime, when the less fortunate *at length* lay down, for a pillow enjoying the gentle inclination afforded by the back of a capsized chair, and so they slept.

"In the midst of their varied dreams of election bets, Joe Smith, Elder Knapp, and pitch-forks, all were roused suddenly by a most singular and startling noise. Fifty heads were popped up from the floor of the now but dimly lighted cabin, state-room doors were opened, there was a protrusion of profiles, and a general inquiry,

"'What the devil is that?'

"Among the very first, the door of the Millerite was flung open, and he appeared actually in his *ascension robe*, a long white gown reaching to his feet. His face wore a very wild expression, but whether with hope of the 'advent' or fear of an explosion we will not undertake to say. After much guessing and wondering what the matter was, and a general admission that it was 'a strange noise,' the heads began to disappear, when the sound was heard again, as sudden and as startling as before. It was something like an escape of steam, yet steam it certainly was not—a sort of cry, but abrupt—short—a sort of explosion of voice, as if the effort, suddenly checked, had burst the breather's windpipe. In the midst of the natural surprise and conjecture came a low chant of voices. The forward doors, opening upon the boiler-deck, were thrown wide, and a singular spectacle presented itself. A brilliant light streamed in upon the dim cabin, and a number of strange, tall figures, 'all in white,' approached along the vista, gliding, as it were, spectre-like, over the mattress-covered floor. Every one was roused and gazing in mute astonishment. The chant continued, and the figures came on. In their midst walked two much taller than the rest, apparently supporting a body of some kind on their shoulders, but what it was no one could tell, for it was also enveloped in long *white* drapery. On they came, solemnly and slowly, forming at length a semicircle round the Millerite's door, who regarded them with an eye of intense astonishment. One of the figures now thrust his arm under the cloth which covered the strange object just mentioned, and gave a turn or two, as if winding up an instrument, when instantly came once more that frightful cry, making the Millerite start back into his room. The chant now swelled more loudly, and its burden became distinguishable:

"'Come forth, oh thou elected,
Millennium is nigh;
Let sinners here rejected
Say now it's all my eye!'

"The figure continued his *winding-up* motion, and the strange cries and screams became absolutely ear-splitting. The Millerite endeavored to escape through the opposite door of his state-room on to the 'guard,' when a heavy object fell thundering at his feet, and in the very act of retreating into the air *a well-grown pig* darted between his legs, carrying him a few yards triumphantly, and finally disappeared headlong down the stairs leading to the lower deck, bearing off with him a considerable spread of the *ascension robe*, which he had stuck his fore legs through.

"Of course every body was up and out, but on their return the strange pageant had disappeared. The Millerite left the boat next morning, and, singular to say, notwithstanding every possible inquiry, nothing was ascertained as to who the wags were. They had evidently resolved not to '*say a word about the pig!*'"

CHAPTER VIII.

MR. MACREADY began the season with us in St. Louis, opening with HAMLET on the 9th of April, 1844. His engagement was not a great success here. Mr. Forrest followed soon after, and his engagement was a very poor one. Being absent nearly the whole of this season, I shall only say that it was pursued

"To a dismal and a fatal end;"

that is to say, it was fatal to the pockets of the managers, emptying them as effectually as *Macbeth's* daggers emptied the body of *King Duncan* of its blood.

After getting the season a going, I proceeded to Cincinnati, Ohio, having rented the National Theatre from Mr. John Bates, leaving Mr. Macready and a portion of the company (J. M. Field and wife, J. M. Weston and others) to follow, and join the forces from Mobile, which were to form the company for the support of the stars engaged for that city. My passage to Louisville was made on the steamer White Cloud. This was a *trial* trip, as will be seen from the following report:

Court of Uncommon Pleas.

Temperance vs. James Green. } *Indictment for whisky drinking out of a jug.*

If the reader has traveled much in the West, he has witnessed the proceedings of self-constituted courts on the boiler-decks of steam-boats. It has been the luck of the writer of this sketch to act as *judge* of many of these dignified tribunals, consequently he has been called on to pass judgment on many of his fellow-travelers during the last thirty years.

In the courts here spoken of the jurisdiction is generally co-extensive with the boats on which they are held, and it is very seldom an individual is found who is foolhardy enough to call in question their powers, hence the sentences are pretty generally carried into effect without resistance.

In the summer of 1844, when all was "hurrah for Clay" and "hurrah for Polk," a *term* of the Court of Uncommon Pleas was "begun and held" on board the good steamer White Cloud, Captain Robards, during her voyage from St. Louis to Louisville.

After the organization of the court by the appointment of judge, prosecuting attorney, clerk, and sheriff, proclamation was made by the latter functionary that all was ready for business. The first case on the docket was the one stated at the head of this report. The defendant, Green, a deck-passenger, had been delivering a temperance lecture in the cabin, and was retiring to his quarters on the lower deck, when he was arrested by the sheriff and brought before the "honorable court." I never saw a "prisoner at the bar," *charged with murder*, manifest more fear than did this poor fellow: the reason will appear hereafter. The indictment was read, charging him, the said Green, being at the time a member of a temperance society, with having, "with malice aforethought," drank whisky out of a jug, contrary to the dignity of the temperance cause and the interest of the bar-keeper of the White Cloud, etc.

"Prisoner, you have heard the charge; are you guilty or not guilty?"

"Not guilty," replied the trembling Green—"that is, not *very* guilty; I did take a little bit of—"

"Prisoner, answer distinctly to the charge—are you guilty or not guilty?"

"Is there any lawyer aboard?" asked the defendant, looking fearfully at the crowd.

"Yes," replied the Court, "there are any number of them on board, going to the Whig Convention at Nashville; you are entitled to counsel, and the Court assigns you L. V. Bogy, Esq., so you can unbosom yourself to *him*."

The worthy gentleman named readily accepted the appointment, and a jury being empaneled, the trial commenced.

The prosecuting attorney (who was no other than my friend Colonel A. B. Chambers, the well-known apostle of temperance) made a splendid "opening." He insisted that intemperance was the unpardonable sin, and demanded that the jury, if convinced of the guilt of the accused, should inflict the severest punishment known to the law.

The evidence all went to show that the accused had certainly committed the damning deed—he had most surely drank whisky—more than that, he had drank it out of a jug! There was no getting round it, or over it, or under it; drank he had—he had drank whisky—and out—of—a j-u-g!

The counsel for the prisoner, finding the *fact* could not be controverted, endeavored to *justify*, and went into a lengthy argument to show that the greatest men in ancient and modern times *had been and were drunkards;* that the greatest literary efforts had been inspired by the wine-bottle; and, so far from the defendant being blamable for what he had done, he, the learned counsel, contended that he was deserving of the highest commendation.

A reply from the prosecuting attorney closed the case, and the jury were about to retire to the pantry to deliberate on their verdict, when the defendant addressed the Court:

"May it please your honor, I want to say a few words, if you've no objections."

"By all means; you shall be heard. The defendant has a right to be heard by himself and counsel; proceed."

Green, trembling from head to foot, mounted a chair (on the intimation of the sheriff), and spoke as follows:

"Mister Judge, and gentle*men* of the jury, I want to say this much—I *am* guilty; I don't justify the drinking of the whisky, I don't. I tried to persuade my attorney not to make that sort of defense, but he *would* do it. I drank a leetle whisky; but *I took it for medicine*, as I have proved to you by the doctor who prescribed it. I know I've done wrong—*very* wrong, and I deserve punishment; but I beg and pray this honorable Court to have pity on my wife and—"

"Hast thou a wife?" interrupted the Court.

"I have," replied the defendant.

"And children?"

"No; no children *yet*, may it please the honorable Court, but *my wife is in a fix.*"

"A fix?"

"Yes; a fix."

"Prisoner, what do you mean by your wife being in a fix?"

"Why, your honor," proceeded the accused, "she will shortly become the mother of a fatherless orphan *if you throw me overboard.*"

"Throw you overboard! What has put that into your head, prisoner?"

"We, the jury, find the defendant *not guilty*, and recommend him to mercy. The sheriff to treat the jury, the attorneys to pay costs, and the judge to *fill the jug* which the defendant drank out of, and which the jury have emptied during the trial."

The defendant, when he heard the verdict read, fell down on his knees in thankfulness, renewed his temperance pledge, thanked the judge and

THE COURT OF UNCOMMON PLEAS. (See page 182.)

"Oh!" groaned Green, in agony, "I know the punishment of my crime; my counsel has told me all about it. I'm to be thrown overboard, to prevent my ever again drinking any thing but cold water!"

Finding the poor fellow took the matter so seriously, there was a general desire for his acquittal.

The judge gave a charge to the jury full of nice points of law, and leaning greatly toward the prisonet. Without leaving their seats, the jury returned the following verdict:

gentlemen of the jury, and in his wife's name called down blessings on the whole crowd.

CHAPTER IX.

NOTWITHSTANDING the great depression in business of all kinds—theatrical business particularly—I had hopes of a good season in Cincinnati, the scene of my earliest attempt in management. I was doomed to bitter disappointment. Macready's houses counted thus: $721, $292,

$430, $377, $295, $406; total in six nights, $2525; average per night, $422, half of which Mr. Macready received. The receipts on Forrest's nights were $360, $286, $142, $135, $207, $426, $175, $422, $140, $241, $426; total in eleven nights, $2960; average per night, $269, half of which went to Mr. Forrest. Is not this a pitiful beginning of a season? But worse remained behind! After the departure of the great stars the business fell down to almost nothing. H. Placide played his great character of *Grandfather Whitehead* to $7 75! Miss Nelson opened to $49! Hackett opened in his great *Falstaff* to $113, and played *Rip Van Winkle* to $78. H. Placide's benefit, $47; Hackett's, $124. You may be sure I was not idle during the engagements of the tragic stars, neither were the artists and carpenters, for they were working day and night on ALADDIN, which was eventually brought out with entirely new and gorgeous scenery by Lehr, machinery by Ellsworth, and two hundred new dresses, to a house of $98!! Next night $111, and the run of the piece continued without attracting any better houses. CHERRY AND FAIR STAR followed, equally well put upon the stage, and the first night yielded but $81. C. A. Logan, a very popular actor and resident of Cincinnati, took a benefit, and was honored with a house counting $61. J. M. Weston, another favorite, had $42; and Miss Randolph, a charming girl and good actress, had $52. The Fourth of July, advertised as, and intended to be, the closing of the season, the irresistible attraction of ALADDIN and CHERRY AND FAIR STAR was offered, to be played in the daytime and at night, and the Cincinnatians managed to contribute for both performances the enormous sum of $547, and were so elated with such a grand success (!) that a request was got up and extensively signed that the manager would consent to the reopening of the house for one night for the purpose of receiving a complimentary benefit! I was fool enough to comply with this request, and was *complimented* to the tune of $171.

I am thus particular in the details of this spring season for the reason that my friends in Cincinnati have since blamed me for not giving their city a fair trial. The total receipts for sixty-three nights, with a better company than had ever visited the place, or ever has visited it since, with the best stars and showy pieces, were $6098, about $96 per night!

Mr. Macready, the principal star of the season which I have just been writing about, is a great actor unquestionably, and, as I believe, a good man. Of his acting I judge by effects. For six nights I have sat and witnessed his personation of *Werner;* and his *King Lear* I have witnessed twice. Macready's *Hamlet* is a masterpiece. He acts *that* part at rehearsal as well as when before an audience. His *Iago* is very fine, but, in my estimation, not equal to that of the late James Wallack. His *Shylock* is immense, and far ahead of the *Shylock* of any other actor I have ever seen. In the character of *Joseph Surface* he was not appreciated by our audience, but he was extremely correct in it. The same may be said of his *Lord Townley*. In *Macbeth* he was great throughout, and I have seen the pit almost rise at him in the fifth act, where he turns from his flight at the taunts of Macduff, and says,

"I will not yield
To kiss the ground beneath young Malcolm's feet," etc.

I could see nothing extraordinary in Macready's *Cardinal Wolsey*. *William Tell* and *Virginius* (his original characters) were very good indeed; but, while playing those characters, he never *could* be satisfied with the support he received in our Southern and Western theatres. In *Richelieu* he fairly reveled in the consciousness that he had no rival who would even *attempt* competition.

In the second act of MACBETH, when he goes off to murder *King Duncan*, Mr. Macready went through the act of stabbing behind the scenes, and the carpenters to this day point out the spot upon the brick wall of the St. Charles where the stabs were made! It is quite true that he entirely forgot the actor in the character he was portraying. When he came to himself between the acts, he was irritable and fault-finding; never satisfied with those who acted with him, sending for this one and that one for the purpose of administering a lecture, and often, until I gave him notice I would not go, dispatching his servant to the manager, to whom he would pour out complaint after complaint, until the rising of the curtain called him to his duties upon the stage.

I have said I believed Mr. Macready to be a good man. I have many reasons to believe so. That he was an active and ardent lover of his art, no one can doubt who remembers that he spent £50,000 more than his receipts while managing the two great theatres of London, Drury Lane and Covent Garden. Of his goodness of heart I have had many opportunities of knowing. He has been called haughty and proud. I never found him so in the least.

The following letter, written (of course) without the slightest idea that it would ever be published, will be interesting to theatrical people, if not to others. It is in answer to a letter I wrote him, mentioning the fact that an old professional associate of his—Mr. James H. Caldwell—complained to me of his (Macready's) cold treatment when he met him in London, and afterward in New Orleans. Mr. Caldwell had told me that on separating many years previously in Liverpool, he had received from Mr. Macready a stage dress as a token of regard. Here is the letter:

W. C. Macready to Sol. Smith.

"Niagara, Upper Canada, June 3, 1844.

"MY DEAR SIR,—Your kind and welcome letter lay some time at New York, awaiting my emerging from a wild, unsettled district in that beautiful state, where I had been to 'hunt the flying deer.' But the deer were dear indeed; I got no venison, but had much delightful excitement—

"'The woods, the mountains, and the sun,
The streams that murmur as they run,
Were there my dearest joy.'

I am now rambling about, half idle, and the other half employed, but still with very little time on my hands, and that is my excuse for replying to you in such an apparent, and, indeed, actual hurry. My arrears of correspondence have grown like a mountain, and now are like an avalanche suspended over and threatening to overwhelm me. You are not the first by several, my dear sir, that have been *taught* to mistake me. No man is more sensible to, nor suffers more from self-reproach for his infirmities and errors than myself; but 'I am richer than my base accusers, who never knew what *truth* meant,' and I know that I *wish* to be just, and justice, in my definition, is as comprehensive as the great scheme of Christianity itself, which is the sublime of justice. It is a *very great satisfaction* to me that you think more indulgently of me than you had been taught to do, for I value the esteem of the estimable at its proper price. In regard to your inquiry respecting Mr. Caldwell, I beg to say that I was never on terms of intimacy with that gentleman; he was a stationary performer, I an auxiliary (a considerable distance in England!) in the Dublin Theatre for about eleven weeks, during which period I rarely saw him, and then only in the greenroom—certainly never addressed him *familiarly* in my life, but showed that courtesy which I endeavored to practice to all respectable actors. I dare say I gave him, with other actors, one of my dresses, as my country wardrobe ceased to be of use to me *after that engagement*, my first London engagement beginning the September following, when the same professional gear would not be suitable to my advanced position, and I gave away nearly my whole wardrobe. I could tell you the names of several to whom I had presented them. I assure you this was a mere civility on the part of a very young man, fond of giving, and merely indulging a disposition. The persons in the Dublin Theatre at the same time, with whom I was on terms of greater intimacy—and for one I entertained a friendship—to these my demeanor never changed during their lives. Without wishing to say an ungracious thing of or to any person, I can not but think that Mr. Caldwell's memory is either not so good as mine, or that he must have construed a mere civility (which a person about to throw his life's fortunes on the hazard is often, I may say *superstitiously*, prone to be lavish of) into a testimony, which was not intended as such. I perhaps should regret more than I do any misapprehension of Mr. Caldwell's if I had not had reported to me his mention of my name at the St. Charles Hotel! I can only assure you that however he may have interpreted any behavior of mine into the expression of a desire to be intimately acquainted, I never had such intention, nor ever meant my manner to convey such an impression. I bowed to him in England, as I should to any gentleman I had only professionally known for a few weeks, after the lapse of so many years. *You know* I do not carry the 'hail fellow well met' address of a greenroom into my circle of acquaintance, and *that disappoints* and *annoys many actors*, and has *been one great means* of sending to you the lessons you had been taught of me. Mr. Stephen Price has told me of this, and I have heard something like remarks to this effect from other theatrical people; but if my education and habits have made me carry the same address into a greenroom that I do into a drawing-room, those to whom it was distasteful have had their revenge, as your preconceived notions of me testify. This I can say, that the good qualities of a man's heart make it a duty to me to grapple that man to me—high or low, rich or poor. I honor and regard him, and am *happy* in the ability to show I do. Should I not see you again, my dear sir, before my departure in October, I leave with you the assurance of my cordial and lasting esteem and regard, subscribing myself in good earnest most sincerely yours, W. C. MACREADY."

We had taken the Cincinnati Theatre for the full season, and reopened on the 24th of August. No use. A dead failure. To help the matter, I felt a fever gradually creeping upon me, and—but, before saying any thing more about this fever, I will say that the fall season was worse, if possible, than that of the summer. Logan, into whose hands I placed the management when I "knocked under," did all that man could do, but all—all in vain. In vain he brought out the FORTY THIEVES, the ICE WITCH, and other attractive pieces. The theatre closed ingloriously on the 5th of October, several weeks earlier than contemplated, and I have not visited Cincinnati managerially nor professionally since. Now, about the fever aforesaid, the truth is, I came very near

Kicking the Bucket.

Pulse 140! — *Whiew!* — *Whurr!*

Reader, did you ever have a fever?—a regular-built, up and down, thumping fever?—a fever that carried you up, as it were, to another existence? I had such a fever in the fall of 1844—September—in Cincinnati. I tried to *put* it *off*. It wouldn't go. I went to Louisville in a steamboat, and endeavored to persuade myself, during the night, while my pulse was rising and my brain was becoming more and more pressed, that *I should be better in the morning*. I endeavored to transact business in Louisville, but my questions and replies were so incoherent that the people stared at me and (for aught I know) thought me tipsy. On the return trip, all was pleasant enough in the afternoon, but at night, and during the long night, thump, thump, thump went my blood again, as though it was determined to burst through and be free.

I found myself at my brother's house on Fourth Street, where a room is always reserved for me. I had purchased some calomel and castor oil on my way from the boat, and I went to taking medicine. It did no good—the fever did not diminish at all. At the request of my good brother a homœopathic physician was called in, who attended me and administered small globules of something or other for a week — *two* weeks, perhaps — probably *three*—"I took no note of time." No change. My brothers and other relations visited me frequently. I could see by their manner they thought I must go. They did not shake their heads, but the expression of their countenances did not at all conform to their words of comfort and encouragement.

My sense of hearing was fearfully acute. I could *hear them look!* It was plain enough I was given up. The doctor (Dutch at that!) said he had been called too late; if he had only been called in before I had taken the calomel all would have been well, but—

With the exception of a headache, which hung to me, it was not a disagreeable month I passed thus. The pressure on my brain caused those about me to take the most fanciful forms and to do the drollest things. The doctor appeared to *dance* into the room, pour his useless (and harmless) medicine into water, and present me the tumbler, dancing all the while; my sisters, my brothers, nieces and nephews, all to appearance about half their real height, danced about the apartment in the most picturesque forms, all bearing a striking resemblance to each other, and all wearing wreaths — rocking, prancing, bending, smiling, and attitudinizing to the tune of—my pulse. It was very pleasant indeed.

I remember every occurrence while under the influence of this fever with the utmost distinctness. About the eighteenth day I called the homœopathic doctor to my bedside and told him I had no farther occasion for his services. He remonstrated—the family remonstrated; but I was firm: I would take no more of those little globules.

My friend Logan came to see me every day. When he found the homœopathist had retired he urged the calling in of one of the allopathic physicians. After some argument I consented, and Dr. Shotwell took me in hand. I could see plainly enough *he* thought the call had been put off too long, but he prescribed for me, and in one week I was able to sit up an hour at a time; in two weeks I could walk, and in less than three I embarked for St. Louis—my home.

When I began to write this article I intended to describe some of my singular fancies, but I shall confine myself to *one* strange fancy I took into my feverish head.

It seemed to me that *possibly* my friends might be right, and that I was doomed to *kick the bucket* sure enough. I was away from home — my affairs were unsettled — no preparations made for such a feat; but yet, I thought, my time had possibly come! The idea was not at all unpleasant. I had shaken off all care of business, having placed it in competent hands, and my only uneasiness arose from the TROUBLE I was giving my kind nurses. I took up the idea that, if I must *kick the bucket*, I might as well do it in the middle of the night, when most of the family were asleep, so that in the morning they would find *all was over with me*, and the disagreeable part of the business would be past. I kept thinking of this, and constantly continued to contrive out ways and means to effect my designs without causing trouble to the family. I knew that if I *asked for a bucket to kick*, they would refuse to let me have it; so I pretended every night that I wanted water to bathe my feet in, and, when I had finished bathing them, I always asked the girl to leave the bucket on a chair beside my bed! And there I lay, night after night, waiting for the time to come when I should kick the bucket without *troubling* any one! In the middle of the night I would laugh heartily at my cunning contrivance, keeping the bucket all the time within kicking distance of my right foot, and chuckling at the idea of what a splash I would make when I should give my *last kick!*

But I recovered in spite of the doctors, homœpathic and allopathic, yet not entirely so until I got home in St. Louis. From the effects of the quinine poured into me by Dr. Short (with the best intentions, of course), I believe I have not yet recovered — and twenty-four years have passed. During my sickness Logan was a constant caller, and had a fair opportunity of knowing all about my "case," and I could perceive he thought the chances were greatly against my ever getting well. It will be seen from the following little sketch, which I cut out of a newspaper in 1845, that the nature of certain medicines were sadly mixed up in my wandering mind:

"FEBRIFUGE AND VERMIFUGE!

"*By C. A. Logan.*

"Sol was so desperately ill in this city last summer that Death and he were for weeks playing at a game in which both parties were so *dead* a match that the slightest false move on either side would have fatally decided the wager. Sol is acknowledged to be an excellent player, but Death has had great experience in his line, and often makes tremendous hits. Sol played, too, at great disadvantage, having to carry on the game on the flat of his back, while his adversary stood bolt upright before him, displaying his *points* in the strongest light. At length Sol became somewhat doubtful about his next *move*, and called in the aid of a celebrated physician—as skillful a man as this or any other city can boast. 'Let me feel your pulse,' said the doctor. Sol stretched out what in better days had been his arm. 'Hum! you should have sent for me before.' 'Do your best now,' replied the sick man. For a whole week there was no appearance of amendment in poor Sol. The doctor would come, feel his pulse, look at his tongue, order him to take—nothing, and depart. Out of all patience, Sol said one morning, 'Give me something, doctor; don't let me lie here and die without an effort to break the fever.' The doctor wrote a prescription. 'What's this?' said the patient: 'I'll swallow no drugs I don't know the ingredients of.' 'It's a febrifuge,' said the physician, briefly. 'A what?' 'A febrifuge.' 'Febrifuge! febrifuge!' repeated the patient, slowly and musingly. 'Hum! and you have been coming here daily for a week, and you now give me a febrifuge. Be good enough to hand me that purse on the table—thank you—how much is your fee?' The doctor stared. 'How much do I owe you, I say? You don't understand my case, and I will insist on your leaving me.' 'Mr. Smith—' exclaimed the doctor, fearing the fever had disordered his head. 'Stop!' said Sol; 'you won't take the money? Then send in your bill and retire, I beg of you.' The physician looked with commiseration on the suffering man, but, observing the fire flash from his sunken sockets, withdrew with a haughty bow.

"Half an hour afterward Logan came in, and found Sol repeating in every variety of indignant tone, 'Febrifuge! febrifuge! the ignorant quack! give me febrifuge! What do you think, Logan? that licensed assassin, after considering my case for a week, has just found out that I'm troubled with *worms*, and has prescribed a febrifuge! Worms! who ever heard of any body but molasses-candy-sucking children having worms?'

"'Febrifuge! worms!' said Logan, in surprise; 'haven't you made some mistake? Febrifuge is *any* medicine intended to cure fevers; aren't you thinking of vermifuge?' 'Oh Lord!' groaned Sol—'vermifuge—that's what I meant; I've made a mistake; call back that doctor—I must beg his pardon. But why, in the name of heaven, don't they give Christian names to their drugs?'"

I close this chapter with a pen-sketch, which, with some other scribblings of mine, has been thought worthy of a place in Burton's Cyclopædia of Wit and Humor.

Tom, "the Man at the Curtain."

(Written in 1844.)

Tom is a character. I remember him when he was a chubby little red-haired boy; he is now a very large, freckle-faced man. I can not call to mind my first acquaintance with him; indeed, I don't believe, when I come to think of it, that I *have* any acquaintance with him. All I know of him is, ever since I can remember, *he has been within call*, and has obeyed every order given with the most scrupulous exactness and at every hazard. Tom is always about the theatre. By some chance or other, he was placed, ten or fifteen years ago, "at the curtain" in St. Louis—that is to say, he was required on some emergency to turn the wheel which draws up the curtain, and he has stuck to that wheel ever since! When I say that wheel, I do not mean *the* veritable wheel that he was first placed at—no; he has followed the company to every place and to all places, and has turned every wheel of every curtain that has been drawn up by order and by the direction of the writer of this sketch, through all the turnings of Fortune's wheel during a series of eventful years. The old theatre on Second Street, commonly called the "Salt-house," was probably the first scene of Tom's official duties. There he was, for years, perched upon a platform about six feet above the prompter's head, grinning at the plays, and ready, without warning, to obey the bell. He was a fixture—always there, and never out of the way when wanted. This was not all. At an early age, I remember he was very watchful of the other officials behind the scenes, and every neglect of duty was duly noticed by Tom, and a juvenile cursing was duly administered to every delinquent. All bore with him—all liked Tom.

A new theatre was built in Mobile in 1835. In the hurry of business we neglected to employ a man to raise the curtain; nevertheless, at the ringing of the bell, the curtain went up—Tom was there. I do not know to this day how Tom in those days obtained his bread. He *slept* in the theatre—up by the curtain wheel.

The new St. Louis Theatre was erected in 1837.

Tom obeyed the bell, and has taken his station at the wheel and drawn up the curtain every night of every season since. In 1840 another new theatre was built in Mobile, and Tom having been detained (with me) on the voyage down the Mississippi, he and I were not present on the opening night, so another man was unthinkingly engaged to raise the curtain. On the second night of performance, while the overture was being played, I heard a slight bustle above my head, and was about inquiring into the cause of the disturbance, when a human body fell at my feet nearly senseless—it was the new curtain man! I looked up, and behold, Tom's face was peeping out from among the pulleys and ropes like a large pumpkin from its own vines.

"Halloo above there!" I hailed.

"Ay, ay, sir!" answered Tom.

"What's the meaning of this?" I inquired.

"The meaning is, sir," replied Tom, "that the fellow who lies there was interloping, sir—pretended he was engaged *in my place!* ho! ho! ho!"

I pacified the knocked-down individual and sent him away, leaving Tom in quiet and undisputed possession of his elevated post.

How did Tom travel? He was always on the boats that I traveled on; always looking out for the freight; always seeing to its embarkation and debarkation, and always cursing those who neglected their duty. He was the last to leave the theatre at the closing of a season, and the first to enter it on commencing a campaign. If any one was at a loss for a key, "Where's Tom?" was the first inquiry. Tom could tell all about the keys; Tom could open every door.

After a number of years' close attention to business, Tom hinted that he was now "big enough" to *receive a salary*—so Tom's salary for raising the curtain was fixed at three dollars per week; but he earned something more by carrying to and from the theatre the bundles and boxes of the performers.

In latter years Tom has been doing a pretty good business. He has earned, on an average, besides his salary for turning the wheel, about four dollars per week. Without orders, he takes the place of any one who happens to be absent, either from sickness or other cause.

On salary-days, Tom's face is seen at twelve o'clock peeping through the banisters of the stairs leading to the director's room.

"Well, Tom, what do we owe *you* this week?"

"Why, sir," replies Tom, "I have been property-man two days, that's three dollars; second carpenter four nights, eight dollars; paint-grinder half a day, fifty cents; back-doorkeeper one night, one dollar; and gas man two nights and part of another, four dollars—in all, sixteen dollars and fifty cents; my salary added, makes nineteen dollars and fifty cents, sir."

"Very well, Tom, there it is."

"Thank you, sir!" Exit Tom, who is immediately after heard down in the vestibule, "Look here, you d—d loafers! See how a *gentleman* is paid for his services. Go up and get your paltry ten dollars a week—you are *actors!* ho! ho! ho! ho! But I'll be liberal; come down with me to the Shades, and I'll treat you all!"

To while away the time on board of steamboats, we have frequently established Courts of "*Un*common Pleas." The mandates of these courts are generally obeyed with alacrity by the passengers; but once in a while a contumacious individual is found who can not enjoy a joke, and who objects to be "fooled with." Whenever it has been my fortune to be appointed judge, I have stipulated that the sheriff should appoint Tom one of his deputies; and woe to the man who attempted to resist *him*. A word from me was enough for Tom. "Bring such a one before the court." Ay, ay, sir," Tom would answer, and a "return forthwith" would be made of the corpus required, sometimes minus a coat, which would be sacrificed in the useless struggle. I verily believe, if I should command Tom to throw a man overboard, he would not hesitate a moment to obey me!

Tom can speak French as well as English, and can read and write very well in both languages, though where he *learned* to do *any* thing except carry baskets for the performers and wind up curtains I can not tell.

Tom's appearance is very much like what we may suppose was that of the "Dougal creature" in Scott's Rob Roy.

A couple of years ago Tom had some money left him by a relative—no one knew till then that Tom ever *had* a relative—and, after dressing himself in the best suit that could be had at Martin's, he spent the whole legacy in *hiring horses!* taking especial care, however, to be at his post in time to wind up the curtain each night.

In the summer of 1843 there occurred a long vacation. On reopening, the bell was rung as usual, and (of course) the curtain rose; but it rose slowly—*very* slowly. "What can this mean?" I asked the master carpenter. "I believe, sir," replied Ellsworth, "Tom is not well—he got in late—he appears hurt." I ascended the winding stairs to the wheel, and there lay poor Tom, holding on to the crank, which he had not been able to make fast, pale and haggard, and his skin hanging about his bones like

—like—I can't think of a simile; but his appearance bore about as much resemblance to his former self as a *raisin* bears to a *ripe grape.* "Why, what's the matter with you, Tom?" I asked, soothingly, after relieving him of the crank. "What *is* the matter with you?"

Tom looked up gratefully into my face, and replied, "Ah! sir, they've played the d—l with my innards—stabbed me in eleven places!"

"*Who* have played the d—l with you? *who* have stabbed you?" "Those cursed Mexicans, sir—the traders. I started with 'em for Santa Fe, just to fill up the vacation; but I hadn't gone more than seven hundred miles beyond Independence when the infernal dark-skinned rascals picked a quarrel with me because I wouldn't worship the Virgin every morning, and all stuck their knives into me."

Poor Tom!

"And didn't you wound any of *them?*" I asked.

"Wound any of 'em?" echoed Tom. "Well, I believe you! I WOUND THREE OF THEM UP! *They'll* never worship any more Virgins in this world, I believe," he answered.

Tom recovered, and he continues to wind up the curtain nightly!

CHAPTER X.

THE New Orleans season of 1844–5, the worst of all seasons I was ever concerned in (always excepting that of Mobile in 1839-40), commenced November 23. As a specimen of the business of the St. Charles, I record the miserable receipts of the first week: Saturday—WIVES AS THEY WERE AND MAIDS AS THEY ARE, with an afterpiece, $184; Sunday—PILOT, DUMB BELLE, and A ROLAND FOR AN OLIVER, $177; Monday—TOWN AND COUNTRY and A LADY AND GENTLEMAN IN A PECULIARLY PERPLEXING PREDICAMENT, $88; Tuesday—(Never acted) MARY TUDOR and NEW FOOTMAN, $68; Wednesday—WIFE and MR. AND MRS. WHITE, $70; Thursday—second night of MARY TUDOR and FORTUNE'S FROLIC, $69; Friday—(Benefit of the author) MARY TUDOR and MIDDY ASHORE, $84. Total receipts for the week, $743—a loss sustained of about $1400! Not very encouraging, you will probably think. But the next week was worse, for it only yielded $660; and the third worse still, $494. I am not going to pursue this theme. After seven weeks it became absolutely necessary that I should go to St. Louis for the purpose of raising funds to carry the season through; so, leaving the reins of management in the hands of J. M. Weston, I started up the river in a boat commanded by Captain Summons, a real jolly old Cincinnatian.

Breaking a Bank.

Captain Summons was a very clever fellow, and the "Dr. Franklin" was a very superb boat, albeit inclined to rock about a good deal, and nearly turn over on her side when visited by a breath of air in the least resembling a gale. Captain Summons was a clever fellow. All steamboat captains are clever fellows, or *nearly* all; but what I mean to say is, Captain Summons was a *particularly* clever fellow; a clever fellow in the widest sense of the term; a fellow that is clever in every way—anxious that his passengers shall be comfortably bestowed, well fed and well attended to, and *determined* that they shall amuse themselves "just as they d—n please," as the saying is. If he happened to have preachers on board, he put on a serious countenance of a Sunday morning, consented that there should be preaching, ordered the chairs to be set out, and provided Bibles and hymn-books for the occasion, himself and officers, whose watch was below, taking front seats and listening attentively to the discourse. Likely as not, at the close of the service, he would ask the reverend gentleman who had been officiating, with his back in close proximity to a hot fire in a Franklin furnace, to accompany him to the bar and join him in some refreshments! If there were passengers on board who desired to pass away the time in playing poker, euchre, brag, or whist, tables and chairs were ready for *them* too—poker, brag, euchre, and whist be it! All sorts of passengers were accommodated on the Dr. Franklin; the rights of none were suffered to be infringed; all were free to follow such employments as should please themselves. A *dance* in the evening was a very common occurrence on this boat, and when cotillons were *on the carpet* the captain was sure to be *thar.*

It sometimes happened that, at the commencement of a voyage, it was found somewhat difficult to reconcile *all* the passengers to the system of Captain Summons, which was founded on the broad principle of equal rights to all.

On the occasion of my voyage in the "Doctor," in December, 1844, I found myself surrounded by a crowd of passengers who were *entire strangers* to me—a very rare occurrence to one who travels so often on the Western rivers as I do. I wished my absence from New Orleans to be as brief as possible, and the "Doctor" was the fastest boat in port at the time of my leaving the Crescent City; so I resolved to secure a berth in her, and trust to luck to find a St. Louis boat at the Mouth.

I don't know how it is or *why* it is, but by strangers I am almost always taken for a PREACHER. It was so on this voyage. There were two Methodist *circuit* riders on board, and it happened that we got acquainted and were a good deal together, from which circumstance I was supposed to be *one of them*, which supposition was the means of bringing me into an acquaintance with the female passengers, who, for the most part, were very pious, religiously-inclined souls. We had preaching every day, and sometimes at night; and I must say, in justice to Brothers Twitchell and Switchell, that their sermons were highly edifying and instructive.

In the mean time a portion of the passengers "at the other end of the hall" continued to play sundry games with cards, notwithstanding the remonstrances of the worthy followers of Wesley, who frequently requested the captain to interfere and break up such unholy doings. The captain had but one answer—it was something like this: "Gentle*men*, amuse yourselves as you like; preach and pray to your hearts' content—none shall interfere with your pious purposes; some like that sort of thing—*I* have no objection to it. These men prefer to amuse themselves with cards; let them; they pay their passages as well as you, gentle*men*, and have as much right to *their* amuse*ments* as you have to *yours*, and they shall not be disturbed. Preach, play cards, dance cotillons, do what you like, *I* am agreeable; only understand that *all games* (preaching among the rest) *must cease at* 10 *o'clock*." So *we* preachers got very little comfort from Captain Summons.

Up, up, up, up we went. Christmas day arrived. All the *other* preachers had holden forth on divers occasions, and it being ascertained that it was my intention to leave the boat on her arrival at Cairo, a formal request was preferred that *I should preach the Christmas sermon!* The women (God bless them all!) were *very* urgent in their applications to me. "Oh *do*, Brother Smith; we want to hear *you* preach. All the others have contributed their share to our spiritual comfort—you *must* oblige us—indeed you must." I endeavored to excuse myself the best way I could, alleging the necessity of my leaving the boat in less than an hour—my baggage was not ready—I had a terrible cold, and many other good and substantial reasons were given, but all in vain; preach I must. "Well," thinks I, "if I must, I must." At this crisis, casting my eyes down toward the Social Hall, and seeing an unusual crowd assembled around a table, I asked one of the brethren what might be going on down there. The fattest of the preaching gentlemen replied, "The poor miserable sinners have filled the measure of their iniquity by opening a FARO BANK!" "Horrible!" exclaimed I, holding up my hands, and "horrible!" echoed the women and missionaries in full chorus. "Can not such doings be put a stop to?" asked an elderly female, addressing the pious travelers. "I fear not," groaned my Methodist colleague (the fat one). "We have been trying to convince the captain that some dreadful accident will inevitably befall the boat if such proceedings are permitted, and what do you think he answered?" "What?" we all asked, of course. "Why, he just said that, inasmuch as he permitted *us* to preach and pray, he should let other passengers dance and play, if they chose to do so; and that, if I didn't like the 'proceedings' complained of, *I might leave the boat!* Yes, he did; and, moreover, he mentioned that it was 11 o'clock, and asked me if I wouldn't 'liquor!'" This announcement of the captain's stubbornness and impiety was met with a general groan of pity and sorrow, and we resumed the conversation respecting the unhallowed faro bank. "It is much to be regretted," remarked the gentlewoman who had spoken before, "that *something* can't be done. Brother Smith," she continued, appealing directly to me, and laying her forefinger impressively upon my arm, "can not *you* break up that bank?" "Dear madam," I answered, "you know not the difficulty of the task you impose upon me; FARO BANKS ARE NOT SO EASILY BROKEN UP as you may imagine; however, as you all appear so anxious about it, if you'll excuse me from preaching the sermon I'll see what can be done." "Ah! that's a dear soul!" "I knew he would try!" "He'll be sure to succeed!" "Our prayers shall not be wanting!" Such were the exclamations that greeted me as I moved off toward the faro bank. Elbowing my way into the crowd, I got near the table in front of the dealer, and was for a time completely concealed from the view of my pious friends near the door of the ladies' cabin. I found the bank was a small affair. The betters were risking trifling sums, ranging from six to twenty-five cents.

"Mr. Dealer," I remarked, "I have come to break up this bank." "The deuce you have!" replied the banker; "let's see you do it." "What amount have you in bank?" I inquired. "Eleven dollars," was his answer. "What is your limit?" asked I. "A dollar," he replied.

"Very well," said I, placing a ragged Indiana dollar behind the queen—"turn on." He turned, and the king won for me. I took the two dollars up and let him make another turn, when I replaced the bet, and the queen came up in my favor. I had now four dollars, which I placed in the square, taking in the 5, 6, 7, and 8, and it won again! Here were seven dollars of the banker's money. I pocketed three of them, and bet four dollars behind the queen again; the jack won, and the BANK WAS BROKEN! The crowd dispersed in all directions, laughing at the breaking up of the petty bank, and I made my way toward the ladies' cabin, where my new friends were anxiously awaiting the result of my bold attempt. "Well, well, well," they all exclaimed, "what success? Have you done it? Do let us hear all about it!" I wiped the perspiration from my brow, and, putting on a very serious face, I said solemnly, "I HAVE BROKEN THAT BANK!" "You have?" they all exclaimed. "Yes, I'll be d—d if he hasn't!" muttered the disappointed gamester, the keeper of the late bank, who was just going into his state-room. In the midst of the congratulations which were showered upon me, I received a *summons* from the captain to come forward with my baggage—we were at Cairo.

Disembarking from the "Doctor" at Cairo, I wended my way, in company with a jolly company of drovers, and in a common road wagon, the only conveyance to be had, through snow, sleet, and rain, over the bleak prairies of Illinois, to St. Louis, which city we reached in five days. Here I remained about a week with my family, during which time I made the necessary "raise" of funds for the New Orleans requirements by mortgaging property.

It happened that the third payment was due the city for the 4½ acres of land I had purchased a few years previously in the city commons, and, on a cold January morning, I started down Second Street for Mr. Provencière's office to pay it. The amount was small, and the payment of that and one more instalment would entitle me to a deed from the city; yet, in my solitary walk, I began to doubt whether I ought to go on and complete the payment! It seemed a hopeless task to attempt to get through the pecuniary difficulties which surrounded me. "All must go," said my evil genius. "All must go—let your land go—let *all* go, and leave this money with your wife to get wood and provisions for the winter, which is going to be a very cold one." I listened to the fiend (I thought of *Launcelot Gobbo* in the play), and actually turned around and commenced walking northwardly toward my home! I had no sooner made this turn than my good genius, "hanging round the neck of my heart," said, "Don't go back without paying that money to Provencière! You are within two squares of his office. Pay it! Times are going to change; it is always darkest before day. Your seven years of ill luck are almost past; there will be a turn in your affairs next year, see if there isn't! Pay Provencière, and trust to luck to get through your theatrical difficulties; this sum is but a drop in the bucket to pay your New Orleans debts with. You have raised several thousand dollars to take South. Take this small sum — the firm owes you twenty times that amount — and secure your commons lot; it is going to be valuable." The fiend tried to get in a word or two, but I couldn't hear him, for at that moment came such a blow from old Boreas that it was impossible to proceed a step farther north for a minute or two, during which minute or two my good genius threw in a few words which decided me. I turned toward Provencière's, and did not listen to a word my evil genius had to say until I had made the payment, and then I laughed at him. I will close up the account of this little land speculation when I come to write of better times.

I went back to New Orleans with a full purse (of borrowed money), and paid off all salaries due, some of which had gone behind eleven weeks.

The only stars that were attractive this season were James R. Anderson and the Seguin Opera Troupe, and their attraction was only moderate. Anderson played *Claude Melnotte* to some tolerably good houses. We produced the FAIR ONE WITH THE GOLDEN LOCKS, DON CÆSAR DE BAZAN, and FAUSTUS in good style—all without avail. The total receipts of the season were only $22,446 (twenty weeks), while the expenses could not have been very much short of $50,000. In debt "deeper and deeper still;" but I felt as if this was our last bad season in New Orleans, and that on the following 20th of November — seven years from the date of the burning of the St. Emanuel Theatre in Mobile—a favorable change would take place in the business, and we should rise from our misfortunes, pay all our debts, and be once more free.

I here give one of several letters received from Mrs. Ewing (formerly Miss Hamblin), the woman who killed her husband in the Mobile Theatre, as related in a letter from Mr. Buckstone in 1842:

LETTER FROM A REPENTANT MURDERESS.

Charlotte Ewing to Sol. Smith.

"New Orleans, May 25, 1845.

"MR. SOL. SMITH: DEAR SIR,—I wrote to you last winter, and sent the letter by Mr. Ewing, my husband's father—the sorrowing and bereaved father. You refused to see me. Had you come, I would have thrown myself at your feet, and, with streaming eyes and a bursting heart, begged you for an engagement—for something to do to support myself and father honestly. And now I beg, as you are a father, a husband—as you have children of your own—oh, in mercy, give me something to do! I may have done wrong, but oh! in mercy, do not you cast me off. Give me, I beg you, a chance to regain what I have lost. If you have cause to complain of me, then cast me off, and give me that name I think I was not born to bear. I am most friendless and heart-broken. You knew me when I was happy—oh! do not desert me in my misery. I have no one to speak for me—no one to say a word in my behalf. I feel as though my heart would break. I do not ask you to believe my simple word, but try me; put me to the test. Let me come and work in the theatre. Give me any thing you please—I will not complain. On my knees I beg and pray you—with heart-broken anguish, believe me. If the whole world curse me, oh! do not you desert me. My heart will break. I turned me on all and every side, and every one shrinks from me as from a leper whose every breath comes filled with pestilence and disease. Tell me, is this the way to win a woman back to virtue? is this the way to succor a friendless and unprotected woman? Oh! what shall I do if you refuse me your countenance?

"Pray, pray write me that you will see me next winter, for I am an outcast and heart-broken woman. I have not a friend in the wide world. Save me—oh! save me from despair, and I will pray God to bless you forever; for I *will* stand firm in the right path, if you will give me an opportunity.

"Respectfully, CHARLOTTE EWING."

Mr. and Mrs. Hart were members of the company this winter season. I had known Mr. Hart in New York State as long ago as 1825. He was my successor in the management of the Georgia theatres and the theatre in Montgomery, Ala. Mrs. Hart was the Miss Carter who, with her father and mother, traveled with me in 1831–2 through West Tennessee, Alabama, and Georgia.

The season at the American Theatre, under the management of Mueller & Place, burst up prematurely, as all seasons had since it was rebuilt.

I don't remember much about the season of 1845 in St. Louis, but there was no very favorable change.

This summer (if I remember rightly—I can't find any memoranda to guide me), leaving the theatrical affairs to be mostly conducted, in the details, by my partner, I spent in the *practice of the law*, confining myself, in a great measure, to the Criminal and Recorder's courts. The circuit attorney, Mr. Hall, being called away on business a week or two before the close of the term then being held, I was appointed temporarily to fill his place, which I did to the close of the term. I did some pettifogging too, as practicing before justices of the peace is called. One case before Justice Walsh I must report.

A Hung Jury.

Many of our old citizens will remember Noah Ridgely, as good and true a man as ever acted as clerk of a boat and collected freight-bills. Wherever the steamer Hannibal made a landing (and where is the landing between St. Louis and New Orleans she has not stopped at?), Noah has been seen and known at some time or other; but in St. Louis—well, there's no use writing how well he was known *here*. And, wherever known, Noah was a favorite—I might say a *great* favorite. He had been clerk of the aforesaid Hannibal for I don't know how many years, and during all those years he went round to the consignees at the end of each voyage to collect the freight-bills. So, as I have intimated, every body knew Noah Ridgely, and liked him.

But to my story. In St. Louis we all know the difficulty of procuring *jurors* to try cases before justices of the peace, it being almost next to an impossibility to get together twelve citizens, "good men and true," who are willing to sit for two or three hours in a justice's office, which is never, by any accident, larger than a moderate-sized bandbox, surrounded by a promiscuous crowd, which always gathers, filling up room, doors, and windows whenever a "jury-trial" is to come off, especially if *lawyers* are employed in it.

It so happened, "once upon a time," that two merchants had a little misunderstanding, which resulted in their "going to law" before Justice Walsh. The amount in dispute was a mere trifle, but each was obstinate, and would not give way a jot, so to law they went. To make matters worse, each must have a lawyer to help him on, and one of the lawyers, determined to make as much out of the case as he could, asserted the constitutional right of his client, and *demanded a jury*. A *venire facias* was accordingly issued, and Constable Busby started off to execute his writ.

At the expiration of about an hour, during which the court, attorneys, and spectators waited with exemplary patience, Busby returned, followed by *one solitary individual*, carrying a huge lot of freight-bills in one hand, and a half-smoked cigar in the other. It was Noah.

"Have you summoned the jury, Mr. Constable?" inquired the justice.

"Yes, sir," replied Busby, throwing down upon the table his writ with the names of twelve citizens inscribed thereon; "I have summoned them, but they won't come."

"Won't come? won't come?" remarked the justice. "We'll see about that. Clerk, write out attachments for these gentlemen. How many are there who refuse to obey the order of the Court?"

"Eleven, your honor," answered the sweating constable. "This is the only one of the lot" (pointing to our friend Noah) "I have been able to scare up, and *he* don't seem much disposed to serve; says he intends to *plead his privilege*."

"What privilege, pray, Mr. Ridgely, have you to plead? What valid reason can you give the Court why you should not serve on this jury?" asked the justice.

"I believe," replied Noah, stretching himself up to his full height, and taking the cigar from his mouth which he had been industriously smoking since he entered the office, "I believe a *fireman* is exempt from jury duty?"

"Certainly, certainly," replied the justice. "But I was not aware you belonged to either of the engine companies. May I ask, Mr. Ridgely, which engine you run with?"

"Which engine? The old St. Louis! You are aware, perhaps, Mr. Justice, that the old steamer St. Louis had *two* engines. One of them constitutes at this time the motive power of the Hannibal, and that is the engine I run with; and when hard pushed for hands, I have, upon occasion, acted as *fireman*, therefore I suppose I'm excused from jury duty."

"Not so fast, my friend," interposed the justice; "this will *not* excuse you—"

"Not!" exclaimed Noah, with apparent surprise. "Then," he continued, taking a seat on the jury-bench, "bring on your case, since I am overruled, and let us get through with it as soon as we can, for I'll be hanged if I stop long."

Busby at this juncture returned from another unsuccessful foray through the neighboring streets and alleys. "Can't scare up a single man," he reported, sitting down and wiping the perspiration from his face with a cotton pocket-handkerchief which he carried in his hat.

"What is to be done?" inquired the lawyers.

"I am sure I don't know," answered Justice Walsh, "unless you choose to take Mr. Ridgely here, and let *him* decide your case."

As the laws of Missouri permit parties by mutual consent to take "any number less than twelve" in civil cases before justices of the peace, the lawyers, finding there was no chance of "scaring up" any more jurors, agreed to *take Noah as the jury*, and, after a few modest objections on his part, he was sworn in, and assigned a seat in the centre of the jury-bench.

"Come, now, boys," remarked the solitary juror on taking his seat, "hurry up these cakes; I've got all these freight-bills to collect, and confound me if I can stay here long for *any* body."

The lawyers made short work of the evidence, "not wishing to fatigue the jury," and proposed to submit the case without argument.

The justice thought this was a very good plan —it was near dinner-time—and suggested that perhaps the jury was ready to give a verdict without leaving his seat, when the jury spoke as follows:

"May it please the court, the jury is *not* ready to give a verdict. This is an important matter —a matter involving but a small sum, it is true, but the *principle* to be settled by our decision here to-day is one which interests the whole city, the state, the United States—I may say the whole commercial world! The jury, at great inconvenience, has been dragged here and compelled to sit in judgment. The evidence being through, this jury would like to hear the argument of counsel."

"Very well," answered the counsel for the defense, and immediately poured forth a torrent of eloquence in favor of the side he espoused, which must have had a convincing effect in the right quarter, for when the learned gentleman resumed his seat, the jury expressed himself ready to render a verdict; but the attorney for the plaintiff now insisted upon being heard, and accordingly set forth *his* view of the case in such vivid colors that the jury, before he had finished his hour's speech, had evidently relapsed into a state of doubt and uncertainty.

"If the court pleases," remarked the jury, "before this last speech a verdict might have been given which would have satisfied *one* of the parties at least; *now*, it is impossible; this last speech has turned every thing topsy-turvy. There are some points on which the jury must request the instructions of the court."

The instructions were given, and it was generally supposed that a verdict would be rendered at once, as the dinner-bells were now ringing out in every direction; but not so; *the jury preferred to retire and consider upon its verdict;* and as all parties, *except the jury*, seemed about obeying the summons of the bells, a hint was delicately given that it would be no more than proper, and, indeed, humane, that the jury should be *furnished with refreshments*. The hint was seized upon by the attorneys, and *two* very abundant dinners were in a few minutes passed in through the window from the neighboring Jefferson House, the justice, constables, lawyers, and spectators having left the office in possession of the jury, according to the custom of those times.

After dinner the crowd gradually reassembled in the street, and through the open window the imperturbable jury was seen with one leg cocked over the knee of the other, looking carefully over the "authorities" which had been referred to by the lawyers; then changing his position, and putting the leg which had been under on top, the upper wall of the room was scanned with great earnestness for a few minutes, after which a large volume containing the statutes of Missouri was diligently consulted, and so on. It was evident, from appearances, that the *jury had not yet agreed.*

At six o'clock, under instructions from Justice Walsh, the constable inquired, as is usual in similar cases, "Has the jury agreed?" A solemn "No" was the response, and soon after candles were brought and placed upon the table by the constable, who, after lingering a moment in hopes of an intimation that a verdict had been agreed on, was waved out of the room by the jury. From a quarter past 6 until 11 o'clock the jury cogitated without any result. At length Busby was ordered to summon the jury into court, which was done by opening the outer door and admitting the justice and crowd into the presence of the jury.

THE JURY CONSIDERING OF ITS VERDICT.

There sat the jury, as undecided as at dinner-time.

"Gentle*man* of the jury," said the justice, majestically, "have you agreed upon your verdict?"

"May it please the court," answered Noah.

with great dignity, "I believe it is customary to *poll the jury* before asking that question."

"Very well," replied the justice, who, it must be confessed, was becoming a little fretful—"poll away."

Busby polled the jury, calling out from his list,

"No-ah Ridgely!"

"Here!" answered the jury.

"All right," reported Busby to the justice.

"*Now*, then—the jury being polled—gentle*man* of the jury," repeated the justice, slowly, "have—you—agreed—upon—your—verdict?"

"May—it—please—the—court—NO!" answered Noah, rising, and shaking his head emphatically

"Is there any likelihood of the jury being able to agree?" demanded Justice Walsh, desperately.

"Not the least ghost of a chance," replied the person addressed: "THE JURY IS HUNG!"

A dismissal of the jury followed, and a new trial was ordered. The hero of my sketch was ever after, by general consent, considered exempt from jury duty.

Having occasion to go to New Orleans during the summer on some law business, I took passage on the magnificent steamer Missouri, Captain Geo. Taylor and Clerk Twitchell. The second day out one of those detentions took place which in those days were frequently experienced by travelers by water in summer time. During this detention I heard (or *thought* I heard) a pitiful story from one who had seen better days, which I will proceed to give:

Bewailing of a Barge.

"Fast on a sand-bar! no getting her off to-night." Such was the remark that passed around among the passengers on board the magnificent Missouri, as her stern swung down stream, while the muddy Mississippi water began to gurgle under her hull, and between it and an old barge fastened alongside. The afternoon was one of decided leisure for the passengers. Some played cards, others discussed the likelihoods of a Mexican war. For my own part, I passed the afternoon in reading a bucketful of old newspapers. I went early to bed, but could not sleep, in consequence of a violent creaking of the barge alongside. It was a kind of mournful creak, and it disturbed me considerably. At length I felt the "gentle influence" coming over me, and I promised myself a good night's rest. Just before I lost myself, however, I thought I heard a knocking at the outer door. "Who's there?" I demanded, rising in my bed. "Come out here," replied a voice which appeared to be a mixture of a groan and a creak; "come out on the guards a moment; I want to *consult* you." I obeyed the summons instantly, "for," said I to myself, "it won't do to neglect the chance of a *fee*." As I opened my door the same voice asked, "You are a *lawyer*, ar'n't you?" I could see no one, but I answered, "Yes, I pass for one." "Well," said the voice, "I want your assistance." "But where *are* you?" I asked. "Here alongside," replied the voice. "Alongside of what?" I inquired. "Alongside of the Missouri—here—don't you see me?—the barge. Hush! Sit down, and I'll tell you my case." I was very much puzzled; I doubted whether I was not dreaming; however, I determined to hear the "case," and, taking an arm-chair, intimated that I was listening. After a creak or two, the voice proceeded as follows:

"You see before you the wreck of what was once the proud steamer Scioto.

"My keel was laid at Ripley, Ohio, in the fall of 1839. Early in the spring of '40 I was launched and towed down to Fulton, where I received my engine and boilers on board. I began to breathe (that is to say, steam was 'let on' me) in June, and proudly I commenced my first downward trip, loaded to my guards with the produce of the Miami Valley, consisting of pork, potatoes, flour, whisky, and some live poultry. Captain Haggerty was proud of me, and at that time I was proud of *him*. I obeyed his every wish; a mere touch of the pilot's wheel was sufficient for me; I was young and active, full of hope for the future, and anxious to perform my duties faithfully and fearlessly, as a good boat ought, not doubting that in my old age I should be taken care of, or at least be suffered to repose at some respectable landing as a wharf-boat.

"I made many voyages, greatly to the satisfaction and profit of my owners. I was contented with my situation, and all hands seemed pleased with me. I never complained of the quick trips the captain compelled me to make, never *blew him up*, never collapsed a flue in my life; I was devoted to the interests of my commander and owners; night and day I kept going, going, and I felt happy that I was enriching those who had brought me into existence. All went on pleasantly for three years. I began to feel the effects of age and high pressure, but still complained not. After a rest of a few days at Louisville I always felt my energies return with full vigor, and as the 'last bell' rang I was *fired up* with new courage, my steam rose high within me, and, if it had not been for Evans's safety guard, I verily believe I should have *burst* through all restraints, and convinced all hands that—I was nearly as good as new.

"Alas! how shall I relate the melancholy casualty which reduced me from a proud Ohio steamer to the miserable wreck you see me? In the midst of my usefulness—in my pride of boathood—with all my 'works' in good order, and on the eve of departure for the lower country, was I cut off and reduced to cinders! A fire broke out in my blacksmith shop, caused by the end of a cigar carelessly thrown by a 'striker' among some rubbish in a corner, and, before the danger was discovered by the watchman, I was all in a blaze. I will not attempt to describe to you, Mr. Attorney, the pangs I experienced that night, but you can imagine what must have been my feelings with an inward fire consuming me. After considerable exertion on the part of the crew, assisted by the firemen of Cincinnati and Covington, who played into my hold an hour or more, I was *put out.* But oh, what a miserable creature I now felt myself to be! My cabins completely consumed—my ruined engines and boilers standing on my cindered lower deck—crowds thronging the levee to witness my burning agony! Let me draw a veil over the distressing picture.

"Before I had done smoking my *lungs* were torn out (I mean my engines and boilers); and I have heard from a flat-boat which lately lay alongside of me at Cairo that they have been transferred to a new boat called the *Good-as-new.* For myself, or rather my remains, I was sold at auction for $300, and towed about at the pleasure of my new owners, carrying enormous loads and doing all sorts of drudgery. At length I fell into the hands of Captain Taylor, and was employed as a lighter for the late Missouri. *She* had known what it was to be burned out as well as myself, and while lying at Cairo, and transferring the leaden cargo from my bowels to hers, or lighting her of her sugar hogsheads, it was a comfort to hear the lengthened sighs she poured out through her 'scape-pipe in answer to my complaining creak. *I became very much attached to that boat.* I had known her when she first came out, and we had always kept up a friendly intercourse. I regretted that some enterprising John Hunt had not got hold of *me*, and by a refitting made me a fit companion for that noble boat; instead of which, I was reduced to the condition in which you now see me, and compelled to be hauled about in a helpless and hopeless state of *bargery!*

"Last fall, as I was busily employed *lighting* my friend Missouri one dark night, I heard the voice of Captain Taylor on the lower deck of that vessel talking to the clerk in a low tone, after all the other officers had retired to rest. The Missouri was fast asleep; her fires were out, and all was still around except a murmuring chorus of deck-hands, who were *taking coffee* from my companion's forecastle to mine. Wishing to hear the conversation going on between the captain and clerk, I drew closely up, and, holding my sides so as to stifle the creaking moans that uneasily burst from me at times, I listened in breathless silence for several minutes.

"'Twitchell,' said the bluff captain, 'we must build a new boat: this is getting behind the times; the "Scott" and the "White" are getting ahead of us.'

"The clerk did not answer for some time, but whistled a sort of reflecting tune for several minutes. At length the captain roused him from his whistling by saying,

"'What do you think of it, Twitchell?'

"Twitchell had now made up his mind, and promptly answered in three words,

"'Well, go it!'

"I felt my fate was sealed! I was to be robbed of the only companionship that had afforded me any comfort for many a day. I could not—I *felt* I could not—bear being hauled about by a *new* Missouri—a Missouri that had never been burned to the water's edge—a Missouri that was intended to 'go ahead' of the *Scott* and the *White*—an entire stranger to me—it was too much! I creaked aloud in utter agony; and as the captain and clerk moved off to their state-rooms, I heard the latter remark that 'the old barge seemed to be near falling to pieces; it won't last many voyages more.'

"'Ah!' thought I, 'I wish I *could* fall to pieces, or sink at once and end my misery.' I felt as heavy as if, instead of taking coffee that night, I had been loaded down with pigs of lead, as I am now.

"I was laid up for a long time—I can not say *how* long; but my repose was doomed to a fearful interruption.

"One day I felt the waves of the Mississippi coming against my sides with unusual force and violence. A large crowd was gathering upon me, and I heard many persons talking of the NEW MISSOURI; and, sure enough, soon that monster boat came booming, and I distinctly heard the voice of the captain say 'there's our old barge!' *Old* barge! So I must be called *old* too! My charred keel and ribs ached with vexation.

"There is no use in my detailing to you what I have undergone since I have been forced to attend on this boat. Suffice it to say that she has nearly jerked the life out of my timbers. I feel I can not stand it—there is no repose for me. If I am left at Cairo while my principal makes a voyage to the Southern capital, I scarcely have time to breathe before she returns and hitches me to her side, and away we go as if 'the d—l kicked us on end!' "

"But what can I do for you?" I asked.

"I want you to get out an injunction against Captain Taylor and Clerk Twitchell," replied the barge, "and compel them to let me lay up for the balance of my life; or, if I must continue in service, sell me to a slower boat, or—for heaven's sake, do *something* for me!"

"Our city council has lately passed an ordinance against *cruelty to animals*," I said, "but how far its provisions can be brought to bear for your relief I can not pretend to say. I'll see what can be done. In the mean time—"

"In the mean time you'd better go to bed," said, in a low voice, my friend Twitchell—"that is, if you have done talking to the old barge," he continued, gently forcing me into my stateroom. * * * *I had been walking and talking in my sleep.*

ACT FIFTH.

1845–1853.

CHAPTER I.

The business of the season of 1845–6 was an improvement on all previous seasons in the new St. Charles. My memory tells me a great and favorable change took place in the fortunes of the new temple—yes, and it commenced on the very night of the anniversary of the burning of the theatre in Mobile in St. Emanuel Street, as I had all along thought it would.

During this season Mr. and Mrs. Charles Kean played forty nights in New Orleans, Mobile, and St. Louis to fine business. Mrs. Mowatt also played a good engagement in each of the three cities. About this time Mr. and Mrs. Farren left our company to go starring, taking with them, with our full consent, several new plays—Mary Tudor, Lucretia Borgia, Catharine Howard, and others, which her great talents had materially assisted in making successful in performance. For some years Mrs. Farren maintained her position as a star, but latterly, I perceive, she is content with stock engagements. Mr. Farren is no longer living. Their eldest son is a scenic artist, the second an actor, and their daughter an actress. All three are married, and our well-beloved leading actress of former years is a grandmother!

Of all the star actors and actresses I have had to deal with, Mr. and Mrs. Kean, separately and together, were the most agreeable and friendly. It was a positive pleasure to have them with us. They gave no trouble whatever, and all were anxious to do whatever they requested in the way of stage business. During their engagements they were so unassuming and kind in their demeanor that, were it not for the immense receipts they attracted, you would not have supposed, to see them, that they were any thing but the humblest members of the stock company.

Mr. C. Kean was always nervous about the success of any engagement he and his wife were to play, and on this occasion, learning that the times were very bad at the South, his expectation of profit was very moderate—so moderate, indeed, that he offered to sell me his share of their forty nights for $8000, which would be $200 per night. I had such confidence in the change for the better which had set in, that I was in favor of taking this risk, and I wrote to my partner at Mobile for his consent to the acceptance of the offer, which he refused. I then wrote that I wished to take the speculation on myself individually, the terms with the Keans not to be changed so far as the firm was concerned, but offering to take their place in the settlement, making up whatever deficiency there might be of the $8000, and receiving the overplus, if any. This my partner objected to and protested against, on the ground that by our old articles of partnership (long since expired) it was stipulated we should have no separate theatrical interests. I was fool enough to yield to this protest, and the engagement went on upon the terms previously agreed on—an equal division of the receipts. The result was this: I was deprived of the opportunity of making $4000 clear money either for the firm or myself, while Kean pocketed that sum in addition to the amount he was willing to take as a certainty. I never think of this without being reminded of a speech of *Old Delph*, where he says to *Mr. Porcelain*, "You're like a dog in the manger; you won't heat yourself, nor let nobody helse heat."

The profits of this season were considerable, and our debts began to melt away before the good business as the mists disperse before the bright sun.

The great feature of the season of 1846 in St. Louis was the engagement of the Keans, who continued their successful career to the end of the forty nights for which they were engaged. Mrs. Mowatt also performed a good engagement. Other stars followed, but I do not really remember who they were.

During the engagement of the Keans, the following whimsical scene was enacted without announcement in the bills:

Where's the Swab?

Gas had not been introduced into St. Louis at this time, and our oil lamps at the wings had a dangerous way of flaring up in a most unruly manner, occasionally threatening to set fire to the lamp-ladders, and thus endanger the building. The lamps were open "floats," with wick-holders coming up from the bottom, and the oil, when heated, would take fire, and burn up in a large flame. To guard against accidents, we had a tub of water placed on each side of the stage, with a large swab or mop in it ready for use at any moment; and scarcely a night passed without a swabbing being required. The wing hands (subordinate stage-carpenters) were instructed to keep a strict watch over the wing lamps, and to use *the swab* promptly whenever occasion might require. Besides these watches, every actor and actress felt a deep interest in the swabbing process, and it was not an unusual thing to see *Richard the Third*, or *Hamlet*, just before entering upon the stage, catch up a swab and dash it upon the rising flames, which, if not attended to, were likely to burn up the Tower of London, or the royal palace of Elsinore.

SCENE IN ROMEO AND JULIET—SWABBING! (See page 201.)

Miss Tree was performing the part of *Juliet*, and had taken her station (Act ii., Scene 2) on the balcony, for the purpose of enjoying the fresh night-breeze after the fatigue of the ball which had concluded in the previous act, and to think of the young pilgrim who had so greatly interested her during the festival, when, casting her eyes over the way, she saw that one of the wing lamps was just beginning to flare up, and all eyes being fixed upon *her*, there was imminent danger of a conflagration. The fair *Juliet* had taken her seat on the balcony, but was observed to fidget and turn in her chair in a most un-*Juliet*-like manner, calling off through the window behind her, in a loud whisper, for "*somebody to get the swab!*"

Romeo, who had entered from the right-hand side, and had not seen the flaring lamp, went on with his speech, interrupted from time to time by the lovely Capulet.

Romeo. "She speaks, yet she says nothing. What of that?"

Juliet. (*Aside.*) Where is Mr. Sol Smith? Will somebody call him?

Romeo. "Her eye discourses; I will answer it."

Juliet. (*Aside.*) Will nobody get the swab? We shall all be burnt up!

Romeo. "I am too bold; 'tis not to me she speaks."

Juliet. (*Aside.*) No; it is to somebody to bring the swab. Where is Mr. Sol Smith?

Romeo. "See how she leans her cheek upon her hand! Oh that I were a glove upon that hand, that I might touch that cheek!"

Juliet. "Ah me!" (*Aside.*) We'd better not go on. Where is the swab?

Romeo. "She speaks! Oh, speak again, bright angel!"

Juliet. (*Aside.*) If that swab isn't brought this instant, I'll come down — I will. Ah! there's Mr. Sol Smith with the swab at last.

Romeo. (Speaks the balance of the speech, unheeded by *Juliet*, who is watching the swabbing.)

Juliet. "Oh! Romeo, Romeo, wherefore art thou Romeo?"

(*Aside.*) Thank heaven, the danger's over; the swab has saved us!

"Deny thy father and refuse thy name"—and so on.

During the existence of the "Reveille" newspaper I contributed to it occasionally. The following sketch of a well-known theatrical character of the time (since deceased) is one of my light contributions:

Old Rowley Marks.

Rowley is a character. I first became acquainted with him in 1830, but his fame had reached my ears as early as 1826, when he formed a part of Mr. Alexander Drake's traveling company in Western New York and Kentucky. Rowley is an Israelite, and has been for many years high-priest of the Jews in New Orleans and parts adjacent, receiving a very handsome income from the chosen people for the performance of marriage ceremonies, funeral rites, and *other* little operations indispensable to the proper starting of young Jews of the male sex into their second week's journey of life.

Rowley is an actor of no inconsiderable talent —that is to say, of a peculiar kind—*very* peculiar, I might say. Comic old men are his hobby, and it would do your heart good to see one of his laughs. I say *see* one of them, for nothing particular is *heard* when he laughs; a sort of turning up of his eyes, a filling of his cheeks with wind, and suddenly letting it burst forth, at the same time giving himself a half turn, stooping as if to spit, indulging in a sly wink at the public, and swinging his cane about—and it is done.

Rowley was once stage-manager in a traveling company under the direction of my brother, and during the whole of a very hot summer he luxuriated in the performance of *Gov. Heartall*, *Old Snacks*, and *Andrew Mucklestane*. Andrew Mucklestane! Ah! how often have I witnessed his personation of this character, which is nothing more nor less than a sentimental Scotch fisherman, very benevolent in his feelings, and ever ready to rescue runaway countesses and drowning children! And to see Rowley sweating through the "business" of this character is a treat to all lovers of the romantic drama. Rowley introduces thirteen *falls* in this performance, and more than once has it been found necessary to *prop* the stage before subjecting it to his energetic manœuvres.

Rowley is well known in the Crescent City, where he has *acted* in various capacities besides those mentioned above. He is a veteran in the fire department, of which he is the poet laureate; he holds, or *did* hold, a lucrative office in the Custom-house, sings in the choruses at the theatres in the winter, and in the summer accepts the "direction" of the *National* Institution at the Carrollton Railroad Dépôt, where plays and farces are "produced" in "rapid succession" and in every variety of style, and performed by actors and actresses who can not obtain, or will not accept engagements elsewhere. In the direction of this *National* Theatre Rowley manages to keep up a constant succession of novelties—*in the bills* —but gives the *same entertainment* every night of the week, thus:

Monday — The "Soldier's Daughter:" Gov. Heartall, Mr. A. J. R. Marks; Widow Cheerly, Mrs. Simpkins. With the "Warlock of the Glen:" Andrew Mucklestane, Mr. A. J. R. Marks.

Tuesday—"The London Merchant:" Governor, Mr. A. J. R. Marks; Widow, Mrs. Simpkins. And the "Faithful Fisherman:" Fisherman, Mr. A. J. R. Marks.

Wednesday—"The Country Widow:" Heartall, Sen., Mr. A. J. R. Marks. To conclude with the "Laird of Glencairn:" Andrew, a fisherman, Mr. A. J. R. Marks.

Thursday—[Firemen's benefit] "The Generous Merchant; or, Pump Away: you may prevent a Conflagration!" Uncle of the Generous Merchant, Mr. A. J. R. Marks; the Country Widow, Mrs. Simpkins. With "The Vassal:" Vassal, Mr. A. J. R. Marks.

Friday—The "Eccentric Governor; or, Heart-all All Heart:" the Eccentric Governor, Mr. A. J. R. Marks; the Daughter of Discipline, Mrs. Simpkins. With the "Solitary of the Heath," in which Mr. A. J. R. Marks will appear.

Saturday—The "Generous Old Uncle:" Uncle, Mr. A. J. R. Marks. To conclude with "A Day in Scotland:" Scotchman, Mr. A. J. R. Marks.

Sunday—[Benefit of the Hospital] "Charitable Widow; or, Say you So, my little Cherub?" The Retired Governor, Mr. A. J. R. Marks; Charitable Widow, Mrs. Simpkins. After which, "I have left him struggling in the Waves; or, the Warlock Laird:" the Fighting Fisherman, Mr. A. J. R. Marks.

By thus ringing the changes a week's business is gotten through, and on the next Monday he is ready with *two other* pieces—we'll say the CASTLE SPECTRE and INTRIGUE—which he presents during the week with the following varied titles: 1. Castle Spectre and Intrigue; 2. Mysteries of Conway Castle and Bath Road; 3. Ghost of Evelina and Married Yesterday; 4. Humors of Father Philip and Tom and Ellen; 5. Hassan the Slave, and the Wolf and the Lamb; 6. Angelina, or Reginald the Imprisoned, and the Jealous Landlord; 7. The Three Earls, or Percy Triumphant, and the Wife's Stratagem, or the Libertines Deceived!

These are but a few of Rowley's alterations of titles during a season. The interesting little drama of the RENDEZVOUS has gone through an extensive variety of changes in the bills, and has been witnessed under the titles of "All in the Dark," "Hide and Seek," "The Robbers of the Heath," "The Cock-ed Hat, or Simon in a Quandary," "Frightened to Death," "Matches are made in Heaven," "Rose d'Amour," "Now let's to Supper," etc., etc. Hundreds of other equally ingenious variations of titles might be mentioned, by which Manager Rowley carries on the National institution to a profitable conclusion of its summer seasons; but, from the above specimens, an idea may be formed of some of the expedients by which a fertile mind may make a great deal out of a limited amount of material. It ought to be observed that Eastern managers of theatres are beginning to adopt the system so successfully introduced by the director of the "National," and it has become next to an impossibility to ascertain, from the newspaper announcements, what play really *is* to be acted in the New York and Philadelphia theatres. Even at the South and West, in other than *National* institutions, we see occasional symptoms of Rowleyism beginning to show themselves. Rowley should obtain a patent, and then prosecute all "acting and stage managers" who "'fringe that way."

In appearance Rowley Marks is a little *below* the middle size, measuring, in his stockings, about four feet and some inches. A gleam of good humor is always beaming on his countenance, except when he experiences a twinge of the gout (unfortunately pretty often), and he is one of the best-natured fellows in existence. Though short in stature, long may he live to officiate as High Priest of the Jews and of the Sun—may he continue to carry out his enlightened views of management in his National establishment, and remain a shining light in the paths of the drama! Good luck to thee Rowley!

CHAPTER II.

THE New Orleans season of 1846–7 witnessed a continuation of the prosperity which had now become an assured fact. Business not only came up to a paying point, but went considerably beyond it. Stars this season, Wallack, Mrs. Mowatt (with E. L. Davenport, a fine actor), Murdoch, Anderson, Collins, and the Ravel family. As stock-stars we also had Mr. and Mrs. James W. Wallack, engaged with the view of making strong combinations with their uncle, but somehow they wouldn't "combine" much, and the three could very seldom be brought into the cast of one play. It made but little difference, however, as, with the exception of a night or two of DON CÆSAR DE BAZAN (a splendid performance!), Mr. Wallack this season played to very thin audiences, whether in connection with his nephew and niece or by himself.

The Keans returned to the St. Charles in the spring, but, in consequence of Mrs. Kean being taken ill, the engagement was shortened to about a week. Mr. Kean offered to make a compensation for necessarily cutting the engagement down to seven nights, but I wouldn't listen to such a proposition. Nevertheless, he left a hundred dollars in the treasury out of the proceeds of his benefit, at which Mrs. Kean was not able to assist.

This season was so prosperous (even Mobile didn't turn out so badly as it usually had) that it was decided to refit and remodel the St. Charles at an estimated cost of $8000, which (of course) went up to $16,000.

The American Theatre on Poydras Street had been opened every season in some form or other, generally collapsing in the middle of winter, and throwing large numbers of people out of employment. This season it was conducted by Messrs. S. P. Stickney and Lucius Place (R. L. Place as his agent) as a theatre and circus, and had escaped the usual collapse.

A "combination" was formed for conducting the ensuing season of the St. Charles, American, and Mobile theatres under one management; that is to say, a board of directors was created, consisting of our firm and Stickney, by which all important matters were to be arranged, and the manager of each theatre to carry out the details. By virtue of our having two theatres to Stickney's one, we had two votes, being two thirds of the whole board; consequently, as my partner was the manager in Mobile, where he resided, the real weight of the management of all three theatres fell upon me. But the yoke was easy and the burden was light, as will be seen presently.

During this season, finding the houses sometimes affected by people staying away to hear expected news from Mexico, I adopted the plan of announcing from the stage any new tidings that might come in from the seat of war after the assemblage of the audience. Being on the best of terms with the editors of the *Picayune* (Kendall was with the army all through the war), I was enabled to obtain the very latest news during the evening, and it came to be understood that the St. Charles Theatre was the very best place for newsmongers to go to if they wanted to be posted up with the war proceedings on the Rio Grande. I remember announcing, on the 20th of March, the great victory of General Taylor over Santa Anna at Buena Vista on the 22d of the preceding month. When the applause and cheers had subsided, I added these words: "I prophesy that General Zachary Taylor will be the next President of the United States," when the applause and cheers were redoubled. I spoke as I *thought*, not as I *wished.* Henry Clay *should* have been elected the following year, but it seems that great and good man had to be thrust aside for "expediency."

On the 27th of February an actor of the American Theatre, by name Collins, departed this life. Attending his funeral on the 28th, it was found that the minister engaged to perform the funeral service could not attend. Being the senior actor present, I was requested to read the service, to which request I unhesitatingly assented, but there being no Liturgy at hand, I sent home for one, and we proceeded to the grave-yard, where my messenger met me with the book, and there I read the services for the burial of the dead according to the ritual of the New Jerusalem Church, all the actors and actresses present joining most devoutly in the ceremonies.

Having occasion to go to St. Louis during this season in the Old Hickory, Captain Stetinnius, I amused myself on the way and pleased my excellent friend Captain Sellars, the pilot, by writing the following account of a public meeting, the idea of which was suggested by an article in the *Louisville Journal*, the whole being intended as a hit at President Polk for his veto of the River and Harbor Bill:

"☞ We understand that as soon as the present high water in the Western rivers subsides, there are to be several meetings of the snags and sawyers in various portions of the Ohio and the Mississippi, to adopt resolutions thanking their friend Mr. Polk for his affectionate regard for them, and also to contrive ways and means for wrecking all the steam, flat, and keel boats that shall have the hardihood to question their right under the Constitution to occupy places in the beds of the rivers."—*Lou. Jour.*

Proceedings of the Convention of Snags and Sawyers, held at the Grave-yard, in the Mississippi River, Dec. 31, 1846.

Delegates were in attendance from Turkey Island, Dog-tooth Bend, Head of Hat Island, Riddle's Point, Number Ten, Devil's Island, Hull's Left Leg, Elk Island, Number Twenty-one, Plum Point, Number Thirty-seven, Devil's Back-bone, Tyawapeta, Hanging-dog Island, Devil's Elbow, Charley's Bend, My Wife's Island, Number Sixty-five, Shirt-tail Bend, Goose Island, Devil's Tea-table, and the Grave-yard.

Several delegates from the most important sand-bars presented their credentials and claimed seats in the Convention, but, objection being made by nearly all of the snags and sawyers present, they were excluded on the ground that, although they were quite useful in *detaining* boats, they very seldom succeeded in *destroying* them.

After the transaction of some unimportant preliminary business, Awful Hull-ripper, Esq., from Devil's Back-bone, was unanimously elected President, and Mr. Terrible Keel-scraper, from Goose Island, was appointed Secretary.

The venerable snag who had been called on to preside over the proceedings of the Convention, on being conducted to his seat, briefly addressed the members in a tone of congratulation upon the occasion which called them together, alluding in feeling terms to the great success which had attended their exertions during the late season of low water. He concluded his very pertinent remarks by suggesting that it would be advisable to confine the action of the Convention to the objects of the assemblage, which, as he understood them, were to pass resolutions thanking President Polk for his paternal care, and to contrive ways and means for wrecking all the steam, flat, and keel boats that shall have the hardihood to question the rights of snags and sawyers, under the Constitution, to occupy places in the bed of the mighty Mississippi.

A delegate in the shape of a very large piece of rock here presented himself at the bar, and claimed a seat in the Convention as a member from the Grand Chain. It was objected by several snags and sawyers that the Grand Chain had no claims to be represented in this Convention, as the notice in the *Louisville Journal*, which published the call, named only "snags and sawyers."

"No claim?" exclaimed the delegate from the Grand Chain; "no claim? I would point out to honorable members the wreck of the old J. M. White, which I had the pleasure of sinking. Yes, gentlemen snags and sawyers, there lies—"

Several members here interrupted the speaker, and suggested that, to save time, a vote should be taken on his claims to a seat, which suggestion being acted on, it was found that a large majority were in favor of according the applicant a place in the Convention. On taking his seat, the delegate was understood to say, in a grumbling tone, that he thought it a pretty thing, indeed, that his right to a seat should be questioned, while he saw around him numerous snags and sawyers that he could remember when they were but young trees—yea, nothing but saplings—long before they took to the water, or thought of establishing themselves as obstructions.

The business of the Convention was resumed by appointing a committee to draft a preamble and resolutions expressive of the sentiments of the meeting.

The committee having retired, several eloquent addresses were delivered by members from the several wrecking stations, which were listened to with profound attention by the assembled obstructions. One member from Plum Point excited the liveliest interest by relating his experience during the last seventy years, having during that time, unassisted, dove into sixty-three flat-boats, twenty-five barges, twenty-eight keelboats, and seven steam-boats. The venerable snag observed, in conclusion, that he had grown rotten in the cause; that he had lost all his limbs, and much more service could not be expected of him in this world; "yet," he continued, "I am encouraged to hope that the younger branches of my family will not disgrace their sire, but, under the fostering influence of the presidential veto, will stand their ground, as I have done."

This address was received with great applause. Several stumps attempted to address the Convention, but the President decided that *stump speeches* could not be permitted, as *politics* were to form no part of the proceedings of the meeting. So the stumps remained silent.

A very tall, healthy-looking snag from Turkey Island now obtained the floor, and called the attention of the members to the growing importance of the place he had the honor to represent, observing that he might point with pride to the wrecks of the Rienzi, Oregon, Levant, Yucatan, and Rubicon as proofs of industry and efficiency.

Some very touching remarks were made by several other members, all tending to show the brilliant prospects which opened to the community of snags and sawyers in consequence of the advocacy of their cause by the present patriotic and conscientious head of the administration.

The committee now returned and reported the following preamble and resolutions:

"*Whereas* the snags, sawyers, rocks, and stumps in the Mississippi River have certain vested and inalienable rights, which should not be invaded—rights of long standing, which will never be surrendered but with life; *and, whereas*, at various times within the last twenty years, attempts have been made, by means of certain contrivances called snag-boats, to pull us up root and branch, and tear us from our homes and families—

"*Resolved*, That we pledge ourselves to each other that we will stick up for our rights while we have a root or limb to hold on by, and we will rip, stave, and tear into eternal smash all flat, keel, and steam boats that we can reach.

"*Resolved*, That we point with exultation to the numerous wrecks in this grave-yard, and in all the other (so called) *bad places* represented in this Convention, as monuments of our power.

"*Resolved*, That our thanks are hereby tendered to the President for his veto on the attempts of Congress to interfere with our constitutional rights, and that he be invited to visit us at our several stations during the low-water season of next year, when we promise him he shall see sights.

"*Resolved*, That, in order to co-operate with the views of our conscientious President, it is expedient that three or four efficient and experienced snags shall establish themselves in eligible positions in the harbor of St. Louis, to be ready for duty during the summer of 1847.

"*Resolved*, That we adopt the title by which we have been called in derision by our opponents, and glory in the name of *Polk stalks*.

"*Resolved*, That the proceedings of this Convention be published in the St. Louis Reveille, Louisville Journal, and such other papers as are friendly to the cause of equal rights throughout the Union."

The resolutions were unanimously adopted, and, after a vote of thanks to the Chairman, and to the Grave-yard for the accommodations afforded to the Convention, an adjournment was moved and carried.

AWFUL HULL-RIPPER,
(from the Devil's Back-bone), *Chairman.*
TERRIBLE KEEL-SCRAPER,
(from Goose Island), *Secretary.*

CHAPTER III.

I HAVE nothing particular to record of the season of 1847 in St. Louis except that it was unusually prosperous—for that place, and that here commenced an engagement which I had much difficulty in making, with the great troupe of Viennoise children, who, under the management of Madame Weisse, were to perform eighty nights with us in New Orleans, Mobile, and this city. Of all the attractions ever offered to the public of these United States, I consider this troupe of forty-eight girls the greatest; and it is not too much to say that their performances were the most artistic and pleasing of any thing ever seen in this country in the way of dancing. The whole people flocked to see them, and there was but one opinion as to their merits.

I here insert a letter from my old and valued friend, Major Noah, of New York, giving that worthy gentleman's views of theatrical affairs in general, and pretty women in particular:

M. M. Noah to Sol. Smith.

"New York, October 11, 1847.

"MY OLD FRIEND,—I saw your name gazetted at St. Louis, and presume you are now home. Having some leisure on hand, I should be glad to correspond with a New Orleans paper of established reputation, furnishing all the foreign and local news, making a useful as well as agreeable correspondence, for which I have all the material on hand, and the experience in such matters. Should you learn that such an opening exists, have the kindness to drop me a line. Madame Augusta tells me she has written to you in relation to an engagement, but has not received an answer. I have known her since her first arrival in this country, and, although a prodigious favorite every where, the numerous adventurers from abroad, of less merit and beauty, ask more reasonable terms, and supersede her. In the aggregate, I doubt whether the economy is the best policy. Old Placide, the Charleston manager, once said to me, 'Give me de prette vimin, and I vill fill my house,' and he had a galaxy of beauty, and so I would have were I manager. Augusta tells me you have engaged Demier. I hope she may take in New Orleans, but I apprehend against Blangy she can make no run. What is to become of the rivalry in New York? I apprehend that, with all the splendor of the Broadway Theatre, the sawdust and horses will come in play during the winter. Simpson, though dreadfully alarmed at first, is recovering from the shock. Music and dancing, however, will overshadow the legitimate, I apprehend, during the coming season.

"We shall lose our election this fall in consequence of the division in the Democratic party, and I apprehend I shall be compelled once more to take the field with the Old Guard, and endeavor to recover the day. Whenever there is a fierce battle to be fought, I am called upon. The moment victory ensues, I am shelved. 'Every puny whipster gets my sword.' If Clay's name is not brought forward until next summer, and he writes no letters and keeps quiet, I think his chance is the best. I suppose you still adhere to old 'Rough and Ready.' It is impossible, in these trying times, when the political elements are all in confusion, to say who stands the best chance.

"Write to Augusta. I think her an excellent card for the South, and I am sure you will want her. Success attend you.

"Sincerely yours, M. M. NOAH."

The good Major Noah and I had known each other for a quarter of a century. As editors, in 1823, we had had several good-natured controversies—he supporting Crawford for the Presidency, and I De Witt Clinton, and afterward Jackson. He was a great friend to actors. For many, many years we held friendly intercourse, and when I went to New York was always sure of meeting him at Niblo's, where we occupied the interval between the performances with a good chat and a good glass of ice-cream in the saloon. Adieu, major! You are gone before; but, if congenial spirits are permitted to meet in the spirit-world, I hope for future communion with you. I shall try to hunt you up, wherever you may be. If there are any theatres there, there's where I shall look for you.

A Lapse of Twenty Years.

[1827.] The elderly and middle-aged residents of St. Louis all remember the theatre on Second Street, between Olive and Locust Streets, commonly known as the *Salt-house.* The "temple" was somewhat limited in size, of a surety; but it was generally well filled with well-satisfied audiences, and I have always contended that a small theatre FULL was far preferable to a large one half empty. No matter for that; it is all aside from the purpose of my story, which is intended to record one of the most singular coincidences I have ever known.

In the summer of 1827, the company of which I was then a member performed with great success a new drama entitled THE GAMBLER'S FATE, OR A LAPSE OF TWENTY YEARS. It took well with the St. Louisans, and was often repeated.

On one occasion, when this thrilling drama was announced, two young men, just enlisted for a trip to the mountains in the Fur Company's service, attended the theatre to witness the performance. At the end of the first act they got impatient at the length of time the curtain was suffered to remain down, and concluded to go out and *take a drink*. Another drink followed, and then another.

"Come, Jim," said one, "let's return to the theatre; the curtain must be up by this time."

"No," replied the other; "look here—just read that bill, will you?—*Between the* 1*st and* 2*d acts twenty years are supposed to elapse.*"

"Thunder and gunpowder!" exclaimed Joe, the liquor beginning to assert its power, "who's gwine to wait twenty years? Let's go back to the Green Tree tavern and retire to our virtuous beds, for to-morrow we start for the mountains."

"Agreed," says Jim, and off they went. They slept off the effects of the "drink," and next day the party to which they belonged moved westward.

* * * * *

[A LAPSE OF TWENTY YEARS.]

* * * * *

[1847.] Two middle-aged individuals are seen reading a large poster at the "Green Tree." Rough-looking customers they are, and look toil-worn and browned by the weather, but hardy and honest. They are our old friends who, twenty years ago, went to see THE GAMBLER'S FATE, and retired at the end of the first act. Singularly enough, there is the same play announced, THE GAMBLER'S FATE, OR A LAPSE OF TWENTY YEARS.

Our trappers agree at once to go and *see the rest on't.*

They make their way up Second Street until they come to about the spot where the theatre stood, and then inquire of a passer-by for directions, which are speedily given, and in a few minutes they find themselves in the vestibule of the theatre on Third Street.

"Halloo! old feller," says Joe, addressing the ticket-seller through a hole, "they play THE GAMBLER'S FATE here to-night, don't they?"

"Well, they don't play any thing else," was the polite reply of the gentlemanly treasurer.

"All right, old feller," replied Joe; "I don't want to *see* any thing else, though I believe you advertise a farce with it. Is the first act over?"

"I believe it is," answered the clerk.

"All right again—we only want to see the second act; we saw the other some time ago. What's the price of tickets *now?*"

"The same as a while ago—seventy-five cents."

"What, *now*—and one act over."

"Exactly—one act over."

"But," expostulated Joe, who did all the talking, while Jim stood a little back and chewed tobacco, "we've paid *once before* for seeing this piece, and only staid for the first act."

"Can't help that, my friend," replies the imperturbable ticket-seller; "we have but one price."

"Well, hand out two tickets for up stairs."

The tickets were handed out, the money being first handed *in*, and the two trappers entered the house. In a few minutes the curtain was raised, and the mountaineers finished seeing THE GAMBLER'S FATE, the first act of which they had seen twenty years before in the same city, though not in the same theatre, and with only one person in the cast who had played in it on the previous occasion. In effect, our *voyageurs* witnessed this play with a "real lapse" of twenty years between the acts.

The season of 1847–8 in New Orleans, which was carried on by a "combination" between the St. Charles and American Theatres, opened auspiciously at the American with Miss Wemyss as the star, the St. Charles, from policy, holding back and yielding the field for several weeks, employing the company at St. Louis until about the end of November. The great card at the American was Mr. Forrest, who played a farewell engagement of thirty nights to an average of $534. His farewell benefit was $802. This engagement of Mr. F.'s was interrupted once or twice by attacks of gout which that gentleman experienced, but, owing to our peculiar facilities, we filled up the gaps with various attractions, so that nothing was lost by Mr. F.'s occasional failure to perform.

The wonderful Viennoise children danced thirty nights at the St. Charles to houses averaging $793, and then went to Mobile, returning to us for a few nights, and afterward dancing at the French Theatre, also at the American for a night or two.

Other stars this season, Mrs. Farren, Julia Dean, Madame Augusta, Madam Bishop (with Reeves and Brough), and (I think—I will not be sure) the Ravel family.

The profits of the combination footed up about $25,000, two thirds of which came to us, and one third to Stickney and Place.

Before the close in New Orleans I proceeded

to St. Louis with the charming Viennoisses, and a very pleasant journey we had of it, the children being all amiable and well-behaved.

At this time (spring of 1848) I purchased a house and lot on Chouteau Avenue—this after PAYING ALL DEBTS (oh, blessed liberty!)—where we have found a happy home for twenty years.

The season of 1848 in St. Louis was opened with the ever-welcome Viennoise children, and carried through, with other stars, to a successful conclusion. After they left us I saw no more of the good Madame Josephine Weisse and her lovely children. She and they soon after returned to Vienna, where the madame, in compliance with her contracts, restored each child to its parents, and then resigned her spirit to her Maker!

I have nothing particular to relate concerning this season except that Mr. Forrest did *not* engage with us. I did not offer him half the receipts, but asked him to fix the sum per night for which he would act, which he declined to do, saying that he never would act again for a sum certain, but must have half the receipts wherever he played. We parted in New Orleans on good terms and in friendship, and I had no idea of any change in his feelings toward me; but I soon found he was arranging, or trying to arrange for an opposition house here. He sent up John Greene to procure a place and put up temporary scenery. John looked about the city and talked with citizens, and—returned to New Orleans without making any arrangements for Mr. Forrest to appear in St. Louis. The next I heard from Mr. Forrest was through Mr. Logan, Bates's stage-manager at Cincinnati, whose letter I give:

C. A. Logan to Sol. Smith.

"Cincinnati, April 16, 1848.

"MY DEAR OLD FRIEND,—I have just received your friendly letter, and hasten to reply, although there is absolutely no news here, and scarce any thing to write about. You, of course, ere this, must be aware that Forrest acted in Louisville, but you may *not* be aware that he received $200 a night for so acting. A melancholy fact: $200 for each night, and on some nights he *played* to a less sum; one night, at least, the *receipts* were but $150, and he got $200, leaving the manager to pay $50 to the star beyond the gross receipts, besides his own expenses! Blessed system! His whole engagement in Louisville was a failure, and he told me yesterday that the houses were a series of thunderbolts to him—his manner of expressing his astonishment at their thinness. He opened here last night to about $700—a far better house than any he had in Louisville, his benefit there being $515. But he gets his $200 a night here too, and asked me yesterday whether, if successful, there would be a chance of renewal. I suppose he would extend the length indefinitely on the same terms. John Greene arrived here a day or two ago to announce his failure in St. Louis, and seek a company for *Galena*, I believe. He could get nobody, and left again for the West yesterday.

"Your only real danger in St. Louis of opposition is from John Bates. I violate no confidence when I tell you that he has serious notions of building there this summer. He declared this to a party of us yesterday (and often before *to me*), among whom was John Greene and, I think, Forrest, and added jocosely that I had better inform 'my friend Sol' of his intention. This I now do, not with any intention of thwarting the views of my employer (for your knowledge of the fact can not work detriment to him), but simply that you may know *there* what is the common talk *here*. * * * *

"Forrest is evidently angry with you for not offering him an engagement in St. Louis. He told me yesterday (but, remember, *this* must not be mentioned as coming from me) that he intended to *pay a visit* to St. Louis. I presume you understand the significance of his *paying a visit.* Some years ago he said to me in Philadelphia, 'Logan, I start to-morrow for Charleston.' 'The devil you do!' I replied; 'you told me only yesterday the manager had refused your terms.' 'True, that's the reason I'm going. When I'm *on thet* SPOT I think I can make him *change his mind!' and he did.* I believe you know I am one of your sincerest well-wishers, and therefore if I speak plainly you will not misunderstand me. Your letter contains some justly indignant denunciations of the starring system. Ask yourself if you are not an active *particeps criminis* in it. John Bates from the first took a strong stand against this monstrous abuse, and all my influence with him was exerted to confirm him in his resolves to resist these ruinous demands. He has constantly said if you will sustain us in this matter we can break it up in the West. But you always pursued the old course, and (as Bates says) endeavored to force certain stars upon him at exorbitant terms. It seems now that he is tired of refusing terms that all other managers give—tired of hearing the people say, 'These performers play in all other cities; why do you not engage them?' Hence Forrest at length has triumphed, and draws from the treasury $200 a night! I rejoice to hear that your Southern season was prosperous. It is quite currently believed that you and the American were in *cahoot.*

"Your letters are always welcome, and I wish you would write oftener. I will always most cheerfully give you any information in my power, or do any thing else to advance your views—'not wronging him I serve.'

"Yours ever, C. A. LOGAN."

So it seemed Mr. Forrest had changed his mind in regard to playing for a "certainty," and I wrote immediately to him, offering the same terms he had with Bates in Louisville. To this I received no reply! I then wrote another letter asking him to name the sum per night for which he would act here for twelve nights. Below will be found Mr. Forrest's reply to one of his oldest and best friends:

Edwin Forrest to Sol. Smith.

"Detroit, July 31, 1848.

"SIR,—I regret I can not appear in St. Louis under your management; no amount of money could induce me to do so. EDWIN FORREST.

"Sol. Smith, Esq., St. Louis."

This was the last letter received from one whom I had cherished as a sincere friend for twenty-six years, and terminated all correspondence between us. I know not to this day what I had done to deserve so curt a reply to a fair business proposition, and I suppose I never shall.

It will be seen from Logan's letter that John Bates contemplated building a new theatre here. Knowing his pecuniary ability to carry out his designs, and believing two theatres could not be sustained, the house we occupied was offered to Mr. Bates, at our instance, by Mr. Collier; but Mr. Bates was bent on building, and it will be seen he eventually carried out his design.

The stars that gave light to this season, which was a prosperous one in a small way, were, besides the wonderful Viennoise children, Yankee Hill, Julia Dean, Mrs. Farren, Winchell, Mrs. Hunt, C. D. Pitt, G. W. Jamison, J. R. Scott, Mr. and Mrs. Conner, Dan Marble, Booth, and Augusta, with her troupe

CHAPTER IV.

I HERE insert a reply I made and published to a sermon on amusements, preached by one of our most esteemed clergymen:

Extract from a Lecture on Amusements, by the Rev. W. G. Elliot.

"It is a fair objection to the theatre, that, as an amusement, it is too exciting—by far too much so for a beneficial influence on the young. It often unfits their minds for serious thoughts and labor. To older persons it may not be so hurtful; but for the young man, I do not know of any habit, in *itself not positively sinful*, which is more injurious, or more fraught with serious danger, than that of theatre-going. It stimulates the imagination too strongly; it awakens dormant passions; it overtasks the sensibilities, and generally makes more quiet and less exciting amusements seem flat and tasteless. It is, moreover, an expensive amusement, much beyond the proper means of most young men; and, unfortunately, it is surrounded with many incidental evils, which, although theoretically not inseparable from it, are always practically attendant upon it, as camp followers are an evil inseparable from the camp. I appeal to yourselves if it is not true that the young man who becomes fond of the theatre is very likely to become immoral and dissipated. Believing that it is so, I feel justified in advising you strongly against it. Select more quiet and less dangerous amusements. At least wait until you are well established in virtue before you subject yourselves to such severe tests; and when you are thus established, the desire to set a good example to those whose principles are not yet equally confirmed may become a still stronger motive for staying away."

At various times during my professional life I have felt called upon to make comments, through the press, upon the strictures of certain reverend gentlemen who have thought proper to denounce the institution of the theatre as demoralizing in its tendency. Among the so-called "divines" (what a title for human beings!) to whom I have paid my respects, I may name Mr. Bullard, of this city, and Mr. Beecher, of Cincinnati. These preachers of the Gospel of Jesus Christ—one on the occasion of delivering a sermon on the death of President Harrison, and the other at a sort of holy triumphant celebration, held on the occasion of the conversion of the Tremont Theatre (Boston) into a church —took upon themselves the offices of judges of their fellow-sinners, and, instead of obeying the command of the Master they pretend to serve, which required his followers to go forth to all the world and preach GOOD WILL TO ALL MEN, passed sentence of unconditional condemnation not only upon the professors of the stage, but upon all who encouraged its representations by their presence in the passive characters of auditors.

It may be asked why I, out of the whole community of actors in this extensive country, should take upon myself the task of defending the theatre. I answer, because I *feel it to be my duty*, and because I do not perceive others, far more able to do justice to the cause, step forward, as it appears to me they should, to defend their profession when assailed.

Being a great admirer of the Rev. Mr. Elliot, whom I *know* to be a good man and an exemplary Christian, I confess I was not prepared to find *him* following so far in the wake of the orthodox gentlemen above named as to advise his young hearers to discountenance an institution which has been advocated and upheld by a vast majority of the great and good men of all ages, and in all countries where civilization and refinement have prevailed to any extent. I thought we had *one* church, at least, in St. Louis whose pulpit was occupied by a man who, while he was strictly faithful to his trust, and watchful over the moral conduct of his parishioners, would rise above the petty prejudices which unfortunately, to some extent, exist against the institution referred to;

and if he could not conscientiously assist in dissipating those prejudices, that he would at least refrain from giving countenance to the war of extermination waged by interested and bigoted clergymen against the theatre, leaving his congregation to exercise their own judgments, and obey the dictates of their own consciences (influenced, if you please, by his excellent general teachings) on the subject of amusements.

Before attempting to controvert the opinions of Mr. Elliot as expressed above, it is with pleasure I award to that gentleman great sincerity and honesty of purpose in all his acts and words. His *language*, correctly quoted at the head of this article, it need not be said, is that of a gentleman, a scholar, and a Christian; and its style is referred to only for the purpose of remarking upon the striking difference between it and that of the language generally made use of by the orthodox "gentlemen in black" gowns who have heretofore taken upon themselves the offices of censors of the stage, and, in consequence, claimed my attention.

I will now state concisely Mr. Elliot's reasons for advising young people to stay away from the theatre:

1. The theatre, as an amusement, is too exciting, and, therefore, fraught with serious danger.
2. It is too expensive.
3. It is surrounded with many *incidental* evils, which are always practically attendant upon it, though not theoretically inseparable from it.
4. It leads young men to become immoral and dissipated.

To be sure, all these are mere *assertions;* but, as they are made in sincerity, and doubtless in the full belief of their truth, let us examine them separately.

It is said that the theatre is "too exciting." Now it appears to me that, if the tendency of stage representations be for *good*, they *can not* be "too exciting;" but if for evil, then the gentleman is right. When the heart throbs with the feelings of patriotism and virtuous indignation against tyranny and oppression; when the eye of youth fills with tears of sorrow for suffering virtue; when the cheek burns with indignation at successful villainy—all the effect of the poet's language and the actor's power—will it be said that these aroused feelings are to be suppressed because they are "exciting?" I say to you, friend Elliot, that, so far from the amusement of the theatre being "too exciting" for the young, it would be better for the moral condition of the world if the excellent sentiments promulgated from the stage could be more universally disseminated than they are. That the cold, formal teachings of the pulpit have their uses is not denied; but the practical lessons *acted* before the auditor at the theatre, from the very fact that they *are* more "exciting," are more lasting, and consequently more useful.

I conclude, then, on this point, that a play can not be "too exciting" if the moral be good, and the tendency of the sentiment ennobling to human nature. Let the pulpit, therefore, confine its censures and strictures to *immoral* stage representations, and cherish those which tend to refine, ameliorate, and improve society.

The second objection to the theatre as an amusement, that *it is too expensive*, may be answered in a few words. Let there be a very general attendance (allowing it to be deserving of support), and the prices of admission can be proportionately reduced. This has already been exemplified in our theatres. Notwithstanding the anathemas occasionally launched forth from the pulpit, the attendance has so increased within late years that the admission fee has been reduced *one half!* so it is not very "expensive," after all. And if young men are moderate in their enjoyment of dramatic amusements, visiting the theatre only once or twice a week, it will not be very "hurtful" to them, I imagine, in a pecuniary point of view (in which view I suppose *this* objection is made), and they will have something left for pew rent, preacher's salary, and the missionary box too. Taking into view the *quality* of the various amusements, it appears to me that there is none so cheap as that of the theatre.

The charge that the theatre is "surrounded by *incidental* evils" I scarcely know how to meet, unless the evils are more particularly specified. In the absence of such specifications, I hope it will not be thought unfair to assume that the lecturer referred to those truly objectionable adjuncts to *some* theatres—the bar-room and the third tier. If I am right in this assumption, it is sufficient to say that *here*, in St. Louis, there has been no saloon or bar-room carried on in the theatre for ten years, and that the third tier is frequented by as honest and virtuous a set of auditors, male and female, as can be found in any community—of colored people.

And here I must complain of the illiberality and positive *unfairness* of all the clergymen in this city who oppose the theatre, as they say, *upon principle;* for while they very willingly and with apparent candor admit, *in private*, that the establishment *here* is an exception to the generality of theatres, and, indeed, that its directors deserve credit for the manner in which it is conducted, *in the pulpit* they do not give us the benefit of this exception, but class all theatres together indiscriminately, and indiscriminately condemn them all!

The fourth objection, that going to the theatre leads young men to become immoral and dissipated, is controverted thus: They learn there the best lessons taught by history and experience; they pass their time pleasantly—commit no sin—and retire to their homes satisfied that they have spent the evening in rational enjoyment. "Dissipation" has no more connection with the theatre than with the church. If a man is desirous of indulging in the intoxicating cup, he can obtain it (and will) as easily after attending a lecture or prayer-meeting as after witnessing a theatrical performance.

Instead of theatre-going being an injury to the young (or the old either, for that matter), I insist that it is a positive benefit; and I hope to live long enough to see the respectable portion of our pulpit orators throw aside their long-cherished prejudices and come out in its support. Come, gentlemen of the long robe, what do you say to a "combination" between the Church and the Theatre against the devil and all his works? Instead of endeavoring to *put down the theatre*, WHICH YOU CAN NEVER DO, suppose you preach against the *abuses* which exist in it—recommend your hearers to witness none but good plays—*moral* plays—plays which *are* plays! Tell the young men to stay away when the trash which managers are sometimes *compelled* to offer is announced, and *crowd the house* when a sterling piece is brought out!

If preachers will follow my advice, and let it be understood that they uphold the good and condemn the bad of the theatre, they can then incorporate into their sermons some of the sentiments of our fine old dramatists, and instead of quoting, as they now frequently do, surreptitiously, some good sentiments *from a play*, and shuffle it over with a half-uttered reference to "the poet," they could quote boldly from Shakspeare, Johnson, Home, and other play-writers, and give them due credit for their sentiments. More than a thousand times have I heard passages from Shakspeare quoted in the pulpit, and never but once did I hear that poet's *name* mentioned there, and then the minister said he valued the plays of Shakspeare *next to his Bible!* The minister here spoken of gave this rule as the proper one to be followed by all Christians in relation to amusements: "*Never to go to any place where you are not willing to die!*" An excellent rule, I humbly think, and one which, if followed by us all (preachers as well as players), might be considered a safe guide through life.

For twenty-five years I have followed the stage as a profession. If I thought it a sinful one I would leave it to-morrow—nay, to-night, though a large family is dependent on my professional exertions for support—my children for their education.

If my own motives and feelings are known to myself, my aim has always been, so far as my limited influence extended, to elevate the drama, or, rather, to so conduct my course in the management of such theatres as have been wholly or partially under my direction as to maintain the STAGE in its proper position among the professions. This I have effected so far as the public would sustain me; and, in conclusion, I invite all who believe that theatre-going is attended with injurious effects to examine well the subject, discard all illiberal prejudices, exercise a Christian spirit toward those who differ with them in opinion, and pause before they publicly utter opinions which, if concurred in by the community in which we live, would consign to want and starvation all who are engaged in the theatre, consisting of no less than sixty or seventy individuals, who, for virtue, intelligence, and honesty (leaving myself out of the party), may safely challenge a comparison with those who seem disposed to deprive them of their bread.

SOL. SMITH.

CHAPTER V.

THE coalition, somewhat modified in consequence of our refusing to take the Mobile Theatre, was renewed between the St. Charles (now enlarged and refitted at an expense of $16,000) and American. Stickney was no longer connected with the latter. We still retained the two votes to the one of Lucius Place in the board of directors. Mr. George Vandenhoff was our leading man in tragedy and comedy, Mrs. Melinda Jones and Mrs. Stuart leading women, W. H. Chippendale stage manager and leading old man.

A "gentleman of New Orleans" desired to adopt the stage as a profession. He was introduced to me by my very good friend S. S. Prentiss, Esq., after whom I have named one of my children:

S. S. Prentiss to Sol. Smith.

"New Orleans, November 7, 1848.

"SOL. SMITH, ESQ.: MY DEAR SIR, —Allow me to introduce to you my very particular friend, J. W. Frost, Esq., a member of the bar of this city. Mr. Frost desires to speak with you concerning a young friend of his who is anxious to go on the stage, and who Mr. F. thinks has a decided capacity for your profession. Mr. F. is an excellent judge, and full reliance may be placed upon his representations.

"If you can further the wishes of Mr. Frost in regard to this young man, you will much oblige both him and your friend and obedient servant,

"S. S. Prentiss."

The young friend of Judge Frost's was Mr. W. W. W. Wood, a lawyer, and a very intelligent man. After due preparation Mr. Wood appeared in the character of *Bertram*. His performance was respectable for a new beginner, but I was satisfied, and told him so, he would never succeed in tragedy; as a low comedian I thought he might in time become a passable actor. He had the good sense to give up all idea of adopting the stage as a profession; nevertheless, it so happened in after years that he became quite a popular low comedian in amateur theatricals. He is not now living.

Another young lawyer from New Albany, Ind., came to me well introduced. *He* wanted to become a comedian. As there must necessarily be new beginners in our profession as well as in all others, I took his application into consideration, and promised him a business interview in a day or two, in the interim giving him the freedom of the theatre. The very first night he went into the house he got drinking with some friends, and became a maniac for the time being, kicking up a general row, and fighting the policemen! Of course, his lodging that night was in the calaboose. Next morning I received a note from the poor fellow—his name was Nunemacher—begging me to visit him instantly, as he was accused of committing a murder! I hastened to the prison, and found him in a cell with a dead man, who bore on his neck marks of having been strangled. "In God's name," said I, "what does this mean?" His answer, through tears, was, "You know as much about it as I do." "Had you a quarrel with this man?" I inquired. "So help me God," said he, "I never saw him before this morning. When I came to myself—for I have no recollection of any thing that passed last night—he was lying dead as you see him, and now I am accused of murdering him." "Do you think it possible that you *could* have strangled him in your delirium?" I inquired. "That's the worst of it," returned he, solemnly. "I *may* have done it, but I can not think I did. I was never drunk before, and don't know what a drunken man may do. Now, Mr. Smith, what I want you to do is to get me a lawyer, and *send for my father.*" I felt sure he was innocent of committing any willful homicide, and investigations since have satisfied me he had nothing whatever to do with the killing. I employed Mr. Prentiss, who joined me in investigating the case. The young man's father arrived in due time, and the innocence of his son was at length made manifest without a trial. The noble Prentiss refused taking any fee, saying that, as I seemed very much interested in the case, it was enough fee for him to partake of the gratification I experienced on seeing the young man set at liberty after a month's confinement in the city prison.

I advised Mr. Nunemacher to go home and "stick to the law," and he promised to do so. We shall presently see whether he was cured of his passion for the stage by the horible scenes he had passed through, not to say his narrow escape from the gallows for a murder he did not commit.

This was the cholera season. My partner retired to his villa in Mobile, and I was left to make headway alone against the horrible epidemic as well as I could. General Taylor attended the theatre on the 1st of December, and drew a tolerably good house. The business, as a general thing, was very bad. C. D. Pitt, a very good actor, played two very poor engagements, the receipts at his second benefit being only $65! Cholera increased at a terrible rate during December. "Old Logan" and daughter played one night, and then fled from the pestilence, and they did perfectly right. A Mr. Flemming (any body would do for a star under such circumstances) played to houses averaging about $40. My partner, by letter, urged me to close. The American was doing considerably better than the St. Charles, and Place proposed we should close the St. Charles *and keep the American open!* This proposition was decided in the negative by a two thirds vote (to wit, *my* vote), and then, not wishing, as he said, to "shoulder his portion of the immense losses the St. Charles was nightly sustaining," Mr. Lucius Place proposed we should each pay up his proportion of the losses so far sustained and dissolve the coalition. "Upon this hint I spake, and, taking a pliant hour," namely, that very moment in which the proposition was made, I wrote out and offered the following resolution, which I need not say was adopted unanimously:

"*Whereas* it is feared that there does not exist in this board an entire unanimity with regard to the policy it is proper to pursue in the present situation of affairs, and during the existence of the cholera as an epidemic in New Orleans, it is unanimously

"*Resolved*, That the coalition between the managements of the St. Charles and American Theatres * * * be, and the same is hereby amicably dissolved, and each theatre shall hereafter be conducted by the respective managements as if no such coalition had existed—the managers of the St. Charles relinquishing all claims on the profits of the American, and the manager of the American, in like manner, relinquishing all claims upon the profits of the St. Charles, and neither party to be responsible for the other's losses; and it is hereby declared that all accounts are settled, and neither party owes the other any thing."

The principal actors and actresses urged me to close, and on the 26th of December there appeared posted in the greenroom a notice for a meeting of the company and orchestra, to adopt such measures as might be thought advisable, under existing circumstances, to relieve the management from farther losses by reason of keeping the theatre open any longer during the prevalence of the epidemic. As soon as I saw the notice I wrote the following and caused it to be put up in the greenroom. I heard no more of closing:

TO THE COMPANY.

Having seen a notice, unauthorized by the management, for a meeting of the company at 12 o'clock this day, and having been informed that the object of the proposed meeting is to submit a proposition that the theatre be closed for a short time, or during the prevalence of the cholera as an epidemic, it is deemed proper to anticipate whatever proceedings may be contemplated by stating—

1. I most cordially thank those members of the company who have called the meeting, believing—indeed, *knowing*—they were actuated by kindly feeling toward the management, and a desire to share in the losses consequent upon the unexpected calamity which has visited the city.

2. All who, from fear of the cholera, wish to leave New Orleans, are hereby released from their engagements: their articles will be canceled to-morrow morning, and they will be paid to the end of the theatrical week.

3. The St. Charles Theatre will remain open every night without interruption, unless, from sickness or desertion under the above permission, the company shall become so reduced that pieces can not be respectably performed.

4. This notice is not prompted by any wish to cast reproach on those who signed the notice for a meeting of the company. On the contrary, the undersigned is satisfied that the movement was instigated by the best of motives.

SOL. SMITH.

December 26, 1848.

I record this as the *only* instance which ever came under my observation of any considerable number of a company of actors and actresses being willing that a theatre should close on account of sickness in a city. They are generally the most fearless people in the world, and entirely willing to risk their lives in the midst of an epidemic, provided the manager is responsible for salaries. I may say that, having my wife and three children with me in New Orleans, nothing would have suited *me* better than to close up and retire from the pestilent city, but I felt that, as the conductor of a public institution, I owed the public and the company a duty which I could not shrink from performing. Besides, I have ever been of the opinion that we are in the hands of God, and under his special care, and there is no use in attempting to flee from cholera or yellow fever; hence I have never hesitated a moment in going into New Orleans when business (duty) called me there in any and all seasons of the year. Yet there are men, and good men, who dare not and will not go where an epidemic prevails, and I do not question their right to obey the dictates of their judgment, prompted by their fears.

In the midst of this gloomy time, the receipts having fallen down to $60, $50, and $40 a night, I heard by accident of Mr. Hackett being in the interior of Louisiana—hunting. The telegraph was put into operation, and he was brought to New Orleans in double-quick time. His arrival was a perfect godsend. An arrangement was made in a very few moments, for we had dealt with each other so many years that but few words were necessary between us, and he appeared as *Jack Falstaff* on the 4th of January to a house counting nearly $400. Some of his houses went even above that, and his benefit was fine. His engagement was renewed, and the business continued passably good to the end of his second week.

Mr. James H. Hackett is the only man I know or have heard of, save David Garrick, who at a single bound leapt into the position of a first-class actor. After receiving a classical education at Columbia College, he began the business of life as a merchant in Utica, N.Y., in 1820, and was so successful that he removed to New York City in 1825, where, with a capital of $20,000 and any amount of credit, he commenced to deal in teas and wines, cargoes of Holland gin and French brandies, for a few months being quite successful; but the summer of that year was remarkable for the great and sudden depreciation of goods in his line, and being caught with a heavy amount of stock on hand, more than his whole capital was sunk, and he found himself a bankrupt! Assistance was offered to "help him through" by many friendly merchants, but he resolved to "stop" and dispose of his stock in trade, in hopes of paying all, or nearly all of his debts, which amounted to some $40,000. His assets proved about $6000 short of the mark. Determined to pay all as soon as he could earn the money in some other business, Mr. Hackett turned his attention to the stage, and in March, 1826, made his appearance at the Park Theatre in the character of *Justice Woodcock* (LOVE IN A VILLAGE), *in imitation of old Jack Barnes!* The imitation was so true in voice and manner that many persons believed it was old Jack himself who was performing before them, though it was with great difficulty his face (being that of a young man) could be "made up" to resemble that of the popular old comedian he was imitating.

Encouraged by his decided success on his first appearance, he adopted the stage as a profession in October of the same year, and in fifteen months thereafter earned and devoted to a full and final settlement with his creditors about $6000, the greater portion of which he cleared by getting up Shakspeare's COMEDY OF ERRORS, old Jack Barnes playing *Dromio of Syracuse*, and Hackett *Dromio of Ephesus*, and imitating the personal peculiarities of Barnes to the absolute confusion of the audience in reference to their proper and respective persons. Although I never witnessed this performance, I well remember the sensation it produced, and I afterward (in 1837, I think) saw Mr. Hackett perform one of the *Dromios*, with Vincent De Camp in the other, with equal success in the imitation.

Mr. Hackett's next attempt, I believe, was in a local sketch entitled the MILITIA TRAINING, in which he personated a Yankee character, *Captain Bunker*, or *Bunkum*. He afterward took upon himself the rôle of *Solomon Swap*, a Yankee, in an adaptation (by himself) of Colman's comedy of WHO WANTS A GUINEA? and this was the beginning of what may be termed the Yankee Drama in this country, leading to the writing of many Yankee plays, in which the Yankee Hills, the Yankee Marbles, and the Yankee Sillsbees had their being as "Yankee delineators." Mr. Hackett, leaving the Yankee characters to the new-comers, procured the writing of the LION OF THE WEST, ... in which he personated *Colonel Wildfire*, a Kentuckian, and a little one-act piece entitled MONSIEUR MALLET, in which he played the part of an old French exile in such a way that no other actor has ever even *attempted* it. RIP VAN WINKLE was afterward added to his short list of characters, and in this (an adaptation of his own from a London play) he has remained without a rival to this day, although a young actor has recently achieved great and deserved success in a *Boucicaulted* version of the same piece. I should despair of finding a man or woman in an audience of five hundred who could hear Hackett's utterance of five words in the second act, "But she was mine vrow," without experiencing some moisture in the eyes.

These few characters, with the addition of *Sir Pertinax MacSycophant*, carried him through many years of successful starring, during which he was studying the character of *Jack Falstaff* as created by William Shakspeare, and carried rollicking through three plays. It is unnecessary to say what he *was* in this great character, for what he *was* he *is*, and the present generation will agree with me that he is *the Jack Falstaff* of the present age, and stands without a rival in the character.

After Hackett came Mr. and Mrs. Conner, Miss Brienti and Brough, and the Heron family, who all helped to keep us going without much loss, if any, until the time when the great feature of the season, MACREADY, was to appear, according to his engagement (being due on the 29th of January); but he was one who did not implicitly trust in Providence for his preservation through an epidemic, and though, as I believe, a truly conscientious and Christian man, he held back persistently. I make no apology for inserting all of his letters written about this time, as I suppose my readers will be glad to read them, if for no other reason than because they are his. You will understand that most of these letters are in answer to my urgent requests for him to come on, which requests were not, however, made until our Board of Health had officially declared that cholera no longer existed as an epidemic.

W. C. Macready to Sol. Smith.

Mansion House Hotel, Charleston, S. C.,
Jan. 10, 1849.

"DEAR SIR,—I have waited with much anxiety the arrival of the posts for an answer to my telegraph to you from Washington, dispatched last week. I need not tell you I have watched with the keenest interest the daily reports of the cholera's progress at New Orleans. To go there while this disease is prevalent would be little short of madness, and of course I can not be expected to incur such a risk.

"I will willingly wait here, or in this neighborhood, any reasonable time for its disappearance; and upon the notification of clean bills of health, will instantly set out on my journey. Can you obtain such information as may afford you a probable guess, from the present state of affairs, when *this is likely to be*, that I may be fully prepared not to lose one day more than is in reason unavoidable?

"Deeply groaning under this calamity, which

touches us both so sorely, but especially myself, I remain, dear sir, yours very faithfully,

"W. C. MACREADY.

P.S.—I telegraphed you yesterday that I could not be with you on the 29th January. This is a grievous disappointment to me."

From the same to the same.

"Mansion House, Charleston, S. C., Jan. 13, 1849.

"DEAR SIR,—Your telegraphic communication I received, dated January 8, with the statement—'*Expect you 29th. Board of Health report epidemic gone.*' Upon which I dispatched by telegraph an answer, suggesting to you the impolicy of *precipitating* such an engagement as this before the return of the people could give any chance or hope of success to it. Nevertheless, impolitic and unwise in the extreme as I should regard such a measure, useless and worse than useless to you, and to me the destruction of all the results looked for from my visit to New Orleans, I should hold myself bound to go *directly* the health of the city justified me in so doing. But the Board of Health must have been betrayed by some deceitful appearance on the 8th, for here is the telegraph of *January 10th*—'*Deaths by cholera* 48 *in* 48 *hours.*'

"Now, while this continues, indeed, until it is clear that the pestilence has left the city, *you must not expect me.* I stay away *in idleness*, and my purpose in this country is frustrated by such a calamity. I mention this to convince you that my holding back is most reluctant, and assented to only under a sense of duty. Yours, dear sir, very truly, W. C. MACREADY."

From the same to the same.

"Mansion House, Charleston, S. C., Jan. 16, 1849.

"DEAR SIR,—Your favors of the 7th and 8th, with the inclosures of slips from Picayune and Bulletin, have come to hand.

"Notice by telegraph of '*10th, N. O.*,' and the inclosed statement from this day's Charleston Mercury, giving accounts to the 9th, make it still questionable here as to the risk to be incurred in going to New Orleans and Mobile under the existence of the cholera in its present condition.

"For perfect satisfaction and correct guidance in the matter, I have taken professional advice, consulting the leading physician here, and I lose no time in forwarding you a copy of the certificate of his opinion, given after receiving information on my habits and constitution.

"It seems needless, my dear sir, to observe to you how much I am embarrassed by this most untoward event, and how anxious I must be to turn to account every moment of my time in this country. You may be assured that I shall not lose a day, upon the knowledge of the disappearance of the disorder, in telegraphing you of my coming on, and of my immediate setting out.

"Had I been circumstanced as you unfortunately have been, I should have closed the theatre, as, under a visitation and calamity so grievous, all ought to bear their portion in its suffering. Believe me to remain, dear sir, always and most truly yours, W. C. MACREADY."

Physician's Certificate.

"Charleston, Jan. 16, 1849.

"Having been consulted by Mr. W. C. Macready as to the risks of cholera attendant upon the fulfillment of his engagement in New Orleans at the present time, I have no hesitation in advising a postponement of his contemplated visit until the evidence of the departure of that disease is more certain than it appears to me to be at this time. JAS. MOULTRIE, M.D.

"(Correct copy. W. C. M.)"

From the same to the same.

"Mansion House, Charleston, S. C., Jan. 19, 1849.

"DEAR SIR,—Your peremptory telegraph of the 15th I have received and answered.

"In such a question—no less, perhaps, than that of life or death—wherein I should peril by my imprudence other persons besides myself, I must be allowed to exercise ordinary discretion, and upon authentic private reports, as well as public documents, together with information of the state of the cities and country through which we have to pass, submit the question of the propriety of going to New Orleans to the most competent medical authorities, and be guided by them.

"Having come thus far, and that almost solely with the object of visiting New Orleans, my interest, and certainly my inclination, will urge me forward directly I can understand that I shall be acting with common prudence in going on; but the justifiable caution I use is strongly urged on me by persons here more capable than myself of deciding on such a step.

"Mr. Wilson and Mad. Weiss have both abandoned *altogether* their intended journey to New Orleans.

"I only wait the needful satisfactory certifications of the departure of the disease from my route and my destination, and I will telegraph you on the instant of my speedy setting out.

"With all good wishes, I am, dear sir, yours very truly, W. C. MACREADY."

From the same to the same.

"Mansion House, Charleston, South Carolina,
Saturday evening, January 20, 1849.

"MY DEAR SIR,—Your letter of the 14th has just reached me. I thank you for sending me the telegraphic letter. The lines have been broken.

"I have just seen a gentleman *direct* from *New Orleans.* He was recommended to come away, and dissuades from thinking of going till the disorder, which he believes to be abating, is gone. By telegraph I have dates 14th and 15th, which give a daily mortality with the disorder that make apparent the reasonableness of the course I adopt. I will (anxiously) wait the departure of this pestilence to the last moment of my power, and DIRECTLY that I can understand from competent persons here that I may encounter the journey, I will telegraph you of my instant preparation to set out. But I must know that my course is clear before I start.

"Believe me to be very truly yours,

"W. C. MACREADY."

From the same to the same.

"Mansion House, Charleston, S. C., Jan. 18, 1849.

"DEAR SIR,—I need not say how heartily I rejoice in all the good news you can send me. It is a selfish subject of congratulation with me. But to the dates you send me—'9th' and '10th' —I have '11th.' '*New Orleans, seventeen interments from cholera.*' By the same intelligence we read of the '*death of Judge Lacy, Supreme Court, at Mobile;*' and it is understood here that the disease is prevalent at *Montgomery, Mobile, and all along the Alabama River!* The opinion of the medical men here, and, indeed, general opinion, is, that I should not be justified in making the journey till more decisive evidences of the subsidence of the pestilence. My health would not warrant the risk of entering boats or houses where infection is. I need not observe to you what a crushing blow to my prospects this disaster is; but there is no help for it. I will wait here in the hope of each day's news rapidly dispersing the obstructions in my way. The telegraph lines have been broken between Mobile and this city; I have heard it suspected—*purposely*. I ended here last night.

"Yours very truly, W. C. MACREADY."

From the same to the same.

"Savannah, Ga., January 25, 1849.

"DEAR SIR,—Your letters of the 15th and 16th I have this moment received, in which you urge the necessity of my coming to New Orleans, and inform me the 'postponement of my engagement can not be *thought* of,' stating the 'cholera is over.'

"I shall be truly sorry if the postponement of my arrival should interfere with my engagement, because it is most reluctant on my part, and I have come thus far upon my route to New Orleans, that city being really the object of my Southern journey. But, losing my time, as I unfortunately am doing here—for this dribbling work is nothing but loss of time—I can not hazard my health (quite weak and uncertain enough already) and the safety of those with me by going into a city where disease is prevalent. You write to me on the 15th of January that 'the cholera is over,' and my accounts at Charleston are—'New Orleans, January 14th, deaths by cholera, 23; January 15th, 17.'

"On Saturday I saw a gentleman of the very first respectability, U. S. N., who left New Orleans on the 12th because he had been advised to do so *on account of the disorder*.

"This delay is at serious war with my interest, but no obligation, legal or honorable, lies on me to go where infection is, or *where it has been, until certified beyond contradiction of its departure.* In the newspapers that give the announcement of the Board of Health that the epidemic has ceased is the enumeration of the interments of cholera patients! If in your view the postponement of the engagement is tantamount to a nullification of it, I shall be truly grieved, because I am prepared to wait to the latest reasonable day for the assurance of safety in proceeding. I am diligent in my inquiries at each place where information can be obtained, and directly I can know that I ought to go forward I will telegraph you to that effect. I can do no more.

"With every kind wish, I am, dear sir, yours very truly, W. C. MACREADY."

From the same to the same.

"Mansion House, Charleston, S. C., Jan. 29, 1849.

"DEAR SIR,—I am in receipt of your two letters, arrived together this morning, dates 21st, 22d inst. In the first you seem to take offense at the expression of my telegraphic notice, which I very much regret, as I would not on any account have used a word that should seem wanting in respect or regard; but I chose *direct terms* in order to convey to you in the least number of words the decision I had taken—and that most reluctantly—after submitting the case of my state of health to the first medical opinion here, and receiving his strong recommendation not to go to New Orleans while the appearance of disease remained. I am sorry you should suppose that I could intend any thing unkind or discourteous in tone or purpose, than which nothing was farther from my thoughts. The delay has been *to me* a serious disappointment and loss, and it is with extreme anxiety I have been watching daily the reports from your city for information that would justify me in advancing.

"My reports of deaths by cholera reach up to the 18th inst. Now, my dear sir, it is not reasonable to expect that *even a person in sound health*, much less one whose system is much shaken, should go where infection is, and in this opinion both medical and the best legal opinions concur.

"In to-day's report I find that the cholera had entirely subsided at New Orleans on the 24th. I shall therefore take steps immediately for such arrangement of my baggage, etc., as may prevent the loss of farther time, and (D. V.) will start by rail on Wednesday morning; but even now shall not be able to go by the river, so that in what condition I may reach you I can not guess.

"Will you oblige me by taking rooms for me—parlor and bedroom? I have my meals served in my own apartments. On my former visit they made an arrangement for me of this kind at Hewlett's, where I received every attention; perhaps they would not be indisposed to do the same again. If they should object I should prefer the St. Charles. Hamlet must be my opening play.

"With every kind wish, I remain, dear sir, yours very truly, W. C. MACREADY."

From the same to the same.

"Charleston, S. C., January 31, 1849.

"DEAR SIR,—Yesterday, on receipt of your telegraphic inquiry, I dispatched an answer that, God willing, you might rely on me for the 12th of February. I had arranged to leave this morning, but am not at all well to-day, having been troubled with serious irritation of the trachea and general derangement of system, which I fancy is attributable to the very great heat we experience here. I shall set out to-morrow morning, that I may, in case of need, take some rest on my journey, or arrive in time to push our business forward by some preliminary rehearsals. I think I mentioned Hamlet for our opening play.

"I trust to meet you in better health than I am at this writing, and that I may be in good condition for my morning's start.

"With kindest wishes, I am, dear sir, most truly yours, W. C. MACREADY."

A letter from "Old Logan," written about this time, will give some idea of the exaggerated reports which went forth from the Crescent City concerning the ravages of the cholera there, as well as some account of theatrical matters in Cincinnati and elsewhere:

C. A. Logan to Sol. Smith.

"Pittsburg, Pennsylvania, January 18, 1849.

"(I believe it's the 18th, but, like Sir *George Thunder*, all log reckonings have gone wrong with me lately.)

"MY DEAR SMITH,—When a merchant receives intelligence that his ship which he thought lost, and, to heighten the picture, having his favorite son aboard, who went out to visit foreign parts, is safe, son, cargo, and all, even so, like unto his sensations, to-day, when I received your most welcome letter, were mine to hear that you were safe, family and all. In this letter you refer to one I never received, else I should tell you now how cruel it was in you not to write—never to pay any regard to the *imploring* tone of the note written to you from Cairo. But I'll say nothing, as you doubtless wrote a letter, which miscarried.

"On reaching home, I found that the eresipalus (I don't know how to spell it) in my wife's face was nearly cured, but her fears for Eliza and myself were so extreme that an observer would have been puzzled to judge from her mingled weeping and laughter whether she was glad or sorry for our safe return.

"Bates holds the scales of justice with an even hand. He very properly allows no extraneous circumstances, such as cholera, or any other thing which is not *business matter*, to weigh a feather in the scale. When I returned to Cincinnati, no offer of immediate employment was made to me. When I left for the South, in December, I myself arranged the business of the theatre in view of my absence for six weeks, and when I returned unexpectedly, of course I could not hope they would alter it. There was a clamor in the town for my new piece, when it was known I had arrived, and it would have *drawn*, but my bosom friend Sarzedas argued that, as Bates had bought a copy of the play, it could be done without me, and 'so save $62 per week, the salary of the family, besides those constantly recurring benefits which' (albeit Bates always took the lion's share of, still) 'injured so much the previous and subsequent nights.'

"I didn't stop to argue the question, but, like *Rob Roy*, I took to the mountain and the glen. Potter, a notorious man whom I had never seen, having heard, I suppose, that I did not return to the National, came to me and offered terms for Columbus, Ohio.

"'Have you a theatre there?'

"'A very fine *hall*," said he.

"'How much will it hold?'

"'We've had $90 in,' said he, boastingly.

"'How much of the receipts will you give me?'

"'Twenty per cent. and half benefits.'

"'Done,' said I; 'done,' said he, and we went.

"We played four nights, and on the fifth Eliza squeezed $119 50 in a room not more than four times the size of the office of your Board. The last theatre we had played in was the St. Charles, the next was the Columbus!

"Eliza said to Potter (imprudently, and I reproved her for the bad taste of the remark) that she had never seen such an apt illustration of the contiguity of the sublime and the ridiculous.

"I resolved not to return to Cincinnati immediately, because I determined not to be questioned by my friends respecting the unusual incident of my being idle. There are many relations between Bates and myself which it is not necessary to enter into a discussion of, or explanation of, to every body one meets in the street, but to YOU I say that, had *his* situation and *mine* been reversed, I should have thrown wide open the door, and said, 'Come in; there's your old seat reserved for you by the fire.'

"Self, self, self! How a man will talk of himself! Pshaw! In looking over what I have written about my own affairs, I feel ashamed that I'm bothering with my trifling grievances my friend, who is in, perhaps, really serious difficulties.

"The editors are all beginning, I believe, to think that I have some morbid idea about cholera, for, when I enter their offices, I at once inquire for the latest dates from New Orleans. This anxiety is to find out whether you are still open, or if any deaths have occurred in your company.

"Later dates than your letter of to-day have reached me. The disease is abating, they say. Whenever you say, 'Logan, come,' I'll start, but I know you will not say this until the proper time. At the same time, I feel it due to myself to say that I hereby release you from any kind of engagement with me or with my daughter. When the city becomes healthy, stars will be apt to crowd on you, and your whole season may be filled up. In such case, do not consider me for a moment. We met in friendship, lived in friendship, parted in friendship, and no mere *theatrical business*, which is so apt to dull all the better feelings of our manhood, shall ever, as far as *I* am concerned, disturb the esteem I feel for you—the esteem of one honorable man for another.

"Murdoch is here, and he asks me to speak to you for him. I devote the next page to his business. I write what he dictates.

"Half an hour has elapsed. Murdoch's business shall be stated on another *sheet*. I wonder how much you'll have to pay for this manuscript! Talking of paying reminds me of the $25 you were kind enough to lend me. If your former letter to me had not miscarried, I should inclose the sum in this. It might be a drop in the ocean of your misfortunes. But if this package, with its inclosure, should be lost, like your first letter, it would be, situated as I am, an increase of my recent ill luck.

"9 o'clock Sunday night, January 21.
"(That's the right date.)

"Just seen Murdoch; frightened at cholera; declines treating for New Orleans at present; asks me to send regrets, etc.

"Just heard that Harry Grattan is dead. Still address me at home; I shall be there before your letter.

"Can't get any better paper, so I had to make this bungling packgage.

"Trusting that you'll keep your health and recover all losses, I remain LOGAN.

"P.S.—If I had a quire or two more of paper, I suppose I should fill them up to-night, and send them to you; but I have written up all the paper in the house, and it's too late to send for more, so I trust you'll excuse the extreme *brevity* of my epistle."

CHAPTER VI.

THE long-looked-for Macready came at last, and opened on the 12th of February to a house of $1304 75! The great tragedian consented to do what he had not done elsewhere—play consecutive nights (except Sundays), thus saving us from the terrible losses of "off nights;" but at the end of the first week he remonstrated as follows:

W. C. Macready to Sol. Smith.

"Hewlett's Exchange, Saturday.

"MY DEAR SIR,—In the most friendly spirit, and with an *instinct* of self-preservation (I mean pecuniarily), I *warn you* against persisting in this suicidal act of playing every night. The feeling of your supporters is AGAINST it. Not even the population of LONDON can sustain it. I will not stop, because I will not make you uncomfortable; but a sense of duty to you and to myself (seeing as I do the possible *destruction* of an engagement that promised such *great things*) obliges me to caution you, and on my own part to protest against the policy you are pursuing. There! I have discharged my conscience, and now do as you please; you shall not have one word more.

"Most sincerely your friend,
"W. C. MACREADY."

But I was obdurate, having so much leeway to make up, and he bravely went through his task, playing to great houses for four weeks! Vandenhoff and Ryder gave Macready a good support, and the rest of the company were fully up to the mark of his expectations and wishes. I doubt whether JULIUS CÆSAR was ever better performed out of London than it was in the St. Charles, Mr. Macready playing *Brutus* to Mr. Vandenhoff's *Cassius* one night, and reversing the cast on the next night; the same with *Othello* and *Iago*.

Mr. Macready, at the close of his engagement, after playing in Louisville, went to New York, and was there unjustly and cowardly driven from the stage of the Astor Place Opera House by a cabal, under the pretense that he had done something the year previously against the interests of an American actor in England! There never was a more unjust persecution than that which he was subjected to, and all decent New Yorkers are heartily ashamed of the whole affair.

I anticipate a little in order to give an extract from a letter written by my stage manager, W. H. Chippendale, relative to the lamentable affair at the Astor Place Opera House in New York. He was, I believe, concerned in the management of that theatre at the time of the massacre.

"MY DEAR MR. SMITH,—Yours received. I give you my address, because I am now out of place, being *stoned* out of my last situation.

"Did you ever play in MACBETH with the theatre in a state of siege? No, you never did! *I* HAVE! yes, sir! I have assisted to sing the beautiful music of that tragedy with a full accompaniment of paving-stones, and the rioters at the stage door keeping indifferent time with battering-rams in the act of bursting it open. The hero of the night behaved as cool as a cucumber, and, indeed, so did all the *corps dramatique*. A few in the orchestra were alarmed, though the leader protested *his* alarm was on account of his fiddle, not himself. I was determined to work the bill out, so the farce was pretty well on when death ensued, and it became proper to stop. Had the mob got possession of the house, my calculation is from two to three hundred lives would have been lost, and the house would have been fired. It was a solemn affair, and solemn has been the lesson.

"At the Broadway Forrest's engagement diminished to nothing, or next to it—some $170 taken the last two nights. It was in bad taste for the management, under the afflicting circumstances of the time, to urge its fulfillment. I feel well assured it was against Forrest's wish."

The Monplaisir troupe followed Macready, and played and danced a tolerable engagement, after which came Julia Dean, who played a fine one. Julia (bless her!) never failed to draw good houses. The season closed with the last performances in New Orleans of Dan Marble, on the 10th of April, *without loss!*

The "American" closed *prematurely*, as usual.

A theatre in Lafayette, a suburb of New Orleans, was opened under the management of a Mr. Oliver this season. The prevalence of the cholera blighted any prospect there might have been of success. The company was composed principally of new beginners, and their salaries were to be paid in various commodities, such as the manager stipulated to receive of the citizens for tickets. It was a stipulation in each article of agreement (so the manager told me) that every actor should take a portion of his salary in *coffins*, should he need any!—that is to say, if he should die during the season, he should be *buried on account;* the style of coffin, number of carriages, and so forth, to be regulated by the amount due at the time of his demise.

I had a fellow feeling for this manager, and when he asked me to act one night for him, assuring me I could fill the house at double prices, I could not refuse him, though I doubted very much whether my acting would add any thing to his receipts. Manager Oliver was right, however, and I had the pleasure of playing the *Mock Duke* in the HONEYMOON to one of the most crowded audiences I had ever acted to. Of course, under the circumstances, I would take no pay for my night's services, though the grateful manager offered me a clear half of the receipts.

The season failed totally, the manager left for parts unknown, and next season, after a vain attempt by one Hicky to resuscitate the drama by presenting some horrible representations (or misrepresentations rather) of Yankee character, the theatre took fire one day and was burned to the ground. Lafayette is too near New Orleans to give an efficient support to a theatre.

As I shall have no farther occasion to make mention of Mr. Macready, all my business connections with him having terminated with this season, I take leave to record here the error to which I think he—the best *Hamlet* I ever saw—commits while performing that character; and not he only, but every actor I have seen attempt the part. I refer to the using of *real pictures* in what is termed the "closet scene." What I have to say on this matter I will entitle

Whole Lengths, Half Lengths, and Miniatures.

"Look here upon this picture, and on this."

At the age of fourteen years I first perused the plays of Shakspeare. The inside of a theatre I had never seen, yet the "situations" of the various characters forming the *dramatis personæ* of the plays of the great author were as palpably fixed in my mind at that time as they were in after years, when regulated by rehearsals, under the direction of capable stage-managers; and now, after thirty years' actual experience in theatrical management, having been in business relations with all the great actors and actresses of the age, and having learned their various conceptions and ideas of "situations" and "effects," as evinced in their respective performances, I am convinced that my first impressions were generally correct, and that many of the traditional stage situations and arrangements, as well as some of the "new readings" of modern performers, will not, in all instances, bear the test of criticism.

At the early age I speak of, Hamlet was my favorite play. I could recite nearly every line of it. My young brothers and myself spent hours, if not days, in speaking the dialogues of this great play. The scene between *Hamlet* and the ghost of his father was an especial favorite with my brother M. and myself, and we became as perfect in the words as we were in the Lord's Prayer, or "Now I lay me down to sleep."

During my early acquaintance with the works of Shakspeare it did not once occur to my youthful mind that *Hamlet* is really a madman. I thought in my innocence that he "essentially is not in madness, but mad in craft" (as he says); but volumes having since been written to prove that he is actually a madman, and, on the other side, that he only assumes madness the more effectually to work out his purposes and encompass the avenging of his father's murder, I suppose there is a doubt upon the matter, and my boyish judgment must have been premature in deciding so summarily what had been then and is still considered so knotty a point; yet I am free to say that my riper judgment confirms that of the boy, and I at this moment side with those who think that Shakspeare's Hamlet, so far from being a madman, is the most sensible, philosophic, sound-minded individual of all the characters created by the immortal bard.

Much has been written during the last one hundred years, and much more will doubtless be written during the *next* hundred years, on the disputed point, raised, I believe, in the time of Garrick, whether, in the closet scene, so-called, of the tragedy of Hamlet (Act iii., Scene 4), there should be large portraits of the late and reigning kings hanging on the walls, or miniature likenesses of those royal personages in the possession of the queen and her son. Commentators differ on this question. Steevens favors the idea that when Hamlet says

"Look here upon this picture, and on this,"

he has reference to two full-length portraits, being part of the furniture of the queen's closet; because, he argues, Hamlet, who in a former scene had censured those who gave high prices for his uncle's "pictures in little" (miniatures), would hardly have condescended to carry such a thing in his pocket.

Modern Hamlets get over this difficulty by carrying their deceased father's "pictures in little" suspended to a ribbon about the neck, while the queen very accommodatingly carries that of her present husband suspended by a ribbon about her neck, ready for her son to seize upon at the proper time.

Malone says: "The introduction of miniatures in this place appears to be a modern innovation. A print prefixed to Rowe's edition of Hamlet, published in 1709, proves this. There, the two royal portraits are exhibited as half lengths, hanging in the queen's closet; and either thus, or as whole lengths, they probably were exhibited from the time of the original performance of this tragedy to the death of Betterton. To half lengths, however, the same objection lies as to miniatures."

I shall never forget the singular sensation I experienced when, on first witnessing a stage representation of this great play, I saw Mr. Collins—it was at the old Columbia Street Theatre, Cincinnati—make use of *real* pictures (miniatures), worn by the actor and actress in the manner heretofore indicated. I laughed outright; I couldn't help it. Seeing Hamlet directing the attention of his mother to the little pictures, the idea instantly crossed my mind that presently, if the scene was to be carried through in the same literal manner, he would be compelled to attempt a somewhat difficult feat; for the queen says:

> "Oh! Hamlet, speak no more:
> *Thou turn'st mine eyes into my very soul;*
> And there I see such black and grained spots
> As will not leave their tinct."

And farther on, when the conscience-stricken queen likened his words to *daggers*, if Hamlet had not in a previous scene given his princely word to the audience that he would "*speak* daggers, but *use* none," I should have expected to see him draw a couple of those efficient stage properties; and again, when afterward the queen exclaimed,

> "Oh! Hamlet, thou hast cleft my heart in twain!"

the vision of a butcher's cleaver actually swung before my eyes!

The truth is, the introduction of real pictures into this scene had never entered into my mind; and though I now find that all actors use them, to me they appear entirely out of place.

This is *my* theory:

The *pictures* drawn by Hamlet for his mother's contemplation—"the counterfeit presentment of two brothers"—are these:

PICTURE I.—HIS FATHER.

> "See what a grace was seated on this brow:
> Hyperion's curls; the front of Jove himself;
> An eye like Mars, to threaten and command;
> A station like the herald Mercury,
> New-lighted on a heaven-kissing hill;
> A combination and a form indeed,
> Where every god did seem to set his seal,
> To give the world assurance of a man:
> This was your husband."

If Hamlet is exhibiting to his mother a *real* picture, why speak of the grace that *was* seated on his brow? Why say that "every god *did* set his seal?" etc. Why not speak of the picture as it appears at the time of its exhibition, and say, "See what a grace *is* seated on his brow?" etc.

PICTURE II.—HIS UNCLE.

> "Look you, now, what follows:
> Here is your husband; like a mildew'd ear,
> Blasting his wholesome brother. * * *
> * * * * * What judgment
> Would step from this to this?
> * * * * * * * * * *
> A murderer and a villain;
> A slave, that is not twentieth part the tithe
> Of your precedent lord; a vice of kings;
> A cut-purse of the empire and the rule,
> That from a shelf the precious diadem stole,
> And put it in his pocket; a king
> Of shreds and patches—"

The filling out of the *second* picture is cut off by the entrance of the ghost of the original of the *first;* but both are so truthfully drawn—in outline, so to speak—that the wife recognizes her two husbands, and beseeches her son to "speak no more." It must be observed that, during the exhibition of those *speaking likenesses* to the queen, there is not one word said to justify the belief that the author contemplated the use of either whole lengths, half lengths, or miniatures in illustration of the scene. On the contrary, when the queen, pricked by her awakened conscience, becomes tired of the pictures called up to the view of her mind's eye by her son, she entreats him—(to take them away? hide them from her sight? no!)—to "speak no more;" and this she does three different times.

According to my reading, the text of Shakspeare affords no authority whatever for the introduction of pictures of any kind as "properties" in the closet scene of the tragedy of HAMLET; and I hope to see our actors break through the traditionary manner of rendering this scene, so long persisted in, and give it in the way the author undoubtedly intended it should be given —drawing the pictures before the mental vision of the queen in words which, "like daggers, enter into her ears," "turn her eyes into her soul," and "cleave her heart in twain."

In the name of all that is reasonable, let us have no more whole lengths, half lengths, nor miniatures, daubed upon canvas or ivory, for this scene, when Shakspeare has given us the two pictures ready to our hand, drawn by his matchless pen, and handed down to us by types and printers' ink. Or, if actors *will* have "real pictures," I must insist that there be also provided a looking-glass of some kind—either a good-sized article to hang against the wall, a pier-glass, or a pocket mirror (perhaps one on the back of a pocket hair-brush would do); for it will be remembered that the prince says to his mother, in the beginning of the scene,

"Come, come, and sit ye down; you shall not budge;
You go not till I *set you up a glass*
Where you may see the inmost part of you."

As a farther improvement, this scene might be illustrated by getting up—"regardless of expense"—a moving panorama of the two royal brothers, the elder, a very commanding figure, standing in a Mercurial attitude, as if

"New-lighted on a heaven-kissing hill,"

and the younger, a very diminutive specimen of humanity (being, as Hamlet avers, not a twentieth part of the tithe of the "precedent lord"), dressed in a shabby suit of "shreds and patches," in a sneaking attitude, and in the act of stealing from a shelf a precious diadem; with a background representing the "mountain" which the queen is asked if she could "leave to feed," and the "moor" she is asked if she could "batten on;" the whole illuminated with blue fire or calcium lights: to conclude with a grand transformation scene!

I will close this chapter with a letter received by me about this time from that noble, generous, genial gentleman, ex-President Lamar, of Texas

Mirabeau B. Lamar to Sol. Smith.

"Galveston, Texas, 10th January, 1849.

"Dear Sol,—If, in consequence of my long silence, you have been induced, as I fear you have, to drop me from your 'list of friends,' I hope you will not deny me the privilege, under fair explanation, of reinstating myself in your good graces. Our acquaintance began at that halcyon period of life when the heart is most susceptible of strong and lasting impressions; and I can assure you, my old friend, that the attachment which then grew up between us, making us two as one man, has not been weakened in me by the flight of years, but, on the contrary, it has rather been improved by time, the great maturer, which converts the flowers of spring into the ripe and pleasant fruits of autumn. My life, like your own, has been somewhat checkered by adventure; but I account it one of the greatest blessings of Fortune that, amid all her buffetings, she has not deprived me of the cheerful companion of my happier days—the 'friend of my soul'—my old Sol Smith. A three-years' entombment of myself in Mexico and the frontier wilds has prevented my receiving your little book, which you kindly dedicated to me, and which now meets my sight for the first time. Its laughing tone and animated stories show that you have not lost the joyous spirit of your younger years; that you are still the man of 'infinite jest,' in spite of all your ups and downs; and surely, my friend, if the ancients were right in saying that a brave man struggling with adversity was a sight worthy of the gods, I know of no claimant more worthy of their favors than yourself—than you, who have contributed so much to lighten the burdens of others while bravely bearing your own. You have 'played many parts' in your time, have played them all well, and most certainly none better than that of the true 'philosopher and friend.' Then 'here's a double health to thee,' old Sol. Long life and a happy one to him who knows how to enjoy prosperity with gratitude, and whose happy alchemy of mind can turn even misfortune into pleasantry. 'All the world's a stage;' but the 'farce, tragedy, and comedy' of life will soon be over. Let us then, my friend, endeavor so to *act* the *parts* assigned us here as may secure to us a good *cast* and full *benefits* in that sublimer THEATRE which will be opened hereafter by the great MANAGER above, when the universe shall be the audience and eternity the curtain.

"Your friend, MIRABEAU B. LAMAR."

CHAPTER VII.

A PRELIMINARY season was made at St. Louis, in the spring of 1849, with the Monplaisir troupe. The dramatic season commenced with Dan Marble as the star. This was poor Dan's last engagement. Cholera prevailing, he was fearful of taking it. His final benefit and last performance on earth took place on the night of Saturday, the 12th of May. The last piece he appeared in was ALL THE WORLD'S A STAGE, in which he personated *Diggory*. It was my intention to go with him to Louisville. He secured berths for us both in the steamer Washington, and seemed highly gratified he was to have my company on the voyage. Something happened to prevent my going, and I shall never forget his despondent look when I told him so. "If you were along I should feel safe," said he; "but by myself, I know I shall be taken down—I know I shall." I tried to encourage him, and to convince him we were in the hands of Providence all the time, whether on land or water, but could not. He wrung my hand at parting, saying, "Sol, I feel as if we shall never meet again. Good-by; you have been a good friend to me. God bless you!" And so we parted, and my eyes never saw Dan any more! He kindly undertook to carry some money to Paducah for me. In due time I received a letter, dated on the Ohio River, informing me that, the boat passing in the night, he had paid the money over to a Mr. Jones, who had promised to dispose of it for me as requested; but three days before the receipt of that letter we had intelligence of poor Dan's death at Louisville! He had been "taken down," sure enough, as his presentiment told him he would be, and, having no friend to tend on him on the boat, the disease (cholera) had got such a hold on him that, on his arrival at Louisville, all medical skill failed in his case. The Rev. Charles Parsons (ex-tragedian) attended on him in his last moments, and administered the consolations of religion; but the last thoughts and words of the dying comedian were of his wife and children. I have been sorry ever since I did not go with poor Dan on that voyage to Louisville. If I could not (under Providence) have saved him, I should at least experience the satisfaction of having done for him all that a man could do for a dying friend.

Melinda Jones played a few nights to poor houses. The cholera had now become an epidemic. Next came George Holland, my worthy old friend and partner in Montgomery, Alabama. And though the houses he drew were none of the fullest, I tried to amuse him as well as I could by driving him around the suburbs; but somehow we met so many funerals, and passed so many grave-yards, that his spirits could not be raised to a very high pitch. Then came the great fire, which was to ruin St. Louis, but did not—quite the contrary, for it was built up better than ever. Mrs. Farren, Mr. and Mrs. J. M. Field, Mr. C. D. Pitt, and the Heron family followed on in the regular course, and Mdlle. Blangy closed the season—not a very profitable one.

The season of 1849–50 in New Orleans began November 10th. Mr. Benedict De Bar was engaged as stage manager, and continued as such during the remaining time of my management. Julia Dean, the ever-successful young actress, played three brilliant engagements. Mr. Buchanan played a week to the worst kind of business. Blangy was moderately successful. The Heron family pleased the sparse audiences who came to see them; and Hudson, a very clever actor of Irish characters, and a worthy gentleman, did very well for a fortnight. Hackett and Murdoch again visited us (the former had been hunting up country somewhere), and were successful as usual. Then came the great card of the season, Charlotte Cushman (supported by Mr. Couldock), who played to great houses for twenty-seven nights. Mr. and Mrs. C. D. Pitt followed, with poor success. Mr. Pitt's benefit receipts (gross) were only $81! The season closed March 29th, with a good balance on the right side of the cash-book. If I remember rightly, the American had a failing season, its manager, R. L. Place (brother of Lucius), dying a few days before its opening. Miss Eliza Petrie, so long a member of our company, had married this Mr. Place the year before, and now became a widow, but inherited nothing from her deceased husband but debts! Miss Petrie deserved a better lot.

My son Marcus Smith became a member of the St. Charles company this season. It was not my intention that any of my children should adopt the stage as a profession, but two of them have done so—Mark and Sol, Jr. After educating Mark as well as my cramped means would allow, I apprenticed him to the printing business; but, for good causes, he soon left the office where I had placed him, and came to me at New Orleans. At his earnest request, I arranged for him to go in a sailing ship to Liverpool, with the view of practically learning navigation. In the voyage outward and back he learned as much as he wanted to of that business. He next became a member of a "Phalanx" in Ohio, which breaking up in about a year after its formation, he went to work with Miles Greenwood, in Cincinnati, to learn the iron-finishing business. Mark next came to New Orleans, and engaged himself to work at an establishment in Algiers, opposite New Orleans. I left him there one spring, but, before I had returned in the fall, the bird had flown. There had been a "strike" in the foundery, and Mark had struck with the rest—while the iron was hot, I suppose. He went to New York City, and not succeeding in procuring employment as an iron-finisher (not trying very hard to do so, I suspect), when his money gave out he applied at the Chatham Theatre for an engagement. Telling the manager whose son he was, employment was immediately given him, and he was rated on the salary-list at $6 per week. With the experience he had had when a child as *Tom Thumb*, *Cora's baby*, *young Count Wintersen*, one of the young *Heywoods*, and sundry *Apparitions* in MACBETH, Mark very soon became proficient in going on in groups, and carrying spears and banners, and shortly aspired to speaking parts in village gatherings and mobs of citizens; he was, moreover, considered one of the best shouters and chorus singers in the company. He rose so fast in the profession that Hamblin engaged him for the Bowery the next season at $8 per week! I have witnessed his efforts at the latter-named house, and, without partiality, I must declare that Mark earned his money. I have seen him toil through a leading heavy part in a drama, and go on in the melodrama which followed in five or six parts! He, in connection with another actor, wrote or adapted a piece for the Misses Denin which was played many times successfully. At last the time came when his frequent applications to be enrolled in my company were to meet with a favorable response. He was engaged for the St.

Charles at $12 per week for general respectable utility.

The following extract from an editorial report of the opening of the St. Charles Theatre for the season of 1849-50 will show that young Mark appeared upon the stage of his native city with a fair chance of attaining popularity:

"FAMILY JARS was then performed, in which Sol Smith, as *Old Delph*, kept the house in a continued roar of laughter. In this character he is certainly unapproachable. Mr. Marcus Smith, as *Diggory*, made his first début before an audience in his native city. He evinces much talent, and is a worthy scion of a worthy stock. They were applauded to the echo, and 'take my hat' was twice the cry of enthusiastic admirers as they flung their beavers at the feet of Old Sol. The Messrs. Smith, Sr. and Jr., when FAMILY JARS were settled, were called for amid an uproar. The former made a handsome speech on the occasion:

"'Twenty-two years ago,' said he, 'before the birth of my son, I trod the boards in this city in the identical character which I have enacted this evening. The kindness with which you then received me has been generously continued throughout my professional career. In the course of nature, it is not probable that I shall remain long among you as an actor, but I leave my son to take my place, and if he be so fortunate as to receive the same testimonies of regard and kind consideration from the inhabitants of his native city which his father has received, he will have nothing to regret. Ladies and gentlemen, I thank you for him and for myself.'"

The other son, who adopted the theatrical profession the very day he became of age (Sol. Smith, Jr.), has, at the time I write (1868), been on the stage about ten years, and is a good actor. He is now performing in New York City, but most of his experience has been had in the Western cities, Boston, and the provincial theatres in England.

One might suppose that the young man Nunemacher, of New Albany, would have been cured of his desire to become an actor by the circumstances by which he became surrounded on the night when he first visited a theatre the year previously. Not so. Read the following letter from that gentleman, written about eight or nine months after his adventure in the calaboose and narrow escape from arraignment before the Criminal Court on the charge of murder:

Vint S. Nunemacher to Sol. Smith.

"New Albany, November 11, 1849.

"Mr. Solomon Smith, New Orleans, La.:

"SIR,—The termination of our short acquaintance during the course of last winter was not of a nature to warrant me in trespassing upon your good nature in the manner I now do, and were it not that, whatever may be your answer, I am assured it will be made in kindness, I would be silent.

"To be brief, I have determined to quit the law and go upon the stage—not because I could not hope for success at the former, but because I could not enjoy myself at it. I am not so presumptuous as to aspire to tragedy. I would rather make people laugh than cry. I know nothing about the stage, but am prepared for all the trials and troubles of an actor's life. I would go upon the stage with the hope and intention of making a fine actor, for I have ambition. I am a perfect novice, but I can be industrious. These are the facts in the case. Am I in the least available? A candid answer is requested.

"Now I can guess very well what you will perhaps say. You will advise me not to be rash, to reflect, and all that. I've done so. You will warn me of the loss of friends, and all that. I'm prepared for it. My true friends will not respect me any the less. I do not care a straw for others. I am going on the stage, now or soon, some way or other, and if you will take me under your wing, it will save me the trouble of applying to some one in whom I can not have one hundredth part of the confidence I have in you.

"So, sir, what say you? You were kind enough to say last winter that, should the opportunity happen, you would be happy to render me any service, and you can do it now. Pardon the gaucherie of reminding you of that, my pen runs on so. If you want me, say the word, and I will be at Orleans and at your service as soon as a steamer can take me there, as I am now settling up my business, and making preparations to go to some place.

"Yours ever, VINT S. NUNEMACHER."

Was not this man persistent in his determination to learn to be an actor? I was equally so in mine to decline receiving him as a learner. He might have become a good actor for aught I know—*has*, possibly, for I have little doubt he tried other managers, failing with me, but, if so, he most likely went on the stage under a feigned name, as many do. I never heard of him again.

The St. Louis season of 1850 was a very fair one, considering that the cholera again paid the city a visit. We had for stars Mr. and Miss Logan, Mr. Hudson, Mr. Murdoch, Mr. Manvers and troupe (opera), Mr. C. D. Pitt, Mr. De Bar, Mrs. Farren, Miss Julia Dean, Charles Burke, and the Bateman children.

Mr. Charles Burke was too good an actor to be very successful. Those who have never seen him (he died young) can see his counterpart in his half-brother, Joseph Jefferson.

During this season my son and I played the *Two Dromios*, in the COMEDY OF ERRORS, on the occasion of Mark's benefit, and we had to repeat the performance several nights. Our "make-up" was so exactly alike that, even in the

greenroom, very few could distinguish one from the other.

Mr. John Bates, after threatening for many years, actually commenced the erection of a new theatre during this summer, which he opened the ensuing winter. He advertised stock for sale in this new enterprise, but not a dollar of it was taken. As a reason for building a new house, he propagated the report (or somebody did *for* him) that our theatre was in danger of falling! There *was* a crack in the building, and had been for years, but I had had a committee of all the best builders in the city to make a survey, and they had published their unanimous opinion that there was not the least danger. Yet this report had its effect, and no doubt injured our business a little. As Mr. Bates took measurements freely at our house (working without a plan, as I have been told, and personally superintending the whole work), I watched carefully the progress of the masonry of the new building up to the very roof, and, on being asked my opinion of the strength of the walls, I told Mr. Bates that *the roof would fall in whenever there came a big fall of snow.* It so happened there was not much snow the winter it was opened, but the *following* winter—wait, and you'll see.

The New Orleans season of 1850–51 opened on the 12th of November with a comedy written by Mr. Leaman (one of our actors), entitled the MILLIONAIRE. Mrs. Farren played twelve nights, earning $777. Then came Julia Dean (successful, as usual), followed by Charlotte Cushman, who was this time a comparative failure. When I say "failure," I mean nothing more nor less than that the "half houses" failed to give the management any profit. Miss C. played to good, but not *crowded* audiences. J. M. Field had the Mobile Theatre this season, and my son Mark was engaged with him. I recollect bringing the latter over to New Orleans to play *Sir Harcourt Courtly* and *Sir Peter Teazle* with Miss Cushman. This was the inauguration of Mark's performances in the line of *old men*, in which he has since become so popular throughout the United States. One cause of the partial failure of Miss Cushman in New Orleans was the expected arrival of the Swedish Nightingale, Jenny Lind, who was to sing at the St. Charles.

Jenny Lind, with a splendid orchestra, conducted by Benedict, of London, and led by Joseph Burk, commenced her series of concerts on the 12th of February. The excitement she (or Barnum) created was unprecedented. Tickets were disposed of at auction at as high a rate as $40 and $50 each. The receipts at the first concert could not have been much less than $25,000, and on no night did they fall short of $10,000, I believe. There were thirteen concerts given, and then she and her troupe (taking two of our best musicians, Waldauer and Kost, with them) took their departure up the river in the steamer Magnolia, which, by arrangement made by Barnum, stopped long enough at Natchez, Vicksburg, and Memphis to give a concert in each of those cities.

The season at New Orleans was continued on successfully with C. Burke, the Bateman children, and the Celestine troupe of dancers (under Eytinge), and triumphantly brought to a close with thirty performances of the Ravel family.

We had to contend this season (in a friendly way) with a new and beautiful theatre—the "Varieties"—built by stock subscriptions, under the management of our old comedian and friend, Tom Placide. The "American" gave us no trouble at all; and at its close the lease was offered to us by the proprietors, and (not very wisely, I *now* think) we took it, and held it for the two remaining years of our management, renting it out to magicians, dogs, "goats, and monkeys," and for political meetings. In this connection I remember being applied to by a committee for a meeting of citizens to receive Kossuth, and of being thought quite unpatriotic because I offered them the house on "sharing terms"—that is to say, I proposed a dollar should be charged for the admission of each citizen, Kossuth to receive half, and our treasury the other half.

At the earnest request of Mr. Barnum, I preceded the Jenny Lind troupe to St. Louis for the purpose of arranging for their reception, having full powers to fit up the theatre with extra seats, to engage a church, or hall, or any building which I should judge to be most eligible for the concerts. I felt a great delicacy in taking Jenny Lind and the large audiences she was sure to draw into our theatre, after the industrious spreading of the reports that the building was liable to fall. Bates's new theatre had been opened, and was in full blast, Miss Cushman playing. James Bates (son of John, the proprietor) was manager of the new house, and kindly offered that splendid establishment to me for the concerts at $500 per night, with the additional stipulation that I should pay Miss Cushman $250 per night for giving up her claim to the nights—$750 in all!—a pretty good rent, *I* thought. I simply declined this offer, and should have been content to have said nothing about it publicly; but that did not suit young Mr. Bates, who undertook to excite indignation against me for inviting the people into Wyman's Hall (which, upon consultation with my friends, I had engaged and was fitting up), when the splendid new theatre could be had! I thereupon "came out" in the Republican with a statement of the exact *terms* demanded for the use of the new theatre, and added that if I could get that building free of rent I would not venture to ask the St. Louis public into it in such crowds as would attend the concerts, for *I did not consider the building safe!* This ended the controversy. The concerts took place in Wyman's Hall, and were grandly successful.

I fully expected this, our last season in St. Louis, would be a sad failure, in view of the opposition of the new theatre; but I was greatly surprised to find, upon our opening, all seemed to desert the new house and come to the old one. Celestine Frank and troupe (with Espinosa), the Bateman children, C. Burke, Collins, Mrs. Farren, Miss Davenport, Macallister, and De Bar, all played to paying business, while the new theatre lingered through a miserable season, playing to a "beggarly account of empty boxes."

On the 16th of June (I was absent—in New York—at the time), while playing the drama of JACK SHEPPARD—a favorite piece of De Bar's, and always performed during his engagements—there happened a most terrible accident, by which an excellent woman was sent into eternity. Mrs. Blanche Shea (*née* Kemble) was performing the character of *Mrs. Wood*, who is killed in one of the scenes. Mr. Harry Chapman was lying sick at his boarding-house, Mrs. Shea boarding at the same place. Mrs. S. had promised Mrs. Chapman, who was playing the youthful house-breaker, that she would go home as soon as possible and attend on Mr. Chapman until his wife should come home. When Mrs. Shea was called for the last scene of the character she was playing, she said to those in the greenroom, "*I am now going to be killed*, and then I shall go right home to sit up with Harry Chapman." She proceeded to the place of her entrance, between the second and third wings, and while standing there a moment waiting for her cue to go on the stage, a counter-weight fell from above on her head and killed her instantly.

Mrs. Lamar, a lovely and amiable young woman, new upon the stage, but giving great promise of excellence in her profession, died of cholera the same day, and the two women were buried in Christ Church Cemetery. I have recently caused the remains of Mrs. Lamar and Mrs. Shea, together with those of poor Dick Russell, who died in 1849, to be taken up and interred in the beautiful Bellefontaine Cemetery. On Mrs. Shea's head-stone are inscribed these words:

BLANCHE SHEA

(Born KEMBLE),

NIECE OF J. P. KEMBLE AND SARAH SIDDONS,

Instantly killed by the accidental falling of a weight in the St. Louis Theatre, during the performance of the pernicious play of "JACK SHEPPARD," June 16, 1851.

AGED ABOUT 30 YEARS.

This stone erected to her memory by

SOL. SMITH,

1867.

After a fair season (under the circumstances), the old St. Louis Theatre closed its doors with a benefit to the ORPHAN'S HOME, the entire receipts going into the treasury of that institution without any deduction for expenses of any kind. The closing play was the HONEY MOON, Mr. and Mrs. J. M. Field playing the *Duke* and *Duchess*, as they had done at its opening fourteen years previously. Being called before the curtain at the end of the performance, I addressed the audience as follows:

"MY FRIENDS,—For nearly a quarter of a century I have appeared before your parents and yourselves as an actor, and during all that time I have never, in a single instance, incurred the displeasure of this public, which fact I am not so vain as to attribute to my deservings, but to your leniency and kindness. As a manager I have endeavored to uphold the respectability of the drama by enlisting in your 'limited service' its most able interpreters. On these boards you have witnessed the acting of Ellen Tree, Forrest, Celeste, Macready, Booth, Julia Dean, the Ravel family, the Viennoise children, and hosts of others, the very mention of whose names would take up more time than I intend to occupy in these farewell remarks. The stock companies have been generally fully equal to those of Eastern theatres, I believe, and plays have been placed upon the stage with the proper scenery and appointments. It is my belief that the citizens of St. Louis will hereafter look back with pleasure on the happy hours they have spent in this house, and speak with pride of the companies which acted before them. Yet, my friends, mixed with the feelings of satisfaction which now fill me, as I look back on my managerial course, there comes up—and I can not help expressing it—a regret that such plays as JACK SHEPPARD and A GLANCE AT NEW YORK were ever permitted to stain these boards. The former I consider a most pernicious stage representation, and calculated to demoralize the rising generation; and I hope that my successors in management here will respect the wish which I now express, that it may never again be represented on the St. Louis stage. With unfeigned thanks for your many kindnesses through a long series of years, I take my leave with my heart full of desires for your future welfare and happiness."

Mr. J. M. Field, on the closing of the old establishment, immediately took measures for building a new theatre by subscription, in which he was successful. By invitation, the writer of these memoirs performed the ceremony of laying the corner-stone of the new edifice, which was called the "Varieties." The theatre is still in existence, but its first and best manager has gone to his rest long ago.

CHAPTER VIII.

THE New Orleans season of 1851-2 commenced November 1 (All Saints' Day) with a prelude from my pen—no, not from my *pen* exactly, but from my brain, the actors taking the words from my mouth at two rehearsals. I never knew an audience better pleased than they were with this little piece. It was founded on the idea of Colman's MANAGER IN DISTRESS, and all, or nearly all of our actors being strangers in New Orleans, the effect was all the greater. Mark Smith personated a Frenchman in the boxes, and made up for the part in such a way that nobody knew him. Mr. Sloan represented an obstreperous Irishman in the pit so well that he was summarily expelled from the house by the police, and it was with some difficulty he was saved from incarceration in the Calaboose! Mr. Perry (our leading actor) played his part so naturally (in the parquet) that he was hissed amid loud cries of "Turn him out!"

The comedy of the POOR GENTLEMAN followed, the entertainment concluding with the ROUGH DIAMOND, in which Mr. and Mrs. Sloan appeared.

George Barrett and daughter Henrietta played a short engagement; then came the ever-welcome Logan and daughter, followed by Celeste after an absence of fourteen years. Her engagement was a failure, though she played as well as ever she did. Julia Bennett (Mrs. Barrow), the Roussett sisters, Mr. Neaffie, and Miss Davenport performed for limited periods. Professor Anderson gave one performance at the St. Charles, and attracted a house of $999! The Heron family, accompanied by the very tall comedian, Sir William Don, played a pretty good engagement, and the season wound up with a series of forty-six performances by the Ravel family.

Our leading man, Perry, a talented actor, turned out to be undependable. "The drink, Hamlet, the drink!" that was what was the matter. "Seeing a friend off" to Mobile, he staid on the boat so long that he was carried off himself—being in the bills for the night. Arrived at Mobile, he telegraphed to know if he might play for somebody's benefit The answer was, "Yes, play for whom you like. You play no more here." And I never saw Perry again. Next spring strong interest was made by Eliza Logan in St. Louis to have him reinstated in the St. Charles. I steadily refused, not believing in his reported reformation, or rather in its permanency. The dear Eliza offered to enter into bonds for his good behavior; she had just been playing with him in Louisville, and would pledge her life on his future good conduct. Just at the moment we were discussing this matter—it was in front of Bates's Theatre in Pine Street—Bates came down the steps, and, catching the subject of our conversation, handed me, over Miss Logan's shoulder, a telegraphic dispatch he had received from his son in Louisville. I cast my eye over the dispatch, and then quietly said to the fair pleader for the absent actor, "So you will pledge your life for poor Perry's future sobriety?" "Yes, indeed I will; I am so very sure he will never get drunk any more." "Very well, Eliza; you take such an interest in the poor fellow, I am inclined—he is such an excellent actor, and so worthy a gentleman when he is himself—to take you as his security and give him another chance; but first read that." Placing the dispatch in her hand, I turned to leave, but had not gone far when I heard her exclaim, "Well, I never *will* speak in favor of any body again—never!" and away she flew up the steps. The dispatch ran thus: "*Had to postpone last night. Perry drunk as h-ll.*"

Perry was one of the best light comedians of modern times, and also a very passable tragedian. I administered to him, at his own request, a most solemn temperance pledge; how he kept it the above paragraph has told.

I spent part of this winter in St. Louis with my family. Mr. Bates was going on with his second season in the new theatre. Field's "Varieties" was going up, and it was to be ready for opening in the spring, when its manager was to return from Mobile with his company.

While at home, at the earnest request of Captain Sellers and other river men, the report of another meeting of snags and sawyers was communicated to the press as follows:

Proceedings of the second Convention of the Snags and Sawyers, held at the Grave-yard, in the Mississippi River, Dec. 31, 1851.

Delegates were present from Plum Point, Turkey Island, Dog-tooth Bend, Riddle's Point, Number Ten, Devil's Island, Hull's Left Leg, Elk Island, Number Twenty-one, Devil's Backbone, Ditto's Tea-table, Hanging-dog Island, Devil's Elbow, Tyawapeta, My Wife's Island, Shirt-tail Bend, Grand Chain, Goose Island, and the Grave-yard. Two sets of delegates from Hat Island claimed seats—one set from the *north* and the other from the *south* side. The attendance was very large, it being a season of leisure, in consequence of the river being closed by ice, and navigation suspended.

The Convention was temporarily organized by calling to the chair the President of the last Convention, Awful Hull-Ripper, Esq., of the Devil's Back-bone, and appointing Terrible Keel-Scraper, of Goose Island, temporary Secretary.

On motion, a committee of three was appointed on credentials, to whom was referred the conflicting claims of the two sets of delegates from Hat Island.

A committee on organization was chosen, and intrusted with the duty of nominating officers for this Convention.

A committee on resolutions, consisting of one member from each wrecking station, was elected by ballot, the names of whom are omitted, on account of the great difficulty in obtaining type with which to spell them, and the positive certainty that if put together they never could adhere in such a singular combination during the process of going through the press for a large edition.

On motion, the Convention adjourned for dinner and other refreshments.

EVENING SESSION.

Precisely at 3 o'clock the Convention was called to order. The Committee on Organization, by their chairman, the Hon. *Plank Splitter*, reported the following officers for the Convention:

President—Tree-top Deck-Sweeper, from Plum Point.

Vice-Presidents—Sudden Wheel-house-Hoister, from Devil's Island, and Sharp-rock Rudder-Loosener, from the Grand Chain.

Secretary—Rotten Log, Esq., from Shirt-tail Bend.

The report having been unanimously adopted, the President was conducted to the chair, and the Vice-Presidents and Secretaries assumed their proper positions in the Assembly:

PRESIDENT'S ADDRESS:

Fellow-Snags, Sawyers, Stumps, and other Obstructions,—Since our last Convention, held at this very spot exactly five years ago, our affairs have remained pretty much in *statu quo*. During the continuance in office of the excellent man who then occupied the presidential chair of this Union, our rights were safe; Congress might (and did) pass bills containing appropriations for "clearing us out," but the Veto was our safeguard and refuge! Fellow-obstructions, there is now at the head of this government a man who, having no regard for our constitutional rights, has recommended to Congress that appropriations be made for the improvement of Rivers and Harbors, which means nothing more nor less than dragging us from our stations, and despoiling us of our constitutional rights.

This recommendation has been seconded by the people and the press with alarming unanimity. To resist this unwarrantable interference with our rights and privileges is the object of this Convention. At this crisis, it is expected that every snag and sawyer will do his duty!

The address of the worthy President was received with considerable applause. The Committee on Credentials, by its chairman, Copper Bottom Piercer, Esq., reported that they had examined the certificates of the claimants from Hat Island, and, considering the great and essential services rendered since the last Convention by the snags and sawyers of that important wrecking station, had resolved to recommend that *both* sets of delegates be admitted to seats. The Hon. Chairman went on to state that Hat Island had become one of the most considerable "places" on any of the Western rivers for wrecking boats, as would appear by a list of wrecked boats furnished by the delegates from that locality, which he begged might be read by the secretary. The list was then read, as follows: The *Josephine*, the *United States Mail*, the *Gen. Jesup*, the *Hamilton*, the *Maid of Orleans*, the *Warren*, the *Monona*, the *Cumberland*, the *Sciota Valley*, the *Duke of Orleans*, the *Simon Kenton*, the *Billow*, the *Western*, the *America*, the *Pearl*, and the *Tennessee Valley*, besides two well-laden *barges*, names unknown.

The report was received, and the members from both sides of Hat Island took their seats amid much cheering.

The report of the Committee on Resolutions was now called for and read.

PREAMBLE AND RESOLUTIONS.

"*Whereas* there appears to be a growing disposition in the inhabitants of the Mississippi Valley, as appears by newspaper articles, to urge upon the Western members of Congress a renewal of the attempts heretofore made in that honorable body to uproot and tear out from our long-established homes the snags, stumps, and sawyers so long and happily established in the bed of the Mississippi River;

"*And whereas* there is, unhappily at this juncture, no Loco-foco President at the helm of state to arrest the attempts aforesaid by the interposition of the Roman remedy, the VETO; on the contrary, believing, as we do, that the present chief magistrate would be glad of the opportunity to sign a bill authorizing our overthrow and ruin;

"*Resolved*, By the snags, sawyers, and other 'obstructions,' in solemn Convention assembled, that we reaffirm our right to remain in our several localities, undisturbed by meddlers in or out of Congress, who affect to believe that we have no right to the homes of our fathers, and would tear us up, root and branch, without the least regard to our rights or feelings.

"*Resolved, further*, That we will resist with steadfast and determined resistance all attempts which may be made to tear us up by the roots; and, if our destruction should be determined on by the government, we will hold on to our moorings to the last gasp, and if conquered in the struggle we will die at our posts.

"*Resolved, furthermore*, That our warmest thanks are due, and are hereby tendered to Western members of Congress generally, for their evident determination to 'hold back' from joining the unholy crusade against us, knowing, as we do, that a *united* effort of Western members would immediately secure our destruction and utter extermination.

"*Resolved, furthermore yet*, That all legal means be adopted by our fraternity to prevent the election of Millard Fillmore as President of the United States (the office which he *accidentally* fills at present), inasmuch as we are firmly impressed with the belief that his election would be a death-blow to the whole boodle of us.

"*Resolved, still furthermore, and finally*, That in case of the passage of any act by the present or any future Congress to expel, drag, draw out, root up, split to pieces, break off, dig into, wrench, extricate, eradicate, or otherwise interfere with or materially injure the snags, sawyers, and other obstructions (so called) in the Mississippi River or any of its tributaries, then the presiding officer of this assembly shall have power, and he is hereby requested, to call another Convention at some central location to determine the 'mode and measure of redress.' In the mean time, we hereby pledge our fortunes and our sacred honors to stave into all the boats that come within our reach, and sink them if we can."

The preamble and resolutions having been adopted without a division, a venerable snag from Goose Island moved the following additional resolution, which was unanimously adopted:

"*Resolved*, That our next Convention be held on the 31st of December, 1857 (unless previously called together under the fifth resolution just adopted), at the head of Hat Island, *where the wrecks of sixteen vessels can be seen at one view.*

"*On motion, Resolved*, That the thanks of this Convention be tendered to the snags and sawyers located on both sides of Hat Island for their meritorious and highly successful efforts in opposition to the boating interests."

The Honorable *Plank Splitter*, from Hat Island (south), rose to return thanks for the last resolution, and said that it was the determination of himself and associates to continue on steadfastly in the good work. He concluded a very stirring address by offering the following resolution, which was adopted with enthusiasm:

"*Resolved*, That we view with scorn and contempt the conduct of Captain Swon and his pilots, Sellars and Duffy, who in the most dastardly manner *steer clear* of us with the 'Aleck Scott,' and dare not 'let her rip' among us, and that the snags and sawyers of the young wrecking station, Hat Island, be, and are hereby constituted a special committee to sink the said 'Scott' as soon as possible."

At this stage of the proceedings (it being nearly dark) the sergeant-at-arms announced that a very large *cake of ice* was approaching from the direction of St. Louis—the same which had the good fortune to pitch into and destroy the "Jewess"—whereupon a resolution was introduced inviting the "cake" to take a seat in the Convention.

This gave rise to considerable debate, some members contending that "ice" could not be properly considered of that class of obstructions entitled to the proposed honor, it being liable to melt away in warm weather; while others insisted that the destruction of the "Jewess" within the very harbor of St. Louis, and within sight of numerous citizens, was, or ought to be, a convincing proof of what ice *could* do when put in motion. A loud "hurrah" from the outsiders interrupted the debate, and it was subsequently found that, before the Convention could pass the complimentary resolution, the subject of it had passed the Convention, and proceeded down the river several miles, answering the "hurrah" of the outsiders by a declaration that, while its hand was in, it intended to have a crack at several boats between the Grave-yard and the Mouth.

The usual resolution of thanks to the presiding officers and secretaries was moved and carried, after which it was ordered that the proceedings be furnished to the press for publication. The Convention then adjourned, and the members immediately returned to their several constituencies, resuming their stations with a determination to do their full share in the work of destruction about to be commenced on the breaking up of the ice.

TREE-TOP DECK-SWEEPER, *President.*
ROTTEN LOG, *Seeretary.*

It is not my province to follow my friend Joe Field through his short career of management in St. Louis. He opened the "Varieties" with a very fine company, and with every prospect of success, while Bates's theatre was comparatively deserted; but success did not attend his efforts beyond the first season, I am sorry to say.

Before briefly noticing our last season at the St. Charles, New Orleans, I will record, with great pleasure, the fulfillment of my prophecy that the roof of Bates's theatre in St. Louis would fall in. It *did* fall in during the winter of 1853. There had been a heavy fall of snow during the evening; the Ravels were performing, and my wife and I had attended, but took care to get our seats very far back in the dress circle. The audience had not been out of the house quite half an hour when the roof came crashing down into the pit and on the stage! Why do I record this event "with pleasure?" you will naturally ask. I will tell you. I knew the roof *must* fall sooner or later, and my pleasure is derived from the fact that it did not fall while the audience were there, and that not a single human life was lost by the catastrophe. The Ravels removed to the "Varieties," and finished their engagement there. The walls of Bates's house were taken down for a considerable distance, and rebuilt in a proper manner.

CHAPTER IX.

I RETURNED to New Orleans to find my son the happy husband of an amiable and lovely gentlewoman, with whom he had formed an acquaintance since my departure for St. Louis.

As I am bestowing "all my tediousness" upon my gentle reader, I make no apology for handing him (or her) to read a letter written in the familiar style which characterized the correspondence carried on for years between "Old Logan" and myself.

Sol. Smith to C. A. Logan.

Theatre, St. Charles, April 3, 1852.

I am very certain, my valued, venerable, esteemed, and *handsome* friend, that you must have missed one of my letters, if not two. Yours of the 27th ult., full of nothing, but fully and poetically *directed*, came to hand this day, and I must also acknowledge the receipt, some weeks ago, of a *paper*, also poetically superscribed, and about two weeks since a tolerably decent letter (I mean, decently filled) from Philadelphia. I am not so certain I answered *that*, but, considering I had written two letters, principally on one subject—my personal beauty, which had been most wantonly attacked, through pure envy, I have no doubt, sorry am I to say it! in which I attempted—feebly, may be, but *attempted*—to set forth those much-slighted personal advantages which the gods have, for some unknown reason, bestowed upon the writer hereof, and to repel the assaults made upon them by one who, however estimable he may be in his feelings and moral qualities, can not but perceive that Nature has, not "smiling," but frowning, withheld the "winning grace" so bountifully bestowed elsewhere. If those letters—particularly that letter written in my little back parlor in Chouteau Avenue, while I was contemplating a thermometer the mercury whereof had sunk down to double G below the stave, and at the same time *burning* under the effects of the unjust aspersion thrown upon my personal appearance by one from whom I expected better things—have reached their destination, I shall expect—mind, I say I shall *expect*—I purposely emphasize the word "expect," expecting you will particularly notice it—an ample—I will not say *apology*, but an ample and amplified EXPLANATION!

* * * * * * *

We are doing immensely with the Ravels. They have played ten nights, including to-night, and averaged over $820!—in Lent, too. Next week (Holy Week) we expect a falling off, of course, but after that, commencing with Easter Monday, we expect great business again. They will stay during the whole of the month—perhaps longer. This engagement is a wonderful "pull up" to our season.

You mentioned Celia had been offered an engagement in Philadelphia. If you engage her at all, and don't engage her to me, I'll—never mind, I won't threaten. Where will you be in June?

I take great pride and pleasure in Eliza's success, you *know*, and I therefore thank you for the bills and papers, which I take care to have *seen*. Thad. is not here with me now, little Sergeant Prentiss being my companion this time. I suppose you heard of Mark's marriage. It took place in January, and I am pleased to say it is the best "engagement" he ever made. It seems but yesterday that he was born—here in this very city, and here he is presenting me a beautiful and amiable daughter.

Joe Field closed his season in Mobile last

night. He comes over to-morrow, and goes immediately to St. Louis to prepare for the opening of his new theatre. I want a good leading actor for next year—no reformed drunkard, but one who has *never been a drunkard.* How would Lester do? Does he play any leading parts in tragedy? "Keep an eye out" for us, will you? You have a chance to see them all. We shall probably make a long season next year. There is to be a Southwestern Agricultural and Mechanical Fair in May.

The theatre in Gravier Street has not been overly prosperous this season. Max Maretzek disappointed the management in January. He was to pay $400 per night for the house, four nights per week. That great impressario is here now with Stefanone, Beneventano, and some inferior secondaries, and has given one performance at the Orleans, and *advertised* another (oh! don't he advertise and bill!), but Stefanone had "von grand malade," and "Relache" was posted on the doors last night. Mark and I had complimentary tickets for the parquette, and, considering the circumstances, we did not demand our *money back*, but kept the tickets for another night. It is said that after three representations among the French, they come up to the "Varieties" and give three more. *We* don't care, the Ravels rendering us (just now) invincible and invulnerable.

Ever your friend, whether you can appreciate beauty or not, SOL. SMITH.

The *address* of this letter was as follows (the superscription of L.'s last letter having been in *rhyme*, and the opinion expressed that I could not follow his example in consequence of the difficulty—*impossibility* he called it—of finding a word to rhyme with his name):

"Beat the drum and sound the slogan!
This letter is for C. A. LOGAN.
The penny-post this man will meet
About the theatre in Chestnut Street—
I mean in Philadelphia City.
If he's not there, why, 'tis a pity;
But if 'tis found that he is gone,
The manager must send it on."

The season of 1852-3 in the St. Charles, the last in which I appeared in the character of manager, opened on the 6th of November with Goldsmith's comedy of SHE STOOPS TO CONQUER, and a farce taken bodily out of a musical comedy entitled THE ENGLISHMAN IN INDIA, and called SKETCHES IN INDIA.

The first star was Booth, who performed six nights on his return from California. These were his last professional appearances on earth! The characters he personated were: 1. *Richard;* 2. *Sir Giles Overreach;* 3. *Pescara;* 4. *Shylock;* 5. *Bertram;* 6. (Benefit and last appearance), *Sir Edward Mortimer.*

At the close of this brief engagement, anxious to join his wife and children at Baltimore, he embarked on board a Mississippi river-boat, was taken sick, and died before arriving at Louisville. Thus passed away a man who had it in his power, if he had possessed common prudence, to share equally with the elder Kean the plaudits of a London audience, *and succeed him.* Booth was nobody's enemy but his own.

In 1820, April 13th, Booth played *King Lear* three times at Covent Garden Theatre, London. He afterward was engaged at Drury Lane, where he was making his way finely, when he took a notion into his head to go over to the other house, and play *Iago* to Kean's *Othello*, which, I think, was the greatest error of his life. There was almost a row in consequence. In August of that year Drury Lane was opened for an extra season "for the express purpose of giving Kean an opportunity of playing his principal characters previous to his departure for America." Booth was announced as being "*engaged for a few nights.*" They played together in the following pieces: RICHARD III.—*Richard*, Mr. Kean; *Richmond*, Mr. Booth. OTHELLO—*Othello*, Kean; *Iago*, Booth. KING LEAR—*Lear*, Kean; *Edgar*, Booth. That same year, in the fall, he played in pieces as follows: OTHELLO—*Othello*, Cooper (not *our* Cooper); *Iago*, Booth. ADELGITHA—*Michael Ducas*, Booth. PIZARRO—*Pizarro*, Booth; *Rolla*, Wallack. JULIUS CÆSAR—*Brutus*, Wallack; *Cassius*, Booth. JANE SHORE—*Hastings*, Cooper; *Duke of Gloster*, Wallack; *Dumont*, Booth. Macready and Wallack seemed to monopolize most of the good parts that season. Booth came over to America. He returned to London in 1826, and played *Brutus*, *Othello*, and *Richard*—three nights in all. His professional career was afterward confined to the United States, where he married and raised a family. His home was on a farm near Baltimore.

I was acquainted with Junius Brutus Booth for about a quarter of a century. When I first knew him (in 1827) he was a truly great actor, and continued so to be until he fell into bad company in New Orleans, and took to hard drink. Then he became undependable, and, "putting an antic disposition on," made many believe that he was crazy. *I* never believed him to be a crazy man except when he was excited by liquor, and that was pretty often—nearly all the time, in fact. I have seen him act *Richard* many times as no other man could or can act it. I have seen not only the pit "rise at him," as it did at Kean in Drury Lane on the occasion of that great actor's first appearance in London, but have seen the whole house—pit, boxes, and gallery—on their feet to do honor to Booth while playing *King Richard.* His *Sir Giles Overreach* (in the last scene) was terrific! *Pescara* he acted perfectly. *King Lear*, barring that he acted from Tate's adaptation of the play instead of the text of Shakspeare, was fully up to his *Richard.* His *Hamlet* was not great, ever. In *Othello* Mr. Booth was very good, but not great; and in *Iago*, according to my poor judgment, very bad indeed, and yet he was always yearning to play the latter. In *Sylla* and *Brutus* he appeared in my eyes to magnify himself so as to look almost a giant in size. He was great in *Sir Edward Mortimer* (the last part he ever played), and cast all others who attempted to play it in this country into the shade. I have seen Mr. Booth play *Jerry Sneak* and *John Lump*, and I could scarcely believe it *was* Booth who was playing them. After Tom Flynn broke his nose he was a different man and an indifferent actor. His face, which had been beautiful and intellectual, became almost disgusting to see; his voice, which had been of great power and sweetness, became harsh and nasal—he was completely changed. The present generation has not seen the Booth that I knew. Yet, with all the disadvantages he labored under during the latter years of his life, *he continued* (as the man said at Kean's funeral) *to draw to the last.*

The other stars of this season were Mr. and Mrs. Barney Williams, Mrs. Mowatt, Madame Thillon, Mr. Hudson, and Julia Dean. The Williamses were very successful, the receipts on their nights averaging well up toward $600 per night. Thillon and Hudson drew very well; Julia Dean excellently, and Mrs. Mowatt tolerably. The Ravel family came and performed thirty-six nights, winding up the season on the 30th of April in a blaze of triumph.

There was a buzzing fellow hanging about the theatres this season named Dr. Northall, who aspired to be a theatrical critic, and who published his lucubrations—puffs for the "Varieties," and abuse for the St. Charles—in the *Delta* newspaper. I don't know if 'twere so, but it did appear to me he must have been a hired puffer of the "Varieties," for he never by any chance spoke of that house except in unqualified praise, while, according to his account, nothing was ever decently done at the St. Charles. When the benefits came on, his name was put up at the "Varieties" for a "complimentary" one, on which occasion he was advertised to speak a poem written by himself. When the time came for him to appear before the very sparse audience which honored him with their presence, he broke down utterly at the second line, and was hissed from the stage. He liked New Orleans so well that he remained there dissipating till he died.

Among the members of the stock company of the St. Charles this season was Mr. John S. Potter, better known as

Manager Potter.

No one can tell with what reverence I write the name of this distinguished individual, a few of whose doings I propose to relate. MANAGER POTTER! The Simpsons, the Hamblins, the Pelbys, the George Woods, even the Dion Boucicaults of the profession sink into utter insignificance when mentioned on the same page with J. S. Potter. There is not a town on any of the Western waters, from Fever River in Illinois, to the Bay of Mobile in Alabama, but has experienced him; not a steam-boat captain, nor a tavern-keeper in any town accessible to theatrical enterprise, but retains notes of remembrance of the hero of my sketch. There is not a star or demi-star inducible to visit any but metropolitan towns and cities but holds Manager Potter in "memory locked."

There was, once upon a time, in a Southern city, an enterprising and honest carpenter, who took it into his head to become a manager. He built a theatre, and opened it with a very expensive company, but he soon *plain*ly *saw* that all his earnings with the *saw* and *plane* were fast frittering away in salaries and other enormous expenses which he had never dreamed of while he remained in a happy state of carpentery. He came to me for advice. I told him I knew but of one way by which he could carry on the theatrical business with any chance of profit. It was this: *abolish the salary-list.* He thanked me, and went his way. Three weeks afterward the new manager came back to me and said he had tried the plan I had suggested.

"Well, how does it work?" I inquired.

"It works well enough," he answered, innocently, "but the actor folk—unreasonable fellows!—*don't much like it;* indeed," he continued, "they talk as though they won't stand it."

He asked me if I had no *other* plan to suggest. I dismissed him with the expression of my belief that unless he could devise some means by which he could *do away with the salary-list*, there was no way by which a person inexperienced in the business of theatrical management could possibly be assured of success. Finding the actors unanimous in their stubbornness, and determined in their resolution to have their pay or quit, the new manager shortly afterward gave up the business in despair, and took to the management of an exceedingly large PIG, with one head, two tails, and six legs! There being no salary-list to bother him, he got along very well with this speculation. This pig exhibition being opened on St. Charles Street, nearly opposite our theatre, Mr. Macready and I went in one day to see the monstrosity. On leaving the booth we were politely handed back the money we paid for admission, the manager remarking, "You are on the free list, gentlemen; *we do not charge the profession.*"

But to return to Manager Potter, who has carried out the plan I suggested to this tyro, with improvements. Many instances of Mr. Potter's unrivaled tact in overcoming and surmounting pecuniary difficulties have come under my notice, a few of which I proceed to relate.

He purchased of Mrs. A. Drake, when she abandoned management in Louisville, her extensive wardrobe, valued at $3000, the purchase-money to be paid at Jackson, Miss. As an inducement for her to give him the desired credit until the arrival of his company at the capital of Mississippi, he offered Mrs. D. a splendid engagement in that city, which she accepted, and off went the whole concern—actors, musicians, *boxes*, and the star to Vicksburg. Arrived at this point, a settlement at the captain's office became necessary for passage and freight to the amount of some hundreds of dollars. Potter actually persuaded Mrs. Drake to become responsible for the whole bill, and she eventually was obliged to pay it, as she informed me, besides losing the whole of her magnificent wardrobe, which she never set eyes on more!

Once upon a time a lawyer named Yeager loaned Manager Potter $50, under a solemn promise that the amount should be returned out of the first night's receipts of the season then just commencing in Jackson. The time passed on until nearly the end of the legislative session and theatrical season, and no sign of the $50 appeared to be forthcoming, though the debtor had been "often requested" to refund. In the mean time, reports of Potter's facility in "putting off" duns reached Lawyer Y.'s ears, and, "in a merry mood," he laid a wager with some friends that he would visit the manager in his box-office, and would not depart without his money. To secure himself against a possibility of failure, the attorney armed himself with a cowhide and a pair of pistols, and entered the sanctum. The friends of Y. had stationed themselves near the premises, and within hearing. The inexorable creditor entered, and the door closed upon the debtor and creditor. At first loud words were heard, but gradually the voices of the dun and the dunned sunk into a low tone of friendly converse. In about twenty minutes longer Y. sallied forth and encountered his friends, who were in waiting, and who showered questions upon him without ceasing until they all arrived at Y.'s lodgings.

"Here, Dick!" exclaimed the discomfited lawyer to the waiter, "bring a basket of Champagne; I've lost."

"Oh, then," asked the friends, "you didn't get your fifty dollars?"

"Get my fifty dollars?" answered the loser of the wager—"get my fifty? I should like to see the man that *could* get fifty out of *him!* Curse the fellow. I went in there determined to have my money or take it out of his hide; and before I left—I am almost ashamed to own it—hang me if he didn't borrow *another* fifty of me!"

In 1844 Manager Potter came to St. Louis with a company on his way to Chicago. The captain of the boat which brought him from Memphis swore the baggage should not be taken away until the passages and freight-bills were paid. This was in the forenoon, and before night Potter had the whole company and property shipped on board a Galena boat, the captain who brought him to St. Louis receiving his notes for his debt, and *indorsing notes for him* to pay not only the passages of his company to Galena, but across the country to Chicago!

It ought to be mentioned that P. has a weakness in a nerve of one of his eyes, from which a *tear* is always involuntarily starting. It is supposed that in this weakness consists Manager Potter's strength, no person having yet been found who could resist it.

How Manager Potter moves from place to place nobody knows; but he *does* move, and he travels incredibly long journeys in incredibly short periods of time. The great Napoleon, in his day, moved his armies from one place to another with some speed—but *he* had means; Potter moves *his* army from one extremity of this vast Union to the other without any means whatever!

Manager Potter deserves success, if any manager ever deserved it. His industry is sleepless, his enterprise untiring. He *engages* to give *any* price to stars and stock actors, pays them *if he can*, and if he can not he does not make himself unhappy about it. I have never heard the complaint made by any of his numerous professional creditors that he ever was known to *have* any cash on hand. For a manager, in hard times, to make use of any money for his own purposes is a sin that no actor *can* forgive. Potter has always kept his skirts clear of any *such* offense, and it is well for him that he has. Hence comes it that, although he owes every body, every body likes him: he would pay if he *could*, poor fellow! but if he *can't*, what is a poor fellow to do?

Manager Potter has built and "fitted up" more theatres than any other manager, dead or alive, and traveled a greater number of miles with large companies than any other manager ever *thought* of traveling. He has played more parts in one play than any other three men that can be mentioned, doubling, trebling, and quadrupling characters to an enormous extent (with the aid of a black cloak and a yellow domino), in tragedies, comedies, and farces innumerable. He assured me once that he took a company of eighteen persons from Detroit in Michigan, to Richmond in Virginia, with but seventy-five cents in his pocket to start with! He has established theatres throughout California and Oregon, Nevada, Utah, and in the Cherokee nation. To China he intends to go with a company as soon as that empire is opened to outside barbarians. At present I hear he is making up a company and arranging with Mr. Vanderbilt for their passages around Cape Horn and up to Walrussa! Success to Manager Potter!

CHAPTER X. AND LAST.

Before concluding this sketchy history of my management in the South and West, I feel it to be my bounden duty to say a few words on

Sunday-night Performances.

When I went to New Orleans as an actor (1827), Sunday-night performances certainly did—at first—appear strange to me, and perhaps slightly out of order; but, upon a careful view of the matter in all its bearings, my mind became convinced that keeping the theatres open on *every* night—with this especial observance, that they are under the management of conscientious, well-meaning directors—must be beneficial to any community. Observation and experience, during a period of nearly thirty years, so far from changing my opinion on this subject, have confirmed it; and I now look back upon no part of my managerial course with more heartfelt approval than the continuation of the policy adopted and practiced by Mr. Caldwell, of affording the American citizens of New Orleans an opportunity of enjoying the beneficial influences of the Drama on Sundays as well as on other nights of the week, thus placing the American theatres on an even footing with the French Theatre in the same city.

In 1831 attempts were made by a portion of the people to "put down" Sunday performances in the American Theatre. One editor was peculiarly urgent in the matter, and went so far as to advise the "authorities" to interfere and put a stop to the "unholy practice" of allowing the citizens to be amused on the night of the Christian Sabbath. Mr. Caldwell addressed the following communication to the editor referred to, which had the effect to silence that battery, and no more was heard in opposition to the Sunday-night performances for several years:

"Mr. Editor,—You have disseminated so many opinions of your own, and published so many of other people's upon the subject of opening the Theatre on Sunday, a practice common on the whole Continent of Europe, in Catholic as well as Protestant countries, whether in English, French, German, Russe, Prusse, Dutch, or Italian—moreover, my name has been so cavalierly used by you and your incognito correspondents, that I claim the privilege of a short space in your columns to say a few words for myself, which words shall smack more of piety than any of the articles which have appeared (which I view as so many anathemas) can boast of.

"I thank heaven I was born in a free country.

"I thank heaven that I am a citizen of the United States.

"I thank heaven that the Constitution of the United States grants to me the liberty of thinking, writing, printing, and acting for myself, as every man ought, though his thinking, writing, printing, and acting should differ from all other men's thinking, writing, printing, and acting.

"I thank heaven that the majority can rule the minority, *as it ought*.

"I thank heaven that the majority is not against me, *as it might*.

"I thank heaven that the minority is not the majority, for fear it would proscribe and ruin me, *as it would*.

"I am happy in the knowledge that the majority of the people of New Orleans think that, instead of an evil, it is a moral good to open the Theatre on Sunday evenings.

"To conclude: I thank heaven that those who think differently from the majority have the right to act as independently as the subscriber to this article, by expressing their opinions. May they live long to express them, and long live the republic to protect them.

"James H. Caldwell."

During my management of theatres in New Orleans, Sunday-night performances were continued, and, as I think, much to the benefit, morally and physically, of the inhabitants of that great city and the strangers congregated therein, until all opposition ceased, except from a few religionists by *trade*, and some keepers of beer-houses, coffee-houses, billiard-houses, nine-pin alleys, and *other* establishments not fit to be mentioned here.

It is not to be denied that in latter years the American theatres were not "fashionably" attended on Sundays; but what of that? The hardy mechanic, with his wife and children, the boatman, the visiting stranger, the apprentice, the clerk—these and others flocked to the theatre to enjoy an innocent recreation, instead of (as in other cities) passing the evening at the resorts mentioned and indicated in the last paragraph.

An honest Irish woman came to the St. Charles one Saturday evening to secure seats for her husband and herself, with "the childer," for the following night. Seeing me writing at a desk in the box-office, she asked the clerk to call me for a moment. She wished to speak to me.

"Oh, sir, Mr. Sol," said she, when I came to the counter, "I want to thank you, sir, for the good you have done to my husband, my dear Pathrick. He has often wished to thank you himself."

"Madam," I replied, "I do not remember of having performed any particular service for your husband."

"Ah! sir," said she, "you have, and many services. In Pittsburg, where we lived till we came here, Pathrick was always at the drinking-houses on Sunday nights, where he spent half the wages he earned during the week, leaving the childer and meself at home worrying and fretting on account of him; and then he was not fit to work on Monday, which he lost entirely, besides getting worser and worser in the drinking way, you understand. Now, sir, blessings upon you and the other managers, we spend our Sunday nights seeing good plays, and Pathrick is always with us except when away at his work, and he is a changed man entirely. And it is so with many others I know. God bless you, Mr. Sol, and prosper your great institootion." With a hearty shake of the hand, the good woman left me, and next night, happening to be standing near the box door as the audience was assembling, I found myself suddenly surrounded by Mr. and Mrs. Pathrick and several little Pathricks, who all became intimately acquainted with me through the introduction of the grateful woman, who attributed the reformation of her husband to the good influences of the Drama. As for Pathrick, he became a prosperous man, and engaged in large contracts with the city government. Whenever he met me he never failed to acknowledge his obligation to the "institootion," insisting that the Church and Theatre are both good in their way. "The Church in the morning—the Drayma at night, is my maxam, Mister Sol, and I'll stick to it!" said honest Pat the last time I met him.

In a pecuniary point of view, I must say that, were it not for the Sunday-night performances, I never could have pushed through the great difficulties which beset my path during the seven unlucky years of my management, from 1838 to 1845.

In justice to myself, I will add that, so far as my influence would go, pieces were always selected for Sunday nights which were unquestionably moral in their tendencies. This assertion may cause a smile upon the faces of some clergymen who consider the pulpit the *only* teacher of morality, while other clergymen will agree with me that the stage *may* be so conducted as to encourage Virtue and condemn Vice.

Lending Money in small Sums.

"I have never yet seen the man that I would not render some assistance to, if in my power. It seems to me no more than a duty; there is no *merit* in it."

The above thirty-four words have cost me hundreds, if not thousands of dollars! They occur in a little book entitled "Theatrical Apprenticeship," page 81, published in 1845. I hereby revoke them, and wish the reading world to understand that there is not one word of truth in the whole sentence—not one; on the contrary, I won't render assistance to any body! It is *not* "in my power." I am a hard-hearted—outrageously hard-hearted wretch, and I wish it to be so particularly understood from this out.

The reader could scarcely believe what I could with perfect truth relate on this subject.

"I haye read your book, Mr. Smith," says the modest applicant; "and as *you* have been in difficulties in your early days, and as you have published the fact that *you never have seen the man you wouldn't render assistance to*, I have come to solicit a small loan;" and he then goes on to explain his situation, which is very bad, to be sure, generally requiring five, ten, twenty-five, or thirty-five dollars to set him on his legs! When I am in New Orleans, the applicant is from St. Louis, Cincinnati, Belleville, Alton, or *somewhere* up the river, and wants to get home very badly. If I am in New York, the applicant is generally an actor, and the theatre where he is engaged is to open almost immediately, and he will be sure to pay me out of his first week's salary; his board-bill is due, and he will be turned out of his lodgings if he don't pay up. In St.

Louis (my home), he is traveling, and his money has given out; he has been sick; his father knew me in Georgia, or Alabama, or Kentucky—had seen me act many a time (his father had); he therefore is emboldened to come to me—has read my book, of course! In London or Paris, it is a fellow-countryman who claims my assistance; only wants money enough to pay his passage home—a *second-cabin* passage. Once in a while a sentimental female sends a letter through the post-office; knows my generous nature; has read my book (confound that book!), and wants only twenty-three dollars, which she *knows* I will willingly and cheerfully bestow upon one who has seen better days, and so forth, and so on.

If these people would ever *pay*, or ever *think* of paying—but they never do. Stop! Let me not be quite so sweeping. A man to whom I once loaned five dollars on board of a steamboat *did* pay it back five years afterward. His name is hereby immortalized—it is Kidd. Henry Ward Beecher says the only one who ever paid back any thing of the many thousands he had loaned in small sums was a negro! The man who paid *me* was an actor!

Now remember, reader, what I said at the beginning of this article—I am a changed man. I make no more loans to distressed wanderers wanting to go home. I pay no more boarding-bills of actors whose engagements haven't begun. No, *sir!* I'm flint—adamant! ☞ and, moreover, I've bought out the copyright of the book containing the above-quoted paragraph, so that no more copies of it can possibly be published.

I promised, many pages back, to give the result of my second purchase (of $4\frac{53}{100}$ acres) in the city commons of St. Louis. According to the promise of my good genius in that cold winter (1845), times *did* change somewhat for the better, and in May of that year I made the last payment on that land, receiving from the city a full title. In 1866 I sold nine of the thirty lots into which the tract had been subdivided for $27,500, and this spring (1868) I have sold the remaining twenty-one lots for $50,000, making *seventy-seven thousand five hundred dollars* for what cost me originally *five hundred and eighty-seven dollars and fifty cents!*

Another land operation I must mention. In 1837 I purchased from Col. John O'Fallon 75 feet of ground on the east side of Third Street, adjoining the theatre, at $110 per front foot. The cash payment and some of the "time" payments had been made, but in the dark days of 1840, '41, and '42, finding it impossible to meet further payments, I requested the good colonel to sell a portion of the land under the deed of trust he held, and pay himself the balance I owed him. He was reluctant to do so, but finally consented at my urgent request, and twenty-two feet of the ground were sold to the city, at $100 per foot, for an engine-house. Mr. Samuel Jacks purchased twenty feet more at $91 per foot, leaving me thirty-three feet out of my seventy-five, on which I afterward built two small houses, in one of which my family resided for several years, and until we removed into our present residence on Chouteau Avenue in 1848. When the cloud of debt cleared away from the atmosphere in which I walked, I purchased from Mr. Jacks the twenty feet of ground he had bought at the trust sale, paying him $400 per front foot for the same, thus becoming possessed of fifty-three feet of the seventy-five feet of ground I had originally purchased from Col. O'Fallon. This land I afterward sold to Messrs. Mitchell, Rammellsberg & Co., for $50,000.

While writing of land, I will say that I made about $10,000 on some land I purchased in Columbus (Ga.) in 1833; and on some lots I purchased in Paducah (Ky.) in 1836, I eventually realized about $8000 profit, after keeping them nearly thirty years. My *Illinois* lands I have told you about.

I am about through. As a manager of theatres, I don't consider that I have been very successful, pecuniarily speaking. It is true that at times I made many thousands of dollars in a single year; but then at other times—these *other* times extending through several successive years (as in 1838 to 1845), all I had made, and more, was swallowed up in losses. If I had quit the business in 1838, when the old St. Emanuel was destroyed by fire, I could have paid all my debts —they were inconsiderable then—and have had something handsome left, say twenty thousand dollars in money and lands, and saved fifteen years of the hard toil I have since gone through. If the burning of the theatre had occurred before I sold out my printing-office, I should probably have resigned the reins of management and taken up the editorial pen; but the conflagration happened a few days *after* my sale of the newspaper, and I was doomed to slavery for many years, for my business then began to sink me into debt, which I did not get entirely out of until 1848, and to be in debt is to be in slavery, as every body knows who has tried it. So I struggled on —on—on, year after year, *all the time dreading that I should die*—IN DEBT, and leave my family unprovided for (and oh! what a thought is *that!*), until at last, under the blessings of a kind Providence, I achieved my liberty!

READER. Well, Sol, I have accompanied you through your managerial pilgrimage, which, I must confess (some parts of it, at least), was rather tedious, though relieved somewhat by your anecdotes as we went along. I now ask you, as we are about to part company, *How did you come out in the long run?*

My reader, I will tell you. I started in the business of management in 1823, about even with the world. I came out of it in 1853, free from debt, my family having been maintained during the time and my children educated, possessing a good house to live in (cost $7000), some money (not much, and what there was I have since lost by lending it without security), and some lands, which have increased in value greatly, and been sold for such prices (as heretofore stated) that I am now considered a man in comfortable circumstances. So I say, "ALL'S WELL THAT ENDS WELL."

Now, as you have been so kind as to keep company with me so long, let me tell you, before we part, that I am blessed with a good but plain home, ditto wife, and am probably about as happy as most of my neighbors. I am the father of seven living sons (Lemuel Edwin, for many years a printer; Marcus, actor; Sol. Jr., actor; Franklin, insurance clerk; Thaddeus Sanford, civil engineer; Sergeant Prentiss, bank clerk; and Asa Wilgus, bank teller), four of whom are married to excellent wives; and I have seven living grandchildren, four boys and three girls. My reader, I give you these particulars of my domestic relations on the supposition that you have become somewhat interested in me and mine by this time, and will be glad to know of our welfare.

In my retirement, happy in the reflection that I never willfully wronged my fellow-actors—meaning all human beings; for hath not our Shakspeare said that all men and women are players?—and that, so far as was in my power, I always aimed to elevate the stage in the estimation of the public, by presenting the legitimate drama, interpreted by the best living masters, though *compelled* by the vitiated taste of that public, *engendered elsewhere*, to descend a little sometimes from the high standard I had set up for myself, I do not look back upon my managerial career with any feelings of regret, but with a reasonable amount of satisfaction; and when reclining on a garden bench under my vines and cherry-trees, with book in hand, I often think over, if I do not speak aloud, the following exquisitely beautiful lines of the great bard:

"SWEET ARE THE USES OF ADVERSITY;
Which, like the toad, ugly and venomous,
Wears yet a precious jewel in his head;
And this our life, exempt from public haunt,
Finds tongues in trees, books in the running brooks,
Sermons in stones, and GOOD IN EVERY THING."

Thanking you, madam (or sir), for accompanying me through the varied scenes of my checkered professional life, and hoping that you have been amused (for to amuse has been my only aim in writing these memoirs), I now ring down the curtain on my

THEATRICAL MANAGEMENT.

EPILOGUE.

1853—1868.

SINCE the close of my management in 1853, I have acted on the stage twelve times: (1.) One night at the St. Charles, New Orleans, for which I received two hundred dollars. (2, 3, 4, 5, 6, and 7.) An engagement at Mobile, for which I received about five hundred dollars (sharing terms). (8.) One night for my son Mark's benefit at the Varieties in New Orleans, my first and only appearance there, and to one of the most crowded audiences I ever appeared before. (9.) One night for the farewell benefit of my valued and lamented friend, J. M. Field, in the Varieties, St. Louis. (10.) One night for my no less valued friend, Mrs. J. M. Field (then a widow), a year afterward, in the same theatre. (11.) One night for the benefit of my son Sol. Smith, Jun., in the St. Louis Theatre, in 1860; and (12.) One night for charity, in connection with Mrs. Farren, in the same house. I gave a "reading" of the *Grave-diggers'* scene in HAMLET on the occasion of the celebration in St. Louis commemorative of the tercentenary anniversary of the birth of Shakspeare, gotten up in aid of the Fund for the Relief of Disabled Soldiers; and at the urgent, flattering, and persistent request of a committee of most amiable gentlewomen (neighbors of mine) I gave an additional reading for the same cause in the Mercantile Library Hall, consisting of scenes from HAMLET, *Jaques's* speech beginning "All the world's a stage," from AS YOU LIKE IT, *Dogberry's* scenes in MUCH ADO ABOUT NOTHING, and (spare my blushes!) several sketches from my own pen. On the invitation of a number of the best citizens of Jacksonville, Ill., I gave two readings from Shakspeare and my own writings, for the benefit of the worthy widow of a worthy clergyman then recently deceased.

In 1861 I was elected, receiving 15,004 votes, a member of the sovereign State Convention of Missouri, which was called by the Legislature with the expectation that it would take the state immediately and bodily out of the Union, but it didn't do any thing of the kind—"quite the reverse." Awful threatenings were made against, and horrible deaths promised us if we didn't *carry out the will of the people* and pass a secession ordinance! But we didn't see it (the people's will) in that light. We had the sovereign power of the state in our hands, and we exercised it by dissolving the Legislature, deposing the governor and executive officers, and erecting a provisional government for the state. This unmaking and making governments (except on the stage) was a new line of business for me, but I *went through my part* regardless of the dire threats, communicated to me through anonymous letters, that my life would certainly be taken if I did thus and so. But I *did* thus and so nevertheless, and here I am alive yet!

In 1855 or 1856 I was offered an engagement by the late Mr. Burton to play a week in his theatre in Broadway, New York, on excellent terms. I declined. In 1861 I was offered $10,000 and all my expenses paid to play *Mawworm* and five other characters which I might select throughout the United States for one year. This offer was made by a gentleman who never saw me act but once, and it was very tempting, I confess, but I declined *that*. I have declined all invitations to appear upon the stage again.

With the exceptions above noted, I have been a RETIRED ACTOR for fifteen years, during which years many changes have taken place in theatrical affairs. The number of buildings for dramatic purposes in the United States has increased at an astonishing rate, and of course actors and actresses are abundant in proportion, such as they are, and some of them are very good ones.

In latter years the legitimate drama seems to have been nearly crushed out by what may be termed BLACK CROOKERY and WHITE FAWNERY, consisting of red and blue fires, a fine collection of French legs, calcium lights, and grand transformation scenes. Negro minstrelsy itself, a modulated form of the drama, has had a hard struggle to maintain its ground, and has only done so by burlesquing the burlesques of the theatres. *Theatres* did I say? Where *are* the theatres? They seem to have nearly all vanished, and in their places we have "Academies of Music," "Olympics," "Varieties," "Gaieties," "Athenæums," and "Opera Houses." The name of *theatre*—plain *theatre*—has been discarded by managers, except in a very few instances. Such an organization as a regular company, engaged for a full year, is now scarcely known in New York City, which is claimed to be the theatrical head-quarters of this country. At Wallack's there is a regular company for from seven to eight months in the year. With this single exception, how are matters managed in the way of engaging companies? About thus, so far as I can learn: Actors and actresses are engaged *by the job*, or during the run of a piece. Mr. D., or Mr. G., or Mr. F. translates a French play, or writes a sensation drama, made up of escapes from trains of cars, burning steam-boats or sinking ships, negro jigs and banjo-playing—walks down or up to the Metropolitan Hotel, which is called the *Rialto* by actors, selects from the crowd, which is always there assembled at certain hours in the day, such performers as will best suit the characters of his piece, and engages them during its "run;" runs his piece until it will run no longer, and then the actors may run where they please, and procure other engagements—if they can. Two of our best tragedians are obliged to make up strolling companies, and roam through the rural districts, in hopes of finding some lovers of the good old drama in villages which have not yet had the love of Shakspeare fumigated out of them by red fires and blue blazes. Occasionally we see a company organized "for one night only" to play in Brooklyn, Newark, Patterson, or Williamsburgh!

The OPERA has no permanent home in New York, but, broken into fragments, scatters itself into the interior towns and cities, where, with scant orchestra and a chorus of eight or ten cracked voices, IL TROVATORE, IL BARBIERE DE SEVIGLIA, and all the other *Ils* of the Italian repertoire, are given to the worthy citizens of Peoria and Detroit at a dollar admission, children half price, and no charge extra for securing seats; while the Academy of Music in Fourteenth Street stands with its doors closed, except when opened occasionally for a single night by some meritorious individual, who hires it for the purpose of giving himself a complimentary benefit.

Is this state of theatrical affairs to continue? Perhaps not—long. I fancy I see a gleam of hope—*two* gleams—*three*, in fact, that a change for the better is at hand. (1.) A young actor is building a fine house in New York, equal to any existing theatre in any part of the world, and that theatre is to be dedicated to the legitimate drama. (2.) Large audiences are drawn together by another young actor (a member of my company when a boy) to see *natural acting*—acting which reminds old playgoers of his grandfather and namesake at the old Chestnut Street Theatre in Philadelphia, when surrounded by the Woods, the Warrens, the Francises, and the Blissetts, and leads them (the old playgoers) to think of and tell their sons and daughters of the happy times they enjoyed at the old Park Theatre in New York, when the Simpsons, Clarkes, Barrys, Masons, Fishers, Hilsons, and Placides acted. (3.) The Western managers with whom I have conversed on the subject are anxiously waiting for the change. They have been obliged to follow the metropolitan managers in the tomfooleries of the time, but they are now sick of Crooks and Fawns—they have had enough of them, and so (it is hoped) have the Western publics.

Let us all pray for this change; and, above all, let us pray that such pernicious plays as JACK SHEPPARD, the performance of which ruins more young men and boys than can be counted, may be banished forever from the stage—if not by the managers, then by the interference of the authorities. An esteemed friend in Philadelphia writes me to-day thus: "I consider JACK SHEPPARD, and other sensation plays of its kind now in vogue, as being the chief cause of the deterioration of the moral drama and increase of crime among a certain class. The theatre and its associations are now looked upon as being the school and play-ground of vice, simply from the fact that the character of the plays produced is calculated to corrupt rather than improve the morals of our youth. During the first month subsequent to the production of JACK SHEPPARD, a magistrate informed me that he committed over twenty young *Jack Sheppards* to prison, or had them sent to the House of Refuge." And yet managers *will* continue to perform the piece!

Since my retirement I have been frequently asked my opinion of theatrical people as a class, and I have not been backward in giving it. So far as I can, in a few words, I here repeat in substance what I have said, and what I really *think* of the members of the theatrical profession (as a class), my opinion being the result of an association with them for fifty years. In the first place, then, there are unquestionably some very mean and despicable men and women—more men than women—who contrive to creep into the profession and disgrace it; but these are rare exceptions. I have intimately known and associated with statesmen, lawyers, doctors, merchants, and preachers—also mechanics and laboring men; I have been honored with the acquaintance and friendship of gentlewomen, the best in the land; I have been thrown into temporary association with *all sorts* of men and women, I may say, and, so far as my observation has gone, I most conscientiously declare that the members of the theatrical profession will compare favorably, as a class, with those of *any* other profession. (Don't shake your head, reverend sir; this is the truth which I write.) I suppose I have had dealings with at least a thousand actors and actresses in my time, and of all that number I can not call to mind more than a score of black sheep out of the whole flock—that is, that were depraved in their natures. On the contrary, I have found in the most of them the Christian virtues—not *professed*, perhaps, but carried into act. There is not a more charitable class of individuals on the earth than theatrical performers. Their means are generally small, but their hearts are large. *Giving* is not of their most charitable acts, for they have precious little to spare in that way; yet I believe they contribute in money as much as any other of the classes I have mentioned, according to their ability. Personal service to the sick and disabled are very seldom withheld by any. It would, perhaps, surprise some readers to know how many actors and actresses are members of the Church—not that I consider them any better for that, or think *professing* religion always makes one religious.

The persecution the stage and its professors have been subjected to from certain ministers of the Gospel, so called—those "I am better than thou" teachers of God's law, who delight in crushing and belittling all professions but that to which they belong — must be stopped, or the stage will be justified in turning the tables upon its persecutors. On suitable occasions I have spoken through the press to the gentlemen with black coats and white neckerchiefs who have assailed us, and in this book I reproduce some of the letters I have written. (If you have skipped them, madam, I would like very much to have you now turn back and read them.) In latter years I perceive the stage has found an able defender, or defend*ress*, if you will, in Chicago, away up on the lakes. Let every actor—yea, and every actress—who can wield a pen—and there are very few of either who can not—turn upon their assailants as that gentlewoman has done, and the bigots will soon cease their railing against the STAGE, which ought to be, and *is* (with all faults of both considered), of equal standing with the PULPIT as a teacher of morality.

But, after all, the good conduct of actors and actresses is their best defense. Let them not only *be* good and virtuous, but *appear* so in the eyes of the world, for there are no people so watched as they are. Let married women be announced by their right names, and let them abandon at once and forever the foolish desire to be called *Misses*—clinging to their maiden names even after becoming mothers of several children, as if they supposed it to be disgraceful to be wives. I know of no custom so ridiculous, so foolish, and so inexcusable as this I refer to. Let me beg the few *American* actresses who follow this despicable custom to consider, only for a moment, the equivocal position they are content to occupy while *living with men, and not bearing their names.* "Oh! shame, where is thy blush?"

For the Men of the profession I have a few words. To each actor I say, Be provident. Lay up something for a rainy day and for old age. (Look at your happy brothers and sisters at Long Branch!) Shun the bottle, your worst enemy—not *yours* only, but the enemy and cause of ruin of many of the wisest and best of *all* professions. *Avoid getting into debt*, and thus avoid being a slave. "Be good, and fear not." Respect yourself, and study to deserve the respect of all good men and women. Respect true religion, and strive to *be* religious, whether you become a *professor* of religion or not. "Do unto others"—you know the rule; ACT on it.

I believe I have done forever with theatrical management in *this* world. How it may be in the world we are all hastening to I know not. I have sometimes had rather hard work *here*, that's certain; for "working out of debt" is about the hardest work I know of; but, taking the "good and ill together" of my "web of life," which our Shakspeare says is "of a mingled yarn," I have abundant cause to be thankful for the many blessings which have been bestowed upon me during my prolonged existence.

Swedenborg tells us that in the spiritual world there are theatres, beautiful and well-managed establishments, devoted (as they should be *here*) to amusement and INSTRUCTION. It is very likely that, if permitted, I may be concerned in the management of one of them. From my long experience in the business, and my extensive acquaintance with artists—those who have already "shuffled off this mortal coil," as well as those who, not having yet been "called," are still playing their parts on *this* stage of life; and having always dealt fairly by and with them—I am not without hope that, if I *do* go into management up there, I shall be able to surround myself with a first-rate COMPANY and an ORCHESTRA of surpassing excellence.

APPENDIX.

APPENDIX.

Murder of an Actor.

Often—very often—I have attempted to write of my brother's murder in Georgia, but could not. Thirty-six years have elapsed since that terrible event, and yet, whenever I put pen to paper with the intention of recording the circumstances attending it, my hand trembles, my eyes become dim, my throat swells as if I were choking, and I push aside the writing materials, and try to think of something else. About eleven years ago I took a seat in the cars at Montgomery, Alabama, with a determination to visit my murdered brother's grave at Milledgeville; but, in the middle of the night, as the train was passing through the old "Indian nation," a chill came over me, warning me to return—and I did. I couldn't go on. Returning by the morning train, I determined in my own mind I *would* write a brief history of that horrible scene in Georgia in 1832, which is always present in my thoughts, and at the same time give some account of the circumstances which preceded and succeeded it. In carrying out this determination, I can only say that what I write shall be strictly the truth, without the least embellishment or coloring for effect. The *reality* is shocking enough—no need of adding one syllable to the sad narration.

My brother Lemuel (the youngest of eleven of us) was twenty-seven years of age at the time he was cut off from the land of the living. He is still remembered by many Georgians as an actor of great promise. Possessed of a good person, handsome and intelligent face and graceful bearing, he was very popular wherever he appeared upon the stage; and being of a genial disposition and pleasant manners, his society was much sought after in private life.

How and where my brother became acquainted with William Flournoy, his slayer, I have never learned. They were together at a drinking saloon at the capital of Georgia on the night of the 12th of November, 1832, and words passed between them on some trifling subject. My brother was warned by a friend, a member of the Georgia Legislature, that Flournoy was a dangerous man—that he was armed, and would use his arms—and he was advised to avoid him; but *avoiding danger* was, unfortunately, what my brother never thought of doing; so he remarked to his friend that if Flournoy wanted any thing of him he might come on—he was ready for him, at the same time pointing to the handle of a pistol (loaded with powder only, as it afterward appeared) which he happened to have in his coat pocket. This remark, it seems, was communicated to Flournoy, and eventually saved his neck from the halter. At the time, and until the trial of the murderer two years afterward, I knew nothing of these particulars. The following I knew: Flournoy came up to him, apparently in a friendly manner, and said, "Come, let us settle this matter," at the same time making a movement toward the bar. My brother, supposing the little difficulty they had had was to be amicably settled, acquiesced, saying, "Very well—with all my heart." "What will you drink?" asked Flournoy. "A glass of porter," replied my brother. "I take brandy," said Flournoy, and they both were served. As they replaced their glasses on the counter after drinking, Flournoy coolly remarked, "This is the d—d rascal who insulted me at Etonton;" then drawing a pistol from his bosom, he cried in a loud voice, "Clear the way, gentlemen!" Two reports, so nearly together that it has never been known which was first, were now heard, and my poor brother fell, shot through the body and mortally wounded. When he saw Flournoy drawing his pistol, he instinctively seized upon his own, and it went off in his pocket before he could draw it forth.

No one, to my knowledge, has ever been able to solve the meaning of the words, "You are the d—d rascal who insulted me at Etonton." My brother had never been in Etonton except to pass through it, and had certainly never met Flournoy there. *My* supposition is that possibly he might at some time have had a difficulty with *some* person, and, filled with liquor as he was, he might have *imagined* his antagonist present at the moment; or that, having had a difficulty with some one at Etonton, he pretended to think my brother was his opponent in that difficulty, and (having no other) gave this as a reason for shooting. I have not heard that he ever gave, or attempted to give, any explanation of the exclamation.

At half past twelve in the morning I was awakened at my hotel, and informed that my brother was shot. I dressed myself, and followed the messenger to the fatal spot, a mile distant, where I found my poor brother weltering in his blood. The murderer had fled, and it only remained for me, with the help of friends, to convey my brother home and see him die—the medical man informing me there was no hope of his surviving more than a few hours. The poor fellow retained his senses to the last, but would give me no particulars of the cause of the difficulty. When asked who shot him, he answered distinctly, "William Flournoy;" but when desired to give the particulars of the quarrel, he said, impatiently, "We had no quarrel; it is all nonsense; let it go." About three o'clock he breathed his last, having suffered great pain for three hours. No one has ever known—no one *can* ever know the agony his brother experienced then, and for years afterward; but *that* is not a part of the history of the case.

The coroner's jury brought in a verdict of "willful murder" against Flournoy, and the governor offered a reward for his apprehension, but he was not taken. During the following summer, while I was absent from the state, he delivered himself up, and, upon such evidence as could then be procured, was admitted to bail in the sum of twenty thousand dollars, to appear and stand a trial upon the charge of murder. In the mean time he had retained the whole bar of the county, so that I was compelled to go to the neighboring county of Bibb for a lawyer to assist the prosecuting officer whenever the trial should come on.

I had never seen Flournoy, to my knowledge; but, knowing almost every body by *sight*, I was fearful, on my return to the state in the fall, that I might meet this man and speak to him, as I did to others—*perhaps shake hands with him!* This dread haunted me continually, and made me very shy of all persons I did not actually know by name.

There were persons who thought that when I should meet the murderer of my brother I ought to shoot him down like a dog. Others, and by far the greater number, considered I was doing my whole duty by prosecuting him on the indictment found against him in the Superior Court. I will not pretend that I had not strong temptations to follow the advice of those who thought I ought to take the law into my own hands; but, without considering the probability of my being killed instead of killing, should I attempt to become my brother's avenger, the idea of taking life, under any circumstances, could never, for any length of time, be entertained by me. The slayer of my younger brother was a rich man; I was as poor as it is possible to be, and live respectably. The chances, I knew, were against a conviction; but my mind was made up to pursue the murderer to the extent of the law, and no farther.

I am now going to relate a little incident which may possibly interest the believers in mesmerism. During the fall of 1833 Major Ward was shot by Mr. M'Comb in an affray one night at the latter's hotel, and it was supposed the major would die of the wound, which happened to be on the very same spot, apparently, where my brother received *his* wound the year before. This affray was the subject of conversation every where the next morning after its occurrence. I had been to see Major Ward, and attentively examined the wound; so, when I saw in a public place a circle of men engaged in discussing the probabilities of his recovery or death, describing the situation of the wounded man, and discoursing generally of the affray, I stepped into and made one of the circle. A man exactly opposite to me was making some statement respecting the situation of the bullet-wound in Major Ward. I did not know him, but, when he finished speaking, I said, "You are mistaken; I know exactly the situation of the wound; it is just here," placing my finger on his velvet vest; and I here declare that at that moment I felt a shock as of electricity, which made me start as if receiving a heavy blow. I don't know that *he* felt a shock, but he started back as if struck too, and we were both seized by the by-standers and dragged away in opposite directions. I instantly became aware, before a word was spoken, that it was my brother's murderer whom I had touched with my finger. He knew *me* well enough, and, prompted by his guilty conscience, he thought I was about to avenge my brother's murder on the spot.

"That is Flournoy," I said to those who were dragging me away.

"Yes," replied one; "but come along; let the law take its course; you shall *not* attack him here; he is always armed, and *you* are more likely to fall than he."

"Gentlemen," I replied, "let me go—release me! I have no idea of acting as you suppose. I did not know him. Now I *do*, and shall avoid him as I would a serpent."

On my word they released me. Casting my

eyes toward the group of which Flournoy formed the centre, I took a good look at him, so that I should know him again. He was very pale.

After various postponements, the cause was set for trial in the winter of 1834. By the advice of my counsel, General Beall, of Macon, I underwent an examination and was admitted to the bar, so that I could assist at the prosecution, having traveled from Montgomery, a distance of nearly three hundred miles, in the dead of winter, and over the worst kind of roads, for the especial purpose of endeavoring to convict this man.

In the course of the trial—the particulars of which I am not going to record—I became aware for the first time of the fact that my brother had shown a pistol when warned by a friend to avoid a rencounter with Flournoy, and expressed himself "READY FOR HIM." I felt very certain then that there would be no conviction of the murderer; it would be urged upon the jury that the affray amounted to a duel—nothing more; and so it turned out.

Having been denounced by one of the attorneys for the defense as one *seeking the life of the defendant* by this prosecution, while, on the other hand, many warm-hearted Georgians having expressed surprise that I did not take the law into my own hands and *shoot the slayer of my brother at sight*, I felt it to be my duty on this occasion to set myself right before the court and jury, which I did in a speech of perhaps twenty minutes, wherein my position was clearly defined. As prosecutor, made so by the law, as well as by my near relationship to the deceased, it was my duty to use all legal means to convict the prisoner, but beyond this I should not proceed one step. Should the jury acquit or convict, there was the end of my mission. My closing remarks were addressed to the prisoner, who sat with his counsel within four feet of where I stood, a table only dividing us.

"Whatever may be the verdict of this jury," I said, "you, William Flournoy, are convicted of murder by your own conscience. You know that my brother intended you no harm—that it was *not* in self-defense you discharged your pistol at his heart. Before God and man, I charge you with basely murdering my young brother. You tremble now and turn pale at the charge. Your peace of mind is gone, never, never to be recovered. The sleep of the innocent will never more be yours. YOU ARE A MURDERER; and I tell you here in this crowded court-room, at this hour of midnight, that, whether convicted or acquitted here, you will evermore carry the mark of a homicide upon your brow; and from this time forth, in this world, YOU WILL NEVER SLEEP AGAIN."

I left the court-room and sought that repose which my journey and the exciting scenes of the trial had deprived me of for three days and nights. When I awakened, late on the following day, I learned that the murderer had been acquitted and was at large.

* * * * *

Two years passed away. I had left Georgia immediately after the trial, and now returned to its borders (Columbus) to attend to some business unconnected with my profession. Some Indian disturbances in the Creek nation were anticipated (this was in the spring of 1836), and, having concluded the business which took me there, it was my desire to avoid the night-traveling in the stage from the Georgia line, in returning to Alabama—to "Elliott's," thirteen miles from the Chattahoochee River. I therefore proceeded to a livery stable and endeavored to hire a horse and buggy, intending to await at Elliott's the arrival of the stage in the morning. Failing to get the conveyance, I was turning to leave the stable, when I was accosted by a stooping, miserable-looking individual, wearing a slouched hat and a great-coat, who held out his hand to me and greeted me by name. Supposing he was a former acquaintance whose face I had forgotten, I was about to take his hand, when, just as my fingers touched his, I felt a shock exactly like the one heretofore spoken of, and I started back, exclaiming, "You are Flournoy!" I felt it was the murderer, though not in the slightest degree resembling that individual as I had last seen him.

"Yes," he answered feebly, and attempting to come near me, "I *am* William Flournoy; and I have been long seeking you. I heard you were here, and I have come from my place on purpose to see you. Do not refuse what I have to ask."

I can not very well describe my feelings. There was the slayer of my poor brother standing abjectly before me, with his hands clasped as if in supplication. I confess my first sensations were those of pity; but conquering them as unworthy to be entertained for this person, I was next tempted to strike him down with my arm, and spurn him with my foot. After a moment's hesitation, I made up my mind to leave him as soon as possible, and thus get out of the way of temptation.

"I want nothing to say to you or do with you," I said, and, brushing past him, walked over into the broad, sandy street, determined to avoid him at all hazards; but, though I did not hear his steps, I felt he was following me. Stopping in the centre of the wide street, I turned suddenly, and, sure enough, there he was, close by me, in the same supplicating attitude as when I left him at the stable door. Looking into his sunken eyes, I asked, angrily, "Why do you follow me?" I shall never forget his despairing look as he answered, in a deep and solemn voice,

"I want you, the brother of the man I slew, to shoot me—here—right here."

Shocked beyond measure by his words and manner, both full of earnestness, I scarcely knew what to say or do.

"No," at length I replied, "it is not for *me* to punish you."

"Ah!" replied he, quickly, "it is not *punishment* I ask you to inflict; that I have received already, in full measure; but it is vengeance I wish you to take—vengeance for your brother's murder, and upon his murderer."

Observing I did not immediately reply, the miserable wretch continued:

"Yes, his murderer; you called me by the right name when you spoke to the jury two years ago. I *am* a murderer! I know it *now! Then*, I endeavored to persuade myself that I committed the deed in self-defense; but I soon found out it was not so. You said, at the trial, I would never sleep more, AND I NEVER HAVE!"

"What!" I exclaimed, "not slept in two years!"

"It is true," said he—"perfectly true what I say; not once have I slept since that terrible night when you spoke to me in the court-room. I have closed my eyes at night, as usual; I have steeped my senses in brandy until unconsciousness took the place of sleep, but that blessed sleep you drove away that night has never returned to me for one moment. My life is a burden to me. I pray you, in God's name and in your murdered brother's, to take it—take it!"

Though not a tear dimmed the homicide's eye, mine began to moisten, and I felt it incumbent upon me to leave this man before he should perceive my weakness. Summoning all my firmness, I said, "Ask forgiveness of that God whose name you invoke. Let your future life be such as to prove the sincerity of your repentance, and—"

"No, no, no!" he said, interrupting me. "No repentance will avail me. Let me die by your hand; *then* I feel that there may be some hope for me—*then* your brother may forgive me."

I could endure this scene no longer. Turning suddenly from him, I walked away, leaving him standing in the middle of the street. "I WILL DIE TO-NIGHT" were the last words I heard him utter, and when I reached the corner I turned and saw the miserable creature standing in the middle of the street with his hands clasped as before.

I started for home in the stage that night, being the only passenger. The driver's name was Green. About six miles from the river we stopped at a log cabin, in a swampy hollow, to water the horses, and saw a party of a dozen or more of Creek Indians *executing the war dance!* The driver, a good jolly soul, wanted to stop and take a turn or two with them; but I persuaded and pulled him away, and we got through safely. The very next night the stage was captured and burnt, several passengers were killed, and that very driver (Green) tied to a tree, his feet cut off, and burnt to death!

* * * * * * * *

"I will die to-night!" said the murderer; and he spoke truly. About a month after the events I have been relating, when the Indian disturbances had been quelled, and the mail could come through safely, my friend James Kevlin, of Columbus, wrote me at Mobile as follows:

"The very next morning after you left Columbus, the body of your brother's murderer was found at his country place, pierced by a dozen rifle bullets and scalped—the first victim of our little Indian War."

Butting an Iceberg.

"*Starboard hard! Stop her!*"

These words, uttered in a loud and sharp voice by the look-out stationed on the bowsprit, were heard by every one of us on deck, and they caused us all to start to our feet, for we became instantly aware there was a vessel or an iceberg—most likely the latter—right ahead of us, and not more than fifty yards off. We were in a thick fog, which had arisen in less than ten minutes—so thick that those who were in the middle of the ship could just see, dimly and more dimly as the distance increased, to the man at the wheel one way, and to the man at the look-out on the other; and when the last-named individual shouted out the words written in italics, we were "brought up all standing"—that is to say, all of us that did not faint, and only one of us, an elderly female, did that.

It was on the 9th of July, 1859, at 1 50 P.M., that we, the passengers in the good but old ship Canada, of the Cunard line, heard that awful cry, which seemed to come from a man in mortal agony—awful to us who knew its import, and found ourselves staring up and down at the two lines of ghosts, as we all appeared to be at the time, waiting for the impending shock. It is said that in such times of mortal peril our thoughts are very active, and I know it to be so, for it seems to me that, in the ten seconds we stood there, I thought of almost every incident of my previous life. I also thought of events in the lives of other people, and of the end of the lives of some. I thought of the steam-ship President, and other vessels which had gone down just as the Canada appeared likely to go; of poor Tyrone Power, the great Irish actor, of Le Grand Smith, and hundreds of others, of whose fate nothing had been nor ever would be known. I thought of home, and the anxious ones who would never know how we perished, if we were to perish, and of thousands of other matters not necessary to mention here. My son and I stood there casting our eyes up and down at the two rows of ghosts in the thick fog.

"Let me go down and get our life-preservers," proposed my son.

"No," said I, quickly, "our only life-preserver now is God."

My idea was, that if the vessel was to sink, my son, being below, would be overwhelmed with the waters first, and I preferred that we should take our fate together; so there we stood, holding each other by the arms and shoulders, looking up and down at our pale fellow-passengers. Once only I turned my eyes aside, and then I saw a boat, hanging by the davits, filled with people, and heard a man, who held an oar uplifted threateningly toward others who were endeavoring to climb up and into the swinging boat, exclaim, "Not another one!" meaning, as I understood it, that the boat would not hold any more than were already in it, and he would knock the brains out of any one who should attempt to force his way into that crowd. I could scarcely refrain from laughing at the young man's earnestness, and I thought to myself, "You are very welcome to the monopoly of *that* mode of preservation; that little boat, full of frightened people, will almost certainly be upset in lowering it to the water; *we* stand right here, and take our chance."

I most solemnly declare that I had no consciousness of fear within me at that most critical moment of my life, and it was the same with my son, I am sure, though I have no doubt we were as pale as any of the other ghosts. There was no time for fear. We were very well aware that in a few seconds the shock would come. The vessel was about 280 feet in length. We were in the centre, and could only see, as I have said, as far as either end of it, consequently the man on the look-out could only see as far ahead into the fog from where he was stationed as was the distance from us to him. When he gave the warning cry, he instantly jumped from the bowsprit to the forecastle deck, and, with the other sailors who had been standing and sitting there, began a precipitate retreat aft, from which movements we knew he and the sailors expected the vessel would immediately strike the impending object, whatever it might be. We were going at the rate of eleven or twelve miles an hour, so we were sure the catastrophe was very nearly upon us.

On the previous day all the passengers had been anxious to see the icebergs, and we had arisen unusually early in order to get a good view of them, Captain Lang having told us we should probably be among them at dawn of day —and we were. The morning was clear and sunshiny, and we had seen and counted twenty-six good-sized bergs, some a mile off, some two miles, and others within half a mile of the ship. We had got by them all, as we supposed, and most of us had disposed ourselves upon settees on deck, reading, when suddenly, as I have related, the fog enveloped us, and the fog-whistle began to sound at short intervals, and then came the warning cry from the look-out.

My son and I had been to England ostensibly to attend the great Handel Festival held in the Crystal Palace at Sydenham, seven miles from London, but, being there, we of course did not neglect seeing all we could see in so short a time (nineteen days) in the British capital. The festival was a grand affair indeed, occupying three days, the music of the MESSIAH, ISRAEL IN EGYPT, the DETTINGEN TE DEUM, and other fine compositions of Handel being given by over four thousand performers, conducted by Costa, and the solo parts sustained by Simms Reeves, Miss Novello, and the baritone singer who accompanied Jenny Lind to this country seven years previously. It was expected the queen would attend the festival on the third day, but she failed to appear, and I must confess I thought a little hard of her for staying away, remembering what a favorite Handel had been of her great-grandfather. However, I must not omit to say that she sent Prince Albert and two or three princesses to occupy the royal box. The attendance on the last day amounted to 28,000 paying people.

We visited the British Museum, Westminster Abbey, Westminster Hall, St. Paul's, the Tower, the Tunnel, the Monument, the Zoological Garden, the parks, and the two houses of Parliament—the last by virtue of tickets kindly furnished by Mr. Moran, secretary of our minister. In the House of Commons about five hundred ordinary-looking people were seated in rows, all wearing their hats except when addressing the chair. Not much business seemed to be doing that afternoon, the session only lasting an hour and a half. In the House of Lords, which was sitting as a court, there were not more than twenty persons in the room, including the lords, of whom there were only three, besides the queer-looking chap who occupied the woolsack. We saw the queen pass in her state carriage through Green Park on her way to open Parliament, and found her to be a tolerably good-looking gentlewoman, with a benevolent but somewhat worried countenance. The coachman who drove the state carriage was a sight to see—fat, lazy, and bedizened all over with gold lace, with such a wig! The Horse Guards were a fine-looking set of men, and their horses (all jet black) were worthy of their riders. We saw her majesty again at Ascot Races.

We witnessed the performance of the TROVATORE at Drury Lane Theatre, with Titiens in the leading part, an orchestra of forty-eight, conducted by Benedict (Jenny Lind's leader in this country), and a chorus of one hundred and fifty. At the Royal Opera, Covent Garden (a guinea admission), we heard the HUGUENOTS performed, with Mario and Grisi in the principal parts, an orchestra of ninety-six, under Costa, and a chorus of over three hundred! At the Standard Theatre, in Shoreditch, we saw Phelps perform *Othello*, and came to the conclusion that when he became jealous he must have been attacked with a fit of chills and fever, under the effects of which he seemed to labor until he stabbed himself in the fifth act. The admission to the Standard Theatre was sixpence only to the pit. At the Princess's Theatre in Oxford Street, we witnessed the great performance of Shakspeare's HENRY V., with Mr. and Mrs. Charles Kean and five hundred people engaged in the representation! At the Haymarket we had the good fortune to see EVERY BODY'S FRIEND, with Charles Mathews, Buckstone, and Compton in their original characters. The CRITIC was also given, Charles Mathews assuming the two characters of *Sir Fretful Plagiary* and *Puff*. "Little Robson" played two of his best characters for us at the Olympic, and Toole, just then beginning to be appreciated, amused us greatly at the Adelphi. At Astley's (generally called Hastly's) we saw a performance of the BATTLE OF WATERLOO, a very tall man taking the part of *Napoleon*. We heard the great Spurgeon preach an excellent sermon, and excellently he preached it, in the hall of Surrey Garden (early admission one shilling), from the text, "Whatsoever thy hand findeth to do, do it with all thy might," and thought his "do it," frequently repeated, was fully equal to the "do it" of Ellen Tree in the HUNCHBACK, in her best days. We went into a coal-hole, or cider-cellar, in the Strand to hear a mock trial, but, finding the speeches were indecent, we "retired early."

We also went over to Paris, where we saw as much, probably, as any other two Americans ever have seen in four days. To accomplish our desire to see all over Paris, we ascended to the top of the Column of July, in the Place de la Bastile. The view was magnificent. Descending from that great height, we pursued our way up (or down) the Rue St. Antoine to the Hôtel de Ville, and from thence over a bridge to the Church of Notre Dame and the Hôtel Dieu; thence back to the River Seine, in which we took a swim, paying one sou each for admission to the bathing-house, but towels, bathing-dresses, dressing-room, and soap carried the price up to about one franc each. Repassing the Hôtel de Ville, we followed the Rue Rivoli till we came to the palaces of the Louvre and the Tuileries (now all one), and into the garden, through which we passed to the Place de la Concorde; after spending an hour in which, and taking a look at the neighboring Church of the Madeleine (outside and inside), and viewing the Grand Column in the Place Vendôme, with the Little Corporal on top of it, we went to dinner, and afterward to the Theatre Française. This was *one* day in Paris. The other days were equally well employed.

It was on the Banks of Newfoundland—why that particular part of the Atlantic Ocean should be called the "Banks" of *any* "land," I can't imagine, for we were hundreds of miles from any shore—on our return voyage, that the event occurred which I am endeavoring to record.

We waited the ten seconds with exemplary patience, not knowing but—indeed, rather expecting—we should all go down in about a minute after we should strike. At length, *c-r-u-n-c-h* it came (the shock), and for a second or two we could scarcely retain our standing positions. The vessel trembled to its centre, and the great monster of an iceberg came booming along on our starboard side, tearing the wheel-house entirely off, but, fortunately, not injuring the wheel, and passing astern into the fog and out of sight almost instantly. It was about as large as a church. The captain came running aft, exclaiming, "The ship is all right!" but it was some time, and not until we had examined for ourselves, that we (the passengers) felt that possibly we might be spared to get into port. On examination, it was found that the bow of the vessel, including bowsprit, keelson, and nearly the whole of the forecastle, had been stove in, leaving an opening as large as a barn-door, extending down to within a foot of the water's edge. The timbers, some of them fourteen inches thick, were crushed up like so many pipe-stems. If the event had occurred ten minutes later in the day (2 o'clock), nothing could have saved the lives of eight sailors, who would at that time have occupied the berths in the forecastle. If the weather had been as it had been the day before, nothing could have saved the vessel; she would have shipped twenty hogsheads of water at every wave. The sheer the pilot was enabled to give her in the ten seconds which intervened between the time when he was warned to put down the helm and the happening of the collision, prevented her meeting the iceberg exactly "head on," and, in fact, saved the ship.

While laying to about four hours, the cargo was changed so as to lighten the fore part of the vessel, and raise it about three feet. Across and around the huge opening made by the iceberg double sails were wrapped and fastened. At about 6 P.M. the fog cleared away, and discovered Old Cruncher about four miles to leeward. All being ready, we started on our course. Next day, being Sunday, we had religious services, and most fervent thanks were given to God for deliverance from our very great danger.

The sea continuing calm, we passed on safely, and on Tuesday, the 12th of July, arrived at Halifax, where a large crowd was assembled on the wharf, attracted by the appearance of the Cunarder as she steered up the harbor with her head cut off and her neck wrapped up in towels.

"Halloo!" hailed a sailor on shore, as we neared the wharf; "what's the matter, and what have you been about?"

"Can't you see?" answered the man with the line, which he was just throwing to his interlocutor; "can't you see? WE'VE BEEN BUTTING AN ICEBERG!"

The Shakspeare Monument in Central Park.

I had intended to give an account in this appendix of the movement for the erection of a monument to Shakspeare in Central Park, and, with the view of collecting information on the subject, I addressed a note to James H. Hackett, Esq., knowing that he had been most active in the business, asking him to communicate to me such facts relative to the origin of the undertaking, which all devotees of the great poet must feel a deep interest in, as were in his possession. Mr. Hackett answered promptly, and I see no better way of placing the facts before my readers than by giving his letter in full, just as it came from his pen:

James H. Hackett to Sol. Smith.

"107 East Thirty-fifth Street, Murray Hill,
"New York, August 19, 1868.

"MY DEAR SIR,—In reply to your note requesting 'the briefest kind of an account of the origin of the Shakspeare Monument,' in preparation for its foundation, located in the mall of the Central Park 23d April, 1864, 'and particularly my connection with that enterprise,' I would mention that, in November, 1863, in a social letter to me from the Earl of Carlisle, chairman of the committee at Stratford-upon-Avon for a public demonstration there, *23d April*, 1864 —the 300th anniversary of the birth of Shakspeare—that gentleman, who, as Lord Morpeth, had visited and been popular in the United States in 1842, suggested that that then coming tercentenary would afford a favorable opportunity for cultivating the good feeling which prevailed between the people of Great Britain and of the United States, and hoped that some of us (Americans) might find it convenient to come and unite in their celebration. Accordingly, the Hon. Edward Everett, Hon. William H. Seward, and the British minister, Lord Lyons, were consulted upon the subject, and it was resolved that an invitation to Americans generally should be sent to the Stratford committee through Lord Lyons, and Lord Carlisle was so informed and highly approved of the course proposed, but, being at the same time (February, 1864) Lord Lieutenant of Ireland and located at Castle Dublin, he dispatched the correspondence which I had sent him to the committee at Stratford, urging their favorable consideration and immediate action in conformity therewith. Owing to the sudden death soon after of Lord Carlisle, or to some other cause not known, the middle of March arrived, and no invitation from the Stratford committee had reached us or been heard of, and, if it had been received here, it would have been *too late* to prove of favorable consequence in seducing *many* Americans over to unite in a celebration *in England;* and *then* the idea occurred to me that, though there were but a few weeks left for the attempt, it was *not impossible* to prepare some suitable demonstration on the 23d of April following, *including a project for the erection of a monument to Shakspeare* in our own Central Park.

"I first sought and communicated to Mr. James W. Wallack my project. He admired my spirit, but pronounced impracticable the initiation of any considerable fund for it within so short a time, and suggested my postponing the attempt until the next *autumn*, when he would give a benefit for the object at his theatre. I then consulted Mr. William Wheatley and Mr. Edwin Booth; both of them cheered me by offering to get up a benefit, the former at Niblo's Theatre and the latter at the Winter Garden, in aid of a fund for the erection of a monument to Shakspeare. Through the friendly aid of the Hon.

Charles P. Daly, a site for it was conceded by the Commissioners of the Central Park; and, calling again upon my old friend Mr. Wallack and reporting progress, he concluded, 'The arrangements of my theatre this spring disable me from giving such fund a benefit, but, whenever I may think you are likely to succeed, I'll put my hand in my pocket and give you a thousand dollars toward its accomplishment.'

"To prepare the foundation for the ceremony of laying the corner-stone on the tercentenary involved some pecuniary responsibility, which I agreed with the commissioners to take, and it was laid accordingly; the honor of wielding the trowel on the occasion was conferred upon me. Some $2000 were obtained by the benefit at Niblo's and Winter Garden same evening. Mr. Wallack added his $1000 soon afterward, and, together with another benefit at Niblo's by Mr. Wheatley and a second one by Mr. Edwin Booth, which netted nearly $3000, and donations from private citizens of New York, the fund had reached last spring upward of $23,000, when a contract with John Quincy Adams Ward, the sculptor, was entered into for the completion of a statue after his model, and which Mr. Ward thinks may be finished and placed upon its pedestal by the 23d of April, 1869. Yours faithfully,

"JAS. H. HACKETT.

"Sol. Smith, Esq."

High Tide at Long Branch.

Roll, roll! dash, dash! What does it all mean, the tide rising to such a height? Such a thing was never heard of before. I was aware that in winter time there were storms; that then the waves rolled over the bluff banks here at Long Branch, and sometimes swept away fences, pig-pens, and small houses; but that in August such an event could occur seemed so unlikely, that when the excellent new landlord of the Clarendon (Watts his name) called out, "Get up, all of ye! the tide is carrying us all away!" which proclamation he accompanied by a severe pounding upon a Chinese gong, I could scarcely credit the evidence of my senses. My room was in the second story of the house, and I thought if *any body* was safe *I* must be. Nevertheless, it must be confessed that my uneasiness was considerable as the gong of warning continued to sound in the distant corridor, and Watts's voice persisted in proclaiming that we should all be "carried away."

It was as dark as Erebus, and I heard, or fancied I heard, a roaring of the waves very unusual to me, my hearing being none of the best, and I began to reflect seriously on our situation—I say *our* situation, for my wife lay beside me quite unconscious of the threatening danger. The gong continued to sound, so I determined to see how matters stood, or at least *feel* my way to the door or window, and take a look out. I stepped out of bed, and, by George! one of my feet found itself in water a foot deep!

"We are inundated!" I exclaimed, as I dashed about the room frantically, and then began shaking my wife furiously to awaken her.

"What *is* the matter?" asked my sleeping partner, laying hold of me in affright. "Is the house on fire, or what?"

"We are drowning!" I exclaimed. "Don't you hear the gong? The tide has risen, and the Clarendon is floating off at this moment. We shall soon be out at sea, and there will be no hope for us."

I hereupon seized my wife, and began to make toward the door—and I must here remark that she is not a light load to carry, even for a strong man, which I am not. The waves seemed to roar louder and louder; the gong sounded more terrifically than ever; the house seemed to be loosened from its foundations, and rolled about in harmony with the moving waters, while "carried away!" was the distant but unceasing cry of the landlord.

"On horror's head horrors accumulate,"

Shakspeare says, you know. I felt as though swimming was my only chance, and I resolved, if I could get out, to do my best in that line, trusting to the buoyancy of my wife to keep *her* afloat, while I propelled. The door was locked, and I had forgotten where I had laid or hung the key.

"Burst it open!" suggested my wife.

"Just so," responded I.

And I receded a step or two to get headway for a big kick at the door, which, in my opinion, would have shattered it to atoms, when we stumbled backward over our large traveling trunk, and there we lay sprawling on the floor—or, rather, *I* did!

* * * * * * * *

The sun was shining brightly into the room, and the gong was sounding for breakfast. My wife stood over me in her new night-cap, smiling benignantly on my prostrate condition, and quietly remarking,

"You have made a horrible muss here, old man—upset the slop-pail, and knocked things about generally. Had bad dreams, I reckon. I told you it was not good to eat crabs for supper."

Complimentary Benefits.

Time was when a complimentary benefit meant something. John Howard Payne, at first a precocious actor, and afterward a translator of French plays in London, and author of the ballad of "Home, sweet Home," received a complimentary benefit in New York. Thomas Cooper, an actor, for a time without a rival upon the American boards, was complimented in a similar way upon his retirement from the stage. These demonstrations took place more than thirty years ago, and the recipients of the "compliments" are now resting in their graves. They were both entitled, by long service, to such a proof of the estimation in which they were held by their countrymen. But how is it nowadays with the "complimentaries" which are given at our theatres? How are they gotten up? Who are the instigators and abettors of these benefits? Is it the people who sign the requests, or is it the actors and actresses themselves, or some particular friend, aided by a newspaper reporter or two (for the sake of the advertising which accrues to the papers), who prepare the "request" and solicit signatures? Are not the letter and answer generally written by the same person? Some busy, meddling individual, wishing to show himself particularly intimate and friendly with a party who is about to close a rather unsuccessful engagement, goes round to his friends and acquaintances—

"Here, colonel (or major, or captain), we are going to give a complimentary benefit at the theatre, and we want your name."

"My name? I don't know the person."

"That makes no difference; you needn't go to the benefit; but let us have your name to the request."

"But, confound it! I don't request any thing of the kind."

"Well, you have no objection to the affair going on?"

"Not at all. It can go on, I suppose, without my name being paraded in the newspapers."

"Oh, hang it, put down your name; it can do you no harm, and will perhaps do some good."

So, after a little more persuasion, another name is obtained. Thus some twenty or thirty citizens are persuaded into publishing their names requesting an individual they have perhaps never seen or heard of to accept of a complimentary benefit! To make the thing more imposing, the canvasser, or the beneficiaire, or the stage manager, or whoever it is that makes out the programme or "correspondence" for the newspapers, after giving the actual signatures to the petition, adds "143 others," and, appending the grateful answer of the recipient of the "compliment," in which the night is "fixed"—by the kind co-operation of the manager—(always happening to be on the very night on which the regular benefit was to take place), out comes the announcement, in all the papers, of the "complimentary benefit of the citizens of So-and-So to Mr. and Mrs. So-and-So."

Did any one ever hear of Macready taking a complimentary benefit? or Ellen Tree? or Charlotte Cushman? or any other truly great and attractive artist? I think not. It is only the twinklers in the dramatic firmament that require such humbuggery to keep them from sinking to their deserved obscurity. The real "stars" of the profession despise such tomfoolery.

It is, unfortunately, not the would-be "stars" alone who resort to this method of bolstering up their fame and fortune. Stock actors — sometimes talented and deserving ones—are occasionally induced by their friends to resort to this disgusting and nonsensical mode of "getting a house," particularly in dull times, when it is difficult to gather an audience. It is within the memory of some that a young actor of promise—one of our own people, raised and educated here (St. Louis), and who had never failed in obtaining a good benefit—was once (in an evil hour) persuaded to take a complimentary. The list of requesters was easily filled up, for the people all liked the young man, and the "correspondence" was duly published. What was the result? A failure. For the first time was the appeal of this favorite actor and citizen neglected. A benefit in the ordinary way would probably have been fully attended; but the complimentary people had taken hold of the matter, and the actor's real friends considered the matter settled—the house would be good "any how," and it being a very warm night, they concluded they would stay at home—and they did. The newspaper proprietors pocketed their advertising fee for the "correspondence," the manager received his expenses, and the favorite actor was out of pocket some fifty dollars! So much for the kindly interference of friends.

Let us hope that this sort of humbuggery and nonsense will be done away with.

Committee on Authors and Amateurs.

As long ago as 1826 there was formed in Cincinatti a "Committee on Authors and Amateurs," consisting of Alexander Drake, Frederick Henderson, A. W. Jackson (afterward manager of the Bowery Theatre, New York), Lemuel Smith, and the writer hereof, the latter individual being then elected *chairman for life!* It is melancholy to reflect that, except the chairman, all the members of this committee have closed their earthly "sittings," and will never more "report" upon the merits or demerits of new plays or would-be actors. Nevertheless, the committee, enlarged by the accession of new members, and with "branches" distributed all through the United States and Canada, has continued to exist and flourish down to this day, albeit the chairman of the parent body, retired from the profession of the stage, and not relishing, perhaps, so much as formerly the usual "proceedings," has called but few meetings in latter years.

To entitle a person to membership, it was not absolutely essential that he should belong to the theatrical profession. The press has been largely represented in it, the law has furnished many members, and the healing art has contributed its full quota to this very droll organization.

The *objects* had in view by the founders of "the committee" were:

1. The *cure* of individuals afflicted with stage madness.

2. To relieve managers of theatres from the sometimes *dangerous* responsibility of directly rejecting worthless pieces offered for representation.

3. To extract (incidentally) from the proceedings of the committee as much fun and amusement as the nature of each case would admit of.

It must not be understood that *all* who applied for admission into the profession, or who submitted new plays for managerial approval, were sent before the committee. A nice discrimination was always exercised in selecting the "victims," as they were called, and it was very seldom a mistake was made in this regard. Persons taken in training were generally "put through;" and very many permanent cures of stage madness have been effected, as could be easily proved by living witnesses, were not their mouths forever closed by the "solemn obligation" they were required to take upon themselves at their respective times of trial.

There are many citizens of New Orleans, Cincinnati, St. Louis, Mobile, Louisville, and other Western and Southern cities who have participated in the doings of this committee, and who still live to remember the rich scenes they have witnessed and assisted in while "sitting" upon the merits of aspiring young *Richards*, *Hamlets*, *Norvals*, and *Romeos*, and during the reading of new plays never destined to be represented on the stage. It would be impossible to convey to the reader any thing more than the faintest idea of these "proceedings," therefore I shall not attempt it. I can truly say, however, that they were always full of fun, and running over. A few isolated "cases," with some letters of application, which I shall give in the exact words of their respective writers, must suffice for these pages.

LETTERS OF APPLICATION.

Without regard to dates, I proceed to give a few letters from aspiring young heroes who would become actors. These letters, with a thousand or two of others of the same kind, having been referred to the "Committee on Authors and Amateurs," are presented as specimens of the style in which managers are addressed by those who have *made up their minds* to adopt the theatrical profession. There is no mistake in the genuineness of the documents, the *originals* being furnished to the printers of these sketches:

A CLASSICAL APPLICANT.

"St. Louie, May 13, 1840.

"MR. SOL. SMITH, ESQ.: SIR, — Although a perfect stranger to you, I do sincerely hope that you will not, in any wise, consider me impertinent on account of my addressing you in this style, anonymous tho' it is and perhaps quaint withall. But the only excuse I am able to offer is that I belong to the present generation, and that you are aware is very quaint. Also, that I may have some notions concerning matters and things, which, to superior understandings, may seem rather unique, instance this affair in particular. Why I do not personally appear before you and verbally state my request, I will tell you on some future day, if an opportunity ever offer. But, to the Point.

"I have long been affected with a mania for mimickry, and never having had an opportunity of Privately having my bump of representation examined by any disciple of Gall, or Spurzheim, I am at a loss to know, whether it is decidedly, or partially developed, or whether it is developed at all; being equally as ignorant of its locality upon my caput, but if it be not developed, even should there be a cavity, where a bump should 'towering rise;' still I imagine that I might soon acquire the 'modus operandi' of acting; the tenets of the above-mentioned worthies to the contrary notwithstanding. But my strange 'un! say you, what meaneth this rigmarole, know'st thou not, that I have else to do than attend to the empty nonsense over which my eyes have glanced? True! true! and therefore I'll have done quick, I will not detain you long. I wish very much to appear upon the stage in the capacity of an actor; and when I have a remarkably strong desire for anything I contrive to gratify my wish, in the most efficient manner possible, and in this emergency I know of no other expedient than to appeal to you. No opportunity has heretofore offered to favor my wishes; the present I hope may be auspicious. I have been an actor in my time; but the wide world was the theatre; and the stage—no matter—I'll tell thee at a future day, where the stage and where the scenery. Now I wish to confine my operations—to compress them into a more narrow space — within the walls of a mimic world, where tragedy and comedy are really nought but fiction, I would bear a part.

"But Sir I did not take up my feathered distaff to spin a long, ragged, jagged, uneven yarn, or tell of things to which one may attach no consequence—but merely to make a simple request; and perhaps you may consider it a very simple request. Well! be it so; it arises from my own peculiarity. My request is, That you would merely enroll me among the members of your corps. I would demand no compensation whatever for my services unless you (yourself being the judge) would think them worthy of compensation; until I might be capable of succeeding 'secundum artem.' But should the prospect of succeeding 'a la mode' be very obscure merely open your mouth and speak in this wise. Non tu es doctissimue Romanorum, non tu es sumæ prudentie, go thy way young knight of the buskin, I'll have none of thee—merely sir give me a hint and I will be minus. I am sir your obedient and humble servant,

"L. M. Dunmore."

I don't remember the result of the above strong appeal. I guess he got the "hint," and was "minus," as he promised to be.

ANOTHER "CLASSICALLY"-EDUCATED YOUTH.

"St. Louis, June 10t, 1844.

"To the Managers: Gentlemen,—A young man in this city, at the age of 20, possessing a classical education, who has paid much attention to the cultivation of the rhetoric art, and has quite a taste for the Dramatic Profession, is desirous of connecting himself with a Theatrical Company, and would Hereby beg leave to ask on what terms, if at all, you would receive him into your Company now in St. Louis.

"A letter addressed 'Don Letrande,' and dropped into the Post Office to day or on Monday would be seasonably Received.

"Very Respectfully."

Probably "Don Letrande" got no answer, as the committee paid no attention to anonymous communications.

A PEARL NOT TO BE CAST AWAY.

"New York, May 25, 1837.

"Mr. Smith: Dear Sir,—Observing an advertisement of yours in the New York Spirit of Times, stating you should be in New York in August, to make professional engagements. Having a great desire to become a performer, and no means to gratify that desire—my friends, although giving their consent, withholding their aid (which is much more desirable than their consent). In this predicament I am forced to apply to you. I have no doubt that if I were to apply to any of our enterprising managers in this city, I should receive their immediate support, nay, I have almost been told so, that by one gentleman, the Manager of the N******l Theatre, but in accordance with the wishes of my friends, I have consented not to make an appearance in this city, and consequently the only means left was to apply to you. I am 14 years of age, and already perfect in the following parts: Richard III., Bertram, Shylock, Hamlet, Rolla, Othello, Carwin, and Beverly, in the domestic play of the Gamester (Ruined), and have been told by several that my conception of these parts was extremely correct, and with a person, as I am told; well adapted to the stage. Should you, however, think this a mere boyish whim, you will see the inconsistency of that in my having persevered in my parts, and at a time when I had but two hours leisure in a day. At the time when Edwin Forrest made his first appearance, he was but a few years older than myself, and if I have been correctly informed, his first prospects were no better than mine. Should you think favorably of it, the terms which I propose are these: the dresses to be found by you, the expences to Mobile or St. Louis to be at my expence, if I should succeed to perform for you (for the privilege and the dresses), one month from the night of my first appearance; should I not succeed, you will be no loser, as I can give security for the amount of the dresses and the expences of the theatre for one night. Do not too hastily decide against me, for perhaps in so doing you throw a pearl away. At all events let me receive an answer, stating what time you shall be in New York, and if I shall call on you. If the terms are not acceptable to your ideas, you can make them so on your arrival in New York.

"You will please direct your answer to Thomas R. Hammond, New York, and be sure at least to answer it, for if you do not answer it, I shall think you have not received it, and write to you again.

"'Not worse the fruit that in the wilderness the blossom blows.'

"Yours Very Respectfully,

"Thomas R. Hammond."

I fear Mr. Hammond was not favored with an answer, and that he was obliged to "blow" on in the wilderness, instead of being transplanted to the sunny South.

A DEMOCRATIC GRADUATE OF S. C. COLLEGE APPLIES.

"New Orleans, 12th Feb., 1843.

"Mr. Smith: Sir,—In 1836 I graduated in the South Carolina College, delivered the anniversary oration of the Clasiosophic Society, and acquitted myself with credit, at least my friends were partial enough to say with applause. I commenced the study of the law, was admitted to practice, located myself in Georgia, where I soon obtained business, more than enough to support me; I am in your city upon professional business. But throughout the whole of my life, from my earliest recollection to the present time I have been haunted with a sort of idiosyncracy, or rather monomania for the stage. I have reasoned with myself, and have a thousand times resolved to conquer my propensity, but am unable. It grows with my growth, and strengthens with my strength. My prospects are good, my business is on the average. I was nominated by the Democratic party as a candidate for the State Legislature, ran ahead of my party by 31 votes, and was beaten but 7 in a strong Whig county. Yet I am willing to forego every thing, fortune, friends, ambition, and devote myself entirely to the stage. Will you accept my services? If yea, have printed on your small bills 'the services of A. B. are accepted'—if nay, destroy this."

"A. B." was not notified in the small bill, and it will be seen "this" was not destroyed.

BROTHER TOM WANTS TO PLAY ROLLO.

"New Orleans, 22d January, '51.

"DEAR BROTHER SOL,—I much regret I have not time at my disposal to see you; yet time runs. Golden locked and hoary headed Time gives me no respite, so light of foot and swift of wing is he or she, by the which gender Sol, doctors disagree; however, we will not, but settle it, to our mutual satisfaction, over a big bellied bottle, some of these dull, rainy nights, when you, Sol, have the blues, and I have the blacks, or if you please the yellows.

"Well, back to old, young and middle-aged Time, I was on the point of saying, fast man, as I am, and you well know that is not what our mamma's washed clothes with.

"In plain, downright, flat footed, democratic way of speaking, I am compelled to leave the city to-day, yes, to-day; business honor requires demands, and nothing but honor first and then a woman; wo-man could serve us now.

"Next Saturday night, please heaven, stages, hacks and steamboats, I will be here to act the character of Rollo, in Pizarò. You Sol, must act the character of Lascasses, for you love 'to hear and to repeat the heroes name.' The deil will let it go.

"Well, now for the ladies, heaven ever bless them. You see Sol I have put them last, last, where they should be, for you know I don't like common things or common notions, or moreover, I put the ladies last, because you know Sol, or I do, that about the last terestial thoughts, my brain, big as it is, will contain, will be relative to a pretty foot and well and gently swelling l—g, pardon, I can't say it.

"Julia must act Elvira, and who Cora, you are ready to ask, well I will tell you, not that I love to hear and to repeat the name, for I own on a time, no matter or when, would get nervous at the very sound of school ——, now that day is past and nerves case hardened sinner. The Count must act Pizaro; that disbursed lover, last on, must act (or play, a better word) rub brackets out, Alonzo; other characters dispose of as you please.

"Well Sol you see I have used the imperative mood which is the only sensible one.

"My object is, 1st the ladies, now 1st their benefit, then to benefit you Sol, then to benefit the Saint Charles theatre.

"And lastly making generally, and the good people of this famous city particularly.

"That night will be my first and last appearance, then Sol you and me will write a play that will pay you and the ladies well in your green old ages.

"It will be 'Tragic Comedy,' you Sol the tragical of course, and in after years Sol you and the ladies will visit my Bachelors (God of Heaven, in tears) Domicil, sea girt, lashed by the tempest, lulled by the billows.

"I send the ladies a small memento and ask in return, for I must have some-thing in return make Rollo a belt, red silk bound green mockasins, consider as if he walked—waded—in the battle field. The balance of his person he will take care of himself.

"You will see nothing of Rollo until about the time he enters the stage, unless you wish otherwise, if so address A. B. C. in Post Office, Saturday eve. from your bro., TOM.

"P.S.—I never overlook letters."

"Brother Tom," whoever he was, received no encouragement from the committee, and the St. Charles audience lost the opportunity of witnessing his "first and last appearance."

There are numerous letters from females—generally young girls—for *they* (the blessed creatures!) are not more exempt from stage madness than young men; indeed, when they are attacked, it is a hard matter to effect a cure; but they require different treatment. The committee, in not a single instance, "sat" upon *their* applications. One of the managers, in *propria personæ*, attended to their cases, consequently none of their letters can appear here.

I will now vary the scene a little by giving the complaint of a father for taking away the "carackter" of his daughter.

LETTER OF COMPLAINT.

"Mobele, Decem. 11th, 1837.

"SIR,—It is with regret to see, things sim to torn out so much to my surprais, and dissatisfaction instad of hoping to mit with som advansmunt for my girl, the only indusmant, what ever maid me com in to your establismant, of taking a situvation, you plaged your word as a man of principall, you would ancarug her, mor so then circomstances would permit at St. Louis, but instad of this, she has bin taken from the only carackter in which you ever gave her an opertunety to display to som advantage, and in which she ganed the generall aprobation of the Ordians; Is it just! is it far! I askt you, to tak the only shanc out hur hands so barburusly and give it to an other, a big wommen, who has allrady the favours and good opinnion of the peple— by havens She is wiping could you stand by camly lik Gentleman of principhall, and sufer this apression, it was not caust by neglians, on hur part not to com suner, for the botte with which she cam was ditand by axcidances, and not her falt, and the moment she arifet she appearet before you. the cast is not yet in the peapers, and I intret for hur sak you will compermis with Mis Petry.

"I am with all due restect your humble

"I HENNINGS."

I do not remember what the result of this touching complaint was, but think it likely we listened to reason, and entered into a "compermis with Mis Petry."

AN EMBRYO STAR—GOOD TERMS TO BEGIN WITH.

"Cincinnati, August 11, 1844.

"SOL. SMITH, ESQ.: SIR,—I have just played Hamlet in the American Theatre, New Orleans, for a charitable benefit, with a success unprecedented. Mr. Kendall, of the Picayune, said he had never seen such acting! and others have expressed themselves the same way. I have concluded to play 6 nights here. Terms, same as Macready's—½ receipts. I am only afraid your company can not support me.

"I shall play 12 nights with you at the St. Charles, New Orleans, next season. Terms the same. I am certain of attracting $1200 each night, so you will make a good thing of it.

"I want to settle the nights here immediately. Those in New Orleans we can arrange hereafter.

"A line from you, appointing an interview for casting the pieces, is desirable.

"Yours Respectfully, M—— B——

"P.S.—I open in Hamlet. I shall require the lady who plays the Queen to be sent to my room, to be taught the business, which is very particular as I do it."

The answer to the above *modest* letter was in the following words:

"Cincinnati Theatre, Aug. 11, 1844.

"To M—— B——, Esq.

"Sir,—Your favor of this date is received. In regard to your acting in Cincinnati, it is impossible, as the company is quite incompetent to 'support' you. It was as much as they could do to support Macready and Forrest; I feel certain they would fail when put in competition with such acting as yours, the like of which has not been seen by that experienced critic, Mr. Kendall; besides, our Queen Gertrude, we feel quite sure, would object to visiting your room for the purpose of being taught business by you.

"As to New Orleans, there being time to remodel our company for such an occasion, I intend to accept the proffer of your services for the 12 nights mentioned (the time to be fixed hereafter), only varying the terms a little, or, rather, changing the mode of settlement, thus: As I understand you are a thriving and prosperous merchant in the Crescent City, you can pay in cash, or give us a Note, satisfactorily indorsed, for $7200, our share of the $1200 per night you are sure to draw, and we resign to you the whole receipts for the 12 nights you play. Respectfully yours, Sol. Smith."

No engagement came out of this correspondence; but the candidate for starring honors became so importunate in reference to the proposed immediate Cincinnati engagement, it was thought advisable to hand him over to the committee, who, after giving him a hearing in *Shylock*, reported adversely to his claims. But the committee must have erred in judgment on this occasion, for see what celebrity the rejected individual has achieved since! In England, Ireland, Scotland, California, and Australia, to say nothing of the Atlantic States, the great West, and the South of this part of the world, the people all agree with the judgment pronounced by G. W. Kendall—*they have never seen such acting* by any other individual—never! He has become, *par excellence*, "*the* eminent tragedian" (see bills), and he plays *Hamlet and the game of poker* with "great success" wherever he goes—except *here*—exemplifying in a very marked manner the true policy of an actor, which undoubtedly is to begin at the *top* instead of at the *bottom* of the ladder. This is the tragedian who produced such effects in rehearsing Macbeth at a Boston theatre that a countryman ran up the steps and through the front door, asking the sweeper *if there was a dog-fight going on!* and who elicited from a critic in this city who witnessed one of his stage spasms in the third act of Othello, the remark that the audience were in doubt whether he should be hissed or subjected to the operation of phlebotomy.

The late John S. Robb (himself a member) gave the following account (in a California paper which he edited in 1854) of the proceedings at *one* of the meetings of the committee:

"ST. LOUIS DRAMATIC BOARD.

"BY SOLITAIRE.

"Every body has heard of Sol Smith, the well known theatrical manager; well, as he has retired from the profession now, we may be permitted to briefly describe an association or critical board of which he was then father and founder. While in St. Louis, during the summer campaign of his company, our friend Sol was very much troubled by stage-struck youths, and, indeed, infatuated middle age, who desired to strut in spangles upon the boards. The manager, occupied by his multifarious duties as lawyer, city councilman, school director, etc., had not that time to devote to the dramatic part of the business which he wished, or which was necessary, particularly in the examination of stage aspirants; he therefore organized a 'Dramatic Board' to assist him.

"One of the rules of the Board, and one which required much effort to observe, was, that no member, on pain of expulsion, should laugh while it was in session. The last examination it was our privilege to be present at was deeply interesting. We had a fat, big-headed policeman to examine, who, from being on duty in the theatre, had imbibed a passion for the stage. I remember that, upon the occasion named, poor Dan Marble—one of the best-hearted men and gifted actors of the American stage—officiated as a member of the board. A magistrate, famous for the paucity of his intellect, was also an invited member of the board. From the invitation sent to the latter, he was led to believe that the members of the board, appreciating his literary acquirements and critical ability, had sent for him to help them out of some difficult case.

"The board having been called to order, the rules read, the theatrical victim was admitted, and without mercy put through one of the strangest examinations that ever bothered the head of a Thespian aspirant. His store of passages from Shakspeare, including all the tragedies, his Norval, his Sir Giles Overreach, and his Sir Edward Mortimer, were each listened to, and, with most serious countenance, commented upon. Sol, the president, listened and looked with absorbing intensity, and his long face remained immovable as marble. We don't mean DAN Marble, for he snorted right out, and was forthwith expelled. When we heard Dan's Yankee 'he-ah! he-ah!' as he retreated down the stairs, it was with difficulty any of us could keep a straight face.

"After Dan's exit, Sol put the policeman through a series of attitudes, during which a very lively discussion was going on as to the correctness of them. The self-satisfied candidate was placed in an advancing posture, with one arm extended, his head fixed in a most unnatural position one side, his eyebrows brought down in a most terrible frown, his mouth twisted into a scathing sneer, while his breast was kept heaving with supposed passion; and from this he was transposed to an attitude of supplication. This was the most ludicrous of all the efforts made in the examining chamber. The attempt of our victim to look imploring was very much like the expression a human being would put on if receiving some violent assault in the rear. His eyes rolled upward, his mouth open, and his face curled like a bad boy's about to receive a licking, was a picture of comic anguish.

"Sol now proposed that we should retire to the stage for the final ceremony, where the candidate was expected to go through a course of motions in costume, which costume was tin armor! Being duly incased therein, he was again put through a series of armed positions; now with the spear, again with the battle-axe, and then with sword and shield. To familiarize him with the stage, and make him capable of finding his adversary or his mistress upon it when darkened, the visor of his helmet was closed, and over its bars a piece of leather was fastened, which completely blindfolded our candidate. In this fix he was rushed about the stage: now charging here, again cautiously stealing along there; again going through a warrior's dying scene, in which he is feeling about for the foe, who has stabbed him in the dark; and then he would be sent to delivering a burst of passion from Romeo and Juliet.

"The final trial was proposed by Sol, after he had expressed commendation on those past. It was represented to the candidate that rushing off the scene properly was a great feature of tragedy, and (like all aspirants), as he desired more particularly to make that his line of business, it was necessary that he should learn to rush off. It was farther represented to him that, carried away by the excitement of the piece, he was liable to run against the scenery, and mar the effectiveness of an entire scene just at what should be its triumphant close, and therefore the profession had adopted the practice of learning to rush off blindfolded, as then, no matter what the actor's state of excitement might be, he being practiced, could without difficulty avoid the scenery. This being fully understood by the novice, he was placed in his position, his visor was closed, and he was then told to take a Richard the Third attitude, as if charging upon Richmond's forces; and Sol, taking position, gave the signal:

"'Upon 'em—charge!'

"The candidate rushed forward, a ring like a tin pan concussion followed, and the next moment the man in armor recoiled from the side-scenes, and fell sprawling on his nether extremity about the centre of the stage. His first desire was to see what he had encountered; but the force of the collision having driven the rim of the tin helmet over his ears, he was, like the dog with his head in the pitcher of milk, imprisoned. The member who held the upright board in the entrance between the scenes, which the policeman rushed headforemost against, laying it quietly down, with the rest of us exhibited commendable zeal in trying to release the candidate from his vile durance. After the practical jokes he had submitted to, it may be guessed that he had a pair of EARS it was not easy to release! We effected it, however, and, having relieved him from his armor, we conducted him up to the room where he was first introduced, and here the manager, Sol. Smith, Esq., addressed him in very flattering terms, commented on his correct reading of many passages, and advised a farther study of the rushing-off movement.

"Sol then called upon the justice to say a few words to the aspirant. The latter, who had not seen the 'board' part of the above-mentioned scene because of his position on the stage, and who believed the whole affair to be a serious preparatory lesson to fit the would-be actor for the profession, delivered a most incoherent echo of the manager's speech, mingled with expressions such as 'great Bard of Avon,' 'immortal Shakspeare,' 'great responsibility resting upon those who choose the great profession of being the great chroniclers of the time,' etc. In short, it was a GOOD speech for a brief one.

"The candidate was now allowed to depart, and Sol commenced enacting the last scene of our comedy. Taking from an antique trunk in his room an old three-cornered stage hat, he presented it to the magistrate as an acknowledgment of the high estimation in which the Dramatic Board held his literary critical ability. The said venerable old tile was represented to be the last one that ever the patriot and sage, Dr. Franklin, wore. The literary justice, in a perfect paroxysm of pleasure, pressed the black cockade upon this relic to his bosom, declared it the happiest day of his life, and vowed that his posterity should preserve it to 'the last syllable of recorded time.'

"The board now adjourned, but we are under the impression that both candidate and the justice are ignorant to this moment of the fact that all stage-struck heroes who came before our association had to butt the 'dramatic board' which stood between the scenes. The last time we saw Manager Sol, he was sitting in his office at the St. Charles Theatre, complacently listening to a Spaniard reading a blank-verse poem, written in English by himself, which the Castilian was reciting in the worst English we have ever heard."

New plays submitted to the management of course received due attention, but I must say that "very few and far between" were the instances of acceptance. Generally the veriest trash constituted the staple offered, and this trash was referred to the committee.

I give here the title, *dramatis personæ*, and one scene—and that's enough—of a play written by one Mr. Davis, of Mobile, who waited eight years for a report from the committee, and then was allowed, on giving bonds, to take a copy of it for transmission to the Theatre Royal, Drury Lane, where he felt quite sure it would be accepted and played at once:

THE COTAGER'S GRANDSON,

OR THE

MURDERD BRUTHER

AND

GOST OF THE MURDERD COUNTISS.

A Orijenel Dramy in three Acts.

(COPPY WRIGHT SKURED.)

NAMES OF CARIOTERS.

Count Elmore, disguised as a Rober.
Count Askins, a Yusurper.
Williamson & Harrison, the Count's Confidence.
Cotager.
Thomas, supposed to be the Cotager's Son.
Duncan, a fisherman.
Jaquise, a Rober.
Grome.
Gost.
Jane, the Cotager's Wife.
Lucy, the dames dotter.
The bride.
Solgers & servants by Supernumeraries and Knumerus Oxhilliraries.

ACT THIRD—SCENE FIRST.

[A Room and A Castle. Count Askins sitting at a table and reading a Book.]

Count Askins raising from his seat and laing a book on a table, Who with in there (enters servant) My lord did you call Yes is Williamson returned yet servant speaking no my lord not yet should any strangers come show them up begone Sir (exhert servant) Count geting up and walking the floor it is it must be and it shall be this must go in force raising his hand nocking on the table it must be and shall be this boy once in my power then all will be saved it must be the boy and he must die villan as I am my villany must not stop here the boy that I saw at the cottage before a nother day must be in my power then powers I defy the and all the can do villan I am and villan I will be until I am satisfied (the doors opens carefully) Enters the Gost a dagger in his right hand with the four finger of the left hand pointing to her bleding stab in her side noble count thou art not satisfied with murdering she that harmed the not but now thee seaks to the life him thou noist not. Noble Count night time is short the count folling on his knees and clasping his hand together most noble and ginerous specter what thou wants what is it that I shall do name it were it in the power of man it shall be done then my requist this you you shall give over they plaus with glaturing they vangence with innocente bloud count speaking thy requist will be as thou wishes it but leve me Gost speaking Rise then tyrant Count raising Gost before forty-eight hours thou shalt be as I am moldering in the dust Count agitated thou saidst I shall die. Gost speaking Yes thou shalt die by the hand of him thou triest to murder he shall revenge his murdered mother No Count Call for they redemer for murcey time is short for he is the only one that can give murcey on the farewell we mete again not in this world but before the Juge of all Juges on hight so farewell repent for they time is short, farewell (exhert Gost) Count agitated O havens that I had not been born to come to this. Exhert Count Sloe moosick.

In the summer of 1841, which was an extremely dull one in our business, among the numerous candidates for theatrical honors, wishing to learn the "trade, art, and mystery" of acting, came one morning a weak, trembling, peaked-nosed individual, who looked as though a tolerable breeze would blow him to pieces. With a hesitating, tender voice, he asked to see the "boss of the show." I instantly discovered a "subject" for the committee, and asked him, in a loud voice, his name.

"Macumber — Jeemes Macumber," he answered, his knees fairly knocking together when he discovered who it was that addressed him.

"What canst thou do?" I inquired.

After a moment's hesitation, and making two or three vain attempts to swallow something, he gasped twice, and got out this answer: "I can speak orations, and I *think* I could learn to act out plays in a short time."

"Speak orations? What orations canst thou speak?"

"Mark Antony's, John Quincy Adams's Fourth of July, Hannibal's Address to his Army, Patrick Henry's Give me Liberty or Give me Death, Clay's speech on the Declaration of War, Washington's Farewell, Webster's Union Speech, Hayne's—"

"Stop!" I cried; "enough—*more* than enough. And you wish to speak these orations on the stage?"

"Ye-es," he answered; "I am told that I can make heaps of money by speaking 'em."

"Are you aware, Mr. Macumber, that before being allowed to step upon the sacred precincts of the stage, you will be obliged to undergo an examination, and be put through certain ceremonies by a committee?" This question I asked in a very solemn manner, of course, and his answer was equally solemn. With tears in his eyes, he answered,

"I—I don't mind, I don't, *what* ceremonies I go through; I am ready and willin'."

"Very well," I said. "Now take off your hat and kneel down." And down he went upon his marrow-bones, hat in hand, without the least hesitation. I then administered a solemn obligation to the candidate, which bound him by the shade of Shakspeare, the memory of Ben Jonson, and his sacred honor, not to reveal any thing which should transpire during his initiation into the mysteries of the drama. [The Sons of Malta, Know-Nothings, Druids, Mormons, Sons of Temperance, all, I suppose, founded upon the ceremonies of this committee, can form a tolerable idea of the "obligation," without a reprint of the same—they are all pretty nearly alike.] Macumber subscribed cheerfully to every thing, kissed the hilt of the Maltese sword held out to him, and, on a signal given, rose to his feet.

"Having taken the preliminary obligation, Jeemes, you will go to your place of sojourn and refresh your memory by reading over the Fourth of July Address of Adams, the younger of that name; refresh your body by sleep, and to-morrow morning, as the Cathedral clock strikes the hour of nine, you will present yourself at the second vestibule door, counting from the south, of this edifice, where you will be received by the committee. Now, Jeemes, begone!"

And he *was* gone—off like a flash.

It was a little doubtful in my mind whether he would return or not. However, as there were several other candidates waiting a hearing, an order was issued through the "Reveille" for an assemblage of the committee the next morning at a quarter before nine. As I passed into the theatre just before the appointed time, I saw our man standing at the door designated. Quickly informing the committee of what was the order of the day, all was soon ready for the reception. The Cathedral clock began to strike, and between the fourth and fifth strokes the door was suddenly opened, the candidate seized by the sergeant-at-arms, drawn quickly within the vestibule, *blindfolded*, and— * * *

The reader will not expect a full account of the "secret ceremonies" which followed. It is sufficient to be informed that Macumber demeaned himself most manfully, and that the trap-doors, pulleys, and travelers worked well; the thunder, lightning, rain, and blue-lights were all in fine order. The candidate was dismissed at a little after 10 o'clock, with directions to present himself the next morning at the same time and place, which directions he scrupulously obeyed. After three courses of training, he was pronounced ready and capable of *appearing before the public.* This was an entirely new course of policy, adopted by the committee in consideration of the great merits of the candidate, the almost intolerable warmth of the weather, and the "beggarly account of empty boxes" nightly exhibited at the theatre.

The first appearance of Macumber was duly heralded by the press (nearly all the editors being members of the committee), and the Fourth of July Oration of Adams chosen for the occasion. Proper scenery and costumes were selected, and, at the appointed time, Macumber, strictly guarded by the sergeant-at-arms, was stationed back of a *cave flat*, which, at a given signal, opened, and the debutant appeared bodily in the presence of the audience, with a bound, amid tremendous flashes of lightning, the flat instantly closing behind him—and *such* an appearance as he made! Dressed in a suit of regimentals "a world too wide," and considerably too long for him, after the manner of Col. Pluck or Bombastes Furioso, flourishing a sabre as long as himself, Macumber stood in an attitude of stern defiance (according to instructions) until the awful yells and shouts which greeted him had in some degree subsided; then, sheathing his sword with a clang, he strutted to the front, made three bows or salaams in the Turkish fashion, gave a stamp with his right foot, and proceeded with the oration, every word of which he spoke, to the very last line, receiving abundance of applause during its delivery from the committee-men stationed in front, as well as from the general audience, all seeming, after a little while, to enter into the "fun of the thing." At the conclusion of the speech, according to orders, the orator placed himself upon a certain place previously chalked out for him, drew his immense sword, and, poising it in the way of a salute, *was let down through a trap*, and so disappeared, a sudden flash of lightning flaming up through the opening in the stage. Cries of "*encore!*" were now heard from all parts of the house, mixed with cries of "Macumber! Macumber!" The will of the public evidently was that the orator should come forward and receive its congratulations on his decided success. This call not having been anticipated—calls were not so common *then* as they are now—no provision had been made for getting him out of the cellar except by means of the very trap which let him down; so an order was hastily transmitted through the speaking-trumpet to place him upon the trap, and to caution him to hold himself firm and steady. All being ready, the signal was given for the trap to rise quickly, when Macumber was projected through the stage and shot up into the air at least two yards! The brave fellow, however, lit upon his feet, and resumed that same defiant attitude, with sword drawn, which had brought down such bursts of applause on his appearance through the flats. After stamping two or three times, and bowing low to the audience, he took his stand upon the chalked square, and was again lowered out of sight.

The newspapers next day teemed with the success achieved by the new-comer, and soon the Eastern papers took up the strain, remarking that "a new tragedian was making a great sensation at St. Louis."

The next effort of Macumber was in "Hannibal's Address to his Army." His appearance this time was in what is called a boat carriage—a board on small wheels, to which the profile of a boat is usually fastened, run upon the floor, but concealed from the audience by a ground or water piece, giving the boat an appearance of gliding through the water. Standing upon this board, the orator was drawn on, appearing to slide or skate along upon the painted water. When in the centre of the stage he jumped out, and, after going through the defiant attitude and requisite number of stamps, proceeded with his oration, which was received by a larger audience than the one of the night before, and with equal enthusiasm. At the conclusion, instead of going down a trap, he was taken up in the car which is used in MACBETH for carrying up Mrs. *Hecate;* and so on through the week, until all the orations in the programme had been spoken by the bold Macumber, changing nightly the manner of his entrance and exit, and also, after his second night, his costume. An account of the week's proceedings would be tedious; enough has been told to convince the reader that we had a good deal of amusement, and, perhaps, that we carried the joke too far, especially in permitting the candidate to *go before the public.* I think it *was* a strong draw upon the good-nature of our audiences; but it was such a dull time, *something* had to be done to wake up the people, and our committee-men felt justified in treating themselves to a hearty laugh, even at the expense of strict dramatic propriety—*and they did*, at the same time permitting (for once) all outside jokers to participate.

After his performance each night, we seated Macumber in one of the private boxes, where, surrounded by guards, he received deputations from outside committee-men. One night I remember a visit he received from the venerable Charles Keemle, who, together with another equally worthy citizen (a great proficient in set-back euchre), and ten others, representing themselves to be the mayor and aldermen of the city, presented a petition, which was immediately granted, that the Fourth of July should be postponed a week or two, in consequence of the inclemency of the weather!

At the end of the week a warrant was made out in due form for the sum of twelve dollars, and Macumber (always accompanied by the sergeant-at-arms) was told to present it for payment to the lord high treasurer, whom he would know by his being the *ugliest man* he should find in the room where he was to be conducted. It happened the whole company, orchestra and all, were engaged in the greenroom, rehearsing the burlesque opera of DON GIOVANNI. Macumber, on looking round when the bandage was removed from his eyes, without the least hesitation kneeled down and presented the warrant to my old leader, Carl Mueller, who solemnly paid him the money in currency. Mac was again blindfolded and conducted to the committee-room, where, another obligation of secrecy being administered, he was dismissed. I have not heard of or from him since. The person who so efficiently performed the arduous duties of sergeant-at-arms during the Macumber engagement was "Tom, the Curtain Man," of whom mention is made in another portion of this volume. By the way, I haven't seen Tom for several years.

During the season of 1844, in Cincinnati, the committee had considerable business on hand.

A member of the medical profession was stage-struck, and applied for an opportunity to appear as *Hamlet.* Being referred to the committee, he had a private hearing one afternoon, old Logan, Falvy Williams, and myself constituting a quorum on that occasion. In the ghost scene the candidate (as *Hamlet*) was instructed in the "start" for at least an hour, the various committee-men acting alternately as the ghost. In the play scene the candidate was advised to *sing* a portion of the text, referring to *Hamlet's* mention of the "pious chanson." He went through to the end, but we could see that about the time he exclaimed

"A rat! Dead for a ducat!"

he began to smell one. The sitting was closed, and the candidate dismissed with the usual obligations of secrecy; but we all felt we had not done with that chap, and, sure enough, in an hour or two the following letter was handed in:

"Cincinnati, 21 June.

"MR. SOL. SMITH: SIR, — Agreeable to appointment, I met with pleasure your honorable Committee, but must confess (and not without shame) I retired with perfect disgust and amediately resolved on giving you amediate notice as to my utter contempt of such treatment and henceforth tak no further notice of the matter. I am somewhat suprised that your power of conception would have suffered you to make sutch a pitiful attempt to make a wanton of one who had imposed uter confidece in you.

"You and your Committee did not exhibit quite skill enough to surpress my disagreable aprehensions—as swearing in one of your hon. body at the out side the door—'knoted and combined locks'—noted down by the chairman of the Committee—opinions as the complixion of the Germans & Danes with french pronunciation —pious chasaw!—by Mr. W—— new and wonderful afect produced by singing certain poetry unanimously concured in—bah—booh—skat—perfect failure gent.

"Sol you enforced secrecy upon me in this mater—I have and will observe to the letter—while the efect produced by a failure mining all all within infects unseen.

"J. E.—The Committee who as you say are sworn to secrecy therefore I need not fear their ill report els I should prefer a bad epitaph.

"Your —— Dupe, HAMLET.

"N.B.—Any response to this through the P. Office shall be cheerfuly & confidentialy regarded. H.

"'Why have you used me thus, I loved you ever.'
"—Shaks."

ANSWER.

"Committee-room, Cincinnati Theatre,
"June 22, 1844.

"DEAR SIR,—Your note of yesterday is received, and we hasten to say that your determination to 'go no farther' is unanimously approved of by the committee.

"The proceedings of yesterday were such as are usual on such occasions, and you certainly passed through the ordeal with considerable credit to yourself. It is but justice to say that, notwithstanding the disadvantage of a CHANGE OF GHOSTS, we have never seen a novice acquit himself so well as you did.

"We must insist that we did no more than our duty in giving you the proper pronunciation of the FRENCH WORDS; and our 'failure' to give the 'original music' of the 'pious chanson' must be attributed to the fact that the members of the committee do not profess or possess very splendid vocal powers.

"We close this reply to your note by copying a resolution adopted unanimously by the committee:

"'*Resolved*, That the injunction of secrecy on the proceedings of Friday, June 21, be made PERPETUAL, and the candidate for histrionic honors be congratulated upon his fortunate escape.'

"Wishing you every success, in whatever profession you may think proper to adopt,

"We remain yours very truly,
"THE COMMITTEE."

So far as I know, we, in this instance, effected a *perfect cure*.

At a sitting in New Orleans, we were "putting through" a candidate in RICHARD THE THIRD, when, just as he started from his couch in the last scene, exclaiming

"Give me another horse," etc.,

a little fiste of a dog flew at him, and, seizing on the seat of his trowsers, hung there until taken off by his master, who was acting at the time as sergeant-at-arms. Of course the would-be tragedian was required to try the scene over again and again, but every time that confounded dog *would* get loose and attack him in the rear! I have no doubt he had been trained to it. At least six times he went to sleep, and old Jack Greene, as the ghost of *Henry VI.*, with a segar in his mouth, repeated the line,

"Wake, Richard, awake! to guilty minds a terrible example!"

and *Richard* every time bounded from his couch, flourishing his sword, and, staggering toward the foot-lights, exclaimed,

"Give me another horse! Bind up my wounds—here's that d—d dog again; CAN'T he be tied?"

The rehearsal was at last suspended—the dog *couldn't* be kept out of the fray.

These few instances of the "proceedings" of the committee must suffice. There are many living lay members in St. Louis who have participated in the meetings at the N. W. corner of Third and Olive Streets, up stairs, and whose sides must occasionally shake while recalling the ludicrous scenes enacted, where the collector of customs now so seriously carries on the business of the general government.

I close this very "loose" report of the proceedings of the "Committee on Authors and Actors" by giving a "pome" which I considered too good to be inserted under the proper date (1837) with the other "Rejected Addresses," written in competition for the prize of $100 offered for the best poetic address, to be spoken at the opening of the New St. Louis Theatre. I give it exactly as written.

ADDRESS TO THE NEW ST. LOUIS THEATRE—ON THE POWER OF EDUCATION.

BY JOHN S. H——, HOWARD COUNTY, MO.

[Respectfully referred by the Committee of Literary Gentlemen to the Committee on Authors and Amateurs.]

O, what a dark, and direful scene, bruded o'er the world! [furled:
Before the glorious light of Education was un-
And diffused with splendour, its golden ray;
With grandeur; converting night to peaceful day.

Which erected on the bosom of chaos a light,
Which contributes to man, a store of sublime delight:
Has untwined the fetters in which he was bound:
And scattered the clouds of ignorance, that hung around. [on every virtue,
Ignorance joined with her sister vice; frowned
And on sweet innocence, her imperious falchion drew. [act,
Which distressfully imprisoned every virtuous
And made the world, with envy and vice compact.
But now, O! now! print the boon of Heaven is diffused; [perused;
And knowledge by Peasants, as well as Princes
The hills rejoice, the plains proclaim peace,
The reign of ignorance, bigotry, and superstition cease. [aside,
All nations, have those rude obstacles thrown
Which, with their intelligence had so long vied:
Ere (Education,) the great fountain of light ushered on,
Ere virtue, her moral, hallowed precepts won.
The prize,* so long fought for, out of peril has arose, [repose,
And on the bosom, of fair Columbia shall ever
Until the last trump, the catastrophe of time shall propose.
This land, fair Columbia's pleasant plains,
Was beat beat by great solitude's awful rains:
And where freedom's pallace, now arises above ire, [tire:
Unaccompanied with disgrace, robed in holy at-
Was a barren wilderness, in space unexplored;
Before the sublime art (education,) upon us poured,
Its briliant ray, the dawn of purity and light;
Which snaches from the hand of ignorance, all might. [the mind,
No more shall the blubbers of ignorance choke
Nor blindness, nor sorrows, veil the sight of mankind; [free,
Come bounteous era! when mankind shall all be
And march to the Altar of union and liberty;
See the Ark of ignorance, and slavery scud away.
Behold the Squadron of right, and justice, arives to-day.
Through the veil of ignorance to smell the flower, [power;
That now smiles on the summet of fame and
That now gilds, and decks liberties lofty tower.
Not by gems of silver, and gold, we were brought [wrought,
For dignity, and eminence education has
And by education, philosophy we are taught.
Yes, education more valuable than rubies, far,
A pharos to our feet; to our minds a gilding star.

* Aluding to education.

Through boundless space we measure the commets flight,
We see the Sun in his glory, the centre of might.
The moons silver orb; that gilds the horrors of night,
That spreads her twinkling beams So bright,
And in kind peace, enlightens this vast globe,
With beauty; and wraps it in one magnificent robe,
And Mercury's, heated, fervent, burning sphere
Too with Jubiter, and Saturn, on vast regions there, [petual blaze,
Mighty moons in splendour roll, and shed per-
Which shines to their great Author's name, eternal praise; [ly spied,
Are by the great tube, (Education,) complete-
Nor can one celestial form, from, the eye of the philosopher hide.
By that heavenly boon, the gift of Education,
We can fly through all ages, in the creation,
Live the lives of all antiquity; see Adam live;
See Socrates, and Plato, to youth advice give,
The siege of Troy, and Jerusalem is exposed to our view, [too.
The sentiments of Uclid, and Newton are ours
Misteries are unfurled, (that bane,) ignorance is sold,
For value, purer than gems of silver or gold;
Wisdom established in its stead, more radiant it shines, [mines.
Than the Diamonds ray, glitring in Golconda's

St. John the Baptist.

In 1843 or 1844 an Englishman died in St. Louis. When the effects of the deceased were looked into by the public administrator, there was found in the false bottom of one of his trunks an old picture, carefully rolled up, of St. John the Baptist and the Paschal Lamb—John holding a staff, in which was fastened a scroll bearing these words: "*Ecce Agnus Deo*" (Behold the Lamb of God). This picture was purchased at the administrator's sale by a Dr. Edgerly (now deceased), and from him purchased by me for the sum of fifty dollars. The truth of the matter was, I thought that picture of St. John might be an "original" by one of the old masters, it looked so old and dim, and, if so, would be worth several thousands of dollars, if not *pounds* to me, which suppositious dollars or pounds I stood very much in need of at the time; and my hopes were founded in part upon the following occurrence, which took place in St. Louis the year before my coming into possession of St. John:

At the corner of Second and Pine Street there

was on exhibition and sale a very fine collection of pictures. Some were purchased by such of our citizens as had any taste in, and appreciation of the Fine Arts; but the sales were few and far between. One morning an Englishman entered the room where the pictures were hanging, and, after carefully examining the collection, opened a business conversation with the proprietor—asked him several questions as to where he had picked up the various paintings, and the prices at which he held them. In the course of an hour the Englishman had selected six or eight of the pictures, and agreed on the price of each, the whole amounting to about two hundred dollars. "Make out your bill," said the stranger. The bill was made out and paid.

"Where will you have them sent?" asked the picture-dealer.

"Don't send them any where at present," replied the purchaser. "When I want them I will call for them;" and he stepped toward the door as if going. "By-the-by," said he, returning, "*this* one," pointing carelessly to one of his purchases—a small, ordinary-looking picture without a frame, which he had previously carefully examined, back and front—"*this* one, if you will please to hand it down to me, I will take *with* me, in my hand, to the hotel."

The picture was handed down, and the purchaser took it in his hand, which was observed to tremble a little as he received it, and his face grew suddenly pale. "What is the matter?" asked the picture-dealer; "are you not well?"

"Never better in my life," replied the stranger, accepting the chair and glass of water offered him by the kind picture-dealer. "Never better—never better," continued the stranger. "This is my picture now, is it not? I have purchased it and paid for it, I think." "Most decidedly you have," responded the other; "you paid me twenty-five dollars for it; it is well worth it, I think." "I think so too; it is a bargain which I am well satisfied with," said the purchaser. "I hope, sir, you are also satisfied with your *other* purchases," quoth the seller of pictures.

"Yes," replied the pale Englishman—"well satisfied with my whole morning's work. Listen: All the pictures I have purchased from you, except this which I hold in my hand, I make you a present of; I don't want them. They are yours as a free gift. *This*, and this only, I keep, and start with it to-morrow for England. *I have been in search of this little picture for four years.* I traced it to Spain, Portugal, South America, Mexico, and the United States, and have at last found it *and purchased it* here in St. Louis." "What! *that* little picture?" "Yes, *this* little picture; it is an 'original,' by Rubens, and I am to receive for it in England, by contract, £4000, besides my expenses during the four years I have been hunting it up!"

"Well," thought I, after hearing this strange story, "if that little picture, which sold for twenty-five dollars, was worth £4000 ($20,000), who knows but this St. John, which cost me $50, may be worth £8000?" At all events, I determined to find out *what* it was worth, and to do that it was necessary to send it to Italy, where there are records by which such questions can be decided. So, bethinking me of the friend of my boyhood, HIRAM POWERS, the great sculptor, I packed up my St. John and sent it to that gentleman at Florence, requesting him to ascertain, first, whether it was an "original," and by one of the "great masters;" secondly, if it *was* one of those immensely valuable works of art, to sell it at what it would bring—but not *less* than $20,000; and, thirdly, to remit the proceeds, after paying charges, to me in New Orleans, where I had debts which that sum would about wipe out.

In due time my St. John arrived at Florence, and my old friend promptly replied to me that —it was *not* an "original"—*not* by any "old master," nor by any known *young* master; in fact, it was a very ordinary picture, which *wanted cleaning and renovating*, and then *might* possibly be sold for twenty or thirty dollars! He also said, if I wanted it cleaned and renovated, I might send ten dollars to our mutual friend Mr. Nicholas Longworth, of Cincinnati, and he (Powers) would have the work done, and hold my St. John subject to my order.

Of course my hopes of a fortune from St. John were at an end; but believing in my heart it was a pretty good picture, notwithstanding its finding no place in the "records" of Florence, I wrote my early friend to have my St. John cleaned up, and to hold on to it until I should send or call for it. I sent the ten dollars to Mr. Longworth, and received the following reply:

Nicholas Longworth to Sol. Smith.

"Cincinnati, Nov. 17, 1845.

"DEAR SIR,—Your letter, inclosing one from our friend Powers, and ten dollars on his account, was duly received. The ten dollars I will hand over to his brother. As you are in the picture line, you should visit New York during the winter season. So little taste is there, in that city of low path streets, for the arts, that you may weekly buy pictures of all the great ancient painters, at public auction, at from fifty cents to ten dollars; and many of them so dimmed by age as to be invaluable. I shall be pleased to see you when next in Porkopolis. When

I last saw you, dyspepsia had deprived me of all my faculties but memory. Of what then passed I retain a perfect recollection. With regard, yours, N. LONGWORTH."

Time passed, and I supposed my saint was quietly reposing—he and the lamb, and staff, and scroll—in the warehouse of the great American sculptor. My debts were paid, and I didn't care so much about the $20,000 which I *didn't* get from Italy, but I always felt a desire to get my St. John back again. I *wanted* it.

In 1859 I wrote my friend Hiram that I was going to London, and requested him to send my St. John to me there, naming a certain address. I went to London, but St. John didn't meet me, nor did I get an answer to my letter—it had miscarried, I thought. On my return home I wrote again, for my St. John I was determined to have. In the spring of 1860 an answer came from my old friend, which—but read it. It is in the Quaker style:

Hiram Powers to Sol. Smith.

"SOLOMON,—Thou hast written to me two letters which I have not answered. I did, indeed, attempt an answer to the first, but it proved only a flash in the pan.

"Thou hast asked me in regard to thy picture of 'St. John and the Lamb.' Thou hast forgotten some things in relation to it. I told thee that thy picture was worthless, that thou hadst been deceived in it, but that I would send it back to thee, if desired.

"I have thy answer somewhere among my old papers, in which thou sayest that thou hast paid $10 (ten dollars) to our old friend Mr. Longworth to my account, but not, as thou now supposest, for 'cleaning and repairing,' but to reimburse me for the freight and other expenses on it to Florence, all of which I had paid. Thou saidst likewise that I need not send the picture back, but might do what I liked with it—so my memory serves me. The picture lay in one of my rooms for several years, when an officer of our navy happened to see it, and I told him the story of it.

"'I know Old Sol,' said he, 'and if you will let me have it, I will take it to St. Louis when I go home, and he shall be surprised with it.'

"I said, 'Take it,' and he cut it out of the stretcher, rolled it up, and that was the last I ever heard or saw of thy picture. I can not now recall the name of the officer, but remember that he was from St. Louis.

"Had it entered my head to suppose that thou wouldst ever require the picture back after so long a silence about it, and after telling me to do as I liked with it, or words to that effect, I should have preserved it with care.

"I read your melancholy history of poor Lemuel's death with great interest. The sad story was well told.

"I have just received the cards of Mrs. J. M. Field and Miss Kate Field, and shall call upon them as soon as possible.

"With many kind remembrances, I am truly your old friend, HIRAM POWERS.

"Florence, March 5, 1860."

There is the letter. My recollection and that of my friend do not exactly agree, and I dare say his is better than mine; but—ha! I got from this letter a clew by which I might get back my St. John, "worthless" though it may have been considered at Florence. An officer of the United States Navy had taken it, under a promise of surprising me by the delivery of it to me. Hiram didn't recollect the name of the officer, but he was "from St. Louis," he "knew Old Sol," and he was doubtless waiting the opportunity of "surprising" me by handing over the (to me) precious picture. I knew of but four officers of the Navy who hailed from St. Louis, to wit: Bent, Radford, Smith, and M'Gunnigle. I was *bent* on having the lost treasure, so I began my search by writing to Officer Bent as follows:

Sol. Smith to Silas Bent, U.S.N.

St. Louis, Mo., March 29, 1860.

Silas Bent, U.S.N.:

DEAR SIR,—"You see before you a man" who has lost a treasure which he hopes to recover through you. I must trouble you with a brief history.

In 1844 (no matter *how*) I became possessed of an old picture—*so* old that I thought and hoped it might be an "original" of one of the oldest masters—representing St. John the Baptist and the Paschal Lamb. In 1845 I sent it to my friend Hiram Powers, the eminent sculptor, at Florence, Italy, with the request that he would ascertain if my hopes were well founded, and, if so, sell it, and remit me the proceeds, be they $20,000, or $50,000, or any intermediate sum, as the case might be, and if found to be *only a copy*, or by a *young* master, to let me know. My friend wrote me on receiving the picture, and after a careful examination of records, that my St. John was not worth much; that he would, however, if I desired it, have it cleaned and renovated, at a cost of about ten dollars American money, which amount I could hand to our mutual friend Longworth, of Cincinnati. I wrote to my friend at Florence desiring him to have the cleaning and renovating done, and then to do what he liked with it, or whatever seemed best for my interest, but if he didn't sell it at some price, to hold on to it till sent or called for. In the spring of 1859 I wrote him to have my St. John packed in a box and sent to me in London, where I expected to be early in June. No St. John came to London, though I gave my address plainly. Soon after my return home, I wrote again to my friend at Florence about my St. John picture, for I wanted it, and was determined to have it, if possible. The answer came to the effect that an officer of the United States Navy, on seeing the picture in question, and learning the story of it, said he knew Old Sol, and would surprise him by delivering it to him at St. Louis when he went home, if Mr. P. would let him take it. He was allowed to take it to surprise me with, but I have seen nothing of him or St. John to this day. Mr. Powers in his letter says, "I can not now recall the name of the officer, but remember that he was from St. Louis."

Now, my dear fellow-townsman, *you* reside in St. Louis when you are at home, and I write to ask if *you* are the officer who so kindly undertook to surprise me with my St. John? Knowing you are a great lover of the fine arts, and have a fine collection of your own, I am tempted to believe you saw at a glance the beauties of my St. John (which the Florentines had failed to discover), and determined to restore that gem of art to its rightful owner, but have been prevented carrying out your benevolent intentions by the exigencies of the service, which may not have allowed you to visit your home (perhaps) since your return from Italy, and (if I am right in my hopes and expectations) you design to "surprise" me by a personal visit to my house, when you intend to hold out the aforesaid to my delighted gaze, and exclaim, "Here, Old Sol, is your St. John!"

I can only say I am anxious, willing, and waiting to be "surprised" in that way. I *want* to be surprised, and, if you can not do it, I beg of you to put me on the track of the officer of the Navy who can. Awaiting your answer, I am very truly yours, SOL. SMITH.

P.S.—I want my St. John!

In due course of mail came the following answer from Mr. Bent, who, it will be seen, entered into the spirit of the St. John inquiry in a style after my own heart:

Silas Bent, U. S. N., to Sol. Smith.

[Address of this letter: "Sol. Smith, Esq., or the man who is in search of his St. John the Baptist."]

"Washington, D. C., April 4, 1860.

"Sol. Smith, Esq., St. Louis, Mo.:

"DEAR SIR,—Your interesting favor of the 29th ult. is just received, and, under less equivocal circumstances, I should extremely regret my inability to give you the 'surprise' you so anxiously covet by the return to your fond hands of your 'St. John the Baptist.' I have a great veneration for the historical character of that worthy man, and not long since traveled all the way over the 'hard road to Jordan,' and waded and swam across the ford of Bethabāra expressly to get upon his tracks. The refreshing sensations I experienced from that matutinal bath were in a great measure owing, no doubt, to the holy influence thrown by him around that spot some nineteen hundred years ago.

"Subsequently, on my return to Italy, I called upon your 'old friend, Hiram Powers, the eminent sculptor, at Florence,' gave him my card, invited him on board the frigate Wabash, and on two several occasions had the pleasure of seeing not only himself, but his family, on board that ship, but he never said 'St. John the Baptist' nor Mr. Sol. Smith to me 'na'ry-a-time;' and if I said 'surprise' to him, it certainly was not in connection with either of those respectable names; and for the verity of which, I am sure your old friend Hiram will readily vouch.

"This was in 1859. I was in Italy also in 1851, and, like every 'true American,' called at the atelier of Mr. Powers, 'the eminent sculptor, at Florence,' but he was equally silent then as upon the more recent occasion in regard to your 'St. John the Baptist,' which you 'want' so badly.

"Therefore, my dear sir, you will have to look elsewhere for your lost 'St. John the Baptist.' Perhaps he took to the wilderness again after friend Hiram had him 'renovated?' But, in case you should be denied the 'surprise' which his unexpected advent would occasion you, I am rejoiced to inform you that I shall shortly receive a large lot of paintings from Italy, and think it not at all unlikely that there may be *another* 'St. John the Baptist' among them, and shall be glad to comfort you by letting you see it—as soon as I can afford to buy a house to hang it in—if the enterprising and obliging individual who took charge of yours from the confiding hands of your 'old friend Hiram' should never turn up, and you will keep me posted as to your whereabouts.

"I know of no officers of the Navy who *reside* in St. Louis, for our good old Uncle Samuel is usually so pressing in his solicitations for us to reside at some of his very interesting dock-yards, or to extend our travels to foreign parts in some of his floating fortresses, that it is rarely the case that officers can find the heart to refuse; but the principal of those, beside myself, who hail from that sainted city are Commodore William Smith (*can* he be of your branch of that distinguished family?), now in command of the navy yard at Boston, Commodore William Radford, in command of the steamer Dakotah at New York, and Lieutenant William M'Gunnigle, at the Naval Academy at Annapolis, Md.

"With sincere sympathy and respect for your grief over your lost 'St. John the Baptist,' I am very truly yours, SILAS BENT.

"P.S.—I greatly doubt if any *naval officer* ever proposed giving you the 'surprise' you represent, though it is not at all unlikely that some person representing himself to be such imposed upon the confidence of Mr. Powers. If he gave your picture to an officer, he can assuredly furnish you with that officer's name. S. B.

"P.S. No. 2.—I have never seen your 'St. John the Baptist,' but 'hope you may get it.'"

The exquisite humor of Mr. Bent's letter almost consoled me for the loss of my St. John.

In conclusion, I regret to say the naval officer who said he was "from St. Louis" has staid away "*from* St. Louis" to this day, so far as I know, and he has not "surprised" me yet—perhaps never will. My only hope now is that the publication of this correspondence (certainly not written for publication) may lead, in some mysterious way, to the restoration (and "no questions asked") of my St. John the Baptist.

New Names for Old Farces.

Managers of modern times have hit upon a novel mode of making out their bills, which, in effect, gives an agreeable variety to the announcements, without in reality making much change in the performances. Old farces are presented with new titles, by which very simple means a half dozen pieces are made to run through a whole season. For example, the neat little comedy of Perfection, has, at a theatre I wot of, been performed for several seasons, two or three times a week upon an average, under various titles, a few of which I give: The Cork Leg; The Maid of Munster; The Daughter of Erin; John, remove the Sofa; The Gentleman hard to Please; Erin is my Home; The Paragons, Father and Son; My charming Kate; The Lady from Cork, etc., etc.

There is another farce (or petit comedy) which has undergone many mutations on the posters. Its true title is, or was, The Dumb Belle. In the hands of our modern caterers for the public amusement, it is now called The Dumb Lady cured; The Bold Dragoon; She can't Speak; Irish Blunders; The Irishman in Petticoats; The Lady in a delicate Situation, and many others equally appropriate.

Buckstone's neat little farce of a Kiss in the Dark is changed to Curiosities from America, which is a very curious change, and farfetched, I think.

The Loan of a Lover is changed to Borrowing a beax; Mr. and Mrs. White to The Whites and Browns; The Rough Diamond to Buttons all over Him, etc.

It is somewhat remarkable that the changes of titles are confined to farces. Why not apply the same system to plays? Othello, for instance, might be announced as The Unhappy Marriage, or The dreadful Effects of Amalgamation; Hamlet could be changed to My Father's Ghost, or Methinks I see him Now; Damon and Pythias would be very attractive, one would think, announced as The Revolution at Syracuse, or the Gallant Gray of Anaxagoras. In the comedy line, many changes could be made to advantage. The School for Scandal should be called The Sale of Pictures, or My two Nephews; The Rivals would show well on the bills as The Absolute Father, or The original Mrs. Partington. Many other changes to better titles might be suggested; but our managers seem pretty well "up" to these things, and require no hints on this subject.

Story of a Head.

It is now nearly forty years since Hiram Powers, the great American sculptor—he was not great then, in an artistical point of view, but he was *good*, and to be good is to be great, as *I* view greatness—was engaged by Mr. Dorfieulle, proprietor of a museum in Cincinnati, Ohio, to mould a set of wax figures, consisting of effigies of Washington, Franklin, General Jackson, Commodores Bainbridge, Hull, and Perry, the Witch of Endor, Louis XVI., Charlotte Corday, Marie Antoinette, Napoleon Bonaparte, several murderers and murderesses, the Babes in the Wood, and various other celebrities; and to manufacture a scene representing the infernal regions, superintended by old *Satan* himself, and attended by all the inferior devils known to heathen mythology; to which was to be added a lake of fire and brimstone, and all the other accessories which modern divines (so called) have pictured as belonging to that dreaded locality. The whole of this work he accomplished in about a year, or a little more. The "Regions" had a great run. Clergymen visited the museum, and testified to the correctness of the picture; children were taken to see the awful "show," that they might know what sort of a place they would "go to" if they didn't behave themselves; and the people generally, from all quarters of the great West, when they visited Cincinnati, considered their sight-seeing incomplete until they had seen h—l in Dorfieulle's Museum. I suppose the getting up of this affair may be considered as the groundwork of Powers's subsequent greatness as an artist.

But, successful as this work was, his next achievement was more so, if possible—a Head of Aleck Drake, a popular comedian of that day—in wax. This head, when conjoined to a ragged suit of stuffed clothes, with a pair of wax hands, sticking out of the arm-holes of the coat, and surmounted by a shocking bad hat, and the whole placed in position, was a most striking likeness of the comedian in the attitude he assumed when singing a popular ballad entitled "Love and Sausages." At a short distance from this figure as it stood, a spectator could scarcely be made to believe it was not the actor himself, instead of being only his "counterfeit presentment." The correctness of the likeness was proved on the occasion of Aleck's benefit at the theatre, when he engaged the figure "for that night only," and advertised in the bills that *he would appear* (not in two *parts*, but) *in two places at one and the same time!* At the proper moment the effigy was placed behind a closed door, and the actor stood in the same attitude behind another door. On a signal given, the two doors were simultaneously opened, and there stood two ragged attitudinizers,

> "The one so like the other
> As could not be distinguished,"

until the *original* walked out of the door and down to the front of the stage to commence his song!

The grand success of this latter work drew the attention of Mr. Nicholas Longworth to the "Infernal Regions," and led to his loaning Hiram Powers a sufficient sum of money to enable him to go to Italy and perfect himself in the art of which he has since become so consummate a master.

In 1830 the proprietor of the museum wished me to "sit" (or *stand*) to Mr. Powers for a wax figure of myself in the character of *Mawworm*, which I had been playing at the theatre with some success. Hiram was quite willing, and I have no doubt it would have been a labor of love to "take me;" but I declined, for the reason that the proposed figure, standing up behind a screen which conveyed the idea of a pulpit, and in the *attitude of preaching*, and labeled "Sol Smith as *Mawworm*," might lead unthinking spectators who did not personally know me (knowing, however, that I was an *actor*) to suppose Sol Smith was making a mock of the forms of religion, which he has never done nor ever will do. I have often wished since that I had sat to the embryo artist in some *other* character, that my name might be handed down to posterity (even in wax) in connection with that of the great sculptor.

An effigy of old Fred Henderson in the character of old *Restive, the enraged Politician*, was talked of, and, though never executed, a small party of Powers's friends were greatly amused by a trick played upon them with the connivance of Henderson. It was given out that the *head* of this actor had been completed in wax, and a small party of friends were invited one afternoon to see it in Mr. Powers's studio. Old Fred, with his face marked to suit the character of *Restive*, with wig and neckerchief complete, was seated under a high table, through the centre of which protruded his head (the table having been prepared for the purpose like a pair of stocks), so that it appeared to be a head resting *on* the table. From the table to the floor hung a sheet which effectually concealed the person of the actor, and a crimson curtain was arranged in front of the head, ready to be drawn aside when all was ready. The party being assembled in front of the supposed wax figure, Powers, whispering to Henderson to keep a steady face, drew aside the curtain.

"Great!" "good!" "exact!" "better than Drake's!" "splendid!" were the first exclamations of the enraptured party, followed by more extended remarks and criticisms. Henderson kept his face wonderfully well at first; but when one of the party remarked, approaching very near him, that the face had not quite *color* enough, considering what a *hard drinker* old Fred was, he was obliged to give Powers a gentle kick as a signal to draw the curtain in order that he might indulge in a hearty laugh. After an interval of a few seconds the wax figure was again unveiled, and criticisms were freely indulged in for some considerable time. At last one remarked, "It looks so natural, and so like Henderson, that I feel almost like asking it to go and take a drink with me."

"Well, suppose you do," said Powers.

The admirer of art then approached very near the table, and said, in a natural and friendly way, "Henderson, old boy, will you go out with me and take a drink?"

The face of H. became very expressive, the lips twitched a little, then moved, and then the answer came, "*Don't care if I do!*"

The farce was ended.

There is a sequel to this "story of a head," which would hardly be entitled to be so entitled were I to stop here.

The effigy of the dead and gone Aleck Drake stood there in that museum, in that very attitude of singing that very old song of "Love *and* Sausages," for considerably over a quarter of a century, until (alas!) very few people remained who knew or had ever heard of the fine comedian it was so fine a likeness of. At last the proprietor of the museum (the proprietorship had changed —changed several times), when asked what ragged old cuss *that* was standing there holding out a dirty pocket-handkerchief full of holes, was obliged to confess he didn't know *who* it was;

and, presently, wanting the ragged clothes to dress up a murderer or some other new celebrity, he dismantled the figure, and the *head* was thrown away among a lot of other heads and hands in a garret, and forgotten.

I was not there, but I had a brother—SAM, a lover of the fine arts, living in Cincinnati. [This brother had under his control, in 1864, a celebrated picture entitled THE CRUCIFIXION, which produced at the Sanitary Fair $1100, and then, the ticket drawing it remaining unsold, was removed to St. Louis, where $2500 were realized on it by raffle at *our* fair, making a total of $3600 for our sick and wounded soldiers. I think it likely he or some other fortunate man may succeed in purchasing it from the lucky individual of Belleville, Ill., who drew it on a ticket which cost him a dollar, and now says he is willing to lose $500 on it—that is, he will sell it for $2000, as he has no house large enough to get it into, and is obliged to *store* it in St. Louis. This by the way.] This only living brother of mine was a warm friend of the living Powers, and also of the deceased Drake, and hearing that the "Love and Sausages" effigy no longer attitudinized in the museum, he instituted a search for the lost figure, but for a long time no tidings of it could be obtained. At length, in the year of grace 1867, his hopes were revived on reading in the *Commercial* one morning that the Museum had "smashed up," and all the curiosities were to be sold at auction to the highest bidder, the *Infernal Regions* included. He attended that auction, and saw Washingtons, Websters, and Jacksons knocked down to the Barnums of the country at astonishingly low prices. The component parts of the "Infernal Regions" were sold in lots to suit purchasers. *Devils* were at a discount. Pitchforks were not in demand. *Demons* of all kinds went for a song. Even old *Satan* himself brought only a dollar and a half! My brother looked on indifferently at these sacrifices, until, toward the close of the sale, a dusty old *head* was produced from a barrel. Could it be *the* head? It *was;* he couldn't be mistaken. It was as bald as a badger, the wig having been stripped off and (probably) used for some other head—possibly sold to some modern comedian; but the veritable head it was, and no mistake about it. Samuel was willing to pay a good price for that head, and expected it would be "run up" on him, especially if any of the company should happen to know whose head it was, and by whom moulded; but he assumed an air of indifference, and appeared scarcely to notice what it was that was up, though he *was determined to have it*, cost what it might. [My brother has never told me exactly the cost of that head, so I have to assume a sum. All he ever told me was that he bought it at a very low figure.]

Auctioneer. What am I offered for this head?

Gentleman. Whose head is it?

Auctioneer. Sir, I don't know *whose* head it is, but it will be *yours* if you purchase it. (*A laugh.*) What-am-I-bid-for-it? Does any body want it? Look at it, gentlemen; it is weeping with sorrow at your want of appreciation of true art. What do you say—shall I have a bid?

A small Englishman (*after a pause*). I will give you twenty-five cents for that 'ere 'ead.

Auctioneer. Twenty-five cents? Why, that wouldn't pay for the wax it is made of. Where's Artemus Ward? Twenty-five cents is bid—twenty-five, twenty-five, twenty-five! Where's Barnum? Twenty-five, twenty-five, twenty-five—

S. S. S. (*disgusted at the smallness of the bid*). I will give ten dollars! (*A general whistle.*)

Auctioneer. Thank you, sir. Here's somebody that understands the worth of statuary. Ten dollars—ten dollars—ten—ten—ten dollars—go-o-o-*ing!* Can I have any more? Let me say twenty dollars for *you*, sir (*to a young man smoking, who puts his thumb to his nose, and with his forefinger brushes the ashes from the end of his cigar, while the other fingers go through the motions of playing the flute*). Go-o-o-*ing!* for ten—ten—ten—ten dollars! It is dirt cheap, gentlemen! Only ten—ten--ten—ten—ten—ten—ten—ten—ten—ten—ten—ten—go-o-o-*ing! Will* you let a valuable head like this go for ten—ten—ten—ten—ten—ten—ten—quick, or you lose it!—ten—ten—ten—ten—can't dwell—going for ten—ten—ten—once—twice—last call—GONE! (*with a gentle rap upon the head*). It is yours, sir, and a great bargain you have got. (*All look round to see who is the purchaser.*) You must have known the person whose head that represents?

S. S. S. (*taking the head reverently*). "I knew him well, Horatio."

Auctioneer. Shall I send it up to your office?

S. S. S. No; I'll take it *with* me. Here's your money; and you will please mark this head "delivered."

And, elated beyond measure, he covered his purchase with a pocket-handkerchief and hastened home. If there were any applications for insurance at his office *that* day, they had to lie over: the President of the Equitable remained at home contemplating the features of his old friend Aleck, and explaining to his family the lucky chance by which he became possessed of the long-lost head; and it *required* some explanation, for not one of his children, now, all but one, grown up to be men and women, nor even his wife, had ever heard of such a person as Alexander Drake, whose head was destined thenceforth to rest upon a bracket, covered with a glass case, in the parlor.

Alas for the mutability of human affairs! A regard for truth will not permit me to leave that head upon that bracket, with select crowds of invited friends gazing at it and giving breath to their ecstatic emotions in words of unbounded admiration. [Between you and I, reader, it must be confessed that the head by itself, without the body, wig, and costume, and, above all, the *attitude*, could not have been a very agreeable sight to strangers—not much more so than the head of St. John upon a charger; but no matter, I must hasten to a conclusion, or I shall tire you.]

A. DRAKE'S HEAD.

When all was ready, and the grim bald head was up, the young folk of the family had a party, and my brother intended to astonish his young visitors by a disclosure which they would remember for the remainder of their lives. A rich crimson shawl was thrown over the glass case, and he intended, when the dancing should be over, to surprise the company with a sight of poor Yorick's head. Being somewhat indisposed that night, most likely from the excitement he had undergone while preparing for the intended "surprise," he did not leave his room until late in the evening, when the dancing had suddenly ceased, as he learned by the house ceasing to shake. "Now," said he, "now is the time for the surprise." In slippers and morning-gown, he crept down stairs and opened one of the parlor doors, when he saw all his visitors huddled together and looking at something on the floor. "Some play they are at," thought he. But it couldn't be a play either, for who ever saw a parlor play where all were silent and sad?

"What's the matter, girls?" asked the invalid, approaching the circle. "You all seem as melancholy as a defeated party after an election. What has happened?"

No answer was given *in words*, but all turned their eyes upward to the empty bracket—yes, the *empty* bracket; *his* eyes followed theirs, which now returned to the floor . . . .

The dancing had jarred the bracket. The head and the glass-case had been shaken off. They had fallen to the floor with a crash, and there lay the glass *and* head, broken into about a thousand and twenty-three small bits!

So, instead of surprising his friends, as he fondly hoped to do, my good brother got very much surprised himself—shocked, I may say.

The Actor and the Phrenologist.

BY JAMES REES.

"Prove all things."—St. Paul.

"In the year 1835, being in the city of New York, it was our good fortune to form an acquaintance with Mr. Sol Smith, which it has pleased that same fortune to keep unimpaired ever since. We long had expressed a desire to meet this eccentric genius face to face; and as we have, as is pretty well known, a *penchant* for every thing of a dramatic character, it would have been high treason in us to have neglected the opportunity of becoming personally acquainted with one so justly celebrated in dramatic annals as is this gentleman. The name of Sol Smith was at that period, and still is with us, associated with all our early recollections of the dramatic history of our country. We have numerous anecdotes of his sayings and doings in the 'mimic world,' all of which, if given with the spirit of their truth, would keep the table in a roar, and reflect, at least upon one member of the profession, the highest degree of credit. We remember certain vocal exhibitions in the old Vauxhall Garden of Philadelphia in 'auld lang syne,' and concertizing, and lecturing in divers places and upon divers subjects—in fact the very name of Sol Smith has a charm for us; it calls up reminiscences of a pleasing and romantic character; and when we refer back o'er the pages of memory, what a host of incidents present themselves, and every memento has a tale of mirthful, and, not unfrequently, sorrowful interest. Memories, however, are but retrogressive shadows—the waking dreams of past realities.

"Sol Smith's connection with the American

stage, and his identity with a most interesting portion of it—the South and West—is of that character which, if published, would be, perhaps, the most interesting and amusing of all his other dramatic sketches. The Drama of the West would be a history of an adventurous band, who, like the early pioneers to the 'dark and bloody ground,' had to contend against obstacles almost as terrible as the wild savages, the tiger, and the bear. Fanaticism, in any country, is a far more dangerous monster to art and science than are the hordes of untamed beasts or armed savages. The Drama, however, flourished; Sol flourished with it, and has ever since maintained its character, and protected and defended it from and against this, its most dangerous enemy.

"Let this pass. To those unacquainted with Sol Smith, there are times and occasions when he may be readily taken for a preacher; indeed, this is not altogether an optical delusion, but a veritable truth; and, if we mistake not, he has on one or two occasions officiated under circumstances which reflected the highest credit on his talents, and zealous exertions in that cause—the cause of truth and of morality. Well, it so happened, just at that time, not far from the Park Theatre, where Sol was playing an engagement, there resided a somewhat celebrated phrenologist—one of those deluded sons of science, who imagined it one, when, in fact, it was and is but a mapped humbug, drawn on the surface of a shadowy skull. Indeed, this disciple of Combe and Gall really thought that he possessed an ethereal spark of divinity, which enabled him to read and expound the mysteries of the invisible world, and the wonders of the human mind. His shingle was at the door, and professions, characters, habits, etc., of individuals were written out for the trifling sum of five dollars each, Empire State currency. Before this door, on the day in question, stood Sol Smith, silent, solemn, sombre, serious, somewhat skeptical, if not superstitious. He looked as much like a preacher as it was possible for a man to look who really wished to be gazed upon as such. Preachers have a sort of human feeling that way—it is natural, nor is there any great harm in it.

"The phrenologist was in his sanctum, and looking forth into the crowded street, not unlike a Peter Funk seeking whom he may devour. In a moment, Sir Oracle of the head read his man, and it so happened that, at the very moment this knowledge entered the brain of the bumpologist, a similar transfer of mesmeric fluid passed into that of Sol; *he, too, read his man.* It was a sort of mutual sympathetic electricity—a communion of souls and thoughts; and although Sol was not then (as we sincerely hope he is now) blessed with many V's, he determined to lessen the alphabet of his cash by that letter at least; so he entered the sanctum, and the man of bumps scratched his head in actual ecstasy, numbering the digits exactly in accordance with the amount of dollars he was to receive.

"The smile, the bow, the greeting being over, Sol was placed in a sort of inquisitorial chair. His head—and a good phrenological head it was and is, apart from the science—was erect; his forehead, high and intellectual, was somewhat marred by a sort of dramatic frown, which rested at its base like a dark shadow on a piece of sculptured marble. That frown should not have been there; but there it was, and those who know the man, and examine that same head, will find that same frown still lingering near and about it. It is, we are afraid, a sort of *fixture.* He, however, sat erect; lips compressed; lines, which are called the 'traces of humor,' diverged from the mouth, and, assuming a sterner form from those which make up the human face divine, were lost in the infixible, if not contraction of every muscle, over which he at times has so much command. The head, then and there, was a model, and the phrenologist gazed upon it with wonder, awe, and veneration. The man of science approached it cautiously; his very lips smacked with the innate chuckle which came up from the hidden caverns of his throat like those of an old hen presiding over the ivory-like prisons of her unfledged young. It was a scientific chuckle—a voluntary action of the organ of joy; it was, however, a chuckle, and we will set it down as one of delight. The man of bumps spoke as he mapped the actor's head; he went on to this effect—it was a perfect eruption of a Vesuvius of science: 'Extraordinary head—veneration the most profound, reverence the most exalted, a mysterious combination of all the elements which make up the model man of God. How they harmonize—a life of study, of piety, and religious observance—a distaste of the vanities of the world. Sir!' he exclaimed, in the excitement of his enthusiastic admiration, 'you have the exact copy of a head of one of the greatest and best of men. Excuse me, sir—ah! here is a bump—Channing has one exactly like it. Here is a line dividing, or rather diverging from a membrane. See how exquisitely, how beautifully it lingers around the base of veneration, and links it with reverence. The mind of man, sir, is endowed with a plurality of innate faculties. Each of the faculties manifests itself through the medium of some particular organ. Sir, I am now looking down into your brain.' [Here Smith winced a little.] 'Be still, sir—all right. The organs of the mental faculty have their seat in the brain, the brain being a congeries of these organs. I am now, sir, in your brain.' [Here another wince.] 'Be silent, sir—I will soon step out. Now I am on the surface —what a surface!' Thus he continued, filling up the time occupied with his examination with all sorts of remarks and technical phrases. Sol suffered the infliction—for it was one—in silence, although it was with the greatest difficulty he could refrain from laughing outright. Immediately across the street there was posted a large play-bill of the Park Theatre, announcing the play of the HYPOCRITE, *Mawworm* by Mr. Sol Smith! After receiving his fee (a V), the bumpologist requested the name of his distinguished visitor, observing that he was always anxious to have gentlemen of his calling on his list. Sol seized the arm of the astonished man of science, led him in silence to the window, and, pointing his finger in a theatrical manner toward the imposing play-bill on the opposite side, and speaking in a slow but decided tone, 'Sir, there—behold my card—my name is Smith—not John Smith, but Sol Smith. I am an actor, and manager of several theatres in the South, and should be most happy to see you at the theatre this evening. Sir, I wish you a very good morning.'

"Sol vanished, leaving the astonished bumpologist a picture of human petrifaction. The last we heard of him, he was engaged in the manufacturing of fine-tooth combs at Deep River, Connecticut, in the extensive comb manufactory of George Read & Co., and, although his hands are no longer employed in looking for bumps on the head, the produce of his labor goes abroad, performing the task in a far more creditable, if not more effective and beneficial manner."

The Prince of Morocco on Horseback.

BY THE LATE M. C. FIELD.

"In the MERCHANT OF VENICE, Shakspeare has several fine, high-born suitors applying for the hand of Portia. There is, first, the Neapolitan Prince, then the County Palatine, the French lord, Monsieur Le Bon, Falconbridge, the young baron of England, a Scottish lord, the young German, the Duke of Saxony's nephew (an ancestor of Prince Albert, perhaps), after whom comes the *Prince of Morocco*, and the *Prince of Aragon*, these two last being introduced personally in the play, while the former respectable individuals are only 'over-named' to her mistress by Nerissa. But as the piece is acted, even these two are 'cut out,' and they are scarcely named in modern performances.

"'Old Sol' Smith was some years since making a circuit of several towns in Georgia and Alabama, where he had theatres, when at one place he was pestered by a persevering country simpleton who wanted to 'come out and act.' Nothing is more difficult than to get rid of one of these stage-struck innocents when once touched by the mania. Sol saw at a glance the character he had before him, and determined to repay himself for the constant annoyance of the young man by extracting some amusement from him. He accordingly told the youth that he might attend when he liked behind the scenes, and some opportunity would perhaps occur when he could come out. This privilege was greedily seized upon by the aspirant, who immediately became almost part and parcel of the scenery, so closely did he scrutinize the actors and lounge around the stage.

"Still pertinaciously he demanded every morning what his part was to be, and when he was to play. Worn out with continual teasing, Old Sol told him one day, during a rehearsal of the MERCHANT OF VENICE, that he should appear that evening, and his part should be that of the *Prince of Morocco*, a personage now wholly unknown in 'Cumberland's Acting Edition.' This new and original cast had its designed effect of raising a laugh at the time, and was then forgotten until the evening, when the stage-doorkeeper was heard in loud words with some one who wanted to come in and act.

"'Who are you?' said the doorkeeper.

"'I'm *the Prince of Morocco*,' said the unsophisticated young gentleman, 'and you must let me in to act.'

"Sol knew the voice, and hurried to quench the disturbance, in doing which his ready drollery and wit at once displayed themselves.

"'Ah! you are here,' said Sol; 'that's right; but, shade of Thespis! what do I behold? Man! man! where is your *red morocco dress?*'

"'Eh?' said the Georgia bumpkin, with a stupid stare.

"'Oh, all the gods at once, and miching mallecho to boot! who ever heard of a *Prince of Morocco* without a full suit of red morocco armor! Go away, sir; I see now you will never do for an actor,' and so Old Sol got rid of the young tragedian this time.

"Months afterward our eccentric manager had his company in another town, several hundred miles away, when the MERCHANT OF VENICE, or, as an old stager would say, 'the *Shylock* piece,' in due time came to be announced, as it was one of the standing stock performances of the troupe. When the actors were assembling for rehearsal, every body was astounded at the apparition of a man *dressed from head to foot in red leather*, standing in front of the theatre, waiting, as he said, to see Sol Smith. Presently Sol came along, recognized his old protegé, went through the operation of a side-splitting fit of laughter, and then commenced studying how to get rid once more of so strange an annoyance.

"'Ah! you are here,' said Old Sol; 'that's right; but, eh? shade of Thespis! where's your horse?'

"'Horse!' ejaculated the gentleman in red, with profound astonishment spreading over his face.

"'Your *horse*,' cried Old Sol, pretending to fly into a tremendous passion. 'Oh, miching mallecho, and all the gods! who ever saw a *Prince of Morocco* on foot? Begone, sir; I see you are no actor.'

"The poor young fellow went away abashed, and Sol concluded his crazy desires were checked, when once again, after a long travel through Georgia to Montgomery, Alabama, one morning, just when the theatre was announced to open for the first time, up rode the young Georgia Cracker, in his scarlet dress, on a wild-looking Indian pony, followed by twenty or thirty boys, just starting out to school, all screaming and flinging up their caps with delight at the strange spectacle.

"Orally, Old Sol tells the story with a droll and irresistible effect, much of which may be lost in our attempt at writing it, but we have never had a more ludicrous occurrence to record. The mirth of the actors and the whimsical manager may be imagined when the tragic tyro from Georgia came riding into Montgomery, armed and equipped according to order, with red leather pantaloons, jacket, and cap, and valiantly mounted, to make his first appearance on any stage as the *Prince of Morocco—on horseback!*

There being a page or two to spare, I fill them, and close my book with

A Defense of the Stage,

BY THE LATE C. A. LOGAN.

From the New Orleans Republican, 1844.

THE THEATRE.

"Sol. Smith, Esq., the worthy manager of the St. Charles Theatre has kindly placed in our hands the following article for publication. Mr. Smith tells us it was written by Mr. Logan, the well-known comedian, in August last, which, we believe, was about the time his own most able and pungent letter to Dr. Beecher was published in the New York papers, and so extensively copied throughout the country. It will be remembered that the Tremont Theatre in Boston was last summer converted into a church, and at its consecration the reverend doctor preached a sermon, in which he assailed with great bitterness plays, players, and all things theatrical.

"The following letter will explain why this 'reply' was not published before:

"'Mobile, February 9, 1844.

"'SOL. SMITH, ESQ.: DEAR SIR,—I cheerfully comply with your flattering request to furnish you with a copy of my reply to Dr. Beecher's sermon, although it is with some reluctance I consent to its publication at this late day. I wrote the reply immediately after the sermon was delivered, and was about to publish it when your own letter to the reverend doctor met my eye. That letter, so admirably written, and so far superior to my humble effort, seemed to cover the whole ground, and leave nothing farther to be said on the subject.

"'Fully agreeing with you that when the Drama is assailed from so many quarters, all its friends should become its defenders, I respectfully submit the manuscript to your disposal.

"'Very respectfully, your obedient servant,

"'C. A. LOGAN.'

"We regret that we have not space for the whole of this 'reply.' After an elaborate exordium the writer thus proceeds:

"'The doctor's text is inappropriate—it means nothing in connection with his subject. He doubtless searched the Scriptures for a motto, and could find nothing nearer his subject-matter than "traitors, heady, high-minded lovers of pleasure more than lovers of God;" and yet he asserts that the Scriptures expressly forbid theatrical amusements. They do not. No sentence that can be tortured into such a prohibition is to be found in the sacred volume. He admits that the Drama is coeval with religion. If so, it must have been well known to the inspired writers, and yet, while no human vice or folly escaped the strictures of these reverend characters, no word of censure, even in parable, was ever uttered against theatrical representations.

"'The doctor enumerates as sinful pleasures "gladiatorial shows, bull-fights, excess of eating, inebriation, and groveling animalism," and says that "the theatre has in all time stood the temple of these Mammon worshipers." Here is a jumble of epithets from which no sense can be extracted. Surely no man ever saw a gladiatorial show, or a bull-fight, or excess of eating, or groveling animalism in a modern theatre. And how can it be called a temple of the worshipers of Mammon? The doctor says afterward that the amusement is too dear to be indulged in except by a few, and surely these few can not be worshipers of the sordid deity of gold, or they would not be there. He can not mean the actors, for if *they* worship gold, verily they bend the knee to an unknown God.

"'We are told that "although the Drama was originally a religious institution, the divinity adored was Bacchus, and the sacrifices, feastings, wine, and songs have come down in unbroken succession to our day." The doctor's knowledge of early history is defective, or he willfully misrepresents the whole matter. In the remoter ages of the world the Drama was the *only* medium of human worship. Bacchus, and Mammon, and the whole host of heathen deities were imaginations of a much later date. The shepherds and husbandmen of the Nile—the earliest worshipers that tradition reaches—invented a sort of sacred Drama, of which the priests were the actors. The "God of the Overflow" was adored in a secondary character—that is, as represented by a sage, whose duty it was to watch the march of the heavenly bodies, and to predict the period of the inundation of the valley. A malignant spirit was also introduced upon the scene who was crowned with a dead serpent of the Nile, and whose dress was composed of the leaves of the withered lotus. This mystery, like the melodrama of the present day, was interspersed with music, and the most magnificent temples were erected for its representation. These were the first churches.

"'Thus it appears that Religion and the Drama were at first identical, but Time has divided them. God has assigned to the one the high and holy mission of promulgating throughout the world his ineffable glory, and to the other he has delegated the power to sway the human heart by striking its subtle and intangible chords—to soften, to refine, and to elevate.

"'Tis true that Thespis on his car at Athens chanted odes to Bacchus; but Bacchus was not held by the Athenians as the God of Drunkenness, as many imagine. He was the God of the Vine, doubtless, but he was honored for qualities distinct from ideas of sensual indulgence. Solemn temples were erected to his worship by a temperate people, and it is thus that with the name of this god the performances of the earliest professional actor are associated.

"'As civilization advanced Æschylus rose—the father of the Drama. He was, like Shakspeare, an actor as well as a poet, and "no Athenian of his day was so honored as Æschylus, for he created the Drama." They bound his brows with laurel, and when he walked forth at noon they sprung arches of oak over his head. Sophocles, Euripides, and Aristophanes followed Æschylus, and some of their works live yet, unapproached by effort—an imperishable and somewhat humiliating proof that whatever strides science may have taken in the world, the sublime genius of letters—mature at its birth—has denied the honor to succeeding generations of adding any thing to its brilliancy.

"'This divine tells us that "the Drama has commenced its retreat, and will soon pass away." Nothing can be more evidently opposite to the truth than both the assertion and the prediction. At no period of the world were theatres and actors so numerous as now. In most of the civilized nations of Europe the Drama is under the special protection of the crown, and in those countries where letters are most cultivated, and where refinement has attained its highest polish, the theatre is supported by the government. In this country, 'tis true, the recent commercial distress, pervading as it did all classes of the community, reached theatrical amusements, and prostrated several establishments whose capital was too slender to bear the shock. The Tremont house was one of these, and Dr. Beecher gloats over the fall of his imaginary foe in a strain of invective that falls harshly from the lips of a disciple of our meek and mild Redeemer.

"'The doctor next refers to his prediction—uttered, he says, at the building of the Tremont Theatre—"that he would live to preach in it." Let me record another prediction, uttered in my hearing at the same time. One day, while the workmen were shingling the roof of the theatre, I ascended to the cupola of the State-house in Boston, and, on reaching the platform, I found the Rev. Doctor —— and two ladies enjoying the fine view of the city. Their eyes at length rested on this splendid temple of the Muses, and the doctor exclaimed, "So they're shingling the house of the devil! I prophesy that in less than *one year* God in his wrath will burn it up with fire!" This false prophet was a divine of no less reputation than Dr. Beecher, and I withhold his name only because, his prognostication having failed, the disclosure might throw discredit on his future predictions.

"'"The claims of the theatre to holiness will not be insisted on." No; the theatre lays as few claims to holiness as the Church does to comedy—each has its appropriate sphere. The Church is built upon the Rock of Ages, and the Drama is built upon the human heart; the divine truth of the one, and the sublime morality of the other, will find a living response in that heart as long as it beats with a single attribute of the Deity.

"The doctor complains that ministers of religion are brought upon the stage to be ridiculed as 'dolts, pedants, or dullards.' The reply is that *there exist* ministers who *are* stupid, pedantic, and dull; and should these be exempt from censure or ridicule more than the rest of mankind? Should 'such divinity hedge' *all* who wear the black robe that they should not be held amenable to the laws by which other men are governed? If there *are* reverend gentlemen who disgrace their holy calling by seduction, adultery, forgery, simony, or hypocrisy, should our awe of the cloth they pollute screen them from the punishment with which the law should visit their crimes, or the satire with which the stage should lash their vices?

"'What school-houses, academies, or colleges has it (the theatre) built?' If the theatre added to its other important powers the building or endowing of educational institutions, it would surpass as an instrument of good all human inventions. But, unhappily, its ability is not equal to such attempts. Its means of doing good are crippled by the pulpit. The fulminations of clerical orators of all grades of intellect, from Dr. Beecher down to the poor mad ranter who desecrates the stillness of our Sabbath by his senseless bellowings in the highways and market-places of this city—all, all have a fling at their great rival, the theatre! Is this unchristian spirit imitated by the theatre? No. Not a sentence—not a syllable is ever heard from the stage that can be construed to swerve from that respect which the Drama ever pays to true religion.

"'What streams of knowledge has it diffused? What science cultivated or explained?' Plays, for the most part, are founded on remarkable events in history, ancient and modern. Of the thirty-seven written by Shakspeare, twenty-four may for our present purpose be called poetical versions of well-authenticated historical passages. From no single historian can a tenth part of the truth of any event dramatized by Shakspeare be gathered. The immortal poet frequently drew his knowledge from sources which have not come down to our day. We can nowhere obtain so clear an insight into the characters, motives, passions, and politics of the men who fought the Wars of the Roses as in the plays of this author. Who ever *saw*, except their own contemporaries, the heroes of antiquity until Shakspeare introduced them to us face to face—the living, breathing, speaking inhabitants of Greece and Rome—their warriors, sages, orators, patriarchs, and plebeians? To the man who reads history only, Marius, Sylla, Nero, and Caligula have none of the features of humanity about them. The chief acts of their lives being exhibited unrelieved by a statement of the means by which their deeds were accomplished, they appear like the grotesque figures in a phantasmagoria—fearful from their indistinctness, horrible from their mysterious burlesque on human nature, and alike hideous whether we laugh or shudder at the monstrous chimera. Turn to the page of Shakspeare, or behold his swelling scene at the theatre, and these men—seen, arriving at natural ends by natural means — teach the eternal truth that the heart of man is the same in all ages, and that vice has produced misery and virtue happiness from the beginning of the world.

"The doctor quotes Plato as adverse to the theatre. Every man who has not forgotten his school-boy classics can quote passages in Plato which would make the doctor feel that he calculated too much on the ignorance of his hearers. And Aristotle, too, the divine drags into the argument. Why, every tyro knows that the only laws acknowledged even to this day for constructing comedies are those of this philosopher, who declares that 'tragedy is intended to purge our passions by means of terror and pity.' And 'Tacitus says the German manners were guarded by having no play-houses among them.' If that be true, the Germans have thought better on the subject since the time of Tacitus; for one of the modern writers of that nation (Zingerman) says, 'We are greatly a dramatic people. * * * Nothing but good can result from the widest indulgence of this taste among us, unless it happen that the sedentary and imaginative student should, through his diseased appetite, draw poison from the stage, as the serpent distills venom from the nutritious things of nature.'

"The doctor next invokes Ovid to his aid. Surely nothing but a design to frighten us with an array of classical names could induce the preacher to bolster his argument with the opinion of the most licentious poet of ancient or modern times. Ovid calling the theatre dissolute! and advising its suppression! Why, 'tis like Satan denouncing heaven from the burning lake, or like a pickpocket advising the suppression of the penal code.

"Next we have a list of the formidable opinions of the early fathers of the Church, who were unanimous in their condemnation of the theatre. Doubtless. So they were in the condemnation and burning of martyrs and witches. However pious were many of them according to their unchristian and ferocious notions of piety, their sentiments on the subject of the Drama are not worth a moment's discussion.

"The doctor here arrives at a point where the stage seems indeed vulnerable. He alludes to the bars for the sale of liquor, and to the third row.

"In reply to the first, I would say, that if men will drink in despite of Temperance Societies, it matters but little where they get the liquor. If there were no bars within the house, the thirsty would most certainly find the stimulant out of doors. And yet bars are no more necessary to the theatre than to the pulpit. I am old enough to remember the time when men would assemble at the tavern nearest the church as soon as the service was over, and there discuss the merits of the sermon and of brandy and water at the same time. The Temperance movement, however, wrought wonders, and I believe the same men do not drink now—at least not until they reach home.

"The other charge is a graver one—the third tier. This evil is no more essential to the Drama than the bars, nor is it 'an inseparable concomitant of the theatre.' The separation *has* taken place in many towns of this country. In Europe, and in the larger cities of this continent, the doors are thrown open to all who pay, and conform to certain regulations. No one has a right to say to his neighbor, 'Stand aside, for I am holier than thou.' The third row is assigned to those who are without the pale of society, and the money of these, 'tis true, is often needful to a treasury impoverished by the absence of persons of enlightened piety, whom clerical denunciations deter from partaking of that elegant amusement, blended with wholesome instruction, which can be enjoyed nowhere but in a well-regulated theatre.

"The 'pants' and abbreviated garments of Fanny Ellsler next fall under the animadversions of the doctor. Of all the dancers that have appeared on the modern stage, this celebrated Terpsichorean is the most modest. In this lies her principal charm. Her dress, necessarily short, to permit the free use of her limbs, is managed with such graceful dexterity, that his imagination must be 'as foul as Vulcan's stithy' who could conceive an impure thought while gazing on her ethereal movement or her classic repose; and what a libel on the ladies of Boston and other cities—the refined, the high, and the pure, who flocked in crowds, night after night, in thousands, to behold this fascinating artiste, to say that 'her dancing might have made the devil blush, and female virtue, *had it been there*, burn with indignation, and hang her head in shame!'

"No woman blushes to see the bold and slightly draped statuary of the great masters. The paintings of our first parents in Paradise suggest no indelicate ideas. Why is this? Because no taint of voluptuousness defiled the mind of the sculptor or the painter in the production of his work. His soul, filled only with sublime notions of the beautiful and the true, chisels or delineates humanity without its earthiness and passion—without its grossness. A rising young sculptor who was in New Orleans a year or two ago was desirous of studying the anatomical outline of the living subject. He made every exertion to induce a woman to sit for him—in vain. He sought out at length some of the abject and abandoned Quadroons, whose scanty meal was gained by the most loathsome infamy, and offered what to them must have been a large sum, to stand before him as a model for one hour. None could be found to do it. *The blush lay in the pollution of their own minds.*

"Our young American, however, had but little right to complain. Two of the greatest masters of antiquity, Apelles the painter, and Praxiteles the sculptor, seemed to have had but one model between them for their respective works—Phryne of Bœsia having been the original of the Venus in oil, as well as of the goddess in stone. Caroline, queen of Naples, sister to Napoleon and wife of Murat, stood as a model for Psyche at the Tribunal of Venus in Paris. The lady in the modern case may be condemned, but it went to show that in her lofty mind no impure thought could be connected with the Fine Arts.

"Dr. Channing happened to remark two or three years ago that much of the *spirit* of the Drama—that is, its purer portions—divested of the necessary dross of bad acting (which seems to be only as shade in a picture), might be condensed into readings or 'lectures;' and, lo! a swarm of lecturers, numerous and noisy as the locusts of Egypt, devoured the land. Men of little education and less character committed to memory a few of the simplest truths of Natural Philosophy, Astronomy, Magnetism, Chemistry, and the laws of general Physics, and advertised to instruct the public at a price for the course of lectures, half the amount of which would be sufficient to purchase at any book-store volumes that contain not only the whole stock of the lecturer's knowledge, but more extended views of the subject than he himself, perhaps, ever read. This mania hurt the theatre a while, but the unnatural excitement was short-lived. The public has already turned from this paltry banquet, and seeks again the wholesome food spread before it by every well-conducted theatre.

"Those periods in history in which the Drama declined are marked by bigotry, violence, and civil war. All the theatres in London were closed by order of Oliver Cromwell, and ten days afterward the head of Charles the First rolled from the block! Terror and gloom hung over the kingdom. The Drama was interdicted—the arts perished—the woof rotted in the loom—the plow rusted in the furrow, and men's hearts were strung to the ferocity of fanaticism. Fathers and sons shed each other's blood; and in the intervals of lust and murder, wild riot howled through the wasted land. Even if permitted by the laws, the theatre could not exist amid such horrors. But the actors were outlawed, and the bigoted Roundheads fixed that stigma upon the profession of a player which illiterate and narrow-minded people attach to it even to this day.

"The pulpit too often depicts Virtue in austere and forbidding colors, and strips her of every attractive grace. The path of duty is made a rugged and toilsome way—narrow and steep; and the fainting pilgrim is sternly forbidden to turn aside his bleeding feet to tread, even for a moment, the soft and pleasant greensward of Sin, which smiles alluring on every side.

"The stage paints Virtue in her holiday garments; and though storms sometimes gather round her radiant head, the countenance of the heavenly maid, resigned, serene, and meek, beams forth, after a season of patient suffering, with ineffable refulgence. Vice constantly wears his hideous features, and in the sure, inevitable punishment of the guilty we behold the type of that Eternal Justice before whose fiat the purest of us shall tremble when the curtain falls on the Great Drama of Life."

EPITAPH.

[TO BE ENGRAVED UPON A PLAIN STONE IN BELLEFONTAINE CEMETERY, ST. LOUIS.]

SOL. SMITH,

RETIRED ACTOR.

1801—18--.

"Life's but a walking shadow; a poor PLAYER,
That struts and frets his hour upon the STAGE,
And then is heard no more."

"All the world's a STAGE,
And all the men and women merely PLAYERS."

EXIT SOL.

FRANKLIN SQUARE, NEW YORK,
October 1, 1868.

HARPER & BROTHERS'

AUTUMN BOOK LIST.

☞ HARPER & BROTHERS *will send the following Works by Mail, postage paid, to any part of the United States on receipt of the Price.*

HARPER'S CATALOGUE *sent by Mail on receipt of Five Cents, or it may be obtained gratuitously on application to the Publishers personally.*

Kinglake's Crimean War.

The Invasion of the Crimea: Its Origin, and an Account of its Progress down to the Death of Lord Raglan. By ALEXANDER WILLIAM KINGLAKE. *Vol. II. now ready.* With Maps and Plans. 12mo, Cloth, $2 00 per Vol.

Whatever opinion may be formed of some of the author's deductions, no one can hesitate to allow that he has clearly devoted the utmost patience to the sifting of a mass of materials by which a less laborious or clear-sighted writer would have been confused, if not overwhelmed. The polished diction and burnished style which first made their author famous are still maintained in this volume; and were the interest of the subject even less momentous, they would be eagerly read as specimens of a literary production of consummate skill.—*Saturday Review.*

By a happy accident the author has acquired extraordinary opportunities and advantages for ascertaining and verifying the incidents of a remarkable episode in history, with which the national honor is inextricably mixed up. He has shown himself willing to undergo any amount of personal sacrifice and responsibility for the adequate performance of what, to him, is both a public and a private duty. He has instituted a careful survey of the localities; he has consulted and collected dispatches and correspondence without end; he has personally communicated with statesmen and warriors, with almost all the leading actors and many of the less prominent characters who have figured on the scene, and he has got together a mass of information perhaps unequaled *in pari materia* for fullness, accuracy, interest, and variety—*Fraser's Magazine.*

(*In regard to the Charge of the Light Brigade.*) Mr. Kinglake, in our opinion, states the case in its different aspects, clearly and impartially, and is disposed rather to extenuate faults than to set down aught in malice. . . . . Mr. Kinglake in his present volume fully sustains his reputation; and this is saying much. Few non-professional men have ever so completely mastered the true spirit of the art of war, or described military events with such graphic power; fewer still can clothe their impressions in such pure and nervous English.—*Examiner.*

Mr. Kinglake has exhibited extraordinary powers as a historian in his account of the Battle of Balaklava. The minuteness with which he traces all the movements of that terrible action—the care and industry with which he weighs the several and sometimes conflicting accounts—the mastery of detail and knowledge of military tactics which he displays—and the general vividness of the narrative, which often seems to glow with the light and echo with the roar of mortal combat, combine to form one of the most remarkable pictures of a great battle which our literature can boast. Sometimes composed in the spirit of military criticism—calm, cool, and observant—and at others in that of some modern prose Homer, who feels the inspiration of the fight, and kindles with the personal heroism of individual actors, it shows throughout the hand of a master in this species of writing.—*London Review.*

Dalton's Physiology.

Physiology and Hygiene. For Schools, Families, and Colleges. By J. C. DALTON, M.D., Professor of Physiology in the College of Physicians and Surgeons, New York. With Illustrations. 12mo, Cloth. (*Just ready.*)

M'Clintock & Strong's Cyclopædia.

Cyclopædia of Biblical, Theological, and Ecclesiastical Literature. Prepared by the Rev. JOHN M'CLINTOCK, D.D., and JAMES STRONG, S.T.D. *Vol. II. now ready.* Royal 8vo. Price per Vol., Cloth, $5 00; Sheep, $6 00; Half Morocco, $8 00.

The Opium Habit.

The Opium Habit, with Suggestions as to the Remedy. 12mo, Cloth, $1 75.

The writer and compiler of the volume has been himself a victim to the habit which he describes, having eaten more than half a hundredweight of the drug and continued in its uninterrupted use for more than fifteen years. He emancipated himself by a short but painful struggle of six weeks, in which he proceeded from 80 grains a day by diminished doses to its entire abandonment. The story which he tells is interesting without being at all sensational; it is minute enough without being tedious, and its moral lessons of hope and perseverance are none the less impressive from the fact that there is not any attempt to state or enforce them. There is no cant nor preaching in the story, and but very little in the selections which follow it; the author judging wisely enough that the facts preach loudly and forcibly enough, and that to the great majority of opium-eaters their own reflections furnish more preaching than they care to hear or can consent to endorse.—*Nation.*

Student's New Testament History.

The New Testament History. With an Introduction, connecting the History of the Old and New Testaments. Edited by WILLIAM SMITH, LL.D., Classical Examiner in the University of London. With Maps and Woodcuts. Large 12mo, Cloth, $2 00.

A valuable and cheap compendium of accurate information drawn from the most recent results of scholarship.—*Advance.*

Those who have read the New Testament only in a desultory fashion, or in the disorderly method in which it is arranged in our version, will find a new light cast upon it by the study of the book in its chronological order, and with such helps as Dr. Smith has here presented.—*Amer. Presbyterian* (Philadelphia).

Very complete and excellent as a book of reference. —*Observer.*

It meets a want which every young student of the Bible feels.—*Cincinnati Christian Advocate.*

Sabbath-school teachers, and the more advanced pupils of Sabbath-schools, as well as intelligent private students of the Scriptures, will find this a helpful and remunerative volume.—*Congregationalist.*

By far the best of its kind of any thing that has yet been published.—*Churchman.*

The chapters treating of the Maccabees and the times of Herod, the sects and several branches of the Jews, and their new forms of worship, are thoughtfully written, though necessarily from a Christian standpoint—but the book is prepared for Christian students, and they will find it exceedingly useful and valuable.—*Jewish Messenger.*

Uniform with the above:

THE STUDENT'S HISTORY OF GREECE. A History of Greece from the Earliest Times to the Roman Conquest. With Supplementary Chapters on the History of Literature and Art. By WILLIAM SMITH, LL.D., Editor of the "Classical Dictionary," "Dictionary of Greek and Roman Antiquities," &c. Revised, with an Appendix, by Prof. GEORGE W. GREENE, A.M. Illustrated by Engravings on Wood. Large 12mo, 724 pages, Cloth, $2 00.

☞ A SMALLER HISTORY OF GREECE: The above Work abridged for Younger Students and Common Schools. Engravings. 16mo, 272 pages, Cloth, $1 00.

THE STUDENT'S HISTORY OF ROME. A History of Rome from the Earliest Times to the Establishment of the Empire. With Chapters on the History of Literature and Art. By HENRY G. LIDDELL, D.D., Dean of Christ Church, Oxford. Illustrated by numerous Woodcuts. Large 12mo, 778 pages, Cloth, $2 00.

☞ A SMALLER HISTORY OF ROME, from the Earliest Times to the Establishment of the Empire. By WILLIAM SMITH, LL.D. With a Continuation to A.D. 476. By EUGENE LAWRENCE, A.M. Illustrations. 16mo, Cloth, $1 00.

THE STUDENT'S HISTORY OF FRANCE. A History of France from the Earliest Times to the Establishment of the Second Empire in 1852. Illustrated by Engravings on Wood. Large 12mo, 742 pages, Cloth, $2 00.

THE STUDENT'S GIBBON. The History of the Decline and Fall of the Roman Empire. By EDWARD GIBBON. Abridged. Incorporating the Researches of Recent Commentators. By WILLIAM SMITH, LL.D., Editor of the "Classical Dictionary," "Dictionary of Greek and Roman Antiquities," &c. Illustrated by 100 Engravings on Wood. Large 12mo, 706 pages, Cloth, $2 00.

THE STUDENT'S HUME. A History of England from the Earliest Times to the Revolution in 1688. By DAVID HUME. Abridged. Incorporating the Corrections and Researches of Recent Historians, and continued down to the Year 1858. Illustrated by Engravings on Wood. Large 12mo, 806 pages, Cloth, $2 00.

☞ A SMALLER HISTORY OF ENGLAND, from the Earliest Times to the Year 1862. Edited By WILLIAM SMITH, LL.D. Illustrated by Engravings on Wood. 16mo, Cloth, $1 00.

THE STUDENT'S QUEENS OF ENGLAND. Lives of the Queens of England. From the Norman Conquest. By AGNES STRICKLAND. Abridged by the Author. Revised and Edited by CAROLINE G. PARKER. 12mo, Cloth, $2 00.

THE STUDENT'S OLD TESTAMENT HISTORY, from the Creation to the Return of the Jews from Captivity. Edited by WILLIAM SMITH, LL.D., Classical Examiner in the University of London. With Maps and Woodcuts. *(In Press.)*

Pictorial History of the Great Rebellion.

Harper's Pictorial History of the Rebellion. By ALFRED H. GUERNSEY and HENRY M. ALDEN. Complete in Two Volumes, with nearly One Thousand Illustrations. Quarto, Cloth, $6 00 each.

This work contains 998 Illustrations. Of these 562 are authentic representations of Scenes and Incidents in the War; 99 Maps and Plans of Battles, among which is a large Colored Map of the Southern States, showing the position of nearly every place of note, together with the great lines of communication; and 337 Portraits of persons who have borne a prominent civil or military part in the war.

I have seen no other History of the Rebellion that seems to embrace so many admirable qualities as this does. I wish that so carefully prepared, beautifully illustrated, and reliable a History of our late Civil War might be placed in the library of every Grammar and High School and Academy in our country.—ABNER J. PHIPPS, *Agent of the Massachusetts State Board of Education.*

This is as valuable a work as ever was compiled on a historical subject.—*Zion's Herald.*

A careful, comprehensive, minute, and graphic record of the origin and progress of the war; and in the size and beauty of its pages and paper, in the profuseness, costliness, elegance, and completeness of its illustrations, far exceeding any other history yet attempted.—*New York Observer.*

A thoroughly well written and complete history of the great war.—*World.*

Clearly, simply, and impartially written.—*London Spectator.*

Many of its illustrative pictures are the best that we have seen in such a work; and some of the numerous portraits of prominent actors in the war are admirable as likenesses and works of art.—*London Athenæum.*

Every thing that relates to the contest is here given —military and naval operations, political matters, financial matters, and so forth—and always in a style that is as clear as it is strong, and with entire impartiality. The criticisms are sound and weighty, and full justice is done to each and every department of the public service, and to the enemy. The great story is told with spirit and fidelity, and in a tone that must be acceptable to all persons of sound taste. . . . . The *Pictorial History of the Great Rebellion* in no sense depends upon its illustrations for its worth, though they are excellent specimens of the art, and help the reader to understand the incidents of the war. The real merits of the work are apart from its engravings. Those merits are a strong and lucid style, a vast amount of well-digested and well-told information, just and well-considered criticisms, and impartial statements of all points about which there are disputes. . . . . Every library should have this work, for it is one of singular value as a book of reference, because of its comprehensiveness as well as accuracy. . . . . As a work of general reading it is of unsurpassed value.—*Boston Traveller.*

Full of interesting matter.—*London Review.*

Bulwer's Prose Works.

The Miscellaneous Prose Works of Edward Bulwer, Lord Lytton. In Two Volumes. 12mo, Cloth, $3 50.

Few books are likely to be more generally popular during the present season than the miscellaneous works of a statesman, essayist, poet, and novelist whose reputation has scarcely for a moment been dimmed by the rise of some of the most brilliant stars of literature, at a time when his fame as a writer had already well nigh reached its zenith.—*Athenæum.*

Harper's Hand-Book for Europe.

Harper's Hand-Book for Travellers in Europe and the East. Being a Guide through France, Belgium, Holland, Germany, Austria, Italy, Sicily, Egypt, Syria, Turkey, Switzerland, Greece, Tyrol, Russia, Denmark, Sweden, Spain, and Great Britain and Ireland. With a Railroad Map corrected up to 1868, and a Map embracing Colored Routes of Travel in the above Countries. By W. PEMBROKE FETRIDGE. Seventh Year. Large 12mo, Leather, Pocket-Book Form, $7 50.

Barnes's Thirty-ninth Congress.

History of the Thirty-ninth Congress of the United States. By WILLIAM H. BARNES, M.A., Author of "The Body Politic," &c. With Eighteen Steel Portraits. 8vo, Cloth, $5 00.

The reader who wishes for a condensed view of the national legislation for the eventful period from December 4, 1865, to March 4, 1867, will find the details of this volume of value and interest. It presents a summary of the debates and their results on the prominent bills brought before Congress during that time, connected by a simple thread of narrative, sufficient for the elucidation of the subject in hand, but never expanding into irrelevant and tedious verbosity. The issue of the work comes at a seasonable moment, and, without aiming at any partisan objects, it throws great light on the usurpations of the Executive and the long-suffering of Congress.—*New York Tribune.*

To the politician and political student the book will be of the greatest value as a summary and digest of two years of the national life.—*N. Y. Com. Advertiser.*

Draper's Civil War.

History of the American Civil War. By JOHN WILLIAM DRAPER, M.D., LL.D., Professor of Chemistry and Physiology in the University of New York, Author of a "Treatise on Human Physiology," "History of the Intellectual Development of Europe," "Thoughts on American Civil Policy," &c. To be completed in three elegant octavo vols., of about 500 pp. each. *Vol. II. just ready.* Cloth, Beveled Edges, price $3 50 per volume.

The leading political questions involved in the national legislation for nearly half a century are amply discussed, and their influence on recent events is elucidated with calmness and impartiality. A certain dramatic aspect is given to the successive steps which preceded the Rebellion, from the movement of nullification to the conflict in Kansas. The novelty of the volume consists not so much in the exhibition of facts before unknown as in the effective grouping of familiar events so as to form a grand historical unity.—*New York Tribune.*

The style of the author is discriminating, terse, vigorous, and makes a most pleasing impression on the mind: now setting forth rich galleries of historic personages, anon cataloguing mighty events, and setting forth their connection and sequences, and always investing his theme with strong human sympathies.—*Pittsburg Christian Advocate.*

With a fluent eloquence, a vast array of facts, a lucid arrangement, and an argumentative skill, the problem of the civil war is solved as an event born of numerous antecedent causes: its principles are laid bare, and we have what can not fail to heal and harmonize—because to enlighten and elevate—a philosophical history of the Southern Rebellion.—*Boston Transcript.*

Professor Draper treats of the causes of our late civil war with great clearness, and in that wise spirit of philosophy and patriotic statesmanship for which he is distinguished. We have not in a long time looked into a book containing so much of pure intellect as this.—*Congressional Globe.*

Very interesting and suggestive, and contains many new and valuable ideas, and the calm, philosophical tone that pervades it renders it doubly enjoyable and valuable.—*Congregationalist and Recorder.*

Dr. Draper is an admirable writer of history. He aims to search beneath the surface of things, to deal with the deeper and hidden causes of national prosperity and national disaster. Dr. Draper's idea of history is the true one, and in carrying it out he shows that he has been a careful and laborious student, an acute observer, and a dispassionate judge. Philosophical breadth of view, and perfect impartiality in presenting facts, are among the qualifications which should be demanded of him who presumes to write history; and these are certainly possessed in a high degree by Dr. Draper.—*Citizen.*

One of the most valuable contributions, if not the most valuable, yet made to the literature of the great struggle.—*Brooklyn Eagle.*

It is animated, picturesque, and eminently attractive in style. He admirably condenses the narrative of events bearing upon our great national struggle, giving each its due prominence, and sketching with graphic effect those which had the most marked influence in hastening the crisis; and weaves in with this the argument of the work with a skill that leads each to aid the interest of the other.—*Roxbury Journal.*

Dr. Draper has great dramatic powers, and his historical pictures are always finely colored. They are not sensational battle-pieces and personal situations merely; but they contain a profound philosophical suggestiveness, bringing out by their skillful contrasts and delicate light and shade the inner meanings of history, and attempting the solution of the great human problems that agitate the world, and are constantly upheaving, destroying, emerging from, and assimilating old and new forms of social, civil, and political life.—*Detroit Post.*

Macé's Physiology for the Young.

The History of a Mouthful of Bread, and its Effect on the Organization of Men and Animals. By JEAN MACÉ. Translated from the Eighth French Edition by Mrs. ALFRED GATTY. 12mo, Cloth, $1 75.

The Servants of the Stomach. By JEAN MACÉ, Author of "The History of a Mouthful of Bread," "Home Fairy Tales," &c., &c. Reprinted from the London Edition, Revised and Corrected. 12mo, Cloth, $1 75.

They are written in the form of letters to a child, and disclose, in a style wondrously clear and fascinating, the hidden wonders of the phenomena of life, the processes by which physical existence is preserved, and mental power and activity maintained. They compose a complete elementary treatise on physiology, which will be read by a healthy child of eight years with more pleasure than the *Arabian Nights*, and with as great advantage as the boy of twice that age, previously uninformed on the subject, will pursue the study at school.—*Methodist.*

Get these two books for your boys and girls, and you'll have a family struggle, yourselves included, as to who shall have the first reading.—*Zion's Herald.*

The "History of a Mouthful of Bread" is more simple in its style than the "Servants of the Stomach," which is designed to follow the former, and develops with wonderful clearness the leading facts of human anatomy. Besides their value as primary text books of science, they abound in useful hints for the preservation of health, and are pervaded by a healthy moral and religious sentiment.—*Evening Post.*

These volumes present important facts in physiology, in a form at once interesting and fascinating, and with a clearness of diction that is remarkable.—*New York Commercial.*

We doubt if two such fascinating and profitable volumes on popular Physiology were ever before written. The author's style is beautiful and quaint—his very quaintness giving the whole a peculiar charm, and enabling him to present facts and illustrations with rare force. He combines knowledge, and entertainment, and wholesome advice, with consummate skill, and makes the whole range of physiological subjects read more like a pleasant romance than a wearying science.—*Physio-Medical Recorder.*

In these two volumes important physiological facts and principles are presented to the youthful mind in a form so lucid and fascinating that the process of mastering them is literally one of "smoothness and delight."—*Boston Transcript.*

Something superior and rare in juvenile literature.—*Observer.*

www.ingramcontent.com/pod-product-compliance
Lightning Source LLC
LaVergne TN
LVHW010549110826
845149LV00003B/608

9781418187682